An Examination of
PLATO'S DOCTRINES

II. PLATO ON KNOWLEDGE AND REALITY

International Library of Philosophy and Scientific Method

EDITOR: TED HONDERICH
ADVISORY EDITOR: BERNARD WILLIAMS

A Catalogue of books already published in the
International Library of Philosophy and Scientific Method
will be found at the end of this volume.

An Examination of
PLATO'S
DOCTRINES

---

by

I. M. Crombie
Fellow of Wadham College, Oxford

II. PLATO ON KNOWLEDGE AND REALITY

LONDON
ROUTLEDGE & KEGAN PAUL
NEW YORK : THE HUMANITIES PRESS

First published 1963
by Routledge & Kegan Paul Ltd
Broadway House, 68–74 Carter Lane
London, E.C.4

Printed in Great Britain
by Fletcher & Son Ltd, Norwich

Second impression 1967

CONTENTS

PREFACE   *page* ix

GLOSSARY   x

1. THEORY OF KNOWLEDGE

   I. *AISTHÊSIS*

   A. *The machinery of sensation*   1
   B. *The epistemological status of sensation (the* Theaetetus)   3
      i. *The discussion of Protagoras*   4
      ii. *The discussion of Heraclitus*   10
      iii. *The equation of knowledge with sensation*   13
      iv. *The perception theory of the* Theaetetus   14
      v. *Our knowledge of the external world*   26

   II. *DOXA* AND *EPISTÊMÊ*

   A. *The concept of* doxa   33
   B. *The contrast between* doxa *and* epistêmê; *introduc-
      tory*   34
   C. *General impressions of the contrast between* doxa
      and epistêmê   35
   D. *Doxa and* epistêmê; *anticipation of conclusions*   41
   E. *Knowledge and belief in the* Meno   50
   F. *Knowledge and belief in the* Republic   53
      i. *In* Republic *5*   53
      ii. *In* Republic *6 and 7*   70
      iii. *In* Republic *10*   103
   G. *Knowledge and belief in the* Theaetetus   105
   H. *Knowledge and belief in the* Seventh Letter   122
   I. *The formal question: "What is knowledge?"*   127
   J. *The material guestion: "What can we know?"*   128

   III. THE DOCTRINE OF *ANAMNÊSIS*   135

   APPENDIX. FURTHER POINTS CONCERNING THE PASSAGE IN
   THE FIFTH BOOK OF THE *REPUBLIC*   148

2. COSMOLOGY AND THEORY OF NATURE

   I. THREE PRESUPPOSITIONS   153
   II. THE *PHAEDO*   156
   III. THE *REPUBLIC*   171

v

CONTENTS

IV. THE *TIMAEUS* 197
   A. *The first section of Timaeus' discourse; the creation* 199
   B. *The second section of Timaeus' discourse; what the Creator had to contend with* 216
   C. *The third section of Timaeus' discourse; what the Creator did about the brute facts* 229
   D. *General conclusions from the* Timaeus *concerning teleology and scientific method* 230
V. COSMOLOGICAL MATERIAL IN THE OTHER POST-*REPUBLIC* DIALOGUES 237
VI. CONCLUSIONS 244

3. METAPHYSICAL ANALYSIS

I. THE "THEORY OF FORMS"
   A. *Introductory* 247
   B. *The chronology of the theory of forms* 252
     i. *Early traces of the theory* 254
     ii. *Did Plato repent of the theory after his middle period?* 257
   C. *Problems about the nature of forms* 261
     i. *The forms as perfect particulars* 262
     ii. *Problems concerning the relations between the forms and the properties of things* 271
       a. *Introductory discussion* 271
       b. *Excursus on forms and craftsmen* 273
       c. *Resumption of introductory discussion* 274
       d. *Forms and vulgar universals* 278
       e. *Imperfect embodiment* 284
       f. *Perfect embodiments* 305
       g. *Imperfect and perfect embodiment; conclusion* 308
       h. *The status of property-instances* 310
   D. *The "classical theory of forms"; conclusion and application to the physical world* 319
II. PLATO ON THE THEORY OF FORMS: THE *PARMENIDES*
   A. *The first part of the* Parmenides 326
   B. *The second part of the* Parmenides 336
   C. *The contribution of the second part of the* Parmenides *to the problems raised in the first part* 347
III. THE RANGE OF FORMS 353
IV. RELATIONS BETWEEN UNIVERSALS 356
   A. *Introductory* 356
   B. *Dialectic and Protarchus' fallacy* 359
     i. *Protarchus' fallacy* 359
     ii. *Socrates on Protarchus' fallacy* 361
     iii. *Collection and division* 368

CONTENTS

C. Dialectic and the letters and syllables of reality 374
  i. Introductory 374
  ii. Letters and syllables in the Cratylus 376
  iii. Letters and syllables in the Theaetetus 377
  iv. Letters and syllables in the Statesman 378
  v. The relation of spelling to collection and division 380
  vi. The relation of spelling to dichotomous definition 380
  vii. A general problem about the metaphor of letters and syllables 383
D. Conclusion of this account of the relations between universals 386

V. THE SOPHIST

  A. Introductory 388
  B. Analysis of the relevant section 388
  C. Problems in Sophist 241–60 401
    i. The nature of the general terms discussed and of the relations said to hold between them 401
    ii. The "vowels of reality"; cohesive and disruptive factors 411
    iii. Participation 416
    iv. What the dialectician can do 417
    v. Who are the "Partisans of the Forms"? 419

VI. THE PHILEBUS

  A. Introductory 422
  B. The concepts of peras and to apeiron 423
  C. Some questions 436

VII. THE UNWRITTEN DOCTRINES 440

  A Theory of number; mathematical numbers 443
  B. Theory of number; formal numbers 447
  C. Mathematical properties and the world; things, forms and numbers 459

VIII. CONCLUSION 471

4. LOGIC AND LANGUAGE

  I. FORMAL AND INFORMAL LOGIC 473
  II. THE CRATYLUS ON LANGUAGE 475
  III. THE PARADOX OF FALSE BELIEF 486
    A. Inconclusive discussions of the Paradox 487
    B. The Sophist on the Paradox 492
  IV. SOME FURTHER PROBLEMS ARISING OUT OF THE SOPHIST: THE COPULA AND EXISTENCE, ETC. 498

CONTENTS

5. PLATO'S CONCEPTION OF PHILOSOPHICAL METHOD

I. GENERAL CONSIDERATIONS — 517

II. HYPOTHESES AND DIALECTIC — 528

    A. *Hypotheses in the* Meno *and* Phaedo — 529

    B. *Hypotheses and dialectic in the* Republic — 548

III. THE CONCEPT OF DIALECTIC — 562

IV. CONCLUSION — 567

INDEX — 571

PREFACE

FOR an account of what I have tried to do in this book I would refer the reader to the Preface and Introductory Notes to the first volume. This second volume contains my account of Plato's treatment of the more technical problems of philosophy. I have tried to make it self-contained; this has entailed some repetition of matters already treated in Volume 1. I repeat the acknowledgments made in the earlier preface. In particular my thanks are due to my colleagues and pupils for what I have learnt from them; to Professor Ayer who kindly read my manuscript and persuaded me to remove some of its faults; to Mr. B. G. Mitchell who read and commented on an earlier draft of Chapter 1; to Mr. J. C. B. Gosling, from discussions with whom I have learnt a very great deal about the topics treated here (though I doubt whether he will agree with many of my conclusions); to Mr. R. M. Hare, whose article on Philosophical Discoveries (*Mind* 1960) has helped me to crystallise some of the things that I wanted to say; to Professor Ryle, whose studies in Plato, published and unpublished, have done so much to breathe life into the discussion of Plato's later work.

I. M. CROMBIE

Oxford

GLOSSARY

The following crude equivalences may be found useful as *aide-mémoire*.

Agnoia, ignorance
Aisthêsis, sense-perception
Aitia, cause, reason, explanation
Akribeia, accuracy
Alêtheia, truth
Anamnêsis, recollection
Anankê, necessity ("brute fact")
Archê, beginning, source, principle
Chôra, space
Diairesis, division, separation
Dialektikê, dialectic.
Dianoia, thought
Doxa, belief, opinion, impression
Eikasia, conjecture, likening
Eikôn, image
Epistêmê, knowledge
Genesis, a becoming, happening, coming to be
Gignomenon, something that becomes

Gnôsis, knowledge
Kalos, noble, fine, beautiful
Kinêsis, change ("motion")
Logismos, calculation, thinking out
Logos, account, definition, argument, proposition, etc.
Meros, part, bit
Nöêsis, intellectual apprehension
Nous, mind, intellectual apprehension
Opsis, sight
Paradeigma, exemplar, illustration, archetype
Pathêma, something undergone
Phronêsis, wisdom
Pistis, belief, grounded confidence
Saphêneia, clarity
Sophia, wisdom
Sunagôgê, drawing together, collection

I

THEORY OF KNOWLEDGE

THE discussion of epistemological questions was begun, I suppose, by the fifth century Sophists and in particular by Protagoras: but there was a good deal left for Plato to contribute. It will be convenient to discuss his contributions mainly in terms of three central concepts, namely *aisthêsis* (perception or sensation), *doxa* (belief, opinion, judgment) and *epistêmê* or *gnôsis* (knowledge or understanding).

I. *AISTHÊSIS*

A. *The machinery of sensation*

Plato was well aware of the difference between a philosopher and a physiologist, and did not feel called upon to offer a physiological account of perception. In the *Timaeus* however (45–6 and 61–8) Timaeus is made to say how he supposes the senses to work. The account which he offers is of the same type as that which is given by a modern physiologist, though of course the details are very different. It is important to have some idea of the physiological picture which Plato thought probable and we will therefore look briefly at Timaeus' account of sight (*Timaeus* 45–6 and 67–8).

There is, then, a certain type of fire which cannot burn—in other words, light. This substance is to be found outside us, and there is also a supply of it inside the body. This internal light flows out through the eye when the eye is surrounded by light outside (it cannot get out at night when the eye is surrounded by darkness). The beam of light which flows out through the eye coalesces with the light straight ahead of it, and forms a sort of solid cone with its point at the eye and its base at the surface of the object which is being looked at. Being solid, this cone of light acts as a sort of rigid body and transmits any motions which there may be at the surface of the object back to the eye of the percipient and thence to his mind.

1

(The movement of this solid cone of light thus does the work of light rays in modern optics in that it stimulates in the eye disturbances which correspond to the disturbances at the surface of the object). The colour of the object seen depends on the size of the particles emitted by the object, particles of different sizes having different effects on the cone of light, and therefore on its effect on the eye.

Plato is not committed to the details of this account, and they are not perfectly clear. But in general the position is that both the percipient and the perceived object must be in a state of activity, the one emitting light through its eyes, the other particles from its surface, and that this activity is not what we see, but the cause of our seeing. Our seeing is a *pathêma* or something which we undergo when the disturbances set up in the eye are large enough to be transmitted to the *psuchê* or mind.

When Plato turns to a philosophical discussion of the problems of perception in the *Theaetetus* he seems, as we shall see, to accept this kind of generalised version of the optics of the *Timaeus* as the basis from which epistemology must start. Epistemological pictures can be crudely divided into cognitive pictures and causal pictures. According to a cognitive picture we somehow use our senses to find out what things are like. The colours and other sense-properties of things belong to them quite independently of our perceiving them; in perception we discover but in no sense create the properties which things have. According to a causal picture on the other hand our sense-data are simply the *results* of the stimulation of our sense-organs. The sensible properties of things are therefore joint products of the activities of the sense-organ and of the perceived object; and in that way colours and tastes and so on are partially created (so to speak) by our sense-organs in perception. The colour of a thing is the way in which it affects our senses and the true properties of the thing are those properties, whatever they are, which enable it to affect our senses in that way. A causal picture is commonly adopted by those who take seriously (or, some would say, naïvely) the discoveries of the physiologists; and it is I think important, if we are to understand Plato's attitude to empirical knowledge, to remember that he seems to have taken a causal picture for granted.

To take only one respect in which this may be important: a causal picture enhances what I will call the formal rather than the qualitative aspect of our sensory information. Thus there is a formal correspondence, but no qualitative resemblance, between the shape of the groove in a gramophone record and the sound which comes out of the loudspeaker; a certain type of sound corresponds to a certain pattern of groove, but a high note (for example) is not in any

2

other way *like* a sharply serrated groove. If our sense-organs are thought of as mechanisms, as gramophones are mechanisms, this might at least make it easier to believe that it is the shapes, sizes, velocities and other "primary qualities" of things which are essential to them as they are in themselves.

(One might illustrate the difference between the causal and the cognitive pictures of perception by the difference between two types of mechanism, a gramophone and a magic lantern. In the case of a gramophone you feed in a series of jolts to a stylus and get out something quite different. In the case of a magic lantern you feed in a picture and get out the same picture enlarged on a screen; the mechanism hardly creates the picture but merely renders it visible to a large audience. If our senses are like magic lanterns, windows or telescopes then clearly the world is very much as it seems; if however our senses are more like gramophones then clearly there is a sense in which we shall be misled if we suppose that they tell us what the world is really like).

B. *The epistemological status of sensation* (*the* Theaetetus)

Plato's discussion of *aisthêsis* or sensation is to be found in one of his most brilliant dialogues, the *Theaetetus*. In form this dialogue is a search for a Socratic definition of knowledge (*epistêmê*), and the search is unsuccessful. In practice however the point of writing the dialogue was not to fail to define knowledge, nor to show that it cannot be defined, but to illuminate certain other matters. Perhaps the chief of these is that our knowledge[1] of the external world is not a matter of undergoing sense-data but of interpreting them. This result emerges from a long and complicated discussion which takes the form of distinguishing *aisthêsis* or sensation (which consists of things which happen to us as a result of the stimulation of our sense-organs) from *doxa* or judgment (which comes about through the comparison of sense-data with each other and which consists in treating them as manifestations of an external world).

The discussion is, as I say, long and complicated. The section we are concerned with is from 151 to 187. It opens when Theaetetus (having begun by defining knowledge in terms of its instances, and having been told that this is not the proper way to define) says that a man who knows anything perceives or senses it and that therefore knowledge is perception or sensation (*aisthêsis*).

Socrates' reaction to this is striking, for he proceeds rapidly to

[1] Here and elsewhere I shall, where convenient, allow myself to use "knowledge" in places where Plato would perhaps regard *epistêmê* as strictly inappropriate.

3

identify this definition firstly with Protagoras' doctrine that there is no distinction (in terms of truth and falsehood) between illusion and reality, and secondly with Heraclitus' doctrine that there is no stability in the world (*panta rei*, or "everything is in flux").

These identifications seem bold, and the second of them far-fetched. In order to understand what is in Socrates' mind we must remember that Theaetetus' proposed definition "knowledge is perception" is to be read as an equation, and therefore as entailing both: "Every case of perception is a case of knowledge" and also: "Every case of knowledge is a case of perception." Now if every perception is a case of knowledge, then evidently there are no illusions, and where there is an empirical disagreement, say between Jones who finds the wind chilly and Smith who finds it warm, both must in a sense be right. On the other hand if every case of knowledge is a case of perception then there must be complete instability and randomness in the world. For if there are constant relations between sense-data, and we can be aware of them, then there are things other than sense-data that we can know, namely the constant relations between them. Therefore if our knowledge consists of nothing but the having of sense-data, these constant relations cannot exist; in other words everything is in flux. It must I think be in this way that Socrates makes Theaetetus' definition imply the Heraclitean doctrine of flux (though it must be confessed that the connection is not made clear in the text).

We must go into this in rather more detail. Since Plato feels that the Protagorean and the Heraclitean doctrines belong very much (at the least) to the same stable, he does not disentangle them completely and we shall not be able to do so either.

(i) *The discussion of Protagoras*

Protagoras' treatise apparently opened with the sonorous aphorism "Man is the measure of all things", and his "relativism" seems to have boxed the philosophical compass. Whatever seems to a man to be so, is so to that man—whether it is a matter of wine seeming sour, or of an institution seeming unjust. There are unusual sense-data and deplorable opinions but there are no illusions and no false beliefs. Plato seems to imply, however, that this general relativism had its roots in a doctrine of perception according to which nobody ever perceives anything but his own sense-data, and grew from these roots into a universal doctrine. This extension may well have taken place in both of two ways. Firstly Protagoras may have felt that all beliefs that a man holds must in the end be based on his experience, so that differences of opinion about, say, politics, or agriculture derive ultimately from different ways of experiencing the world.

4

Secondly, and perhaps more importantly, the words for *seeming* in Greek as in English (*dokein* and *phainesthai*) are ambiguous in having both a sensory and a non-sensory use. Thus the wine may seem sour in the sense that it tastes sour, or it may seem to be stolen in the sense that it is reasonable to believe that it is stolen. It is possible then that Protagoras began by asserting that all sense-data are in the same ontological boat; the wine really has as many different tastes as there are people to whom it tastes different. It is not the case that the wine is really sweet, though it tastes sour to Jones; rather it is really sweet-to-Smith, sour-to-Jones, tasteless-to-Green and so on. Expressing this in the form "whatever seems to a man is to that man", Protagoras may have felt obliged to go on to say that all opinions are equally true, just as all sense-data are equally valid, simply because an opinion too is something which "seems to a man".

However this may be, we can distinguish in Protagoras what we may call his central and his extended thesis, his central thesis being that all reports of immediate perception are equally valid, his extended thesis that all beliefs whatever are equally valid. This distinction Socrates gradually draws in the course of the present discussion.

Theaetetus, then, proposes (151) that knowledge is perception, and Socrates tells him that this amounts to the Protagorean doctrine that man is the measure of all things. This doctrine in turn, he says, rests on the further doctrine that: (*a*) there are really no individual things having properties of their own (whatever seems to have one property can also seem to have the opposite property); and (*b*) everything is a product of motion and activity. Thus the whiteness of an object, for example, is "a resultant of the contact of the eyes with the appropriate motion" (153 e 6). Since this can be applied to every property of a thing, the objective existence of things is dissolved away and we are left with a world of sense-data, each private to a given percipient. We know from our own experience that a thing which looks one colour on one occasion may well look another colour on another occasion; *a fortiori* we can infer that what looks one colour to one man may well look different to another man. There is therefore no reason why any sense-datum should be regarded as more veridical than any other, and thus the distinction between reality and illusion is done away with as Protagoras' thesis requires.

What has happened is this. Theaetetus has suggested that knowledge is perception. But if that is so then there is truth in every perceptual judgment. Yet perceptual disputes occur; the stone which one man finds warm seems cold to another. Therefore we can only say that both of these perceptual judgments are true, if we say that what each man perceives is private to himself—the warm stone private to the one man, the cold stone private to the other. Each man will be correctly reporting the properties of his private stone. But we cannot have an indefinite number of private *physical* stones in the same place at the same time. The only way therefore in which this can be rendered plausible is to get rid of the physical stone. If the stone is nothing but a collection of the sense-data which lead us to speak of the stone, then there is no reason why one man's sense-data of the stone should agree with another's. The only physical thing involved in the transaction is some process or other whose interaction with our bodies gives rise to the sense-data which we take to represent the stone to us. Physical things are thus got rid of in favour of physical processes and the sense-data begotten of their interaction. This is justly said to be a Heraclitean conclusion.

We know that Plato was influenced by Heracliteanism in his youth; and according to Aristotle he never fully shook it off. It is not surprising therefore that Socrates goes on (153–5) to find things to say in defence of this doctrine. The first is the general observation that activity is beneficial and sloth harmful; this presumably gives some measure of support to the view that nothing in nature is at rest, since it shows nature to be on the side of activity. More seriously Socrates next observes that if a sense-property such as whiteness were located in the object it is difficult to see how it could ever seem any other colour; while if it were supposed to characterise the visual sense of the percipient he would presumably see white all the time. It seems inevitable to regard the whiteness as a product of the inter-action between the object and the percipient. These arguments are of some weight and as Plato produces no answer to them it is natural to suppose that he accepted the sense-datum theory to which he makes them point. Then finally Socrates is made to observe that the conventional view that properties belong in an absolute way to the objects to which they are commonly ascribed gives rise to paradoxes. For if A is larger than B or more numerous than C, it can without change in itself become smaller than B (if B grows) or less numerous than D (if D is a larger group). Needless to say if this is meant as an *argument* in favour of the view that sense-properties are products of interaction it is a very bad one, for whiteness is not at all the same kind of property as largeness. Perhaps however it is intended not so much as an argument, but more as an *apéritif*. Get a man to admit that Jones's shortness does not belong absolutely to Jones, but exists only as a relation between Jones and the average man, and you will have him in a more amenable state for persuasion that the stone's whiteness belongs not absolutely to the stone, but is begotten of the intercourse of the stone with the percipient's sense-organs. Common-sense holds, does it, that stones are really grey? But it also holds that Little Tich was really short.[1]

Socrates now goes on (156) to reveal what he calls the Mysteries of the Protagorean and Heraclitean thinkers. A philosopher's "Mysteries" must be doctrines which he never published, and so we may infer that what Plato offers us under this title is the theory of perception which he took to underlie views of this kind. It is roughly as follows.

Nothing exists except *kinêsis* (activity, change, process). There are two kinds of process, the one capable of affecting, the other of being affected—that is of sensing. (This distinction as Socrates says is only relative. B may be an object in one transaction but a subject in another. When I see Jones, Jones is the object, but when Jones sees the tree he is the subject). But processes may be divided not only into subjects and objects, but also into slow and fast. Both subjects and objects—percipients and the things they perceive—are slow processes, but when a subject and an object come together, two quick processes occur. There are, as Socrates says, "twin offspring of the intercourse" of the two slow processes, namely a sense-quality (e.g. whiteness) and the perception of it; and these "twin offspring" travel rapidly between the two parties so that the stone (for example) becomes white and the eye comes to see it. Every sense-datum exists only as the object of a particular act of sensing and every act of sensing only as the correlate of that particular sense-datum. There is nothing continuous in the stream of sense-data nor in the sensings which are correlated with them. Every pair of "twin offspring" exists only momentarily having no necessary relation to its predecessors or successors, and owing its character entirely to the momentary condition of the two "slow processes" involved in the transaction.

This theory, Socrates goes on to observe, deals admirably with the phenomenon of "illusion" or perceptual disagreement—with the sick man to whom wine tastes bitter or with the mad man who sees things which are not there. What we see, hear or otherwise perceive is always a sense-datum, and sense-data owe their qualities to the momentary state of the two interacting processes. It is not to be wondered at, therefore, if a piece of physical environment which produces nothing but an image of a blank wall in the visual field of a sane man produces an image of a scarlet toad in the visual field of a madman. We have no access (this seems to be essential to the theory, though it is not explicitly stated) to the real nature of the other "slow

[1] The idea that Plato failed to see that such properties as shortness are relational, or that he confused relational with non-relational properties seems to me groundless. *Phaedo* 102 where he is sometimes said to treat shortness as a non-relational property seems to say the opposite (see 102 c 7).

process" whose interaction with our own produces our sense-data, but only to the sense-data which are the "twins" to our acts of sensing. This being the case, the external world to which we have access is a world of momentarily existing sense-data only; physical things are simply "collections" of these (157 b 9). The result of this is that while, as a matter of fact, our sense-data are normally regular and can be "collected" into what we call men or rocks, there is none the less nothing ontologically inferior, so to speak, about the irregular sense-data suffered by people in abnormal conditions. All are equally "true", all perception is infallible (since there is nothing to check it against, no reality apart from each man's private reality); and therefore all perception is equally knowledge.

(We may notice in passing that this is a somewhat cavalier treatment of the phenomenon of "illusion". The water which feels hot to a cold hand is easily explained in this way, but Socrates is surely wrong to include, as he does, dreams and complete hallucinations under the same umbrella. Given that when I am asleep I am not in the same condition as I am when I am awake; but what is it that is supposed to be interacting with my sleeping organism to produce the marble halls I seem to see?).

Socrates has now (161) completed his exposition of the Protagorean theory and of the Mysteries which he deems it to rest on, and he turns to criticism. Plato was extremely conscious in his later years of the facility and danger of criticising *au pied de la lettre*, and he goes out of his way in a number of places to denounce it. This is one such place, for he makes Socrates offer a number of criticisms which he then condemns on the ground that they rely either on appeals to emotion or on unsympathetic interpretation of his opponent's words. There is however one important point which emerges from this criticism. Socrates says that when one hears people talking in a foreign language, one hears, but does not know, what they say; and to this Theaetetus replies that one hears and knows the sounds, but neither hears nor knows their significance (163). He is commended for this reply and it is left on one side. It is of course a pointer to Socrates' essential objection to the view that knowledge is perception, namely that to acquire information about the external world we need not only to have sense-data but to interpret them.

The Protagorean thesis which Socrates has expounded is what we called Protagoras' central thesis, namely that all reports of immediate perception are equally valid. When, however, Socrates turns to serious criticism it is the extended thesis, that all beliefs whatever are equally valid, that he attacks. He begins by putting into Protagoras' mouth an ingenious "pragmatist" answer to the obvious objection that some men are surely wiser than others. That this is so Protagoras concedes, but he is made to reply that the wisdom of a wise man consists not in the truth of his beliefs but in their beneficial character; a wise man is one who can make his plants or his farm stock or his fellow humans experience their environment in a healthy and fruitful way. Whatever a man thinks right "is right to that man" (whatever exactly that means); but the things that some men think are right are bad and unprofitable things, and it is desirable that these men should be brought to see things differently.

Socrates' reply to Protagoras' extended thesis makes two main points. The first is that the thesis is self-refuting, for, by claiming that all beliefs are true, it is forced to concede truth to the almost universal belief, that some beliefs are false. Protagoras must concede then that at least some error is possible, namely the error of his opponents. This established, Socrates goes on to admit that Protagoras' relativistic view of morality is not repugnant to common sense. It is commonly held that opinions about right and wrong are no more capable of being corrected in the light of an objective standard than are reports of immediate perception. The man with eccentric moral views, like the man with some abnormality of sense, is out of step with the majority but cannot be said to be wrong. Though he admits that this doctrine is not repugnant to common sense, Socrates does not of course accept it. He does not however attempt to refute it. Rather he meets it with a long and splendid passage (172–7) contrasting the litigious and practically-minded man with the speculative and practically incompetent philosopher. The upshot of this praise of the philosophic life seems to be that men in general fail to understand the true reward of virtue and punishment of vice. The common conception of justice is a querulous conception based on self-seeking, and it is no wonder that this is thought to have no objective foundation. But the man who realises the sordidness of material ends will have a motive for goodness—escape from sordidness and assimilation to the divine—which could not be dismissed as merely conventional. However, as Socrates says, this will cut no ice with the tough-minded, so he allows that it is tenable that "what a man or community thinks fair and right is so to him". But he denies that what a man thinks beneficial is so to him. "Beneficial" as he says means "likely to do good" and his point is a general one about prediction. To allow that all reports of present experience are equally valid is one thing, to allow that all predictions of future experience are equally valid is another. Every man can tell whether he is enjoying his meal, but it takes a cook to know whether a meal is likely to be enjoyable.

This establishes a large class of beliefs—beliefs about what is likely to do good, beliefs about what is likely to happen—within which the

9

beliefs of the expert are much more likely to be right than the beliefs of the non-expert. That is why the expert is trusted. In this sphere at least the distinction between true and false beliefs is needed, and therefore Protagoras' extended thesis fails.

Plato has his pulpit moments and his philosophical moments. In his pulpit moments he calls down universal curses on any line of thought whose tendency he distrusts. This is decidedly one of his philosophical moments, for this criticism is very economical. Protagoras' extended thesis goes too far, but Socrates concedes that the central thesis is left untouched. "Concerning what happens to a man at any given moment, and the sensations to which that gives rise, and the beliefs based upon these sensations—it is not so easy to show that these are not true." Perhaps beliefs based on present experience have the "clarity" which entitles them to be called knowledge (179 c). To decide whether this is so it is necessary to examine the Heraclitean doctrine of the instability of all things.

(ii) *The Discussion of Heraclitus*

Socrates begins his discussion of instability by distinguishing two kinds of it, namely motion and change (181). He then reminds his hearers that the doctrine they are examining is: that when contact is established between subject and object, a twin progeny is begotten, namely a sense-quality (e.g. whiteness) and the appropriate sensation; and that these travel between the two parties so that the object becomes white and the subject comes to see it.

Now, he continues, if the instability doctrine confined itself to asserting that everything is in motion, all would be well. For in that case a given thing might persist in, for example, "flowing white". Or, in other words, it does not matter making the sensible properties of things resultants of motion so long as you allow that the motion in question conforms to a stable pattern in such a way that the object continues to manifest the same sensible properties for a reasonable period of time. In that case it will be possible to describe things. However incessantly active the plate may be behind its placid appearance, so long as the activity, by virtue of which it "flows white", persists unchanged, it will be possible to call it a white plate. But the Heraclitean cannot allow this, for he asserts that everything is unstable. But there is no point in saying that everything is unstable if you merely mean that everything results from instability; for if you allow that the instability of objects conforms to a stable pattern so that the same sensible property is manifested over a period of time, then you have admitted that something is stable, namely the pattern and the sensible property in which it results. Therefore the Heraclitean must either reduce: "Everything is unstable" to the tame

10

doctrine: "Some things are unstable and some stable", or else he must claim not only that things "flow white", but also that "whiteness itself is in flux", or in other words that sensible properties not only result from, but are themselves subject to, continuous change. But to say this is to say that neither percipient subjects nor perceivable objects are ever in the same condition in any respect in two consecutive moments. But in a world in which that was true all propositions (except perhaps negations) would be false (183 a–b). A plate cannot be said to be white if it is the next moment some other colour. Nor would there be in such a world such a thing as perception; for "sight", for example, is presumably the name of some constant and unchanging activity. There is therefore this dilemma for the Heraclitean:—either his thesis is tenable but trivial, or he is committed to a world in which there is no such thing as a describable object, nor such an activity as perception, nor therefore (if perception is knowledge) such a thing as knowledge. (See below pp. 27–33).

The blunder, which has led the Heracliteans (if there were any) who embraced the latter alternative to this absurd conclusion, is that of confusing: "All properties result from change" with: "All properties are subject to change". Perhaps an illustration would help. An electric bulb glows (we will suppose) because of some kind of incessant activity in the filament. But although the glowing is a process which *results from* activity or change it is not in itself a process *of* change, in the way in which a continuous flickering could be said to be a process of change. The Heraclitean doctrine which Plato is refuting amounts to the doctrine that, since the incandescence of the bulb is due to activity in the filament, there can never really be a steady glow but only a flickering one.

The argument establishes that whatever views you may hold about the nature of the mechanisms underlying the phenomena, it cannot seriously be disputed that there are many constant phenomena in the world. The comment which Socrates makes upon this result is: "this emancipates us from Protagoras; . . . we cannot agree that perception is knowledge, at any rate along the lines of the doctrine that everything is unstable" (183 b–c).

This is an odd comment. Socrates had said that beliefs based upon present perception might be true and might count as knowledge; the doctrine of instability would have to be examined to decide that. Now it has been examined and found wanting, and Socrates concludes that "Perception is knowledge" fails, meaning presumably thereby that beliefs based upon present perception cannot count as knowledge. This may seem plain sailing; Protagoras' central thesis entails Heraclitus' thesis; Heraclitus' thesis is false; therefore Protagoras' central thesis is false. But in fact it is not so simple as that.

11

With Heraclitus, as with Protagoras, one can distinguish two theses, which we will call normal and rampant. Normal Heracliteanism asserts that all properties result from activity, rampant Heracliteanism draws the absurd conclusion that there are no stable properties. Now in the discussion of Protagoras his view had been shown to require something like the normal Heraclitean thesis. The denial of illusion makes sense only if all sense-data are momentary resultants of the interaction of two processes. But Protagoras' view has not been shown to require (and does not require) the rampant Heraclitean thesis. Yet in the discussion of Heraclitus the normal thesis has been treated as tenable, and only the rampant thesis refuted. But since Protagoras does not require the rampant thesis, the refutation of the latter should leave him unscathed. What has happened?

The truth is, I believe, that Socrates has not yet given his reasons for denying that beliefs based upon present perception can be counted as knowledge. His reasons, to be given in the sequel, are that a belief which was based strictly and only on present perception would be simply an expression of one's private sensations and would have no reference to an objective external world. How then does rampant Heracliteanism come into the picture? Only, I think, because *if it were* true, we should *have* to concede the status of knowledge to beliefs based on present perception. Protagoras does not entail Heraclitus, but Heraclitus does entail Protagoras. In the actual world, in which there is in fact considerable stability, I cannot be said to know anything on the basis of my present perceptions alone. To know that there is a white plate on the table is a good deal more than to know that there is a round white patch in my visual sense-field. It is at least to know also that such a white patch has been and will be available to myself and others at this and other times. What can be called belief (and *a fortiori* what, if anything, can be called knowledge) about the external world is something much more than awareness of present sensations. But in a rampant Heraclitean world this would not be so. There being no constant patterns in such a world, there would be nothing whatever to know except present sensations, and no point in reserving the title "knowledge" for something else. In the actual world expressions such as "true" and "knowledge" must be kept to characterise beliefs not about sense-data but about real things (however precisely these may be related to sense-data); in the world of rampant Heracliteanism there would be no real things and therefore no such use for these expressions. The destruction therefore of the rampant Heraclitean thesis does not directly destroy Protagoras' central thesis; rather it takes away the only prop which could sustain it against the criticism which is forthcoming.

12

The position then so far is as follows. Theaetetus' equation of knowledge with perception has been shown to involve the Protagorean denial of the distinction between reality and illusion; and it has been argued that this denial can only be sustained on the basis of some kind of a sense-datum theory of perception. Protagoras' extended thesis has been discussed, and it has been shown that while parts of it are acceptable to common sense parts of it are certainly untenable. Protagoras' central thesis however has so far been left untouched, and so has the theory of perception which was worked out to support it. The theory of perception has also survived the scrutiny of Heracliteanism; for it is more or less equivalent to what we have called the normal Heraclitean thesis, whereas Socrates' criticisms were directed against the rampant thesis alone. There are therefore two extremist theories refuted at this stage, and two (Protagoras' central thesis and the perception theory associated with normal Heracliteanism) still in the field.

(iii) *The equation of knowledge with sensation*

Having disposed of the authorities whom Theaetetus might have invoked in defence of his equation of knowledge with sense-perception, Socrates turns to discuss the equation in its own right (184–7). His reason for rejecting it is essentially that what the senses give us, strictly speaking, is no more than sensation, and that we do not know anything about the real world by having sensations, but only by interpreting their significance.

He begins by saying that we ought strictly to say that the mind perceives the external world through the medium of the senses. The senses are not independent receptors of information, "located in the body like the Greeks in the belly of the Trojan Horse"; they are abilities or tools through which the mind becomes aware of the world.[1] Each sense has its own proper range of sense-qualities; thus sight is correlated with colours, hearing with sounds and so on. But we are capable of noticing other things beside the proper objects of a particular sense; we can for example notice about two of the latter that they both exist, are not identical with each other, and do (or do not) resemble each other. These additional facts concerning existence, identity, number, similarity and so on are not the objects of any particular sense but are noticed by the mind without the aid of the senses. Goodness and nobility, similarly, with their opposites, "are pre-eminently things whose existence is observed . . . by the mind, by a process of reckoning up past and present in relation to the future". Any animal, however young, can perceive bodily disturbances (*pathêmata*) which penetrate into consciousness; what needs

[1] 184 c–d. I think that this is the correct account of this rather obscure passage.

13

to be learnt is the necessary calculations (*analogismata*) which have to be made concerning these with reference to "existence and utility" (186 c 3). However without this process of calculation the perceptions of the organism do not make contact with existence, and hence cannot be called true, nor count as knowledge. "Knowledge therefore is not to be found in the sensations we undergo, but in our thought about them; it is only by the latter that we make contact with existence and truth" (186 d).

What this amounts to is, I think, as follows. If we suppose an organism merely to have sensations, then all we can say of it is that it has sensations. Unless it notices that they are occurring (this I take to be what is meant by "noticing their existence"), discriminates them, notices which resembles which, and the patterns in which they recur, it will be completely without information. Its sense organs will be undergoing things and it will be in a sense conscious of what they undergo, but it cannot be said to be in a state of knowledge or belief. Things are happening to its consciousness but it is not intelligently aware of them. Intelligent awareness is something which only arises when one critically surveys the significance of what happens in consciousness.

To put it at the lowest, the point is being made that there is a non-sensory component in empirical knowledge. This seems quite clear. There are however difficulties in detail about the interpretation of Plato's version of this truth which we shall consider in the next section. Meanwhile we can round off this section by giving the conclusion of the discussion, which is that knowledge is not to be looked for in the sphere of sensation but in the sphere of "properly mental activity about the world" (187 a 5); and this, Theaetetus says, is called the sphere of *doxa* or judgment.

(iv) *The perception theory of the* Theaetetus

The concept of *aisthêsis* or sensory activity has now been discussed in relation to *doxa* or judgment and *epistêmê* or knowledge, and it has been shown that *aisthêsis* is essential to, but not identical with, *doxa*. Meanwhile it seems that a theory concerning the status of the objects of perception has been implied in the discussion, and we must now consider what this theory is.

There are two places where a theory is stated or implied. There is firstly Socrates' account of the Mysteries of the Protagoreans and Heracliteans (153–60, and a repetition, 182), and there is secondly the passage we have just considered (184–7) where the relation between judgment and its sensory component is discussed.

The question arises whether Socrates is committed to the theory outlined in the first of these two places. The answer seems to be that

14

he is not. He says, and rightly says, that Theaetetus' definition requires some such theory, and this is a sufficient reason for his stating it. On the other hand the rejection of Theaetetus' definition leaves the Mysteries untouched. Unless therefore it can be shown that the theory of the Mysteries is implied in the final and constructive discussion, it seems to be impossible to determine Socrates' attitude to the Mysteries. From the fact that Socrates gives a sympathetic and plausible account of the theory, and subsequently offers no refutation of it we can no doubt infer that Plato was at least not hostile to it; but we cannot at the moment go further than that.

Is it the case then that the theory of the Mysteries is implied in the constructive discussion at the end of the section? We must look at this discussion more closely.

The argument, as we have seen, is that the senses do not (by themselves) inform us of the existence of their objects, and that that which makes no contact with existence makes no contact with truth, so that there are no truths which we owe to the senses alone. So far, so good, but what is meant by "the existence of their objects"? What does Socrates mean when he asks: "With what sense do we notice the existence (and also distinctness, number and similarity or otherwise) of a sound and a colour?" (185 a–b)? One is tempted to suppose that the point is that sense-data are subjective occurrences, and that we do not therefore, by having sense-data, get into touch with an objective physical world. The contribution of the mind on this view would consist in referring our sense-data to the external world, in treating them as manifestations of independent entities; the mind would get us across the gap between a subjective world of Lockeian "ideas" and an objective world of physical things. Sensory activity by itself would not get us into touch with the real world, but only a world of private experience, and the "protocol-sentences", such as "I am now sensing a red patch", which would express its meagre information would be without "ontological commitment", and hence would not deserve to be called true. *Epistêmê* or "knowledge", and with it *alêtheia* or "truth" are reserved for awareness of a reality independent of oneself.

Socrates may mean this, but his words do not bear this interpretation. What the mind notices according to him is not that the colour belongs to an independently existing object, but that the colour exists. The mind also notices that the colour is not identical with the sound, and that it does or does not resemble it; and if we interpret "that the colour exists" as "that the colour belongs to an independently existing object", we shall find it impossible to give a parallel interpretation of these two additional observations (for a colour and a sound do not necessarily belong to two distinct objects). Therefore

15

the distinction that Socrates is making seems to be the distinction between (*a*) passively undergoing sense-experience, and (*b*) noticing that it is occurring, distinguishing its items, detecting resemblances between them and so on. It is this contribution which the mind makes, and it must be this which is enough to bring us into contact with *ousia* or reality and to give our observations the status of true beliefs. In that case a man who takes a detached and observant attitude to the events of his dreams, while not knowing that he is dreaming, could presumably be said to be making contact with reality.

This conclusion seems odd; so odd that, while I think that this is what Socrates says, I have admitted that it may not be all that he means. There is however a way of escaping this conclusion. We may say first that Plato is not talking about dreams but about sense-perception, and that although he has himself raised "the old chestnut: 'How do we know we are not now dreaming?'" (158 b 8), he is not himself troubled by this kind of Cartesian doubt. Then we can say next that Plato talks, not about "sense-data" or anything of the kind, but about sounds and colours. If then we suppose that Plato takes a Naïve Realist view of sense-perception, according to which the colours which we see are normally "parts of the surfaces of material objects", the situation is saved. On this view when we notice that a colour exists we are not noticing that we are having a visual sense-datum, but that there is a coloured expanse out there in the physical world. What we sense then on this view is not sense-data but physical things. The contribution of the senses is to put us *de facto* into touch with physical things, the contribution of the mind to make us aware that we are in fact in touch with them.

This line of escape is attractive, but has its difficulties. For Socrates distinguishes not only seeing colours from noticing their existence, but also suffering *pathêmata* or undergoings from "reckoning them up with reference to existence and utility"; and it seems clear that these two distinctions are roughly the same, and in particular that colours, sounds and so on are identical with the *pathêmata* which we suffer. But a Naïve Realist who speaks of the things we see and hear as *pathêmata*, or things that happen to us, is surely giving away his case. As recent writers have argued, to treat perception as if it were a form of sensation (in the way in which a pain or a tickle is a sensation) is to take the high road leading to sense-datum theories of perception. But there are without doubt places (e.g. 186 c 1) where Plato writes as if he took the objects of sensory awareness to be, or to be the results of, bodily disturbances which penetrate into consciousness, or in other words as if he took awareness of a colour to be analogous to awareness of a tickle or a pain. "New-born men and animals," he says in that place, "are endowed by nature with the ability to perceive such *pathêmata* as reach through the body to the mind." But if the objects of vision and of the other senses are, or result from, bodily disturbances stimulated by the impact of external objects, then the question surely arises: How are these immediate objects of experience related to the external objects which stimulate the senses and thus give rise to them? And in the context of the *Theaetetus* it is difficult to believe that Plato would have overlooked this question, since it seems to be so germane to the theory outlined in the Mysteries.

In the *Timaeus* (61–8) Plato seems to treat the colours, tastes, smells and so on that we are immediately aware of as things which arise in the mind as the results of bodily disturbances; and this, as far as it goes, supports the view that *pathêmata* in the present passage are to be understood in the same way. Again in the *Theaetetus* itself, in the discussion of Protagoras, Socrates treats the awareness of cold, burning, pleasure, pain, desire and fear (156 b), and also apparently memory (166 b) as if they belonged to the same class as the five senses, and as if their objects were the same sort of thing as colours and sounds. It is true that this occurs in the discussion of Protagoras, for whom of course this was so; but the point is that Socrates makes no bones at all about lumping together these different things, and it is difficult to believe that a writer who meant us, a few pages further on, to take a Naïve Realist view of the five senses would do nothing to mark the discomfort which he would be bound to feel at this "assimilation of the concept of perception to the concept of sensation"—and indeed to that of emotion as well.

We seem then to have two possible interpretations of the theory of sensory awareness which Socrates relies on in order to distinguish the latter from judgment; and each of them has its difficulties. The one interpretation gives us a Realist theory. Through the senses we are directly aware of physical objects, or their sensible properties, and the contribution of the mind is to recognise them as such and to assess their significance for us. The other interpretation gives us a theory which is compatible with Phenomenalism or with a Lockeian Causal Theory of perception. According to this interpretation what we are aware of in sensation is sense-data, and the contribution of the mind lies in noticing that they are occurring and in constructing, so to speak, an objective external world by observing the patterns in which they occur. The empirical world in this view (as in Phenomenalism and in the Causal Theory) is the orderly system of sense-data which we experience. In neither of these interpretations, it may be noticed, does the mind enable us to cross the gap between private sensations and physical objects. The one interpretation begins with physical objects, and the other ends with private sensations. The third

17

interpretation according to which we begin with private sensations and end, through an act of the mind, with physical objects had to be rejected because it did not conform to the text.

Which of these interpretations ought we to take? The sense-datum interpretation, according to which this account of perception is in line with the theory of the Mysteries, or the Realist interpretation according to which it is not? Here, as so often, the truth may well be that it would be historically inaccurate to choose. The truth may well be that Plato was not completely clear in his own mind and that the theory is an unstable amalgam. If however I were forced to choose, the interpretation I would reject is the Realist interpretation.

Provisionally, then, the theory implied in this passage is some form of sense-datum theory; and this conclusion brings what we have taken to be Plato's own views more or less into line with the theory which he calls the Mysteries of the subtle thinkers. We must now look more closely at this latter.

The theory is stated in terms of *kinêsis*, a word for which I have used various equivalents, such as "change", "process", "instability" and "activity". "Process" is perhaps the most convenient in this place. There are then four kinds of processes mentioned, namely two kinds of slow processes, that which can affect, and that which can be affected, and two kinds of quick process, namely that whereby an object comes to have some sense-quality, and that whereby a subject comes to sense it. Let us try to interpret this.

We will suppose that the two slow processes involved in a perception-transaction are the perceiving subject (say Jones) and the perceived object (say a stone). To describe Jones as a slow process would indeed be a strictly improper use of the abstract noun *kinêsis* (Jones's life might be a process, but not Jones himself); but this I think is not an impropriety which would have worried Plato very much. Jones and the stone are called processes, we will suppose, because for perception to occur each must be in a state of activity. Jones, we might say, must be emitting light from his eyes and the stone particles from its surface, as in the *Timaeus*. And anyhow since the theory is being stated in a Heraclitean context a thing can well be called a process as a concession to Heraclitus. Here, then, are our two slow processes, Jones and the stone, and they are slow because, in themselves apart from anything that they do, they remain much the same over a period of time. But when they get near enough to each other their two gradual and placid activities impinge on each other and create some kind of a disturbance. Jones's cones of light from his eyes, perhaps, collide with the particles given off by the stone, and this sets up a rapid two-way process, or pair of rapid processes, by which Jones comes to see and the stone to be white.

18

It is easy to see that on this interpretation the theory given as the Mysteries is a generalised version, uncommitted as to physical and physiological detail, of the account given in the *Timaeus*. But there are difficulties in this interpretation.

Firstly this is not a Phenomenalist account of perception, but a version of the Causal Theory; it mentions two physical objects, namely the two slow processes, Jones and the stone. Now if Jones and Smith both look at the same stone, the same physical object is interfering with, and giving rise to sensations in, both of them. In one sense they have a common object. No doubt their sense-data are private, and Jones sees the stone as grey whereas Smith, who has jaundice, sees it as khaki; but it is the same stone which affects them in these different ways. Now at times in his exposition Socrates talks as if this was the picture he is trying to paint; but at other times he does not. When talking of wine which tastes sour to a sick man (159) he speaks of the same object interacting with different subjects, the normal and the sick, and thus begetting different progeny. But there are other places where he speaks in different terms. Thus in 157 b–c he says that men and stones and other objects ought strictly to be spoken of, on the theory, as collections (*hathroismata*) of the things which come into existence only momentarily and in relation to each other; and it is clear from the context that these momentary entities are sense-data and the awareness of them. But this whole Heraclitean denial that there are any persistent things which exist in their own right, but only a world of momentary sense-data and their correlative sensations, is, verbally at least, inconsistent with the Causal Theory. According to the Causal Theory my glimpse of the stone, indeed, exists only in relation to me, but the stone itself exists in its own right and endures through time whether anybody is seeing it or not. It does not come into existence when it is seen; it has to be there beforehand in order to cause the seeing.

Now this objection may not seem very serious. It is true that, on the Causal Theory, there do exist enduring and independent objects constituting the physical world, but it is also true that we can never be directly aware of them. As Locke saw it is necessary to locate the causes of our sensations in space and to attribute to them some kind of activity; but as Locke also saw[1] it is logically incoherent to ascribe to them any sensible properties. (This is the point of the famous distinction between primary and secondary qualities, and it is also the reason why the Causal Theory, though taken for granted by many scientists and by educated common sense, is seldom popular among philosophers). But if we cannot attribute sensible properties to the physical objects which are postulated as the causes of our

[1] Though not, perhaps, quite clearly.

19

sensations, then obviously they form no part of the world of our experience. As Berkeley said, even if you suppose that they exist, you have to admit that our experience might be precisely the same though they did not. Therefore it might be argued that, when Socrates says that, on the theory he has outlined, there are no enduring and independent objects, he is speaking loosely but perfectly naturally. For the independent objects that the theory postulates never enter into our experience. When we talk of the tree, we are talking of the tree as we experience it, not of whatever it is that causes our experience; and the tree as we experience it is a collection of momentarily existing sense-data. Provided that "the world" means "the world of experience" it is perfectly true that the world contains nothing but collections of momentary entities.

This is all very well, but one would have expected Socrates to throw a sop, now and then, in the name of accuracy to the enduring physical objects that the theory postulates, if that is indeed the correct interpretation of the theory. And there is worse than that. Not only does he often speak of the world as if the causes of our sensations did not exist, there is one place where he actually says about the causes things which ought only to be said about their effects. This is 160 c 4–5, where Socrates says: "Therefore, since that which affects me" (*to eme poioun*, the phrase which, on this interpretation, means "the cause of my sense-data") "exists to me only, I also alone perceive it."

I do not want to make too heavy weather of this. No doubt it can be dismissed as a slip. But surely it at least suggests that if Plato intends an interpretation along the lines of the Causal Theory he is not perfectly clear in his own mind of the logic of his theory.

But there is a further difficulty about this interpretation, and it concerns the rapid processes. For Plato talks of two rapid processes, and, though I tried to conceal it in my exposition above, we have really only found one. If the rapid processes are the effects of the two objects on each other, the effect of the stone on Jones is clear—it gives him a sense-datum—but what is the effect of Jones on the stone? No doubt his cones of light could be thought to cause some disturbance at its surface as they collide with the particles it gives off; but this is clearly a negligible effect, and anyhow it is not the effect which Socrates describes.

What precisely does Socrates say about the rapid processes? He says the following (156–7): "the slow process or activity carries on its activity (*kinêsis*) in the same place and in relation to its environment". This means, I think, not that the slow processes never move, but that their activity does not consist in moving; and that their activity consists in their effects upon their neighbours. Then he says

20

that when two of these slow processes come together their inter-course begets a twin offspring, and that these twin offspring are quicker, travel, and exercise their activity in travelling. Thus, he goes on, when an eye meets an appropriate object (*summetron*) they beget a sense-quality, e.g. whiteness, and the corresponding sensation; and the sight travels from the eyes and the whiteness travels from the object, so that the eye becomes full of sight and sees, while "the other parent of the colour" is filled with whiteness and becomes white.

Looked at close to, this is a very odd account. One puzzling feature is the use of the abstract nouns "whiteness" and "sight" as names of things that travel between the two parties. For Plato is writing carefully here; thus he troubles to say that the eye becomes "not sight, but a seeing eye", while the object becomes "not whiteness, but white". Clearly then when he uses the words "whiteness" and "sight" he uses them on purpose, whatever he means by them. "Sight" is perhaps not too troublesome, for the stream of light is referred to in the *Timaeus* (45 c 3) as *opseôs reuma* or a stream of sight; but what can "whiteness" stand for? If we make "sight" stand for the light flowing in one direction, what is supposed to be flowing in the opposite direction and to be called whiteness? No doubt it is the particles given off by the object; but these are odd candidates for the name "whiteness". Then again there is something odd about the direction of travel. For sight travels *from* the eyes (*pros* with the genitive; it seems hard to translate this "towards") and whiteness *from* the object, and the result of this is that "the eye therefore becomes full of sight and sees at that moment, and becomes not sight but a seeing eye, while the other parent of the colour is filled with whiteness and becomes, not whiteness again, but white" (156 e 2–5). But if the whiteness travels *from* the stone, why does the stone thereby become filled with whiteness? If water travels from a tap it is the bucket and not the tap that gets filled.

Perhaps the best we can do towards a physical picture is the following. When the *Timaeus* comes to talk of the perception of colours (67–8) it speaks of colour as "a flame flowing off from every object, having its particles appropriate (*summetra*) to sight in relation to perception" (67 c 6–7). The theory seems to be that different kinds of fire correspond to different colours, the different kinds of fire having particles of different sizes, some of them being larger, some smaller, and some the same size as the particles constituting the *opsis*, the stream of light from the eyes called sight. As the *opsis* and the flame of colour flow through each other in opposite directions, the jostling effect of their particles on each other varies with the variations of the particles constituting the colour-flame, and that is how we see different colours. Clearly in that case it would not be too

21

far-fetched to use the word "whiteness" as the name of that kind of flame whose particles are such as to make us see white. Then whiteness, in the sense of the appropriate flame, would travel from the object along the beam of sight, and the beam of sight would travel from the eyes to the object. But this still leaves us wondering why the eyes are filled with sight and the object with whiteness, and not the other way round. Obviously if "the eyes are filled with sight" is simply a florid way of saying "the eyes see", and if "the stone is filled with whiteness" just means "the stone looks white", all is well. But if we take that interpretation we make Plato use "sight" and "whiteness" to stand for two different things (streams of particles, and the sensations that their interaction results in) in consecutive sentences in a passage in which he makes almost a parade of precision.

This is unsatisfactory, and it tempts one to abandon a physical picture in favour of a metaphorical one. For the stone, as we have just seen, can easily be said to be filled with whiteness in a metaphorical sense.

Let us then try a picture more in accordance with Phenomenalism, or Russell's Neutral Monism, than with Locke's Causal Theory. In this picture the two slow processes are not two physical objects in a state of steady physical activity, but two sets of sensory phenomena. Jones is a gradually growing biography of sense-perceptions, and the stone a gradually growing history of sense-data. Jones is the sum of his experiences and the stone is the sum of the experiences of which it would ordinarily be called the object. To talk of the stone is to talk of the views, pressures and so on that people have of it, to talk of people is to talk of the experiences that they have. In this picture "when two slow processes come together" means something like "when their histories intersect". The rapid processes which thereupon occur are no more than Jones's view of the stone. This is indeed the same thing as the coming together of the two slow processes, but in a metaphorical account this does not perhaps matter. Jones's view of the stone, which occurs instantaneously when Jones sees the stone, is described as *two* rapid processes because the sight of something can be analysed into two, logically distinct, components, the sense-datum and the sensing of it. Sight is said to travel from the eye because of course it is the eye that sees, and whiteness to travel from the stone because the whiteness seen is thought of as "coming from over there". The eye is filled with sight in an easily understood metaphorical sense, and the stone is filled with whiteness analogously. Since the travelling of the sight and the whiteness is purely metaphorical the difficulties about the direction of travel no longer arise.

This picture has the advantage that it abolishes the physical objects.

22

If this seems too daring, we may remember that Plato denied the status of *onta* to material things; and there seems to be one place (*Symposium* 207 e–208 b) where he is prepared to treat human minds as consisting of nothing but the sum of what would ordinarily be called their acts and experiences, where men are nothing but a stream of transient thoughts, feelings and sensations. This interpretation, then, is not too daring for Plato; and of course it suits the present context very well. For as we have seen the Causal Theory of perception does not strictly allow one to say the Heraclitean things which Socrates deduces from what he says in this passage. The meta-phorical interpretation, by giving us a Phenomenalist or Neutral Monist picture, does indeed delineate a world in which nothing en-dures (except in the way in which a stream endures) nor exists in its own right, but everything is a collection of momentary entities, such as sense-data and sensings of them, existing only in relation to each other.

This is a strong argument in favour of the metaphorical inter-pretation of the doctrine of the Mysteries, but the interpretation is, nonetheless, untenable. The trouble is this. When Socrates turns to refute rampant Heracliteanism he first carefully distinguishes *kinêsis* into motion and other kinds of change. He then recalls the doctrine of the Mysteries in words which make it perfectly clear that the travelling of the sense-quality and its appropriate sensation between the object and the subject is supposed to be a case of motion (182 a 3–6 and c 9 and d 5). In face of this it is impossible to maintain that the metaphorical interpretation tells the whole story.

We are forced therefore to fit the slow processes and the rapid processes into a physical picture. No doubt the two slow processes will have to be Jones and the stone, described as slow processes because they exert a steady effect on their environment. And no doubt the two rapid processes, being cases of motion, will have to be the streaming of light from Jones's eyes and of the flame of colour from the stone. The picture is still a blurred picture, both for the reason given above, that the eyes are filled with the "sight" that streams *from* them, and also because the only travelling that we can find, namely the travelling of the two sets of particles, is surely not something that "is begotten", and rapidly *happens*, when the two slow processes approach, but something that *goes on all the time*. We still want, for the rapid processes, something that happens instan-taneously when and only when perception occurs. The *interference* between the two sets of particles is no doubt such a happening; but how do we make this into two processes, each travelling rapidly in the opposite direction?

What happens rapidly or instantaneously when a subject and an object come into range is that the object is perceived and that the subject perceives it; and this is how we naturally want to take the two rapid processes. But if we do take them in that (metaphorical) way the conclusion follows that Plato's doctrine is inconsistent with itself; and that is probably the right conclusion.

Perhaps the following is the best account of the matter. What Plato intends to put forward is a version of the Causal Theory, but he does not fully understand the logic of the theory, which requires two sets of terms, one to stand for things as they are in themselves, the other for things as they are perceived. Let us call the stone as it is in itself the physical object and the stone as it is in perception the empirical object, and let us make a similar distinction between Jones as the physical subject and Jones as the empirical subject. This duplication of terminology does not of course mean a duplication of entities; it only means that there are on the theory two ways of considering every object. We are supposing that there is some kind of activity located at a certain point in space which causes in us the sense-experiences which we call views or feels of the stone, and this activity is not perceived (we do not see the particles which are supposed to stream off the stone; we see the grey expanse which they cause us to see). And similarly there is some kind of activity going on in ourselves by virtue of which we are enabled to perceive, and this activity again is not itself an object of perception.

Now when the physical subject and the physical object are in a certain spatial relationship to each other the physical activity of the one interferes with the physical activity of the other, producing various disturbances in the nervous system, and ultimately in the brain of the physical subject. The result of this is the birth of a "twin progeny", namely the sensing by the empirical subject of a sense-datum belonging to the empirical object. Since, on the theory, our sensations are *due to*, but are never *of* the physical activity of the physical object, it follows that no sense-qualities can be ascribed to this physical activity. One cannot talk, for example, of the emission of white particles, but only of the emission of the kind of particles which produce white sense-data in normal percipients. The scientist who wants to advance a detailed explanatory hypothesis to account for perception will want to offer some kind of description of the type of physical activity correlated with a particular type of sense-datum; but he will find that he can only do so, at best, in terms of *primary* qualities—shape, size, velocity and so on. This Plato does in the *Timaeus* in terms of shapes and sizes of particles, and the modern physicist in terms of wave-lengths, frequencies and so on. Primary-quality words such as "triangular" may therefore be usable both on the physical and on the empirical side, but secondary-quality words

24

such as "white" must be confined to the description of empirical objects.[1]

Plato however fails to observe this rule. He allows himself to talk of whiteness travelling when he intends to refer to the travelling of a certain kind of particle. Instead of saying something like: "when the appropriate particles travel from the physical stone a white sense-datum of the empirical stone is sensed", he says: "when whiteness flows from the stone the stone is filled with whiteness." This is puzzling language in itself, and what is worse it confuses the physical with the empirical stone. This is dangerous for the following reason. There are certain sentences in which the expression "the empirical stone" can function as subject which are harmless enough when taken in the right way; for example: "The empirical stone exists only when it is being perceived." Rightly understood this sentence expresses a tautology, since it is no more than a round-about way of expressing the definition of "the empirical stone" as "the stone as it is in perception". But if the distinction between "the empirical stone" and "the physical stone" is not drawn, trouble results. For "the stone exists only when it is perceived" seems to be an acceptable way of saying that the (empirical) stone is only filled with whiteness, hardness and its other observable properties when it is sensed. Yet it also seems to imply that there is no independent and enduring (physical) stone. Thus the lack of a distinction between the "physical" and the "empirical" stone allows the Causal Theory to topple over into Phenomenalism, and encourages Plato to think that the Causal Theory is able to bear the Heraclitean superstructure which he builds upon it. It would seem therefore that the hypothesis, that Plato intended to put forward a version of the Causal Theory, but failed to conform to the logical requirements for doing so, explains all the difficulties which we found in his account of the doctrine of the Mysteries.

This conclusion also allows us to bring the doctrine of the Mysteries into line with the account of perception which is drawn on by Socrates when he comes to describe the relationship between sensory activity and judgment. This is obviously a desirable result; for unless we were allowed to draw on the former it would be difficult to understand what Socrates meant by referring to sense-experiences as *pathêmata* or undergoings in the latter. There is then only one theory of perception in the *Theaetetus* and since it is presupposed by Socrates

---

[1] That Plato did in fact understand the relation between primary and secondary qualities in this way is clear from the *Timaeus* (see below pp. 221–2). See also an incidental remark in *Laws* X, 897 a, where he makes sense-properties such as warmth and whiteness *consequent upon* physical activities of increase, diminution, separation and combination.

25

when he is arguing in his own person we may conclude that Plato intends us to accept it as his own.

(v) *Our knowledge of the external world*

What then is Plato's conception of our knowledge of the external world? The activity of the things around us interferes with the activity of our bodies, thereby setting up *pathêmata* or disturbances in our bodies. These disturbances we are said to perceive, and this is *aisthêsis* or sense-perception (186 c 1). This again is loose language, for it suggests that we perceive the electrical impulses in our nerves or whatever it may be that is set up by external stimulation. It is, however, the same kind of looseness as that which we have just been considering, for it consists in combining the physical and the empirical vocabularies in an illegitimate way. We shall therefore confidently emend it, and say that we do not perceive the disturbances caused in our bodies by external stimulation but that we do perceive the sense-data to which they give rise. This I think is not only what Plato ought to say, but also what he means. This perceiving of sense-data is common to all organisms, and it does not constitute knowledge of the external world. Knowledge of the external world only arises when we notice the occurrence of our sense-data and, by comparison of one with another, assess their significance as pointers to our future experience, when we notice for example that we are perceiving the kind of objects to which we have learnt to give the name "black clouds", and conclude from this that we shall shortly experience what we have learnt to call rain. This means that knowledge of the external world is always knowledge of the significance of our experiences and of the patterns to which they conform. Of the real physical activity of the real physical things which give rise to our experience we can have no knowledge, but are confined to plausible conjecture such as that given in the *Timaeus* (which repeatedly stresses the conjectural nature of its doctrine).

The name which Plato gives to the having of sense-data is *aisthêsis*, the name which he gives to the activity of determining their significance is *doxa*. It follows from this definition that *aisthêsis* does not by itself give rise to any propositions about the world, and that predicates such as "true" cannot be used of it. It is simply something that happens to us and can be used as the raw material of true (or false) judgments. *Aisthêsis* therefore cannot be identified with *epistêmê*. *Epistêmê* is to be looked for in the sphere of *doxa*, in the sphere where "the mind concerns itself with things that are, itself according to itself " (187 a 5).

(Verbally this is a bad description of *doxa*, for it suggests that *doxa* or knowledge of the external world is something that the mind achieves by its own resources; and this suggests the picture of *aisthêsis* and *doxa* as parallel "faculties", the former putting us in touch with sensible objects, the latter giving us some kind of intellectual intuition of *onta* or things that are really real. However congenial this may be to certain conventional pictures of Platonism it must be rejected. There is no reference in this passage to any knowledge of supra-sensible entities and hence the idea that the sphere of *doxa* is a sphere in which the mind dispenses with *aisthêsis* is quite out of place. Reality and truth are attained to by *use* of sense-data, and it is within this "properly mental activity" that *epistêmê* is to be looked for).

Note on the refutation of the extreme Heraclitean thesis.

Something must be said to justify the view (whose truth I have assumed above) that the *Theaetetus* contains an intended refutation of what I have called the rampant Heraclitean view of the natural world. For it has often been held that this is not the case, but that the *Theaetetus* resists the equation of *aisthêsis* with *epistêmê* by conceding to the Heracliteans that the natural world (which is the object of *aisthêsis*) is radically unstable, while hinting that there exist other entities (viz. the forms) which are, being stable, fit objects of knowledge. So far as I know this view was first effectively challenged in recent times by Mr G. E. L. Owen in *The Classical Quarterly* for 1953.

In the vital passage (182 c 9-d 5) Socrates says: "If everything was in motion only, but not changing, we should be able to say what-like sorts of things the objects in motion flow. . . . But if[1] not even this is stable, namely that that which flows flows white, but this too changes, so that there is flux of just this thing, whiteness, and change into some other colour, in order that it may not be caught staying the same, how then will it be possible to name any colour so as to speak of it correctly?". I have taken this to mean that Socrates has no objection to an account of apparently stable entities which makes them consist of particles[2] in continuous motion or something of the kind, provided that their continuous activity is such as to permit them occasionally to manifest stable sense-properties over a period of time, this proviso being a necessary condition of the describability of physical things, and of there being such a thing as *aisthêsis* for *epistêmê* to be identical with. This interpretation may be challenged on the ground that Socrates has earlier said (154 a 7–9 and 159 e 7–160 a 3) that no two sense-perceptions are ever exactly alike, from which it might seem that we can infer that he does not believe that anything ever does manifest stable sense-properties. An alternative interpretation of the crucial passage may be preferred as follows. Socrates is not concerned with the describability of the physical world. Physical things, and even the activity of perceiving, may be totally in flux; but knowledge is not. He is not concerned to say: "I don't mind inconstancy on the microscopic level so long as I am allowed reasonable macroscopic constancy." He is willing to consign the physical world, and ourselves as sentient beings with it, to the Heracliteans; he only wants stability in the realm of the intellect. His argument

[1] Literally "since" (*epeidê*). But Socrates must mean "since, on the theory which I cannot accept, . . .", for Socrates is now introducing the view which leads to the unacceptable conclusion that all that one can ever say of anything is that it is not-P.

[2] For the introduction of particles see the last but one paragraph of this note.

is not that we could not describe a totally fluid world, but that we could not describe with totally fluid predicates. The "flux of whiteness" which he speaks of as something which it would be difficult to allow is not what I have taken it to be (namely that the plate is never on two successive occasions the same colour); rather it is that *whiteness* is always changing into some other colour. The flux in fact that Socrates cannot agree to is not an inconstancy in the whiteness of a white thing, but an inconstancy in whiteness itself. We must insist that whiteness is always whiteness[1] though we need not insist (indeed should deny) that anything is ever continuously white. What would happen if whiteness were not always the same is not that we could never describe any physical thing (it is strictly the case on Heraclitean principles that we cannot in fact do this anyhow) but rather that we could never "name" or "speak of" (*proseipein* and *prosagoreuein*, d 4–5) any colour. The argument is in fact: "We have names for colours; therefore colours must be constant", and not: "We speak of plates as e.g. white; therefore the whiteness of plates must sometimes be constant." Things, that is, can be indefinitely unstable, but properties cannot be unstable at all. It might be added by those who favour this interpretation that, although whiteness and other colour-properties are doubtless not themselves forms, one of the purposes of the demonstration that properties cannot be unstable is to remind us that forms have the stability which is common to all properties, and hence are fit objects of knowledge. In this way we can link up the view that what Socrates is doing in these sentences is to tell us that properties cannot change with the "conservative" interpretation of the *Theaetetus* according to which one of Plato's main purposes in writing it is to hint to us that knowledge is always of the forms.

It must be allowed that this reading of the crucial sentences fits the text very nicely at certain points. Socrates asks for example (182 d 4–5): "how then will it be possible to name any colour so as to speak of it correctly?", and not: "how then will it be possible to name *anything's* colour . . . ?". (The view that we are following has to take "any colour" to mean "anything's colour"). I agree also that Plato wants to make the point that properties are not themselves subject to change. This is probably what Socrates is getting at in 182 a 3–b 7; and it was of course a necessary part of the task of extricating the notion of a property that the point should be made that things change their properties, and that properties are what change is *from* and *to*, and not what *changes*. But I do not think that this is all that Plato wants to tell us in the passage under consideration, though it is possible that he did not see clearly that the two points are distinct.[2] Like its rival, the interpretation that we have followed can also be said to fit the text very nicely at certain points. For example in 182 c 9–10 the words: "If everything were in motion only but not changing, we should be able to say what-like sorts of things (*hoia atta*) the objects in motion flow" seem to say: "Let A be in motion; provided it is not also changing qualitatively we shall be able to describe it", where this lends itself to the interpretation that things which are in motion (in some sense) can be said to be, e.g. white if neither their motion nor the motion of their particles nor anything else causes them to cease to be white. Again in d 1 the words "that that which flows flows white" (which are used to express a proposition which is denied by the Heraclitean view under discussion) suggest not that whiteness stays white, but that some admittedly flowing thing stays white—e.g.

---

[1] This is of course logically necessary, in that the notion of whiteness becoming some other colour makes no sense. It would be anachronistic to say in so many words that this is Socrates' point, but on the interpretation that we are considering this will be the modern version of his point.

[2] For it might be rather easy for him to confuse "whiteness is constant" with "*Cases of* whiteness are constant".

this plate. These words suggest, then, that Socrates is attacking a view according to which things which flow do not go on flowing in the same manner, i.e. is arguing that things may flow, and yet flow in such a way as to be, for example, continuously white. These words, then, seem to support our interpretation, even if the succeeding words ("so that there is flux of just this thing, whiteness, and change into some other colour") might seem to support its rival. And yet these last words do not support the latter very strongly, for it is surely not too difficult to take "flux of ... whiteness" as "flux of ... the whiteness of S". This is the easier when we remember that "flux of ... whiteness" is advanced as the alternative to "that *that which* flows flows white".

It seems then that neither reading fits the words of the text perfectly and that each fits it tolerably. We shall have to try to decide between them on general grounds. Perhaps the three most potent considerations which can be advanced against the reading of this passage which accords with the "conservative" interpretation are the following.

1. Whatever Socrates is doing here, it ought to be relevant to the truth of Protagoras' central thesis, for it is this that the examination of Heraclitus' doctrines is designed to test. On the conservative interpretation Socrates is consigning the physical world to the Heracliteans. It might seem that this gives us all the relevance that we need, on the ground that if the physical world is as the Heracliteans say it is, then presumably all statements about it are strictly speaking false, and then presumably none of them, not even those based on present perception, will be true, nor count as knowledge. If this is acceptable (about which I have doubts) it establishes the required connection between what Socrates says and what he is supposed to be trying to show; but the overall result seems to be very much out of key with what Plato is trying to do in this part of the *Theaetetus*. For he seems to be trying to examine rather carefully how we get the information that we possess about the material world, which of our beliefs about it are to be regarded as "objective", and so forth. To this end the general statement that no empirical judgment is strictly true is of no use whatever. The blanket condemnation of all empirical judgments is just as anarchic as, and in the end little different from, Protagoras' blanket endorsement of them all. "All judgments about the natural world are false because each implies a permanence which does not in fact obtain" and "All judgments about the natural world are true because each is about just one momentary private sense-occurrence" come to very much the same thing, and neither fits well with, for example, the doctrine that the expert is more likely to be right about the future than the non-expert. Plato seems to want to tell us that we derive our information about the natural world not from just having sense-experiences but from intelligent "reckoning-up" of the patterns into which they fall. To this purpose it is helpful to point out that the instability of the natural world is not total; it is not helpful to concede that it is.

2. The doctrine that objects are inconstant with respect to colour, but that colours themselves are constant, must be allowed to be very mysterious. For whiteness, for example, must surely be identified with the colour of white things. It is unplausible to suppose that it is the archetypal white patch in the visual sense-field of Eternal Reason. (The case would have been different if Plato had given as his example of something constant an "intelligible" property such as circularity, for we could then have supposed that circularity was something other than the property common to objects generally called circular). This mysterious doctrine could, I suppose, be understood in either of two ways. We shall have to suppose that things which apparently stay white actually fluctuate within a band of similar but not identical shades, and we shall have to suppose also *either*

that "whiteness" is the name of just one of these shades (with the result that nothing is ever continuously white), *or* that "whiteness" is the name of the band of shades within which an object is allowed to fluctuate without forfeiting its title to the description "white" (with the result that things can stay white, but that "staying white" does not entail "staying just the same"). The constancy of whiteness will have to consist *either* in the fact that "whiteness" is the name of just one shade, *or* in the fact that, although a number of shades fall under it (as a number of visual appearances fall under the description "dingy"), nevertheless the shades that fall under it are always just those shades; a word which is to be of any use can be indefinite in meaning in that what falls under it may be a range which includes considerable variation, but it cannot be indefinite in meaning in that what falls under it is now one range, now another. It is true that the doctrine that things are inconstant in point of colour, but that colours themselves are constant, *can* be understood in either of these two ways (only the first of which, incidentally, allows the point that Socrates is now making to contain the refutation of Protagoras' central thesis which we suggested above); but it is not true that Plato gives us any indication how we are to understand his point, on the assumption that this is the point that he is making. We are left to puzzle out for ourselves how whiteness can be something constant when things are inconstant in respect of colour.

3. On any view Plato does not make it clear quite how he thinks he has shown that we cannot "agree that *epistêmê* is *aisthêsis*, at any rate along the 'everything is unstable' road" (183 c 1 sqq.). On the interpretation we have followed the point is that there are entities other than sense-data to be known (namely the patterns into which they fall), this suggesting the conclusion that reports of present sense-experience are on the wrong logical level, so to speak, to count as cases of knowledge. It is true that this point is not clearly brought out, though it has been fairly well indicated that Protagoras' views require a world of disconnected, atomistic sense-data, and that this requires that the world be as inconstant as the rampant Heracliteans say it is. But it is a sound point; it is entirely consistent with what was said earlier about hearing people talking in a foreign language, and with what is to be said later about reckoning-up our sense-experiences with reference to existence and utility; and it would seem to be about the only way in which Plato could show that *judgments based on present perception* are not all true and do not count as knowledge—for we have been allowed to get the impression that these are incorrigible, so that it is only if truth involves something more than incorrigibility that we can deny them truth. And it does depend on showing that the physical world is not totally inconstant. But on the conservative interpretation what are we to say are Plato's grounds for denying that such judgments count as knowledge, and thus finally getting rid of Protagoras? If his grounds are to be valid they cannot really be what I suggested earlier that they might be, namely that the objects of *aisthêsis* are inconstant and hence cannot have true statements made about them. For "This is now pink to me" can be true however inconstant "this" may be. In other words, if we are considering the hypothesis that all judgments based on present perception may be true since such a judgment commits its maker to nothing about the future, or the past, or any other sense-experience whatever except the one that is being currently described, then it will not do to dismiss this hypothesis by arguing that such a judgment *would* be false *if it did* imply constancy, i.e. *if it did* commit its maker to something about the future or the past or someone else's experience. If therefore we are to find for Plato a valid reason for denying that such judgments count as knowledge, it cannot be, I think, that the *objects* of *aisthêsis* are inconstant; it must be that *aisthêsis itself* is inconstant, and therefore cannot be a kind of

epistêmê, this being assumed to be something constant. Now on the conservative view Socrates does not argue that, if the natural world is inconstant, sensory activity must be so also, for what he is saying at 182 d 8 sqq., on that view, is that if whiteness itself (as opposed to white things) were inconstant, then sensing itself (as opposed to sentient activity) would, by parity of reasoning, be inconstant also; and this does not come to the same thing.[1] But it could be said that this has sufficiently hinted that percipient subjects are in the same boat with the objects of their perceptions, from which we could no doubt conclude that if the natural world is unstable, then our sensory apparatus is so also. It must be allowed, too, that the conservative view can argue with some plausibility that Plato might well have assumed that readers who would not boggle at the inconstancy of the bodily function of perceiving would boggle at that of the spiritual function of knowing, and therefore reject the linking of the two; but two difficulties remain. The first is that it is necessary for the argument that it should be *shown* that everything changes in every way all the time; it is not enough that it should be conceded that this *may* be so. It is only if *aisthêsis is* inconstant that it cannot be a kind of *epistêmê*. But Socrates does not in the least seem to argue that everything in the natural world, including our sense-apparatus, *does in fact* change in every way all the time; the most that the conservative view can claim is that he argues that *even* if this is so, still properties themselves cannot change. But this is not enough to show that sensing, being inconstant, cannot be a kind of knowing. (A version of this objection also holds against the view that Plato's reason for denying that *aisthêsis* is a kind of *epistêmê* is that the objects of *aisthêsis* are inconstant; for the most that can be claimed is that it is conceded that it is possible, not that it is said to be true). And secondly it is very difficult to believe that when Plato subsequently comes to discuss the contributions of sensing and of reckoning-up to our acquisition of empirical information, he writes as if he thought that what goes on in our bodies is something totally inconstant.

The conservative view can get a measure of support from the fact that there are other places in Plato where the natural world is said to be a theatre of change, and where this is held to put difficulties in the way of our describing it. But it is perhaps significant that in the *Timaeus*, for example,[2] Timaeus does not object to describing things adjectivally; it is merely the application of substantives that he finds strictly misleading. However this may be, the considerations we have advanced tend to show, so far as this passage is concerned, that if Plato's purpose is to deny, on the ground that the natural world is totally inconstant, that *aisthêsis* is a kind of *epistêmê*, then his argument is somewhat incoherent. Since there are other interpretations which attribute to Plato a more coherent (and less silly) train of thought, it seems that the conservative interpretation is to be rejected. What then is to be said about the two passages (154 a 7–9 and 159 e 7–160 a 3)[3] in which Socrates seems to say that the content of one sense-experience is never identical with that of any other? The answer will have to be that what Socrates is here saying is that each sense-experience is independent of every other, in that the parties interacting in the one are always different from those which interact in the other. If, that is, I look at the table, and then look at it again, both the table and I will have changed, in small ways at least, on the second occasion, so that it cannot be assumed that the content of the two experiences will be identical; and indeed if one includes enough in what counts as one

---

[1] On any interpretation this particular sentence is counter-factual, i.e. is part of what Socrates cannot allow.

[2] *Timaeus* 49–50; see below p. 217.

[3] I am grateful to Mr. J. L. Ackrill for forcing me to clear my mind about these two passages.

sense-experience, and demands sufficiently high standards of identity, it can almost be assumed that the two contents will not be identical (something will have moved, the noise of the wind will have changed, my ear will have started to tickle, or . . . or . . . etc.). And the reason why Socrates is saying this is that he wants to argue that perceptual disagreement between two different percipients is not surprising, and that Protagoras is right, with certain qualifications, in holding that in such a case we cannot say that the one percipient is right and the other wrong. Each is having the sense-experience which was bound to arise from the interaction of just those factors which are interacting, each pair of factors is a unique pair, and therefore identity of offspring between one interaction and another (i.e. identity of content between two sense-experiences) must be the exception rather than the rule. If it is thought that I am putting rather a deflationary interpretation upon Socrates' words, I can perhaps retort that in the earlier of the two passages at any rate (154 a 7–9) we must deflate what he says a little, since Theaetetus accepts it without demur. Socrates and Theaetetus agree without argument that nothing can ever seem the same to someone else as it seems to oneself; indeed, they say, nothing can ever seem the same to oneself as it seemed on another occasion, on the ground that one is in a different state. But if this is accepted without argument, it must be meant as something fairly mild—that no two sense-experiences will ever be *totally* identical, or that it cannot be *assumed* that they will. It is very difficult to believe that they suppose themselves to be assenting to the paradoxical and dogmatic statement that the same thing never looks exactly alike on two distinct occasions. Perhaps we can conclude, then, that Socrates does not, in these two passages, mean to deny to the empirical world the element of stability which we took him to be attributing to it in 182.

It may be asked finally whether it is legitimate to construe "if everything was in motion only " in 182 c 9 as I have construed it, namely as if it were "if everything consisted of particles in motion only". I think that it is, for the following reasons. Firstly I can see no point in considering the hypothesis that everything[1] is in motion as a whole, for, in relation to the earth at any rate, this house for example plainly is not. It seems more worth while, therefore, to consider the hypothesis "that this house is in motion" in a form in which it is not plainly false, i.e. in the form in which it means that the house consists of nothing but moving things. It is the easier to take Socrates' words in this way in that, when he recently distinguished *kinêsis* or activity into motion and qualitative change, he reminded Theaetetus (182 a 5) that the sense-qualities of a thing depend on the motions which pass between subject and object; a thing's "becoming white" on being seen was a resultant of motions, the moving objects being, we decided, the particles constituting the *opsis* given off by the beholder, and those constituting the flame of colour given off by the beheld. In this context the hypothesis "that everything is in motion" is very naturally taken to be the hypothesis that everything consists of particles in motion. If it is objected that there will be on the theory certain entities which may well be at rest (e.g. the stone whose surface gives off the white flame), the answer must be that we have already seen that it is characteristic of this whole section of the dialogue that Plato is a little uncertain about the status of entities such as the physical stone. Certainly it is inaccurate to say that we never see anything but swarms of particles, but this is just the kind of inaccuracy which has troubled us throughout this argument.

I think we can conclude, then, that the purpose of this passage is to argue that the sane parts of the doctrine of the Heracliteans do not justify the multitudinous enigmatic apophthegms which, as Theodorus says at 180 a, these

---

[1] *Panta* from c 4 seems to be the subject of the verb.

philosophers are wont inconsistently to shoot at one, without staying to give an answer.[1] In other words, it is intended as a refutation of rampant Heracliteanism.

II. *DOXA* AND *EPISTÊMÊ*

A. *The concept of* doxa

What Plato has to say about *doxa* is mostly said in the course of contrasting it with *aisthêsis* on the one hand or with *epistêmê* on the other. We cannot of course assume that the word means precisely the same in these two contrasts. A man who in one place contrasts, say, feeling with thinking, and in another place thinking with knowing may, without equivocation, easily intend "thinking" to be taken in two rather different ways. "Thinking as opposed to feeling" may be a wider notion than "thinking as opposed to knowing", just as "animals as opposed to vegetables" is a wider notion than "animals as opposed to men".

Doxa then is a term which is employed primarily in contrasts; Plato says little about the meaning of the word on its own, and perhaps there is not very much that can be said. There is however what follows.

In the passage we have just been examining *doxazein* the verb and *doxa* the noun stand as we saw for the activity of assessing or interpreting the significance of material; or rather, for the decision in which that activity culminates. Socrates says a little further on (189–90) that thinking (*dianöeisthai*) is silent discussion and that *doxazein* is the decision which the discussion comes to. A *doxa* therefore is something one asserts to oneself, and it is based on some kind of assessment of material.

That a *doxa* is based on silent discussion is not always an essential part of the word's meaning. Commonly elsewhere (e.g. *Theaetetus* 201) it is said to be a mark of a *doxa* that one can be induced, persuaded or jockeyed into holding it. Knowledge must be taught but *doxa* can be induced by any method which secures the victim's assent to a proposition. *Doxa* in other words, like "belief", does not strictly imply the existence of grounds.

On the other hand there are one or two places (e.g. *Theaetetus* 189) which suggest that the verb *doxazein* is nearer to "judge" than to "believe". For "judge" implies (more clearly than "believe") that something is being assessed or interpreted; and so it is, I think, with

[1] One gets strongly the impression from this speech of Theodorus' that Plato thinks that some of the Heracliteans are rather silly. There is also the general impression that he is mediating between the Heraclitean belief in total instability and the Eleatic belief in total changelessness. These impressions militate against the conservative view.

doxazein. The word is etymologically connected with the notion of seeming (*dokein*) and retains some flavour of "putting an interpretation upon". This I suspect helps to create the problem of false beliefs which puzzled so many Greek thinkers. For when I believe something false, I, in one sense, "judge what is not"; but yet when I judge I must judge something, so that I must in another sense "judge what is". You cannot construct this contradiction with "believe", for I believe what is not, but I believe it *about* something that is.[1]

Doxa, then, though it is the general word for "belief", tends to carry with it the hidden, but sometimes operative, implication that the belief in question is an assessment of something. This is an important clue to the contrast of *doxa* with *epistêmê*, to which we must now turn; for *epistêmê* implies that the object is not being interpreted or assessed, but grasped.

B. *The contrast between* doxa *and* epistêmê. *Introductory*

A great deal hangs on the contrast between *doxa* and *epistêmê*. Indeed some will tell us that the fallacious distinction between these two concepts is the root error from which the whole of Platonism grew. What Plato did, they will say, is to notice that *doxazein*, "to believe", does not mean the same as *epistasthai*, "to know". What he failed, very naturally, to see is that this is only because, when I say that Jones knows that S is P, I commit myself to the truth of "S is P", whereas I do not do so when I only say that Jones believes this proposition. Therefore I cannot say: "Jones knows that S is P; but he may be wrong." Hence it appears that to know is to do something which is infallible (cp. *Republic* 477 e 6–7). Deceived by this appearance, the argument runs, Plato assumed that believing and knowing were the exercise of two different faculties, each with its appropriate kind of object. He looked therefore for an infallible faculty, and for objects upon which it could plausibly be exercised. Since our beliefs about ordinary things can always be wrong, special objects, having a special affinity to the mind, had to be invented to become the objects of knowledge. For various reasons universals and mathematical entities seem best fitted to play this role, and hence a special brand of self-subsistent universals, and perhaps mathematical entities, had to be invented. This is the origin of the belief in forms.

I do not deny that Plato may have thought along these lines, but I think that we shall find that there is a good deal more to it than that.

A contrast between two intellectual levels is very pervasive in Plato's writings from the *Gorgias* to the *Laws*. The word for the

[1] For further discussion of the Paradox of False Belief see below, pp. 486–98.

34

lower level is fairly constantly *doxa*, though in the *Gorgias* (454, 462–5 and 501) the words *pistis* ("conviction") and *empeiria* ("experience") turn up instead. *Epistêmê* is commonly used for the higher level, but we also find its near-synonym *gnôsis*, and also such words as *nöêsis* (which rather implies "understanding") and *sophia* (commonly translated "*wisdom*"). The looseness of language is of course typically Platonic, but it is also perhaps due to the fact that the higher level consists in the attainment of the intellectual goal, which can be looked at in more than one way and called by more than one name, whereas the lower level consists in a practically adequate approximation to it.

The major discussions of *doxa* and *epistêmê* are to be found in the *Meno*, *Republic* and *Theaetetus*; and there is an illuminating discussion of *epistêmê* in the Seventh Letter. Before we turn to detailed examination of these passages we shall describe certain general impressions which can be got from them and also from the shorter discussions in other dialogues.

C. *General impressions of the contrast between* doxa *and* epistêmê

1. Knowledge (if I may use the English words without necessarily intending their English meaning) is of course superior to belief, and its superiority seems to reside (*a*) in the *directness* (*Republic* Books 6 and 7) with which a man who knows is related to what is really the case, and consequently (*b*) in the *infallibility* of knowledge. On the whole what Plato seems to have in mind by "fallibility" is the tendency of something which we only believe to let us down when we come to apply it to a particular situation (cp. *Meno* 96–8, discussed p. 52 below). This suggests that he is chiefly, though not exclusively, thinking of his contrast as one which is useful in the context of pieces of *general* information; for it is general information which can be applied in various situations.

2. Knowledge is bound up with understanding, and hence has to be conveyed by teaching whereas belief can be induced by training, persuasion and so on. We have already quoted this point from *Theaetetus* 201, and it comes out in the discussion of the courage of the soldiers in *Republic* 429–30. In this connection there is a noteworthy passage in the *Timaeus* (51–2). Here Timaeus has been making use of forms in his account of nature, and he pauses briefly in order to justify doing so. Some, he says, hold that particulars are the only realities, the universals of which they are said to be instances being only "expressions we use" (*logoi*). His reply to this (which he admits is summary) is that, if *nous* or intelligent understanding is not the same thing as right belief, then there must be something which can be grasped by the mind, though not by the senses, to be the object

of the former. But in fact these two states of mind are different. Intelligent understanding is a rare state which can only arise through teaching, involves an accurate account (*alêthês logos*),[1] and is not dislodged by persuasion. Right belief on the other hand is something all men share in, is not rational, and is inculcated, and thus can be destroyed, by persuasion. Therefore understanding and belief are distinct, and therefore there exist self-consistent universals as the object of the former, and changeable sensible particulars as the object of the latter. This passage can clearly be used by those who hold that the forms were invented to give knowledge an object. Meanwhile, however that may be, it emphasises that knowledge (if we may identify *nous* and *epistêmê*) is something which exists at the rational level whereas belief is confined to the level (or levels) at which sense-perception is decisive and at which emotional appeals can be effective. Knowledge then is connected with understanding.

3. In particular it is connected with understanding why what is the case must be the case—with insight into necessity. This is said in *Meno* 96–8, though it might be held that doubt is cast upon it in the last section (201 onwards) of the *Theaetetus*.

4. A conflicting general impression. In some places it is implied that what we can believe we can also come to know. In other places it is implied that this is not so, that belief and knowledge have different "objects" or spheres of operation.

Thus in the *Meno* one can believe *or* know a proposition like that which describes the road to Larisa (97); and indeed the *Meno* gives the recipe for turning belief into knowledge. Similarly in the *Theaetetus* (201) it is said that an eye-witness may be the only person who can know the facts though the court may be induced to believe in them. These two passages allow knowledge and belief to have the same objects, and indeed allow that matters of empirical fact can be known.

Elsewhere, however, and perhaps predominantly, this is not so; knowledge has special objects, and matters of empirical fact are not among them. The *Meno*, as we shall see, is hardly consistent with itself and says things which make one wonder how it is possible, on its terms, to know the road to Larisa. The *Republic* speaks quite happily (Books 6 and 7) of the "sphere of belief", which seems to be at least closely related to the empirical world. In the passage from the *Timaeus* which we just looked at belief was connected with sensible particulars, and knowledge with universals. The same thing is said earlier in the same dialogue (*Timaeus* 27 d–28 a), where Timaeus begins his discussion by distinguishing "that which is at all times,

---

[1] This surely means an account which gives the reason for the fact in question, an account which gives insight.

and never becomes" and "that which becomes at all times, and never is", of which the first is "graspable by understanding (*nöêsis*) with rational insight (*logos*), being always the same", whereas the second "can only be judged by judgment (*doxa*), with non-rational perception (*aisthêsis*), since it comes and goes and never really is".

The same point, that that which changes cannot properly be known, is made in the *Philebus* (55–9). Socrates is examining the various branches of knowledge to test their purity, or in other words to see how much real knowledge each involves. To do this he puts branches of knowledge in order of *akribeia*, a notion which involves accuracy, but also more than that. Perhaps "finality" or "unrevisability" would do. At the bottom go practical arts, those like carpentry which involve mathematical techniques being preferred above those like music which do not. Pure mathematics is on the floor above, but the top stage is occupied by philosophy (*dialektikê*), which alone is unadulterated knowledge. The subjects on the ground floor are put there (59 a) because they rely on beliefs; not only music and architecture, but also cosmology, are belief-ridden subjects because they concern themselves with changeable particulars.

In the *Epinomis* (or thirteenth book of the *Laws*), however, cosmology is promoted. In the first book of the *Laws* it is said that a community needs some guardians of its laws who walk by wisdom (*phronêsis*) and some who walk by true belief. The astronomer-philosophers of the Nocturnal Council are provided to supply the former need. When the Athenian Stranger comes to consider the education these men are to receive, he asks himself what branch of knowledge entitles a man to be called wise (*Epinomis* 974–6). Every other branch of knowledge is rejected for one reason or another (in the case of medicine and rhetoric the reason being that these subjects rely on beliefs) except for an astronomico-mathematical brand of philosophy which involves a grasp of the perfect harmony of the motions of the heavenly bodies. Here therefore it is clearly allowed that certain changeable particulars can at any rate be the objects of something higher than belief.

5. In one or two places it seems to be implied that knowledge involves something like direct acquaintance, and thus goes beyond the ability to describe correctly. The point is perhaps made in the *Theaetetus* (208–9) in terms of a distinction between knowing *who* Theaetetus is, and knowing only *what sort of* man he is; and a similar distinction is made in the Seventh Letter (342–3). The idea that knowledge is to be thought of after the model of direct acquaintance could be made to take care of the man in the *Meno* who knows the road to Larisa and of the eye-witness in the *Theaetetus* who knows what the prisoner did.

To sum up these general impressions, then, knowledge is infallible; involves understanding in some sense, perhaps insight into why what is the case must be so; is commonly, though not always, confined to the sphere of things which do not change, which is a sphere from which facts about the empirical world are excluded; and finally it can be conceived after the model of direct acquaintance.

One view, then, is that we can only know things which do not change, and that this means that we cannot know the physical world. It is in the *Timaeus* that this view is most prominent, and it is to be noticed that in this dialogue three classes of objects are identified: (*a*) that which can be understood, (*b*) that which does not change, and (*c*) that which cannot be grasped by the senses. Moreover the *Timaeus* seems to argue that it is *because* physical things come into and pass out of existence that they cannot be known; and the *Philebus* seems to agree with it on this point.

This raises two problems. Firstly we remember that the *Theaetetus* argues that, although it may be true that physical things are in flux, the manner in which they are in flux does not make it impossible to describe them; for the flux results in the stable manifestation of properties such as whiteness. Now, whether or not the *Theaetetus* is earlier than the *Timaeus*, it is almost certainly earlier than the *Philebus*. But by the time of the *Theaetetus* Plato has seen that the kind of change which can plausibly be ascribed to the physical world does not render it indescribable; why then, one wants to ask, should it render it unknowable? Is the position of the *Theaetetus*, that the physical world may be impermanent, but is none the less describable, consistent with the position of the *Timaeus* and *Philebus* that its impermanence renders it unknowable?

The second problem which arises concerning this latter position is one of interpretation. What does it mean to say that the physical world is unknowable? If we are being told that there is no such thing as (for example) "knowing the sun", what is it that is here being denied? And similarly what is it that is being said to be impermanent, to "become and perish"? Is it the sun itself which becomes and perishes; and if so does this mean only that it is not an eternal object, or does it rather mean that its material is continually consumed and renewed? Or is it that *nothing about* the sun endures, that its size fluctuates, its path wanders, its temperature varies, and so on?

There are three rather tempting ideas which suggest themselves in the light of these difficulties. The first of these is that the *Timaeus* does not mean to tell us that we cannot know *facts about* the sun (to continue with that example), but only that there is no such thing as "knowing the sun". Things are what we can perceive, and they change; facts about things cannot be perceived by the senses but can

38

be grasped by the mind; and facts about things, even about changing things, do not themselves change. We can therefore know in what path the sun travels, though we cannot literally see this; and we can see, but cannot literally know, the sun itself. This is an attractive idea. The conception that the senses put us into touch with things, but that the mind puts us into touch with facts about them, reminds us of the distinction between *aisthêsis* and *doxa* in the *Theaetetus*. But unfortunately there are two fatal objections to this idea. Firstly if physical things are what we perceive, and if facts about physical things are among the things that we know, what is it that we believe? This objection may perhaps be answerable, but the second is not. It is simply that the use Timaeus makes of his distinction between knowledge and belief does not at all correspond to the suggestion we are considering. That the sun is of such and such a size or travels in such and such a path is not at all the sort of thing that Timaeus describes as "something that always is, and hence can be known". He introduces his distinction precisely in order to explain why his account of physical nature is and must be conjectural. Facts about nature therefore are exactly that which can only be believed. It is the rational necessities which must have determined the creative activity of the divine Craftsman that can be known.

The second tempting idea is that physical things are not *gignomena*, or things that become and perish, in the sense that they change, but in a different sense, the sense in which this and allied notions were used in the description of the Protagorean-Heraclitean Mysteries in the *Theaetetus*. In this sense natural objects are *gignomena* in that they only come into momentary existence when they are perceived; the tree as we know it only "becomes" when there is someone in the quad, and "perishes" when he goes away. The real physical activity which gives rise to the sense-data which constitute empirical objects is inaccessible except to conjecture; and the best that we can manage with the natural world is a knowledge of the patterns to which sense-experience conforms—in fact what the *Theaetetus* calls *doxa*.

The trouble with this suggestion is that it is far-fetched. "Change and decay in all around I see" is the natural reading of Timaeus' language about becoming and perishing, and it is difficult to believe that we were meant to understand anything else. It is *possible* that if we knew more of the things that were written and said by Plato's philosophical contemporaries we should see that "become and perish" could naturally be taken in some other way; but we cannot assume that this is so.

The third suggestion is on a rather different plane. It is that the *Timaeus* should not be taken too seriously. The dialogue is more a piece of cosmological speculation than of philosophy; the tone is

39

lofty and hierophantic and the philosophical issues it raises get rather summary treatment. How would it be then to say that Timaeus uses what looks like a clinching argument in order to make as briefly as possible a point which does not in fact depend at all upon that argument? Plato's real point is somewhat as follows:—Observation and theories based upon it can never put us into touch with the realities of nature; it can give us information about things as they affect our senses but not about things as they are in themselves. If we want a picture of things as they are in themselves the best we can have is a conjectural one. The conjecture will be a kind of bridge resting at one end on things that we can know and at the other end on things that we can observe. We can know the intelligible necessities which must have determined the Creator's ends but we cannot know how he may have set about realising them in the material available. This we can only conjecture by constructing hypotheses to explain the observed phenomena. Thus we can know that irregular shapes are offensive to reason, and we can know how many regular solids there are. We can know from this that the shapes of any three-dimensional particles there may be will be from among the regular solids. Reason will have decreed this. On the opposite bank we can observe, for example, that fire burns. Between these two ends we can build a bridge by supposing (as in *Timaeus* 56) that fire is made of pyramidal particles and owes its destructive powers to the sharp corners of the regular pyramid. However confident we may be of such a theory it must remain an explanatory hypothesis, and the intelligible facts (geometrical and other) which we can know are somewhat remotely related to it. We do not need to *suppose* that this is Plato's real point about certainty and uncertainty in the *Timaeus*, for it is clear that it is. What we will suppose is that Timaeus in the preface to his discourse wants to convey that what follows is a conjectural edifice, and cannot, without anticipating what he is going to say, describe the precise roles played in it by intelligible necessities, facts of observation and hypotheses linking the two. But there lies ready to hand what seems a clinching argument to show that cosmology must be conjectural: cosmology is about the world, the world is subject to change, and what changes cannot be known.

It may be felt that "what changes cannot be known", as applied to the world, rests on a fallacy exposed in the *Theaetetus* and that therefore in the *Philebus* at least Plato should have known better. One might perhaps reply to this that "what changes cannot be known, and therefore the physical world cannot be known" is the sort of error which is so natural that it can only be got rid of by frequent refutation. Whatever Plato may have done in the *Theaetetus* the error is hardy enough to reappear in the Sixth Book of Aristotle's *Ethics* (*E.N.* 1139 b 22).

We shall have to return to this later when we have examined the three major discussions of knowledge and belief. Meanwhile we can note that this preliminary discussion has the following result:—The doctrine that the physical world is impermanent and hence cannot be known (*a*) may perhaps represent an over-simplification of Plato's real thought into which he sometimes slipped and (*b*) is an unclear doctrine in that we are uncertain both in what sense the physical world is said to be impermanent and also what precisely it is said that we cannot know.

D. *The contrast between* doxa *and* epistêmê; *anticipation of conclusions*

The three major discussions of knowledge and belief are so complicated that a thread is needed to guide one through them. I shall try to provide such a thread in this section by anticipating the conclusions which I hope to come to.

The question: "what can human beings feed on?" admits of a formal and of a material interpretation. Formally interpreted, the answer expected is something like: "Any thing which can be absorbed through the digestive tract and used to build and maintain the tissues." But this formal answer having been given, the question can still be put materially by asking: "Well, and what kinds of things are these?"

So with the question: "What can we know?" The answer to the formal version of this question will lay down the conditions which anything must satisfy in order to be knowable: the answer to the material version will tell us what things satisfy these conditions. A good deal of confusion can get into the discussion of what Plato says about knowledge and belief if this distinction between the formal and the material version of the question is not kept in mind.

Next we must remember that some of the things which Plato says are said in terms of what is to us an unfamiliar picture of the relationship between the knowing subject and the thing known. To avoid unnecessary confusion it is important to get the right picture. Firstly, what we would naturally claim to know are propositions, truths. What Plato would naturally claim to know are things. We would tend to say of a mathematician that he knows *that* triangles have such and such properties, or indeed that he knows *how* to multiply or to integrate. Plato would tend to say of him that he knows triangles and numbers (cp. *Theaetetus* 198). Secondly, Plato tends to think of the process of learning as one of acquiring or devouring (see again the image of the aviary, *Theaetetus loc. cit.*). Thirdly, what the learner needs to acquire or devour is some part of the real objective world. Knowledge then, being the achievement of learning, is the devouring of something real. The mathematician who knows all about triangles (who "knows the triangle") has devoured triangularity; triangularity has become part of his mental equipment. The school-boy on the other hand who can assert some, but not all, of the truths about triangles, and who can do so with a measure, but not a full measure, of understanding, he has devoured not triangularity but a likeness of it only; and his state is one not of knowledge but of belief. The difference between the two states is that in knowledge what has been devoured is an objective entity, whereas in belief what has been devoured is no more than a likeness of such an entity. This is important so we will repeat it in a little more detail.

There are really three states we are concerned with, namely knowledge, belief and what the *Republic* calls *agnoia* or ignorance. Now to decide whether my state on a given occasion is one of knowledge or of belief or of ignorance what you have to ask is what it is that I have in my mind. Take the case of knowing Jones. Let us suppose that my conception of Jones is faithful in all respects, so that Jones himself, we might say, lives in my mind. What the Jones whom I conceive of would do or think or say in a given situation is identical with what the real Jones would do or think or say; there is no discrepancy between the Jones in my mind and the Jones in the real world. My Jones is identical with the real Jones; and yet there are not two Joneses, one in my mind and one outside it, so perhaps we had better say that what exists in my mind *is* the real Jones. My mind in this case has absorbed a real thing. This is a case of knowledge.

But now let us suppose that my conception of Jones, though based on the real Jones, is all the same distorted, blurred, defective. I can tell for example the *kind* of political views which Jones tends towards, but I do not know him well enough to be able to say just what he thinks about nuclear weapons; or perhaps I think I can say, but am wrong. What exists in my mind now is not Jones, but an *eikôn*, an image or picture, of Jones—something that owes its broad outlines to his outlines, but is deficient (schematic and two-dimensional, whereas he is in the round) and also perhaps distorted. This is a case of *doxa* or belief, and in this case what exists in my mind *is not identical with, but is based on* the real thing of which I am forming a conception.

Finally let us suppose that there is nothing in my mind which can be called a picture of Jones. Here my conception of Jones is nothing, and here my condition with regard to Jones is one of *agnoia* or ignorance. This can happen in either of two ways; either because I have never heard of Jones and hence would not claim to have any conception of him; or because the conception of him which I do claim to have is so completely false that it cannot be called a conception of Jones at all, but a complete figment, where the man whom I conceive under that name has no existence outside my mind. (Similarly there may be no picture of the Marble Arch in my sketchbook either because I have not tried to draw it, or because, although I have tried to draw it, the result is so hopeless that it must be dismissed as "not a picture of the Marble Arch at all". When is a picture not a picture? When it is hopelessly unlike).

That to know something is to grasp or absorb some piece of reality is of course only a picture. If we approach the consideration of cognitive states in terms of this picture (as I am suggesting Plato did) it will give rise to certain difficulties, of terminology at least, which it will be worth our while to look at. We begin from the position that he who comes to know something thereby absorbs part of the world; starting there it is natural to go on to ask what it is that has been absorbed by the man who is in a state of belief or ignorance. To see the answers that might be given to these questions we must consider in a little more detail what these two states consist of.

The distinction between knowledge and belief which we sketched above is roughly this. When I know something, say that Jones has a moustache, there exists a complex in the external world, Jones-having-a-moustache, or (we might almost say) Jones's moustache; and this complex is actually before, or in, my mind. When I only believe that Jones has a moustache I am not in direct touch with Jones's moustache, or with the state of affairs Jones-having-a-moustache. The position is rather that I affirm the existence of a state of affairs which belongs to a certain range of states of affairs, namely that range the existence of any member of which would render true the proposition that Jones has a moustache. I am out of touch with the actual individual condition of Jones's lip,[1] though I very likely imagine some individual lip-condition and impute this to Jones with the reservation that his actual lip-condition will resemble, but may not be identical with, the lip-condition that I imagine. For my belief that Jones has a moustache to count as a true belief it is necessary that there should be a reasonable degree of resemblance between the actual condition of Jones's lip on the one hand and on the other the condition that I impute to him in my imagination, or rather perhaps the typical condition with which a proposition to the effect that some man has a moustache is correlated. A belief can be regarded as reasonably reliable so long as

---

[1] cp. *Theaetetus* 209 c 4–9, discussed below, p. 113.

43

such a resemblance holds; in a sufficiently complicated case a belief may be of some service even if there is a certain amount of positive discrepancy between the actual situation and the expectations which the belief leads one to form, even if the actual situation falls in some ways outside the range of situations which is such that one of these situations must be the case if the proposition which expresses the belief is to count as perfectly true. Analogously a picture will be recognisable even though it misrepresents its subject in certain respects.[1] I shall not say that you are totally out of touch with the actual situation just because the type of situation which falls plumb under the meaning of the proposition to which you assent differs in some ways from the actual situation. We do not therefore reach the borders of *agnoia* or of being totally out of touch with what is going on until we transgress the bounds of reasonable resemblance. With regard to any topic, I may be said to be totally out of touch with it if none of the contents of my mind has any reference to that topic, or if some of the contents of my mind do claim to refer to it, but totally misrepresent it. As we have seen we do not get a case of this latter just because I say that Jones is clean-shaven when the truth is that he has not in fact shaved for three days; but we certainly will get a case of it if I say that Jones is clean-shaven when the truth is that his moustache is and has been for years the pride of the Sergeants' Mess. What happens in this case is that I assert a proposition such that there is correlated with the truth of that proposition a range of situations such that the actual situation falls clean outside the boundaries of that range however tolerantly they are construed.

We have then certain factors which we can distinguish and which we can use if we wish in the analysis of the cognitive relationship between a man and a topic. We have first the mental state of the man with respect to that topic. This may be one of knowledge, of true belief, of false belief, or of being totally unaware of the topic. We have next the mental correlate, or content, of the state in question. In the case of knowledge, the absorption-picture requires that we should say that this is the topic itself. In the case of true and false belief it will be what we should call a proposition. In the case of total unawareness it will of course be nothing. Next we have the actual state of the topic, the actual condition of that to which the mental state relates. In the case of knowledge this will be identical with the content of the state. In the case of true belief it will be a state of affairs which fits more or less comfortably under the meaning of the proposition which expresses the belief. In the case of false belief it will be a state of affairs which falls outside this range. In

---

[1] *Cratylus* 430 affords an example of the use by Plato of the notion of a picture in this kind of context.

the case of unawareness it will neither fall nor fail to fall within the range of the proposition believed, for there is no such proposition. Finally in addition to the actual state of the topic we have what we may call the alleged state of the topic. In the case of knowledge the alleged state is of course identical with the actual state of the topic, and this in turn is identical with the content of the knowledge. In the case of true belief the alleged state of the topic is the class of states of affairs each of which would, if it existed, suffice to render true the content of the belief, the actual state of affairs being one of these. In the case of false belief the alleged state of the topic is again the class of states of affairs each of which would, if it existed, suffice to render true the content of the belief, but in this case the actual state of affairs is not a member of this class. In true belief therefore the actual state falls within the alleged state, in false belief it falls outside it. There is of course no alleged state in the case of total unawareness.

We have then four factors: a mental state, its mental correlate or content, and two objective correlates, the actual and the alleged state of the topic to which the mental state in question relates. Our purpose in distinguishing these four factors was to use them in trying to see some of the difficulties which might arise if we were to start from the principle that that which is before the mind of the knower is some actual state of affairs, and go on to ask what it is that is before the mind of a man who is in a condition of *doxa* or *agnoia*.

Today we tend to say that what is before or in the mind of the believer is a proposition, true or false. But as we have seen Plato tended to speak of knowing, not propositions, but things; and it seems that he tended also at one stage to speak of that which is before the mind of the believer and of the ignorant as if it were some kind of thing. More accurately, perhaps, he tended to use the syntax of *connaître* for the case of knowledge, and to use the same syntax for the other cases; and some of the difficulties in his account in the *Republic* in particular can be construed as difficulties which are due to thinking of belief and ignorance in this syntax. This gives the impression that belief and ignorance are epistemologically inferior faculties whereby we become acquainted with ontologically inferior objects. One can of course assimilate the logical syntax of *savoir* to that of *connaître* by treating a *that*-clause as the name of a complex entity. This in itself gives no trouble; trouble arises when we treat as names of complex entities the *that*-clauses which occur in false-belief statements. "That Jones has a moustache" can be regarded as the name of a state of affairs so long as Jones has a moustache; if however he is clean-shaven there is no such state of affairs for it to

45

name. Reflection on false belief thus induces us to introduce the notion of a proposition as something distinct from a fact, event, state of affairs or what you will. (This does not mean of course that it induces us, necessarily, to believe that there exist propositions which serve as intermediaries between minds and facts. That it may induce us to believe this is the objection to the notion of a proposition, for the idea that propositions are intermediaries has notorious difficulties of its own. But reflection on false belief is likely to induce us at least to introduce the term "proposition" as an analytic tool).

It was Plato's achievement to make clear in the *Sophist* (and to hint perhaps in the *Theaetetus*) that we need the notion of a proposition for the analysis of false belief.[1] But at an earlier stage he appears to have followed what seems to have been the practice of his contemporaries and to have tried to manage without it. Let us try to see where this would have got him to. The question was: "If some part of reality is what is before the mind of a man who knows something, what is it that is before the mind of a man in an inferior cognitive state?". We will start with the case of false belief. The man in a state of false belief has taken into his mind a proposition, and this proposition is one which would be verified by the existence of any one of a range of states of affairs, none of which exists. For the sake of simplicity let us speak as if there were just one state of affairs ("the alleged state of the topic") whose existence would verify a given proposition. In this simpler language we can say that the false believer has taken into, or has before, his mind a proposition which would be verified only by a state of affairs which does not exist. Telescoping this by leaving out the proposition we can say that the false believer has before his mind something which does not exist, a non-entity. Notoriously this is what many Greeks did say, for it is this which leads to the Paradox of False Belief—since there are no such things as non-entities, it would seem that the false believer has nothing before his mind.[2]

We will take next the case of true belief. If we bear clearly in mind that there are many different states of affairs each of which is sufficient for the truth of a given proposition, and only one of which, at most, exists, we shall say, as we have said, that the alleged state of the topic in the case of true belief consists of a range of states of affairs such that the actual state of affairs is a member of that range. But we might fail to bear this clearly in mind, especially perhaps if we did not make use of the notion of a proposition. Without this notion

[1] See pp. 492–8 for an account of the discussion in the *Sophist* and pp. 490–2 for an account of the possible hints in the *Theaetetus*.

[2] For the Paradox of False Belief see Chapter 4, pp. 486–98.

46

we shall tend to say that belief affirms the existence of a state of affairs. Since this "state of affairs" will have to include within itself all the various possibilities which are compatible with the truth of the belief, it will be an odd sort of entity, a kind of highest common factor of the range of possibilities. If we ask how this "state of affairs" is related to the actual state of affairs, we shall say perhaps that it resembles it or that it is an image or representation of it. True belief therefore affirms the existence of a state of affairs which is an image of the actual state of affairs. If the man who knows has in his mind the actual state of affairs, the man who truly believes has in his mind an image or likeness of the actual state of affairs. What he has in his mind therefore is something which comes in between the real entity which is grasped by the knower and the non-entity which deludes the false believer. It is neither an entity nor a non-entity, but something in between.

We can of course avoid this paradoxical result if we clearly insist that there is no such thing as "the state of affairs which the true believer believes". We do not believe states of affairs, we believe *that* so and so; and the relationship between the *that*-clause or proposition and the world is that the rules of the language we are using are such that the proposition would be true if the actual situation fell within a certain range, false if it fell outside it. The state of affairs which the believer believes, the thing which is neither an entity nor a non-entity, is something which we only get if we, so to speak, treat the *that*-clause as if it were a state of affairs. It is this which makes us try to find an ontological status for it in between those states of affairs which do, and those which do not, exist—or rather to use language which makes it seem that this is what we are trying to do. It is the treatment of *that*-clauses as if they named some complex in the world that makes us treat the *that*-clauses which are the objects of true belief as if they named complexes in the half-world, and to treat those which are the objects of false belief as if they named complexes in the non-world.

Finally we may round this discussion off by considering the case where my ignorance of X consists in my being totally unaware of it. Here clearly what exists in my mind with respect to X is nothing whatever. If we are thinking of cognitive states in terms of the degree of contact between the subject and the object it may well seem that being deluded about X and being unaware of X are more or less the same thing. The difference between them is that in the case of delusion there is a reference to X (or more strictly to that locus which is in fact occupied by X); but so far as contact with what is going on is concerned this is equally missing in the case of unawareness and in the case of delusion. It will be argued later that the *Theaetetus* shows

47

Plato becoming aware of the importance of the topic of reference,[1] and he is certainly aware of it in the *Sophist*. But if in the earlier period he attached no great significance to this relationship, it might well have seemed to him that delusion and unawareness could be treated together under the title of *agnoia*, the common factor of the two cases being that nothing with respect to X is present in the mind of the man who is either deluded about it or unaware of it; and (if delusion was the one of these conditions which attracted more of his attention) it might well have seemed to him tolerable to use of both of these kinds of nothing the title "non-entity" which belongs more properly to a figment, i.e. to that kind of "nothing with respect to X" which occupies my mind when I am deluded about it rather than to the blank space opposite X which exists in my mind when I am unaware of it.

I need not remind the reader that in recent paragraphs we have been speculating about the sort of language which Plato might have found himself using if he had thought of cognitive states in a certain way—that is, if he had thought of them in terms of the degree of contact between mind and state of affairs which is present in each of them. This speculation, I own, has not been entirely disinterested; it has been guided by the interpretation which it seems to me necessary to put upon certain texts, especially those in the *Republic*. But I do not claim that in these paragraphs I have been reporting doctrines that Plato explicitly advocated; and I hope that I shall not be accused of saying, for example, that Plato anywhere tells us in so many words that knowledge is full contact between mind and object; that he thought that what occupies the mind of the believer is, in favourable cases, an image of the object; that he lacked the notion of a proposition and thought that *that*-clauses were the names of states of affairs, real, unreal or half-real; or any other things of this kind. I have done no more than try to show what might have happened if he had thought about certain topics in certain ways, in the hope that, when we come to consider some of the things that he said, we may find that the conjectures throw light on the facts. The proposition which is essential to these speculations, namely that in knowledge the known state of affairs exists in the knower's mind, is not, let us say it frankly, to be found in Plato's writings. We do find it explicitly stated by Aristotle, but not by Plato. I do not even say that it is a proposition to which Plato would have given his assent. He might have found it, as we find it, a proposition to which it is difficult to attach a clear meaning. It is no part of my argument that Plato thought that he knew what knowledge was but kept it as a secret which he passed on to Aristotle to publish. Being less in-

[1] See below pp. 110–11.

48

clined than Aristotle to believe that philosophical problems can be solved by formulas, he may well have found himself to the end puzzled about knowledge and unable to say what it is. I suggest no more than that the proposition in question gives expression to the picture which Plato took for granted in his reflection about knowledge and its inferior states.

Remembering then that these are conjectures, let us take them a little further. From those which we have made so far we are in a position to extract an answer to the formal interpretation of the question: "What sorts of things can we know?" Since, when I know something, I have in my mind the thing itself and not just a representation of it, the things which can be known will be presumably those which can be grasped or absorbed by, or which can exist in a mind. But now the material interpretation of the question arises in the form: "What sort of things can exist in a mind?" In our discussion so far we have used various examples—triangularity, Jones, Jones's possession of a moustache, the road to Larisa. Are all of these things which the mind can absorb? Is it, for example, possible for a man to have the road to Larisa in his mind?

Metaphorically of course it is. The man who has often travelled to Larisa certainly has the road in his mind. There is no significant difference between his conception of the intervening country and the intervening country as it is in reality. But literally the road to Larisa is a stretch of earth and rocks and trees and not a system of logical necessities. Literally therefore a man cannot have the road to Larisa in his mind but only a conception or series of pictures of it. What he has in his mind logically cannot be more than an *eikôn* or image of reality. In the case of triangularity this is not so. Triangularity is something more like a system of logical necessities, and as such it is a *nöêton* or intelligible entity, something which can itself be absorbed by the mind. Strictly therefore in the case of triangularity what a man has in his mind and the reality that he is thinking about can be identical, whereas in the case of the road to Larisa they cannot. Yet while in the latter case we strictly have to confess that what is in the mind is an *eikôn*, it may be an *eikôn* which is capable of no improvement. A perfect *eikôn* is not identical with its original, but if it is perfect there is no point in stressing this. It follows from this that, in terms of the conception of knowledge that we have outlined, it will be perfectly natural, but strictly incorrect, to speak of knowing the road to Larisa. The conception of the road which exists in the mind of the man who has merely been told how to get there is an *eikôn* in a far more significant sense than that of the local inhabitant, so that if you want to bring this out you will say that the visitor has correct belief and the local inhabitant knowledge.

49

The same point may be made in a different way. To want to know is to want to have insight into what really exists in the world. In one sense the road to Larisa is one of the things that really exist in the world, and therefore the man who is familiar with it can be said to have achieved the goal of knowledge. But in another sense, used at a more theoretical level of discourse, the road to Larisa is no more than a complex of empirical objects; and, as we have seen more than once, to be familiar with an empirical object is not to be in touch with something ultimate. An empirical object is "in flux" in all the senses which can be attached to that phrase. If we want to be strict we shall reserve the title of an *on*, or of an ultimate reality, for that which determines that the flux shall take, in any given case, the form that it does. In this way therefore it is strictly true that the man who is familiar with the road to Larisa is familiar with something derivative, something that can be called an *eikôn*.[1] Clearly therefore if we are to reserve "to know" for insight into ultimate realities the man who is familiar with the ordered series of sense-experiences which constitutes the road to Larisa cannot be said to know. Equally clearly however it would in some contexts be pedantic to insist on this point. The upshot therefore of these last two paragraphs is that it will not surprise us if we find Plato using a strict sense of *epistasthai* in which we cannot be said to know physical objects and a relaxed sense in which, under favourable conditions, we can.

E. *Knowledge and belief in the* Meno

The first of the major discussions of knowledge and belief is to be found in the *Meno*. The topic pervades the whole dialogue but it is to be found in concentrated form from 96–8. The context of the passage is this. If goodness were some kind of knowledge, it would be teachable. It seems that it must be knowledge, for goodness is valuable, and therefore must involve knowing how to make use of potentially valuable endowments. Yet in fact goodness does not seem to be teachable. Socrates gets out of this dilemma by saying that it is in practice just as useful to have right belief as it is to know, and that it may be impossible sufficiently to inculcate right beliefs about life.[2] If then goodness depends on right belief, rather than knowledge, we can understand both why it is useful and why it cannot be taught.

In detail Socrates says that one man may have done the journey to Larisa and hence know the road, but that another man who has not done the journey, and therefore does not know, may be an

---

[1] This of course is a different use of *eikôn* from that in the last paragraph. For this double use of the word compare *Phaedo* 100 a.

[2] The implication is of course that knowledge always can be taught.

equally good guide provided that his beliefs are correct. Right belief is just as effective towards right action. Meno objects that right belief does not always work, and Socrates retorts that it always works when it is present, but that it does not always stick. It runs away—and needs to be tied down. This can be done by "working out the explanation" (*aitiâs logismos*), which Socrates calls recollection (*anamnêsis*). When a belief is tied down in this way it is turned into knowledge, which persists. Socrates adds that he is sure that right belief is not the same as knowledge, but is only conjecturing the difference between them. This is a significant comment, for it suggests that Plato's starting point in the whole business was the conviction that there is one state of mind which involves insight and hence is unshakable, and another which does not.

Knowledge then must be teachable, it must involve understanding, and for that reason it is not liable to "run away". A belief can be converted into knowledge by "recollection", that is by working out the explanation of the fact. What Socrates means by "teachable", and why understanding the explanation of a fact is called recollection has been explained earlier in the dialogue (80–6) where Socrates gives an instance of how to teach by getting an uneducated slave to prove a geometrical theorem simply by asking him the right questions in the right order. The slave is thereby enabled to gather from his own resources insight into the logical necessities of the theorem (it is because the insight is gathered from within that the process is called recollection).[1] The false beliefs that he had on the subject are thereby expunged, and his true beliefs (this seems to be the point) are converted into knowledge by being strung together in such a way that they afford him understanding.

It is noteworthy that in this account "knowledge" and "belief" are used to classify two attitudes of mind and not two classes of proposition. There is no suggestion that only propositions about universals can count as knowledge, propositions about particulars counting as belief. In 86 a 7 the right answers that the slave gave are called "true opinions" and it is said that they were turned into "knowledges" (*epistêmai*) when they were "awoken by questioning". The implication of this is that what the slave tentatively put forward, as what seemed to him the probably correct answer, became something of which he could be certain as the course of the questioning showed him that no other answer was possible. Knowledge then is the state of mind in which you are certain because you have seen why the answer must be right. As in the *Gorgias* (501) and elsewhere

---

[1] This is complicated by the additional doctrine that the resources which we draw on when we understand something were garnered before birth. See below, pp. 135–47.

experience or luck may enable you to give the right answer, but unless you can "give account" (*logon didonai*) you cannot be said to know. Any belief, however, can be converted into knowledge by working out the reason for the fact.

This catholicity is perhaps a little puzzling, for if the typical instance of knowledge, and of insight into necessity, is given by the understanding of a geometrical theorem, one wonders how it is possible to know the road to Larisa. There could not be a theorem proving with geometrical rigour that one must turn right at the pond. No doubt it is true that the man who knows the countryside can give account of why one has to follow a certain route, but we shall still have to say that in this dialogue the notion of insight into necessity which is used to characterise knowledge is a very wide notion embracing the understanding of theorems and the understanding of terrain. What the spotlight is trained on is not any particular type of understanding nor any particular class of intelligible entities, but rather the certainty that a man is entitled to have concerning something that he understands in any sense.

Understanding not only justifies certainty, it also prevents knowledge from "running away". Our discussion of the *Protagoras*[1] has suggested that its doctrine is that people yield to temptation because they do not understand the reason for their moral rules, and thus find it easy to deceive themselves about their application to particular cases. In the language of the *Meno* this is probably a case of a belief "running away". The *Republic* (413) offers two other causes for the loss of a belief in addition to temptation, namely persuasion and simple forgetting. The point probably is that what a man merely believes is no more than an impression that he has formed or a lesson that he has learnt by rote. It has not been built into his mental outlook nor is its true significance grasped, and for this reason its applicability to a present situation can easily be ignored. The man who merely believes that stealing is wrong without understanding why it is wrong is in a better position than the man who has thought the matter out to persuade himself that what he proposes to do would not be a case of stealing.

Finally, although the *Meno* stresses the importance of understanding to the notion of knowledge, it also, by citing the example of the road to Larisa, gives some place to acquaintance. Perhaps we ought to say that understanding is thought of after the model of acquaintance. The man who knows, not by hearsay, but by following the demonstration, that the square of the hypotenuse equals the sum of the squares of the other two sides, has seen for himself these features of squareness which bring this about.

[1] See above, pp. 241–3 of Vol. 1.

F. *Knowledge and belief in the* Republic

The contrast between *epistêmê* and *doxa* pervades the *Republic*. There are two main passages where it is explicitly discussed and one important subsidiary passage. The first main passage is at the end of the Fifth Book (474–80), and the second runs from the concluding pages of the Sixth Book almost to the end of the Seventh (504–34). The subsidiary passage is in the tenth book (601–2). Something has already been said about these passages in the chapter on the *Republic*, but they are difficult enough and controversial enough to call for further treatment. I shall not attempt to do justice to the controversies they have provoked or to justify my interpretation by scholarly standards; but I must try to indicate what seems to me to be the correct approach.

(i) *Knowledge and belief in* Republic 5[1]

Having declared that philosophers must rule, Socrates tries, towards the end of the fifth book, to distinguish true philosophers from "lovers of sights and sounds"—a derogatory title used to describe learned persons as well as those who cultivate novel experiences. The mark of philosophers is that they love *alêtheia*. This word includes the idea of truth, but also a good deal more. The central notion is something more like reliability, and therefore one can talk of the *alêtheia* of things as well as of propositions. The word carries a suggestion of getting behind appearances to something ultimate and unrevisable (it was probably in this spirit that Protagoras called his epistemological treatise *Alêtheia*). We are being told therefore that the philosopher is the man who wants to get down to bedrock, who will remain dissatisfied until he sees things precisely as they are. That the beliefs of the unphilosophical lack *alêtheia* does not mean that they are *false* in the natural English sense of the word. That heavy objects fall is not false though the lover of *alêtheia* would think Newton's Inverse Square Law a much better statement of the matter.

So much for what *alêtheia* is. Philosophers desire to have it, and this, Socrates says (475 e) is dependent upon acknowledging the existence of universals. The philosopher knows that beauty or weight is a distinct thing with a nature of its own, and is concerned to understand it in itself; and this he does not do by inductive observation of its instances. For any given universal is a single common quality present to all the things which exemplify it; but qualities are met with in the physical world only as the qualities of particular things and not in isolation but "combined with each other". For

---

[1] My view of this passage owes much to discussions with Mr. Gosling; see his article in *Phronesis*, Vol. 5.

this reason it is impossible to come to know what, say, beauty or heaviness is by collecting facts about "the multifarious beautiful or heavy things".

Those who try to do this—"the lovers of sights and sounds"— are said to be living in a dream. This is a common Platonic metaphor, and in this place he says what he means by it (476 c 5–7). The essence of dreaming, Socrates says, is to mistake A for B when A merely resembles B. Thus (I suppose) when I dream of St. Paul's I have an experience which is *like* seeing St. Paul's, and mistake it for an experience *of* seeing St. Paul's. Thus to concern oneself only with "the multifarious beautiful things" and not with beauty is to make the former identical with the latter when in fact they are only similar to it.

This is important, but not clear. There are two problems in particular: what does Plato mean by saying that a universal resembles the class which is correlated with it, and what precisely is the error of which the non-philosophical learned are accused?

Similarity-language is not uncommon in Plato in the context of the relation between a common quality and its instances.[1] Such language obviously cannot be taken literally, and this Plato points out in the *Parmenides* (132).[2] Although he finds it necessary to make this point, the absurdity of saying that animality (for example) literally resembles the multifarious animals is so gross that one cannot suppose that he is castigating a mistake he has himself made. To see how such language arises, take an architect's plans for a house, and take two houses built to those plans. The two houses will resemble each other, and there will be some kind of affinity (we should call it conformity) between the houses and the plans. Nor would it be too far-fetched, especially in certain contexts, to speak of the conformity in terms of likeness. Thus, to choose a phrase which is paralleled in the *Timaeus* (e.g. 31 b 1), we should understand what the builder meant if he said he had tried to make the houses "as like the plans as he could". Something like conformity then is presumably the relation intended by the similarity-language which Plato uses about common qualities and their instances.

This being so, what precisely is the intellectual error described as identifying the two? Plato is trying, I think, to diagnose a logical blunder which he takes to be implicit in contemporary thought-processes. The blunder is too gross to be explicitly committed, and

---

[1] It is especially common in the *Timaeus*, a dialogue written in a lofty tragical manner. The references can be found in Ross: *Plato's Theory of Ideas*, pp. 228–30.

[2] The same point is obliquely made in the *Republic* itself (597). We shall have more to say of all this in a later chapter, below pp. 267 sqq., 332 sqq.

therefore I say that he is trying to diagnose a hidden confusion. I shall try to state the blunder clearly and I dare say that, if I succeed in making it clear, then I shall have taken the analysis a little further than Plato had taken it, and in this way my account of his meaning will be historically inexact. The blunder then is that of supposing that, when it is true that S is P, the property P-hood is identical with the properties of S which make us say that S is P. Thus many objects (cp. *Phaedo* 100 d 1) owe their beauty to bright colouring, and in the case of these objects bright colouring is the property which makes us call them beautiful. Heavy objects observably tend downwards, and it is because they tend downwards that we call them heavy. Beauty then (according to the blunder) is bright colouring, heaviness is a tendency downwards. Yet of course in the case of many properties to follow this method of (we will say) "collecting universals inductively" is to run into contradictions. A is beautiful because of its bright colours, but bright colouring would spoil B's delicate outlines. In the case of B then beauty is not bright colouring, but delicate outline. Although this trouble does not arise in the case of heaviness (for all heavy objects in our experience tend downwards), there is another trouble which does; for, as Plato points out in the *Timaeus* (62), "downwards" has no meaning in a spherical universe, and therefore "tending downwards" gives no insight into the nature of weight. Therefore the practice of collecting universals inductively leads to either or both of two unfortunate consequences. The first is that we refuse to believe in the existence of single self-consistent properties. There is no such thing as beauty which is present in all its instances; there are as many different beauties as there are sets of properties which make us call things beautiful. The result of this is that we do not try to discover what is common to them all. The second unfortunate consequence is connected with this, namely that we rest content with practically adequate but intellectually opaque definitions such as "heaviness is tendency downwards". It is clear that such definitions might have stultifying effects on thought (relativity theory would not have developed if Einstein had not seen that it will not do to say that two events are simultaneous if they happen at the same time). And it is not too far-fetched to say that these effects would come about from identifying, e.g. the multifarious beautifuls with beauty, from thinking that the various general statements that can be made about the "beauties" of the multifarious beautifuls are the most that can be said about beauty. The cure of the error is to realise that whatever can be called beautiful can also in certain circumstances be called ugly. For if a thing which looks bright and therefore beautiful in one room looks harsh and out of place in another, then its colouring is responsible both for its beauty and for its ugliness; and obviously therefore it cannot be identical with either.

The point then is that nobody can be called a philosopher if he is content with inductively collected accounts of properties. Since such accounts are collected by noticing *apparent* (sc. obvious) features of classes of objects, this means "if he is content with *doxai* or judgments based on what is apparent".

Philosophers are awake, whereas ordinary men are asleep and dreaming. This means that the thought of philosophers deals with realities whereas that of ordinary men deals with some kind of images. Socrates allots the names "knowledge" and "belief" to these two states of mind respectively, and then proceeds to offer a proof that the unphilosophical cannot be allowed to claim knowledge. This is one of many places in Plato where he could probably have been more convincing if he had tried to elucidate his point rather than to offer a formal demonstration of it.

Socrates' methods are conversational and in setting his argument out I shall slightly alter the order of exposition. Since much turns on how we translate these key expressions, I shall use without translating: *on* (plural *onta*), literally "that which is" and *mê on* (plural *mê onta*), literally "that which is not". The argument then is as follows:—

(1) A man who knows knows an *on*. (2) That which is fully *on* is fully knowable; that which is totally *mê on* is totally unknowable. (3) Anything which was both *on* and *mê on* would lie between the two, and the state of mind corresponding to it would lie between knowledge and ignorance. (4) Belief and knowledge are different functions (*dunameis*), for the latter cannot be wrong, and the former can. (5) Two functions are different if (*a*) they do different things, and (*b*) they do them to different objects. (6) Therefore the objects of belief are different from the objects of knowledge. (7) The objects of knowledge are *onta*; but the objects of belief cannot be *mê onta*, for a man who believes must believe something, and a *mê on* cannot properly be called something. (8) Since belief is a state of greater darkness than knowledge and of greater light than ignorance, it ought to be located between them, and its objects between *on* and *mê on* (see step 3). (9) Take the multifarious so-and-so's which the unphilosophical believe to be the only realities, and which are not changeless like universals. Now for any predicate P and its opposite -P ("beautiful" and "ugly", "heavy" and "light"), it is always the case that things which one has reason to call P can also be found to be -P. None of the multifarious P's is definitely P and in no way -P. Should they not then be said to be between *on* and *mê on*, "darker than *on* but better lit than *mê on*"? (10) "Therefore the

56

multifarious conventional opinions of ordinary men about beauty and other such things roll about between *on* and *mê on*": and these must be the objects of belief.

This argument is not easy to interpret. We may begin by clarifying its purpose. This is to show that ordinary men cannot ever claim to possess knowledge, and that the reason for this is that their opinions, however correct, are always "inductive" (in the sense used in recent paragraphs), and therefore have the status of *doxai* or beliefs. It tries to show this by assuming (step 4) that since knowledge is infallible and belief is not, knowledge and belief must be different "functions" (*dunameis*) and therefore must have different "objects". The purpose of this is to establish a logical chasm between knowledge and belief, in terms of a difference between their "objects". The rest of the argument is devoted to rendering this plausible by finding suitable "objects" for belief, and by showing that the opinions of ordinary men are concerned with these "objects".

What does Plato mean by "functions" and "objects"? We can begin by noticing what seems to be a fatal flaw in the argument. Two functions are the same if they do the same thing to the same objects, and two functions are different if they do different things to different objects (447 d).[1] But what, one asks, are we to say about functions A and B such that they do *different* things to the *same* objects (as, e.g., sight sees apples and pears, and smell smells them)? Plato is trying to prove that knowledge and belief have different objects on the ground that they do different things (knowledge doing something infallible and belief something fallible). But if the two functions can have the same objects and yet be different functions (as sight and smell are surely different functions) then the argument will not work. Knowledge and belief might have the same object (say the world) although the one recorded it infallibly and the other fallibly.

If this is a mistake, it is a very gross one, and one looks for a different interpretation. Fortunately there is one to hand. If we assume that the "object" of a function is an "internal accusative", the case of A and B which do a different act to the same object does not arise.[2] Thus the internal accusative of "see" is "sights", of "smell" is "smells"; and it is true that sight and only sight sees sights and nothing but sights, that smell and only smell smells smells and nothing but smells. With this conception of "what the function does" and "what it does it to", Socrates' definition of sameness and difference of function becomes correct. The possibilities are now only two in number and the definition exhausts these.

[1] The phrase for "object" is "that which the function is *epi*". *Epi* is a preposition which bears the general sense of "onto" or "on".
[2] Nor does the case of C and D which do the same act to different objects.

It seems therefore worth considering whether that to which a faculty is *epi*, the "object" of a faculty, may not, in this passage at least, be its internal accusative. If we adopt this suggestion, then the "objects" of belief and knowledge becomes beliefs and bits of knowledge, and in that case it will be beliefs themselves and not their subject matter, which are said to be between *on* and *mê on*. Or rather, to use a phrase which we used above in our preliminary discussion, it will be the mental correlates of the state of belief; that which is between *on* and *mê on* will not be that which the belief is about, but that which the believer's mind has grasped. This, as we saw above, will not be precisely a proposition, or rather we shall not expect Plato to speak of it in the language appropriate to propositions. We shall expect him to speak of it as if it were that of which a *that*-clause is the name; and in the case of true belief, as we saw, this is just the sort of entity which we should expect to inhabit a half-world. The *that*-clauses of knowledge name realities, those of delusion figments; and those of respectable opinion ought to name something in between. It seems then worth considering seriously whether the objects of these faculties may not be their "mental correlates" in this sense. Textually indeed it is not at all far-fetched to suggest that that which is between *on* and *mê on* is something of the approximate character of a belief or proposition, for this is entirely in accordance with what Socrates says in step 10 in drawing his conclusion. It is the multifarious conventional opinions of ordinary men which he argues must roll about between *on* and *mê on*, and these are what we should call beliefs. How it can be that beliefs can perform the extraordinary feat of "rolling about between" (this perhaps means "occupying some point anywhere on the scale between") "the existent and the non-existent" has I hope been made clear above. I certainly cannot imagine how the subject-matter of beliefs (the things that we have beliefs about) could do anything of the kind. That beauty is a matter of bright colouring is perhaps one of the multifarious conventional opinions of ordinary men about beauty, and the "quasi-fact" which this clause stands for (namely beauty's being a matter of bright colouring) is not a fact or a reality, but on the other hand it is not a complete figment either. It is between being a fact or reality and being a figment, just as the corresponding state of *doxa* is between grasping perfectly and being completely out of touch.

Using this as a clue we can reconstitute the argument as follows:— (*a*) The mental correlate of knowledge is something which really exists (=step 1 of the original argument). (*b*) Anything which really exists can be a mental correlate of knowledge; any mental correlate which is totally a non-entity must be a correlate of ignorance and not of knowledge (=step 2). (c) Any mental correlate which is and yet is not a reality will lie between these two extremes, and the corresponding state of mind will lie between belief and ignorance (=step 3). (d) Belief and knowledge are different functions, the latter being infallible and the former not (=step 4). (e) Therefore (from the definition of difference of function) the mental correlates of belief and knowledge are different (steps 5 and 6). (f) The mental correlates of knowledge are realities. The mental correlates of belief cannot be non-entities, because a believer must believe something, and a non-entity is not something (=step 7. The present step is clearly fallacious and this will be discussed below). (g) Since belief is a condition of illumination intermediate between knowledge and ignorance, its mental correlates ought to have a status intermediate between that of realities and that of non-entities (=step 8). (h) We need therefore to discover mental correlates having this status. Bearing in mind that anything which is e.g. beautiful is also in suitable circumstances ugly, and *bearing in mind that conventional opinions about beauty and so on are inductively based*, we shall see that these conventional opinions do indeed have that status (steps 9 and 10, the clause in italics being introduced to bridge the gap between them).

Two questions arise. (1) What about step *f* of the reconstituted argument? (2) What about the gap between steps 9 and 10 of the original argument? Or in other words:—How does step *h* of the reconstituted argument work?

Step f *of the reconstituted argument* (478 b 3–c 1)

That which can be believed cannot be that which is, for that which is is that which can be known. But one cannot, either, believe what is-not. The believer must bring his belief to bear on something—one cannot believe, and yet believe nothing. But if the believer must believe some one thing, and if what is-not is not some one thing, then the believer cannot believe what is-not. This is the argument, and it seems to be clearly fallacious, for it seems to argue from the premise that every belief must have some content to the conclusion that the content of a belief cannot be a non-entity, or in other words a falsehood.

About this step there are two points which strike one. The first is that it is fallacious, the second that it proves too much. For this is a standard argument, deriving, it is said, from Protagoras, to show that there can be no such thing as meaningful false belief, that every meaningful belief must be true. But it is clearly no part of Plato's purpose at this point (or indeed anywhere else) to assert this. What he wants to show is that the beliefs of plain men cannot be called fully true; to do this he has no need to deny that some beliefs are totally false. Rather the reverse indeed, for one has the impression that he wishes to make palatable the view that the beliefs of ordinary men cannot count as knowledge by conceding at the same time that they need not count as ignorance either. But in that case surely there must be some beliefs the holding of which *does* count as the opposite pole from knowledge, and these beliefs will have to be false. It is therefore positively inapposite to have at this point an argument showing that there can be no false beliefs.

Therefore we are not intended to find such an argument here. But that is to say that, within the terms of this passage, what we should call in English a false belief does not count as a *doxa*, nor the entertaining of it as *doxazein*. *Doxa* in this passage is what is elsewhere called *orthê doxa* or right belief.

One can begin to see how this happens if one translates *doxa* by some such word as "interpretation" or "representation". To *doxazein*, we might suggest, is "to represent something to oneself as". Using language of this kind we can see that in the case of every *doxa* there are two terms, the thing represented (beauty or whatever it may be) and my representation of it. But there comes a point when a representation of X can no longer be called a representation of X at all, but of something else, Y. Therefore when I totally misrepresent beauty to myself, what I have in my mind is not a *doxa* of beauty at all. Therefore whenever a man has a *doxa* in his mind, what he has is not a total misrepresentation—a total misrepresentation is not a representation, and therefore not a *doxa*.

This explanation of the use of *doxa* in this passage may seem unconvincing. If it is, some other explanation will be needed, for whatever the explanation it seems clear that in this passage *doxa* bears the sense of "tolerable belief". If false beliefs belonged to the sphere of *doxa* they would not belong to the sphere of *agnoia*, i.e. they would not belong to the sphere of that whose correlate is *mê on*. But it is clear from many passages that it was the standard practice to correlate falsity with *mê on* (arguing for example that he who says what is false says a *mê on*), and this standard practice Plato does not depart from, though he tries to rescue it from the paradoxes which it sometimes bred.[1] To me it is incredible that he should have correlated false belief not with *mê on*, but with that which is between *on* and *mê on*. It seems to follow that false beliefs are excluded from the sphere of *doxa* as Plato is using the word in this passage. It would not indeed be to his purpose to include them, since what he

[1] See the discussion of the Paradox of False Belief in Chapter 4, pp. 486–98. Greek-speaking readers will notice that I treat *mê* and *ouk* as interchangeable for our purposes.

is trying to tell us is that the *best* that can be achieved by non-philosophers must fall within the sphere of *doxa*. He is not trying to tell us that blunders fall short of the status of *onta*, but that this happens even to the highest achievements of the inductive approach. Therefore his subject is respectable beliefs, beliefs which "have something in them". If it is thought that this is not in itself enough to explain how he could allow himself to use an argument whose effect is to show that no *doxai* are false, some other explanation will be needed, and this is what I have tried to supply.

This explains, then, why the argument does not prove too much. It does not prove that there can be no false beliefs; rather it refuses to call false beliefs *doxai*. A belief about, say, justice which deserves the label "false" cannot count as a representation of justice to oneself and is therefore excluded from the sphere of *doxa*. It need not perturb us that the sphere of *doxa* is elsewhere extended to include false beliefs. To take a somewhat analogous case, if I mistake that rabbit for a stone, do I or do I not see the rabbit? One might sometimes give the one answer, sometimes the other.

So far so good, but the step is still fallacious. Plato could perhaps have drawn validly the conclusion that he wanted to draw. If he had made explicitly the point that we have just imputed to him, namely that if I totally misrepresent something to myself my state cannot be called *doxa* (but must be called *agnoia*), he could have argued that, if a state is one of *doxa*, its content cannot be a *mê on* or figment. But he does not do this. The premise that "the believer (*doxazôn*) must bring his belief to bear on something; one cannot believe, but believe nothing" (478 b 6–8) cannot be taken to mean that every *doxa* must be a version of some reality; the reader could not be expected to get this meaning out of this terse sentence. What we have here as premise must be the logical truth that every belief must have some content. But of course to say that every belief must have a content is not to say that no belief can have a figment or non-entity as its content. Socrates' statement (478 b 12) that a *mê on* is properly called nothing is false in the sense in which it has to be taken. When I wrongly believe that Jones has a moustache, what I believe is a non-entity (the non-fact that Jones has a moustache) and yet it is also something (the proposition that Jones has a moustache); so a non-entity can be the content of a belief.

Clearly, in that way of setting it out, there is an ambiguity in "what I believe"; it may be used to refer to what we called the alleged state of the topic or it may be used to refer to the proposition which makes the allegation. The former of these is a figment, a non-fact, a non-entity. The latter is false, but it is not a figment or a non-entity— it is a certain proposition, namely that Jones has a moustache.

61

Evidently what has happened is that, in the absense of a clear distinction between the proposition and the state of affairs which it alleges, Plato has allowed himself to confuse together the predicates which belong with logical propriety to each of these, and so he has allowed himself to argue that if I believe something what I believe must be something and therefore cannot be nothing and therefore cannot be a non-entity.

He is not of course alone in this confusion. It was the standard drill of the Paradox of False Belief. But as we have seen it is not to his purpose to propound the Paradox here and we should not say that he is doing so. Rather we should say that he wants a reason for refusing to correlate *doxa* with what is-not. This he wants because the state of mind which he is calling *doxa*, or which he is primarily thinking of under that name, is not a state of total misrepresentation. It is mental furniture such as sound but un-philosophical conceptions of justice that he is trying to locate between *on* and *mê on*. Wanting a reason why *doxa* should not be correlated with *mê on* he finds one ready to hand in the Protagorean armoury of arguments purporting to show that whatever is believed is true. Because in this passage he is making *doxa* bear a sense narrower than "belief" he is not disconcerted by the thought that the argument shows that there are no false beliefs because it seems to him only to show that there are no false *doxai*. Nor, on this occasion, does he notice that the argument is fallacious, for it seems to him to have a healthy result, and he is without the clear distinction between proposition and alleged state, given which the argument must have jarred on his logical conscience. When used by Protagoreans to show that every opinion must be true the argument worried him, but it was to be some years yet before he began to see what was wrong with it, and he did not do so before he distinguished the *logos* or proposition from the subject that it "names", "belongs to" or refers to and from the *rêma* or allegation that it makes.

This explains, I hope, the fallacy which we found in step *f*, both how it occurred and how it escaped detection. It is an instructive slip because it does a good deal to show us what conceptual weapons Plato is using.

We may conclude this section by drawing a comparison between this passage and Symposium 202 *a*. Socrates is there arguing that that which is not noble is not necessarily base; there is something in between. Similarly, he says, there is something in between wisdom (*sophia*) and folly or ignorance (*amathia*). This is *orthê doxa*, right belief. "To believe what is correct", he says, "without being able to give account is, as you must know, not *epistêmê* (for how could something irrational be *epistêmê*?), and it is not *amathia* (for how could that which does not fail to hit *to on* be *amathia*?). *Orthê doxa* therefore is something which is of this nature, and is between *phronêsis* and *amathia*." If we may assume that in this passage Plato has used as a parallel to his point about nobility and baseness something which he thought to be a fairly obvious point about wisdom and folly, then we can perhaps argue that the passage in the *Symposium* throws light on what Plato took for granted when he wrote the passage in the *Republic*. To do this however is to support the view that *doxa* in the *Republic* stands for correct opinions; for it is *orthê doxa* in the *Symposium* which comes between wisdom and folly. It can also, I think, be argued that to bring the two passages together is to strengthen the interpretation of *agnoia* for which I am about to argue—namely that *agnoia* in the *Republic* is primarily delusion. For the corresponding term in the *Symposium* is *amathia*, a word which perhaps tends to connote intellectual coarseness (cp. *Sophist* 229 c, where it is used for the kind of *agnoia* which consists in the possession of deluded *doxai*); and the phrase "for how could that which does not fail to hit *to on* (*to . . . tou ontos tunchanon*) be *amathia*?" might perhaps be said to imply that *amathia* is something which aims at *to on* but fails to hit the target. But this is something which could be said more happily of delusion than of unawareness.

What is agnoia?

Agnoia is correlated with (*epi*) that which does not exist (*to mê on*). We have argued that that which a mental function is *epi*, in this passage, is its mental correlate. Some say however that that which a mental function is *epi* is that segment of the universe which it is competent to deal with. They take *to on* to stand for the forms, and they say that the doctrine that *epistêmê* is in the *epi*-relationship to *to on* means that *epistêmê* is competent to deal with, and confined to, the forms. That which is between *to on* and *to mê on* they take to be the physical world, which occupies this position on the ground that it is only half-real; and it is *doxa*, on this view, which is the mental function which is competent to deal, albeit fallibly, with the physical world. We have seen above[1] that there are passages in Plato, particularly in the *Timaeus*, which support the allocation of the functions of *epistêmê* and *doxa* in this way. But it is highly improbable that the first readers of this section of the *Republic* could have read the *Timaeus*, and I do not believe that the innocent eye could extract this meaning from this passage. I do not believe that the spheres-of-competence view correctly interprets the primary meaning of this passage, though I think I do see how Plato could

[1] See pp. 35–41.

have got to his formula about spheres of competence through putting together what he says in this passage with what he says elsewhere (roughly by putting together the formal and the material answers to the question: "What can we know?"). More of this elsewhere;[1] meanwhile an argument against finding spheres of competence in this passage can be got by reflecting upon the position of *agnoia*. For on this view the sphere of competence of *agnoia* will have to be that which is unreal. But we surely cannot say that there is a mental function or state whose *sphere of competence* is the unreal. We can say that there is a state whose *content* is the unreal, but to say that is to take the view which I am advocating. If we want to find a sphere of competence for *agnoia*, then, we shall have to say that it is the non-existent, or in other words that *agnoia* has no sphere of competence, that whatever exists belongs either to the sphere of *epistêmê* or of *doxa*. This last is harmless; but if we treat *agnoia* and *to mê on* in this way it has the result that Plato's triadic structure is fraudulent. He appears to be asking us to consider three different mental functions or states, each of them being correlated with its own correlate, but in fact, on this view, he is only really asking us to consider two. There is no such thing as a state of mind whose province is the non-existent any more than there is one whose province is the unreal. The things that we are ignorant of are ordinary existent things coming presumably from the province either of *epistêmê* or of *doxa*. To say then that *doxa* is between *epistêmê* and *agnoia* and its objects between *to on* and *to mê on* is simply to say that it is not quite ignorance and its objects not quite non-existent. This would no doubt be a possible thing to say,[2] but it has about it the awkward feature that the *epi*-relation in the case of *agnoia* does not relate a state to a special class of entities as it does in the other two cases; saying that *agnoia* is in the *epi*-relation to *to mê on*, if it is not to tell us that there exists a class of fit objects of ignorance, must simply be telling us that nothing is a fit object of ignorance, or in other words that everything is a fit object either of *epistêmê* or of *doxa*. The view that the *epi*-relationship holds between a state and its mental correlate preserves the triadic structure—*epistêmê* corresponds to facts, *agnoia* to figments, and *doxa* to things which are neither quite facts nor quite figments. The view now under attack fails to preserve this structure.

This argument is plainly not coercive; Plato might have failed to see that his triadic structure was spurious, or seen and not bothered. But I think it has some weight. So far as it goes however it is an

[1] See pp. 49–50, 128–35.

[2] Supporters of the view now being attacked can quote *Timaeus* 52 c 4 "clinging somehow to existence" in support of this notion of being not quite non-existent.

argument against taking *agnoia* to mean ignorance in the sense of unawareness. Does this matter?

Verbally there is no doubt that *agnoia* can mean simply "not knowing", but there is equally no doubt that it can also be used to stand for the kind of ignorance which consists in false belief (e.g. *Sophist* 229 c). There is equally no doubt that *to mê on*, which is here correlated with *agnoia*, is a standard correlate of false belief. There is therefore nothing forced in taking *agnoia* to stand for false belief. Indeed the use to which (as we have argued) Plato is putting the word *doxa* in this section might well make him hesitate to employ the phrase *pseudês doxa* for false belief, and that would drive him back on some such word as *agnoia* to express his meaning. Again he might be led to avoid the phrase *pseudês doxa* by the thought that the use of it would embroil him with the Protagoreans. It seems then perfectly possible that false belief should be comprehended under the meaning of *agnoia*; on the other hand it would be odd if unawareness were excluded from its meaning, as the correlation with *to mê on* might seem to suggest that it is.

The answer to this has been sufficiently given, I hope, in our preliminary discussion. The basic idea of the passage is that of the subject's degree of contact with reality in each of the three states. From this point of view delusion and unawareness come to the same thing, for in each of these states the subject is totally out of touch with the reality in question. Therefore Plato does not trouble to distinguish them. It may still be asked however why Plato gives as the correlate of this two-fold condition of *being out of touch* a correlate which belongs to one of its forms rather than the other. We might reply to this that the correlate Plato gives is the one that he wants for his triadic structure; he wants to tell us that *doxai* are superior to figments rather than that they are superior to unawarenesses. But why does he want to do this? Possibly the answer can be found if we remind ourselves of the topics the grasp of which he is concerned with in this passage. For he is thinking after all about our grasp of entities such as justice and beauty, and these are entities about which many of us are grossly deluded, but few of us totally unaware. He is talking of matters, being totally out of touch with which consists normally not in never having heard of them, but in having gross ideas about them. He is telling the unphilosophical cultured, as it seems to me, that though they cannot claim to know what justice is they need not suppose that they are, like the tyrant or demagogue, totally ignorant of it; and the ignorance of these latter consists in wrong ideas, not in no ideas at all. This might explain why, in the context, he assigned to the condition of *being quite out of touch* the correlate which belongs to delusion rather than to unawareness. He might also, of course, have done this the more easily under the influence of the fact that the nothing which I have in my mind with respect to S when I am unaware of S is after all not something which exists, and can therefore be comprehended under *to mê on* with propriety if not with felicity.[1]

For these reasons it seems to me quite feasible that Plato should have used a word from whose meaning "unawareness" cannot be excluded to stand primarily for "delusion". On the other hand it is no part of my purpose to argue that Plato intended with perfect clarity to say just one thing in this passage. My purpose is to diagnose his "dominant" intention, by which I mean the nexus of ideas which led him to write the passage. I do not have to say, and do not want to say that he would consistently have distinguished the interpretation that he primarily intended from other possible interpretations of his words. Anybody who has ever written any philosophy knows how easy it is to fail to do this. In particular I would suggest that he might well have been deceived by the ambiguity of the resounding phrase with which he introduces the discussion (477 a 3–4): "That which is altogether existent is altogether knowable, that which is in no way existent is altogether unknowable." We have taken this to mean: "That which is without qualification a fact is without qualification a proper object of knowledge, whereas that which is without qualification a figment is in no way a proper object of knowledge." But on the other hand this formula could be (indeed usually is) taken to mean that things which exist can be known, things which do not exist cannot be known. We have argued that this second interpretation cannot be the only correct one, because, if it were, we should have to find a place for the objects of *doxa* "between existence and non-existence"—and that means nothing. But it may well be that Plato did not nicely analyse what he meant by *to mê on* nor therefore what he meant by making *agnoia* correspond to it. The "unknowableness of the unreal" may have comprehended both the fact that it is only non-entities that we are utterly incapable of

---

[1] *Agnoia* of justice might well include at least two things. One is the holding of mistaken theories such as those of Thrasymachus and Callicles. The other is the complete inability to distinguish the just from the unjust which is characteristic of us all in so far as we are prisoners in the cave of *Republic* 7. Aristotle for example seems to imply (*Eth. Nic.* 1110 a 26) that Alcmaeon in Euripides' play offered totally spurious justifications of his murder of his mother. Those of his audience who were taken in (as Plato supposes theatre audiences to be commonly taken in) by such spurious justifications would be totally gullible in the matter of instances of justice, and this might be thought to mean that they were totally out of touch with justice. To stress this interpretation of *agnoia* is to bring it into close contact with *apaideusia* or boorishness in *Republic* 7, and thus into close contact also with *eikasia* in one sense of that word.

grasping, and also the fact that falsehoods cannot be known (for entertaining them is not knowledge, in however lax a sense of the word, but delusion). This would have made it easy for *agnoia* to cover both the mental vacancy which properly corresponds to things which do not exist and also the delusion which we suffer when we accept falsehoods.

The gap between steps 9 and 10: step h of the reconstituted argument

The next question we had to ask concerned the connection between steps 9 and 10 of the original argument, or in other words the cohesion of step *h* of the reconstituted argument. We want in fact to know how, having defined the class of approximations, Plato succeeds in showing that the opinions of ordinary men fit the definition. Every one of the multifarious beautifuls (etc.) can also seem ugly (etc.); therefore the multifarious beautifuls are between being and not being; therefore the multifarious conventional opinions of ordinary men about beauty and so on roll about between *on* and *mê on*. This is the argument, and at first glance it seems a *non-sequitur*. That it has some coherence none the less, I hope I have already implicitly shown. Put to a plain man the question "What is beauty?" (especially in Greek, where you will probably word it "What is the beautiful?") and he might reply (for example): "Well, Regency furniture is beautiful."[1] "Why," you ask, "is it beautiful?" "Well, it is so delicate." "Is delicacy then beauty?" "Yes it is." Or, to take another of Plato's examples, ask the plain man: "What is it for one quantity to be twice another?" (in Greek "what is the double?"). "Well," he might reply, "8 is twice 4, 10 is twice 5, and so on." Now in each of these cases the thing which the plain man was asked to define is not without influence on his mind; his grasp of it is enough to make him give answers which are at least not inapposite. But he has of course no abstract understanding of it. His conception of beauty is an amalgam of the various properties which are in suitable circumstances relevant to the beauty of classes of objects; his conception of duplicity consists of various successful performances in the twice-times table. That his conception does not amount in either case to "knowing the beautiful" or "knowing the double" can be shown by prolonging the conversation. There are contexts in which a Regency piece, being a delicate object, would be out of place; therefore delicate objects are not always beautiful, and delicacy is not beauty. Again 8 is just as much half 16 as it is twice 4; doubles are also always halves. Therefore a conception of duplicity which amounts to the ability to produce a string of doubles cannot be said to be a case of "knowing the double itself according

[1] See the *Hippias Major* for answers of this type to this question.

to itself ". In general, because a thing which is P can always be shown to be in some way not-P, therefore the man who says that P-hood is identical with the various properties which make us attribute P-hood to things cannot be said to know it, although, if his attributions are in general correct, he is not ignorant of it either. His state of mind in relation to P-hood is between knowledge and ignorance; his judgments occupy the ground which lies between *on* and *mê on*.

This seems well enough, but this is a simpler argument than Plato's. From the premise that every one of the multifarious beautifuls can seem ugly we have inferred the conclusion that the opinions of plain men about beauty fall between knowledge and ignorance of it; and the link we used to join the premise to the conclusion was the manner in which plain men form their ideas of general terms, namely by identifying the multifarious beautifuls with beauty in the manner discussed above. But this is not the link that Plato uses. From the premise that every one of the multifarious beautifuls can seem ugly, he infers that each of the multifarious beautifuls is between being and not being (479 c 6), and it is apparently from this that he infers the conclusion.

That he says that each of the multifarious beautifuls is between being and not being is the bastion of those who hold that Plato believed that the physical world does not really exist. But it is a cardboard bastion. He certainly denied to physical things the status of *onta*, but this as we have seen does not mean that he denied their real existence. Nor is this denial really apposite in the present context. No doubt, writing an ambiguous language, Plato might often in some degree have in mind all the various possible interpretations of his words; but it is that interpretation of any given sentence which makes it relevant to its context which is presumably responsible for the writing of the sentence and which should therefore be called its meaning. What is relevant here is not that a given beautiful object is (like any other physical object) no more than a stable pattern manifested in the flux of nature, but that it is and is not beautiful. For that reason we surely ought to say that it is the predicative and not the existential sense of "to be" which is uppermost when Plato says that physical things are between being and not being. They do not lack existence *tout court*, they lack existence-as-beautiful-things/heavy-things or whatever it may be. In other words they are and are not beautiful, heavy and so forth. This of course may have awkward implications. It may seem to imply the (surely empty) notion that there is something which can be said to be beautiful without qualification; and this something must be beauty itself.[1] How Plato came

[1] Whether this implication is really present will be discussed below, pp. 263–5, 309, 334–5.

to write as if it made sense to call beauty beautiful is something we must consider in a later chapter. If this blunder cannot be made intelligible, that will no doubt cast doubt on the current interpretation. Since however I think it can be made intelligible, this does not trouble me. We conclude therefore that the argument is: (*a*) that any given beautiful thing is also not beautiful; (*b*) that therefore any given thing is and is not whatever it is; and (*c*) that therefore conventional opinions about beauty and so on are between *on* and *mê on*; and the link between (*b*) and (*c*) must be that which we supplied above.

Let us try to see the significance of this passage whose interpretation has cost us such a long discussion. Firstly Plato is not concerned here with the question whether we can know facts about the physical world. His purpose is to show that there are certain common states of mind which cannot be classed as knowledge. People who do not ask themselves the counter-inductive, abstract question "What is beauty?", but collect their ideas of beauty from observing the significant features of beautiful things cannot be said to know what beauty is. This is so not only in the case of beauty, but in the case of an indefinitely wide range of other properties. Plato does not say whether he supposes his argument to apply to all properties. His examples are all of properties such as beauty, justice, largeness and so on in the case of which it is plausible to say that a thing which has one of these properties also has its opposite; but he says nothing which suggests that he saw that the argument might be less plausible in the case of other properties. Can something which has the property of being a table also in suitable contexts have the property of not being a table? There is perhaps a passage in the Seventh Book which suggests that Plato thought that his argument did not include "substantival" properties such as that of being a finger (523 d). This is perhaps not very important, for even if it is possible, as the passage just referred to suggests, to collect an adequate idea of a finger inductively, the fact that one cannot do this in the case of such things as beauty, justice, size, weight and so on means that those who collect their universals inductively are deprived of full insight into the principles on which the world is ordered and on which they must themselves order anything of which they are in charge. And the immediate consequence of this is that they are not fit rulers for society.

The material version of the question "What can we know?" is not therefore answered in this passage. Formally speaking we are told (it is taken for granted) that knowledge is the direct grasp of something real, and on the basis of this we learn that in the case of beauty and similar entities it is not possible to have knowledge of them unless you first admit the existence of these universal properties as single self-consistent entities. We are not told whether it is possible to have knowledge of the road to Larisa, nor what form such knowledge would take, nor whether it is available to locals or to philosophers, nor anything of this kind. We are told something about the knowledge of universal properties and how this differs from the indirect apprehension of them in the *doxai* of the ordinary man; and the point of telling us this is that we may see why ordinary men are not fit to rule—eschewing abstract philosophical thought they have no insight into principles.

One final comment. "None of the multifarious justs but is also unjust." Does this mean that there has never been a perfectly just action? I think not. The type/token distinction is not drawn. When Jones pays a debt his action may have been perfectly just. But to make justice consist of debt-paying and other similar activities is not to have achieved insight into justice (and such a *doxa* will be impotent—will "run away"—in a novel situation to which no traditional rules apply). This is so not because Jones should have acted rather differently, but because "what Jones did" (namely a debt-paying) is not always just. Token debt-payings may sometimes be incontrovertibly just. Debt-paying as a type is not always so.[1]

This point can be put in a simpler way. I suggest that the phrase *ta polla kala* should be translated not only "the multifarious beautifuls" but also "the multifarious beauties", because I suspect that it connoted both of these to Plato. When Socrates asks Theaetetus to define knowledge,[2] Theaetetus responds by citing many knowledges —of pottery, woodworking and so on; and Socrates comments: "How generous you are; I asked for one thing and you give me many." So the man who, when asked "What is the just?", cites truth-telling, debt-paying and so on, has given "many justs". If we translate "the just" in the question into normal English as "justice" we can similarly express our comment on the answer by saying that it cites many justices. And each of these many justices will also be unjust in the sense that it will contain unjust members—for example a token debt-paying which it would not, in the reigning circumstances, be just to make. In this way each of the many justices is also unjust.

(ii) *Knowledge and belief in* Republic 6 *and* 7

The main purpose, then, of the discussion in the Fifth Book has been to contrast the inadequate conception of X-hood which can be

[1] A further discussion of this section, including a justification of the point made in this paragraph, will be found in a later chapter. See below, pp. 293–5.
[2] *Theaetetus* 146 d 3.

70

derived by identifying X-hood and "the many X's" with the adequate conception which can only be achieved by what is shortly to be called dialectic—by relentlessly "asking what X-hood is". The contrast has been drawn by assigning to an inductively derived conception of the former kind an ambiguous status (between *on* and *mê on*); and great stress has been laid on the negative point that an adequate conception of X-hood cannot be had so long as one identifies X-hood and the many X's.

When Plato returns to these matters in the passage which begins towards the end of the Sixth Book and continues through most of the Seventh, it is not surprising to find that he illustrates his meaning by making great play with entities of ambiguous status (namely shadows, reflections, echoes and puppets). At the same time it is not surprising that the negative emphasis of the Fifth Book is less prominent. We have been told that no man can govern well unless he achieves an adequate grasp of beauty, justice and other such entities. We have also been warned that such a grasp cannot be achieved by attending to "the many so-and-so's". We want to ask how we can hope to achieve such a grasp, if we cannot do it inductively, and why the achieving of it will assist us in practical tasks. In my judgment it is part of Plato's purpose in the Sixth and Seventh Books to try to answer these questions, to tell us how we can pass from familiarity with the natural world to an understanding of the abstract principles of order, and to explain how it is that such principles are applicable to the understanding and control of our environment and ourselves. Obviously some metaphysical doctrine about the relationship between the forms and the natural world will be involved in any such explanation.

The passage which we are about to examine is extremely controversial. The controversy may perhaps be said to hinge upon two questions. First of these is the question how we are to interpret the entities of ambiguous status, the images as we may collectively call them, which play such a large part in Plato's exposition. How precisely is he employing the notion of an image? To put the same question in a different way, is Plato engaged in stating the metaphysical doctrine which must, as we said, underlie his attempt to answer how we can come to know the forms, and turn our knowledge to practical use, or is he rather expounding an epistemological thesis and leaving the metaphysics alone? Or is he perhaps doing a little of both and to some extent confounding the two? When he puts before us the picture of various layers of objects so arranged that each layer contains images of the entities which figure in the layer above, does he want us to believe that there exist in the world various grades of objects of such a nature that the humbler objects are in some ontological sense images or copies of the superior, or is he rather telling us that there are various states of mind which are related to each other in such a way that the content of one of these states is in some epistemological sense an image of that of the state above it?

The second question on which the controversy hinges is the question how positive Plato is really being, to what extent he is genuinely trying to tell us how true knowledge is after all attainable. This too could be expressed as a question about how we are to interpret the notion of an image. We can be deceived by images if we mistake them for originals, but we can use them to tell us something about the originals if we do not let them take us in. When certain things (whether entities in the world or conceptions in the mind) are said to be images, is the primary meaning that they are deceptive or that they are suggestive? Or (which is perhaps the right answer) does Plato mean to tell us that they *are* deceptive in that they take in most people, but that they *can be* suggestive to those who treat them properly? One might I think say that Plato's failure to make clear in what way he intends the notion of an image to be taken is the main cause of the difficulty of this passage.

I have already[1] given a sketch of the interpretation which I want to put upon this passage. Here I shall only recount its barest outlines, and then proceed to discuss in more detail various particular problems.

The passage begins in 505 where Socrates says that the philosopher needs to know what goodness is. This leads him on to the simile of the Sun in which he tells us that goodness is in the intelligible world what the sun is in the visible world. It is goodness which provides the light whereby we are enabled to know the other forms, and goodness is also responsible for their existence. In order, ostensibly, to illustrate what he means by this, Socrates next passes to the simile of the Line in which he puts before us the contrast between shadows and reflections on the one hand and originals on the other, and tells us that the same contrast holds between *doxa* and *epistêmê*, and that it also holds, "in the intelligible realm", between what he calls *dianoia* and what he calls *nöésis*. We took him to mean that if we liken the man of *doxa* and also, at a higher level, the man of *dianoia* to the man who has before his eyes an image, we may also liken the man of *epistêmê*, and in particular the man of *nöésis*, to the man who has before his eyes an original.

Socrates next passes to the simile of the Cave, which draws together the points made in the previous similes and adds to them in

[1] In Chapter 3 of Vol. 1.

various ways. One of the additional points made by the Cave is that we are all very inclined to rest content with images, and that the darker, and therefore the intrinsically less visible, things are, the easier we find them to look at. In particular although goodness provides the light by which we do all our abstract thinking, and although it is, like the sun, supremely visible, it is the last thing that we are able to see. Another of the additional points made by the Cave is that the contrast between looking at an image and looking at an original may also be drawn within the sphere of *doxa*, and that we need to draw it if we are to see how truly dreadful is the general intellectual condition of mankind. Of these three similes, then, the Cave may be said to apply the implications of the other two to the problem of how we can get from where we are to where we ought to be, to describe the resistances which we shall meet with on our journey, and in general to draw the pedagogic moral from the metaphysical and epistemological doctrine. Plato's positive point might have emerged more clearly if he had forced himself to forego the opportunity of being rude about the mental condition of mankind.

If we could assume the correctness of the interpretation which I have sketched, it would not take us long to state the contribution which this part of the *Republic* makes to Plato's epistemological doctrine. But unfortunately there are a number of points which must be looked into in more detail. Plainly the three similes belong very intimately to each other and to the educational programme to which they are prefixed. However, the comparison of the status of goodness to that of the sun raises problems which belong more to cosmology than to epistemology, and I shall defer these to the next chapter. I shall defer also any detailed consideration of the proposed educational programme. This will leave for immediate attention problems concerning the similes of the Line and of the Cave.

We can take it that the "simile" of the Line consists of the formula $a:b :: c:d :: a + b : c + d$. It says therefore that the relationship between certain pairs of terms is identical with, or at any rate similar to, the relationship between certain other pairs. An "analogy" of this kind is most commonly used when the relationship between one of the pairs of terms occurring in it is known to the hearer, and the purpose of the analogy is to acquaint him with the other relationship by telling him that it is like the known one. It is probable that this is what Socrates is doing in this case. It should therefore be worth while asking which of the relationships (that between a and b, that between c and d, or that between $a + b$ and $c + d$) Socrates takes to be known and uses as the base of the analogy. To do this let us see how Socrates assigns values to his variables.

73

He begins by assigning to *d* shadows and reflections, and to *c* the originals of which these are images. He then however says that *b* is a certain mental condition, namely that wherein we have to use hypotheses as if they were first principles; and that *a* is another mental condition, namely that wherein we use hypotheses as bases from which to set out in search of first principles. This of course is a heterogeneous set of values—two sorts of visible objects and two states of mind. Shortly however (511 d–e) he offers a homogeneous list by assigning to each segment of his line, or to each variable, a "condition of the mind". *a* becomes *nöêsis*, *b* *dianoia*, *c* *pistis* and *d* *eikasia*. When he subsequently reverts to the analogy in 533 e–534 a he gives a slightly modified version of this homogeneous list, and I think we can assume that these four homogeneous terms are the terms of the relationships between which the analogy is supposed to hold. We need not therefore rack our brains to see how *nöêsis* could stand to *dianoia* in the relationships in which things stand to shadows. *Nöêsis* stands to *dianoia* in the relationship in which *pistis* stands to *eikasia*, where *pistis* is a state of mind correlated with looking at things and *eikasia* a state of mind correlated with looking at shadows (*etc.*).

The analogy says, then, that *nöêsis* stands to *dianoia* as *pistis* to *eikasia*, and as the sum of the first two terms stands to the sum of the second two, where *epistêmê* is taken to be the sum of the first two, and *doxa* the sum of the second.[1] On the assumption that one of these relationships is being used to illuminate the others, which is the relationship that we are supposed to understand already?

We know roughly by this stage what the words *epistêmê* (or *gnôsis*) and *doxa* mean. What about the other four words? *Eikasia* ought to mean something like "conjecturing" or "representing by a likeness". *Pistis* means something like "trust" or "confidence", though it can be used to mean "proof" or "ground of confidence".[2] There is therefore a clear difference of meaning between these two terms. The difference between *dianoia* and *nöêsis* is not so clear. *Dianoia* ought to mean something like "thinking" and *nöêsis* might well have been used more or less synonymously with it, though evidently that is not the case here. It is fairly clear, then, that we could not know what the relationship between these two terms is by attending to the meaning of the words used to name them. When we turn our attention from the meanings of the words to the natures of the states that they name, we get a similar result. We have some idea, but we would like more, of what Socrates takes *epistêmê* and *doxa* to be and of the relationship between these states. On the other hand it is

---

[1] This is inaccurate as we shall see below (p. 90–101). *Doxa* is not the sum of *c* and *d* but it is related to *c + d*.

[2] *Laws* 965 c 7, and perhaps *Phaedo* 70 b 2.

clear that Socrates could not and does not expect us to see at once what he means when he speaks of the state of mind in which we have to treat hypotheses as first principles, and contrasts this with the state of mind in which we use hypotheses as bases from which to seek for first principles. But we are of course familiar with the difference between seeing a thing and seeing a shadow or reflection, and we can use our common sense to work out the epistemological relationship between these predicaments. Furthermore we are helped by the application of the two terms *pistis* and *eikasia* to these predicaments in a way in which we are not helped by the term *nöêsis* and *dianoia*[1]. It is obvious that if I can see something I have grounds for confidence about it, whereas if I am only looking at a shadow I am reduced to conjecturing. It is fairly clear therefore that Socrates is intending to throw light on the relationship between *nöêsis* and *dianoia*, and that he is getting the light either from the relationship between *epistêmê* and *doxa* or from that between *pistis* and *eikasia*. Since this last relationship is the only one which is familiar to common sense it is probable that this is the one which is intended to throw light. This conclusion is reinforced by the reflection that there is little point in bringing into the story the intrinsically rather unimportant relationship between seeing things and seeing shadows unless it is brought in to illuminate the other two, much more interesting, relationships. The reasonable conclusion seems to be that the analogy is meant to tell us that the relationship between *nöêsis* and *dianoia* and the relationship between *epistêmê* and *doxa* may be likened to the relationship between a man who is looking at a thing and a man who is looking at an image. A further argument in support of this conclusion is that throughout this section Plato is using well-known facts about visual experience to illustrate what he wants to say about thought.

What is not so clear is whether the description *eikasia* or "conjecture" is being used in a subjective or in an objective sense. That is to say, it is not clear whether the man who has before his eyes an image is aware of this fact and is using the features of the image as clues to the nature of the original, or whether on the contrary he is deceived by the image and assumes that he is looking at a genuine thing. In the former case he would be conjecturing subjectively; in the latter case we might say that he was conjecturing objectively, and say it with pejorative intent. If Plato wanted to speak kindly of *doxa*

---

[1] Indeed Glaucon seems to imply (511 d 2) that Socrates has chosen the word *dianoia* because he wanted a word which could go between *doxa* and *nous* (or *nöêsis*); and in 533 d Socrates seems to say that he chose the word because it connotes more clarity than *doxa* and less than *epistêmê*, and adds that we must not argue about the choice of a name. This suggests that the choice was, linguistically speaking, somewhat arbitrary.

and *dianoia* he would liken them to the state of mind of a man who does the best that he can with the kind of indirect information that an image gives us of its original; if he wanted to speak ill of them he would liken them to the condition of the man whom the image deludes. In fact, I think, Plato wants to do both of these things, in that he wants in particular to tell us that the entities which are studied at the level of *dianoia* (namely mathematical entities) *can be* used as clues to enable us to grasp the forms, but at the same time that they *are in fact* wrongly treated by mathematicians, who do not attempt to get back behind them. For this reason we probably ought to say that the condition described as *eikasia* is neither that of shrewdly conjecturing nor that of being deluded, but more generally the condition of having the kind of second-rate knowledge of a thing which we have if we can only see an image of it. *Pistis* by contrast will be the condition in which we are entitled to be confident because we can actually see the thing about which we are judging.

This account of the meanings of the terms *eikasia* and *pistis* will have to be revised at a later stage of our discussion, because it is part of my argument that the meaning of these two terms changes subtly in the Seventh Book with the complication which is introduced by the subdivision of empirical thought into two grades in the simile of the Cave. Strictly speaking these two grades are related to each other as *eikasia* is related to *pistis* (in the sense in which these terms were introduced in the simile of the Line), but Plato speaks as if the two grades *were eikasia* and *pistis*. But this complication must be deferred until we have looked at the Cave.

Meanwhile so far as the Line is concerned *eikasia* seems to mean "having only an image to go on", and *pistis* seems to mean "having grounds for confidence because the thing itself is before our eyes". When he first assigns images to *d* and their originals to *c* in 509 d 9, Socrates says that he is dividing his line in terms of "clarity and unclarity" (*saphêneia* and *asapheia*), and this surely draws attention to the difference between the good view that I get of a thing that is before my eyes and the poor view that I get of a thing of which I only see a shadow or reflection. This, then, is the fundamental contrast, and it is used to illuminate the contrast between *nöêsis* and *dianoia*, which two terms, it is clearly implied in 511 e 3, also differ in *saphêneia* or clarity.[1]

Our next question therefore must be that of the identities of *nöêsis* and *dianoia*. On this topic I shall not say very much in this chapter.[2] I take it that the process which Socrates calls *nöêsis* is the

[1] I suspect that *saphêneia* connotes both goodness of view and directness of confrontation, the two being thought to amount to the same thing.

[2] See Chapter 5, especially pp. 548–62.

same as that which he calls dialectic, though the word *nöêsis* (which probably means something like "seeing with the mind") really refers to success in this process. It is the process whereby we try to "arrive at just what each thing is" (532 b 1) without the aid of the senses, or to "grasp the intelligible account (*logos*) of the essential nature (*ousia*) of each thing" (534 b 3). It culminates in the vision of goodness, which also provides the light which has been used all along. The word *dianoia* is made by Socrates to stand for the mathematical disciplines which he describes. He does not tell us in so many words that there is no other branch of thought which deserves the title *dianoia*, but he gives no indication of the identity of any other. If there were any other discipline which could be called *dianoia* we would expect it to have the following characteristics, which are derived from Socrates' and Glaucon's descriptions of *dianoia* in the account of the Line. It would be a discipline in which we have to "seek from hypotheses" (510 b 5), and go not towards an *archê* (beginning, first principle or source) but towards a *teleutê* or end. It would make use of physical things in the manner in which mathematicians talk about the shapes of physical things, such as a drawn square, although they are not thinking[1] about the drawn square but about "the square itself" which the drawn square "resembles" (510 c 5–8). It would be unable to get beyond hypotheses (511 a 5) and it would not attempt to "give account" of the things that it hypothesises (510 c 6). Its subject matter would consist of things which are "intelligibles given an *archê*" (511 d 2) and it would deserve the title *dianoia* (implying that it comes between *doxa* and *nous*) because although its subject-matter consists of things which have to be investigated by the mind and not by the senses, it fails to achieve *nous* or understanding of them by reason of the fact that, lacking the *archê*, it has to use hypotheses (511 c–d).

It is not too difficult to see what this means in terms of mathematics. Mathematicians do not get out their rulers to prove that the square on the diagonal of a given square is double the area of the square on whose diagonal it is. They do not do experiments with bundles of matches to prove that $7 \times 7 = 49$. They use their minds and not their senses to prove their theorems. They lay it down that the units that arithmetic is concerned with are indivisible and equal each to each (which is true of no ordinary units such as cattle), and are therefore entities which can be grasped with the mind but not with the senses (525 d–526 a). In fact, to do mathematics we have to make an effort of abstraction. But mathematicians do not take this

---

[1] Subjectively or objectively? Does Socrates mean that they know that they are thinking about "the square itself", or that that is in fact their topic though they do not fully realise this? In my view the latter is nearer the truth.

to its logical conclusion and explicitly allow that they are dealing with totally abstract entities. In geometry they do not try to ask what squareness is; they take this to be "evident to all men" (510 d 1), and therefore their talk has to mention entities which one can only represent to oneself as shapes of physical things, boundaries of physical surfaces. Though Plato talks mostly of geometry it is clear that he thought that something similar applied in the case of arithmetic. I suppose that what he had in mind must be of the following kind: we tell ourselves that the units, which can, for example, be paired off in even but not in odd numbers, are not physical units; nevertheless, because we have no abstract conception of what unity is, we have to represent our arithmetical unit to ourselves as something like a small and featureless pip (the Pythagorean "marbles"), and no doubt we have to represent the pairing-off as a physical process of setting side by side. We have no *Principia Mathematica* to tell us how to construct arithmetical operations such as division out of notions which belong to general logic, i.e. have no special application to the kind of entities which have to be visualised. Therefore our mathematical thought has an essential connection with physical entities, which connection is improper and indeed allowed to be improper by the procedural rules which mathematicians lay down.

Dialectic is the process by which we travel from *dianoia*, I think, to *nöêsis*. Dialectic "makes its way destroying hypotheses" (533 c 8), or in other words doing that which the mathematicians leave undone when they "allow their hypotheses to remain undisturbed, and cannot give account of them" (*ibid.* c 2). The feature of *dianoia* which is here referred to, I believe, is that whereby mathematicians take for granted such things as the division of numbers into odd and even or the classification of angles into three kinds as "evident to all men". Taking such things for granted is objectionable and has to be disturbed, but not primarily because there is any doubt of the truth of the propositions which are involved in these "hypotheses". It is objectionable because the entities which mathematicians take for granted are "intelligible given an *archê*". That is to say an opportunity is missed when we take for granted such a notion as that of an even number and do not try to give account of it. We can indeed proceed towards the *teleutê* or end (that is to say, we can deduce the consequence of our hypotheses, or prove theorems) without giving account, but we cannot get towards the *archê*, source or first principle. We cannot do so because unless we try to give account of such notions as *even number* we cannot discern the source of the division of numbers into odd and even, the abstract principle which, in its application to aggregates of units, entails that the number of every alternate aggregate should be even. We therefore have to accept it as a matter of fact that all numbers are either odd or even, and we lose the chance of seeing the rationale of this, although it is intelligible given an *archê*, i.e. it is the kind of thing whose rationale ought to be discoverable. It is also the case I think (Plato nowhere explicitly says this, but it seems to be the natural interpretation of his language on several occasions) that it is *because* we do not attempt to seek the *logos* or rationale of the things which we take for granted in mathematics that we are forced to represent them to ourselves in sensuous terms. The thought underlying this, I believe, is that we ought to be able to achieve an abstract understanding of principles like squareness or circularity, and that if we could do so we would not have to represent such entities to ourselves in terms of the boundaries of physical surfaces, and that so long as we cannot do so we must think of them in that way. This is the sense in which *dianoia* is compelled (510 b 5) to use hypotheses and to rely on sensibles. The compulsion is not exercised by the nature of the subject matter of mathematics, but by the mathematicians' unwillingness to seek to give account. One might almost say that the compulsion is logical, in that something which did not rest on hypotheses would no longer be *dianoia*. *Nöêsis*, being what we attain to when we do dialectic and disturb our takings-for-granted, will involve understanding the rationale of the distinctions, classifications and so on which *dianoia* takes for granted, it will culminate in the apprehension of the supreme rational principle, the nature of goodness, and it will exempt us from all reliance on sensibles. How it achieves this must be left for another chapter.[1]

We can see now that it would not be easy to imagine a subject other than mathematics which could deserve the title *dianoia*. To be *dianoia* a subject has to be semi-abstract in the way in which mathematics of the kind which Plato is describing is semi-abstract. Mathematics depends upon the act of abstraction whereby we arrive at the notions of space and quantity, and work out rules of procedure which enable us to talk about physical things without reference to any of their physical qualities. It is easy to see that we might be tempted to say that in mathematics we are talking about physical entities *only in so far as they are ordered* (this is a deliberately loose use of the notion of order), and that we might therefore come to think that mathematics offers us a unique range of "images" of the abstract principles of order whose imposition upon physical things renders them susceptible to mathematical treatment.

This brings us to the question how it is that *dianoia* stands to *nöêsis* as *eikasia* to *pistis*. The meaning must be that in the state of *dianoia* a man has before his mind images of the objects which he perceives directly in the state of *nöêsis*. It is made clear enough that

[1] Below, Chapter 5, pp. 548–62.

79

the objects which *noêsis* directly perceives are forms (whatever these may be); and therefore the proximate objects, as we might call them, of *dianoia* must be images of the forms. If *dianoia* is identical with mathematics, this ought to mean that the things which mathematicians talk about (squares and circles, perhaps, odd and even numbers, and similar entities) are images of the forms. He who has reached the level of abstraction at which he can talk about circles as opposed to plates, rectangles as opposed to tables, has reached the level of "conjecturing about the forms", which he perceives indirectly because he has their images before his mind.

This ought to be what the Line is meant to tell us about the relationship between *dianoia* and *noêsis*. What does it mean? Roughly, I think, the meaning is that which I indicated at the end of the last paragraph but one. Plato's view was, I believe, that the form, structure, principle or what you will which constitutes a mathematical entity such as a circle has no essential application to space. Such principles can be expressed in spatial embodiments, but in themselves they are prior to such embodiments and in no way dependent on them. Furthermore they are capable of other embodiments which are not spatial in kind. The spatial embodiments of the forms have the advantage over all other embodiments that they are especially close to the originals in that the "matter" of the embodiment—space—is something abstract, something having no properties of its own which might compromise the purity of the embodiment or distract attention from it.

How did Plato come to have such views? We have already suggested that he might have followed a train of thought similar to that which, we conjectured, underlay the Pythagorean definition of justice as the number 4. Justice is reciprocity; 4 is the first square. But in 2×2 the first number treats the second in the same way in which the second treats the first; each doubles the other. Likewise when you hit me and I justly retaliate each of us does to the other what the other does to each. There is therefore an identity of structure between the arithmetical operation of squaring and the human operation of retaliation.[1] Incidentally the same structure would presumably be common also to a geometrical square. Plato stresses that the man who is to do dialectic must bring his mathematical studies together and see their kinship (531 d), and it may be that he thought that it was when we could see the identity of structure between an equal-sided rectangle and a number whose factors are $n \times n$ that we should be ready to detach the structure from its embodiments and entertain the notion that it might have other, non-mathematical embodiments.

[1] I am not suggesting that Plato would in fact have thought this an adequate account of justice. The Pythagoreans chose too simple a mathematical image.

There are other instances of principles which have mathematical and also non-mathematical embodiment. Equality is a mathematical relationship which exists in two forms, "arithmetical" and "geometrical", and these two forms of equality are also to be found in human society. The *Gorgias*, indeed, makes the point that a knowledge of mathematics will help the politician to distinguish the two kinds of equality in society (*Gorgias* 508 a). There is also the passage in the Tenth Book of the *Laws* (*Laws* 897–8) where the Stranger speaks of the circle as an image of intelligence; the same principle of self-consistency which constitutes intelligence also expresses itself in spatial terms in the form of motion in a circle. There are then examples such as these of structures or principles which can be expressed in spatial or numerical terms to give us entities or relationships with which mathematicians are familiar, but which appear to be capable of non-mathematical embodiment. Such examples might very well have suggested the thought that wherever we find precise relationships between spatial or numerical magnitudes we are dealing with an order which reason has imposed. But reason for Plato is something which is independent of the existence of space or physical objects. It might therefore seem that the order which reason can impose on such entities must also be something which is independent of them although capable of embodiment in them. But if there apparently exist structures (such as circularity) which are, so to speak, neutral between their mathematical and their non-mathematical embodiments, this might be taken to confirm the idea that "in themselves" these structures are independent of all embodiment. It is natural to think that something which can exist either in this form or in that must also be capable of existing in no form at all, but simply "in itself". It was entities existing, in this way, "in themselves" which we were to know at the level of *nöêsis*, and it was their mathematical embodiments that we were familiar with at the level of *dianoia*. It was because the things that we were familiar with at this level are in fact images of pure principles of reason that students have to do mathematics before they can attempt dialectic.

A modern philosopher might allow that some analogy can perhaps be detected between equality in mathematics and in political theory, but he would go on to protest that it would be an idle dream to suppose that we could ever come to know something called "equality itself" which is the pure essence of the mathematical and political embodiments. My suggestion is that Plato did not think this an idle dream. There are two points which may perhaps make this suggestion easier to swallow. One is that it may be that Plato primarily wanted to make a simpler pedagogic point that did not carry with it the notion of "equality itself" and other such entities. This is the point which is made in effect in the passage in the *Gorgias* (508 a) cited above. It is that you can teach a man in the unemotional atmosphere of mathematics to draw distinctions which excite passion in politics. A man can learn in mathematics that there are two kinds of equality, and a man who has thoroughly learnt this will be unable to suppose that "equality" can have only one meaning in politics. There is therefore pragmatic value in the proposal to train future rulers in mathematics. But Plato might have thought that if this was so it must be due to the fact that the two equalities are embodiments of "equality itself", and so on with whatever other examples he had in mind. This pragmatic point might have conspired with his cosmological belief in a reason independent of the physical world to make him think it necessary to postulate entities such as equality itself. But the second point is that it is not certain that Plato did want to postulate such entities in the most offensive way. He did indeed believe, if I am right, in the possibility of knowing things like "equality itself", but it does not fully follow that he thought that this was, so to speak, an essence which we could extract from its embodiments and put a label on. That is to say, knowing equality itself according to itself does not necessarily involve being able to *say* what it is; it might be enough to be able to *see* the analogy between the embodiments. There does not necessarily have to be a *logos*, definition or account, which is the *logos* of pure equality. We shall see later in this chapter that at some stages at any rate Plato may have doubted whether you can always say what you can be said to know; a certain skill in handling attempted refutations may perhaps sometimes count as knowledge.[1] He does indeed speak in this passage several times of "giving a *logos*" as something that a dialectician must be able to do, and he does indeed say in one place (534 b 3) that the dialectician grasps the account of the essence of each thing. But he also says that it is by trying to give account of the entities which mathematicians hypothesise that we come to know the forms. It is conceivable therefore that he thought that to come to know a form was to achieve an understanding that could not be expressed in a formula, and that in this way "knowing equality itself" was not very different from understanding the analogy between its various embodiments. We have to steer between the twin dangers of taking Plato's language too literally, thus burdening him with too much ontology, and of bringing his thoughts too much into line with ours by an over-flexible interpretation.

Whatever exactly the experience of "knowing equality in itself" is to be thought to consist in, our view is that such an achievement is what counts as *noêsis*, and that the mathematical embodiment of

[1] See below, pp. 122–6.

equality which is familiar to us at the level of *dianoia* is an image of the form and can be used to "conjecture" it. This is how *dianoia* stands to *noēsis* as *eikasia* to *pistis*. The question now arises whether *all* forms have their images at the level of *dianoia*. There may be readers who will agree, more or less, with what has been said so far but will want to add that of course it is only some of the forms that have images which we can study at the level of *dianoia*, at any rate if mathematics and *dianoia* are the same thing. It is only "mathematical" forms which can have mathematical images. I think that this view is wrong, but there are two arguments in its favour. One is that in the *Republic* Plato seems to believe in all kinds of forms, including those of artefacts like beds and tables; and it is absurd to believe that there are images of bed-hood and tabularity among the entities of mathematics, as there would be if *dianoia* involved familiarity with images of all the forms. The second argument for the view that it does not involve this is that in the simile of the Cave there are three sets of *simulacra*. There are the shadows on the back wall, which are what the vulgar believe in, there are the reflections in the pool outside, which are plausibly regarded as the things that mathematicians talk about, but there are also the puppets that cast the shadows; and what are these? These could be accommodated if we thought that whereas forms like squareness and equality had mathematical images others like justice and bed-hood had less abstract, more sensuous images, images which were grasped by the senses and therefore properly located in the cave and represented as puppets—as puppets because these are realities in comparison with the shadows, as befits the images of forms, but derivative realities, as befits images.

I shall not attempt to meet this second argument until we have dealt with the Cave, and I shall only offer a sketch of an answer to the first. The argument depends, really, on the question how much is involved in "believing in the existence of a form of so-and-so". There is no doubt that in the Tenth Book of the *Republic* Plato evinces belief, in some sense, in the existence of a form of beds and of tables; and if this means that in addition to entities such as justice and circularity he believed also in an independent principle of bed-hood, then it would be very difficult to suppose that this last could have a mathematical image. However as we shall see elsewhere[1] Plato had at least a tendency, at least at some periods, to regard "adjectival" forms such as equality as more important than "substantival" forms such as bed-hood. Perhaps he felt that "what it is to be a bed" could be regarded as a complex function of the properties which beds have to exhibit. We can after all give some account of what beds ought to

[1] See Chapter 3, pp. 353–6.

83

be like by mentioning properties such as rigidity, rectangularity and so forth. The context in the Tenth Book does not require that bed-hood should be a totally independent form; it only requires (and the same is true of the form of a shuttle in the *Cratylus*) that a principle of organisation should be prior to the things which are organised in accordance with it.

However this may be, I should want to urge that in the Sixth and Seventh Books of the *Republic* when Plato talks about forms he is not thinking of particular principles of organisation such as that of beds, but of altogether more general principles, principles which will be involved in the organising of anything whatever. I have suggested that this can be reconciled with what is said of beds in the Tenth Book. If it cannot, I should prefer to fall back on the hypothesis of disagreement between the two parts of the *Republic*, rather than to allow that it is only mathematical forms whose images the mathe-maticians are familiar with. For it is clear from the Line, and also from Plato's educational proposals, that he does intend us to believe that mathematics is in a unique position, not only with respect to coming to know mathematical forms, but also with respect to coming to know what we need to know in order to govern our lives and our cities. It is therefore a mistake to say that there are mathematical forms and ethical forms and that only the former have their images among the proximate objects of the mathematicians. There are not mathematical forms and ethical forms; there are just forms, or principles of order, all of which, for all that Plato says to the con-trary, have their mathematical and also their non-mathematical embodiments, and may be relevant equally to the study of ordered quantity and of ordered lives.

It may be retorted that, even if we decide somehow to ignore bed-hood and tabularity, it is still absurd to say that all the forms have mathematical embodiments. What is the mathematical embodiment of that whose presence to something makes that thing beautiful, or morally good? Shall we be hearing that triangles are images of beauty, pentagons of virtue? Half of the answer to this is that it is not as absurd as it sounds, so long as we do not look too carefully. We must remember how large a part notions like harmony and pro-portion played in Plato's ethical, political and aesthetic theories. It is not difficult to suppose that he might have thought that mathemati-cians were familiar with harmony and proportion in their mathe-matical forms. In this way he might have come to think, what he would anyhow want to think on *a priori* grounds, that every principle whose application results in something definite and ordered, is cap-able of application to space and quantity and therefore has mathe-matical embodiment. But the second half of the answer to this

84

objection is that we do not need to hit upon a tenable idea in order to find a correct interpretation of the simile of the Line. For Plato does not repeat elsewhere the things which he says in this passage about the special part played by mathematics in the process of coming to know the forms; and it is at least possible that the reason why he does not do so is that he had given here an outline sketch of a train of thought which seemed to him promising, but which he was never able to make good in detail. It may be that the difficulties which trouble us also troubled him.

To sum up, then, the interpretation that I am offering of the simile of the Line is that just as the objects of vision have their shadows which can on occasion delude us, but which can be used to give us clues of a kind to the nature of their originals, so the objects of the mind, the forms or principles of order, have their images with which we can rest content, but which we also can and should make use of as clues to the nature of the principles whose images they are; and that this is so because every principle of order is applicable to the ordering of space and quantity, and is therefore met with in such applications in the course of the mathematical sciences. The entities of mathematics are not pure principles; they are embodiments of such principles, but abstract embodiments, the discipline of mathematical study having purged out of them all the material element with the exception of space and quantity. All that we need therefore, to grasp the formal element in its purity, is to carry the process further and to get rid of this residual material element. This is why mathematics plays a special role in the training of those who need to grasp the formal element in its purity in order to recognise it in its moral and political embodiments, and to bring these about.

We pass now to problems connected with the simile of the Cave.
There are two stages within the cave, that of the prisoners who can see nothing but shadows, and who represent, as Socrates says, "ourselves", and that of the reluctantly liberated man who is forced to look at the puppets and recognise that they are the origin of the shadows. The cave represents the visible world, and this would seem to mean that whatever happens in it represents some kind of use of the senses. Any stage of enlightenment which consists in the exercise of abstract thought is represented by something outside in the daylight. Therefore if there are two stages within the cave this means that Plato is distinguishing two grades of empirical thought, the lower of which is said to be characteristic of "ourselves".

Now the two grades are related precisely as seeing shadows to seeing originals; and since just this relationship has been the motive power of the Line, it is too much to ask us not to interpret the present passage, a page or so further on, in the light of the earlier. This has puzzled many people, for they say that Plato cannot seriously mean to tell us that the depth of unenlightenment from which we all start consists in seeing nothing but shadows and mistaking them for realities. In our account of this passage we allowed that this was just, and dealt with the difficulty by saying that Plato is still analogising. That is to say, just as in the Line he told us that there are two grades of abstract thought which are related to each other by the relation which obtains between seeing shadows and seeing things direct, so here he is to be taken as telling us that there are two grades of empirical thought between which the same relation holds. What the prisoners do on their bench stands in the *eikasia/pistis* relationship to what the man does who is forced to look at the puppets. We decided also to characterise the state of mind of the prisoners on the bench as that of "the aesthete", that of the man who sees the puppets as that of "the craftsman". Something must now be said to explain and justify this.

What primarily requires explanation is Plato's use of phrases like "the realm which is revealed through the sense of sight" (517 b 2) to describe that of which the inside of the cave is a likeness. For it is fairly generally agreed that Plato's primary interest in the prisoners in the cave is paid to their moral and political and not their visual illiteracy. There are shadows of justice and so on on the back wall and it is primarily these that the *illuminati*, who have seen the originals in the outside world, help the prisoners to identify (520 c). It is our proneness to moral and political, not to optical, illusion that is relevant. Why then does Plato speak of "the world revealed by sight"?

The answer is: for no good reason, but from carelessness. Plato knows quite well that we do not literally see with our eyes that it is wrong to steal as we see with our eyes that the coffee-pot is empty. I have complained before of Plato's habit of talking loosely of the senses when he means something more like common sense; now is an occasion to justify these complaints. For we can confirm the suspicion that Plato is lumping things that are in no sense visual under "the sense of sight" by looking at the Tenth Book. In the passage in question (600–4) Plato is talking about painting and poetry. He refers to the phenomena of illusion, such as the straight stick which looks bent in water, and he significantly describes them as "shadow-drawing". He claims that, in painting things as they look, painters exploit our natural propensity to be deceived by this shadow-drawing; and he tells us that our available defences against this propensity are such techniques as measuring, counting and weighing. These techniques are of course those which the craftsman employs, and it is with the craftsman that the painter is contrasted. The painter is concerned to represent what a bed looks like from one angle, and indeed to paint what the uninstructed vulgar regard as a "beautiful" bed. The craftsman is concerned to find out from those who use the things that he makes what they ought to be like, and to make them like that. For him the *kallos*, beauty or fineness, of a bed lies in its fitness for its function; and he wants the bed that he makes to be, and not merely to look, fit for the job. He is said to be concerned with the *alêtheia* or truth of beds, and the painter with *eidôla* or images (600 e etc.). To this is added the comment that it is the user of an object who has *epistêmê* of what it ought to be like, and that the craftsman, by consulting the user, comes to have *pistis orthê* or *doxa orthê* (correct *pistis* or *doxa*). The painter, however, the maker of images, has neither of these things; he simply imitates whatever the vulgar think beautiful.

In this discussion Plato seems to bring against the painter two charges which are distinct but which he does not trouble to distinguish. One is that the painter paints (and the poet depicts) appearances, where this means that the work of art has only to look like that which it represents from a given point of view, in a given light and so on (and *mutatis mutandis* for the poet). In this way the artist is a reproducer of images. This is one charge; it is the charge which brings the notion of an image into the discussion, and it is the charge which is connected with the phenomena of optical illusion, but it is not the main charge. The main charge is that in order to please his clients the painter does not need to know what a bed ought to be like nor a poet how a battle ought to be fought; they only need to be able to reproduce something that the vulgar admire. Contrariwise the craftsman has two distinct virtues; he uses measuring techniques instead of relying on appearances, and he is concerned with fitness for function rather than with fashion. On one side of the contrast is a set of practitioners who are concerned only with how things "look" (whether literally in the case of painting or metaphorically in the case of poetry), and who are trying to please those who are concerned only with how things "look". Such practitioners produce "images", and to be skilful producers of images they need no accurate ideas about the nature of what they depict, and they have no technique for acquiring such ideas. On the other side of the contrast, the craftsmen (whether they are carpenters making the beds which painters paint, or generals fighting the battles which poets depict) are concerned with the *alêtheia* or reality of things, have to have accurate ideas about what they ought to be like, and have to learn techniques for making them so.

We may notice also that although Plato stresses the analogy

between painters and poets in that he fits them under a common formula (they are both "makers of images"), he is also perfectly well aware that it is only an analogy, that painters and poets do not make images in quite the same sense (603 b). The images of justice, warfare and so on in which the poet deals are not the same as images of beds on canvas, because they do not do the same sort of harm to those who indulge in them. Poetry hypertrophies the emotions, whereas painting panders to the tendency to judge by the eyes rather than by the set square. The two arts are differently damnable, but they can be attacked together because of the strength of the positive analogy between them. This lies in the type of person to whom they both appeal. He is the man who is only interested in how things look, who is satisfied of the beauty of anything which looks convincing, and who is to be sharply contrasted with the practical man who demands good workmanship and who identifies soundness of design with serviceableness.

It is fairly easy to see the application of this to the parable of the Cave. We have here a contrast between two levels of empirical thought. The craftsman, though he "looks towards" the form, does not know it; that privilege is reserved for the user, who would of course be the philosopher in the case of the most important kinds of craftsmanship such as government. The craftsman is still "in the world revealed by sight" in that he relies on his senses, although he helps them out with measuring techniques, knowing, as the aesthete does not know, that things are not always as they seem. Furthermore it is a common feature of both passages that although Plato does most of his exposition in terms of the sense of sight he is really more interested in moral than in optical illusion. We have seen that this is true of the Cave, and it is also clear that the energy of Plato's attack in the Tenth Book is directed against poetry and not against painting. I do not believe that Plato really hoped to convince us that people who admire pictures are more likely than the rest of us to be taken in by straight sticks which look bent in water. It is poetry that troubles him, as the end of the discussion makes clear (605–8), and what troubles him about poetry is the moral misjudgment that it encourages. In both discussions therefore Plato tells his story in terms of the sense of sight, but what he is concerned with is the moral blunders to which a certain class of persons is prone. These persons are those of whom the man who is interested only in visual appearances is treated as characteristic. This man is taken as a kind of paradigm of those who are not concerned with the reality of things. He is described as a maker or appreciator of "images", a description which is much more immediately intelligible in its application to him than in its extended application to the moral sphere. In both passages therefore the notion of images is brought into the story by means of introducing the visual analogue to moral carelessness, and in both passages the sense of sight is used to illustrate what Plato wants to say about morals. He seems to have supposed, quite mistakenly, that he would thereby make his meaning clearer. Plato's purpose in the Cave is to castigate the general condition of mankind by attributing to us all a faith in the reality of "images". This is to attribute to us all the disease which, in the Tenth Book, he attributes especially to artists and their public, but which he no doubt supposes to afflict us all to a greater or lesser extent except in so far as intelligence has effected a cure by the use of quasi-mathematical techniques. Plainly Plato is going further than he really means to go when he says that the prisoners in the cave are "like ourselves", if that implies that none of us resemble the man who has been made to look at the puppets. Probably however he intends only to tell us that the condition of the prisoners is our natural condition, out of which we can be, and many of us have been, forced to rise by the education which has been given to us. In so far as we have not risen, our condition is one of being content with "images", or with the appearances of things, whether the things in question are objects of vision, objects of moral judgment or something in between.

We can now see that we can say if we wish that the puppets are images of the forms. This will mean that a well made bed or a well fought battle will be a genuine embodiment of what it is to be a bed or a battle, a truly just transaction will be a genuine case of the just. However it seems to be Plato's purpose to tell us that we ought not to try to conjecture the forms from images of this kind, but rather from those which we encounter on the mathematical level. Probably his reason is that every just act embodies many other principles besides that of justice. (We remember that in 476 a 6 he tells us that it is because forms associate with each other in their instances that we find it difficult to discern their unity). It is because well built beds and truly just acts can be described as images of the forms that they are represented by puppets, but they are not the primary images for his pedagogical purposes, nor are they the only images which some forms possess, the reflections in the pool being the only images to belong to others. Both puppets and reflections are replicas of the contents of the outside world, but replicas of different kinds.

In the simile of the Line there occur two terms, namely *doxa* and *epistêmê*, to which we have so far paid little attention. It is also the case that Socrates recapitulates and amplifies the Line in the Seventh Book (533 d–534 a), and in doing so introduces certain complications. We must now attend to these matters.

89

The first appearance which the terms *doxa* and *epistêmê*, or rather *gnôsis*, make in the simile of the Line is towards the beginning (510 a 9). Socrates has told Glaucon to remember the distinction between the visible and the intelligible, has assigned one major part of his line to the visible and one to the intelligible, has proceeded to divide the two major parts in terms of *saphêneia* or clarity and its opposite, and has progressed with this to the extent of assigning shadows, etc., to one sub-section of the major part concerned with the visible, the originals of the shadows to the other. "Would you agree," he continues, "that the line has been divided, in terms of truth and not-truth, in such a way that, as the believable is to the knowable, so the semblance is to that which it resembles?" Glaucon accepts this. Now there are two things which Socrates may intend by his question, and one that he cannot intend. It is sometimes thought that he is using the word *doxa* to refer to the two states which he is about to name *eikasia* and *pistis*, *gnôsis* to refer to the two which are to be called *dianoia* and *noêsis*, and that his question means: "Would you agree that the ratio between the bits of line representing *doxa* and *gnôsis* respectively is the same as the ratio between the bit representing *eikasia* and the bit representing *pistis*?" This is what Socrates cannot mean, and the reason why he cannot mean it is that this question is not worth asking. For practically all that Socrates has said so far is that the line is to be divided in such a way that the answer to this question must be "Obviously yes". It follows from this that we cannot say that Socrates has so far said that *gnôsis* is equivalent to *noêsis* plus *dianoia* and *doxa* equivalent to *eikasia* plus *pistis*; and it is a good thing that he has not said this, because it would upset all our ideas about *doxa* if we learnt that it comprised nothing but looking at physical things plus looking at their shadows.

There are two interpretations of Socrates' question which make it worth asking. What these are we must defer for the moment in order to look at the complications which Socrates introduces when he recapitulates and amplifies the Line in the light of the Cave in 533–4. Having said that the word *dianoia* will do for the name of the mathematical disciplines, since all that is necessary is to have for the various states names which indicate their relative status in respect of *saphêneia* or clarity, Socrates continues: "It will be good enough, then, to say what we said before, and call the first segment *epistêmê*, the second *dianoia*, the third *pistis*, the fourth *eikasia*; and the first two together *noêsis*, the second two together *doxa*." There are two noteworthy points here. The first is that Socrates is not, of course, saying what he said before, because he earlier called the first segment *noêsis*. It may be that Plato has deliberately made Socrates commit this inconsistency in order to underline the point that the names do not matter, or it may be that he has simply forgotten what he said in Book 6. In either case the inference is that the words *nöêsis* and *epistêmê* are more or less interchangeable in Plato's mind. Therefore the second point about this passage is that Plato does now in effect say that *nöêsis* and *dianoia* add up to *epistêmê* (though he puts it that *epistêmê* and *dianoia* add up to *nöêsis*), and that *pistis* and *eikasia* add up to *doxa*. What this means we shall enquire in a moment. Meanwhile Socrates goes on to say: "*Doxa* is concerned with *genesis* (becoming) and *nöêsis* with *ousia* (reality); and as *ousia* is to *genesis*, so *nöêsis* is to *doxa*, and as *nöêsis* is to *doxa*, so *epistêmê* is to *pistis* and *dianoia* to *eikasia*."[1]

We must defer for the moment those parts of this which are concerned with the relations between states and objects and consider what is said about the mutual relations of mental states. This is, firstly, that a and b together are *epistêmê* and c and d together *doxa*; and secondly that $a+b : c+d : : a : c : : b : d$. (The second of these points follows of course from the original formula). What does all this mean?

To understand this we have got to allow that the words *pistis* and *eikasia*, as I indicated earlier, have undergone a change of meaning. They no longer bear the rather restricted sense which they bore when they were introduced in the simile of the Line, but have taken on a new sense from the distinction which is drawn between two grades of empirical thought in the Cave. *Pistis* now refers to our state of mind when education forces us to admit the reality of the puppets, or to care, in the language of the Tenth Book, for the *alêtheia* of things, *eikasia* to our state of mind while we are still tolerant of "images". As we have seen, the relation between these two states is analogous to the original *pistis/eikasia* relation. The "aesthete's" conception of a table or a just action is an "image" of that with whose *alêtheia* the "craftsman" is concerned, in that all that the former knows is what the thing in question "looks" like. Since this is a consequence of what the thing in question is like, the "aesthete" may be said to perceive a sort of shadow of that which the "craftsman" perceives direct. Therefore the craftsman/aesthete contrast is analogous to the original *pistis/eikasia* contrast. What has now happened is that, in the light of this analogy, the words *pistis* and *eikasia* have been made to stand for the two states of mind which are in this way analogous to the conditions for which the words originally stood.

If this is allowed it can be seen that it is harmless to say (what it would not have been harmless to say in the Sixth Book) that *eikasia* and *pistis* are collectively *doxa*. For *eikasia* and *pistis* now amount

---

[1] All of this appears to be still within the ambit, strictly speaking, of "it will be good enough, then, to say what we said before . . . ".

respectively to careless and to careful judgments upon physical objects, moral actions and the rest of the things which are "revealed by the sense of sight"; and it is not grievous to say that these together constitute *doxa*. It might be possible to try to drive a wedge between this use of *doxa* and that which we found in the Fifth Book; for we thought that in the Fifth Book Plato was primarily thinking of such things as a *doxa* or conception of justice, whereas here, it might be argued, he is primarily thinking of a *doxa* or judgment on a particular just act. But I think that we can stop this wedge by reflecting that though non-theoretical people mainly talk about particular instances, an observer can nevertheless comment on their conception of some general term; Jones can have a conception of justice although his possession of it consists in the particular comments he makes. This wedge therefore does not drive asunder. Jones is a man of *doxa* because he gets his conception from thinking about particulars only. His *doxa* will be *pistis* if he does it well.

The equation of *epistêmê* and *dianoia* with *nöêsis* is also harmless; for these two together constitute the pure activity of the mind, and that I suppose is what *nöêsis* means here. Had Plato said that *nöêsis*, or the grasp of forms and *dianoia*, or traffic with their shadows, together constituted *epistêmê* we should have had to say that this was a rather tolerant use of the word *epistêmê*. This perhaps is one reason why Plato does not in this passage abide by the terminology of the Sixth Book. He has however just observed before this passage opens (533 d 4) that the activities comprised under *dianoia* are often complimented with the title of *epistêmê*. The interchange of *nöêsis* and *epistêmê* is therefore not essential; and that perhaps is why he did not think it necessary to alter what he had written in Book 6.

We can now see what Socrates means when he says that as *nöêsis* is to *doxa* so *epistêmê* is to *pistis* and *dianoia* is to *eikasia*. In each relationship the second term is inferior to the first, and we are confined to the second term if we do not trouble to seek what is ultimate, but content ourselves with images. An inductive conception of a general term is an image of that general term, and we are confined to the level of *doxa* if we are content with inductive conceptions (our possession of which will be mainly or wholly manifested, as we saw, in making particular judgments). Within the level of *doxa*, or within the level of mental activity which does not aspire to an abstract grasp of general terms, we are confined to *eikasia* if we are content with images in the sense of the Tenth Book. Within the level of *nöêsis*, or the level which does so aspire, we are confined to *dianoia* if we do not attempt to do dialectic.

So far we see that the Line has been mainly concerned to sketch the part played by mathematics in the work of coming to know the forms, or of achieving an explicit understanding of the source of the light by which we do our thinking; that the Cave is mainly concerned to add to this that the base-line from which we all have to start is a very long way back from the goal; and that in the passage of recapitulation which we have just been examining Socrates brings these two points together explicitly under a common schema. We must now turn to the question of the "objects" of the mental states which Plato has distinguished.

We have three passages to consider. The first (510 a 8 sqq.) is Socrates' question to Glaucon which we have already mentioned: "Would you agree that the line has been divided, in terms of truth and not-truth, in such a way that, as the believable is to the knowable, so the semblance is to that which it resembles?" The next comes at the end of Socrates' first account of the Line (511 d–e). Here he allots the four names *nöêsis*, *dianoia*, *pistis*, *eikasia* to the *pathêmata* or conditions in the mind which are correlated with (*epi*) the four segments of the line, and continues (if we accept a standard correction of the manuscript reading):—"Arrange these four conditions proportionately, and understand that they partake in *saphêneia*, in the way in which the things that they are correlated with (*epi*) partake in *alêtheia*." The next passage comes in the recapitulation of the Line in the light of the Cave, and consists firstly of that part of what we have so far quoted which we have not considered, namely that *doxa* is concerned with (*peri*) *genesis* and *nöêsis* with *ousia*, and that as *ousia* is to *genesis*, so *nöêsis* is to *doxa*; and secondly of Socrates' concluding words, that "we must dismiss the question of the proportion which holds between that which these states are correlated with (*epi*), and the question of the division of the opinable and the intelligible (*doxastou kai nöêtou*), or we shall involve ourselves in discussions many times longer than those which we have had" (534 a).

In the earlier chapter summarising the *Republic* I sat on the fence with regard to the question whether this part of the dialogue is concerned to grade entities which correspond to the mental states which it names, or whether it is merely concerned to grade mental states by grading their "contents". I must now try to justify this posture by showing that these, which are the crucial passages, are not at all easy to interpret.

We may begin by noticing that the notion of an object or correlate is conveyed in these passages in three different ways: (1) by phrases like "the believable" (*to doxaston*); (2) by the preposition *peri* or "about" used for the relation of *nöêsis* to *ousia* and *doxa* to *genesis*; and (3) by the preposition *epi* or "in relation to". Of these three locutions *peri* is fairly unambiguous; it must I think stand for the relation which *nöêsis* and *doxa* have to their subject-matter, and this is confirmed by the fact that the other term of the relation is *ousia* and *genesis* respectively. The meaning must be that you call it *nöêsis* when a man is concerned with eternal truths, *doxa* when he is concerned with changeable physical processes. A phrase like *to doxaston* however is not so clear. "The believable" might mean "that *about* which one can have beliefs", or in other words "the physical world", or it might mean "that which one can believe", or in other words "beliefs". Likewise, as we have seen in commenting on Book 5, the preposition *epi* might stand for the relation between a mental state and the objects that it is concerned with, so that *dianoia* would be *epi* circles and *pistis epi* plates; but it might also stand for the relation between a mental state and its contents, so that *dianoia* would be *epi* the theorems of mathematics and *pistis epi* my reports of what I can see. In the third of our passages *epi* is used in such close proximity to *peri* (they occur two lines apart) that it is difficult to think that Plato expected us to give each a different meaning; and the same reasoning would suggest that he expected us more or less to identify *to doxaston* with *genèsis* and *to nöêton*, the intelligible, with *ousia*. Socrates' meaning would then be:—"*Nöêsis* is concerned with *ousia* and *doxa* with *genesis*, and *ousia* is to *genesis* as *nöêsis* is to *doxa*; but whether we shall want to sub-divide *ousia* and *genesis*, and what relationships, if so, we shall want to assert between the sub-divisions are questions we cannot now discuss. *Epistêmê* is to *pistis* as *dianoia* is to *eikasia* and so on, but I am not necessarily saying that there is a part of *ousia* which corresponds to *epistêmê*, and which stands to the part of *genesis* corresponding to *pistis* in the same relationship in which the part of *ousia* which corresponds to *dianoia* stands to the part of *genesis* which corresponds to *eikasia*. I am not even necessarily saying that *ousia* and *genesis* are to be sub-divided at all." I think that this is what Socrates means in this place, but it does not follow from this that we must put an analogous sense on the phrases *to doxaston* and *to gnôston* and on the preposition *epi* in Book Six.

It does not follow that we must do this, and it may even seem that it would be undesirable to do it if we notice that there is an apparent inconsistency between the present passage and the second of our three passages. For in the latter Socrates tells us that as his four conditions are arranged in terms of *saphêneia* so the things which they are *epi* are arranged in terms of *alêtheia*. But *prima facie* this looks as if Socrates is doing that which he subsequently says it would take him an impossibly long time to do, namely subdivide that which the states are *epi* and say what relationships hold between them. There are no doubt a good many ways out of this inconsistency. We could say for example that in the later passage Plato had forgotten that he had written this sentence at the end of the Sixth Book, just as he had also, perhaps, forgotten how he used the word *nöêsis* there; or we could say that what Plato is now refusing to do is to *identify* the parts of *ousia* and of *genesis* which correspond to the parts of *nöêsis* and of *doxa* or to explain what he means by saying that one part of *nöêsis* is superior to another in *alêtheia* just as *epistêmê* is superior to *dianoia* in *saphêneia*. Too much therefore must not be made of this inconsistency. Still, such as it is, it exists so long as we suppose that *epi* refers to the same relationship in both passages, and this may make us wonder whether in fact it does, and encourage us to try to settle the meaning of the earlier passage on its own merits without reference to that of the later.

What then does Socrates mean in the second of our three passages, that from the end of the Sixth Book? He says that as the states vary in possession of *saphêneia* so the things with which they are correlated vary in possession of *alêtheia*; and two interpretations of this seem quite natural. The first interpretation makes the preposition *epi* refer to the relationship between a state of mind and its content. *Eikasia* would be the state of mind of a man who has before his eyes an image, and that which this state of mind is *epi* would be the "conjecture" (whether it is a cautious guess or a confident blunder) that he comes to; *pistis* likewise would have as its object, or that which it is *epi*, a report on something of which I have a clear view, *dianoia* a piece of mathematics and *nöêsis* an apprehension of a form. A man who is conjecturing about something is in an unclear cognitive relationship to it compared with a man who has the thing under his eyes, and correspondingly a report based on conjecture is rough and unreliable in comparison with a report based on a clear view. We can therefore grade the states in terms of *saphêneia* and we can correspondingly grade their correlated judgments in terms of a perfectly acceptable sense of *alêtheia*. It is not quite so easy to see why the judgment of a mathematician lacks *alêtheia* in comparison with the insight of a philosopher, but one feels that it is the sort of thing that Plato might say. Since we have not been told that *pistis* and *eikasia* together constitute *doxa* we have not got to grade *doxa* and *epistêmê* in terms of *saphêneia* nor their correlates in terms of *alêtheia*. Nor have we to do this for the terms *pistis* and *dianoia*, for the relationship between the segments c and b corresponding to these two is not the same as that between d and c and between b and a. (In fact from the data c and b must be equal). Therefore this interpretation gives us both of the comparisons in terms of *saphêneia* and in terms of *alêtheia* that we have to provide.

The other natural interpretation perhaps deals more satisfactorily with *alêtheia*. According to this interpretation that which a state is

95

epi is that to which the man in the state is directly related. The man in a state of *eikasia* is directly related to a shadow, the man in a state of *pistis* to a physical thing. *Eikasia* has less *saphêneia* than *pistis*, not because one cannot clearly perceive shadows (this would not be true), but because one cannot clearly perceive things when one can only see their shadows.[1] Shadows have less *alêtheia* than things in the sense that they have less genuineness or real existence. (There is an obvious sense in which this is true enough). When we come to *dianoia* the case is a little complicated, because Plato says three times over (510 b 4; 510 e 2, 511 a 6) that the mathematician is directly related to physical things. He "uses physical things as images"; in fact plates are to him what shadows are to the man who conjectures from these the nature of their originals. But Plato also makes it fairly clear that the mathematician ignores in his physical things everything except their mathematical properties, their shapes and so on. It seems possible therefore to say that what the mathematician is directly related to is things like shapes, special mathematicians' entities which are arrived at by abstraction from physical things. These could be said to fall short in *alêtheia* in comparison with forms in roughly the same way in which shadows do so in comparison with things; or at any rate Plato would presumably be willing to say this, since it is the theme of the whole passage that the entities that mathematicians "hypothesise" are as it were images of the forms. This interpretation also, then, seems to deal satisfactorily with the necessary gradings of the states and their objects, and it is not easy to choose between the two. But whichever we choose it seems fairly clear that Socrates is not here doing that which he refuses to do in his recapitulation, for neither version provides us with something the exposition of which would involve a Marathon.

On the whole it is probably best to accept a compromise interpretation of this second passage. I argue elsewhere[2] that Plato tended to accept a "photographic" conception of thought according to which the distinction between the content of a thought and its subject-matter becomes blurred. Probably therefore Plato did not ask himself too insistently whether, when he told us that the objects of *eikasia* compared ill in point of *alêtheia* with the objects of *pistis*, he meant that the content of an act of *eikasia* lacked reliability or that the image that it was based on lacked genuineness. For content and image, being as alike as sitter and portrait, would share each other's bad qualities.

---

[1] The fact that *eikasia* has less *saphêneia* than *pistis* makes it fairly clear that Plato thinks of *eikasia* primarily as perceiving a thing through an image, and not as being deluded by an image. For delusion lacks *alêtheia* rather than *saphêneia*.

[2] See pp. 296 sqq.

What then is it that Socrates refuses to do in his recapitulation? The probable answer is that he is refusing to be more precise than he had been at the end of Book Six with regard to the relation between the objects of *nöésis* and of *dianoia*, and also conceivably that he is refusing to say anything about the relation between the objects of *pistis* and *eikasia* in the later sense of these terms. For ontological questions arise at any rate about the first pair. We have been told that the objects upon which mathematical thought is intended lack *alêtheia*, and we want to ask, as we have been asking, what these objects are, in what sense they are "objects", and what kind of *alêtheia* they lack. It is conceivable that we might want to ask similar questions about the objects upon which the eikastic thought of the vulgar is intended, the semblances of justice and so forth. Are the objects of mathematics entities in the sense in which forms are entities, or will it do to say that they are images of the forms which have their existence only in the minds of mathematicians? But it would not help Plato's exposition if he got involved in these questions. He wants to explain how we can use mathematics as a base from which we can conduct our exploration of the rational principles which are imaged in its concepts; and for this purpose the weaker thesis will do. It does not matter for the sake of this explanation whether the entities that the mathematicians hypothesise exist (or "subsist") as real but low-grade members of the intelligible realm, nor does it matter what such a question would mean. It is enough that we know what the rules are which govern talk about triangles, numbers and similar entities.

The main topic then which is dismissed in the third of our passages is the topic of *mathêmatika* or "mathematicals", the intermediate entities such as circles, non-physical like forms but plural like things, in which, as Aristotle tells us, Plato believed, at any rate in later years. Socrates is not going to tell us whether it is necessary to postulate these. It is wrong therefore to say that a belief in mathematicals is taught in the *Republic*. Indeed one is tempted to say that the whole tendency of the argument is in the opposite direction from that which leads to mathematicals. One is tempted to feel that Socrates is telling us that nouns like "number" and "triangle" are not the names of entities, and that we shall only suppose that they are if we get stuck half-way along the path of abstraction which leads from ordered things to the order which they exhibit. Geometers' objects are spatial, and yet they lack the physical properties which things need in order to occupy space; numbers are aggregates of units, but what is a unit but the ghost of a pebble? Gross minds suppose that talk about circles is talk about plates, talk about numbers talk about bundles of matches. The mathematician has got so far as to forbid such grossness, but he has not gone to the logical conclusion and seen that what he is really talking about is not things at all, whether coarse or rarefied, but properties which can be embodied in things, principles of order to which ordered things can conform. Mathematicians' entities are images in the sense that they are figments which we create in order to pursue a discipline at a midway level of abstraction. This is an attractive line of interpretation, but it raises difficulties the chief of which, perhaps, is to see how, having once pursued such a line of thought, Plato could ever have relapsed back into a belief in mathematicals. It is safest to say therefore that the *Republic* neither sponsors nor repudiates belief in the "real existence" of such entities, but refuses to discuss their status.

The remaining question about our third passage is the question what Socrates means when he says that *noêsis* is concerned with *ousia* and *doxa* with *genesis*, and that *ousia* is to *genesis* as *noêsis* is to *doxa*. The first part presumably means that abstract thought is concerned with the intelligible principles which inform our thinking and underlie the world's order, and that no thought which is directly concerned with what goes on in the world can rise above the level of *doxa*. I do not believe that this is primarily intended to forbid us to call an erroneous statement about justice a *doxa*, or to call an accurate piece of empirical observation a piece of *epistêmê*, though Plato's language doubtless allows us to deduce these vetoes. Plato is not thinking about natives who know the way to Larisa nor about eye-witnesses who saw the assault. He is still thinking primarily about people's approaches to what are, logically speaking, theoretical questions such as the nature of justice, and he primarily wants to tell us that in so far as we achieve any success in understanding abstract principles we do so by proceeding counter-inductively, and that in so far as our conceptions are formed inductively they count as *doxai*, because they are very indirect and inexplicit apprehensions, whether they are respectable, as in *pistis*, or shoddy, as in *eikasia*. The second of Socrates' points (that *noêsis* is to *doxa* as *ousia* is to *genesis*) means I suspect little more than that, for every respect in which the first member of either pair is superior to the second, there is a corresponding respect in which the same superiority holds within the other pair. Thus the principles which constitute *ousia* are changeless whereas the events which constitute *genesis* are changeable, and similarly *noêsis* is stable while *doxa* must fluctuate. If we feel that we must bring the notion of an image into the object side of the analogy, we can add to this that *genesis* is an image of *ousia* in the sense that the course of nature reflects the principles whose imposition on chaos renders it nature.

There remains the first of our three passages, that from the beginning of Socrates' exposition of the Line. Socrates asks whether the part of the line corresponding to the visible realm has been so sub-divided, in terms of *alêtheia* and the absence of *alêtheia*, that as the believable is to the knowable, so the semblance is to that which it resembles. There seem to be two feasible interpretations of this. Which we choose will depend on whether we take the believable and the knowable to be the same as the visible kind and realm and the intelligible respectively. If we do make this identification we shall make Socrates ask the following: "I have divided a line into two parts; I have assigned one to the visible kind, one to the intelligible; and I have sub-divided the parts in the same ratio. This means that the same relation must hold between the two minor parts of either major part as holds between the two major parts. Now I have assigned shadows and things respectively to the two minor parts belonging to the major part which represents the visible kind. Do you agree that this yields a correct doctrinal interpretation? Do you agree, that is, that shadows stand to things[1] as the visible kind stands to the intelligible?"

This interpretation is not identical with that which I earlier said was untenable. That view (which no one perhaps would explicitly take, but some seem to assume) says that the entities which Socrates mentions constitute the whole of the visible kind and that the states which correspond to them constitute the whole of *doxa*. The present view does not say that reflections, shadows, etc., along with animals, plants and artefacts together constitute the whole of the visible world,[2] nor that seeing them is the whole of *doxa*. It says rather that these two sets of things are the representatives of the visible world in the simile. *In* the visible world certain entities (which do not make up the whole of it, for mountains for example have no place in Socrates' list) are so related to each other that their relationship, and that of the cognitive states correlated with them, can be used to illustrate certain other relationships. On the interpretation which we are con-sidering the major part which Socrates refers to as "belonging to the visible" stands for the visible world as a whole, but the values of its parts belong to the visible world in the sense that they are drawn from it, not in the sense that they together compose the whole of it.

---

[1] It might be thought that it ought to be " . . . that *eikasia* stands to *pistis* . . ." rather than ". . . that shadows stand to things . . .". The ground for this would be that Socrates has allotted values to the minor parts in terms of *saphêneia*, the relation which holds between mental states. However the values allotted are in fact objects and not mental states, and I think that we have now crossed to the object-side. We are talking about relationships in terms of *alêtheia*.

[2] It is pretty clear that "the visible kind" means the visible or physical world. In 509 d 3 Socrates implies that *ouranos* or "the heavens" would have done as the name of the visible kind.

This is superficially awkward because the two sub-segments of line do of course compose the whole of the segment, and it is a little diffi-cult to use "$a + b$" as the name of a class of which a and b are not the only sub-classes. But it can reasonably be said that this is no more than the sort of difficulty which we run into when we try to make graphical illustrations of philosophical points, and that nothing should be hung on it. Socrates' question then, is whether it is true that the image/thing relationship holds, as his formula makes it hold, between the visible realm and the intelligible; is the visible realm an image of the intelligible?

If this interpretation is correct, Glaucon's affirmative answer to this question presumably carries the same message as Socrates' later statement, in the third of our three passages, that *ousia* stands to *genesis* as *nöêsis* stands to *doxa*. Such as they are, there are two difficulties in the way of accepting this interpretation. It is not easy to see why Socrates changes from "the visible kind" to "the believ-able", and one does not feel quite confident that at this stage in the discussion Plato could have expected his readers to understand "the believable" to mean "the world about which we can only have *doxa*" and to identify this with the visible world. Secondly on this interpre-tation Socrates' question introduces a complication which is un-necessary, and which, one would have thought, would have required more elaboration if it was to be mentioned at all. It does not seem to be essential to Socrates' argument at this point to say that the physical world is an image of the forms, and if this is to be said it would come more intelligibly in the place where it probably does come, namely at the end of the whole passage.

Some might prefer, for these reasons, the second interpretation that does not so completely identify "the visible kind and place" and "the believable". According to this view "the believable" means "that which we can believe", "the knowable" means "that which we can know". The former will be the class of opinions, bits of informa-tion and so forth which count as *doxa*, the latter the intelligible principles. On this interpretation the point will be as follows. Socrates has chosen certain sets of entities out of the visible world on the principle that the cognitive state of a man confronted with one set is less clear than that of a man confronted with the other. What he wants to know is whether he has chosen these entities in such a way that the relationship between them in terms of their *alêtheia* is the same as that between that which a man has in his mind in a state of *doxa* and that which he apprehends in a state of *gnôsis*; or, in other words, is a *doxa*-version of, say, justice, an image of justice itself?

This interpretation makes superiority in point of *alêtheia* hold between the contents of mental states. It would therefore naturally go with the interpretation of the second of our three passages (that from the concluding lines of Book Six) which does the same. The advantages of this interpretation of the passage we are now considering are that it does not require that we should understand *to doxaston* to mean "the physical world", and that it does not introduce an unnecessary complication. For the point that is now made is of some small assistance to the future development of the argument, in that we really need it if we are to see why the puppets in the Cave are puppets; but more importantly it ties the present argument on to the discussion of *doxa* and *epistêmê* in Book Five. Glaucon is being asked on this view whether being in a condition of *doxa* stands to being in a condition of *epistêmê* in the same way in which being in a state of *eikasia* stands to being in a state of *pistis*; and it is apposite that Socrates should elicit that this is so before going on to say that the same relation also holds between *dianoia* and *nöêsis*. However, this interpretation has two disadvantages. One is that it is perhaps rather difficult to keep apart the pair: *to doxaston* and *to gnôston*, and the other pair: the visible kind and the intelligible kind, which Glaucon has just been told to bear in mind. (This of course answers the point that the reader could hardly be expected to identify *to doxaston* with the physical world. The point and the answer seem to me about equally valid). The second disadvantage is that if we take this interpretation we deprive Socrates of a chance of explaining why he has taken one line and divided it into two major parts in the same proportion in which he has also sub-divided the latter. The reason will emerge with the shift in the meaning of *eikasia* and *pistis* after the Cave, but it has not emerged yet. For on this interpretation there is no compelling reason why we should take the relationship between the two major parts as a symbol of the relationship between *doxa* and *gnôsis*. We only get that if we somehow implicate the first of the major parts with *doxa*, either by identifying *eikasia* and *pistis* with *doxa*, or by identifying the visible kind to which shadows and their originals belong with *to doxaston*. However it is not difficult to provide a tolerable answer to this point if we say that the reader will obviously remember that *doxa* is bound up with reliance on the senses and will therefore associate with *doxa* the major part which has to do with the senses. The first major part will represent *doxa* not in the sense that the two mental states which are on it together compose *doxa*, nor in the sense that *to doxaston* is the nickname of the physical world to which the entities located on it belong, but in the looser sense that there is an intimate connection between *doxa* and relying on one's eyes.

To the question which of these interpretations is right, as to some of the other questions which I have mentioned, I do not intend to try to say which is the right answer. Indeed I think that it might be wrong in principle to do so. For to do that would be to try to force from Plato answers to questions which perhaps he had not formulated. Our perplexities take the form of asking: Is this a doctrine about levels of thought only, or does it also involve a grading of entities? In my judgment Plato was not unaware of this point. In refusing to discuss the inter-relations of the objects of the four mental states in our third passage he means more, I suspect, than that he does not intend to get embroiled in the topic of mathematicals. He is showing some awareness of the fact that he has not given an explicit account of the metaphysical doctrine underlying the things that he has said; and this, so far as it goes, points in favour of preferring wherever possible a plain epistemological interpretation, without ontological commitment, of the texts that we have been examining.

It is time to ask what contribution this whole passage makes to the epistemology of the *Republic*. The answer seems to be that what we get is rather little in comparison with the trouble which it takes to get it. We learn, from these two books, of the cosmological presupposition which underlies all Plato's epistemology. This is that the forms or eternal counterparts of reason are in some way the originals of the principles which inform our thinking, and also of the order and distinctness which characterise the physical world, and that it is the business of philosophy to achieve or "recover" an explicit understanding of these principles of order. We learn also that mathematics has a special part to play in this process, for the reason that the entities which mathematicians study by abstracting from physical things all but their spatial and quantitative features are peculiarly clear images of the forms. Apart from this we can extract from this passage more clearly than from some of Plato's other writings the view that the physical world is something of which we cannot have *epistêmê*. It is of course possible to write this off to a considerable extent. We can say that what is indisputable is that Plato correlates *doxa* with "the world revealed by sight" and that the world revealed by sight is not identical with the physical world but only with the view of the physical world which we get if we look at it but refrain from thinking about it. "Sight's world", so to speak, can be construed as logically similar to "Sartre's world" or "Proust's world"— not a special world but a special account of it. We can say that Plato thinks it harmless to hypostatise "sight's world" in this way both because it is anyhow an intelligible way of talking, and also because the language proper to the photographic conception of thought happens to have become habitual with him. I have some sympathy with this line of interpretation and believe that we must rely on it to some extent when we are wondering how Plato managed to reconcile the view that the empirical world is a sphere of *doxa* with the view that a rider can *know* what a bridle ought to be like or an eyewitness *know* what the accused did. But I am afraid that we should be relying on it too far if we said that Plato's thoughts on this topic were perfectly clear and that it is only his language which is, to us, a little confusing. He used language appropriate to the photographic conception of thought not because it had, as it happens, become congenial to him but because he was not innocent of that conception.

(iii) *Knowledge and belief in* Republic *10*

There are three triads in the tenth book, a triad of makers and a triad of skills. The triad of makers (596–8) consists of: God who makes the form of an object (e.g. a bed); the craftsman, who makes the object, "looking towards the form"; and the artist who makes an image of the object. The triad of skills (600–2) consists of: The skill which consists in using an object; the skill which consists in making it; and the skill which consists in imitating it. The man who uses an object has knowledge of its "beauty and rightness", the man who makes it acquires right assurance on this point from consulting him, and the artist is only concerned with what passes for beauty and rightness among the vulgar. In a rather similar passage in the *Cratylus* (389) the craftsman is said to make objects "looking towards the form", and here the form of the object in question is identified with "that which is naturally fitted to do the work of the object". Presumably therefore the form of an X which God creates is that which an X ought to be like; or the form, we might say, is the function and the demands which this makes upon whatever is to fulfil the function. But this of course is much the same as the "beauty and rightness" of an X. Accordingly in this passage we have a somewhat odd situation. Knowledge (the knowledge which e.g. a horseman has about bits) is indeed knowledge of a form, but at the same time it is knowledge of an eminently practical kind, knowledge of the physical world.

Otherwise the passage is straightforward enough. The subject in question being: what bits ought to be like, the user, who is directly acquainted with this, has knowledge. The maker, who is directly acquainted, not with this but with a representative of it, namely the user's instructions, has no more than belief. This is familiar enough. The interest of the passage lies in the licence which it gives us to evade what appears at first sight to be the plain sense of passages which seem to tell us that knowledge is of the forms and not of the physical world. For this passage suggests that these are not exclusive alternatives. It favours indeed something like a view which I explored earlier and abandoned,[1] namely the view that although we cannot *know things* we can *know facts about things*. That, as we saw before, is to go too far; but it seems that it is at any rate an over-simplification to say that we can divide the world into the two classes of "that which does not change and can be known" and "that which changes and cannot be known", with general terms going in the first class and physical things in the second. For this passage makes it clear that we can know what bits and shuttles ought to be like, an achievement which must involve some understanding of the physical world; and at the same time it is obvious that bits and shuttles themselves are subject to change. How then are we to classify them? Certainly as objects which change; but it seems difficult to classify them as objects which also cannot be known if at least one very important fact about them, namely what they ought to be like, *can* be known. It would seem to follow that we cannot infer from the premise that bits are subject to change to the conclusion that bits cannot be known. If we are to talk of "knowing bits" at all, this language could surely only refer to such achievements as understanding what they are for, knowing what they ought to be like, and so forth. But these, apparently, are things which we can know, despite the changeableness of the entities which such knowledge is about.

But of course this passage says nothing about changeableness and changelessness; it proceeds along the other road and takes for granted that direct apprehension is knowledge. It is possible however that it is easier to take this for granted in a case, like the present, where what is directly apprehended is something functional. The reason for this we have already sketched. Essentially the point is that whatever is knowable must be capable of being absorbed by minds without remainder. Physical things in their concrete existence are not so capable; that anything should be subject to the physical conditions of change and decay is something which intelligence has to accept as a brute fact and cannot absorb as something intelligible. Order and purpose are essentially the concerns of mind; the orderliness and purposefulness of physical things are therefore absorbable and knowable, their brute physical existence is not. Along this line of thought a good deal could be known about the physical world.

However this may be, the present passage at least shows that the *Republic* does not single-mindedly support the view that there is no knowledge of the physical world; for here is a place where the *epistêmê/doxa* distinction is drawn, and not drawn in that place.

---

[1] See above, pp. 38–9.

G. *Knowledge and belief in the* Theaetetus

Theoretically the second half of the *Theaetetus*, which discusses *epistêmê* in relation to *doxa*, ends in failure. The attempt to define knowledge fails. It had been shown at the end of the first half that knowledge is to be looked for in the sphere of "properly mental activity about realities; and this is *doxa*" (187 a; see above, p. 26). Yet though knowledge is to be looked for in the sphere of *doxa*, it is quickly shown that it is not identical with the latter (201), and the attempt, which occupies the rest of the dialogue, to identify it with *doxa* plus something else fails.

There are various possible views about this negative result. The simplest is that Plato is as puzzled as he represents Socrates and Theaetetus as being. Another view holds that he does not allow his characters to make a serious attempt at defining knowledge. Some who would agree with this would go on to say that the reason why he does not is that it ought to stare us in the face that *epistêmê* is on a different level from *doxa* and cannot possibly be defined as *doxa* plus something else; and that this is what Plato is hinting at. Others, who would agree that he does not make a serious attempt to define knowledge, would hold that the reason is not as simple as that, but that Plato has various doubts and reservations concerning his earlier accounts of knowledge, that he is not yet in a position to offer a better account, but that he tries out some of the ideas which are troubling him. This would incidentally account for the oddly disconnected structure of this part of the dialogue.

On the whole the third view seems to me the nearest to the truth. I would agree that Plato does not make a serious attempt (and does not therefore fail significantly) to define knowledge as *doxa* plus something else. The reason for this is as follows. The formula for which Socrates and Theaetetus try to find an acceptable meaning is: Knowledge is right belief plus *logos*. Now the *Meno* had said that belief could be turned into knowledge by *logismos aitiâs*, by working out the explanation. Knowledge is the understanding of what belief accepts as a brute fact. The phrase *logismos aitiâs* is of course etymologically connected with the word *logos*, and the notion of rational insight is commonly part of the meaning of the latter. Yet when Socrates and Theaetetus try to find senses of *logos* such that knowledge may be right belief plus *logos* they almost ostentatiously ignore this one. It would be very difficult for any reader who had read the *Meno* not to ask himself: "Why do they not try *logismos aitiâs*?"

A possible answer to this question is that given by the second of the three explanations of the failure to define knowledge which I quoted, namely that we are meant to recall that knowledge and belief are on different levels, so that the former could not possibly amount to the latter with the addition of anything. Plato had indeed said in the *Meno*, it might be argued, that beliefs can be turned into knowledge by *logismos aitiâs*; but even this formula does not imply that a piece of knowledge is a belief plus something else—it merely lays down how a man may be lifted from the one level to the other. In the meantime however Plato had come to see that knowledge and belief result from two quite opposite approaches. Only a philosopher is potentially capable of knowing anything, and the philosopher explicitly repudiates the inductive approach which leads to the formation of beliefs. Therefore the suggestion of Theaetetus that a man who has acquired a belief can turn it into knowledge by adding something to it is radically wrong.

This is true enough, but it does not explain the way the *Theaetetus* goes. For unless Plato lets Theaetetus try out the interpretation of *logos* in terms of *logismos aitiâs* he cannot expect the reader to conclude that the reason why the attempt at defining knowledge as true belief plus *logos* has failed is that it could not possibly have succeeded; for one is bound to feel that its only chance of success has been wantonly withheld. Furthermore this explanation presupposes that *epistêmê* and *doxa* are being used in the *Theaetetus* in a strictly technical sense, derived from the fifth book of the *Republic*; and it is far from clear that this is so.

If these arguments are sound one falls back on either of two explanations of the failure to define knowledge in the *Theaetetus*. The first is that Plato is not seriously trying. He has made clear what he thinks knowledge to be elsewhere; the bulk of the *Theaetetus* is concerned with the relation of sensation to judgment, and he fills in the next twenty odd pages by stringing together some thoughts on other topics more or less connected with his theme. This is not an impossible explanation; but it may seem to do less than justice to the bearing of some of these thoughts. So one comes eventually to the explanation already mentioned, that Plato has come to have various more or less specific doubts and reservations about his earlier account of knowledge. (I mention these two explanations together because I think they are both tenable, and each blunts the edge of the other; it is only if the second can establish itself convincingly that the other is ruled out).

What would these doubts and reservations be? I suggest a rather mixed bag.

Firstly I have argued that Plato has hitherto conceived of knowledge as primarily *knowing S* and only secondarily *knowing that S is P*. The ideal condition is to know (say) triangularity; when that condition is achieved everything that is true about triangularity is synoptically seen. The man therefore who knows a few facts about triangles has *doxa* only and not *epistêmê*. But now, I suggest, Plato may have found reason to doubt this. He may have come to feel that it is necessary to distinguish knowing S (*connaître*) from knowing that S is P (*savoir*), and that it is an abuse of language to withhold the title of knowledge from the latter.

Secondly in the *Republic* it was implied that to know S implies being able to give a *logos* of it; and he may have come to feel that he had made use of the phrase "to be able to give a *logos*" without enough hold on its meaning.

Thirdly it may well have struck him that there was something positively wrong with the notion that to know is to be able to give a *logos*, even in the sense he primarily intended. Broadly speaking, I think, the man who can give a *logos* of, say, evenness or justice in the *Republic* is the man who can "say what the thing in question is". This means providing a Socratic definition, or resolving the complex into its elements. It also means (I think) achieving this in such a way that the *logos* or account which is offered *logon echei* or makes sense. This means both that there is nothing opaque in the definition, and also that it is impossible to pick holes in it, to show that it leads to contradictions. There are two troubles here, of either or both of which Plato may have become conscious. The one (and for myself I see less evidence that he was troubled by this one) is that it is presumably not possible to go on resolving complexes into their elements indefinitely; in the end one must presumably get to elements which cannot be further analysed. The other trouble, which I think Plato may have felt, is that it may not, in an indefinite number of cases, be possible to give a *logos* which holds water. Parmenides and his followers had attempted to show that one cannot make sense of any but a wildly paradoxical account of the world. There is evidence that Plato became increasingly aware in his later years of the strength of the Parmenidean criticism of common assumptions, and it is possible that he was driven by this, not to accept Parmenides' views, but to a position which held that nothing is incontrovertible and that the perception of the truth does not therefore depend on argument alone.

To see whether there is any value in these suggestions we must look at the text of the second part of the *Theaetetus*. I shall give a rapid summary of the course of the argument, and then return to comment upon its significant features.

Summary of Theaetetus *187–end*

A. 1. It having been agreed that knowledge is to be looked for in the sphere of mental judgment or *doxa*, Theaetetus suggests that it is true *doxa.* Socrates does not immediately dispute this, but questions the division of judgments into true and false. His initial and fundamental argument against the possibility of false judgment is that you cannot believe anything about something which you do not know, while you cannot believe something false about something which you do know. This is expressed in the form that you cannot confuse two known terms, nor two unknown terms, nor a known with an unknown (187–8).

2. This is then developed by briefly advancing the Parmenidean-Protagorean arguments against the possibility of false belief, and meeting them roughly in the way which is to be developed in the *Sophist*. The argument is: granted that he who believes what is-not believes something false, how can one believe what is-not? For, just as, to see, one must see something, so, to believe, one must believe something; and what is-not is nothing. Therefore false belief cannot be believing what is-not, but believing something other than what is the case; it must consist in transposing two realities and accepting the wrong one (188–9).

3. Against this Socrates develops a rather obscure argument to the effect that one must entertain at least one of the two transposed terms and believe something about both of them (viz. about each that it is the other). But in that case one must be believing something of whose falsity one is plainly aware—as e.g. that the odd is even or that the cow is a horse. But a man cannot believe anything of the kind (189–91). (This argument seems to be a development of that in the first paragraph—if S is unknown to me I cannot believe anything about it, but if it is known I cannot falsely believe that it is P).

4. The argument so far is that false belief can only occur if two things are transposed in the mind, and that they cannot be transposed. Yet false belief plainly occurs and Socrates proceeds to explain it by invoking memory. This he does by the image of a wax tablet. Every experience or thought that we have makes an impression on the wax, and some of these impressions persist. To judge that this is Jones is to judge that this present visual impression corresponds to the memory impression of Jones. But suppose that I either have a bad view of the man before me or a hazy memory of Jones, then I can clearly make a mistake. Error can therefore occur through the faulty fitting of sense-impressions to memory-impressions (191–6).

5. But this does not cope with errors, such as thinking that $7+5 = 11$, which do not involve a present sense-impression. To cope with these within the terms of the rubric that one cannot believe anything, true or false, about something that one does not know, Socrates distinguishes between *having acquired knowledge*, and *currently having it*. If I have acquired knowledge of S then I can believe some-

thing about it; but in order to be right I must recapture my knowledge, and I may make a mistake here and recapture a piece of ignorance, so to say, instead of a piece of knowledge. This Socrates expresses in terms of an aviary; everything that I have learnt is a bird that I have put in my cage; when I want to use something I have learnt I have to catch it, and I may catch the wrong bird (196–9).

6. But this solution has the paradoxical result that I fail to recognise my bits of knowledge; and how can I be said to know something if I cannot recognise it? If I mistake a bit of ignorance for a bit of knowledge, then I am confusing something which I know with something that I do not know; and this was agreed (A.1) to be incomprehensible. No explanation of false belief has been found.

B. 1. Socrates then says that they ought to have decided what knowledge is before they raised the question of false beliefs. (Why? This rather suggests that to believe is to be relatively successful in the enterprise complete success in which is knowledge. One should see what one is trying to do before asking what happens when one fails) (199–200).

2. It is then shown that knowledge cannot be true belief; for an advocate can quickly convince a jury of the truth of facts of which only an eye-witness could have knowledge (200–1).

C. 1. Theaetetus then suggests that knowledge is true belief plus *logos*, and mentions a theory that he has heard to the effect that things which have a *logos* can be known (201).

2. *Socrates' dream.* Socrates then suggests that this is the same as a theory which he has heard in a dream (i.e. it is a post-Socratic theory and Plato's historical conscience is pricking him). The theory is to the effect that there are "letters" and "syllables", or elements and complexes, and that there cannot be a *logos* (here meaning "statement") of an element. For a statement is a complex of names, and mentions (*legei*) the things whose names it contains. Therefore a single element cannot have a statement or *logos* belonging to it. Elements can be named, but nothing can be said about them and they cannot be known. Complexes can be both stated and known (201–2).

3. Socrates commends this theory for tying up knowledge with *logos* and with right belief, but questions the possibility of making complexes knowable and elements unknowable (202–3).

4. Of this possibility he gives a neat refutation. Either the "syllable" is the sum of its "letters", in which case if it is knowable they are also; or the "syllable" is something unitary which results from the combination of the "letters", in which case, if they are unknowable because they are unitary, then it by parity of reasoning must be

unknowable also. Elements and complexes can be both knowable or both unknowable, but the other two combinations are impossible (203–6).

D. Socrates then points out that *logos* is ambiguous and offers three meanings which it might bear in "Knowledge is right belief plus *logos*" (a formula which he had tentatively supported in C.3). These are:—

1. "Plus *logos*" means that the believer can express his belief. But belief is silent speech and therefore every belief can be expressed. "Plus *logos*" would therefore add nothing (206).

2. "Plus *logos*" means that the believer can specify the elements of the thing. But I may correctly specify the elements of something (e.g. spell a syllable right) by accident and without knowledge, as may be evinced by my getting it wrong on another occasion. (207–8. Notice that "*dispositionally* to be able to specify the elements" would meet this objection).

3. "Plus *logos*" means that I can identify the thing—its *logos* is its *differentia*. Thus the believer without *logos* may be able to put a thing into its right class (he may be right in thinking that Theaetetus is snub-nosed) but unable to pick it out within its class (to tell Theaetetus from Socrates). But unless I can identify S I cannot believe anything about it (for the belief is not about *it*). Therefore "plus *logos*" will again add nothing to "right belief" unless it is thought that one must have not right belief, but knowledge, about the *differentia*. But in that case "To know X is to have right belief plus *logos*" becomes a circular definition: "To know X is to have right belief about it, and to *know* how it differs from everything else."

E. At this point Socrates concludes the dialogue by telling Theaetetus that it is good for one to have one's bad ideas refuted. It will improve any subsequent ideas one may have, and if it renders one sterile for the future, at least it will make one less of a bore.

Discussion of the above summary of Theaetetus 187–end

To see the possible significance of this we shall isolate certain important ideas which are canvassed in it.

Reference and identification. The idea of reference is pervasive. Throughout, the point is made that to state one must refer, and in D.3 the point is made that to refer to X one must be able to identify it. The topic of referring can of course be treated as a logical topic, and Plato's discussion of it in that manner is reserved for another dialogue (the *Sophist*—officially a resumption of the conversation in the *Theaetetus*). Here the notion of reference makes itself felt not explicitly, but in terms of the impossibility of believing anything about an unknown.

Kinds of knowledge. To make a statement about something, I must know enough about it to be able to use an expression to refer to it; to make a mistake about it, I must know less than everything about it. If the expression "Nehru" means nothing to me (if I am in this sense totally unacquainted with Mr. Nehru) I cannot wrongly believe him to be President of the United States; and if I know all about him I cannot do so either. To believe wrongly that Mr. Nehru is the American President I must have some correct information about him, enough to know whose name "Nehru" is, but not enough to guard me from error. A distinction between *being acquainted* (in this sense) *with X* and *being familiar with X* would clear away some of the problems in A.1, A.3, A.5 and D.3, and it is probably fair to say that Plato is working towards it. The distinction that he actually introduces in A.5 is the less helpful one between *having learnt about* and *currently knowing*. To see that this is a less helpful distinction consider the child who says that $7+5=11$. One would hesitate to allow that the child (in Plato's language) "knew 7 and 5" if the child could not for example count groups of five and seven objects; and a child in this condition who said "Seven and five make eleven" would be parrotting and not making a mistake. But a child who satisfies the tests for "knowing 7 and 5" may still think their sum 11; for it would not be reasonable to include among the tests for the intelligent use of a numerical expression the ability to state correctly the sum of the number for which it stands and any other number. (Consider the false belief that $931+127=1,066$). Therefore the child who "knows 7 and 5" may never have known that their sum is 12, and we do not (as Plato implies) have to choose between the alternatives: that either the child has never known 7 and 5 or he cannot correctly recapture the knowledge that their sum is 12. It would seem then that consciousness of the problem of referring has made Plato aware of the necessity of some distinction within the field of knowledge, but he has not got it right (or, if he has, he does not tell us, but offers us another and shows that it does not work).

Propositions. The idea of a proposition or statement is involved at various points. It is clearly involved in the passage describing Socrates' dream (C.2), the discussion of which I shall reserve for the moment. It is also involved in the demonstration that we cannot transpose two terms (A.3). The suggestion is that when we make a mistake we put one thing in the place of another, and Socrates argues that we cannot do this, because to do this would be to say

111

something like "the odd is even" and this no one (who knows what the words mean) ever does. But this of course is wrong. When I believe that the product of nine and eleven is an even number I do not say that the odd is even. I say *of* something (which is in fact odd) that it is even. Since the product of nine and eleven is in fact an odd number there is a sense in which I am committed to believing that a certain odd number is even, but not in any paradoxical way. For I refer to this number by using the description "the product of nine and eleven", and not (for example) the description "the odd number between 98 and 100". Or, to take a simpler example, when I falsely believe that Jones has a moustache, I believe *of* something clean-shaven *that* it has a moustache; I am not in the impossible situation of believing *that* something clean-shaven has a moustache.

In other words we need three terms and Socrates has only given us two. The two terms that are transposed are predicates, and we are able to pick the wrong one because we are not predicating them of each other but of a third term, the subject. When Socrates goes on to meet his own difficulties by introducing the image of wax-tablets (A.4) he implicitly introduces the notion of the subject. For the situation he is envisaging is something like this:—I see a man across the road. He is in fact Jones, the Labour agent, but I do not know Jones well (or not at all), and I do not see this man clearly. Accordingly I take him for Smith, the Conservative candidate, whom I have seen but do not remember perfectly. What I say is:—"That man is Smith." Here we need three terms—the man I see, Jones and Smith; and I make the mistake by identifying the first with the third instead of with the second. (It is of course more clearly put in the formal mode. There are three descriptions, "that man", "Jones" and "Smith"; and I wrongly think that the first and the third apply in this context to the same object).

In this way Socrates implicitly introduces the notion of the subject, but he cannot be said really to know what he is doing, for the same point can be made to take care of "$7+5=11$" (A.5). For this error can only be made to seem paradoxical if we assume *either* (as above) that someone cannot be said to "know" seven, five and eleven unless he knows that the last is the sum of the other two, *or* that the child who says that $7+5=11$ is saying that eleven is twelve. Plato could therefore have dispensed with his aviary if he had been clear that the correct analysis of the false belief situation is: A believes about S (which is in fact not-P) that it is P. He was clear about this by the time he wrote the *Sophist*, and I think that perhaps it was beginning to make itself felt at this time. However I shall say some further tentative things about the aviary in a moment.

Analysis. The idea of resolving complexes into their elements is of course canvassed in Socrates' dream (C.2) and also in the second of the three meanings of *logos* (D.2). In the latter place we are apt to think that Socrates is not being serious when he suggests that to be able to give the *logos* of a thing is to be able to give a list of its components, and suggests that a man who can only itemise a thing into "syllables" is at the level of *doxa*, a breakdown into "letters" being necessary for *epistêmê*. But on reflection one remembers that in the *Republic* knowledge was achieved by dialectic, and that perhaps one thing that dialectic does (in the *Republic*) is to analyse a complex into its simple parts. In this light it is interesting to notice Socrates' reaction to this sense of "plus *logos*". Of the other two senses (D.1 and D.3) he says that the phrase thus interpreted adds nothing. Of this interpretation he does not say that, but rather that one can sometimes correctly perform the feat of analysing a thing into its elements by accident, and therefore without knowledge. In other words the ability to "give account" is not sufficient evidence of the possession of knowledge. It is true that, as Socrates develops his criticism of this sense, it could be met by arguing that the man who *always* spells the syllable "The", or carries out some other itemising performance, correctly can be said to know. But it is possible to cap this retort by arguing that a man might by correct instruction be able regularly to list (say) the parts of an electric circuit without any understanding of what he was describing; and that one would hesitate to say of this man that he knew his subject. It is possible therefore that the criticism of this sense of "plus *logos*" may represent serious doubts about something taken for granted in the *Republic*.

Knowing Theaetetus and knowing what he is like. It is suggested in the discussion of the last sense of "plus *logos*" (D.3) that one cannot know something or someone (Theaetetus and the sun are examples taken) unless one can uniquely identify it; and it is possible to think that it is implied that knowing Theaetetus (in this sense) goes, and must go, beyond the ability to describe him. True it is suggested that if you can describe the sun as the brightest of the heavenly bodies, then you have its *logos* (and hence *ex hypothesi* might be said to know it); but when Socrates is discussing what it is to grasp what distinguishes Theaetetus from other similar men he uses language which might be developed into the view that knowledge must always go beyond the ability to describe. For it is said that to describe Theaetetus as snub-nosed is only to classify him (and, the implication is, I can have correct belief of his proper classification without knowing him); and I cannot believe anything which is unambiguously about *him* until "his particular snub-nosedness has left its own private mark on my memory, and all his other components also" (209 c 5–7). If this language is pressed it could be taken to mean: that

113

nothing propositional (whether you call it belief or knowledge) can ever be strictly about X unless the person who makes the proposition is directly acquainted with X, and retains in his memory an impression of X which transcends his ability to describe it. For one can only describe by attaching predicates, and however many predicates I string together it is always logically possible that there is something else, Y, to which they apply equally well.

As this stands it raises the familiar point about reference (that in order to refer to X I do not need to know it intimately), and unless that point is made it is intolerably cramping, for it forbids us to say that anything (for example) that I say can ever be about Julius Caesar, since I do not know him in the required sense. Let us suppose then that we are meant to make the point, and let us make it; but the hint of an important position still remains. This is that I cannot be said to *know* something unless I am directly acquainted with it; that therefore, in default of this acquaintance, no truths that I may utter about it can be said to proceed *from knowledge*; and knowledge goes beyond the ability to describe correctly, so that conversely the ability to describe perfectly correctly is not evidence of knowledge. Something like this is maintained in the *Seventh Letter*.

Before leaving this point we must notice that it could be argued that no great significance should be attached to what Socrates says. For what he says is said in terms of knowing a man, and is broadly true of knowing a man, but could not possibly be true of (e.g.) knowing triangularity; and that Socrates has not noticed, or has forgotten, that what applies to knowing men does not apply to "knowing universals". Indeed it is only Plato's unfortunate tendency to talk about "knowing triangularity" and so on that has blinded him to the narrow application of his point. This may be true; I have already conceded that in looking for doctrinal hints in the second half of the *Theaetetus* we may be looking for what is not there. But it could be retorted that Socrates could hardly be allowed to take the case of knowing a man as typical of knowledge in general *by oversight*; for the oversight is too gross unless it proceeds from a general belief that knowledge of universals can properly be conceived on the model of direct acquaintance. (The ambiguities of the *know*-family might be *responsible* for the belief; that is another question).

Socrates' dream. The question what, if any, hints are dropped in the discussion of Socrates' dream (C.3 and 4) depends on the interpretation of the dream-theory itself (C.2); and of this two opposite views can be taken.

The dream-theory says that elements have no *logos* and are unknowable whereas complexes have a *logos* and are knowable.

114

Socrates' refutation shows that you cannot make elements unknowable and complexes knowable, but it does not tell us how we are to resist the arguments of the theory which purports to show that you must. They can be resisted in two ways. "That X is an element implies that it has no *logos*, and that X has no *logos* implies that it is unknowable" can be met by challenging either of the implications—by showing that an element can have a *logos* or by showing that a thing which has no *logos* may yet be knowable. Plato does not tell us which of these lines of attack we are to take, though he makes it clear that we must take one of them. By making Socrates in C.3 commend the theory for tying up knowledge and *logos* he perhaps indicates a preference for the former; but if we want a clearer light we shall have to see what the theory is.

One view holds that the theory is drawing our attention to the fact that there must be some indefinables. Elsewhere (e.g. in the *Sophist* and *Statesman*) Plato uses the metaphor of letters and syllables in a certain way.[1] A complex and therefore comparatively specific universal (such as *angling*) is said to be a syllable, and the process of defining it is said to be one of spelling it out into its letters. The letters will each occur in numerous syllables (as *animality* occurs in *cathood, doghood*, etc.) and will therefore be comparatively generic. Now it seems reasonable to suppose that if the process of spelling syllables into their letters is continued long enough it will eventually come to a stop by producing some universals which are letters in an absolute sense, which can no longer be analysed into their components. *Unity* for example might be such a universal, *existence* another. Now since defining is often spoken of as "giving a *logos*" it is natural to suppose that when the theory speaks of elements which have no *logos* what it has in mind is highly generic and indefinable universals. Essentially therefore the theory is warning us that it will not always be possible to "give account" of universals, for some of them must be too simple to be defined.

It cannot be denied that the theory *speaks* of its elements as if they were physical elements (they are said to be sensible 202 b 6); but of course what applies to physical elements in so far as they are elementary will apply to any other elements that there may be. On this view therefore the theory is *stated* in terms of physical elements, but intended to *apply* to elementary universals such as unity. On this view what Plato has against the theory would be its passage from the legitimate claim that elements have no *logos* to the illegitimate claim that they cannot be known. His view, on this interpretation, is that knowledge does not always entail the ability to give a *logos*; that some knowledge is "intuitive" and not "discursive".

[1] See below, pp. 374–88, 411–16.

This interpretation is attractive at first sight, and it may be part of what Plato intended. In refuting the theory by leading it into a dilemma he of course avoided the necessity of declaring for or against any particular criticism of the theory. The chief argument, to my view, for this interpretation is Plato's use of the letters and syllables metaphor, which is elsewhere (and, on the whole, subsequently) used of universals. But I do not believe that this interpretation captures what he primarily meant.

On the other view the theory under attack is essentially a confused account of the nature of a proposition. What it holds is as follows:—To know X entails to be able to make a statement about X. Since every statement contains at least two terms, and is in fact the name of the complex consisting of these two terms (e.g. "Man is mortal" is the name of the complex entity, man's mortality), no statement can ever be the name of, and we can therefore never make a statement about, a simple element. Therefore nothing can be said about elements, and therefore they are unknowable.

But if this is what the theory holds, plainly it is uninstructed on the subject of reference, or the *about*-relationship; and this as we have seen was one of the topics in Plato's mind at this time. The theory thinks of a proposition as a complex name of a complex situation, even such a simple proposition as "X exists" or "This is X". It is from this that it infers that nothing can ever be said about an element, and that elements can therefore only be named (see especially 202 a 6–8).

It might be thought that the theory as I have described it is too silly to be seriously held and that this interpretation must be ruled out on this score. This I think is a mistake. The theory is the natural result of a tendency which certainly existed to regard the identity-statement ("A is A") as the type of the true statement. For the only informative identity-statement that can be made is about a complex, and consists of its analysis. "Social democracy is . . . (a, b, c)" is the "private *logos*" (202 a 7) of social democracy, for it mentions nothing but social democracy and its components (which add up to it). Given the tacit assumption that all statements which are not identity-statements are false, then it follows that true statements can only be made about complexes—if we neglect uninformative utterances such as "Jones is Jones". (It is true that the theory talks about statements and not about true statements, but of course "the *logos* of a given situation" means the *true* statement of it. Those who regarded statements as complex names regarded false statements as "non-names" and could not see how they could signify—see *Cratylus* 429).

If this account of the theory is correct, as I think it is, then in view of what happens in the *Sophist* we might expect Plato to want to say

116

that the theory has not shown that an element cannot have a *logos*. To take the metaphor literally, when I say of the letter *S* that it is a sibilant I am making a statement about a simple element. This is something that we would expect Plato to want to say, and I think he even hints at it by putting into Theaetetus' mouth a patently ridiculous reason for saying that consonants have no *logos* (viz. that they have no sound—203 b 5). But he may well have been still far from clear on this point, and this may be why he avoided a direct attack on the theory.

We cannot say, then, that the criticism of the dream-theory shows that Plato was aware that the process of giving a *logos* would eventually have to stop when it came up against indefinables. Indeed if it did show that, I think it would be unique in Plato's writings. Whether or not Plato *ought* to have conceded that there are some indefinables, I know of no place where he did so. I have argued and shall argue again that there are places which suggest that he thought that the ability to give a *logos* is not a *sufficient* condition of knowledge, but I suspect that he always held that it is a *necessary* condition. This is plainly the case in the *Seventh Letter*, which is the passage which provides the proof texts for the view that the ability to give a *logos* is not a sufficient condition. This we shall discuss in a moment. Meanwhile we shall have to say that the significance of Plato's criticism of the dream-theory is uncertain, but that it probably shows once more that he was already unhappy about the current logic of propositions.

One other interpretation of the dream-theory ought perhaps to be mentioned, one that gives it a rather Lockeian flavour. This is that the letters are, or include, "simple qualities" of a sensible kind, and that the syllables are complexes of simple qualities; and that the theory is that you can name a simple quality such as greenness, and can also of course sense it, but cannot give a *logos* of it; giving a *logos* is something which can only be done to a complex entity such as a horse, and it consists in naming the simple qualities which constitute the complex entity. I do not find this interpretation very convincing. I doubt whether Plato could have expected the metaphor of letters and syllables to be understood in this way; and this interpretation does not seem to do sufficient justice to the point that a *logos* is a complex of names corresponding to a complex of entities (202 b 2–5). In the statement (*loc. cit.*) that "a *logos* is essentially a complex of names" I find it very difficult to resist the view that *logos* means "proposition"; and indeed it is largely for this reason that I prefer the interpretation which I mentioned second.[1]

---

[1] Socrates seems to bring forward considerations in favour of the theory which he heard in his dream ("How could an element have a *logos*, and how could that which has no *logos* be knowable?"), and at the same time he seems to

Further reflections about the aviary. The passage about the aviary (A 5 in the summary above) is not at all easy to interpret. For one thing it is not possible to be sure what is represented by the "birds" (the pieces of knowledge which I have acquired in the past, and which I am unsuccessfully trying to recapture in the present when I make a mistake). Are the birds propositions, such as that 7 plus 5 equals 12, or are they terms such as 12? A possible interpretation however is as follows. The birds are neither terms nor propositions, but terms thought of as identical with the true propositions in which they figure. To be able to make a statement about 12, I must have this bird in my aviary; that is to say I must at some time have learnt about it. Now on the assumption that "to know 12" is to know it as everything that it is (the sum of 7 and 5, the product of 4 and 3 and so on) I must, if I am to be able to make statements about 12, have known at some time that it is the sum of 7 and 5; and I must still have this knowledge by me. Now if, when I need the sum of 7 and 5, I go to recapture this knowledge, and lay my hand instead on 11, offering that as the answer, I commit myself to the view that 11 is the sum of 7 and 5. This, as Theaetetus suggests, looks more like a bit of ignorance than a bit of knowledge; so that perhaps we ought to say that we have bits of ignorance in our heads as well as bits of knowledge. But the fact remains that, whether we embroider the simile in this way or not, the use of the simile to explain mistakes runs up against the difficulty that I cannot really be said to know that it is 12 that is the sum of 7 and 5 if I assert that this sum is 11. Therefore the (valid) distinction between having acquired information and having it at one's finger-tips does not help to explain mistakes. I cannot be said to be recapturing knowledge that I still somehow retain if I fail to notice that I have captured something else. My failure to notice that what I have captured is something else shows that I no longer know what I once knew, and that throws us back on to the other horn of

---

show that the theory leads to a dilemma which is fatal to it. Presumably therefore there is something wrong either with the arguments which seem to support the theory or with those which seem to refute it. My discussion has proceeded on the assumption that there is something wrong with the arguments which seem to support the theory, and I hope I have shown what this may be. It is, however, possible that Plato wanted rather to create doubts in our minds as to the validity of the dilemma with which Socrates seems to refute the theory. He might for example have wanted us to argue that a syllable is more than the sum of its letters (though Socrates does not seem to favour this possibility), but that this does not make it a further letter; if the syllable is something unitary which results from the combination of the letters, we cannot reason that, because they were unknowable because they were unitary, therefore it must be unknowable also. I believe that Professor Ryle has an interpretation somewhat along these lines, and it makes Plato make a very good point; but I am not convinced that it was the one he intended to make.

the dilemma. Since the man who says that the sum of 7 and 5 is 11 evidently no longer knows either 11 or the sum of 7 and 5, how can anything that he says be intended to refer to either of these entities? For I cannot refer to that of which I am ignorant.

If this is how we are supposed to understand the passage about the aviary, what are we meant to learn from it? We have assumed that the arguments in this part of the dialogue are meant to discredit, or at least throw doubt on, whatever is responsible for Socrates' inability to see how it is possible to make a mistake. We must ask therefore what are the presuppositions which make it impossible for him to get very far with the *prima facie* valuable distinction between having acquired knowledge and currently possessing it. There are two which obviously suggest themselves. One is the subordination of *savoir* to *connaître*, the other the view that if I know something I know it fully. If we subordinate the knowledge of facts to the knowledge of individuals we shall tend to think that knowing 12 (for example) is primary and that knowing truths about 12 is somehow contained in this. This will make us want to think that a man who knows 12 will *eo ipso* know all the true propositions into which 12 enters. (Such an assumption would be more plausible, perhaps, in the case of "knowing triangularity" than in the case of "knowing 12", for it might seem that there is only a limited number of *a priori* truths about triangles for acquaintance with triangularity to entail. That perhaps may be the reason why Plato chose an arithmetical example, by means of which to demonstrate that knowing X cannot be thought to carry with it knowing all the true propositions, nor even all the *a priori* true propositions, into which X enters. An arithmetical example makes it very clear that there must be something wrong). If we further suppose that I either know something or am ignorant of it, and that when I know it the thing itself (in this case 12-as-the-sum-of-7-and-5, -as-the-product-of-4-and-3, etc., etc.) is in my mind, whereas when I am ignorant of it the thing is outside my mental grasp altogether, and all its bag and baggage with it, then it will be easy to see that either I must be infallible about any given matter, or else I am unable to refer to it. For either the matter with all its ramifications is in my head or I am out of touch with it.[1]

We can conjecture then that what creates Socrates' perplexities in this passage is the two assumptions that what we know are always terms (the true propositions about these terms being somehow con-

---

[1] Compare Leibniz' doctrine that in a true proposition the predicate is contained in the subject. This creates analogous difficulties; for if Peter is the sum of his predicates, then it might be argued that a proposition which ascribes to Peter a predicate which he does not in fact possess is not in fact a proposition about Peter.

tained in them), and that knowledge and ignorance are related as black would be to white if there were no shades of grey in between. We might suggest therefore either that Plato is himself perplexed about the nature of mistakes of the kind which he discusses because he is guilty of these assumptions, or of something like them; or else that he is using Socrates' inability to account for mistakes on a picture of knowledge which depends on these assumptions to hint that they cannot be made. Or, between these two extremes, we might suggest that the truth is that Plato sees the harm that the picture does without being able to say precisely what is wrong with it.

It may be objected to this account that Plato could not have wanted, at this stage, to say that there was something wrong with treating *knowing fully* and *being totally unacquainted with* as exhaustive alternatives, since he had long ago put *doxa* in between these two terms. But this is not perhaps so conclusive as it may seem. For on the view that what we know is terms (entities such as 12, justice and so on) the insertion of *doxa* between *epistêmê* and *agnoia* does not tell us what to do with the principle: either I know X or I do not— at any rate if *knowing* is thought of as *being in touch with*. For when I have a *doxa* (even a true one) about X, what I have in my mind is not X, but a *doxa* of X, an entity between *on* and *mê on*. In other words, so long as *knowing* is thought of as *grasping* (the entities grasped being terms) it is impossible to give a satisfactory account of *doxa* as that which comes between knowledge and ignorance, for the reason that the mental content of a *doxa* is not identical with the object grasped in *epistêmê*. And that a satisfactory account of *doxa* requires a re-examination of the nature of *epistêmê* is Socrates' comment on this part of the argument.[1]

On what may underlie the second half of the Theaetetus

Let us try to make sense of all this, and let us begin with a simple point.

Plato was a declared enemy of formulas in philosophy, even if they came from Socrates or himself. This hostility is re-stated in the last section of the dialogue (E of my summary). It is very likely that "knowledge differs from true belief by the presence of *logos*" had degenerated into a formula among his followers, and that a prime purpose of the second half of the *Theaetetus* was to make trouble for those who used the formula without knowing what they meant by *logos*.

[1] I suspect that I have learnt a lot about this part of the *Theaetetus* from the essays of pupils who have attended the lectures of Professor Ryle. How much of this discussion I owe to him and how much he would repudiate with scorn I do not know.

But perhaps there is more to it than that. We have seen that Plato was probably dissatisfied with the current propositional logic, and that he may have seen (dimly perhaps) that the correct analysis of the false-belief situation is:—A believes about S (which is in fact not-P) that it is P. To see this is to see that we cannot cope with false belief in terms of grasp of realities, for false belief is not well described as grasp of a non-reality. But we saw in discussing *Republic* 5 that Plato's vocabulary was modelled on the case of knowledge or true belief, that is on the case which we *can* describe as grasp of a reality; and we saw that his language about states inferior to knowledge was for this reason awkward. The awkwardness was accepted there, we thought, because of an instinctive feeling that the language used about the inferior cases ought to parallel the language used about the ideal case. Now suppose this feeling to persist, and suppose that Plato is beginning to see that this language is intolerable in the case of incomplete or erroneous grasp of facts, that in these cases the notion of a proposition (of a *that*-clause) has to be introduced. In this situation he might well feel that the notion of a proposition had to be introduced into true-belief situations as well.

This would not of course necessarily entail anything about the analysis of knowledge. But if it were combined with doubts about whether it is reasonable to treat *knowing that S is P* as a consequence of *knowing S*, it might lead to a feeling that there are two different senses of "knowledge", one for each of these two. Such doubts might easily have arisen, for example in connection with arithmetic. As we have seen, if language about "knowing numbers" is adopted, it is unplausible to say that Jones does not "know" 931 and 127 unless he knows that their sum is 1058. It is indeed a consequence of what I have to grasp in order that the expressions "931" and "127" should have meaning for me that $931+127=1058$, but I do not have to know the consequences of everything that I know.

If doubts of this kind had led to the feeling that *knowing S* is to be distinguished from *knowing that S is P*, further doubts might have been excited. How much, for example, must be included in *knowing S*? More perhaps than is needed in order to refer to S (tenuous acquaintance is enough for this); less perhaps than would be needed in order to be infallible about S. And if *knowing S* does not lead automatically to *knowing that S is P*, what is the relation between these two states? Doubts about points such as these might well have led Plato to discuss the topics raised in the second part of the *Theaetetus*.

But there is a further point connected with *knowing S* where S is a universal. If Plato had come to think that it is not always possible to give a *logos* of every universal in such a way that the *logos* cannot be

121

shown to give rise to contradictions, then he might have come to have serious doubt about the precise role played in knowledge by the ability to give a *logos*. Should we say that the ability is necessary, but that a correct *logos* can sometimes be shown to give rise to contradictions? Should one hold to the view that a correct *logos* cannot lead to contradictions and allow that of some universals a *logos* cannot be given? Or what should one say? One way or another Plato might have come to think that there is something in some sense "intuitive" about the grasp of a universal.

That there is some substance in these last suggestions will emerge I hope from consideration of the *Seventh Letter*. The conclusion meanwhile is that the failure of the *Theaetetus* to define knowledge may be an indication of certain fairly specific doubts.

H. *Knowledge and belief in the* Seventh Letter

The passage runs from 341–4. The context is that Plato is protesting against the alleged publication by Dionysius II of Syracuse of a treatise expounding Platonism, and Plato is explaining why he has never published such a treatise himself. To this end he insists that the intellectual goal is a kind of insight which cannot be communicated in speech or writing, but can only be brought about in the pupil by long travail.

What Plato says is this. With respect to any reality (he takes the circle as his example, but he insists that any other universal would do as well), there are four things which are concerned with it, but which must be distinguished from it, and from each other. Firstly there is "knowledge and right belief and understanding (*nous*)", which exist in minds and are not to be distinguished for the present purpose. Then secondly there are the three things through which knowledge has to be brought about, namely the word ("circle"), the *logos* or definition ("the figure all points on whose boundary are equi-distant from the centre"), and actual physical circles (whether diagrams, plates or what-not).

What this means so far, I think, is that if a man knows the word "circle", can give the correct definition of what it stands for, and can recognise instances, then he must be said to have knowledge, right belief or understanding of "the circle"—i.e. circularity. But only in a sense. For Plato goes on to say that without these four (i.e. knowledge in this sense and its three components) you cannot achieve true knowledge of the reality,[1] but that even with them you do not necessarily achieve the knowledge that you seek. For what these four

[1] He says that you cannot achieve the reality. See note at the end of this section, p. 124.

give you (i.e. what knowledge in the inferior sense gives you) is the answer to the question: "What kind of thing is X?" whereas what you want is the answer to the question: "What is X?" (343 c 1). To know the word, to be able to define the thing and to recognise instances of it is to have knowledge in an inferior sense, and this knowledge is a necessary but not a sufficient condition of knowledge in the fullest sense which enables you to grasp the thing.

Plato gives reasons for this. Physical instances are always "full of the contrary nature"—round things for example "touch the straight at all points" (343 a 7). Words again lack fixity: "circle" could be used to stand for squares or triangles. And definitions, being constructed out of words, are tarred with the same brush.

To invoke the conventional nature of language at this point seems to provide a very lame argument. However I daresay that better arguments could be brought for the view that language cannot infallibly communicate insight. But perhaps Plato's own arguments are stronger than they seem, if we interpret them liberally. Because language is conventional we have to rely in the end on ostensive definition; we have to learn what "circle" means by reference to circular objects or diagrams. But if these physical instances are always "full of the contrary nature", then it is embarrassing to realise that in the end we have to rely on them.

However good or bad Plato's reasons for saying that words, definitions and instances cannot communicate insight, what follows is of the greatest interest. He begins by telling us that whatever we can say or point to can always be confuted by empirical evidence. He goes on to say that a man who has not been trained to seek the truth, but is content with any image of it that he can pick up, can very easily be made to look a fool by anybody who can handle the four instruments of knowledge—that is who knows in the inferior sense "what sort of thing" something, say a circle, is.

With the well-deserved humiliation of this man Plato seems (he is too angry to be clear) to contrast the ill-deserved humiliation of another, namely of the man who really knows in the full sense, and who is called upon to expound what he knows. For even he has nothing at his disposal but the four instruments of knowledge—he can only name the thing, give its definition, and point to instances of it—and these are essentially inadequate. This being so he too can easily be made to *seem* a fool by anybody who is a skilful picker of holes. Those who do not realise the inherent limitations of language and of instances for showing what something is will feel that the expositor's ignorance has been revealed. But this is a mistake. Words and instances cannot communicate knowledge; it is only by a laborious process of taking the pupil through and through these over and over again that knowledge can be brought about, and even then only in a man who has an affinity to the subject.

This last point Plato develops briefly in terms of moral knowledge, arguing that this can only come about in a man who has both mental ability and also an affinity to the subject. For virtue and vice can only be grasped together, and only together with what is true of reality as a whole. To understand what is right and wrong, in other words, is to understand the conditions of human life, and this can only occur as part of an understanding of the universe as a whole. This, he continues, can only be brought about by a long and laborious process of "rubbing together" words, definitions and empirical observations. This "rubbing together" must be accompanied by the practice of co-operative refutation through the asking and answering of questions. The end of all this is the sudden shining out of wisdom and of understanding which strains to the limits of human power.

There is a great deal in all this (343 c–344 c). For our purposes two things stand out. Firstly, although grasp of the truth has an intellectual aspect, it is not purely intellectual; for the truth is one and for certain parts of it at least the right spiritual outlook is required. Secondly knowledge in the inferior sense cannot communicate insight, and this is connected with the fact that however skilfully we try to communicate the truth by language or the use of instances, what we say or point to is always liable to empirical confutation.

(*Note*. The account in the *Seventh Letter* is made the more difficult to follow by the fact that Plato in some places speaks of: the three instruments of knowledge, knowledge, and fifthly the thing known; cp. 342 a 8. Elsewhere however—cp. 343 c 1 or d 1–2—he speaks of the first four of these in a slighting manner and treats the fifth term as if it were not the thing known but the knowing of it. On the whole he uses the words *phronêsis* and *nous* for this ambiguous fifth item. I have tried to streamline the account by distinguishing "knowledge in the inferior sense", this being the fourth item, and "true knowledge", this being the fifth).

The passage as a whole seems consonant with passages in Plato's earlier writings.[1] It is consonant for example with the doctrine of the *Republic* that something dramatic, of universal significance, will happen when we learn what goodness is. It is consonant also with the passage in the *Phaedo* (99 e–100 a) where Socrates says that the accounts we give of things are as much reflections of realities as are physical instances. Until the goal is reached the forms are only

---

[1] But the manner of argument seems to me very reminiscent of that of the philosophical passages of the *Laws*.

mirrored in our minds as they are only mirrored in nature. As for the reaching of the goal, Plato is prepared to insist on the possibility of insight into the rational order, but he also insists that insight cannot be infallibly communicated. He is not saying that the truest statements we can make are only partially true, so much as that there is no true statement but can be misunderstood. The truth is in a sense ineffable, not in the sense that there is something non-rational about it, but in that we cannot with certainty communicate it.

Who is the man who knows "what sort of thing a circle is", and what are the criticisms which seem to make a fool not only of him, but even of the man who knows "what a circle is"? I suppose that the first man is one who knows that a circle is an even curve, and that therefore no part of its circumference can be straight. But when he says this we can make a fool of him by showing that a straight line can touch the circumference of a circle. But for one thing to touch another is for them to have part of their boundaries in common. Therefore if a tangent can touch a circle, it must be the case that some part of the circumference is a straight line. (This is apparent when you lay a straight edge against a physical instance of circularity; you see at once that it is "full of the contrary nature"). If our man tries to defend himself by saying that contact occurs over a distance less than the smallest finite distance, then (perhaps with Zeno's aid) we can show him that there is no such thing. Therefore we have a plain contradiction in the notion of a tangent, a contradiction by which the man who knows only "what sort of thing" a circle is may well be perplexed. From contradictions of this kind an Eleatic might conclude that there cannot really be such a thing as circularity, and even perhaps that the whole idea of space is hopelessly incoherent.

The condition of knowing "what a circle is", as opposed to "what sort of thing it is", comes about, I suggest, when we are fully aware of antinomies of this kind, but remain perfectly convinced that there is such a thing of circularity; when we, so to speak, acknowledge the existence of the contradictions, and yet know how to remain unperturbed by them. And the point is that this imperturbability is not achieved by seeing how to resolve the contradictions; for they cannot be resolved. Rather it comes about when we achieve a kind of direct acquaintance with the nature of circularity, analogous, *mutatis mutandis*, with the direct acquaintance which we can have with an individual, when we *know* Theaetetus and do not merely know what sort of man he is. How this direct acquaintance comes about, Plato cannot tell us—"the light is kindled" is his phrase. When it has come about we. have, so to speak, got out beyond the antinomies which are inescapable at the propositional level. We cannot resolve the antinomies because they arise in some way from the conditions of language and of the empirical world; but they cease to trouble us when our knowledge no longer depends upon language or upon the production of instances. Teaching must take place through these media, and therefore to have the correct *logos* and to be able to recognise instances are necessary conditions of knowledge and indispensable means of communication. But what teaching seeks to convey must transcend the media, and that is why knowledge cannot be taught.

It seems to me that something of all this may have been stirring in Plato's mind when he wrote the *Theaetetus,* and that it may have made him feel that the important thing was not to give a correct statement of what knowledge is, but to make difficulties for those who suppose that it is an easy matter to characterise the apprehension of something by the mind.

The *Seventh Letter* can also be read back with profit into others of the later dialogues. The *Parmenides* for example is a sustained confrontation of the reader with the antinomies connected with unity; and perhaps part of the purpose of writing it was to familiarise the reader with the "refutations" which can be brought against any account of the nature of unity, so that if he dwelt long enough on its arguments he would come to see what unity is.

Then again there is the antinomy which Plato mentions in the *Parmenides* and again in the *Philebus,* the antimony of the unity and multiplicity of universals. Of these and other antinomies we are tempted to suppose that Plato must have thought, as we think, that they are resolvable, that in any contradiction at least one side must depend on a bad argument. But this is to suppose that Plato was clearly possessed of the notion of a bad argument, and this may be wrong. To some extent I believe he thought of arguments not in logical but in rhetorical terms. An argument is something by which a hearer is liable to be convinced. We think that the way to defend oneself against being convinced by the wrong arguments is to make sure that the arguments one accepts are valid. No doubt Plato thought this too; he obviously thought that a great many arguments are not valid. But perhaps he thought that to say that an argument is not valid is to say that nobody who listens to the argument and to a criticism of it will be taken in by the argument any more. An invalid argument would then be one whose persuasive power was feeble compared with that of the criticism of it. But now suppose an argument and a counter-argument such that even an intelligent hearer is convinced by both of them, and cannot develop a convincing criticism of either. Both arguments will now be valid. If therefore this situation ever arises (and it does seem to arise in connection with the circle for example) then we can no longer defend ourselves from error by giving our assent only to valid arguments. In this predicament the only remaining defence, the only way of telling which of the arguments is right, will be a direct apprehension, transcending argument, of the subject under discussion. Conceivably this was what Plato thought.

I. *The formal question: "What is knowledge?"*

I think that we have now looked at all the places where Plato says something about the formal question: "What is knowledge?". The answer can be simply given: it is the apprehension by a mind of a reality, and is to be contrasted with the inferior condition in which we merely know (in our sense of the word) truths about the thing in question. Though the answer can be simply given, Plato does not think that this apprehension can be cheaply bought, nor does he think that it is easy to answer the question: "But what is it for a mind to apprehend a reality?". For the obvious answer to this question is something like: "To have apprehended some reality is to be able to give correct answers to questions about it, to be able to point to instances of it and so on." Wanting to say that all this is something less than knowledge, Plato has left himself with little that he can do in answer to this question but to make use of metaphors such as vision and direct acquaintance, and to hope that by use of such metaphors, and by the continual contrast of knowledge with the inferior conditions, in the end "the light will break". This is why he is so consistently enigmatical on this subject.

This account of Plato's answer to the question "What is knowledge?" is given of course in terms of the latest of all the relevant writings, the *Seventh Letter*. But I do not believe that there is very much development on this point. Where there is development is in connection with the inferior state. In the earlier writings (for example the *Timaeus*)[1] it is taken for granted that knowledge can be conveyed by teaching, and the inferior state opposed to knowledge is *doxa* which comes about through the uncritical inductive use of the senses. In the *Seventh Letter* however Plato is interested in a different contrast, that between the kind of knowledge which "plainly arises in minds and is not identical with the thing known nor with its instruments" on the one hand, and the kind of knowledge which he speaks of as if it *were* the thing known on the other; and of the first of these he says (342 c 5) that that which "plainly arises in minds" is one

[1] See *Timaeus* 51 e 2. It is not, of course, certain that the *Timaeus* is earlier than the *Seventh Letter*.

thing, whether you call it *epistêmê* or true *doxa*. What is new here is
not the importance of the distinction between insight and the ability
to recite the correct formula—that was there from the beginning.
What is new is the thought that in comparison with this distinction
the distinction between "knowledge", lying at the end of an *a priori*,
avenue, and "belief", lying at the end of an empirical avenue,
becomes unimportant. Perhaps even non-existent. For although
Plato obviously never held the absurd view that you can achieve
knowledge without the use of the senses (nobody could hold this
view), he sometimes spoke as if he did. Perhaps to some extent the
hard and fast distinction between the *a priori* and the empirical
avenues depends on this misleading way of speaking. The distinction,
which he really wanted to draw, between what I have called the
counter-inductive and the inductive approaches, is a matter of
degree with regard to the use of the senses; it is not a question of
whether you use them, but of the point at which you use them, how
critically, and so on. Perhaps this was becoming clear to Plato; and
perhaps, realising that the senses make a contribution to every
degree of enlightenment, however lofty, he saw that the old distinction between *epistêmê* and *doxa* was not a hard and fast distinction,
and that the important distinction depended simply on whether what
existed in a man's mind was the actual thing which he claimed to
know, or merely a correct account of it in terms of propositions and
the ability to produce instances.

The stress that Plato lays in the *Seventh Letter* on the part played
by sense-experience in the long process of friendly refutation which
must precede the kindling of the light rather suggests something of
this kind. But it would be a mistake to place too much weight on this
passage. For one thing it is short; and for another Plato is plainly
hurt and angry at the insolence of Dionysius in publishing a hand-
book to the truth, something which "had I thought it possible to
write, I would have been greatly privileged to undertake—and more
competent than anyone else" (341 d—a rough paraphrase). In this
state of mind he is naturally concentrating his energies on the task of
explaining why he has always thought that the truth cannot be
communicated in handbooks.

J. The material question: "What can we know?"

On the subject of Plato's answer to the material question: "What can
we know?" I have already put the evidence before the reader, and
raised some of the questions. Briefly the position is that there are
places (early and late) where Plato speaks seriously of knowing
matters of physical fact, but that the predominant position (again

both early and late) is that we cannot have knowledge of the changing physical world. I have argued that this position may perhaps be one that Plato fell into rather than one that he particularly wanted to take up. This sort of contention cannot of course be made good. However by reminding ourselves of the considerations which may perhaps have weighed with Plato in this region we may be able to form a juster conception of the nature of his beliefs. I shall try to rough out a list of such considerations in what follows. It will be found that they constitute a mixed bag. In particular the tendency of some of them will be to *explain how* Plato came to think that we cannot have knowledge of the physical world, whereas the tendency of others will be to *explain away* the dicta which suggest that he believed this.

1. *Concentration on general terms.* When we discussed the *Republic* we saw that Plato was interested in knowledge of universals or general terms and not (for example) in questions such as whether we can ever be justified in being certain about matters of empirical fact. He is not primarily interested in the question whether we can justly claim to be certain either of a particular matter of fact (what the defendant said to the plaintiff) or of a general rule (such as the phases of the moon). He does indeed make observations which seem to imply that we cannot rightly be said to know things of this kind (at any rate in the case of general rules), but he is not primarily concerned with such questions. His primary concern is to contrast the counter-inductive approach to the knowledge of general terms with the inductive approach. But (as we have seen) he is accustomed to speak loosely of the counter-inductive approach as if it consisted of pure thought, and of the inductive approach as if it consisted of nothing but the use of the senses. Underlying this, perhaps, is the soul/body contrast of the mystery religions which is to be found in the *Phaedo*[1] and which leads Socrates in that dialogue to speak of our knowledge of empirical matters as if it were one of the tiresome consequences of having a body. However that may be, whatever the origins of this way of talking, so long as it persisted Plato could say to himself that we do not acquire knowledge of general terms by the use of the senses. Now if (his attention being concentrated on the topic of general terms) the qualification: "of general terms" were to drop out, he would be left telling himself that we cannot acquire knowledge by the use of the senses. In this way he could come to say, and in a sense believe, something which he might not wish to believe if he thought of it on its own merits.

Yet why might he not wish to believe it? Why should we find it difficult to allow that Plato thought it impossible to have *epistêmê*

[1] cp. *Phaedo* 65–6, 79–80; discussed above, Vol. 1, pp. 309–15.

of matters of empirical fact by the use of the senses? Could it not be argued that it is only so long as one puts the English word "knowledge" in place of the Greek word *epistêmê* that difficulty seems to arise? To some extent it could. Nevertheless we have the following three points:—Firstly that Plato does sometimes allow us to have *epistêmê* of matters of empirical fact. Secondly that if *epistêmê* stands for the optimum mind-thing relationship, it seems odd to deny the title to direct perception in the case of matters of fact (for what relation to an empirical fact could be more intimate than direct perception?). Thirdly there is the rather obvious consideration that if uncertainty infects our empirical judgments then it is unreasonable to suppose that there can be any certainty in our apprehensions of general terms; for it is undeniable that if I can never be sure that this is (say) a horse, then I can never be sure that I know what it is to be a horse. In so far therefore as the reason why Plato withholds the title *epistêmê* from something is that he wishes to say that the state of mind in question is not one of justified certainty, to that extent to deny *epistêmê* of matters of empirical fact is to make *epistêmê* of general terms incomprehensible.

So far then we have found in Plato's concentration on the topic of the knowledge of general terms something which might explain how he came to conclude that there can be no knowledge of matters of empirical fact. At the same time we have found three reasons for wanting to argue that this conclusion must have been inadvertent rather than deliberate. In the considerations which follow I shall modify this last point by arguing that on Plato's presuppositions the second and third of these reasons are less potent than they may seem. In other words, I have tried to explain away the appearances which suggest that Plato denied the possibility of empirical knowledge, and I am now about to try to explain how nevertheless it is possible to believe that he did deny precisely this. I shall begin by listing four considerations which undermine the second of the reasons which make belief in this denial difficult. This was that direct perception is, in the case of matters of empirical fact, the optimum mind-thing relationship and that it therefore deserves the title of *epistêmê*.

2. *The causal theory of perception.* In the *Theaetetus*, as we have seen, Plato expresses the belief that we do not in perception get into direct touch with what is really there. What we experience is sense-data produced by the interaction between our bodies and the environment. Perceptual knowledge therefore, even if it is the most direct relation in which a mind can stand to a physical thing, is still a gravely indirect relation. We have no resources except conjecture for getting behind sense-data and arriving at the ultimate facts of the physical world. There cannot therefore be *epistêmê* of physical

things, for the immediate objects of perception are *gignomena*, momentary private entities, and not *onta* or independently existing things; and the *onta* in question, or the physical things, can only be got at by conjecture. Thus so long as Plato held the causal theory of perception (and it is natural to suppose that his primitive thoughts on this topic were in line with the developed theory of the *Theaetetus*), he would be tempted to say that there cannot be *epistêmê* of matters of empirical fact, whether particular or general. It might however be retorted to this that it is in the *Theaetetus* itself just after the exposition of the causal theory that Plato allows that an eye-witness can properly be said to know what took place. I have already suggested that the answer to this may be that there is a relative and an absolute use of the *doxa/epistêmê* contrast. The best relationship in which I can stand to a physical occurrence is that of having witnessed it. In comparison with those whose knowledge of the occurrence is from hearsay, the eye-witness has *epistêmê*. In some contexts however it is apposite to make the point that knowledge of this kind deserves the title *epistêmê* relatively but not absolutely. The causal theory therefore could provide a reason for denying that there can be *epistêmê* in the strictest sense either of particular matters of empirical fact or of empirical general truths.

3. *Cosmological considerations.* We shall be discussing Plato's cosmological views in the next chapter. Meanwhile we all believe it to be roughly true that Plato thought that the world owes such definiteness as it possesses to the ordering work of mind, and that the world tends to fail to live up to the order which mind has imposed upon it. This failure would provide a reason for denying that there can be *epistêmê* of natural regularities such as the phases of the moon. Doubts such as those expressed in the *Republic* about the capacity of a heavenly body to run to time would entail the doubt whether there exists such a regularity to be known. Even however on the hypothesis that the regularity exists Plato might well have doubted whether our observations could be thought sufficiently reliable to assure us of its nature. It seems clear that his confidence in the accuracy of observations was low (as indeed it was right that it should be before the development of the experimental method). In this situation he might well have come to think that in the sphere of natural science the only things of which we can ever be certain are the considerations which must have weighed with the cosmic reason in the work of imposing order on the chaos.[1] But these of course are general terms. Neither the details of the order imposed upon nature nor the closeness with which things actually conform to it can be known. There can be no *epistêmê* of natural regularities in that there

[1] This certainly seems to be the view of the *Timaeus*.

131

can be no certainty that any regularities are actually conformed to by physical things, and in that, even if in fact they are, there can be no certainty about their nature.

4. *The fallacy of timeless truths.* Reflections on the uncertainties of scientific conclusions might have been reinforced by confusion concerning the principle that something which can be known must be true at all times. From this principle it is possible to conclude (fallaciously) that it is impossible to know a particular matter of fact, and that it is impossible to know general truths about things which change. The point which is made in the *Theaetetus*, that describability does not entail complete changelessness, might have served to indicate that these inferences cannot in fact be drawn, but we have seen that there are grounds for thinking that neither Plato nor Aristotle ever got the matter quite straight. Both of them seem to have thought that the fact that it is now raining is not the sort of fact that can strictly be known, on the ground that the sentence "It is now raining" does not always express a truth. That it is now raining, therefore, lacks the timelessness which one looks for in an object of knowledge. Likewise that the sun travels in a circle, being a statement about a changing thing, cannot strictly be known.

5. *Form and matter.* I considered earlier, and rejected, the suggestion that what Plato meant to tell us is that that which we perceive is physical things and that that which we know includes facts about physical things. This suggestion stays rejected. Nevertheless we have seen that in the tenth book of the *Republic* Socrates was made to speak as if I can see but not know a bridle, whereas I can know but not see what a bridle ought to be like; and it is a natural development of the thoughts described in the last paragraph to say that when I know something about the physical world what I do is to pick out a plum of form from the transient pudding of matter. When I know or understand a tune, what I hear is a changing series of momentary sounds, what I know or understand is the pattern to which the sounds conform.[1] In this way what I perceive is not the same as what I know, and this may have been among the thoughts which led Plato to say that we cannot know the physical world. If this point were correctly appreciated it would not amount to the point that there can be no *epistémé* of the physical world, but to the point that such knowledge should not be called "of the physical world", but "of a pattern manifested by the physical world". The suggestion is however that Plato may at times have exaggerated, rather than correctly appreciated, the significance of this point.

The last four considerations have been such as to undermine the second of the three reasons of which I said that they ought to make us

---

[1] cp. *Theaetetus* 163 b–c, mentioned above, p. 8.

uncomfortable about saying that Plato intended to deny that we can have *epistêmê* of the physical world—the reason, namely, that perceptual knowledge, being the optimum cognitive relation to a physical thing, deserves the title of *epistêmê*. I come now to offer considerations calculated to undermine the third of these three reasons, namely that which says that if Plato denied that we can have *epistêmê* of particular empirical facts, then he made it incomprehensible how we can have *epistêmê* of the nature of general terms.

6. *Neglect of Cartesian doubts.* It may be observed that none of the above considerations requires us to say that we cannot be *certain* of a particular matter of fact—as, for example, that this is a horse. Those which withhold the title *epistêmê* from a judgment of this kind do not do so on the ground that we ought (always) to have *doubts* of its truth. The fact is that Plato was not interested in Cartesian doubt —in asking "Can we ever *be really sure* that there is a chair in the room? Or that the litmus paper turned blue?" He was well aware of perceptual illusion, but he was not unduly perturbed by it. In *Theaetetus* 158 b the Cartesian doubt whether we may not now be dreaming is treated as a commonplace which is of interest only because the similarity between waking and dream life requires an explanation; no *sceptical* capital is made of it. On the whole it is probably true to say that Plato's view was that measuring and other techniques can protect us from the effects of perceptual illusion.[1] But if Plato was not interested in Cartesian scepticism, then in denying that I can properly be said to have *epistêmê*, e.g. that this is a horse, it would not occur to him that he was telling us that we can never be certain that we have a horse before us. In that case the question "How then could we ever come to know what it is to be a horse?" would not arise.

7. *Recollection.* We ought however to remember that the question which we have just mentioned would not have seemed to Plato such an obvious question as it seems to us. To him the important part of the achievement described as "knowing what it is to be a horse" is not accomplished primarily by looking at horses. We do not understand what a horse is until we understand what possibility of animal existence is represented by this system of organised material known as the horse. But in the bringing about of this understanding sense-experience offers no more than cues. What, say, the observation that horses are fast runners does towards giving us an understanding of horse-hood is to activate the thought that rapid evasive motion is one way of preserving life. The observed fact puts us in mind of a possible sub-division of the general term *self-activating physical thing*— namely the sub-division *self-activating physical thing which preserves*

[1] cp. *Protagoras* 356, *Republic* 602.

its life by running away from its enemies. We are able to conceive of this possibility (and thereby enabled to interpret the fleetness of horses) because we are able to sub-divide highly generic general terms by multiplying them, so to speak, by each other (*animal* by *swift-moving* in our example) and thus can conceive, antecedently of experience, of the relatively specific general terms which are embodied in concrete things. To put the matter more picturesquely, Plato does not have to believe that we arrive at a knowledge of general terms by abstraction from particulars, because he believes in "the homogeneity of mind". Mind is responsible for the order of nature, and we too, who try to discover that order, are minds; and a mind is something which can grasp the possible ways of existing. Inferior minds we may be, and our inferiority is especially due to the vividness of the impact made upon us by sense-experience, and our consequent tendency to judge by appearances. This is something which we must control by getting away from the senses and the desires that go with them (cp. *Phaedo* 65–6 and 83). Inferior minds that we are, if we do try to control the tendency to rely on appearances, and thereby fall back on the citadel of rationality within us, we are falling back on something which is in sympathy with the mind responsible for the cosmic order. The eternal intelligence designed, figuratively speaking, "looking to the intelligible forms"; and what is intelligible to one mind is intelligible to any. The intelligible principles perfectly grasped by the eternal intelligence can never perhaps be perfectly grasped by us. But since mind is homogeneous, in the end what makes sense to any mind must make sense to any other, so that, if we ruthlessly pursue the policy of discarding what fails to make sense, we shall get as near as we possibly can get to discovering the principles underlying the order of nature. This being so, why waste time on the laborious collection of empirical data? In the light of this we can see both that Plato would have set a low value on observations of particular matters of fact or empirical generalisations (and hence might have been tempted to deny them the title *epistêmê*); and, more particularly, that he would not have felt the force of the argument that, if there is no knowledge of particular matters of fact, there can be no knowledge of general terms. For our knowledge of general terms is not, for him, built up out of the knowledge of particulars. The mind is furnished (potentially) with its store of general terms, out of its own resources.

What is the conclusion of all this? We reminded ourselves in paragraph 6 that Plato would not have agreed that we acquire a knowledge of general terms by abstraction from their instances; paragraph 5 reminded us that in denying that there is *epistêmê* of matters of fact

Plato is not committed to denying that we can ever know for certain the truth of some empirical matter. These two points together undermine the contention that Plato cannot have meant to deny that there is *epistêmê* of matters of fact on the ground that he would have thereby made *epistêmê* of general terms incomprehensible. Paragraphs 4–2 meanwhile have suggested reasons why the title *epistêmê* should have been denied to empirical knowledge; roughly speaking, in empirical knowledge, whether particular or general, we have not got the fast grip of an ultimate constituent of the world that *epistêmê* connotes—either because the grip is not fast or because what it grips is not ultimate. These points together make it credible that Plato should have denied that we have *epistêmê* of the physical world; and all that makes us hesitate to say that he did make this denial is the fact that he did not always do so. The road to Larisa in the *Meno*, the eye-witness in the *Theaetetus*, the user of gadgets in the *Republic*—these cannot be ignored. We accommodate them best by arguing on the one hand that the *doxa/epistêmê* contrast can be made both relatively and absolutely; and by remembering on the other hand the point made in paragraph 1, namely that Plato's interest was not in whether there is empirical knowledge of physical fact but in whether there is empirical knowledge of universals—for a negative answer to the second question may well have expressed itself in words appropriate to a negative answer to the first.

If the answer is wanted in a nutshell, we must say that Plato often, but not always, denies that we can have *epistêmê* of physical facts; that in this *epistêmê* must be construed as a technical term; and that Plato has no special desire to tell us that we cannot, in the ordinary English sense of the words, know matters of empirical fact.

III. THE DOCTRINE OF *ANAMNÊSIS*

Everybody who has heard of Plato has heard of the doctrine of *anamnêsis* or recollection. It is indeed an essential part of Plato's philosophical outlook. It is however not quite so easy to say what precisely the doctrine is.

We may observe by way of introduction that the doctrine of recollection is at any rate a close cousin of some of the things that are said about goodness in the *Republic*. It will be remembered that the culmination of dialectic is the apprehension of the nature of goodness, that goodness is the source of the existence and of the intelligibility of the other forms, and that until we apprehend goodness we cannot be certain of the correctness of any of our earlier dialectical achievements. It will be remembered also that goodness provides the light in which we see whatever we are able to see "in the intelligible realm", whether at the level of *dianoia* or at that of *nöêsis*. But this seems to mean that as we make philosophical progress we get nearer to grasping as a coherent whole the system of universal natures, from which are in some way derived the conceptions that we use and the distinctions that we draw in abstract thought. Therefore in doing dialectic we are advancing towards an explicit grasp of the system of intelligible natures an implicit awareness of which has guided our progress. It is easy to see that this might be described in terms of bringing to the forefront of the mind something which lies at the back of it, or of recapturing a memory which we hazily retain. We shall discover that the doctrine of recollection is very much along these lines.[1]

However the Seventh Book of the *Republic* speaks of using a light whose source we cannot yet see, and not of recapturing a dimly retained memory. The passages where the latter notion is expounded are *Meno* 80–6, *Phaedo* 72–7 and *Phaedrus* 247–50.

The passage in the *Meno* opens significantly, because it shows the connection between the doctrine of *anamnêsis* and the question: How do we make philosophical progress? Socrates has baffled Meno, and, when Meno protests at this, Socrates says that he is baffled too and that they must seek the truth together. Meno retorts that seeking is impossible, because if you knew something you could not seek it, whereas if you did not know it you would not know when you had found it. How, in fact, if you are really trying to solve a problem, do you know that you have got the right answer?

Socrates says that he has often heard this argument and does not think much of it. He proceeds to meet it by quoting what he has heard from "priests . . . who are concerned to be able to give account of their priesthood, and from inspired poets". Their doctrine is that the soul is immortal, and goes to Hades and returns to earth, learning everything in the course of its wanderings. Therefore it is not surprising that it can be reminded of virtue and of other matters, since it has previously known them. "Since the whole of nature is akin, and since the soul has learnt everything, there is no reason why we should not, on being reminded of one thing (or 'learning' it as men say) rediscover all the rest if we have the strength to persevere" (81 c 9–d 4). This last sentence needs some comment. By "nature" Socrates presumably means "the natures of things", or the answers to such questions as what virtue is. The word for "learn" (*manthanein*) can doubtless be used for learning matters of brute fact, but it also means "understand", and "come to understand" is probably the best translation here. Socrates does not want to tell us that we have learnt, at some time, that Peking is in China or that mules are sterile, but that

---

[1] More of this will be found in a subsequent chapter, pp. 558–61.

we have come to understand such things as the rationale of the division of men into virtuous and vicious. Whether he only wants to tell us that the things of this kind which constitute "nature" are akin to each other (c 9–d 1), or whether he also wants to say that they are all akin to the soul is not clear to me. Nor do I know quite what he means by saying that if we are reminded of one thing we can by perseverance re-discover the rest. The sequel suggests that he means that a man may need help from another in the initial stages to put him on the right track, but that he can then carry on for himself if he cares to do so. There does not seem to be any suggestion that there is some one essential clue which a man has got to be reminded of before he can begin. At any rate there is no indication what this essential clue would be—unless it were that learning is recollection. I think however that the point is that we need only to be started off by another's help.

For in order to convince Meno that to come to understand something is to recollect it, Socrates takes a slave who has never had any mathematical teaching, and, roughly speaking, gets the slave to prove a geometrical theorem. The problem that Socrates sets to the slave could be put in the following terms: "What is the construction for a square twice the area of a given square?" In answering this question the slave has the wherewithal for proving the theorem that the square on the diagonal is twice the area of the square on whose diagonal it is. They begin by agreeing on a (rough) definition of a square. Socrates then shows the slave how to reckon the area of a rectangle, and soon elicits from him the answer that a square of side $2n$ will be double the area of a square of side n. This Socrates refutes by reckoning the area of two examples, and Socrates and Meno agree that the slave has benefited by the destruction of this error. The destructive work done, Socrates now proceeds roughly as follows. He takes four equal squares and puts them together so that they form one large square. The resulting figure is a square with a St. George's Cross on it. He then joins up the tips of the arms of the cross so that it is enclosed in a diamond. Each side of the diamond is a diagonal of one of the original squares, and the diamond is composed of four triangles, each of which is half one of the original squares. Since the diamond contains four of these triangles, and the original squares contain two each, the diamond (it is taken for granted that its angles are right angles) is obviously a square double in area to any of the original squares. All this the slave is made to see, simply by being asked the appropriate question at the appropriate time. Naturally Socrates' methods of proof are not rigorous; it is for example accepted as obvious that all diagonals of squares of equal area are of equal length. Nor is the slave entirely ignorant of mathematics; for instance

137

he has learnt to multiply. But of course it would be possible for Socrates, if time was no object, to prove in the same kind of way the things that he takes for granted. It is not true, as it is sometimes said, that Socrates' methods are empirical. He does not, for example, get out a foot rule. His proof works as mathematical proofs should work, by extracting the consequences of things previously agreed to, though some of the steps are omitted.

Socrates' account of what he has done is that the slave, although untaught, had in him all the right opinions; but since they had to be elicited (those which tumbled out of their own accord being mostly wrong ones) he could not be said to know. The asking of the right question at the right time has activated his true beliefs, and enabled him to "recover knowledge from his own resources—which is what we call recollecting" (85 d). Since he did not acquire these true beliefs in his lifetime, he must have got them before he was a man. Socrates then (86 a 6–b 2) offers a very odd proof of immortality, and adds that the only part of the argument that he is confident about is its moral, namely that it is not, as Meno's argument had suggested it was, a waste of time to pursue the truth.

There seem to be two different strands in this argument, one of which leads towards religious notions about pre-existence, the other towards logical notions about the status of necessary truths; and these strands are difficult to disentangle.

Thus in what I called his "very odd" proof of immortality Socrates seems to say that true beliefs can at any time be activated in a soul, whether in or out of the body, by questioning, and that therefore the soul must always at all times *have* learnt all truth (86 a 8). There is therefore no moment, whether here or in Hades, at which the act of learning occurs; the soul is always in the condition of having learnt. (Once again, it seems obvious that by "all truth" Socrates must mean, not every true statement, but all the truths of philosophy, mathematics and so on, in fact all necessary truths; what he is telling us is that it is always possible for us to recover a grasp of these if someone or something will "remind" us of them).

But if we stress the point that a man can always at any time recover a grasp of intelligible necessities and that therefore he must at all times be in a condition of having already learnt them, difficulties arise. For one thing, we wonder what the process of learning is supposed to be if it is always something that has already occurred. For another, we wonder how we have a proof of immortality. Pre-existence is required, and brings with it a proof of immortality, only if our ability to understand a geometrical theorem depends on actual geometry lessons which we were given at some time in Hades, and which we dimly remember on earth. If we are always in a condition of *having learnt*, then there was never a moment at which we did learn; and if there was never a moment at which we did learn, what can be meant by saying that we are always in a condition of having learnt, except that we are always capable of coming to understand? But that does not imply that we existed before we were born; to get that implication we need to say that the time before we were born was the time at which we did learn.

The idea that necessary truths have to be learnt, but that we are conveniently taught them before birth, conflicts not only with the saying that the things that we can know are things that we are at any moment in the condition of having learnt; it conflicts also with the example of method which Socrates has given. For what the slave is made to do is to extract the logical consequences of things which he has already agreed to, and which are logical consequences of the initial data or of the constructions which are made, the function of Socrates being to take the slave step by step, and so prevent him from confusing himself. There does not therefore seem to be much that the slave could have been taught in Hades. He does indeed utilise such facts as that 4 is twice 2 in coming to see the conclusion, but this is not something that has to be learnt in the way in which we have to learn that Berlin is in Germany. Socrates could presumably have brought the slave to see that 4 is twice 2, if it had been necessary, by his method of questioning. What the slave does is to deduce the consequences of premises, and no additional information is necessary to perform a valid deduction. Not only is this true, it also looks very much as if it is the point of Socrates' demonstration. Following this line of thought one comes to the conclusion that the lesson Plato means us to derive from this passage is that a soul is at every moment of its existence capable of reasoning, and thus capable of arriving at all necessary truths out of its own resources; and that this is figuratively called recollection because both this and recollection proper are cases of bringing something up out of one's hidden resources.

But then one remembers that there is supposed to be some connection with immortality in all this; indeed a proof of immortality. No doubt we might say that Plato independently believes in immortality; and believes that the soul enjoys the contemplation of the rational order in the discarnate condition, so that when we discover and contemplate a rational truth on earth we are enjoying again a pre-natal experience, and that this is another reason for talking of recollection. But the fact that Socrates is allowed to talk as if he were offering a *proof*, and the fact that the proof would only be a proof if something like pre-natal instruction were involved, must make us hesitate to say that all that Plato wants to tell us is that every

139

soul is potentially capable of valid reasoning. To say that would be to over-simplify.

One is tempted to wonder whether, when Socrates says that all nature is akin, he means to tell us that all universal natures are akin not only to each other, but also to the soul. This would seem to offer an answer not only to the question what the learning process is supposed to be like, but also how Plato thought that he had here a proof of immortality. We should get the answers roughly as follows. That all universal natures are akin with each other would mean something to the effect that they all form a coherent system. That they are akin to the soul would mean that the concepts which we are naturally prone to form, and the inferences which we are naturally prone to make with these concepts, correspond to these universal natures and to the relations between them. The proof of immortality would lie not in the fact that a time has to be found for pre-natal geometry lessons, but in the presumption (explicitly stated in *Phaedo* 77–80) that if the soul is akin to eternal entities such as universal natures it too must be eternal. To elucidate what I mean when I speak of our concepts and inferences corresponding to universal natures and the relations between them, let us take some such notions as *squareness* and *circularity*. We are naturally prone to notice that there is an important difference between square things and round things; *square* and *round* are headings under which any man will readily classify objects. We naturally see, also, that round things are more likely to roll than square things; we can see some of the consequences of roundness and squareness. We are not likely to see all the consequences; we may, like the slave, think that a square of side $2n$ will be double the area of a square of side n. Nevertheless, if there is somebody present to check us, we can see that this is wrong, and we can eventually work out what is right. We have the ability to discover this aspect of squareness from our own resources. Our natural tendency to classify things as round or square corresponds to the difference which obtains between roundness or squareness as they are in themselves; our tendency to infer that a round thing will roll corresponds to the fact that circularity entails the equidistance of every point on the circumference from the centre. We are naturally inclined to classify things into kinds which reason sees to be genuinely distinct, and we are naturally inclined to see some of the consequences of our classifications, and able to discover the rest. The way our minds work corresponds to the way things are, and this is the kinship of the soul to "universal nature".

However to read all this into the *Meno* is to import into it what the text does not plainly contain. It is also, incidentally, to bring the *Meno* more into line with the *Phaedo*. Since the opening of the passage in the *Phaedo* suggests that it is offering an alternative version of the same doctrine as that in the *Meno*, this is satisfactory so far as it goes. It is possible that one cause of the difficulties that we have found is as follows. In both dialogues *anamnêsis* is supposed to provide an argument for immortality, and in the *Phaedo* the argument is presented as if it were independent of the argument from the soul's kinship with the forms. To be independent, the argument from *anamnêsis* must be thought to involve some sort of pre-natal experience; but as we have seen the *Meno* makes it difficult to see what experience this could have been and when it was provided. Might it not be, then, that Plato intended to impute to Socrates in both places an argument which did depend on pre-natal experience, but that he had himself rather more sophisticated ideas than those which he imputed to Socrates and that he inadvertently spoiled Socrates' case by making him say things which really only accorded with Plato's? This seems to be a possible explanation of the fact that the *Meno* both insists on pre-natal experiences and also fails to find a place for them.[1]

We come now to the passage in the *Phaedo*. As we have seen it begins with what looks like a reference to the *Meno* (*Phaedo* 73 a 7). Kebes suggests that the argument from recollection proves that souls have discarnate existence, and says that the argument rests on the fact that if you question people cunningly they give the right answers, and that this is very clearly seen in geometry. Socrates then offers an alternative version of the argument, saying that if the one does not convince, the other may. The new version is as follows.

1. Whenever there is any connection between two objects A and B (B may be like A, be a picture of A, a familiar piece of A's property, and so on) the sight of the one may remind me of the other. If the connection between A and B is that they are alike, then for B to remind me of A, I must notice not only the resemblance, but also the difference (otherwise I should mistake it for A).

2. Now there is such a thing as equality, and we understand what it is. But where does our knowledge of it come from? In one sense it must come from experience of equal physical objects; and yet equality is not the same thing as equal physical objects; for physical things can seem equal to one man and unequal to another, whereas "the

---

[1] I suppose that it is possible that the immortality argument in the *Meno* is meant to be simply: "If we at all times have learnt, the learning must have taken place infinitely long ago. Therefore the soul has existed since that infinitely distant moment and will presumably exist until an infinitely distant moment in the future, i.e. for ever." But we should still want an explanation of Plato's finding this use of the "actual infinite" convincing.

equals themselves can never seem unequal, nor equality inequality".
There are then two sets of things, equality and equal physical objects, [1]
and these are different from each other, whether or not they are
unlike. (In other words the question of the exact relation between
universals and particulars is dismissed; all that is necessary is that
they should not be identified).

3. Now equal physical objects are, and are seen by us to be, less
equal than equality. We have agreed that there is a sense in which we
derive our knowledge of equality from equal physical objects, but
since we realise that equal physical objects fall short, always, of the
standard of equality, we cannot have derived our knowledge of the
standard from things which admittedly always fall short of it. The
natural thing to say therefore is that we have knowledge of equality
independently, and that what equal objects do is to remind us of it.
This is the sense in which our knowledge of equality is derived from
equal objects.

4. Finally the fact that equal physical objects are equal (though
"less equal than equality") is detected by the senses. Since our senses
always tell us that physical instances of equality are imperfect, we
must have become aware of the standard before we came to enjoy
the use of our senses, i.e. before we were born. It cannot be said that
we have retained this knowledge of equality, because a man can give
account of what he knows, and few men can give account of equality
or anything else. Therefore it must be the case that we forget the
knowledge of equality and the other intelligible natures [2] on coming
into the body, and that we are put in mind of them by experience; and
to be put in mind of one thing by another is recollection.

The general picture presupposed by this argument is familiar to us
from the fifth book of the *Republic*. There are precise analysable
universals, and there are physical instances which must not be confounded with them. The latter do not perfectly exemplify the former,
in the sense that we cannot gather an adequate understanding of the
former from a study of the latter. The reason which is apparently
given for this (para. 2; 74 b 7–8), namely that two physical objects
may seem equal to one man and unequal to another, is a feeble one as
it stands, and I am not sure that this translation is correct. However
we cannot go into this now, [3] so we must leave it that, whatever the
reason, the point is made that universals must not be confounded

---

[1] I shall not here discuss the question whether "the equals themselves" means
the same as "equality". See below, pp. 302–3.

[2] "The things we entitle 'what the thing itself is' in our conversations" Socrates
calls them (75 d 1–3). He means the things whose definitions he habitually seeks.

[3] For a detailed discussion of this passage see below, pp. 295–303.

with their instances and that the instances do not give us the knowledge that we possess of their universals, though they do play some role in relation to it.

The *Republic* says, of course, that what the instances do is to give us a *doxa* of their universals, an idea of how they seem. To decide what the present passage says we must clear up an incoherency in the argument. For it begins by saying that we do of course all know equality and the other natures "whose definitions we seek", but it ends by saying that very few people can be said to retain their pre-natal knowledge, for very few can give account of equality or whatever it may be. The reason for saying that we know equality is, roughly speaking, that we know what the word means and can thus tell that two sticks or stones are not perfect cases of the thing, whereas the reason for saying that we do not know equality is that we cannot give account of it.

Looking at these contradictory positions in the light of the reasons for them and in the light of the *Meno*, one is inclined to wonder whether the doctrine is roughly as follows. What we retain is a true belief concerning the nature of equality. This enables us to see that these two peas are not a perfect case of it. This is not knowledge, and it is not a full-blooded revival of the pre-natal vision of equality. For equality is something that can be grasped abstractly, and of which a *logos* or analytic definition can be given; it is thus that the mind grasped it out of the body, and it is only when this theoretical grasp is re-activated by the question-and-answer technique of Socratic definition that full knowledge is achieved. What experience does, strictly speaking, is to revive not our knowledge of equality, but the true belief which is all that we retain until it is converted into knowledge by philosophical methods.

We can see now that there are two *prima facie* differences between the accounts in these two dialogues; and on reflection neither of them is important. The first is that, textually at any rate, what the *Meno* makes us remember seems to be propositions, whereas the *Phaedo* makes us remember universals. This is not an important difference, for no doubt Plato would say, along the lines of our recent discussion, that to remember squareness is to remember the theorems that flow from it, or the inferences which we can make with this concept. Indeed we found ourselves wondering whether the *Meno* itself did not really intend that what we retain is a grasp of the universal natures which are, so to speak, the archetypes of the concepts which we find ourselves employing. The second difference is that the *Meno* says that we retain true beliefs, in the sense that we shall tend to give the right answer if a questioner asks questions in the proper order and thereby saves us from confusing ourselves; and that it is not this implicit retention, but the conversion of it into full understanding which is to be called "recollection". In the *Phaedo* on the other hand "recollection" is not used for the conversion of true beliefs into knowledge. "Recollection" in the *Phaedo* is the name for what happens when our implicitly retained true beliefs about universals are activated by experience of instances. But this too need not be an important difference. The *Phaedo* uses a more "dispositional" or "behaviouristic" sense of the word "recollection" than the *Meno*, but this does not imply any doctrinal difference.

It is possible however that there is some doctrinal difference, though it does not show itself in any positive discrepancy. This is that the *Phaedo* insists at one point, as we have seen, that knowledge has not been regained until one can "give account". This emphasis on the importance of "giving account" is not to be found in the *Meno*. In talking about the process by which beliefs are converted into knowledge (the process by which knowledge is recovered out of one's own resources, the process which it calls recollection) the *Meno* says: "and if he is questioned about these same things often enough, and in enough different ways, in the end he will come to have knowledge about them as exact as anybody's" (85 c). In other words if you go over a theorem or group of theorems often enough, taking the steps in a different order perhaps, and so forth, the result of this repetition is to confirm your beliefs until they qualify for the status of knowledge. It is true that later on in the same dialogue it is said that belief is turned into knowledge by "the working out of the explanation", but at this point nothing of this kind is stressed. We are allowed to get the impression that experience can restore our knowledge to us provided we are helped by somebody who puts the proper questions to us in the right order. It is not said, though it is not denied, that knowledge necessarily involves theoretical insight. This is not a positive contradiction, but a possible difference of emphasis. When we were discussing knowledge and belief we found a similar difference of emphasis between the *Meno* and the *Republic*; and we have recently seen that the *Phaedo* seems to be in tune with the *Republic* on the subject of this distinction. Since the chronological order plainly is *Meno*: *Phaedo*: *Republic*, this constitutes a coherent development.

It seems then that the *Meno* and *Phaedo* come fairly well into line with each other, the residual difference being that the *Phaedo* insists that to know one must be able to give account. The passage in the *Phaedrus* follows the earlier accounts as far as it goes. It is short however, and it comes in the mythical section of the dialogue, and therefore we cannot perhaps get very much out of it. It tells us that all human souls have seen at least some of the intelligible realities, because no soul can become incarnate in a human body unless it can by reasoning gather together "the so-called form" which is present in many instances (249 b 6). In other words a human mind must be able to abstract the common quality in multifarious instances, and this power depends on recollecting the vision of the forms as they were seen before birth. It is by virtue of this power of recollection that the philosophic propensities are powerfully excited in the finer spirits. Beauty in particular is more luminous in its instances than justice, and the other things that we revere, and hence it is primarily by beautiful objects that the soul can be fired to desire to re-possess itself of the pre-natal vision of reality.

Here evidently what we are put in mind of is universals, and it is by seeing instances of them that we are put in mind of them. Plato's purpose at this point is to explain how sexual passion can elevate the mind: this being so it is probably unwise to try to wring too much epistemology out of what he says. But if we were to try to do so we might think that the doctrine of the *Phaedrus* is simpler and bolder than that of the *Phaedo*. For the *Phaedrus* appears to tell us that the power of generalising as such is due to the pre-natal vision of the common natures which we abstract when we generalise; and in the context of what the *Phaedrus* says about dialectic, we would expect these to include such common natures as animality. The *Phaedo* does not go so far as this, in that the *Phaedo* makes its point in terms of equality, an example with respect to which it is plausible to say that we cannot get to know it from its instances. It does not indeed explicitly allow that there are some general natures (e.g. that of being a helmet) that we can extract from their instances, but it does not appear to exclude the possibility as the *Phaedrus* might be taken to do. However, the answer to this no doubt is that the account in the *Phaedrus* is perfunctory and that Plato is obviously thinking primarily of terms like beauty. Nevertheless it is possible that Plato would have been prepared seriously to defend the connection between the power of generalising and that which he calls recollection. We suggested that the doctrine of recollection can be construed as a way of putting the point that the fundamental distinctions that common sense is inclined to draw correspond to real differences which reason recognises between general terms. Bearing in mind what the *Republic* and the *Cratylus* have to say about forms of artefacts we would expect Plato to argue that even such a concept as that of a helmet is a complex function of such fundamental distinctions. For he who separates off helmets from hats is drawing on notions such as rigidity, protection and so on. Obviously it would seem possible to produce a kind of scale of general terms putting at the top those like equality and justice which it would be plausible to say we "bring to experience" and at the bottom those like concepts of artefacts which it would be plausible to say we "get from experience"; and Plato would have to allow that experience plays a larger part in the genesis of those at the bottom than in that of those at the top. Still, it might be that he would wish to make the point that all concepts, except perhaps those of sense-qualities, do depend on the critical use of experience, or in other words on the application to it of the fundamental distinctions, our ability to use which is a "memory" of the forms.

Having looked at the passages in which the doctrine of *anamnêsis* is put forward we ought to look at one in which it appears to be denied. This is the passage in which the *Theaetetus* talks about the process of learning and compares it to capturing birds and putting them into an aviary (*Theaetetus* 196–9). For here Socrates explicitly says (197 e) that the aviary into which we put the birds that we catch is empty at birth. Nor is this because he is discussing the learning of particular matters of fact, for he is not; mathematical facts are explicitly included among his birds.

This need not amount to a contradiction of the doctrine of *anamnêsis*. In the language of the *Meno* we have learnt at all times that $7+5=12$, but we do not fully remember this until we have been reminded of it, and the *Meno* also uses "being reminded of" and "learning" as equivalents. What we recollect in the full sense we can be said to learn at the moment of recollection, though of course in another sense of "learn" we had learnt it already, always. But the child who has not yet "been reminded" that $7+5=12$ has not learnt this fact in the former use of "learnt" and does not yet know it. This therefore is a bird that the child still has to catch and put into the aviary. In other words if we suppose that Socrates means the process of capturing birds to stand for the process of coming consciously to know something then we should expect the aviary to be empty at birth; for the doctrine of *anamnêsis* does not require us to possess any actual as opposed to potential knowledge before we are reminded of it.

On the other hand if the *Theaetetus* did intend to deny the doctrine of *anamnêsis* this would not be surprising in view of what we might almost call its empiricist theory about the formation of concepts. This may be illustrated by looking again at the argument in the *Phaedo*. Wanting to show that knowledge of equality must have been acquired before birth, Socrates argues that we have enjoyed the use of our senses since infancy, and have always been able to sense that physical equals are not adequate instances of equality. But there is a serious flaw in this argument. Because we have been able to sense since birth, it does not follow that we have been able since then to sense that A and B are roughly but imperfectly equal. In the language of the *Theaetetus*, we are never able to sense this; we judge it on the basis of sense-data, and of course infants cannot make such judgments. Once it is admitted that we *learn* to use such notions as equality, it is not difficult to go on to see that such notions are of completely empirical origin. We use "unequal" to mark gross discrepancies, "equal" where we do not notice discrepancy. Then, having said that A, B and C are equal, we notice that there are in fact discrepancies between them, and so we form the notion of "perfectly equal" to stand for the postulated case of two entities such that there is no discrepancy between them. We may or may not believe it possible to find two such entities, but that is not important. The fact that a concept is without empirical application ("more beautiful than Helen", "more tiresome than Jones") does not imply that it is not of empirical origin.

How far the *Theaetetus* would be prepared to go in this direction is uncertain. As we have seen, it insists that whereas the power of sense-perception is innate, the ability to make judgments has to be learned. The stress which it lays on similarity as one of the items contributed by the mind to a judgment, and the things that it says about comparison of sense-data could be developed into an empiricist theory of the formation of concepts, or at least of empirical concepts. If the mind is endowed with the power of detecting resemblances it can frame concepts for itself, and this power is all it needs to bring into the world. I think however that it would be a mistake to suppose that Plato would ever have been willing to go so far as Locke and Hume. An empiricist theory of the formation of concepts leads in the end to the view that reasoning is the manipulation of material supplied by experience, and this in turn to the view that reason is inoperative in the absence of material upon which it can be exercised. It is true that Plato provides the forms to be so to speak the objects of reason, but an empiricist would want to say that these are not "objects" in the required sense. You cannot just contemplate equality, for it is nothing but a relationship which things have to each other. In so far therefore as Plato wanted the forms to be independent of things (and this I think is something that he always wanted) he would have tended to shy away from a full-bloodedly empiricist theory of the formation of concepts. He would always have wanted to say that forms can be "known" even without a world of things to partake in them. But this amounts to saying that entities like equality have, so to speak, a nature of their own; and so long as you say this you will be likely to wonder how our concept of equality comes to conform to the nature of equality; and that is the question to which the doctrine of *anamnêsis* is an answer.

I suppose that the standard interpretation of this passage is that which takes Plato's meaning to be that the forms are the sphere of competence of *epistêmê*, and that they are real; and that the material world is the sphere of competence of *doxa*, and that it is in some sense only half-real. Leaving aside this use of the notion of "reality", I have indicated that I do not wish to deny that Plato might, if asked, have replied that he intended in this passage to tell us that these were the spheres of competence of these cognitive functions. I certainly admit that he elsewhere made this allocation. My argument however is that we get this allocation if we put together what he here says about the nature of knowledge (viz. that it is the grasp of an *on*) with what he is sometimes at any rate willing to say in answer to the material question: "What can we know?" (viz. that we cannot know physical things because they are not *onta*). I contend also that he is not here primarily concerned with the material question (though how clearly he disentangled it from the formal question I do not profess to know) because he is here interested in distinguishing different levels of apprehension of entities such as justice, and does not want to tell us that we can never know for certain that this is a just act, but rather that we shall never see clearly what justice is so long as we think of it only as the common feature of various (types of) acts.

Essentially my reason for taking this view is a subjective one, that I cannot now read the passage and believe that it is saying anything else. But there is an objective difficulty in the way of any interpretation which depends (as the spheres-of-competence interpretation must depend) on making *to on* mean "the forms". This is that it is not easy to see how the contemporary reader could have been expected to understand that "that which is" means "the forms".[1] As a desperate expedient we could suppose that *Republic* 5 in the form in which we have it was published after, say, the *Timaeus*, though it seems certain that some version of the *Republic* must have preceded the *Timaeus*. But if the reader of *Republic* 5 had not read *Republic* 6 and 7, had not read the *Timaeus*, and had not read books about Plato's theory of forms, could Plato have been sure that he would identify "that which is", or even "that which really is" with the forms? To be sure such a reader might have read the *Phaedo* and derived such an identification thence. But on the whole Plato does not write his dialogues as if they were a serial work; there are cross-

---

[1] The reader who understood by *to on* "that (whatever it is) that is real" would get something out of the passage, but he would surely be rather perplexed.

148

references, certainly, but on the whole it is Plato's custom to make his meaning clear in the current work without depending on some other. The identification of *to on* with the forms in the present context, moreover, would have been especially precarious since in contexts somewhat like this one it appears to have been common practice to correlate *epistêmê* (or anyhow true belief) with *to on* in the sense of "the facts" without any metaphysical preconceptions about what sort of facts there may ultimately be. (*Euthydemus* 284 provides a case in point. Here the Sophist Euthydemus, assuredly no Platonist, uses *on* and *mê on* simply to stand for "fact" and "figment" in developing a form of the Paradox of False Belief; he does this before an audience who seem to find such language familiar).

It may be retorted that the words *epistêmê* and *gnôsis* which Socrates uses in this passage are solemn words, that the same is true of phrases like *to pantelôs on* (477 a 3), and that these are indications from which the reader might have guessed that something was up.[1] I think that he might have guessed that something was up, but the question is: Could Plato reasonably have expected him to diagnose what that something was? Certainly *epistêmê* and *to on* can, but need not, connote profundity; there is a suggestion that the former delves, and the latter dwells, beneath appearances. But this is not always so, as the *Euthydemus* shows for *to on*, and as many passages show for *epistêmê* and the verb *gignôskein*, if not for the (less common) noun *gnôsis*. And the *to on* which dwells beneath appearances need not be Plato's forms, it might be Parmenides' one substance or the water which some Ionian physicist thought to be the ultimate stuff of nature. A reader might well have thought that a passage which correlated *epistêmê* or *gnôsis* with *to pantelôs on* was talking about the ultimate grasp of ultimate realities, and if he remembered his *Phaedo* he might have remembered that in the case of the author he was at present reading ultimate realities were forms; but I do not believe that Plato would have presumed all this. He knew that people read Parmenides' writings, and those of the Ionians, as well as his own.

I allow then that Plato might have expected the reader of this passage to conjecture that *epistêmê* was not the sort of thing one has of transient phenomena, being a more penetrating mental function than that. But I hesitate to allow that he would have expected the reader to see that *epistêmê* is what we have of the forms and that the forms are what we have *epistêmê* of. But I may be told that Socrates has just been talking of the forms on the previous page (476), speaking of "beauty itself" as something which is "one", and as something which only philosophers believe in, and that the contrast between

[1] But see e.g. *Sophist* 240 e 5 for almost equally solemn language without solemn meaning.

149

on the one hand entities like beauty and on the other hand its "participants" could not fail to put the reader in mind of the Platonic theory of forms. I am not so sure of this. What is the theory of forms, and where do we get it from?[1] Having found it in later dialogues and in Aristotle's writings we can detect traces of it in Plato's earlier works; and I must allow that there is a good dose of it in the *Phaedo* and in *Republic* 6 and 7. But does what Socrates says about "beauty itself" in the present passage clearly imply what we mean by the theory of forms for the present purpose—that is to say a doctrine according to which the forms are the only *onta* and physical things cannot be admitted to that status? I am not sure that it does. Socrates has drawn a distinction between those who do and those who do not believe in beauty itself as one unitary thing not unambiguously detectable in its participants, but this does not require that beauty should have any special ontological status. It requires that beauty should be a unitary general term of which a Socratic definition can be given, and that there should not be as many beauties as there are types of beautiful things. It requires the doctrine that every genuine concept corresponds to just one universal common nature. This may be a view which has seemed obvious from the days of Aristotle until the other day, but it was certainly not a view which Plato could treat as obvious. It was therefore a view which non-philosophers could be quite well represented as denying. But it does not require "the Platonic theory of forms" if this phrase stands for a view which asserts the reality of tabularity but denies the reality of this table. It was, after all, a view that Aristotle would have subscribed to in the case of most concepts, though it did not in his case carry with it the view that universals existed otherwise than "in" their instances.

Were it not for the precariousness of taking *to on* to mean "the forms" there is another interpretation of this passage that would seem to me to have merit. It certainly has the merit of not making Plato impugn the reality of physical things. This is the interpretation that says that *to on* stands for the forms, not so much because each of them really without qualification *is*, as rather because each of them really without qualification *is itself*. P-hood is an *ontôs on* not because it exists without question but because it is without qualification P. The forms are those entities each of which is without qualification what it is, and this is how they can be collectively referred to as that which is. *Epistêmê* is set over those entities because beauty and so on are precisely the entities which the mind can grasp. Just as *to on* is those entities to each of which there belongs without qualification a certain predicate (namely itself), so *to mê on* will be that to which there belongs no predicate at all. This will be something like

[1] Serious answers to these questions must be deferred to Chapter 3.

the *chôra* or "space" of the *Timaeus*, the substratum in which properties inhere, which has no properties of its own, and which cannot be
grasped by the mind except by bastard reasoning. Aristotle tells us
(*Physics* 192 a 6–16) that Plato called that in which properties exist
to mê on; and Leucippus had used the phrase to refer to empty space,
which he believed to be real but to have no character. It seems possible then that the phrase could bear this meaning. Since an entity of
this kind can only be grasped by bastard reasoning (i.e. we can see
that it must be postulated but cannot see what it is) *agnoia* seems an
appropriate cognitive function to correlate with the substratum.[1]
Finally ordinary particulars will be between *on* and *mê on* in that they
consist of the characterless informed by that which is fully characterised. Understanding grasps the element of form, *agnoia* answers to
the element of matter; judgment, coming between understanding and
agnoia, deals with entities whose definiteness is due to form and
whose changeableness is due to matter. This is an attractive way of
making sense of this passage, but it cannot be its primary meaning
both because of the difficulty already mentioned about the understanding of *to on*, but also and more decisively because of the greater
difficulty over the meaning of *to mê on* which would almost certainly
have beset those who had read neither the *Timaeus* nor Aristotle.

Lastly, if we accept the spheres-of-competence view, must we say
that Plato here impugns the reality of physical things in a way which
is inconsistent with the rest of his views, for example with the view
that the body is real enough to have disastrous effects on the soul?
The answer to this is a little complicated. Because on this view *to mê
on* has to mean "the non-existent" we shall have to say that in putting
physical things between *to on* and *to mê on* Plato was *logically
committed* to impugning their reality in a dangerous way. But we
need not say that he had any intention of honouring this commitment. We can say that he habitually said that physical things were
not *onta*, meaning thereby not to deny them existence and reality,
but to deny them stability and (in some sense) ultimacy. They were
not *onta* because they were *gignomena*, things that "become".
Gignomena are real and exist but they are not *onta* precisely because
einai[2] and *gignesthai* are the two poles of a contrast which is drawn
within the class of existent things. But Plato might have failed to see
that it is one thing to contrast *einai* with *gignesthai* and another
thing to contrast it with *mê einai*. He saw this in the *Sophist* in what
some regard as a penitent passage.[3] Here however he could have felt

---

[1] See *Cratylus* 440 a 3, where it is said that "no knowledge knows what it
knows except as having certain properties".

[2] The verb whose participle gives us *to on*.

[3] See below, Chapter 3, pp. 419–21.

that he was doing no real harm saying that physical things were "not quite *onta*" even in a passage in which the contrast was between *onta* and *mê onta* and not between *onta* and *gignomena*. After all *mê onta* means "not *onta*", and *gignomena* will seem to be that until you detect (and *Sophist* 243 c 2–5 seems to suggest that there is some novelty about the detection) that *einai* is ambiguous.

2

COSMOLOGY AND THEORY
OF NATURE

THE topics I shall discuss in this chapter will centre round two questions: (1) To what extent and in what sense did Plato believe the natural world to be rationally ordered? and (2) What recommendations does he offer concerning the proper way of studying the natural world? The principal documents for these topics will be the *Phaedo*, *Republic*, *Timaeus* and *Laws*.

There is a view which holds that Plato thought that the natural world is a deplorable place, and that the only proper way of treating it is to ignore it and study "the ideal world" instead. This is an absurd view, and I shall not waste time disputing it. I hope that its falsity will sufficiently emerge.

I. THREE PRESUPPOSITIONS

I shall argue that the earlier documents (*Phaedo* and *Republic*) cannot be understood without reading back into them doctrines which are only explicitly stated in later writings. These doctrines (or embryonic forms of them) are in my view presupposed in the earlier writings, and I shall begin by giving a rough statement of these presuppositions.

Firstly then the natural world is ordered by intelligence; and this rational ordering consists in the gathering up of disorderly material into kinds. The state of the natural world without its ordering would be that of "an infinite sea of dissimilarity" (*Statesman* 273 d 6)—no definite things, and therefore no likenesses between one part of it and another, no regularities for science or common sense to observe, nothing but nothing-in-particular everywhere. The existence of distinct kinds of things is due to the ordering done by mind; and the behaviour of the natural world is due to the natures of the kinds into which it is ordered.

153

Secondly the ordering is *rational* and not arbitrary. Precisely what this means Plato may perhaps never have decided, but at least it will mean something like this:—For a thing to be rationally ordered, it must be possible to see that it *had* to be ordered like that. If I arrange things in one way, and they could equally well have been arranged differently, then my choice of my arrangement is arbitrary and not rational. Therefore the order which is imposed, the kinds that there are and the relations between them, is an order which *had to be*; and that can only mean that the kinds and the relations between them are given—not products of the ordering mind, or its dispositions would be arbitrary and not rational, but intelligible necessities, given as much to the supreme mind which orders as to our minds which try to understand. Therefore the order which the Craftsman (in the language of the *Timaeus*) imposes is something with which he is already confronted when he comes, mythically speaking, to the work of ordering the primal chaos. It is already given by "intelligible necessity" which kinds of things there can be; and the causal relations which will subsist between the things are given by the necessitation relations which exist between the kinds.

Ordered existence has from eternity, of rational necessity, its finite list of kinds; and the act of ordering does not create the kinds, it creates instances of them. What the kinds of ordered existence are, and why there are just these and no others, is of course perfectly known by a perfect divine mind. The kinds of ordered existence are imperfectly reflected in the products of this mind's ordering, because these products are physical; and they are imperfectly reflected also in the minds of human beings, because human minds (until purified by philosophy) are prevented from becoming pure minds by the association with the body and by the almost invincible temptation to identify things as they affect our senses with things as they really are. But although physical things imperfectly reflect their kinds, none the less their behaviour, in so far as it is orderly and capable of scientific study, does depend on the natures of the kinds to which they are conformed. Therefore in order to understand what really happens in nature we must purify our minds as best we can by trying to discern what X-hood really is, and what relations hold between X-hood and W-hood and Y-hood. This is the only way by which we understand how W, X and Y things affect each other.

The third presupposition we have already mentioned; it is that the natural world does not conform perfectly to the order imposed upon it. This presupposition is evinced in odd phrases in various places; for example in certain phrases in the *Timaeus* which we shall encounter, or in a phrase in the *Phaedo* (75) where Socrates speaks of physical things "trying to be equal and failing". But it comes out most clearly in the myth in the *Statesman* (268–74), and this we shall briefly look at here. Sometimes, then, the universe rotates one way, sometimes the other. It goes one way, winding up so to speak, when God is in charge, and in that period all things are ordered by the Gods. But then God resigns the helm and lets the universe unwind. At first, even without divine guidance, all goes moderately well; but the universe gradually forgets its former state, and unbalance creeps in. This goes on until the universe has almost sunk into the infinite sea of dissimilarity, to save it from which God resumes the rudder and orders things once more. We live in the running down phase, and that means that the universe as we know it "remembers", but only imperfectly, the original divine order.

Let us try to sum up these three presuppositions and the lesson that they involve for the proper study of nature by the scientist in an allegory which we have used already. Imagine a library and imagine that the books in it are not only ordered, but rationally ordered. That is to say, not only does every book have its place, but also the whole arrangement makes sense; the man who drew up the plan of classification drew it up with his eye on "intelligible necessities", and in consequence it is not only *a* plan, but an *excellent* plan. Imagine next that over the years the books have been a little disordered, and then imagine a man who wants to find his way about it. He will have to rediscover the original plan, and this is something he will never do if he simply passively observes where the books now are; for some of them are in the wrong places. He will have to combine observation with the presupposition that the library owes such order as it has to the imposition upon it of a rational plan. He will look at a book and ask how reason would classify it; not as a red book, nor as a book of such a size (for a rational librarian does not classify in these ways), but as a work of seventeenth century ecclesiastical biography for example. But the section devoted to seventeenth century ecclesiastical biography, ought to be a sub-section of the section devoted to ecclesiastical biography, and that in turn ought to be a sub-section of the section devoted to biography. Or perhaps this is wrong. Perhaps the section devoted to seventeenth century ecclesiastical biography ought to be a sub-section of the section devoted to seventeenth century church history. Or . . . It is only when these questions are answered that he can decide the significance of the observation that this biography of Laud is on shelf L.3. For either it ought to be there, in which case its neighbours ought to be books on . . . (whatever rational reflection decided to be the proper classification of a biography of Laud), or else it has got into the wrong place and should be disregarded as a stray. If its companions turn out to be, in the main, what reason suggests they should be, then that is evidence

155

that it is in the right place and can be used as a clue to the heading of the section in which it is.

The man who tries to reconstruct the library in this way is reasoning as Plato wants the scientist to reason. If this were not ordered (he is saying to himself) it would be a complete jumble, which it is not. If it is ordered, the order will be coherent. What order then can we discern, which, without doing gross violence to the appearances, shall satisfy the mind as a sensible way (or rather as the rationally necessary way) of ordering the universe?

Without these presuppositions the things that Plato has to say about the relations of observation and theory make complete nonsense; with these presuppositions they make sense. That to my mind is evidence that he really did presuppose these things.

II. THE *PHAEDO*

The relevant section of the *Phaedo* runs from 96 to 107. The context is this. Kebes concedes to Socrates that there are grounds for thinking that the soul is altogether superior to the body, and has the power to keep the latter alive; but he questions whether this entails that the soul is immortal. Powerful though it must be, it might eventually lose its power. Socrates says that this raises the whole question of the cause (*aitiâ*) of coming into existence and perishing, and offers to give an autobiographical account of his own attitudes to the problem.

No doubt the account which follows was believed by Plato to be a historically accurate account of Socrates' intellectual development, but there is also no reason to doubt that Plato believed that the pilgrimage he described had led Socrates in the right direction; and therefore I shall take it that, while the episodes are episodes in the life of Socrates, the conclusions are shared by Plato as well.

It is a complicated passage, raising more hares than it can really manage. The clue to it is to bear in mind that Socrates is discussing "the cause of coming into being and perishing". His problem in other words is: "What is a cause?" or: "What is an explanation?". It goes as follows:—

1. Socrates begins by confessing his deep interest, in his youth, in scientific questions. He thought it would be grand to know why things come into existence and perish, and so he studied scientific problems—of physiology and physics—until he became convinced (this is Socratic irony) of his own incompetence. For things which he had thought himself to understand perfectly well, he no longer understood at all—e.g. how men grow. Fifth century science, in fact,

so far from explaining, made things seem more difficult, and therefore there must be something wrong with it.

2. He then goes on to describe similar inexplicabilities in the field of mathematics. How, for instance, when two 1's are added together can either or both of them become 2? So no more in mathematics than in science could Socrates understand "the reason why things come into existence or perish along these lines; and so he muddled through to the construction of a different method of his own, and abandoned the other".

3. But then he heard of Anaxagoras, and of his doctrine that mind ordains, and is the cause of, all things. He was delighted with this, and took it to mean that Anaxagoras would settle such questions as the shape and position of the earth by showing the reason why it was best for it to be as it is. For presumably mind would ordain that things should be as it is best for them to be.

4. But in fact Anaxagoras let him down, and offered ordinary causal explanations in terms of efficient causes. This treachery of Anaxagoras' Socrates characterises as the extremely common failure to distinguish the *aitiâ* (cause or reason) from the *conditio sine qua non*, or that without which the cause could not operate. Thus Socrates would not be sitting in prison unless his legs could bend (the *sine qua non* of his sitting there); but he would not be sitting in prison unless he had thought it wrong to escape (this therefore is the real reason why he is sitting there, the fact which should be cited in explanation). It is because of this confusion that scientists postulate whirlpools and other explanatory devices in order to explain facts which could be sufficiently explained by demonstrating why it is best that they should be as they are.

5. Betrayed, then, by Anaxagoras, and unable to discover for himself or to learn from anybody else how "the best" serves as the supreme cause, Socrates evolved for himself a second-best approach to the search for the *aitiâ*. His account of this "second-best" is that he gave up looking directly at things, and turned to look at their images in *logoi*, in the accounts we give of them, or the things we say of them; "in our concepts of them" might almost hit the mark. At this point (99 e–100 a) he interpolates the comment, which we have already noticed, that physical things are just as much images as are *logoi*, from which it follows that he was really turning not from realities to their images, but from one kind of image to another.

(I shall here interject the comment that the charge that physical occurrences are images surely implies the doctrine that the world is rationally designed. Why else should they be images?).

6. Socrates then goes on to make two points somewhat jumbled together. The first point is that he decided to proceed hypothetically

in his reasonings. He does not explain until a page or so further on (101 d) what he means by this. Since the hypothetical method is not our concern in this chapter we will pursue this no further here.[1]

7. The second of the two points which Socrates jumbles together is an example of a hypothesis which he provisionally adopted in accordance with his hypothetical method, namely his provisional account of what constitutes a cause or explanation. This, Socrates says, involves something very familiar to his hearers, namely universal common natures or forms—beauty itself according to itself and so on. Strictly the hypothesis which he adopted concerning what counts as an *aitiâ* is: that there are forms. But this is immediately taken to entail a rule: that nothing is to count as an explanation of why S is P, except the presence of P-hood to S, S's participation in P-hood, or however you like to describe the form-particular relationship. It is not its florid colour, nor its shape, which makes something beautiful, but only beauty. Socrates goes on to amuse his audience by working this out further in terms of the arithmetical conundrums which he had propounded above. Two is not created by addition or by division (it had seemed queer that the same result—a given number—could be produced by these apparently contradictory methods) but only by the presence of two-ness.

8. This being established, Socrates goes on to his main proof of immortality which we have already examined.[2] What we must now notice is that, in order to make his proof, Socrates relaxes his stringent provisional rule about the nature of an explanation. The concession is that if there is something, Q, such that the presence of Q entails the presence of P-hood, then Q can be said to cause S to be P just as much as P-hood can. We thus get what Socrates calls bolder answers to the question: "What causes S to be P?" Fire is now allowed to explain the warmth of things, the unit to explain the oddness of numbers, soul the activity of bodies.

9. Eventually it is shown that since the soul is that which brings life, there is just as strong a relation of incompatibility between death and the soul as there is between death and life. In other words, it has been shown that something cannot happen, namely that souls cannot die.

What are the lessons of this long and complicated passage? In particular what are its criticisms of the current procedure of scientists and mathematicians, what is the type of explanation recommended, and what is the attitude here taken up towards teleology, or the view that physical things are as it is best that they should be?

[1] See below, pp. 539–48.   [2] Vol. 1, pp. 318–23.

a. *Socrates' criticisms*

Socrates has in fact two complaints against the explanations offered by his predecessors, and he makes these complaints in two different contexts, though he neither specifically distinguishes the two complaints nor allots one to the one context, the other to the other. The first complaint is that the pre-Socratics failed to offer teleological or for-the-best explanations. This complaint Socrates makes in the context of cosmology; and his comment on it is that those who sinned in this way failed to.distinguish the *sine qua non* from the cause—the implication being that all true causes are for-the-best causes. Socrates' second complaint is that the pre-Socratics advanced confused, incoherent, or self-contradictory explanations, and the examples of this failure are mathematical.

Presumably Socrates believed that the provisional rule which he adopted (para. 7) concerning the nature of a cause would deal with both of these complaints at once. It is evident that it would get rid of confused, incoherent and self-contradictory explanations, but it is startling to find that it is apparently taken for granted that wherever this is achieved something like a teleological explanation will be forthcoming. Certainly in the dialogue: "Why is Laura so beautiful?" "Because she has beauty", the answer does not strike one as a teleological explanation.

However that may be, it also seems likely that one criticism that Socrates is bringing by implication against his predecessors is that of impetuosity. He is accusing them of jumping to the first conclusion that came into their heads. Unless this criticism is implied there does not seem to be any great relevance in Socrates' telling us (para. 6) that he himself decided to proceed hypothetically. This is surely a methodological recommendation designed to avoid the blunders caused by the impetuosity of his predecessors.

To return to the two complaints which Socrates specifically makes, let us ask what he means by saying that his predecessors commonly confused a *sine qua non* with a cause. The position is probably something like this. The Ionian scientists asked such questions as: "What keeps the stars in their courses?" and gave (to Plato) the impression that they would have been happy if there were visible chains which stopped the stars escaping from their orbits; there being no chains, they postulated other physical phenomena, such as whirlpools in space, to do the work of the chains. This they did because they did not realise that "it is goodness that must hold the heavens together" (99 c 5),[1] or in other words that the order of the universe maintains itself because it is good that it should be as it is. They could not

---

[1] Or perhaps "it is goodness and necessity that holds . . .".

realise this because they took for granted that such a question as: "Why doesn't X fall?" must be met with such an answer as: "Well, look at this bracket that it is resting on." That is, they took for granted that you explain a physical phenomenon by pointing to physical apparatus, and for that reason they postulated unnecessary physical apparatus. To them Socrates retorts the counter-example of himself remaining in prison—a counter-example which is of course highly tendentious unless it is granted that the physical universe, like Socrates' body, is operated by mind. This granted, however, the example shows that another kind of explanation is not only possible but superior. Physical apparatus explains in some cases how, but in no case why something happens. (Indeed in the case of the stars there is no apparatus to explain even how they behave as they do, and this no doubt is why they are divine; they, like Socrates, behave as they should simply "under the impulsion of their estimate of what is best"). Thus when Socrates a little further on (108 e–109 a) comes to explain why the earth does not fall, he does so by saying that since the universe is homogeneous there is no reason why it should fall; i.e. there is no better place for it to move to, and so it stays in the middle. This is the kind of explanation of a physical fact which Socrates evidently believes in.

When we turn to Socrates' second complaint (this is the criticism which is made in the context of mathematics) it is not so clear either what it is or what he wants. Two lines of criticism suggest themselves. One is that mathematicians explain mathematical phenomena in terms of physical operations such as cutting in half and putting side by side. The other is that in statements such as "2 is produced by division" (analogous to "Beauty is produced by bright colouring") one does not get the universal correlation required in an explanation. Two is not the quotient in every division, nor is division the only way of arriving at the number 2; some brightly coloured objects are not beautiful, and some beautiful objects are not brightly coloured. The only way of ensuring the desired universal correlation is to say that the only "*aitiâ* of a thing's coming into existence" is its form: thus 2 is only produced by twoness, beautiful objects only by beauty.

Putting together these various points, it seems that Socrates is accusing his predecessors of advancing explanations which have all or some of the following faults:—

They postulate unnecessary physical apparatus in order to explain physical phenomena.

They confuse the apparatus which explains in some cases how a thing happens with the reason why it happens.

They neglect teleology.

They commit "type-transgressions" (as by advancing physical processes to account for mathematical entities).

They explain, at best, particular cases of a phenomenon, but not the phenomenon in general.

As his remedy for these defects Socrates seems to offer:—first a general recommendation to proceed tentatively; and then the particular rule that only the presence of P-hood can explain why S is P. He seems to suggest that compliance with this advice will avoid all these defects, and enable us to give satisfactory explanations of how things come to be and perish; and (remembering the remoter context) he seems to suggest that this will enable us to deal with such questions as whether the soul is immortal.

b. *The type of explanation Socrates recommends*

This is all very puzzling. With the criticisms of the pre-Socratics we must feel some sympathy (assuming that the pre-Socratics were as Socrates describes them); but how on earth are Socrates' recommendations meant to help?

The hypothesis that there are forms, and the "consequence" of it, that only the presence of P-hood to S can explain why S is P, does not seem likely to guarantee adequate explanations. Surely if we adhere to this "safe rule" we shall avoid giving incoherent explanations, if only because we shall avoid giving any kind of explanations whatever. It certainly does not seem at all obvious that we shall arrive at teleological explanations along this route; and indeed it is often supposed that Socrates has given up the hope of arriving at such explanations. He does not however say that he has done so (99 d 1). He does not say that he has given up seeking for "the best" as *aitiâ*, but that he has adopted a different method of seeking the *aitiâ*.

Let us ask then what Socrates is really recommending. At first and at second glance Socrates' rule is a very stupid one. At first glance we say something like this:—Socrates is frightened out of his wits by the confused attempts at explanation of his predecessors, and he prescribes the panic remedy of abandoning the attempt to explain. He justifies to himself the burying of his head in the sand by a fallacious argument resting on the ambiguity of such words as "makes" in such questions as: "What makes Laura so beautiful?" In some contexts we should be seeking for her distinctive kind of beauty, and so the proper answer would be: "Her delicate colouring." In other contexts we should be reflecting on the nature of feminine beauty in general, with Laura merely as an example, and so the proper answer would be something I shall not try to conjecture. And there are just one or two contexts (for instance when we are teaching someone the use of abstract nouns) in which the expected answer to: "What makes

Laura so beautiful?" would be "Her beauty". So a question beginning "What makes . . . ?" or "Why . . . ?" is ambiguous, and, we may feel, Socrates has not noticed this fact. In particular he has not noticed the difference between the general question about feminine beauty and the particular one about Laura's. And so he feels that "Her delicate colouring" is simply a wrong answer to the question, whereas in fact it is a right answer to one interpretation of it. He feels it is a wrong answer because delicate colouring is not, after all, what makes Celia so beautiful (for she has black hair and a white complexion); and therefore delicate colouring is not what makes people beautiful, and therefore it is not what makes Laura beautiful. As we saw, the idea that Socrates is guilty of this confusion is suggested by his arithmetical examples. For he objects to the view that 2 is made by addition on the ground that addition can make other sums, and 2 can be made in other ways. Thinking all this, then, and seeing that it is the business of scientists to give general explanations, he gives them a safe rule for general explanation (cite nothing but P-hood in explanation of the fact that S is P) which loses the baby with the bath-water; and this is all very reactionary and stupid.

So much for first glance. At second glance a worse thought strikes us: perhaps Socrates has been misled by his metaphors about particulars trafficking with universals. Perhaps he is advocating not no explanation, but a mad kind of explanation. He is attributing to universals a magic power; what they lay their hands on is conformed to their likeness; what beauty touches becomes beautiful, pairs spring up where two-ness lays its finger.

But if we look again more closely we can perhaps find something sensible for Socrates to mean. Firstly we must remember that Socrates' rule does not forbid us to answer the question: "What makes S P?" by giving the definition of P-hood. If we could answer the question "What is beauty?" in a way satisfactory to Socrates, we should have insight into the nature of beauty, because we should have analysed it into its elements, and that would enable us to see its connections. Given this insight we could give answers to: "What makes S P?" which should both remain within the framework of Socrates' rule and yet also convey information. If one remembers Socrates' general insistence on the importance of answering such questions as "What is beauty?" we can see that the effect of his rule would be to confine explanations within a framework but not to render them impossible.

But secondly we may observe that Socrates' rule is only provisionally put forward, and its rigour is shortly modified. Perhaps then Socrates does not mean to confine us to saying: "It is beauty that makes Laura so beautiful", nor even to confine us to saying: "It is a, b, c which makes Laura so beautiful" (where "a, b, c" gives the definition of beauty). This is the incontrovertibly *safe* form of explanation, and we are allowed to venture a little outside it when we can see equally safe ways of doing so. The modification which Socrates in fact makes ("Q may be said to explain why S is P if Q entails P-hood") is not a very large one, but the reason for this may be that it is enough to give him all he wants for his proof of immortality. Perhaps he thinks it possible that even more adventurous steps might be made if each step was tested before it was taken. (This may be another reason for the mention of hypothetical procedure in para. 6).

And indeed his modification, small as it seems to us, might have seemed quite large to Socrates. One is reminded of something that Aristotle says of Socrates (*Metaphysics* 1078 b 23–25): "he rightly sought definitions, for he wanted to syllogise, and a definition is the starting-point for a syllogism." What Aristotle means by syllogising in this connection is, I think, the process of drawing the conclusion that whatever is S must be P, from the premises that S-hood entails M-hood and M-hood entails P-hood. Aristotle certainly thought, and Socrates I suggest thought also, that it is possible to arrive at new truths about "things that cannot be otherwise" by syllogising. We know that this is wrong,[1] but it is not unplausible. After all in mathematics we find necessary connections between what seem to be totally distinct natures. To be a three-sided plane figure is not at all the same, we feel, as to be a plane figure whose internal angles are equal to two right angles; to be the square of 5 is surely not at all the same thing as to be the fourth part of 100. Yet in each case wherever you find the one property you find the other. And indeed it is not only that the connection is invariant; it is also intelligible. The proof that establishes the fact also shows *why* it must be so. Geometry and arithmetic consist of such intelligible necessities, and yet they seem to give us vital information about the world. Geometry tells us of the structure of space, arithmetic of what divisions, combinations and other arrangements of objects can be made. Is it not then likely (the ancients may well have thought) that there are other sciences, or developments of these sciences, which consist of intelligible necessities, and yet give us further information about how things can behave? If geometry tells us about the structure of space, why should there not be some other science which teaches us how things can move about in space? After all geometry itself tells us that a thing can travel in a straight path, and then in another straight path at right-angles to its previous path, and then in another straight path at

[1] "Wrong" is perhaps too strong. It depends on how you define "new" in "new truths".

right angles to each of its previous paths; but that it cannot then travel in yet another straight path at right angles to all three previous paths. This may well seem to constitute a restriction upon freedom of movement imposed by rational necessity and discovered by the study of rational necessity in geometry.

If we allow that there are necessary connections of this kind, then we can begin to travel along them; and there was no knowing for Plato and Aristotle how far we might be able to travel. But of course, as Aristotle says, a definition is the starting-point of a syllogism. You need to know what S-hood and M-hood are (in the sense of being able to analyse them) in order to spot the connection which binds them together. It was not absurd to believe that, if we could fulfil the Socratic programme of analysing such natures as beauty or justice or triangularity into their components, we could see what necessary connections hold; and that, if we could see what necessary connections hold, we could swing ourselves from branch to branch along them until we understood the order of nature; and if we did that (to anticipate) we should see how mind had disposed things "as it was best for them to be".

Naturally enough there are no very convincing examples of such journeys from branch to branch in Plato or anywhere else, because they are not in fact possible. But examples of a kind can be found. One is under our noses, for Socrates goes on to discover that souls cannot die. This he does by an implicit analysis of what it is to be a soul, by which he discovers that the correct answer to "What is a soul?" is "A bringer of life". This reveals a necessary connection between souls and life, and the conclusion follows (if we do not look too closely). In this way analysis shows us what to syllogise, and by syllogising we discover an important new truth. Or we might think of the passage at the end of the *Philebus* (64 onwards), where Socrates shows that goodness depends on balance, from which he infers that it is bound up with beauty, and eventually arrives at certain conclusions about thought and pleasure.

All this has got a good way away from the text of the *Phaedo*. The suggestion is that Socrates' rule for explanation is a condensed statement of Plato's methods for constructive philosophising, which are essentially that you can only establish a conclusion about the relations of X and Y things by analysing X-hood and Y-hood and seeing what connections hold between them. Socrates does not tell us positively that we are to follow this method (probably Plato could not at this stage state what the method was). He lays down a rule which prevents us from straying outside the confines of the method, and he follows the method himself (albeit loosely and informally) in his proof of immortality. But although Socrates does not delineate the method, I think we have to choose between two alternatives. Either Socrates is telling us that "Opium makes us sleep because it has a *virtus dormitiva*" is the model of all valid explanation, or he is telling us, not how to make sound explanations, but the confines within which we are to keep if we wish to avoid giving unsound ones, and arriving at false conclusions. But if he is doing the latter, then he must have some idea at the back of his mind about how we are to move within these confines; and what can this idea be but some version of the doctrine I have tried to describe?

Assuming that this reasoning is correct we can put Socrates' point in something like the following way. Kebes had said that, for all he could see, souls might die. Socrates replies that this raises the whole question of the *aitiā* of coming into being and perishing. The reason for this is that Kebes' problem is of the form: "Can X happen to an A?". And to this Socrates wants to say that those and only those things can happen to an A which neither are nor entail the contrary of A-hood. The copper-bottomed rule is that an A thing cannot, while remaining an A thing, become either non-A or something else which entails non-A-hood. To decide therefore for certain whether X can happen to an A it is necessary to analyse X-hood and A-hood in order to see how they are related to each other. The result of such an analysis (informally carried out) in the case of *death* and *the soul* is the conclusion that a soul cannot die.

c. *Teleology*

I have suggested that what Socrates has in mind is the programme of "syllogising", or of making one's way along a chain of necessary connections. So far I have argued for this interpretation chiefly by asking what else Socrates can have had in mind when he advanced the rule that only the presence of P-hood can explain why S is P (the rule from which he extracts the principle that an S thing can only become P if there is no incompatibility between S-hood and P-hood).

We will turn now to the question whether Socrates is abandoning the hope of teleological explanation which arose in him when he read of Anaxagoras' doctrine that mind orders all things. I think the examination of this question will strengthen the view that Socrates has the programme of syllogising in mind.

The crucial paragraph is 99 d 4–100 a 8 (para. 5 of our summary above). Just before the paragraph opens Socrates says: "Shall I give you a demonstration of the second voyage to the search for the *aitiā* in the way I devised?" The phrase "second voyage" (*deuteros plous*) is said to stand for rowing when there is no breeze; in other words for a more laborious way of getting to one's destination. If Socrates were using the phrase strictly in this sense here, then he would be telling us that the procedure he outlines is a more laborious way of arriving at teleological explanations than that taken by Anaxagoras. However one does not always use such metaphorical expressions very strictly, and there is certainly one place in Plato where this one is used to mean no more than "next best thing" (*Philebus* 19 c 2). So we cannot hang anything on this. Socrates may be offering us a less direct method of reaching teleological explanations, or he may be offering us a method of explanation which is not so satisfactory as teleological explanation would be if only teleology were within reach of our powers.

He then goes on to contrast: looking at things and looking at their images. He takes the figure of a man blinding himself by staring at the sun during an eclipse, and compares to the predicament of this man his own failure to achieve teleological explanations by looking at realities. With it he contrasts the wiser policy of watching eclipses in their reflections in water, likening to this his new procedure of looking at things in their *logoi*. So far we are left with the impression that he has decided to give up science and turn to something else—methodology perhaps or even metaphysics—instead. But then we recall that he tells us that the figure of the sun and its reflection is misleading; for the things he looked at after his change of policy are no more images than the things he looked at before it, as the figure implies. At this point we also notice that he employs a different contrast (99 e); no longer between looking at things and looking at their images, but looking at things *with the senses* and looking at them *in the logoi*.

If he simply said: "I turned from things to *logoi*" we could well believe that his meaning was that he gave up his interest in the physical world and went over to logic or some other discipline. But he does not say this. When he says: "From things, to their images, namely *logoi*", he is ironically adopting his opponents' account of what he did. His own account of it is: "From things through the senses, to things in *logoi*." But in this formulation "through the senses" and "in *logoi*" are in parallel with each other. It is as if each of the things he was previously interested in (e.g. the sun) had its empirical phenomena and also its *logos*, and that Socrates abandoned the former for the latter. But if this is right, Socrates is not telling us that he turned over to *logoi* in some general sense (this would be logic or methodology), but to *the logoi* of whatever things he happened to be studying; and in this case "*the logoi*" must mean something like the accounts, definitions or concepts of the things in question.

But does the notion of studying the physical world in "accounts, definitions or concepts" make any sense? One could study the history of ideas, surely, in this way, but one could not do science. But yet it does make sense, on Plato's presuppositions. The idea is that when one is considering whether, for example, the sun travels in a circle, or whether the soul is immortal, one does not rely (solely) on observation. One first tries to find a satisfactory *logos* of the sun or of the soul. How the achieving of a *logos* will settle the question in the case of the soul we have already seen. In the case of the sun, how about the following argument: the sun is a self-moving and therefore spiritual being; but the circle is the motion proper to intelligence; therefore the sun moves in a circle?[1]

I do not think that Socrates means precisely and only this by "looking at things in *logoi*". For just after using this phrase he says (100 a 2): "I always hypothesise what seems to me the strongest *logos*", and then goes on to give the hypothesis relevant to the present discussion which is: that there are forms. And of course "that there are forms" is not a *logos* of anything in the sense which "bringer of life" is a *logos* of the soul. I cannot therefore claim that my interpretation does precise justice to everything that Socrates says. But it does do justice to the parallelism between "through the senses" and "in the *logoi*", and this is important. For the rest, the passage is evidently very compressed, and I would argue that Socrates is passing from one sense to another of *logos* without noticing the transition. Perhaps he is helped to do this by the fact that the use which he proposes to make of the hypothetical *logos* that there are forms and that only the presence of P-hood can make S P, will, as we have seen, draw upon the *logoi* of the entities (life, death and soul, or whatever it may be) that he is discussing. This *logos* is a *logos* which requires us to study things in their *logoi*.

Suppose we say then that Socrates is not telling us that he gave up his interest in questions of physical fact, but that he came to see that it was at any rate no worse to decide them *a priori* than to decide them by relying on observation. The question remains whether this *a priori* procedure is a more laborious method of arriving at teleological explanations, or whether Socrates has given up the hope of arriving at this goal.

To help us with this question let us ask what Socrates had in mind when he expected Anaxagoras to decide whether the earth was in the middle of the universe by demonstrating whether it was better for it to be there (97 e). Surely he must have envisaged some such argument as the following:—The earth is the noblest of the heavenly bodies because it is the home of intelligent beings. The place of privilege in a sphere is the centre. Therefore the proper place for the earth is the

---

[1] This argument is constructed out of something in the Tenth Book of the *Laws*. See below, pp. 240–1.

centre, and for that reason, since there is no more appropriate place for it to move to, that is where it will stay (and without the help of chains, whirlpools or any other physical apparatus). This is the kind of explanation, surely, that Socrates wanted and Anaxagoras failed to provide.

But then surely this is precisely the kind of explanation which Socrates' method of looking at things in their *logoi* will lead to. If this is right, then, what Socrates is proposing is not the abandonment of cosmological and other speculation, but the abandonment of the idea that questions of this kind can be settled by looking and seeing. The kind of science which is to result from attention to *logoi* is the kind of science which Socrates expected from Anaxagoras, and which Anaxagoras could not provide, simply because he relied on observation helped out by wild *ad hoc* hypotheses (whirlpools and so forth) instead of asking himself the crucial question, namely what the entity whose behaviour he is studying really is. Socrates does not want to abandon science, but to do it in a less empirical way.

But even so, will this bring him teleology? If he is going to do science by "syllogising", will he thereby discover that things are arranged as it is best that they should be? If he discovers that it is impossible that souls should die, will this tell him something about the cosmic power of good?

The answer to this surely is that the whole programme of syllogising makes sense only if things are disposed by mind; and clearly "the best" is identical with that which reason approves of. A common word in Greek (especially in Aristotle) for logical impossibility is *atopon* which properly means "absurd" or "bizarre". An impossible arrangement is conceived of as an absurd arrangement, such as will not be allowed to arise in a well-ordered universe. To us it is clear that there *cannot* possibly be round squares, and that there *should not* be functionless organs in animal bodies, and that what cannot be and what should not be are two totally different things. But we must get rid of the idea that Plato would be clear about the gulf between the two. Rather for him, I think, what cannot be is a gross case of what should not be. We feel that by "syllogising" one can discover logical impossibilities, but not teleology. I do not believe that Plato would draw this line. If we carry out his programme of asking how we should conceive of the sun, and settle the nature of its orbit in the light of the answer to this question, then we shall be giving ourselves a picture of the world in which we see things behaving in the manner appropriate to their natures; and to see this is to see them behaving as it is rationally satisfactory that they should; and of course what is rationally satisfactory is good. This is the kind of teleology which Socrates wanted of Anaxagoras, and which his own recommendations were intended to provide. Socrates has not abandoned his hope of seeing that things are arranged as it is best that they should be; he has merely abandoned the idea that empirical observation can get us to this goal.

Some further points about the Phaedo

1. It is common to feel in Plato's writings that his point is better than his reasons for his point. So here. However true it is that what underlies Socrates' rule: "Only the presence of P-hood can make S P" is the programme of syllogising, it is also true that he is made to *argue* for it as if the point were that no other pattern of explanation can explain *every* case of something's becoming P. To this argument one is of course inclined to retort: If you stipulate that the cause of something, say death, has got to be the same in every case, then of course you reduce yourself to tautologies of the form "People die because death is present to them". But the stipulation is quite unreasonable.

There is no doubt that the use of the notion of *aitiâ* in this passage is very crude, and that quite different topics are jumbled together. How there can come to be two objects, how one thing can come to be taller than another, how things can come to be warm or alive—there is no classification of such topics into distinct kinds. Phrases like "the putting of one alongside one is not the cause of the occurrence of two" (101 b 9) are used without any clear indication whether the question is: "Why are there two things here?" (to which an answer in terms of putting one thing alongside another would be appropriate); or whether the question is: "How does the number 2 arise?" This failure to distinguish topics makes it easier to argue that every case of a phenomenon must be given the same explanation as every other. For there is a sense in which one would agree that the number 2 does not sometimes arise by division and sometimes by addition (if only because the number 2 is not the sort of thing that "arises" at all). But if the question "How does the number 2 arise?" is thought to be the same sort of question as "How does life arise?" or "How do eclipses happen?", then this will help one to dismiss, as absurd, answers in terms of anything but "formal causes" ("S becomes P only when P-hood becomes present to S").

It would be possible to say therefore that this section of the *Phaedo* is simply a nest of confusions, and that its only philosophical interest is to show us what can happen if one, for example, jumbles mathematical and non-mathematical topics together, and fails into the bargain to distinguish different senses of such notions as "through" and "in virtue of". This is quite true, and it would be a useful elementary exercise to make a list of such confusions in this passage. But "one finds bad reasons for what one believes on instinct", and the question is, not only what mistakes did Plato make, but also what ideas had he which made the mistakes seem plausible. That is the question I have tried to answer.

2. There is something about Socrates' proposals for *a priori* science which must strike any modern reader. We might grant that if a man believes that the universe is a product of intelligent and comprehensible planning, then to ask the question: "What sort of entity is the sun, and what behaviour is proper for an entity of that sort?" may be a sensible move towards a *hypothesis* about its behaviour, but we should insist that a hypothesis arrived at in this *a priori* fashion would then have to be tested by observation. But Socrates only mentions observation to disparage it. The most he can hope for therefore is to construct for himself a beautiful picture of how things *might* be disposed for the best; whether the picture depicts reality he cannot possibly tell.

To this there are various partial answers. Firstly Socrates has his eye mainly on questions which cannot be settled by observation, or which could not be settled by Greek observational technique—questions of cosmology, of the immortality of the soul, and so on. Secondly Plato is seldom a cautious writer. If his current purpose is to exalt the role of theory at the expense of observation in the framing of hypotheses, he is quite capable of exalting the role of theory at the expense of observation *tout court*. But thirdly there probably is a place for observation in Socrates' procedure anyhow. For every *logos* which is to be advanced is advanced hypothetically, and its "consequences" are to be tested before it is taken seriously. Now the things that Plato says about the testing of "consequences" are obscure and will have to be examined in a later chapter.[1] Plato certainly does not say that empirical tests are included, but he does not say that they are excluded, and I do not think that they are. But in that case if we take the *logos* that the sun is an intelligent being, then it might be a "consequence" of this that it will have the motion proper to intelligence. But then surely the testing of this *logos* might involve ascertaining whether this "consequence" conflicts with evident facts. There are plenty of examples in the dialogues of a *logos* which comes to grief by conflicting with what might easily be called observed facts. But if Plato is proposing that observation should be invoked at this stage, then his point about observation is not that it has no place in science, but that it has negative work to do. He may well have thought that in the case of the topics he has in mind observations are ambiguous. The planets appear to move irregularly, but clearly it is possible that by some system of compound motions their behaviour can be reduced to order. Our problem therefore is

---

[1] See below, pp. 539–42.

what to do with observations when we have got them. This being the case the most that observation can ever do is to show that a theory is untenable. The choice between theories which clear this hurdle will have to be made on other grounds; and at this point (at which the modern scientist invokes such considerations as simplicity) Plato invokes the presupposition that the world is rationally designed.

III. THE *REPUBLIC*

We return now to the *Republic*. The material which concerns our present purpose is to be found in the Sixth and Seventh Books, but particularly in the simile of the Sun in Book 6 and in the proposals for the education of the philosopher-rulers which are made in Book 7. For the general outline of what is said in these places I must refer the reader to the chapter on the *Republic*.[1] Here we shall be chiefly concerned with two questions: (*a*) whether the *Republic* believes in teleology, and (*b*) what it has to tell us about scientific method. Some readers may want to say that these questions are inapposite, since the *Republic* is not concerned with the material world, but with the forms. The short answer to such a dismissal of the questions that we want to ask is that the negative part of this proposition is false and that the positive part does not entail the desired conclusion. The *Republic* is concerned, in the relevant passages, with the material world, for it is concerned with the question how to train men for government; and, while the text indeed talks about the structure of the system of forms, it remains the case that, on almost any view of the relationship between forms and things, statements about forms must entail corresponding statements about things. (To give a crude example of one kind of correspondence, if bee-keeping is a kind of stock-raising, Jones, being a bee-keeper, must be a member of the class of stock-raisers). It is indeed often difficult to decide just what statement about the material world we may infer from some statement about forms; but it seems obvious that any statement about the relationships of the forms must tell us something about the material world and about the proper study of it.

a. *Teleology in the* Republic

The data for considering the question of teleology are mainly to be deduced from the things that are said about "the form of the good", or in other words about goodness. These are to be found in the simile of the Sun and in its graphic elaboration in the simile of the Cave. The general outlines of my interpretation of these passages are to be

---

[1] Vol. 1, Chapter 3.

found in the earlier discussion of them;[1] here we shall be concerned with the more detailed discussion of certain points.

I shall however recapitulate what seems to me to be the essential point. This is that while all abstract thinking is done (as the Cave makes clear) in the light shed by goodness, nevertheless (a) goodness is the last form which we are able to discern, but (b) it is also the first that we are able to discern with absolute certainty; since it is the *anhupothetos archê* of all the others, it is that the discernment of which is no longer a case of supposing or taking for granted. I have taken this to mean that an account of the nature of goodness is somehow presupposed in all the concepts that we form; that in the formation of concepts we are dimly discerning, or "recollecting" a system of distinctions or classifications which somehow owes its nature to goodness. To understand what this might mean I used as a parallel the principle of classification of a collection such as a library. This principle, which could be stated in such a phrase as "that the library should be rationally or properly arranged", is the *telos*, the end or good, which gives the classification its point. It is also something of which any intelligent person can fairly soon get the hang, and of which anybody must get the hang before he can find his way about the library. We might also imagine (though here perhaps we are straining plausibility for the sake of the parallel) that it is impossible really to understand the principle of classification without first seeing how it works out—that is to say that we have to see what sections and sub-sections the classification produces before we can fully grasp the principle of it, and, perhaps, that there is no way of stating the principle except by stating the arrangement in which it issues. It would also of course be the case that the principle is responsible for the existence of the various sections and sub-sections, in that such a section as, for example, Medieval European Costume would have no place in a classification whose principle was colour or weight. The merit which I claim for this parallel is that it gives us some idea of how Plato might have supposed that goodness was responsible for the existence and intelligibility of the other forms and of what he might have meant by telling us that we use all along the light, which comes from a source the nature of which cannot be discerned until we have discerned all (or at any rate very many) of the forms, and which is in some sense decisive of the rightness and wrongness of the discernments of others which we believe ourselves to have made.

If we accept this line of interpretation we can see that the statements about *to agathon* or "the good" in the *Republic* do not bear the same meaning as the statements about *to agathon* or *to beltiston* ("the best") in the *Phaedo*. When *to agathon* is said in the latter

[1] Vol. 1, Chapter 3, pp. 105–27.

dialogue (*Phaedo* 99 c 5) to hold the world together this simply means that the laws and dispositions of nature are as they are because it is good that they should be so; the power of *to agathon* to determine the shape and position of the earth (*Phaedo* 97 d–e) is simply the fact that, through some agency or other, the earth has the shape and position which it deserves. This is not the same as the power whereby *to agathon* in the *Republic* is responsible for the existence and intelligibility of, say, equality. For this latter notion does not mean that, through some agency or other, equality has been given the nature which is best for it, and rendered intelligible because it is good that it should be so. It means rather that equality is a member of a system of differentiations which is due to goodness in the sense that it is the articulation of that which commends itself to reason; and that we cannot form any, even rough, concept of equality unless we have at least some implicit grasp of the system, and therefore of that of which it is the articulation. This does not mean however that there is necessarily any dispute between the *Phaedo* and the *Republic*. It means rather that the two dialogues have different topics. That of the *Phaedo* is teleological explanation of natural phenomena, while that of the *Republic* is roughly the much more abstruse question how we can purify our concepts so that they become identical with the objective distinctions between natures, a dim "memory" of which is responsible for the formation of concepts. This puts the discussion in the *Republic* on to a more abstract level than that in the *Phaedo*. Roughly we might say that, whereas in the *Phaedo to agathon* means "that (arrangement, disposition, etc.) which is acceptable to reason", the same phrase in the *Republic* bears something more like the sense of "*acceptability* to reason", or in other words that it names the feature of "intrinsic reasonableness" or "goodness" which is common to all dispositions which are acceptable to reason. When we learn, as the *Republic* hopes we may, what *to agathon* is, we do not learn what astronomical and other dispositions are acceptable to reason, but rather what acceptability to reason is. Obviously however if we want to know which dispositions would be good, then, if there is such a question as "What is goodness?" this will be prior to the questions that we want to ask; and we shall have to draw upon the answer to it in attempting to deal with them. It is therefore at least possible that Plato thought, when he wrote the *Republic*, that one reason why we need to come to understand the nature of goodness is that we cannot otherwise confidently answer such questions as those which Socrates wanted to answer in the *Phaedo*. We ought not to say therefore that *to agathon* in the *Republic* has nothing to do with the natural world. We have seen that it is possible that it has a good deal to do with understanding the latter; indeed this is probable, or even certain, for a number of reasons. One reason for saying that the discussion of *to agathon* has a good deal to do with the natural world can be seen from the manner in which the whole topic is introduced. For we are told that it is necessary for practical purposes to know what goodness is, since a man who does not know this is in danger of accepting apparent goods in life in place of real goods; and this no man wants to do (505 d). If *to agathon* is later responsible for the existence of the other forms, it is also, in its introduction, the common characteristic of those ends which are truly worth pursuing. It is indeed clear from its name that it ought to have this practical relevance. Phrases like *to agathon* or *hê tou agathou idea* ought after all to mean "that which is common to all cases of something's being good"; we obscure this from ourselves if we use the uncouth phrase "the form of the good" to translate them, but that is our own fault. Therefore coming to know what goodness is is an essential preliminary to coming to know what is a good so-and-so.[1]

Another reason for saying that *to agathon* in the *Republic* has at least an oblique relevance to the study of the natural world is the following. It seems reasonable to suppose that when Plato says that goodness is responsible for the existence of the other forms, he comprehends under "the other forms" not only the rarefied examples such as squareness which he actually mentions in this passage but also more down-to-earth specimens such as the forms of beds and tables; for elsewhere in the *Republic* these seem to be included in the class of forms. But this would naturally seem to mean that there will be forms of products of nature such as stars as well as of products of men such as beds among the entities for whose existence and intelligibility goodness is responsible. (Compare *Republic* 601 d 4–6: "The excellence, nobility and rightness of any artefact or living creature or action is related to nothing but the utility in relation to which it was made by man or nature" as a passage which treats natural objects and human products as equally the fruits of intelligent design). But if goodness is responsible for the existence of starhood, that presumably means that, in so far as something is a star, it is what it is and does what it does because it has been organised into a pattern which conforms to the demands of reason. This might seem to show that the position of the *Phaedo* is not only consistent with, but even a consequence of, that of the *Republic*. We can see also from this example how it is that the goodness of this or that thing is part and parcel of goodness as such, and thus how it comes about that

---

[1] Those who suppose that *idea* in this passage is essentially a technical term might observe 507 e 6 where light is described as "a not un-important *idea*". This is a typical use, significant because it comes from the present context, of *idea* to mean "nature", "reality", "kind of thing".

that which is the cause of the existence of the other forms is also the common feature of all genuinely good things. For if an X is any product of man or nature—a table, a horse or a star—then a good X will of course be an X which behaves in accordance with the end to which it was designed ("its excellence . . . is related to nothing but the utility in relation to which it was made" *loc. cit.*). But this will be an X which conforms to the principle of organisation imposed upon that piece of material by man or nature, and this principle of organisation is determined by that which is acceptable to reason. Therefore, ultimately, the feature common to all good X's will be that they behave conformably with the pattern which it is acceptable to reason that X's should follow; and that is how I cannot be sure that this is a good X until I know what acceptability to reason is; or rather, perhaps, that is why, when I judge confidently and rightly that this is a good X, I am presupposing an "account", which I could not explicitly give, of the nature of acceptability.

The argument of the above paragraph is of course summary and has neglected a number of problems which do not deserve neglect. It will be worth raising one of these problems to guard against a possible misconception. If we say that goodness is responsible for the existence not only of entities such as equality but also for forms of artefacts such as beds, or natural objects such as stars, ought we also to say that goodness is responsible for forms of misbegotten products such as nuclear weapons? If we do say this, will it mean that we are saying, paradoxically, that misbegotten products ought to exist? And if we do not want to say this, can we evade doing so by saying that there are no forms of misbegotten products?[1] I do not know what the correct answers to these questions are, but it is worth observing that we could say, and perhaps ought to say, that goodness is responsible for the forms of misbegotten products without thereby incurring the consequence that it is good that misbegotten products should exist. For one cannot infer directly from the proposition that goodness is responsible for the existence of X-hood the conclusion that it is good that there should exist X things. There is an ambiguity here that we must guard against. To revert to the parallel of a library classification, the principle of classification by subject matter requires that Pornography should be a section, but it does not require that there should be pornographic books; the principle creates the heading (for Pornography would not be a section in a classification by colour) but it does not create the things which fall under it. To say that goodness is responsible for the existence of some form, say P-hood, is to say that, in distinguishing between P and non-P things,

---

[1] We can of course say that A is a good X without therefore having to say that it is good that there should be X's.

we are attending to a distinction which is not arbitrary (like that between Greeks and barbarians, perhaps), but which is grounded in the nature of existence and which has to be recognised by any system of concepts which can serve the purpose of understanding. But in that case there can perfectly well be forms of misbegotten products, and for the existence of these forms goodness can perfectly well be responsible. For the distinction between nuclear weapons and things which are not nuclear weapons is not an arbitrary distinction like that between Greeks and barbarians, but a distinction which we have to draw in accordance with the method of classifying things which is acceptable to reason. This does not mean that it is desirable that nuclear weapons should exist, but only that the common nature of these entities (whether or not there actually exist any instances of them) is one whose existence is necessitated by that which is acceptable to reason. To put it in a different way, there is no objective universal corresponding to the concept of barbarian; the practice of thinking in terms of Greeks and barbarians is not one which assists understanding because it does not correspond to a real distinction. And a real distinction is a distinction which has to exist, one the non-existence of which would be unacceptable to reason, or bad. It seems to follow that there is no reason why there should not be forms of undesirable entities, and no reason why goodness should not be responsible for the existence of these forms. There can be a form (and goodness can be responsible for the existence of the form) of any class of entities such that the concept of that class corresponds to a real property such that it is rationally necessary that that property should exist. Conversely those classes of entities to which there cannot correspond a form are factitious classes created by the application of a concept which does not correspond to a genuine common property. These will be classes of objects whose members are heterogeneous except from some irrational viewpoint (such as that of the Greek who treats as similar to each other all who have in common only the negative property of not being Greeks), and also perhaps classes of things or occurrences such as storms and fevers which have no genuine common structure but only a common type of disorder.[1] This seems to leave room for the existence of classes of things, such as nuclear weapons, which are homogeneous and of a definite structure, but which are undesirable; and it would seem that there ought to be forms of such things if there are forms of beds and tables and that goodness ought to be responsible for the existence of these forms; but this does not mean that it is good that they should have instances.

[1] These latter will be the entities to which the word *apeiron*, in one of its uses, is applied in the *Philebus*; see below, Chapter 3, pp. 432–3.

If this line of reasoning is correct we shall not be able to derive the doctrine of the *Phaedo* from that of the *Republic* in the manner in which we derived it above. We made the derivation by saying that "if goodness is responsible for the existence of star-hood, that presumably means that, in so far as something is a star, it is what it is and does what it does because it has been organised into a pattern which conforms to the demands of reason". We tacitly took this to mean that reason demands that there should be stars, that reason sees, let us say, that it is better that there should be, not just odd bits of fiery material occurring sporadically in space, but rather spherical fiery objects travelling in regular orbits. But we now see that we are not strictly entitled to say this; that reason requires the existence of star-hood does not entail that reason requires the existence of stars. Stars might be, like works of pornography, something for which the system of classification must have a heading, but a heading under which there would best be no entries.

Logically then it would seem that, if the parallel of a principle of classification and the articulation into classes and sub-classes which it creates is adequate to the relationship between goodness and the other forms, we cannot derive from the premise that goodness is responsible for the existence of the other forms the conclusion that things are as they are because it is best that they should be so. We should need the additional premise that there exist no classes such that the members of those classes (*a*) have an ordered common nature, but (*b*) are undesirable. This however does not entitle us to say that Plato did not intend us to derive the teleological conclusion from what he said about the relation between goodness and the other forms. It may be that in drawing the parallel with the principle of classification we have done injustice to Plato's meaning. It may be, even if we have done no injustice, that he failed to see that the conclusion does not follow from the premise; or it may well be that he wished us to understand the additional premise that, so far as nature is concerned at any rate, ordered and consistent patterns of behaviour are not to be found except where reason has imposed them, and that therefore there exist no common natures of a determinate kind except those of things whose existence reason sees to be desirable. That physical nature is of its own accord disorderly, heterogeneous and indeterminate seems entirely consistent with Plato's cosmological outlook.[1] It would be foolish to try to be too rigid about the exegesis of doctrines which are stated in extremely vague terms, but I confess that it seems to me probable that Plato intended us to derive from his statements about the relation of goodness to the other forms the

---

[1] I hope that this will emerge in the course of this chapter. See also certain conclusions about the *Philebus*, below, pp. 435–6.

conclusion which Socrates wished to see established in the *Phaedo*. A phrase which might be cited as a proof-text of this is to be found in 511 b 7 where goodness is described as "the *archê*" (source, principle, starting-point) "of the all". Here it might be argued that the phrase "the all" (*to pan*) would most naturally be understood as referring to the cosmos. Further support might be derived from the language which Socrates uses about the sun. Treating the sun in this passage not only as the illuminator but also as the creator and maintainer of the physical world (509 b 2–4), Socrates calls it the *offspring* of goodness "which goodness has begotten proportionate to itself" (508 b 12; also 506 e–507 a). Commentators tell us not to pay too much attention to the word "offspring"; they say that Socrates means only that the sun stands to the physical world in an analogous relation to that in which goodness stands to the other forms. But commentators can be disobeyed, and it seems to me natural to suppose that when Plato used the notion of an offspring he meant, not indeed that goodness had actually created or begotten the sun, but that the sun, and with it the ordered cosmos which the sun is here thought of as maintaining, had been brought into existence because reason saw that it was best that it should be as it is.[1]

The conclusion then that seems to follow so far is that the simile of the Sun does not precisely commit Plato to the kind of teleology that Socrates desiderated in the *Phaedo*, but that it is probable none the less that we ought to understand it as the background of his remarks. Perhaps the truth is that Plato's attitude to the proposition that the natural world has been ordered in accordance with the demands of reason was still at this stage one of hope rather than of faith.

Before we leave this topic we must try to understand a little more sharply what Plato means by telling us that it is the nature of goodness which provides the light in which we see the other forms and which is also responsible for their existence. Socrates says the following (508 d 4–9): "Think of the eye of the mind in this way: when it is brought to bear on that on which *alêtheia* and *to on* are shining, it understands, it knows, it seems to exercise sound judgment (*noun echein*). But when it is brought to bear on that with which darkness is mixed, that which comes into being and perishes, it can only see dimly, being kept at the level of opinion, indeed of shifting and inconstant opinion, and falls back into the likeness of a fool." What are we to understand by this picturesque saying? If dark things are those which become and perish, illuminated things, I suppose, are those which do not do so; and therefore it would seem that the *alêtheia*

---

[1] How arbitrary an art is exegesis! It will be seen that I regard as figurative the treatment of goodness as a creative agent (its identification with God), but that I take seriously what remains of the notion of a begetter when this is subtracted.

and *to on* which are described as "shining upon" the things which we can understand, know, and exercise sound judgment about must be the stability, changelessness, ultimacy, genuineness and so forth which Plato commonly speaks of as characterising the objects of understanding. This is not the place to inquire quite how an "object of understanding" can be said to manifest such characteristics as these. What is to our immediate purpose is to notice that that which makes the objects of understanding visible to the mind's eye is simply those properties which are regularly said to be characteristic of these entities. In other words general terms such as equality do not share with "the many equals" the embarrassing instability (whatever that may be) which prevents us from "knowing" the latter, and this is the reason why the eye of the mind can focus clearly on entities such as equality. Therefore what makes the objects of understanding visible is simply that they possess the properties which Plato always attributes to them. There is thus a kink in Plato's parallel, at any rate on a realist view of perception according to which physical objects are still there in the dark and still have the properties which the light shows but does not create. We must not think of the objects of understanding as being somehow there all along, but as being invisible to the mind until it sees them in a special sort of light. When we achieve the vision of goodness, it is not that what is thereby rendered explicit is some special sort of clue which we have made unconscious use of all along. There seems to be no room for a special sort of clue of which abstract thinking makes use—no room in this part, at any rate, of Plato's text, any more than in reality.

Surely then there is no significant difference between saying (1) that goodness makes the other forms intelligible, and (2) that it is responsible for their existence; for it seems that it makes them intelligible by making them what they are. The special status of goodness, then, in relation to the other forms seems to amount to something like this: that the forms which there are are those which there must be, goodness being what it is.

Before trying to see what this might mean we must meet a charge of inconsistency which may be brought against this whole discussion. We began, we may be told, by taking as our clue the proposition that goodness provides the light which we use in all our abstract reasonings. Since the only light which we can plausibly be said to use in all our reasonings is a conception of what makes sense, or of what is congruous to reason, we went on to assume that, if goodness is something akin to the light which it provides, goodness must be congruence with reason. Now however we seem to have decided that there is no special light which goodness provides. But, if we decide that, we are throwing away our clue, and we shall be lost in the labyrinth, totally unable to conjecture what sort of thing the nature of goodness may be.

I see the critic's difficulty, but I am reluctant to abandon the view that goodness is somehow that by which we see; this is so important a feature, especially, of the simile of the Cave. But I am also reluctant to abandon the view that if the illumination which goodness bestows on, for example, equality is simply the latter's "truth and reality", then this can hardly be thought of as light of a special kind.

Perhaps the short answer to this is that congruence with reason is hardly light of a *special* kind. If we give that answer we shall find ourselves in a dilemma, but it is perhaps a dilemma that is inescapable. It is that if that which goodness provides is something quite ordinary, then it is incomprehensible what it could be like to discover what goodness is; whereas if the discovery of the nature of goodness is the key to all the puzzles, surely the light with which it has all along been providing us must have some special character of its own.

Perhaps Plato's way out of this dilemma would be to say: "Yes, it is of a special character, and yet it also is quite ordinary. The whole point of this passage is that we need to gain insight into that which is quite ordinary in the sense that we use it all the time. We need to understand why it is that we find convincing the reasonings that we do find convincing."

We may be able to see a little more clearly if we take a different approach. So far in this discussion we have not laid much stress on the fact that goodness is the *anhupothetos archê*, the unhypothetical starting-point. I shall have more to say about this in a later chapter,[1] but some of the conclusions of that discussion may be useful here. "Dialectic" is the name of the process which leads us to the *archê*, and dialectic consists in trying to gain insight into the concepts which we find ourselves using, the distinctions which we are impelled to make, and the inferences which depend on these. More accurately, it is the process of trying to gain insight into the objective natures of which our concepts are representations or "recollections". To try to give account of some general term is, I think, to try to see what it is that we are paying attention to in employing the corresponding concept. To give account of justice is to see what it really is that "justice" stands for, and how this is related to the things that other words stand for. We have the notion of justice, we call men just and unjust, but we need to understand the rationale of this contrast, to see what we are really doing in drawing it. The position of goodness as the keystone of the system of forms, the *archê anhupothetos* of our apprehension of them, amounts, I think, to something like this, that what we are really doing in drawing such contrasts is something of

[1] Below Chapter 5, pp. 558–62.

180

which the nature of goodness provides the rationale. In calling men just or unjust, or in dividing numbers into odd and even, we are doing things which we would not do if we did not possess some awareness of the nature of goodness; and the reason why this is so is that distinctions such as these (unlike, for example, distinctions of colour) belong to a system of classification in which reason as such is interested. Goodness, or that which is congenial to reason, begets such distinctions in that it is these distinctions which are congenial to reason. In making use of them we are being illuminated by that which is congenial to reason; in clarifying our understanding of them we are getting into a better position for seeing what this latter is; and when we achieve this final feat it is natural to suppose that we will thereby confirm, in the only way possible, that what we have been doing hitherto has truly been that we have been seeing more and more clearly and systematically that which is to be seen from the standpoint of reason—for we now see what the standpoint of reason is.

The essential thought, then, of the doctrine of goodness in this passage could be expressed in the formula that reason has a standpoint; that this standpoint we, being imperfectly rational, imperfectly share; that in so far as we share it we see by the light of goodness and we see the things that goodness has begotten; and that when we fully share it we know what goodness is. The conviction that reason has in this way a distinctive standpoint must, of course, be an empty conviction, and that perhaps explains why we do not meet this doctrine outside the *Republic*. The tone of Aristotle's attack on the form of goodness in the *Nicomachean Ethics*[1] is not to my ear that of an attack on a position long-abandoned by the enemy, and perhaps Plato never dropped the belief that we can find out what goodness is. But if he continued to stare into the crystal, he never seems to have deluded himself into thinking that he knew what was at its centre.

Finally we must ask why the name "goodness" should be used for that which is congenial to reason. One way of answering this question, I suppose, is to say that Plato conceived of goodness in terms of rational order—virtue in a man or sharpness in a knife were similar to elegance and cogency in a theorem in that each was a matter of the proper and efficient disposition of the parts with respect to the end. The good life was the life of order, the life which it is rational to live. The doctrine of this passage is that if we are to be certain just what the rationally ordered life involves we need to come to understand the abstract principle of rational order which is mirrored in the study of ordered magnitude (mathematics), and discoverable by dialectic. Since what we discover is what we need to know in order to

---

[1] Book 1, Chapter 6.

tell what ends are truly worth pursuing it is natural enough to say that what we discover is the nature of goodness.

It remains to ask how the doctrine of this part of the *Republic* compares with that of the *Phaedo* with respect to teleology. We have seen already that the discussion in the *Republic* is the more abstract and that the teleology which Socrates hoped to get from Anaxagoras is not strictly entailed by it. We have also decided, however, that Plato probably intended us at least to feel that the two passages are in sympathy. The chief difference which remains between the two discussions is concerned with the doctrine of the *Republic* that the nature of goodness is something which needs to be discovered. In the *Phaedo* Socrates at least allows us to believe that we know perfectly well what goodness is; our difficulty lies in telling which arrangements are for the best, and for this hesitation there might be many causes. This difference however is in no way a disagreement. Socrates in the *Phaedo* could quite well have gone on to say that one reason why he was unable to work out the kind of explanations that he wanted was that he did not know how to decide which dispositions would be congenial to reason, and the *Republic* of course allows that when we discover what goodness is we do no more than discover explicitly the principle which has determined to a greater or lesser extent all our abstract thought. We have used the light of goodness long before we can look at its source. Certainty therefore as to what dispositions are best must attend on our accomplishing the dialectical programme, but reasonable conjectures are already within our power.

One footnote will be desirable. The teleology which we have been considering is not a form of what is sometimes called Optimism of a Leibnizian or Panglossian kind—it does not entail the belief that this is the best of all possible worlds. Plato's belief in the *Timaeus*, as we shall see, is that reason has done the best that it can with a physical cosmos, but not that life in a physical cosmos is a life congenial to rational beings; and there is no reason at all to suppose that the *Phaedo* and the *Republic* go any further in the direction of Optimism than this. A librarian who has made an orderly and rational disposition of the books under his care may be proud of the excellence of his arrangement, but it is open to him to believe that books are so much lumber. If they exist, he may think, they need to be ordered, but they ought not to exist. Something like this seems, on occasions at any rate, to have been Plato's attitude to the material world.

b. *Scientific method in the* Republic

If there is anything about scientific method in the *Republic*, it will be found in the curriculum for the further education of his rulers which

Plato lays down in Book 7. We must therefore remind ourselves of the salient points of this.

The Curriculum. 1. The official reason for the training is that it is necessary to turn the mind from that which becomes towards that which is (from *to gignomenon* to *to on*). Since the senses naturally attract the mind towards that which becomes, this amounts to a purification of the mind.

(Clearly "that which becomes" could mean "the physical world", so that we could say that the purpose of the training is to make us lose interest in science. But the discussion of the question of knowledge of the physical world in the last chapter made it clear, I hope, that we must be careful here. It might be that *to gignomenon* means the world as a series of happenings and *to on* means or includes the order manifested in the series—*to gignomenon* is the succession of notes and *to on* is the tune. On that interpretation a conversion from an aesthetic to a scientific attitude to nature would be consistent with the purpose of the curriculum).

2. The studies likely to turn the mind towards that which is are said to be those topics in which the senses are incapable of unambiguous decision. Such conundrums as one can pose by asking a man whether his fourth finger is large or small cannot be settled by looking to see (for it is larger than one of its neighbours and smaller than the other), but only by clearly distinguishing largeness and smallness in thought. It is only by abstraction that we can understand the incompatibility between such predicates as "one" and "many", "hard" and "soft", "small" and "large". The senses often discover both of a pair of incompatible predicates in the same thing.

(We have to be rather careful of this contrast between the senses and thought, for we would hardly express Plato's point in this way. The point seems to be that common sense uses terms of this kind in an imprecise way, so that if one's conception of—say—hardness consists in the ability to conform to common-sense usage in the use of this word, then we shall find ourselves calling the same thing hard and soft, and will thus blunt the opposition between these two terms. This invites us to ask ourselves what hardness and softness are. Hardness we might say is a tendency to resist penetration, softness the absence of this tendency, so that a thing which is sometimes called hard and sometimes soft will be a thing which has this tendency to some degree. If we are offered three objects each harder than the other, and asked whether the middle one is hard or soft, feeling it will only induce us to say "Well, both", and feeling it again more carefully will not help. We can only settle a conundrum of this kind by asking—as we should put it—what we mean by "hard". But if this is Plato's point, as I think it is, then what is here blackguarded under the title "the senses" is not what we should call the senses at all. It is something more like the unreflective use of concepts. In fact the contrast is the old *doxa/epistêmê* contrast between inductive and counter-inductive concepts).[1]

3. Socrates then prescribes arithmetic as the first subject in his curriculum, on the ground that unity is a pre-eminent example of something whose presence or absence "the senses" cannot unambiguously detect (one man or many members? and so on). In arithmetic however units are subject to discipline. Every arithmetical unit is indivisible and equal to every other, so that it is at once obvious that the units of arithmetic are not physical units like horses. Arithmetic is therefore a science useful to the purpose of purifying the mind and diverting its attention towards that which is.

4. Socrates next prescribes plane and solid geometry, making some remarks which seem to suggest that plane geometry is a development of arithmetic and solid geometry a further development. (This is probably bound up with the fact that irrationals can be given geometrical expression. Thus $\sqrt{2}$ can be represented as the length of the diagonal of a square of side 1 unit of length).

5. He then prescribes astronomy, which he describes as the study of solids in motion, and about which he says some very odd things.

6. He then says that motion has many forms, two of which are obvious, namely the motion of the stars and that which corresponds to it (*antistrophon*). This he explains by saying that as eyes are adapted to astronomy, so ears are to harmonious motion; wherefore astronomy and harmonics are sister-sciences. This is the way in which he prescribes harmonics as the final part of his preliminary course.

7. All this is said to remain on the level of *dianoia*, and is to be supplemented by dialectic, or the process of challenging hypotheses, dispensing with the senses altogether, and discovering "what each thing is". The culmination of the dialectical climb upwards is the discovery of what goodness is.

The significance of the curriculum. Socrates is sometimes made to speak as if the preliminary studies—arithmetic to harmonics—were simply chosen because they have in fact the power to put a man into the right frame of mind for doing dialectic—in such a way that if it were by chance discovered that deep-breathing or doses of tar-water or Latin prose were equally potent purifying agents, well, these would do instead. But this is by no means the whole story. The practice of these subjects is *dianoia* (which drinking tar-water is not), and at the level of *dianoia* one grasps images of the forms. Since the purpose of dialectic is to grasp the forms, the preliminary studies are

[1] This section is further discussed below; see pp. 291–2.

plainly those which are thought to handle their images, and this is why these studies are chosen. The man who decided to drink tar-water instead, however much the effect of this on the brain was to distract the mind from that which becomes, would still be at a hopeless disadvantage because he would be without the images from which the forms are to be conjectured.

This, as we have seen, is because the forms are principles of order which are embodied in mathematical relationships. We therefore expect to find mathematics included in the preliminary training—the simile of the Line has taught us this. But what about astronomy and harmonics? What are they and why are they here? If they are literally astronomy and harmonics we shall have to say that the forms are embodied not only in mathematical relationships, but also in the way in which the stars move and strings vibrate.

What are astronomy and harmonics? These are said to be sister-sciences on the ground that they are both concerned with kinds of motion, the one visible and the other audible. It is implied that there are further sister-sciences in the family, concerned with other kinds of motion. This is in itself a puzzling notion, for in what sense harmonics is concerned with "harmonious motions which are adapted to the ears" is not clear. Perhaps the point is that although we cannot *see* the string moving (as we can see the sun moving), none the less we can *hear* it moving. If so, it is a bad point. More trouble faces us if we try to imagine what the sister-sciences would be. Plato speaks (530 d) as if these two sisters are distinguished by the fact that one of them deals with visible and the other with audible harmony of motion. If so, would other sisters deal with harmonies of motion detectable by the other three senses? Did Plato think that one day some Pythagoras would do for smells and tastes what the historical Pythagoras had done for sounds—namely discover that a mathematical relationship which pleases the mind is correlated with phenomena that please the senses? These are attractive speculations, but perhaps we had better see what is said of each of these sciences.

(a) *Of the one called "astronomy"* (528–30). First Socrates tells us that it is concerned with "the solid in motion" and therefore ought to be studied after solid geometry. Then that none of the subjects in his curriculum consists in trying to learn about sensibles, but about "what is", and that therefore the astronomy he proposes cannot be learnt along the current lines. The pretty things (*poikilmata*) in the sky are the noblest of such things, but, being visible, "fall far short of the true motions with which real speed and real slowness travel in relation to each other in the true manner and in all the true shapes, and carry their contents as they travel, which can be grasped by *logos* and *dianoia* but not by sight" (529 d 1–5. The phrase for "real

185

speed" is *to on tachos,* and correspondingly for "real slowness". It could be "*the* real speed"). The celestial phenomena should be used as a geometer uses the most exactly executed diagram, that is by not expecting it to contain the truth of any mathematical relationship. The true geometer will treat the heavens in the same way. He will think that the heavens and their contents have been put together as cunningly as such things can be, but that it is unreasonable to suppose that the periods and other relationships of visible physical objects should be always constant without any wavering.

(b) *Of the one called "harmonics".* After the remarks which we have already considered about "astronomy" and "harmonics" being sister-sciences, Socrates complains that the best current practitioners of harmonics behave like current astronomers; they "seek the numbers in the harmonies they hear, but fail to rise to problems and ask what numbers are consonant and what are not, and why in each case".

What does all this mean? The remarks about "harmonics" seem the easier, so we will begin with them. The Pythagoreans had discovered that there is a correlation between certain agreeable intervals and simple numerical ratios. Thus the octave is correlated with the ratio 1 : 2 in the sense that if two similar strings under the same tension produce notes an octave apart, one must be twice as long as the other. What those whom Plato is criticising seem to have done is to try to discover further correlations by taking pairs of strings of different lengths, twanging them, deciding whether the result was agreeable or not, and, if it was, measuring the strings. First you discover a consonance by ear, then you look for a "number" in it. Against this Plato seems to argue that there must be some theoretical explanation of the consonance of sounds, and that it must lie in arithmetic.

What he has in mind here is not at all clear. He seems to try to offer an explanation of consonance in the *Timaeus* (67 b, 80 a) and it is possible that he is thinking of something of the kind here. The explanation in the *Timaeus* seems to be roughly of the form: sounds are consonant when the combined vibrations which they set up in the ear are rhythmical. If two strings are sounding together and one is twice as long as the other, their combined vibrations will have a simple rhythm, since the shorter string will have two vibrations for every one of the other's. This would not be so if their lengths were, say, $5\frac{1}{2}$: 7. This being so there will be a branch of arithmetic which enables us to tell whether the combined vibration of any given set of strings is rhythmical. Perhaps Plato is taking for granted some acoustical theory of roughly this kind, and inviting us to work out the pure mathematics involved in it. That is, he may be assuming that an agreeable series of pulses is a rhythmical series, and that the time intervals in a rhythmical series will constitute some kind of a progression. Discover what progressions there are (arithmetical, geometrical, harmonic, and any others there may be), and you will have the mathematics you need for musical theory. Perhaps then this is an invitation to develop a branch of pure mathematics which will be needed for musical theory. If so, he seems to have overlooked the fact that you would not know that you want this branch of mathematics except on the basis of a theory derived from observation about the nature of acoustics.

Let us leave "harmonics" there and return to "astronomy". Two questions seem to arise:—If astronomers are to treat the heavens as geometers treat their diagrams, what does this tell us? And what is the meaning of the dark saying about real speed and real slowness?

Geometers do not prove that the base angles of an isosceles triangle are equal by getting out their protractors. Two reasons might be advanced for this. Either that the diagram may be slightly inaccurate, or that measurement of a particular instance can only tell us something about that instance; giving no insight into a necessary connection between equal sides and equal angles, it cannot show us that what applies to this isosceles triangle applies to all. Which, if either, of these points has Plato in mind? On the whole his language suggests the former—the true geometer will realise that the stars, being physical, are not likely to "draw their diagrams" perfectly. But of course he may have intended the other reason also.

So we are forced back on "real speed and real slowness". One natural interpretation of these phrases is that they mean "speed as such" and "slowness as such". But does it mean anything to speak of the stars "falling short of the true motions with which speed as such and slowness as such travel in relation to each other in the true number and in all the true shapes, and carry their contents as they travel"? The most that it could mean as far as I can see is that if you reflect on what speed and slowness really are, then you will see certain true numbers and true shapes in which rapidly and slowly moving things must travel. This in turn could only mean something like this, that if you reflect on the nature of velocity, you will see that things can only travel in regular paths at regular velocities. But it is difficult to believe that you will see anything of the sort, or that Plato would have supposed that you will.

"Speed as such" then will not do for *to on tachos*. It looks as if we must fall back on "the real speed"; and this seems to give a good sense. It might help to remember that the early astronomers did not picture stars as running round a track, but as being carried round on the rim of a wheel. This of course is only a picture, but the point of it is that it involves the notion of something carrying the star. Plato's phrase "and carry their contents with them" conveys the same suggestion. Now if Plato is using this picture (as a manner of speaking only, no doubt), we could ascribe to him this idea:—Reason has set in the heavens certain speeds and slownesses, or in other words motion-propensities; and in these, as if they were wheels, it has set the stars. The "numbers" and "shapes" of these motion propensities are "true" in the sense that they are regular. (Regular motions and shapes are called "true" because it is presupposed that we are speaking of motions for which reason is responsible, and any irregular motion is not "true" to reason's intention). Their regularity consists in the fact that the ratios between the velocities of these motion propensities are arithmetically elegant, and in that their paths trace out regular shapes. A similar picture is used in the *Timaeus* (35–8) where the Craftsman first makes the "soul" of the world, or in other words its self-movingness, and then puts the stars into the various orbits into which the "soul" is subdivided.

This is only a picture, because the real speed and real slowness are said to carry their contents with them, whereas the point is that the stars are *not* precisely carried as they should be. We are not therefore being asked to imagine as it were currents in space carrying objects round with them, and the stars trying to keep in step with the objects. We are asked to imagine the stars failing to comply with reason's intentions for their motions. "The real speed and the real slowness" stand for the velocities which the stars *ought* to have.

". . . and carry their contents with them" certainly suggests that the stars do in fact travel with the real speed and slowness, and this leads one at first sight to wonder whether Plato's point concerns real and apparent velocity in the sense that the sun appears to move, although it does not really do so. Then the point would be:— Observed astronomical phenomena are chaotic. This is so however because of compound motions. In fact every heavenly body is moving regularly, though some of them are moving in a medium which is itself moving (like a man walking along the corridor of a moving train). This leads to the impression of chaotic motion, but this impression belies the facts.

There is a famous challenge ascribed to Plato on moderately good authority.[1] He is said to have urged the astronomers to say "what uniform and orderly motions can be postulated to save the appearances in the matter of the motion of the planets". Eudoxus met this challenge (after the time of the *Republic*) by making the planets travel in spheres which were already in motion, thereby achieving

[1] That of Eudemus, commenting on Aristotle's *de Caelo*, as quoted by Simplicius.

tolerably regular paths for them. There seems to be a reference to such ideas in the *Laws* (821–2) where it is said that the apparently erratic behaviour of the planets is bound up with the blasphemous belief that the body which is in fact the fastest travels the slowest. This suggests the idea of a number of bodies travelling at different speeds in one direction in a medium which is travelling faster than any of them in the opposite direction—like swimmers unsuccessfully trying to swim upstream. In this case the swimmer who makes the best progress upstream will seem to make the worst progress downstream. Evidently then in his later years Plato felt that the heavenly bodies could be made to behave regularly by postulating compound motions. No doubt it was Eudoxus' relative success in this which made Plato feel confident of it. But if we suppose that Plato's challenge was issued before Eudoxus succeeded in meeting it, we could argue that Plato was already disposed to assume, as he well might, that the heavens could only be reduced to order in this way. If it is true that Eudoxus came to Athens because he found Plato's ideas interesting, that suggests that fruitful astronomical suggestions were already known to have come from Plato. This might lead us to think that the use of compound motion to explain the difference between the real and apparent motions of the stars is what the *Republic* suggests.

But unfortunately this will not do. For Socrates tells us that the true geometer will think it unreasonable to suppose that "the proportion of night to day and of these to the month, and of the month to the year, and of the other stars to these periods and to each other's will always occur constantly and never waver, the stars having bodies and being visible" (530 a–b). Here the implication clearly seems to be not that the apparent behaviour belies the real, but that, the stars being physical, their actual behaviour falls short of their intended.

On the other hand we have seen several times that Plato uses in the *Republic* very unsatisfactory language about the senses and the physical world, and it is possible that he confused together the apparent and the actual behaviour of the stars. In that case it is conceivable that he had in mind simultaneously both the idea that compound motion would deal with the apparent irregularities, and also the idea that there are certain intended regular motions to which the stars fail to conform perfectly. Indeed if he had the planets in mind it is rather likely that he intended both of these points. For the irregularities of the planets are so gross that to explain how they behave by saying "Well of course they are physical objects" is to explain very lamely. It is only if one intends to invoke compound motions as well as a little vagary and incompetence that the planets can be got into the picture.

189

We are to work out then, let us suppose, the rational pattern which the speeds, positions and orbits of the stars are intended to trace out; and in so doing we are to make use of compound motions where we need them. But how are we to proceed?

There seems to be a wide variety of possible positions which we might ascribe to Plato, ranging between the following two extremes. On the one hand he might have thought that we could work the whole thing out *a priori*, that if we thought hard enough we could work out how many stars reason must require there to be, moving in what orbits, with what velocities. This must seem to us a ridiculous idea, but it may not have seemed so to Plato. After all when reason came, so to speak, to the work of ordering, it must have had a free hand. It was faced not with a definite number of heavenly bodies, but with a mass of disordered physical material which could be made into any number of heavenly bodies and disposed in any manner. If there is no reason for the number and dispositions chosen, then the decision will be arbitrary and not rational. If there is a reason, then it might be possible for us to reconstruct it. Indeed Plato might possibly have thought he could catch a hint of some of these reasons. Thus (just for the sake of illustration) there are eight things that travel round the earth (sun, moon, five planets and the "heaven" of the fixed stars); cubes are bound up with three-dimensionality; and eight is the first cube. It might, just possibly, have seemed that there is something significant here, that if we understood more about number and proportion we ought to be able to see *a priori* that the number of things travelling round the earth ought to be the first cube.[1]

That is the one extreme. The other is that Plato thought that if we observed the actual behaviour of the heavens on the presupposition that our observations were inaccurate and that the bodies observed behaved rather imperfectly, then a man with sufficient mathematical skill to cope with compound motions and other such devices would be able to see that there is in fact a rational pattern to which the stars more or less conform (where "rational" in this case means not "that could have been worked out *a priori*", but "that satisfies the mind when it has been discovered"). There is a remark in the *Timaeus* (40 c–d) to the effect that the celestial phenomena turn those who cannot calculate into astrologers. This rather suggests that those who can calculate can readily see how the various combinations and so forth come about, and therefore do not take them as portents. On this view then when Plato tells us to "neglect the heavens" when

[1] But Plato would not, surely, think that we could do this until we knew what goodness is. That is he would not expect his students to be able to do this at the stage in the curriculum at which they study "astronomy".

doing astronomy, he means us to look at them, but as a geometer looks at his diagrams—not as containing within themselves "the truth" of the "numbers" and so forth involved. We are to derive clues, on this interpretation, from the observed behaviour of the heavens, as the man trying to understand the arrangement of a rather disordered library would derive clues from the present position of the books; but we are to remember that it is more certain that the intended pattern makes sense than that the actual phenomena occur as they should. We are not to rack our brains trying to make sense of an observation that may merely record a delinquency on the part of the observed body.

There is perhaps another position between these two extremes, which fits better with the tentative conclusion we came to in the case of "harmonics". This is that Plato is neither telling us that we can work out the motions of the cosmic dance *a priori,* nor that we can get it out of the observations if we treat them with a high hand; rather he is inviting us to work out the pure mathematics which an astronomer requires for his work. This interpretation is perhaps suggested by Socrates' description of "astronomy" as "the solid in motion", and by the fact that he treats it almost as a development of solid geometry, without giving any hint that he is passing from pure mathematics to applied.

There is then a variety of possible positions which we might ascribe to Plato, and I do not think that his language is clear enough to allow us to choose with confidence between them. There is however one interpretation that is sometimes offered and which I think can be ruled out, and that is that Plato is proposing a kind of rational dynamics, an *a priori* version of something like Newton's Laws. This will not do because Plato is not telling us how bodies *must* move (for he says that they do not move in the ways to be studied), but how they *ought* to move.

I think that something like the following is perhaps near the truth. Start with the view that Plato is inviting us to develop further branches of pure mathematics, using the name "harmonics" for those which will be needed in musical theory, "astronomy" for those which will be needed in astronomy. Then add to this the observation that he does not just ask us to develop pure mathematics in general, but those parts of it which are needed if we are to observe the order which does in fact obtain (allowance being made for the imperfect docility of physical things) in certain sectors of nature. Explain the significance of this observation by supposing that Plato has two ideas in mind for the training of his philosophers. He wants to put before them the widest possible range of mathematical embodiments of the principles of order, as the simile of the Line has taught us, and he also wants (for reasons which I hope I have made clear in the chapter on the *Republic*)[1] to convince them that reason is supreme in the universe. That is why he specifies the two departments of mathematics which can in fact be made use of in scientific explanation.

Along this line there are two further things that we can explain. One is the vagueness of Plato's language. He is uncertain both how much of nature is ordered, and also how close may be the conformity of the actual behaviour of the ordered sector of nature to the intended behaviour. He is not prepared to say that the stars do behave more or less as they should, though he hopes that this is the case. Perhaps he is also unclear about the logic of the distinction between mathematics and science, putting on the side of mathematics any discipline in which the emphasis is on theory rather than observation. For these reasons he writes enigmatically and, as it seems to us, incoherently.

The second thing that we are probably in a position to explain is the identity of the other sister sciences concerned with other kinds of motion. The movement of the stars and the phenomena of sound are two departments of nature in which order is detectable. There may well be other departments in which it is detectable also. The mathematics which will be required to detect it, and the sciences which will make use of this mathematics (these two perhaps being confounded together) constitute the other possible sciences which will discover further kinds of harmonious motion. What these are Plato does not care to predict. (He speaks of "kinds of motion"[2] because he assumes that the phenomena of the natural world are or result from motions as sounds result from the motions of strings and air. Order in the natural world will therefore show itself in ordered motion).

It is interesting however to notice that the cases of astronomy and harmonics are not in fact parallel. In harmonics we have certain empirically harmonious sound patterns, we observe that these are connected with arithmetically neat ratios between lengths of strings, and by constructing a conjectural acoustical theory we correlate them with mathematically harmonious motions. There are also empirically discordant sound patterns, and these are similarly correlated with mathematically discordant motions. But in astronomy the position is not like that. You could indeed say that there are empirically harmonious sky-patterns (the sun seems to travel in an arc) and also empirically discordant ones (the planets seem to wander), but this leaves two differences between the case of astronomy and the case of harmonics. In the first place we do not in astronomy postulate orderly motions to explain the harmonious patterns, for the harmonious patterns *are* orderly motions. In the second place it seems clear that Plato does not mean to tell us that it is the business

[1] Vol. 1, pp. 75, 133. [2] *Phora.*

192

of astronomy to explain only these harmonious patterns that meet the eye. For these harmonious patterns meet the eye, and need no mathematics whether to discern or to explain them. The subject called "astronomy" exists not to enable us to see the orderliness of the empirically orderly phenomena, nor to explain it, but to enable us to see that *all* the heavenly movements are more or less orderly, or to see the orderly paths which *all* the heavenly movements are intended to follow, both those which produce orderly appearances, and those which produce disorderly appearances. It does not need "astronomy" to tell us that orderly appearances in the sky are produced by orderly motions. The two sciences are therefore far from parallel to each other. In astronomy, though the phenomena are not all apparently orderly, we can by making suitable corrections convince ourselves that we are observing bodies which are in more or less orderly motion, or which are at least intended to be in orderly motion. In harmonics however there are no corrections that we can make which can convince us that a discordant pattern is or is intended to be a product of orderly motion. The lesson of harmonics is that orderly motions produce phenomena which seem orderly to the senses, the lesson of astronomy is more like the opposite of this, namely that orderly motions need not produce phenomena which seem orderly to the senses.

It is possible if one uses vague enough language to make the two sciences seem parallel; for instance they may both be said to "discover the underlying order". But this covers important differences. Harmonics discovers that orderly motion underlies empirically orderly phenomena (where "underlies" means "causes"); astronomy discovers that orderly behaviour underlies empirically disorderly phenomena (where the meaning of "underlies" is not so clear). What harmonics does, in fact, is not to bring *order* into the story (in so far as that is there it is there from the start), but motion, and with it *mathematics*. What is more it does so only on the basis of empirical observation (about the lengths of string required to produce given notes) and acoustical theory (about vibrations). You do not need to be a mathematician to know that some sounds are orderly: you only need a musical ear. You do need to be a mathematician to see that in this sphere also the order apparent to the senses is a product of something which is susceptible to mathematical treatment, namely orderly motion; and to see this you do not only have to be a mathematician, you have to know some matters of empirical fact about acoustical phenomena.

It rather looks as if Plato made these two sciences sisters simply because they both reveal the importance of mathematical skill for the discovery of order, and did not notice that it comes into the story differently in the two cases. In astronomy mathematics enables us to discover order where we suspected disorder; in harmonics mathematics enables us to discover "genuine" (i.e. mathematical) order where we had hitherto discovered "mere empirical" order. Astronomy helps us to see that the cosmos is (or is meant to be) more orderly than it seems, harmonics helps us to see that order is always expressible in mathematical terms. Both of these could be expressed by saying that wherever reason is operative mathematical order is to be found. This was to Plato an important result, so important that he overlooked the important difference. This is that in astronomy you *presuppose* that reason is operative and thereby deduce stellar behaviour which bears its mathematical regularity on its face, whereas in harmonics you *discover* by experiment that correlations obtain between agreeable sound-patterns on the one hand and arithmetically elegant ratios on the other.

The relevance of the curriculum to scientific theory. It should be plain that Plato is not trying to tell us in this place how to discover what does in fact go on in the world. He wants his philosophers to come to understand the principles of order so that they may be able to order human society, and he wants them to become familiar with the mathematical "images" of these principles. However he also seems to hope that in certain departments of nature we may be able to find actual expressions of these images in the behaviour of things. There is therefore a concrete interest in the curriculum as well as an abstract one. The pupil not only learns on what principles an ordered world would be constructed if there were such a thing; he also learns that this is to some extent an ordered world. This being Plato's purpose it is wrong to say that he advises us to do science *a priori*, for he is not telling us how to do science. There are however certain implications about how to do science that we can perhaps extract from this passage.

We can begin by distinguishing the model of Thales and the model of Pythagoras.[1] Thales invented astronomy not by being the first man to look at the heavens, but by taking the mass of observation records produced by the Babylonians and by asking how the stars move, not as pin-points on a black screen but as three dimensional objects in space. No doubt he also took for granted that: "How do the stars move?" meant: "In what regular paths do they move?" for unless the purpose is to produce a *coherent* picture the answer to the question: "How do the stars move?" would be given by pointing to the observation records and saying "Like that". Theory in fact only comes into celestial geography when one notices that certain recur-

[1] According to the legend, the inventors of astronomy and harmonics respectively.

rences turn up in the records, assumes that more are discoverable, and so tries to construct a system of regular motions which will explain the observed recurrences and enable one to predict others. The Thales-type scientist therefore does the following things:— (a) he brings to the phenomena such notions as he has as to what constitutes regularity; (b) he discerns hints of regularity in the phenomena; and (c) he tries to construct a model according to which the objects in question both behave in a regular manner and also thereby produce something recognisably like the observed phenomena.

Pythagoras on the other hand invented harmonics not by observing hints of regularity and looking for more, but by the lucky accident of hitting upon a correlation between one type of order and another. The Pythagoras-type scientist therefore does the following things:—(a) he too brings to the phenomena such notions as he has as to what constitutes order or regularity; (b) he discovers in the phenomena correlations between one type of order and another; (c) he seeks for an explanatory hypothesis to account for the correlation, being guided by his conception of what constitutes order in his choice of a hypothesis (he will, for example, if he postulates sound-waves, make them travel at a constant speed or with constant deceleration etc.); and (d) he seeks for further correlations under the guidance of his explanatory hypothesis.

What Pythagoras does is therefore more complicated than what Thales does (whether or not Plato was aware of this), but the following things are common to both of them. Firstly neither of them would make any progress unless he assumed that something which to his mind constitutes regularity is to be found in his material. Secondly each of them has to begin with data based on observation. Thirdly each of them has to conjecture a theory on the basis of his data. And fourthly each of them has to confirm his theory, if at all, by observation. Conjecture, observation, and a notion of order are common to them both.

In the *Republic* Plato is concerned with the notion of order almost exclusively. Does it follow from this that he would deny the role of conjecture and observation in science?

Take observation first. Now Plato plainly could not deny that if a man is trying to explain certain phenomena he must first observe the phenomena in order to know what he has got to explain. If he seems to ignore this in the *Republic* the reason is that he is not there concerned with explaining phenomena, but with amplifying and purifying our notions of order. But observation comes in not only to give us our data but also to check our theories; or so we would say. But with this Plato need not agree. If he believed that, although there

195

would be no distinct behaviour patterns in the world without the work of reason, none the less things do not always behave as they should, then he could believe that it is never possible to be sure of the significance of an observation. If an eclipse occurs at the wrong time, then the theory may be wrong or the sun may be late; and there is the same ambiguity if the eclipse occurs at the right time. Theories therefore cannot be confuted or confirmed by observation.

The weight which observation ought to carry can be put, instead, in either or both of two places. Either we can lay heavy emphasis on the fact that all scientific theories are conjectural, or we can say that we can confirm them *a priori*. (If we can show that it is repugnant to reason that the phenomena in question should occur in any but one way, the theory which makes them occur in that way is confirmed *a priori*).

We saw that it was possible that Plato thought in the *Republic* that theories could be deduced *a priori*, but we were not clear about this. What is however clear is that in the *Timaeus* he did lay heavy emphasis on the conjectural nature of all scientific theories; and the more weight this horse is made to carry, the less need be laid upon the *a priori*. Possibly then the truth is that Plato did not think that we could confirm scientific theories either empirically or *a priori*, but that we could not confirm them at all. This is consistent with the idea that the only point of taking any interest in nature is to get hints about the patterns that ought to be there.

However we have seen reason to think that Plato believed in an orderly sector in nature and a disorderly. The idea that astronomy and harmonics are two of an indefinitely large group of subjects concerned with forms of harmonious motion strongly suggests this. But if there is an orderly sector in nature, that means that what goes on in that sector is satisfying to reason, either in the strong sense that it can be worked out *a priori*, or in the weak sense that, when discovered, it gives satisfaction. Now if what happens in the orderly sector is satisfying to reason in the strong sense, then of course science is possible, on an *a priori* basis, in that sector. But if what happens is satisfying to reason only in the weak sense, then science will still be possible as a system of conjectures. The confidence that a man is entitled to have in his conjectures will presumably vary with the profundity of his notions about what constitutes order, with the accuracy of his conception of what is truly satisfying to reason; in fact with the extent of his ability to see by the light of goodness. A man whose mind was a duplicate of the creative reason would presumably sympathise with all the dispositions of this force and hence would know the patterns to which that sector of nature was meant to conform. Since the failures to conform are due to the inadequacy of physical things, that is as far as any one can hope to get. A man with a less purified mind, a man who could not confidently say what goodness is, would be forced to rely more on the congruence between his theory and observed facts; and as we have seen this must mean that our theories are in practice no better than conjectures. However a theory which was congruent with the facts and which postulated a pattern highly satisfying to the mind could presumably be advanced with fair confidence.

So much for the orderly sector. What about the disorderly? Here it would be a waste of time to speculate. Presumably a theory explaining how disorderly phenomena have to occur might be possible. But it is not even clear that Plato believed that there was a disorderly sector. The most one can say is that he seems in the *Republic* to have kept the possibility open as a useful waste-paper basket for things which could not be explained.

This discussion of scientific method may seem very speculative in the light of the *Republic*. It will serve however to conduct us to the *Timaeus* to which we must pass after a brief summary of our conclusions about the *Republic*, and its views on scientific method.

C. *Conclusions concerning the* Republic *on scientific method*

As we have seen Plato is not primarily concerned in the *Republic* to tell us how to do science; he is interested in training men for government. In telling us how to do this latter thing, he tells us that we must study mathematics in order to see the various relationships in which are embodied the principles of order which will determine the activity of any rational organiser—whether it is a cosmic *nous* organising the world, or a philosopher-king organising his state. In telling us this he allows us to collect the impression that he believes that the physical world has been ordered, at least in part, in accordance with these principles. From this we are able to infer that a man who is endowed with an accurate conception of what constitutes order will be able to make conjectural reconstructions of the physical activity which underlies the phenomena; and this is the most that anybody can do.

IV. THE *TIMAEUS*

Plato's main cosmological essay is the *Timaeus*. In form this is chiefly a discourse by Timaeus of Locri, a character who may or may not have enjoyed historical existence, but who is clearly depicted as at least a fellow-traveller of the Pythagoreans of South Italy. The plan is elaborate, for it is intended to be the first of three dialogues. The parties to the conversation are supposed to have heard Socrates on the previous day giving an account of the best constitution. Socrates recapitulates his discourse, and what he gives is in fact a summary of the first five books of the *Republic*. But, Socrates complains, all this is dry bones. He wants somebody who has the gift to depict such a city engaged in the supreme trials of war and foreign affairs—it must show its mettle. It is therefore agreed that Timaeus shall describe the genesis of the universe down to the nature of man, and that Critias shall then take over and describe the exploits of Athens nine thousand years ago, when the city, under Athene, was organised on the principles of the *Republic*, and defeated Atlantis. There is to be a third speaker, Hermocrates, but we are not told what he is to talk about. Plato gives us Timaeus' discourse, and ten pages of Critias', which consist of a beautiful description of Atlantis. At that point, for some reason, Plato dropped the plan.

It is an odd plan, and it is not difficult to imagine why Plato failed to carry it out. It was the task of Critias to relate a historical narrative designed to show just how the education described by Socrates would inevitably, in the world described by Timaeus, enable a city to give a glorious account of itself. Even Plato's imagination failed to construct a suitable narrative. What is not so clear is what the *Timaeus* is supposed to tell us about the *Republic*. It cannot be without significance that Socrates recapitulates the first five books, and no more than the first five books. The suggestion seems to be that the *Timaeus* is in some way to be regarded as substitutable for the metaphysical books of the *Republic*. But in what way—as correcting its doctrine, for example, or as elucidating it? I would choose the latter. Let us suppose that Plato had encountered criticisms of the *Republic* along the following lines:—"You propose to educate your rulers in the principles of order. But unless the world in which they are to work, and the human nature which they are to control, is a product of rational ordering this education will be of no use to them in their practical tasks. But plainly the world, and human nature, are not products of rational ordering." How could Plato meet such a challenge? He could not demonstrate that the world is in fact a work of reason—at best he could offer probable grounds for such a faith. But what he could do is to offer a conjectural account of how the world came into existence, and how it works, which should demonstrate that it is quite conceivable that, if intelligence were faced with the problem of ordering a given state of affairs, what would result would be something recognisably like the world we live in. This would show that it is perfectly possible that the world is in fact rationally ordered. The proposals of the *Republic* only make sense if the world is rationally ordered; the purpose of the *Timaeus* is to show that this may well be so. For this reason Plato is not committed to the details of Timaeus' conjectures (and indeed he makes Timaeus reiterate that they are no more than that); what he is committed to is firstly that an account such as Timaeus offers is perfectly possible, and secondly that the method which Timaeus follows is the only method which can give an insight into the workings of nature—for if we cannot presuppose rational ordering then we can have no idea what the machinery underlying the phenomena may be like.

There is something else which we must bear in mind when looking at the *Timaeus*. That is that the treatment is "mythological". The dialogue is even written in the taut and heightened style which Plato reserves for his myths. It is Plato's habit in his myths to convey a moral by giving an account of something (say the judgment after death) about which he knows himself to be ignorant. We are expected to understand that the moral significance, so to speak, of the myth is to be taken seriously, but no more than that. If we apply this to the *Timaeus* we shall expect that there may be parts of it which we are not in the least expected to take seriously, even as probable conjecture.

Some knowledge of the contents of the *Timaeus* is necessary to an understanding of Plato's thought, and I shall give an outline sketch of it—no more than an outline sketch. The dialogue falls into three parts. In the first of these Plato tries to explain the rational necessity of the universe—why it is good that it should be as it is. In the second he tries to describe what we may call the "factual residue"—the data which the designer had to contend with. Then finally he tries to describe the interaction between the designer's ends and the necessities imposed upon him by the data.

A. *The first section of Timaeus' discourse; the creation*

The first section runs from 27 to 47. Timaeus begins by laying down general principles very much in the spirit of the *Republic*. We are to distinguish "that which is, and does not come into existence or change, and is to be grasped by rational thought" and "that which is always coming into existence, but never is, and which is the object of belief and perception"—in our model of the library, we are to distinguish the principles of classification and the books. Nothing, he continues, comes into existence without a cause, or in other words a maker. If the maker uses as his model the unchanging and intelligible pattern (*paradeigma*; cf. 28 a 7, 29 a 6), an instance of which he is making, his product will be good; if he simply copies another instance it will be bad.[1] The universe, being a physical object, must

[1] Cp. *Cratylus* 389 b, and the contrast of craftsman and artist in *Republic* 10.

have come into existence and therefore has a cause or maker "hard to find, and impossible to declare". (It was already disputed in antiquity whether the notion that the universe had a first moment is or is not part of the myth. The dispute continues, the balance of opinion being that it is; i.e. that Plato believed that there had always been an ordered universe. I feel that I would vote with the minority).[1]

Being good, Timaeus continues, the universe must be modelled after an intelligible pattern, and is therefore an *eikôn* or image. About intelligible patterns certainty is possible; about their images we can produce only probable conjectures. (It is instructive that Timaeus takes it for granted that it is "blasphemous even to suggest" that the universe is not *kalos* or good; and hence it obviously is an image of a form. 29 a 4).

Why then did the divine Craftsman make the world? This Timaeus answers by saying that "the visible", or matter, was in a state of disorderly activity before the creation of the *kosmos* or ordered universe. (It is clear that Plato believed that matter is eternal, whatever he believed about the ordered universe). Since disorderly activity is a bad thing, and since the "generous creator" wished all things to conform as closely as possible (30 a 3) to his own goodness, he reduced its activity to order. Since, further, intelligent objects are preferable to unintelligent objects, he gave it a soul. In the light of our earlier discussion[2] of the meaning of the word *psuchê* or "soul", we can translate this: seeing that self-activating objects are preferable to objects which have to be activated from without, he gave it the power of activating itself.

But, Timaeus tells us, the universe already has a body, so that if it is given a soul it must become a living creature (*zôön*). Therefore the model to be employed in its fashioning is the generic universal *living-creature-hood*. It has to be the *generic* universal, because the universe is to have contents, and the generic universal contains its more specific universals within itself. Likewise, since the generic universal is unique, there can be only one universe, or the image would not share the uniqueness of the original (31 b 1). (It would seem to follow from this that since, say, bedhood is unique, it is a pity that there exists a plurality of beds. I do not suppose that Plato means us to draw this inference. Uniqueness is a formal property of the model, and it is tactless of him to make the image share in the formal properties of the model).

Timaeus now returns to the body of the universe (31–2), to tell us in what way the Craftsman ordered "the visible". I find it difficult to take what he says seriously. He tells us that the universe must be

---

[1] Which includes Aristotle.
[2] See above, pp. 337–41 of Vol. 1.

visible and tangible, and therefore must contain fire to be seen and earth to offer resistance to touch. So far so good, but there are traditionally four elements, and Plato wants (I suspect) to give us a reason for the existence of the other two. This he does by saying that two quantities require a third as a geometrical mean between them to bind them together ($a:b::b:c$; this progression constitutes a unity). But in the case of three-dimensional objects two means are required to bind the extremes together; in other words we need a geometrical progression of four terms. Therefore the Craftsman put air and water between fire and earth in such a way that fire is to air as air is to water, and air is to water as water is to earth. By virtue of this proportion the universe becomes a unitary whole which could only be dissolved by its maker.

Does Plato mean us to take this seriously? It seems unlikely. No doubt some mathematical thought underlies the suggestion that a two-dimensional object can manage with only one mean, whereas a three-dimensional object needs two. But Plato deprives us of any chance we might have of collecting a clear idea of the whole passage by failing to tell us between what the proportions hold—is it the total volume of the elements, their weight, the size of their particles, or what? I suspect that this passage should be intoned in a mock-solemn manner, and only its moral taken seriously; this is that there are reasons of a mathematical type for the number of the elements and for the relations between them.

The body thus compounded was shaped into a sphere and made to rotate (it was given "the motion proper to intelligence". 34 a). The reason for the spherical shape of the universe is two-sided. Firstly a sphere is the most self-consistent and the best shape; and secondly the universe, being all there is, has no use for protuberances. Aesthetic and utilitarian reasons nicely blended, the thought perhaps being that reason will only tolerate a non-spherical shape when there is some functional justification for it.

Meanwhile the universe needs a soul and so the Craftsman makes one for it (34–7). Here too in the description of its making doctrine is conveyed by incantation rather than by plain statement. First for the ingredients of the soul. There is indivisible existence and divisible existence, indivisible sameness and divisible sameness, indivisible difference and divisible difference. What the Craftsman did was to take each of these three pairs and make in each case a blended version—blended existence, blended sameness, blended difference. These three entities he mixed together, and this is the dough, so to speak, from which the soul was rolled out.[1]

[1] Reading, with Cornford and others, the manuscript text, and altering Burnet's punctuation.

What are we to make of these strange ingredients? Various conjectures suggest themselves. A memory of the *Sophist* (which treats
not-being-P and not-being-Q as "parts of difference" and which says
that difference is fragmented into many parts) might suggest the
following interpretation of sameness and difference.[1] Sameness is
one thing and difference is another; this is their indivisible existence.
Yet though difference is one thing, there are nevertheless many
different differences (difference from beauty, difference from heaviness and so on) and likewise many samenesses (A's identity with A
being different from B's identity with B); and divisible difference is
difference-from A, difference-from-B and so on, divisible sameness
sameness-with-A, sameness-with-B and so on. It would be consistent
with this line of interpretation to suppose that "divisible existence"
(*ousia*) refers to the "parts of existence", just as "divisible difference"
referred to the "parts of difference". A meaning which we might
attach to "parts of existence" is that being P is one part of existence,
being Q another. Indivisible *ousia* therefore would be existence,
divisible *ousia* would be being so-and-so. This interpretation, however, though suggested by the *Sophist*, might well be thought to lean
too heavily upon it. It is difficult to see how such a sense could be
got out of the words by one who did not recall the relevant passage
of the *Sophist*; and, apart from any theories about the relative dating
of the two dialogues, it is unusual for Plato to write in one dialogue
words that can only be understood by the aid of a *specific passage*
in another. Furthermore this interpretation does not seem to do
justice to certain details of the present text. When Timaeus introduces
indivisible and divisible *ousia* (35 a 1 sqq.) he says: "between indivisible *ousia* which is always the same, and divisible *ousia* which
comes into being (*gignomenês*) *in relation to* (*peri*) *bodies* . . ."; and
in speaking a few lines further on of sameness and difference he
says: ". . . of that of them which is indivisible and of that which is
divisible *according to* (*kata*) *bodies*" (a 5 sq.). These phrases seem to
connect the divisible versions of existence, sameness and difference
in some way with the physical world; but the fact that being is one
thing indivisibly in itself and also many things in its parts does not
depend on the physical world, and the same is true of the analogous
facts in the case of sameness and difference. In "A is different from
B and B is different from C" we mention two parts of difference, but
we can of course put designations of forms in the place of the variables—e.g. "activity is different from existence and existence is
different from inactivity". Indeed the *Sophist* makes this clear.

We seem to need then an interpretation which makes the divisible
version of these three entities exist "at the level of bodies". One is

[1] The relevant passage in the *Sophist* is discussed below, pp. 399–401, 411–16.

put in mind, now, of Socrates' remark in *Republic* 5 (476 a 5 sqq.) to the effect that each general term is in itself unitary, but takes upon itself an apparent multiplicity in association with "acts and bodies" and with other general terms. Justice, for example, is a single principle, but if this single principle is to be embodied in "acts and bodies", then it must take upon itself (or appear to take upon itself) many forms—the justice of paying one's debts, the justice of telling the truth and so on. That what is in itself unitary becomes diversified when it is embodied in physical instances seems to be a familiar Platonic notion, and to give us the sense that we require for the present passage. A further Platonic notion with which we are familiar is that every general term, or at any rate every form,[1] can be said to possess *ousia*, to be identical with itself, and to be different from every other. It is no doubt in the *Sophist* that these points are made the most of, but they are undoubtedly to be found in earlier dialogues.[2] But if every general term exists both as something unitary in itself and as something multiple in its embodiments, then its *ousia*, self-identity and difference from everything else may presumably be said to exist both in a unitary ("indivisible") and in a multiple ("divisible") form. It is therefore a highly general fact about the nature of forms that each may be said to possess *ousia*, self-sameness and difference, both indivisibly in itself and divisibly in its embodiments. Whatever the world may be like, so long as it contains embodiments of general terms this must be true of it; this is an ultimate logical or metaphysical truth.

What its cash value may be however it is not so easy to see. The case of *ousia* is perhaps the easiest. Since universals exist both in themselves as unities and "torn apart" in their instances,[3] the being of circularity, for example, is both an indivisible and a divisible being. For circularity exists as one distinct shape—indivisibly—and it exists also—divisibly—in innumerable circular objects. The existence of circularity is thus a "blend" of divisible and indivisible existence. (Note that what is here blended is not *being*, the mode of existence of universals, and *becoming*, the mode of existence of particulars, but two kinds of *being*, the mode of existence of universals).

It is also fairly easy to see what might be meant by ascribing to general terms indivisible sameness and difference. Every universal, as we observed above, is of course identical with itself and different from every other. It seems to be suggested in the *Republic*, for

---

[1] I take it that every form is a general term, but that not every general term is a form. *Being eaten on a Monday*, for example, lacks this status.

[2] For an account of their treatment in the *Sophist* and a discussion of its significance see below, *loc. cit.*

[3] cp. *Parmenides* 131 b 1 sq., discussed below, pp. 330–5.

example, and in the *Parmenides*[1] that whereas it may seem to be the case that we encounter at the level of embodiments co-existences of incompatible universals, nevertheless in itself every universal is glacially self-identical and therefore utterly different from every other. Therefore the self-identity of circularity is one unitary thing, and so is its difference from, for example, squareness. This perhaps is enough to take care of indivisible sameness and difference. How we are to understand divisible sameness and difference is more difficult. Vaguely perhaps we might say that every embodiment of justice is, in so far as it is such an embodiment, to that extent the same as every other; but that these samenesses which hold between various pairs of embodiments are not the same as each other, so that the self-identity of justice becomes, at the level of embodiments, a thing of many disparate parts. The identity of this debt-paying with that debt-paying is one identity, and the identity of this requital of injury with that requital is another, and indeed the identity of this third debt-paying with this fourth is yet another; and yet each of these identities is a case of the self-identity of justice, for each of these acts is an embodiment of justice. Again when we distinguish one case from another, treating the first as an embodiment of one principle and the second as an embodiment of another, and when we subsequently draw the same distinction between two further cases, then although in one sense we have here one difference (for case A differs from case B in the same way in which case C differs from case D), nevertheless in another sense we have two differences, for the A/B contrast and the C/D contrast cannot be precisely identical if A is not just the same as C nor B as D—a condition which will never be fulfilled at the level of embodiments. Jones's offence was libel and therefore different from Smith's, which was slander, and the same difference holds between Green's offence and Robinson's. But the difference between Jones's offence and Smith's is not quite the same as the difference between Green's offence and Robinson's (and analogous things can be said of the similarities which obtain between the offences of Jones and Green and of Smith and Robinson), because the four cases, though classifiable as two libels and two slanders, were nevertheless very different each from each. When we re-apply the same principle which we applied on an earlier occasion (whether to show that two things were alike or to show that they were different) the re-application cannot be, so to speak, a case of mechanical repetition, because the concrete situations cannot be exactly alike. If sameness is what makes A, B and C all instances of the same general term, and difference that which distinguishes D, E and F from each other, then each must be made up of infinitely

[1] *Republic* 523–4, *Parmenides* 129–30.

many parts. This not for the reason that the difference between L and M is one difference and that between N and O another (for that as we saw holds when L, M, N and O are forms, and is therefore not a "divisibility" which comes into existence in relation to bodies), but for the reason that the two differences cannot be identical in kind since the things between which they hold are always, in the physical world, disparate.

That the perception of samenesses and differences in the physical world is never mechanically repetitive but always requires an element of judgment is, I believe, a Platonic thought, and it is also, as we shall see, one which is relevant to Plato's concerns in this part of the *Timaeus*. Possibly therefore we have found an acceptable interpretation of divisible sameness and difference, and can claim to have identified all the ingredients from which the soul of the world was made. But perhaps the account so far has been too exclusively concerned with the contrast between the indivisibility which universals possess in themselves and the divisibility which they take upon themselves *in their instances*. I shall argue below that in his later years Plato was at least as much concerned with the relation between more generic and more specific universals (e.g. with the relation between genus and species) as he was with the relation between universals and particulars, and that he did not clearly distinguish these relations, calling them both "participation".[1] It may well be, then, that part of what he meant by the indivisible existence of, say, animality was its existence as a generic universal, its divisible existence being its existence in the relatively specific universals cathood, doghood and so on. Along this line of thought indivisible sameness and difference would be, as before, the self-sameness of every universal and its absolute difference from every other. The divisible sameness of a general term would be its ability to preserve, so to speak, its identity throughout its specific versions,[2] its divisible difference its ability to preserve its distinctness from any other even at the level of specific versions. Thus animality is still one and the same thing (though "divisibly") in cats and in dogs, and it is still "divisibly" different from vegetablehood in the difference between being a cat and being a cabbage. To see that cathood and doghood have (and cathood and cabbagehood have not) something the same portioned out among them would be to discern divisible sameness (and difference). To perform these acts of "collection" and "division" which constitute dialectic we have to discern similarities which do not consist in the presence of a simple common feature among the similars, and differences which do not depend on the absence of such a feature. We

---

[1] Below, pp. 366–8, 416–17.
[2] cp. *Sophist* 253 d 5 sqc., discussed below, pp. 417–19.

cannot, as it were, look for one and the same thing in all animals, nor expect every animal to present the same contrast with every vegetable, still less with every non-animal. The difference between being an animal and being a vegetable, though of course abstractly stateable as one difference, works itself out at the level of subordinate kinds as a multitudinous series of differences holding each between one sub-kind of the animal and one sub-kind of the vegetable.[1]

It probably will not do to say that this contrast between the indivisibility which a term possesses in itself and the divisibility which it manifests in its specific versions is the whole of what Plato means at this point, for this divisibility has no special connection with "bodies". To bring bodies firmly into the story we need to think not only of the pluralisation which animality undergoes when it is expressed in cathood and doghood, but also of the pluralisation suffered by cathood when it retains its identity throughout the range of individual cats with all their accidental similarities and differences which serve to conceal the common nature and to blur the essential difference between it and other common natures.[1] (Two dissimilar objects—say a cat and a dog—can accidentally have very many predicates in common. Both may be black, for example, and on the mat. To think scientifically is to pick out the similarities and differences which matter from those which do not). I have brought in the first kind of pluralisation not because I think it was all that Plato had in mind in this passage, but because I doubt whether it was altogether absent from his mind.

We may conclude then that it is perhaps best to say that in blending together that part of existence, sameness and difference which is indivisible with that part which is divisible what Timaeus' Craftsman did was to make the soul of the universe out of a blend between the manner of existence which a universal enjoys "in itself" with the manner of existence which it enjoys "in its particulars", and also out of a blend between the manner of existence which a universal enjoys "in itself" with the manner of existence which it enjoys "in its sub-kinds", both particulars and sub-kinds being conceived of as "parts" of the general term under which they fall. Finally, obscure though the details are, the general point seems clear. Whatever is intelligible must be differentiated into distinct kinds, and this differentiation is both a clear and simple differentiation at the level of abstract principles and a blurred and complex differentiation at the level of their concrete embodiments. An intelligence, therefore, needs to be made, figuratively speaking, of these ingredients in order that it may apprehend the differentiation of that which it seeks to understand.

[1] cp. *Philebus* 16 e 2, discussed below, pp. 361–8.

Let us hope that we have correctly identified the ingredients; now for what the Craftsman does with them. First, then, he rolls them out into a strip, and then he proceeds to mark the strip out into intervals (imagine a steel tape-measure with lines drawn across it at specified intervals). The intervals are arrived at in what seems a very odd way. Geometrical, arithmetical and harmonic progressions are combined together to make them. You start with the two geometrical progressions 1, 2, 4, 8 and 1, 3, 9, 27 mixed together: 1, 2, 3, 4, 8, 9, 27. Thus the second stretch of strip is twice as long as the first, the third three times . . . and the last twenty-seven times. These unequal stretches are then divided into smaller stretches, some of these further sub-divisions being achieved by finding the arithmetical, some by finding the harmonic mean. When the process of marking out is complete the length of every interval in the strip has a "rational" arithmetical relationship to the length of every other. What is more, according to the experts, the whole series of intervals thus marked out corresponds to four octaves and a major sixth of the diatonic scale.

The strip is now marked out in such a way that the ratio of every interval to every other is the result of arithmetical principle, and so that the whole is of musical significance. So far we are reminded that the ingredients of agreeable concatenations of sounds are correlated with arithmetically simple ratios. The Craftsman's next action has astronomical significance. He splits the strip lengthwise into two strips, and makes them into two rings or wheels by joining their ends. These wheels he puts one inside the other with their planes almost at right angles, like the equator and a meridian. (We remember that the earlier astronomers imagined the orbit of a star as a wheel which rotated and carried the star with it). One wheel we must imagine slightly larger than the other, and it has a single spoke. At the middle of the spoke there is the hub of the smaller wheel, the plane of the smaller wheel being almost at right angles to the plane of the larger. The smaller wheel is thus free to rotate inside the larger wheel, and if the larger wheel rotates it will carry the smaller wheel round with it. The smaller wheel will thus have two rotations: it will rotate on its own centre, but at the same time it will be spun round about[1] its own diameter (like a penny spinning on edge) by the movement of the larger wheel. On closer inspection however the smaller wheel is not a single wheel; for the Craftsman has made it into a nest of seven wheels of different (but rationally related) sizes, rotating in different senses and at different (but rationally related) speeds. The larger wheel is said to have "the rotation of sameness", the smaller wheels "the rotation of difference".

[1] Or rather "almost about", for the two wheels are not quite at right angles. This is said to represent "the obliquity of the ecliptic" by the experts.

207

This is obviously meant to be an astronomical picture, though not a detailed one. The larger wheel is the orbit of the heaven of the fixed stars, and the seven smaller wheels are those of the seven objects (sun, moon, and five planets) which move round the earth. The earth itself therefore is at the centre, not stationary (40 b), though whether rotating on its axis or moving in some other way is not clear. The picture is no doubt meant to convey no more than the general point that if we allow that there exist compound motions we shall be able eventually to see that the movements of the heavenly bodies, even the planets, are in fact regular in spite of the appearances.

The soul of the universe and its body are next joined together; in other words physical objects made of elements bound to each other by geometrical proportion are located within the circles or pre-established orbits which we have just been hearing about. These physical objects are "divine living creatures" which the universe had to contain because it was modelled upon the universal *living-creature-hood*, and this contains within itself its more specific versions (36–7).

The rest of the first section of the discourse is mainly concerned with the creation of human beings. Before he comes to them however Timaeus makes the Craftsman create time as "a moving image of eternity". The universe cannot be an eternal object, because "eternal" is taken to imply changelessness. But it can be the kind of object which goes on without ceasing, and such it is made to be, in order that the image should more closely resemble the original. The sun, moon and planets are made to mark the passage of time. (If we were to be heavy-handed about this we might find here an "absolutist" theory of time. The movements of the heavenly bodies mark rather than constitute equal periods of time. By returning to the same place the sun shows that a year has elapsed, but the statement that a year has elapsed does not mean simply that the sun has returned to the same place. First time is made and then the heavenly bodies are made to move in such a way that we can tell it accurately by observing their motions. But it is probably unreasonable to try to squeeze too much doctrine out of this short passage) (37–9).

Timaeus now (39–40) goes on to describe the creation of the divine living creatures or "created Gods". Some think that he means the stars (the Olympians and similar anthropomorphic deities are dismissed with a quip—40 d), though I take him to refer to the planets and the earth also. There is evidence on both sides. He then comes to the creation of terrestrial living creatures or men. The Craftsman, it will be remembered,[1] makes only their immortal souls, after the pattern of the soul of the universe and from the same in-

[1] See above, p. 333 of Vol. 1.

gredients. Their mortal souls and their bodies are then made by the divine living creatures, and this I take to mean that they develop by natural processes out of the stuff of the planets and earth.

For our purposes what is of most interest in the account of the creation of men is Timaeus' account of the senses (45-7). He begins with his theory of optics, of which I gave an account in the last chapter,[1] and then recurs to an old distinction familiar from the *Phaedo*. The physical facts are not the cause of sight, etc., but their *sine qua non*. The cause of sight and hearing, or the reason why they exist (*aitiâ*), is the good that they do, and this consists in the fact that they allow us to apprehend harmony, to engage in rational discourse, and so forth. The distinction between a cause and a *sine qua non* leads up to the next section of Timaeus' discourse, or his account of the brute facts with which reason had to contend in creation.

The significance of the first section of the discourse

The *Timaeus*, we agreed, is a rationalist manifesto; that is, it undertakes to show that the belief that the world is rationally ordered is tenable. "Rational", however, is a word of many shades of meaning. We must now ask in what sense or senses Timaeus' world is rational.

We may begin by reminding ourselves that the Craftsman is not responsible for the existence of the physical world, but only for its good order. He is therefore somewhat in the position of the librarian who does not believe in books, but who does believe that if one has books on one's hands they had better be arranged. Indeed he is perhaps in a worse position than this; for the librarian, though not himself a bookman, will consult the needs of bookmen in devising his arrangement. Timaeus' Craftsman is (or may be) more like a charwoman tidying some of her employer's possessions, of the purpose of which she knows nothing. She cannot arrange, say, the papers on his desk according to an arrangement dictated by the significance of the papers, for to her they have no significance. Her conception of an orderly arrangement will have to be external, so to speak, to the significance of the objects arranged; in fact she will stack them in neat piles with Income Tax returns and notes on French Grammar jumbled together. So with Timaeus' Craftsman. His conception of an orderly arrangement is likely to be external in this sense to the things arranged. His criterion of what is rational is likely to be a highly abstract criterion, one which can be applied even to a universe in which nothing physical exists. That there should be X's (where X's are physical things) cannot be a demand of reason, but only that, whatever things there are, they should exhibit characteristics A, B and C (where A, B and C are characteristics which are not

[1] Above p. 1 sq.

209

confined to physical things). Thus, to make this discussion more concrete, if Plato consistently applies the view that the Craftsman is not responsible for the existence of the physical, we shall expect to find him holding that reason requires that there should be rational beings, but not that reason requires that there should be men.

Sure enough we find that among the considerations that move the Craftsman one is that regular shapes and regular patterns are preferable to irregular. One sense therefore in which Timaeus' world is rational is that it contains spherical objects travelling in circular paths at arithmetically elegant distances from each other. This could be called an aesthetico-mathematical kind of rationality ("aesthetico-" not being meant to imply that the point is that round objects look nice). The strange business whereby the Craftsman marks out intervals on the strip of mingled existence sameness and difference from which he makes the world's soul seems to be concerned with aesthetico-mathematical regularity. But more of this shortly.

Meanwhile there also seems to be what we might call physico-mathematical rationality in the building of the world. I refer to the doctrine that the constitution of the world's body is as it is because a group of items will always form a coherent unity when geometrical proportion holds between its members. I call this "physico-mathematical" because it looks as if Plato is here putting forward (perhaps light-heartedly) a physical doctrine, to the effect that geometrical proportion will always be found to hold between some aspect of the members of a coherent group; and, if he is doing so, one suspects that he would claim that this fact is in some way due to the fact that geometrical proportion has the mathematical properties that it has. On this interpretation the Craftsman is constrained to order his material into four elementary kinds, with geometrical proportion holding in some way between them, by the fact that they would otherwise lack cohesion, the explanation of this fact being ultimately mathematical. On the other hand I am not very confident of this interpretation (though I can find no better); for in this part of his discourse Timaeus is supposed to be describing not the necessities imposed upon the Craftsman by the existence of physical material, but the values, so to speak, which determined what he did with it; and a fact of the kind which I have described would seem almost more at home in the first of these categories, and therefore in the second section of Timaeus' discourse. (Indeed as will be seen we shall read it in there; see below, p. 225). On the other hand we might say that an inescapability of a mathematical kind does not constitute a *brute* fact, and that the facts which compose the second section are brute.

Next we find the Craftsman allowing force to what appears to be a third kind of reason. Having before him physical material he orders it (order being better than disorder) and thus finds on his hands something that can be called a body.[1] Since an intelligent thing is better than an unintelligent thing, and since an intelligent thing must have a soul (30 b 3) he provides it with a soul, and thus has before himself a living creature. This being done, the model to which he has to look in determining the details of creation is *living-creature-hood*; and so the universe has to be unique as the generic universal is unique, and it has to contain within itself subordinate living creatures as the generic universal contains within itself specific universals.

The literal interpretation of this is that there is a third sense of "rationality", namely that in which a physical thing is rationally ordered if it "resembles" a form. Probably however the thought is as follows. Mind is essentially aware of all the possible ways of existence, and among them it is aware that one way of existing is to exist as a living creature. Mind is also aware that this possibility can be realised in numerous different ways. Accordingly when ordering a physical chaos what mind would do would be to actualise the various possible ways in which it is possible to exist as a living-creature. It is impossible to actualise the generic possibility of living-creature-hood in a specific kind of living-creatures, for they would have to be *generic*—neither celestial nor terrestrial, neither fiery nor earthy . . . but all and none of these at once. The generic possibility can only be realised in the creation of a system of specific kinds of living creatures. By some kind of principle of impartiality it becomes convenient that all the possible versions of living-creature-hood should be actualised to constitute the system which actualises the generic possibility; in creating some but not all of the specific versions reason would be exhibiting bias. Having therefore embarked on the creation of living creatures, reason is committed to actualising the whole range of possible versions of this kind.

It would be wrong however to leave it like that, for that implies that the decision to create living creatures was arbitrary and that the Craftsman might equally well have actualised some quite different range of possibility. On the contrary however it is clear that living-creature-hood has a special place in Timaeus' scheme. Plainly reason has an interest in the creation of living creatures; or in other words it commends itself to mind that there should exist intelligently self-activating beings.

To sum up our conclusions so far, Timaeus' world is rational in three ways. Firstly it contains two things in whose existence (given that something physical is to exist) reason has an interest, namely living creatures, and the orderly shapes and other patterns which

---

[1] This word (*sôma*) being used not to mean something physical, but some *unitary* and *systematic* physical thing.

characterise the constituents and behaviour of their bodies. Secondly it is rational in that it conforms to the "principle of impartiality" according to which the whole range of possibility is to be realised through the realisation of all its specific versions and their binding together into a self-activating system. Thirdly (perhaps) it is rational in that it acknowledges the force of the physico-mathematical necessities which govern the creation of physical bodies. An incompetent universe-builder, so to speak, might have forgotten that geometrical proportion must be conformed to, and such a universe would have kept going only with continual tinkering; this is not the case with ours.[1]

Further light on the senses in which Timaeus' universe is rational can be got from considering the significance of the creation of souls. We may begin by remembering that the soul of the universe, and the souls of the subordinate living creatures within it, are created of the same ingredients (existence, sameness and difference) and according to the same pattern. The marking-out of the strip into intervals, and its division into two rings, one of which is further sub-divided, is characteristic of all the immortal souls made by the Craftsman. Of these two rings Timaeus says, speaking of the soul of the world (36 c–d), that the Craftsman gave to the one the motion of sameness and similarity (for he left it one and undivided) whereas to the other he gave the motion of difference by splitting it into seven orbits. Furthermore he goes on to assign functions to the rotations of sameness and difference (37). What he actually says (37 a 2–c 5) is very obscure, but the drift of it seems to be roughly as follows. Because the soul is made of existence, sameness and difference, and because it is subdivided proportionately, it is able to discern correctly where and how the relations of sameness and difference hold, both in the case of changeable particulars and in the case of intelligible objects. Knowledge, or the discernment of these relations between universals, is the responsibility of the rotation of sameness, whereas right belief, or the discernment of divisible samenesses and differences between sensible particulars, is the responsibility of the rotation of difference; that is, the orbit of the fixed stars is responsible for knowledge, the orbit of the planets for right belief.

Some of this is relatively easy and some of it is very difficult. The function of the soul is intelligent self-activation, and for this purpose a soul must both grasp the principles to which it must conform and the particular situation to which from time to time it must apply them. It needs therefore "knowledge" and "right belief". To know, say, justice, is to grasp it as something real, to see what makes it what it is and what differentiates it from everything else; it is, there-

[1] The *Statesman* myth seems to take a different view; see above, p. 155.

fore, to grasp its indivisible existence, sameness, and difference. To apply the knowledge of justice to particular cases is to be able to see what justice means when it is embodied in an action, to be able to detect its presence in other similar actions, and its absence from actions which are dissimilar in this respect. The power of right belief depends therefore on the recognition of the divisible existence, sameness and difference of universals.[1] Therefore knowledge and right belief can be said to consist in the apprehension of indivisible and divisible existence sameness and difference, and that is why these are the ingredients of that which is to do the knowing and believing. In the case of the soul of the universe the exercise of these powers consists presumably in its conforming in its behaviour to the demands of reason, which requires that it should "be aware" both of the laws governing the behaviour of its members, and also of their present situation at any given moment.

However it is not only by virtue of its ingredients that the world's soul is able to discharge its cognitive functions, but also by virtue of its "proportionate sub-division". (37 a 4). This presumably refers to the marking-out of intervals on the strip. What strikes one at once here is that the significance of these intervals seems to be musical in the sense that this particular set of ratios seems to have been chosen in preference to any other coherent set because it is to be found in the diatonic scale. But what does the capacity of the universe to activate itself intelligently have to do with music? The stars have to travel in circles, they do not have to sing. Presumably the answer to this question is along the following lines. The diatonic scale is the material out of which ordered or "harmonious" strings of sound can be constructed. On the presupposition that empirically discernible order depends upon some underlying order which is stateable in mathematical terms, we can conclude that the set of ratios correlated with the diatonic scale constitutes such an underlying order. From this we can conclude that anything ordered in accordance with these ratios would exhibit "harmony" in its behaviour. Presumably therefore these ratios are somehow embodied in some feature of the disposition of the heavenly bodies.[2] What feature, Plato does not

---

[1] "Right belief" in this context should mean more than the accidentally correct identification of a particular. We are talking about the powers of the immortal part of the soul. We are not therefore concerned with what might on occasion enable Jones to recognise a just action, but with what will enable him to recognise just *actions* generally.

[2] Strictly this argument involves an illicit conversion. That whatever conforms to these ratios is harmonious does not entail that whatever is harmonious conforms to these ratios; i.e. there could be other systems of underlying order. I imagine that Plato would not argue that any underlying structure discernible in music must be discoverable in all other cases of "harmony"; I imagine he thought

tell us (having drawn lines on his strip, he makes no further use of them). By having "harmony" in itself (in some way or other) the soul of the universe is able to recognise and conform to its demands. The significance therefore of the division of the strip into intervals lies not in any musical nor in any astronomical significance that the intervals may have, but in the fact that being itself "harmoniously" sub-divided, it is thereby enabled to respond to "harmony". In the case of the soul of the world it seems to be the case that the sub-divisions represent some astronomical feature, whereas in other souls of course this cannot be so. "Harmony" will be expressed in the self-activation of human beings not by any system of circular orbits nor even exclusively by the production of music but by all these activities which are "harmonious" because they in some way embody the principles of order which are also embodied both in the dispositions of the heavenly bodies and in the lengths of the strings required to produce the notes of the diatonic scale. We see here therefore a further case of something we have noticed before, namely the idea that the same formal principle can have more than one material embodiment.

We have now accounted for the ingredients in the soul and for the intervals on the strip. We have still to ask why the strip is split into two, and formed into two rings one of which is further sub-divided, why the one ring is said to be given the rotation of sameness and the other the rotation of difference, and why the rotation of sameness is given charge of knowledge, the rotation of difference that of right belief. The obvious answer to the first question is that the soul of the world is its orderly self-activation, and that in the self-activation of the world there is the orbit of the fixed stars which carries round with it the orbits of the other heavenly bodies. The "soul" therefore consists of these two orbits. This is not a complete answer, because these rotations are a feature of all souls, and there is nothing in the self-activation of man which corresponds to the movements of the heavens.[1] Presumably therefore the two rotations are only metaphorically present in the human soul (not to mention that of the sun). But how are we to cash the metaphor? The answer to this is no doubt given by the fact that the rotation of sameness (I wonder whether Timaeus really meant to say "indivisibility") has charge over relations between universals, whereas the rotation of difference ("divisibility"?) has charge over relations between particu-

[1] I believe that some think that this is connected with the two "hemispheres" in the brain. Even if it is, the "hemispheres" do not rotate.

that if one "rose to problems" (*Republic* 531 c 2) one could see *a priori* why this set of ratios must characterise all "harmony" musical, astronomical or whatever it may be.

lars. The two "rotations" in the human soul are two intellectual functions, the single act whereby we see that X-hood is self-consistent and utterly different from Y-hood, and the multitudinous fragmented acts whereby we recognise X things and tell them apart from Y things. (Or perhaps—or "and perhaps"—the fragmented acts whereby we recognise and tell apart X-hood and Y-hood in their specific versions). So far so good. But why does Plato call the orbit of the fixed stars the rotation of sameness, the orbit of the other bodies that of difference? Again the obvious answer is that there is one self-consistent revolution of the heavens which carries the fixed stars, whereas the revolution which occurs within this revolution is sub-divided into the seven orbits of the sun, the moon and the planets, so that the first revolution is self-same or undivided, whereas the other is divided, a "unity in difference". But if that is all there is to it there is only the most tenuous connection between "the rotation of sameness and difference" used of the soul of the world and the same phrase used of other souls. It is little more than a pun.

Surely it is more than a pun. Surely the idea is something more like this. Perfect self-identity is characteristic of the things which the mind has to apprehend, but so is their diversification in their embodiments (in itself, beauty, for example, is utterly self-consistent; as it exists in its instances it is diversified). Corresponding to these two features of universals there exist the two intellectual functions which enable us to know universals both "in themselves" and "in their embodiments"; we might call them the unitary and the diversified function. This being the case it is in some sense proper that these two functions should be *expressed* or *symbolised* in the self-activation of the universe, or in other words in its movements. The orbit of the fixed stars is called the rotation of sameness not only because it *is* single and self-consistent, but because *being* single and self-consistent it symbolises the self-consistency of the unitary function just as the diversity of the orbits composing the smaller wheel symbolises the logical features of the diversified function of thought.

If this point is put the other way round, what it tells us is that the Craftsman made the heavens perform the dance that they do perform because the formal properties of the dance, with unity dominating over diversity and carrying diversity round with it, symbolise the formal properties of intelligence. Here then, at last, we have arrived at another sense in which Timaeus' world is rational. It is rational in that the formal features of rationality are symbolised in its over-all pattern. This same notion that symbolical propriety is a consideration which weighs with an intelligent creator is also to be found at 33 b where the Craftsman is said to give to the living creature which is to contain all living creatures the fitting and kindred shape, namely the shape which contains all shapes. In other words the world was made spherical because all the regular figures can be inscribed in a sphere, so that the spherical shape of the world symbolises the fact that it is the container of everything.

To sum up this discussion, we have found four senses in which Timaeus' world is rational, four sorts of consideration which may be expected to have weight with an intelligent creator.

Firstly the world contains things in whose existence mind has an interest; souls, regular shapes, and the "harmonies" whose expression is guaranteed by the building of harmonious ratios into the soul. (Their expression is impaired in man, as Timaeus goes on to tell us in 42–4, by the shock of incarnation, but we can and must regain harmony in our souls. In the heavens the fiery bodies of the stars offer no hindrance to the expression of harmony).

Secondly the world conforms to the principle of impartiality according to which, if any living-creatures are to be created, all should be.

Thirdly the world conforms to any physico-mathematical necessities there may be.

Fourthly the design of the universe is such as to give outward symbolical expression in its motion to the two-sided, unitary and diversified, existence possessed by universals or objects of thought once it is given that they are to be embodied in multitudinous particulars.

B. *The second section of Timaeus' discourse; what the Creator had to contend with*

The second section of Timaeus' discourse runs from 47 to 68. This section is concerned with what Timaeus calls *anankê*. He has described, he tells us, "things made by the craftsmanship of reason", and now he must describe "that which comes about through *anankê*". For the genesis of the ordered world is a matter of reason persuading *anankê* so that the greater part of what happens is led towards the best. The word *anankê* is correctly translated "necessity". Since however we have used that word to stand for rational necessity, or what is best, it seems convenient to use such phrases as "the given" or "brute fact" for *anankê*. Timaeus is distinguishing what ought to be from what cannot be got away from, or those things which exist because the Craftsman meant them to from those things which exist because of the nature of the material he had to work upon.

Timaeus describes brute fact as a "wandering cause". Just as to wander is to travel without rhyme or reason, so, he intends us to understand, there is no rhyme or reason in what is due to brute fact.

216

Thus if you ask a carpenter why he planes in one direction and not another, there will be two components in his answer. One is that he wants to produce a certain result, the other that wood has certain properties. As far as the carpenter is concerned there is a reason for planing with the grain (the desire to produce a smooth surface), but no reason for wood to be as it is; that is simply something that cannot be got away from. The principles of carpentry thus depend on an interaction between what is desired and what cannot be got away from, or between the good and *anankê*. This is how Timaeus intends us to understand the contribution of *anankê* to the creation of the world.

He now proceeds (with many protestations about the obscurity of the subject and the uncertainty of his conjectures) to introduce a new basic entity to which he eventually gives the name *chôra* or space. Hitherto he has managed with two kinds of basic entities, universals as exemplars and particulars which in some sense "imitate" or conform to them. Now he needs a third entity, namely that in which change takes place, its "recipient", "nurse" or "place".

Essentially Timaeus' reason for this is that nature is a theatre of change in which processes are always going on. You cannot, he says (49 d), point to a thing and say "This is fire", because the elements change into one another. You can find an instance of fire and say: "Fire is like that now is", but you cannot say of a changing thing that it is fire; fiery, yes, but not fire. A universal can be momentarily instantiated in a particular, but it cannot *be* a particulaı. The *this* which is referred to in "This is fire" is not the universal *fire*; rather it is *something* which is, for the moment, fiery. No doubt it would be apposite to explain to Timaeus that the "is" in "This is fire" is not like the "is" in "This is Jones" (for it does not imply identity). However he would probably feel that something of his point remained. This is now fire, but it may change. Yes, but what changes? Fieriness does not change; it departs. Yes, but from where? From the thing that was fiery. But what was that? Since by changing it can lose all its properties, what is the "it" which changes? We seem to be able to infer from this by, as Timaeus says, "bastard reasoning",[1] that we must postulate something which has no properties of its own (for it has to be capable of receiving all properties), and whose parts constitute the permanent entities which undergo change. It is therefore as if there were in nature a plastic material which is

---

[1] Why is the reasoning "bastard"? Not, I think, because the inference is illegitimate, but because the mind cannot "grasp" or understand the entity which it has to postulate. We can neither understand what "space" is nor dispense with it. Compare the things which Locke says about his "something, I know not what" (*Human Understanding* Book 2, Chapter 23).

continually being moulded into different shapes. The properties which, from time to time, are to be found in an object are imitations or reflections of universal properties; that in which these reflections arise is the property-less plastic material of which we are, or should be, speaking when we point to something and say "this", "it", or some other word implying substantiality or permanence. When a man moulds gold or wax into squares and circles, he is not doing anything to squares and circles, although from time to time he produces tolerable instances of these shapes. What he is working on is his material, which must be distinguished from the shapes he moulds it into. So it is with nature.

But gold and wax are definite things, each with a nature of its own which can be known and not "grasped by bastard reasoning". The notion of something in which instances of properties arise, but which is the ultimate material of all things and hence has no properties of its own—this is an altogether different notion, and one which naturally suggests the idea of space. For space too is something and nothing. Nobody can deny that it exists, and yet it cannot be seen or touched; indeed it "is not there"—anything which is there is something in space. Space thus shares the ambiguous character of Timaeus' recipient of properties. Again Timaeus is trying to isolate that feature of the given which makes it necessary that there should be a *physical* world—and he would not be the last philosopher to make extension the essence of the physical.[1] It is probably for reasons such as these that Timaeus eventually calls that which "provides the room" for the occurrence of instances of properties by the title "space".

But when he comes to describe the condition of things before the creation of the ordered universe (to describe, in other words, the element of brute fact) we begin to wonder whether the word "space" is not metaphorical. For space is simply a system of relationships, whereas Timaeus' "third force" seems more like a thing; for it exercises effects on its contents.

In the beginning, according to Timaeus (52 d) there was *to on* or that which is, a phrase clearly used in this place to refer to the universal properties or forms. There was also space; and in space there

---

[1] If this is an anticipation of Descartes, there follows a fascinating passage (52 b–c) which seems to anticipate Kant. Timaeus seems to warn us of "the persistence of spatial forms in our thought". We cannot help believing that whatever exists must exist somewhere, and this, he seems to say, leads us to give real existence to physical objects. Instead of this, he seems to say, we ought to realise that physical objects are images and that an image is no more than an appearance of something other than itself (as a mirror-image is the way a mirror looks). We ought therefore to think of the medium (i.e. "space") as more real than the image. The ultimate entities are the originals and the "reflecting media", not the images.

were happenings (*genesis*). These happenings were without order or arrangement. From time to time, but sporadically, there would arise momentarily a faint resemblance to an occurrence of fire, water or another of the elements. These momentary and random happenings would not be tolerable exemplifications of fieriness or whatever it may be; they would bear no more than "traces of themselves" (53 b 2), traces, in other words, of the natures which the elements would display when they owed their existence to the ordering work of reason rather than to the random agitation of space.

So far, then, we have an extended "plastic medium" called space, not consisting of the four elements but throwing up from time to time rudimentary occurrences of the properties which the elements are to have when the ordering work is done. Meanwhile space is to be thought of as shaking all over (and this is one reason why it can hardly be *space*). This jostles its contents, and the consequence of the jostling is that like tends to congregate with like. All the rudimentary occurrences of fieriness tend towards the same region, and so with the embryonic forms of the other elements. The distribution however is "without ratio or measure" (53 a 8).

This is the element of brute fact with which reason was faced when it came to its creative work. It is upon this unsatisfactory and disorderly condition that the Craftsman acts. What he does is to "separate the chaos by imposing pattern in kinds and numbers" (53 b 5). His manner of doing this seems to be roughly as follows. Firstly where there are rudimentary occurrences of fieriness (or one of the other elements) the Craftsman takes the hint and turns the rudimentary occurrences into genuine ones—he makes the quasi-fire into real fire, the quasi-water into real water, and so on. Or at least this is what he does, so far as possible; for the whole work is done "as excellently as it can be out of ingredients which are not excellent". Then secondly, space having thus been shaped out into the elements, he organises these elements into determinate relationships with each other (as we learnt in the first part of the discourse, when Timaeus spoke of the creation of the world's body) so that they cohere to make a unitary whole. All this work is "ordering into kinds".

To understand what this involves we must ask on what principles the Craftsman works. The answer seems to be given in the second half of 53, and to be as follows. The universe is a three-dimensional object, and its contents must be three-dimensional solids. This is a consequence of what is given (*anankê*). On the other hand reason demands that these solids should be regular solids. Therefore, if the universe is to be composed of elements, the particles of each element must be a regular solid. If moreover reason is interested in the production of objects which can change and inter-act with each other according to natural laws, then the shape of the particle associated with one element ought to be capable of being resolved into sub-particles which can be re-combined to form the particle of another element. Therefore Timaeus begins with two two-dimensional sub-particles and constructs four three-dimensional particles out of these. The two sub-particles are triangles, the one the isosceles right-angled triangle, the other that formed by dropping a perpendicular from the apex to the base of an equilateral. The regular solids which these two triangles can severally be made to compose are the pyramid, the cube, the octahedron and the icosahedron. (The first of the two triangles makes the cube, four triangles being used for each face; the second triangle makes the other three solids). The four regular solids are the shapes of the particles of the elements (the pyramid being that of fire, the cube of earth and so on). The four regular solids are therefore Timaeus' molecules, the two triangles being his fundamental particles.

(Timaeus does not actually say why he chose these two fundamental triangles and these four regular solids. However it seems very probable that he did so, as I have said, with a view to the possibility of chemical change. This is made more probable by the fact that he constructs his solids out of his triangles in what is, from the point of view of geometry, an unnecessarily elaborate way. Cornford has convincingly argued that this elaboration makes sense in terms of the forthcoming account of chemical change. See his *Plato's Cosmology*, pp. 230 sqq.).

So far then the given nature of space makes three-dimensional objects necessary and the demands of reason make it desirable that the ultimate three-dimensional particles should be regular solids capable of inter-acting with each other. Therefore the Craftsman acts by ordering space into such regular solids. In so doing he creates the elements. We must think therefore of the creation of fire as the creation of regular pyramids; and in so far as primitive occurrences of fieriness were thrown up in the chaos before it was ordered we must think of these as rough pyramids. Space therefore in its primordial condition must be thought of as forming itself irregularly into rough triangles, these in turn combining from time to time to form crude approximations to the regular solids. The reason presumably why Timaeus has space behaving in this way in its primordial condition is that he wants to hint to us that the Craftsman was not altogether free not to create the four elements. To order space in this way was to comply so to speak with the demands of its nature as well as with the demands of reason.

So far then the irregular configurations in the chaos have been made regular and disposed proportionately. It is out of this material that physical things result, and in order to tell us how the latter arise Timaeus goes on to describe a kind of physical chemistry. He gives a good deal of detail, and produces quite a convincing account of natural change at what must seem to us a Heath-Robinson level. Interesting as it is, we will not follow him into detail. Broadly speaking, he proceeds as follows. He uses two fundamental principles. The first of these is the motion of space, already mentioned. This tends to separate out the molecules into their kinds (it was already doing the same thing to the primordial crude molecules), the model Timaeus uses to illustrate this process being the winnowing basket in which you shake the corn in the husk so that the grain and the chaff tend to separate because of their difference in weight. The motion imparted to the molecules in this way goes on indefinitely because the universe is a finite sphere, and therefore molecules which get out to the circumference have to come inwards again. This perpetual motion is the mainspring of natural change (52 and 57-8). The second principle, brought into operation by the first, is the dynamical properties of the shapes of the molecules. Thus fire is the most cutting or destructive of the elements because a pyramid has sharp corners which can damage whatever it collides with, while earth is the most stable because its molecules are cubes, and a cube is the most stable of the regular solids (55-6).

In terms of these two principles Timaeus can account for chemical change. Molecules are in motion because of the shaking of space, and, as they collide with each other, they tend to cut each other into triangles, which tend to recombine into whatever regular solid there is most of in the neighbourhood (57. I imagine that the reason for the last point is geometrical. It is probably thought that in a region mostly occupied, say, by tightly packed and jostling octahedrons, an octahedron is easier to accommodate than some other solid. However Timaeus is very obscure at this point).

One more complication is now invoked, namely that the fundamental particles, and hence the molecules, are of different sizes. This means that there are different kinds of fire and of the other elements (57 c). These points taken together allow Timaeus to explain the constitution of the whole range of natural objects. The ordinary properties of things can be represented as resultants of motion, of the dynamical properties of the molecules, and of the chemical changes which these beget. Thus hardness is unyieldingness, which results from stability of molecules. Weight is due to a thing's tendency to move towards the region occupied by kindred substances, from which it comes about that fiery things tend to move towards the circumference, earthy things towards the centre. The taste of a thing is due to its effect on the tongue, its colour to its effect on the rod of light from the eye[1] (58–68). And so forth.

This has been a very summary account of the second section of the discourse, that devoted to brute fact. The third section is to be devoted to the co-operation between mind and brute fact, and its contents are mainly physiology, psychology and ethics. It would seem then that the brute facts with which mind has to contend are the physical and chemical properties of matter, or, to speak a little more precisely, those physical and chemical properties which a mind devoted to order is able to confer upon matter in view of the given nature of matter. What mind brings about by contending with these data is the goodness of the universe, especially as it is manifested in the living organisms which it contains.

Some points concerning the second section of the discourse

(a) *What is "space"?* "Space" is shaped into triangles, these triangles are combined into regular solids, and out of these regular solids physical things are made. How then, we are bound to ask, ought we to conceive of "space" and of the triangles which are made of it?

The answer is ambiguous. On the one hand the triangles are simply triangles, the molecules simply configurations in space. If we are tempted to ask: "Triangles of what?" we must resist the question. They are simply triangles.

We are inclined to find this incredible. Triangles and pyramids, we are inclined to say, are geometrical entities, and it does not make sense to say that physical things are literally made of geometrical entities, of pyramids and cubes which are just pyramids and cubes, and not pyramidal or cubical volumes *of something*. We want the pyramids to be pyramidal volumes of fieriness, the cubes cubical volumes of earthiness. A geometrical entity, we say, is simply a region which might be occupied by a body of suitable shape. It makes no sense to suppose that bodies are composed of geometrical entities. We want to imagine an elementary fieriness which exists inside but not outside the boundaries of the pyramid, the boundaries being constituted by the difference in quality between what is inside them and what lies outside them, just as the boundaries of a cricket ball are constituted by the change from the leather within to the air, or whatever it is, which surrounds it.

To understand the *Timaeus* we must resist this demand. We must suspend disbelief and allow that Timaeus is trying to explain nature in terms of the shapes, and nothing but the shapes, of his particles. All properties are represented as resultants of shapes in motion. Fieriness is nothing but the way a pyramid behaves on collision. If

[1] See above, p. 21.

222

you suppose that the pyramid is itself a pyramid of fire, as a cricket ball is a sphere of leather, then this fire will owe its fieriness to the sharp corners of further pyramids, and so *ad infinitum*. Furthermore if a pyramid was a pyramidal volume of fieriness it could not be cut into triangles (fiery triangles?) which could re-combine into a molecule of water. There is no mention of any properties which could fill the volumes of Timaeus' molecules and thereby constitute the difference between what is within them and what is without, and indeed there *could not* be such properties without destroying Timaeus' account of chemical change; for this depends on the possibility of splitting a molecule into its component triangles and re-combining them in a different molecule, so that the triangles must be neutral as between the various basic properties. The triangles therefore are simply triangles and the volumes simply volumes. Plato's fundamental notion is that of configurations in space, configurations which space is prone to take on of its own accord and into which it is more perfectly formed by the Craftsman when he makes the rough regular.[1]

This may seem incredible to us, and it may have historical roots in Pythagorean mathematics (the Pythagoreans had units which did double duty both as components in numbers and as components in things). But it is not simply a primitive failure to distinguish between geometry and physics. Before we condemn it as that we may remember two things. Firstly that any description of the nature (as opposed to the behaviour) of ultimate particles tends to run into trouble; and secondly that the notion that configurations in space can be accepted as ultimates figures in some popular expositions of relativity to this day.

We are asking whether Timaeus' "space" is space. So far, so long as one is prepared to suspend disbelief, and allow that things can be made of volumes, the answer is "Yes". But there are considerations on the other side which make us want to say that some such word as "matter" would be more appropriate. It is not only that physical things are formed of the shapes which the "recipient" takes on; it is also that the "recipient" has a life of its own—for its motion is an essential part of the whole story.

The truth surely is that Plato has got himself into a position where there is not much logical room to manoeuvre; and what there is he makes the most of. The "recipient" is needed because instances of properties have to exist in something, and it has to be as nearly as possible nothing because it has to be neutral as between all properties. (Timaeus compares it to a base used by a scent-maker,

[1] I ought to warn the reader that this is disputed; e.g. by Cornford. See his *Plato's Cosmology*.

which has to be odourless in order that it may serve as a base indifferently for any scent. 50 e). But on the other hand it has to play its part in explaining change. Timaeus indeed says (*loc. cit.*) that it is "shapeless" and "outside all kinds". But this can hardly mean that it is absolutely without properties of any kind whatsoever (for then it would become simply space, and space cannot do anything), nor can it mean that it is absolutely without shape (for it forms itself into rough configurations). The notion of a plastic substance, which Timaeus also uses, gives another side of his ambiguous meaning. The recipient lacks determinate shapes and it lacks intelligible properties, and is in that sense "outside all kinds". It can only be grasped by bastard reasoning, though it plays some part in explanation; a compromise entity, the ghost of the Pythagorean "unlimited", the germ of Aristotle's "matter" and of Locke's "something, I know not what". But at the same time it is also just space.

(*b*) *What is the element of brute fact?* Did the Craftsman create cubes and pyramids because that was a tidy way of organising space, and then proceed to do the best he could with the properties resulting from the method of tidying? Or were the shapes which are imposed on space chosen because they can conspire to produce the natural world? Is the part played by brute fact simply the existence of space, or is it the properties of the elements?

Here too I suspect that the answer is ambiguous. One is inclined to answer that *ananke* consists in the properties of the elements, these being the materials of which things are made. After all, the properties of the elements are described in the section devoted to *ananke*, whereas the section devoted to the co-operation of reason and *ananke* describes how men and other organisms were built up out of these elements. On the other hand what reason was faced with at the start was not the ordered elements, but simply space. If the Craftsman made the elements, how can they figure among the data which confronted him? One might answer this by observing that space was already, in the beginning, showing "traces" of the properties of the elements, and that this forced the Craftsman's hand. But this is not a complete answer, for one can cap it by asking why Timaeus postulates the "traces".

The question is: what is it about the natural world that Plato regards as brute and unintelligible? Is it the fact that there are extended things, or the fact that things are made of earth, air, fire and water? To the question put like that one is inclined to choose the former answer. It is space, and not fire, which can only be grasped by bastard reasoning, and earth, air, fire and water are simply what you get if you shape space into regular solids. They are therefore products of ordering and not that which is ordered. Yet this answer conflicts with the evident fact that the elements are described in the section devoted to brute fact.

Perhaps the position is this. The Craftsman is confronted with three kinds of necessity, factual, physico-mathematical and teleological. The factual necessity consists in the existence of a chaotic three-dimensional continuum. Anything which is to be made has got to be made in it. The physico-mathematical necessity consists in the ways in which a three-dimensional continuum can be filled with regular solids, and in the dynamical properties which any chosen solids will possess. The teleological necessity consists in the constraint on the Creator's will exercised by such facts as that order is preferable to disorder, and that intelligent beings are preferable to inert matter. Because order is preferable to disorder, and because he is faced with a three-dimensional continuum, he is forced to create regular solids in it. This means that he will be faced with some set of particles, and with the behaviour pattern correlated with the chosen set. However, he retains room to manoeuvre in two ways. Firstly (one would have supposed) he is free to choose what set of regular solids to create. Thus he might have created spheres, cubes and dodecahedrons, or nothing but spheres. But secondly he is free to determine the ratios between the elements (how much fire, how much earth and so on) and also their initial distribution. Now when Plato speaks of intelligence co-operating with *ananke* he seems to have in mind the second only of these two freedoms. The Creator is free so to dispose earth, air, fire and water as to produce the best results. The first freedom Plato does not seem to recognise as that. Why not?

One can piece together an official explanation of this. We learnt earlier that to make a three-dimensional unity we need geometrical proportion holding between four terms. This physico-mathematical fact will require the use of four regular solids in the ordering. But there are only five regular solids which can be inscribed in a sphere, only five solids therefore to choose from. Of these the Craftsman uses four, and there is a reason why he does not use the fifth (the dodecahedron). This is (55 c) that the dodecahedron was already used for the shape of the universe (the universe is a sphere, and a dodecahedron is reasonably spherical). But this means that the Craftsman had in fact no choice of which set of regular solids to create; there had to be four of them, and of the five possibles one was already booked. This explains why it can be taken for granted that if reason is faced with a three-dimensional chaos it will without more ado have to organise it into earth, air, fire and water; and that is why the existence of these is part of the given.

But this explanation is obviously very lame. There is clearly no convincing reason for not creating dodecahedral particles,[1] even if we allow that it was necessary to have at least four kinds and that they must all be inscribable in a sphere. Clearly it is necessary to supplement this official explanation with an unofficial one. This surely is that whatever set of regular solids were chosen the choice would have to be arbitrary. At the aesthetico-mathematical level reason sees that things must be tidy; at the teleological level it sees that there must exist rational animals. But there are many ways of tidying things, and also (for all Plato knew) many ways of making rational animals. The question: "How can I design a rational animal?" cannot be grappled with until I know what I have got to make it out of. Given one set of elements I shall produce one design, given another set I shall produce another. The specification "rational animal" is too abstract to entail one particular design and with it one set of materials. Therefore before reason can get to work on the teleological level "persuading *anankē*" to allow the production of rational animals, it has to know what materials it has got to work with. But the aesthetico-mathematical requirement of tidiness does not specify the materials, for there are many tidy arrangements. Therefore the set of materials is not specified from either end. Therefore the Craftsman's hand must be forced in the choice of this set; and that this is the case Timaeus indicates by endowing space with a primordial proneness to take on the shapes of the four chosen elements. This leads to the odd and rather confusing result that the Craftsman is represented as apparently performing a free act of rational creativity in ordering the elements, whereas the results of this free act form part of the brute facts with which reason is confronted in its creative work. The solution of the puzzle is that the creation of the elements is so much a matter of course given the initial nature of space that the Craftsman is not free at this stage.

One might put Plato's dilemma in this way. If he makes space before the creation consist of earth, air, fire and water, then he attributes to matter in its own right the power of orderly self-disposition. But this is to make matter rational. On the other hand if he makes the choice of these elements a purely rational act, then he has to explain why these elements were chosen; and to explain this would be to attribute to reason an interest in the existence of earth, air, fire and water; and that would never do. The most reason can be interested in at that level is tidiness. Therefore Plato tries, rather half-heartedly, to make the interest in tidiness issue inevitably in the existence of earth, air, fire and water. This inevitability he is naturally unable to make good. The root of the trouble is the belief

[1] The dodecahedron cannot be constructed out of Timaeus' triangles; but then he might have chosen some other fundamental particles.

that reason is too high-minded to be concerned for the existence of physical things.

There is a very obscure passage in the *Laws* (903 e 3–904 a 4) which we might notice before we leave this point. Here Plato seems to say that the existence of physical and chemical laws makes the work of moral government of the universe not harder but easier. For if anything could come out of anything, there would be an infinite variety of possible combinations. The actual position, in which change takes place only by dissolution and composition (i.e. such processes as Timaeus describes), makes things much easier by limiting the possibilities. In fact the existence of natural laws in one way constricts but in another way facilitates the realisation of moral ends. Therefore although it is a matter of brute fact that the four elements exist (and with them the laws of physics and chemistry), this is a matter of brute fact simply in the sense that their existence is something in which reason is not interested. It does not follow from this that their existence is a positive obstacle to reason's purposes.

(*c*) *The motion of space.* How does space manage to move of its own accord? For surely it is only souls that can start things moving? This has led some to suppose an irrational element in the soul of the universe to be responsible for the disorderly motions of chaos. But in terms of the myth this is impossible; Timaeus has chaos in disorderly motion before the soul of the universe is created. The irrational element would have to be an irrational counter-Craftsman, and of such a Zoroastrian doctrine there is no mention at all. It is better to say that here Plato attributes some motion to matter in its own right, and in so doing contradicts his own principle that matter is inert and only spirit active. How then does this come about?

Surely the answer is that Plato is in a dilemma similar to the one we have just been considering. For either space is inert, in which case it does nothing, and reason, having nothing to contend with in creation, is absolutely responsible for the physical world; or else matter has to be allowed some activity in its own right. The way out of this dilemma is to allow it disorderly activity, and to make orderly activity the prerogative of spirit. Plato feels able to do this, no doubt, because what really impresses him when he sees a physical object in motion is not: "How does that inert thing come to be doing something?" but: "How does that un-thinking thing manage not to deviate?" In other words the marvel is not motion, but regular motion. Motion in itself is simply change of place, and that is not very wonderful. Because Plato felt mildly that motion needs explaining, he sometimes said that all motion is due to spirit. Because he only felt this mildly, he did not notice that he had contradicted this principle in the *Timaeus* by ascribing disorderly motion to matter in its own right.

(*d*) *The treatment of colour.* There is an illuminating remark at the end of Timaeus' discussion of colour which is important for Plato's view on the relation between theory and observation (68 d 2–7). Timaeus has been explaining colour (or rather visual texture, for brilliance is one of his "colours"). He does so by saying that different objects emit particles of different sizes, which have different effects on the rod of light coming from the eye by which we see. Believing that nature is an economical mechanism, he manages with as few physical effects as he can, and therefore he has certain "primary colours" (black, white, brilliant and red) and constructs the rest out of mixtures of these. Then he makes the comment in which we are interested: "Anybody who thinks to test this in practice does not understand the difference between God and man; for God can combine and separate, whereas man can do neither of these things." In other words: "Don't get out you paint boxes and try it, for it won't work. But that doesn't invalidate the theory."

The question is, why does Plato allow Timaeus to shield his theory from falsification in this way. Assuming that he is being serious[1] the implication must be somewhat along these lines. Since the universe is rational, nothing can be arbitrary. It is therefore not arbitrary that certain colours exist; it must be the case that the phenomena of colour are a necessary consequence of the general laws of nature. Therefore we are entitled to work out a plausible theory by which we can derive the range of colours from the physics and physiology of vision. But suppose we test such an account in the laboratory and it lets us down; what are we to do? Abandon it? No, for we have much better grounds for confidence that things do work as it is "rational" that they should work than we have for supposing that we can construct proper experimental tests. Perhaps for example "man cannot combine", cannot, let us say, by any amount of stirring, produce a homogeneous mixture of pigments and hence a homogeneous emission of particles such as would produce the theoretically predicted colour. We shall therefore hang on to our theory, despite laboratory falsification, as the best conjecture until somebody can produce a more plausible theory. But what makes a theory plausible? The answer is that a theory is plausible if it conforms to the presupposition that nature is efficiently designed. If one theory represents the author of nature as a more efficient designer than another, then the former theory is more probable than the latter.

---

[1] Serious in allowing Timaeus to use the shield. I do not mean that Plato thinks that Timaeus' account of colour must be right.

There being no grounds for confidence in experimental tests, how else can we proceed?

C. *The third section of Timaeus' discourse; what the Creator did about the brute facts*

We need not spend long on the third section of the discourse, in which Timaeus tells us how the Craftsman realised his ends in the material at his disposal, in particular by creating man.[1] All that we need is a specimen or two of his exposition.

Here then is his account of the head. Flesh is insensitive, I suppose because it is yielding and hence does not transmit motion. It is therefore a good padding, but on the other hand it interferes with the operation of sense-organs. Therefore the Creator had to choose, the physical nature of his materials imposing the choice upon him. Either the head could be well padded and less vulnerable, or it could be an efficient seat for the sense-organs and more vulnerable—the choice of longer and duller or shorter and more intelligent life. Naturally the creating mind chose the latter alternative (75).

And here is Timaeus' account of hair. Its efficient cause or *sine qua non* is the fact that fire cuts holes in the skin as it makes its way out of the body, and that moisture escapes out of these holes and hardens into hair. But the true cause of hair is the reason why this physico-chemical process was deemed acceptable and allowed to occur, and this is that it provides a protection for the brain. Likewise the occurrence of nails is due to a similar efficient cause, but the true cause of their existence is that women and brutes, who are to be made from men, will need claws—a frivolous use, no doubt, of the serious distinction between the cause and the *sine qua non* (76).

Timaeus has a great deal more to say about the detailed functioning of the body, the creation of animals and plants, and the proper conduct of life. Throughout he works (as far as his invention will allow) on two levels: what good end is served by the existence of the liver, or whatever it may be; and what it is made of, or how it came to arise. The examples I have given will serve to show the principles on which he goes. In general his purpose is to display familiar objects, and in particular men, as a product of two factors: the physical facts brought about by the patterns imposed on the chaos, and the ends to which the Creator attached value, the chief among them being the existence of rational animals. Man is to be exhibited as what you get

---

[1] Strictly speaking the Craftsman does not create man. He creates the immortal parts of man's soul, leaving the mortal parts, and the body, to be created by the "created Gods". Since however they "imitate" him (69 c 5), I imagine this makes no difference of principle.

if you try to design a living creature which can inhabit the earthy parts of the universe.

If you confine yourself to designing living creatures to inhabit the fiery regions, your problem is simpler and your product more satisfactory; for there you have only to make stars. Why then, one might ask, were terrestrial living creatures produced at all? If there is an official answer to this in the *Timaeus*, I suppose it is to be found in the principle of impartiality according to which, if any kind of living creature is to be produced, all should be. Unofficially however it is quite possible that Plato simply thought it self-evident that men ought to exist.

D. *General conclusions from the* Timaeus *concerning teleology and scientific method*

This recapitulation of the cosmological teaching of the *Timaeus* must be prefaced with a reminder. This is that in my opinion Plato did not mean us to take everything in the *Timaeus* seriously. The dialogue is offered as a concrete illustration of the kind of account of the world Plato believed we ought to look for. It is to be taken seriously in principle but not in detail. In detail it creaks, and inevitably. No one even in Plato's day could seriously hope to account for everything in a hundred pages. Some of the creaks we have already noticed; for example, the explanations of why there are four elements, and of why there are these four. There are plenty more. For instance in the account of chemical change the molecules of one element are allowed to break up those of another, but they are not allowed to break up each other. The sharp corners of the pyramid are allowed to slice cubes into their component triangles, but one pyramid cannot damage another (57 a). Yet it is impossible to imagine why not. But I think that it would be a mistake to worry over points such as these. It does not matter whether Timaeus' account is tenable so long as it serves to exemplify what it would be like to exhibit the world as a rationally satisfactory system.

(i) *Teleology*

What, then, would it be like to exhibit the world as a rationally satisfactory system, and to what extent does Plato's attempt to do this conform or depart from the positions of the *Phaedo* and the *Republic*?

Timaeus' world is a rationally satisfactory system in the four ways previously described. That is to say, it is devised to house entities and to exhibit properties in whose existence reason has an interest; it does this according to a principle of impartiality; it conforms to physico-mathematical necessity, and it gives symbolical expression in its behaviour to the nature of intelligence and of its objects.

To these four ways in which Timaeus' world is rationally satisfactory we may perhaps add a fifth, which is that the world is an economically designed machine. This emerges, I think, in Timaeus' account of physical chemistry. Why does Timaeus feel bound to offer this account? No doubt we would answer this question as follows. Timaeus has to explain why in a world governed by reason there exist not just rational beings, but men, creatures, that is to say, much of whose constitution has nothing obvious to do with the purposes of reason. Why these elaborate animal bodies if men ought really to be thought of simply as rational beings? To answer this question Timaeus has to show that the Craftsman had a range of ineluctable facts with which to contend, and which are responsible for the complexity of the design. You may think that the liver or the hair are irrelevant excrescences in rational beings. If however you bear in mind the nature of the materials, you can see that men would not really have been better designed if these features had been left out.

To make this point, Timaeus has to show that the materials have a nature. However, he could have said this very briefly (it is said very briefly in the passage in *Laws* 903-4, quoted above). I have the feeling that Plato makes him go into so much detail because he wants to show that it is quite conceivable that the multitudinous phenomena of nature result from the inter-action of a small number of general laws. Plato had a most un-Wordsworthian mind. He could not have found something far more deeply interfused in the light of setting suns just by responding to the impression made by the light. That would be rank aestheticism. A sunset to Plato would be evidence of a rational creator only if it could be shown that in terms of some simple and satisfactory mechanism the light had to be the colour that it is. It is significant that although he is prepared to allow that other harmonies exist, the only harmonies he is prepared to identify are those of music and astronomy, in which sensuous harmony is not the point or not the whole story. Certain arrangements of colour may please us, yet unless we can think that in responding to such an arrangement we are responding to something non-sensuously harmonious, then such pleasure ought to be suspect. But if this is Plato's approach to nature, then the existence of nature could never be justified by its appeal to the senses, and he could not, like a Romantic, infer a cosmic mind from the beauties of the cosmos. Indeed the reverse; the existence of all this frippery would argue against the belief that reason is responsible for the order of nature. If however things cannot help being (for example) coloured, because they have to give off particles, and these inevitably affect our eyes, then the scandal of the frippery is disposed of. For this reason Plato would be eager to show that nature, as Wordsworth gaped at it, is the inevitable resultant of the functioning of an efficient machine. That would make nature a work worthy of intelligence.

Mechanical efficiency, then, is probably a fifth way in which Timaeus' world is rationally satisfactory. Does all this mean that everything is disposed as it is best that it should be, in the spirit of the *Phaedo* and the *Republic*? Surely it does. We have already seen reason to believe that "best" in the earlier dialogues means "in accordance with the demands of reason". There is however one way in which the *Timaeus* goes beyond the earlier dialogues, and that is that it makes it clear that the designs of reason had to be realised *in a given material*, and that for this reason we have to bear in mind not only what reason is concerned to produce but also what it has to contend with.

(ii) *Scientific method*

Timaeus does not recommend a method; he follows one. If we want to see the method which his practice can be taken to advocate we shall have to reconstruct it for him. Perhaps it is as follows.

He begins by presupposing that the world is rationally designed. This he derives from the declaration (29 a) that it is blasphemous to deny that the world is a noble thing. Evidently then a good deal of observation[1] goes on before science starts—enough to convince us of the nobility of the world.

The next step seems to be a double one. You ask on the one hand what reason would be concerned to produce, and on the other hand what there is about the existing world which reason could not be concerned to produce. Such things as rational beings and harmonious motions[2] form the answer to the first question, "space" the answer to the second. (What is wrong with the physical world is the fact that it is physical).

Having thus isolated the ends of reason and the nature of the datum, you next ask how reason would work upon this datum to realise these ends. No doubt if this question was put in the void you would not know how to answer it. But of course it is not put in the void, for you know that the answer has got to produce a world which we can recognise as the one we live in. The question therefore becomes something like this: "What mechanism can we postulate such that (*a*) it could be expected to produce the familiar phenomena

---

[1] Chiefly, I suppose, in the fields of astronomy and music.

[2] Strictly, since you cannot have motion without space, what reason cares for is the *harmony* of the motion.

of nature; and (b) it can be seen that in doing so it is doing all that can be expected to bring about the ends of reason?" This in turn excites the further question: "What primordial properties can we attribute to the given such that, in terms of these properties and of the known predilections of reason (for regular figures, etc.), it can be seen that the postulated mechanism would be the one that it would be natural to construct?"

How would one decide that one had got a good answer to these questions? It is hard to say, though the features of bad answers are more obvious. Presumably any answer involving an unnecessarily complicated mechanism would be a bad answer because it would represent reason as a clumsy artificer. Presumably also any answer which attributed *complicated* primordial properties and behaviour patterns to the given would be a bad answer; for the more complicated you make the given the more it looks like something organised and hence a product of reason and not a datum. Perhaps it would be possible to think of other similar features of a bad answer. But how one would choose between two theories which were equally successful in avoiding such defects, which involved an equally economical mechanism and an equally simple primordial state, I do not know. Presumably within these limits all speculations are equally plausible.

It can be seen that if this is the procedure Timaeus would have the scientist follow, then it is governed by two factors. One of these is empirical observation. As the above account shows this operates at two points. It is needed first to assure the scientist that the world is a work of reason; and it is needed again to tell him what he has got to explain. For he has to explain how the hair grows and why metals melt when heated (58–9); and he could not know that he had to explain these facts unless he had observed that they are facts. It is wrong therefore to say that Plato was so foolish as to think that we can find out about the world without using our senses. The senses tell us what our problem is; what they do not do is to solve it for us.

In one way this is correct. The scientist does not solve his problems by using his senses. What is missing from Plato's account of scientific method in this respect is that he fails to see that the senses by themselves *do not* tell us what the problem is. That is to say, he fails to see that there is any work to be done in ascertaining the facts which have to be explained. He takes it for granted that the facts are obvious to any normally educated man. What modern experimental science has shown is that the facts that we are all familiar with are only a small sample of the total, and that a theory which accounts for the familiar facts may very well fail to account for others which can be discovered under experimental conditions or by more careful observation of normal occurrences. This is the better way of expressing the criticism of Plato's conception of scientific method. One might also be inclined to express it by saying that Plato fails to advise us to use observation to check our theories. But this is not quite right, for no doubt he takes for granted that a theory which fails to account for *evident* facts will be non-suited on that ground. Thus if Timaeus' theory had shown why wood does not burn, that would show it to be a bad theory. What Plato fails to do is to advise us to use experiment and disciplined observation to produce new facts, so that we can see whether the theory accounts equally well for these.

Observation, then, is one factor which should govern scientific method in Plato's view. The other is an opinion about the ends of reason. This operates, we may observe, on two levels, which we might call the cosmic and the microscopic. At the cosmic level reason is to be supposed to have certain grand ends, such as the existence of men or circular orbits for the stars. At the microscopic level it is also to be supposed that the predilections of reason are effective in bringing it about, for example, that the shapes of the molecules are symmetrical. Between these two levels utility is naturally allowed to intervene. Thus men are allowed to have asymmetrical bodies because it is more efficient so. No doubt here too the general ends of reason would be effective so far as utility permitted; thus of two equally efficient arrangements no doubt the more elegant would be chosen.

An opinion about the ends of reason might be described in the language of the *Republic* as an opinion about the nature of goodness; and we remember that the *Republic* tells us that although we make use of the light of goodness in all our abstract reasonings, few or none of us know what it is. Does the *Timaeus* also believe that the question "what is goodness?" is a question of substance and the last question we can answer?

This is not an easy problem to settle. A man who does not know what goodness is will be unable to say confidently what reason will do in any given situation; he will be reduced to conjecture. Now Timaeus repeatedly says that he is only conjecturing. But this does not give us our answer, for we can go on to ask why he is only conjecturing; is it because he does not know what reason would do in a given situation, or because he does not know what situations are given? Unfortunately we get no clear answer to this further question. His official reason why his account is conjectural is given in 29 b. It is that the world, being a changing thing, cannot do more than resemble an intelligible object, and that of such a semblance one can only tell a probable story. There is a pun in the Greek (*eikôn* and *eikos*) which makes this seem plausible; without the pun it is not easy to see what we are to make of it, particularly since "resemble" in this context is plainly metaphorical.

So we are forced back on impressions. My impression is that there is nothing tentative about Timaeus when he is telling us what reason would do about a given situation. He seems to know what the ends of reason are. If this is right, then what he does not know is the problem with which reason was faced. In that case either Timaeus has done his dialectic and seen what goodness is, or else the idea that the nature of goodness is a secret has been dropped. One thing is quite certain however, and that is that Timaeus does not think that we can reconstruct the order of nature *a priori*. He invokes *a priori* considerations in his reconstruction, but what he gets is admitted to be a string of conjectures.

We remember that in discussing the *Republic* we wondered whether Plato believed in an orderly and a disorderly sector in nature. There was astronomy and harmonics, and there might be other sciences concerned with other kinds of motion. This seemed to suggest that some happenings came into the sphere of sciences whereas others did not. How does the *Timaeus* stand on this?

Certainly Timaeus does not use a dichotomy between the orderly and the disorderly. His distinction is between what is desirable and what is inescapable, and this is a distinction not between classes of facts but between factors in the production of facts. Every fact is begotten by the desirable upon the inescapable. Furthermore every occurrence is governed by law. Or this is almost true; there is a discussion of smells (66) which suggests that perhaps these are somewhat haphazard. The theory seems to be that smells are given off by things in process of change (melting, decomposing, etc.). The idea probably is that in such circumstances it is triangles broken off from molecules and not yet recombined in fresh molecules which get loose and cause irritations in the nose. However that may be, Timaeus says that "in smell there are no kinds" (*eidê*), and that there is no proportionality (*summetria*) such that a given kind (of what?) has a given smell. If this means that you cannot predict what a given thing will smell like, then this would amount to saying that smells at least are not governed by law. However, it may be that Timaeus is only saying of smells what he might have said of colours, namely that they cannot be classified, that they shade off into each other. Smells then may perhaps constitute an unimportant exception to the principle that all occurrences are governed by law.

If then a disorderly sector is a sector not governed by natural law, the *Timaeus* does not seem to believe that there is a disorderly sector of any significant extent. Everything, or almost everything, is a proper object of science in the sense that one can speculate about the laws governing it. Yet there are two distinctions between heavenly and earthly phenomena which are important and which might lead one to call the former orderly. These two distinctions are that heavenly things and happenings are (*a*) stereotyped and (*b*) symbolical, whereas earthly things (broadly speaking) are neither of these. There is such a thing as *the* shape of a star, and this shape is a sphere because that is a fitting shape, symbolising the true nature of a star. There is no such thing as *the* shape of a human body, except in a very general sense, because human bodies are of infinitely various shapes. The general design of human bodies, as we know, is determined by the working out[1] of the Craftsman's purposes in terms of the behaviour-patterns of his materials. The particular shape of Jones is governed by natural law in the sense that it has been brought about by regular natural processes, and it is governed by reason in the sense that these processes are allowed to operate because a viable human organism can be produced by them. But these processes do not operate to produce a stereotyped human body; the problem of constructing a living creature for a terrestrial environment is too complex for that. Because it is so complex, also, human beings must have many features (such as the hair) which are pragmatically necessary but symbolically meaningless. For this reason if you want to see the glory of God declared you must look for it in the heavens. It is there that motions occur that simply manifest harmony. If a "science of motion" is a branch of knowledge which enables one to apprehend the harmony of certain motions, then astronomy and music remain the only sciences of motion that can be identified.

If then we interpret the *Republic* by the *Timaeus* we shall probably say that Plato did not believe in a disorderly sector in nature if that means believing in a class of happenings not governed by natural law. For the *Timaeus* seems to think that all or almost all happenings are governed by natural law. The distinction is not between that which is regular and that which is irregular, nor between that for which there is a reason and that for which there is no reason. In the *Timaeus*, at least, everything (or almost everything) is regular, and for everything (or almost everything) there is in some sense a reason. The distinction is between that which is "harmonious" or overtly declaratory of reason's ends, and that which is not so. A science of motion in that case would not be a body of conjecture about the laws governing events; it is a body of knowledge enabling us to apprehend the harmony of that which is harmonious.

Finally, how does the *Timaeus* stand with regard to the position of the *Phaedo* that it is a mistake to look directly at the phenomena, that we ought rather to study them in *logoi*?

If Socrates meant by this that reflection on the *logos* of X-hood will tell us everything about X things, then I suppose that the

[1] By the "created Gods".

Timaeus denies this. But presumably Socrates never intended quite so much. Perhaps the best thing to say is that by the time of the *Timaeus* Plato had at least recognised the limitations of the method proposed in the *Phaedo*. In practice one might say that reflection on the *logos* of X-hood still seems to play a vital part when X-hood is something like *being a star*. For in so far as questions about the stars are decided at all they are decided in terms of what is fitting. Reflections on the *logos* of X-hood where X-hood is something like *humanity* still play a part, but a subdued part. We cannot know the true cause why we have livers or lungs until we know what a man truly is (we can then see that the function of the lungs is to control the beating of the heart in violent emotion, thus restraining the emotion; and that the liver has an analogous moral function; 70–1); but we cannot of course deduce the precise shape and position of the organs from reflecting on the nature of man. For the nature of the materials has determined the details of the design.

One might put this in terms of the myth by saying that in the sphere where the Craftsman did the work himself the "syllogising" programme of the *Phaedo* is vital, whereas in the sphere where the work was done by the "created Gods" it is much less so. This, I imagine, is part of the significance of this division of labour.

V. COSMOLOGICAL MATERIAL IN THE OTHER POST-*REPUBLIC* DIALOGUES

A. *The* Statesman

We have already referred to the myth of the *Statesman* (268–74; above, p. 155). Here it will be enough to remind ourselves that we found in it the notion of imperfect conformity to law—the notion that things do not behave as they should. This contrasts to some extent with the *Timaeus*. Timaeus talks as if chaos were ordered (as well as possible) once and for all in the remote past, and has been supplied with a sufficient number of souls to keep it orderly. The *Laws*, on the whole, seems to agree with this. There is a sort of spiritualisation of nature, in fact, in the *Timaeus* and *Laws* which allows the universe to carry on without external tinkering. The *Statesman* contrariwise seems to revert to the earlier view that nature is brute and can only be kept from sinking back into chaos by periodic divine intervention. The intelligent beings of the *Statesman* are less "deeply inter-fused" than those of the *Timaeus* and *Laws*.

B. *The* Philebus *and the* Laws

(*a*) *The doctrine of flux.* Plato not infrequently refers, often light-heartedly, to the dispute between the Heracliteans who maintained that everything is in flux and the Parmenideans who maintained that everything stays as it is. There is, as we have seen, a serious discussion of the doctrine of flux in the *Theaetetus*, and here Plato seems to insist that properties themselves are of course not in flux, and furthermore that it must often be the case that a given property is stably manifested by a given thing for an appreciable period of time.[1] He also seems to make these two points, or at any rate the first of them, at the end of the *Cratylus* (439–40).

However, while not giving unqualified assent to the principle that everything is in flux, Plato does seem in these places to allow that things are ceaselessly active at some level even when the activity produces an appearance of inactivity. For this reason, among others, he refers to physical things as *gignomena*, things that become. Aristotle tells us (*Metaphysics* 987 a) that Plato continued to believe in flux. However there are certain passages in the *Philebus* and the *Laws* which might suggest otherwise.

Thus in *Laws* 893 c 1, in a context in which he is speaking of physical things (for he says that rest and change both take place in space) he says flatly that some things change and others do not; and a little further on (894 a 6) he says that so long as things do not change they are *ontôs onta* or really real, stable entities. Two things are not clear about this passage. Firstly it is not perfectly clear that he thinks that any physical things do in fact comply with the not-changing condition, and hence qualify as *ontôs onta*;[2] and secondly when he says that some physical things do not change it is not clear at what level he is speaking. He may only mean that some things such as rabbits obviously change and move in ways in which other things do not. On the other hand it rather looks as if he wants to deny altogether the doctrine that everything is ceaselessly active and that hence all physical things are *gignomena* and not *onta*. After all the Heracliteans cannot have had very conclusive reasons for their opinion.

An anti-Heraclitean attitude seems perhaps to be detectable also in the *Philebus*. Here (26), speaking of such conditions as health and other right states of things, he uses the phrases "development into stability" (*genesis eis ousian*) and "developed stability" (*gegenêmenê ousia*). And further down (54), in distinguishing between a process and its culmination, he uses the word *genesis* for the former and

---

[1] See above, pp. 10–11, 27–33.
[2] He is in effect defining *gignesthai*, to become.

ousia for the latter (his example of a process is ship-l
ship being the *ousia* in which it culminates).

Perhaps there is no new nor anti-Heraclitean doctrine
term *ousia* is taken loosely enough, it is obvious that a s
and inactive in comparison with the activity of buildin
in truth its nails and timbers are themselves theatres
activity. None the less the anti-Heraclitean interpretati.. .. these
phrases is tempting. For to Heraclitus change was the law of the
universe, and it was an illusion to suppose that a state of equili-
brium could ever be arrived at, at which things would stay as they
were. To Aristotle on the other hand many changes have as their
objectives balances or right states, and when these are attained
there is some chance of persistence in them. It rather looks as if some
such view is to be found in the *Philebus*. For it looks as if Plato is
prepared to call states such as health "realities" as opposed to
processes, and to say that processes exist for the sake of realities
(e.g. 53 d 4). This might seem to carry the implication that change
goes on until a balanced state is arrived at, but that when this is
attained it will persist until it is upset from outside. Nature (under
the impulsion of reason, no doubt) strives towards, and occasionally
attains, stable states.

If this is the position of the *Philebus*, it certainly seems to be a new
doctrine, but it does not entail a recantation of the flux doctrine in
the form in which that is maintained or at least tolerated in the
Theaetetus; it can be reconciled with a physico-chemical doctrine of
ceaseless activity. For there is a sense in which the solar system, for
example, does not change, although its components are active.
Again a man in a state of health is a theatre of activity (circulatory,
respiratory, digestive, and so forth) although his condition does not
change. A sickness develops from day to day, while health stays the
same. It would be perfectly possible for Plato to decide to use the
word *genesis* or "process" to refer to developing conditions, *ousia* or
"reality" to refer to stable conditions, and at the same time to hold
that both processes and realities are maintained by activity which
goes on below the level of appearance.

There seem then to be traces of an "Aristotelian" and anti-
Heraclitean conception in the *Philebus*, and this leads to a new use
of the terms *genesis* and *ousia*. It does not however follow that Plato
had abandoned the doctrine underlying his old use of these terms,
though of course he may have done so; and the passage we considered
from the *Laws* gives some support to the view that he had.

(*b*) *The cosmology of the* Laws. We return to the passage of the
Laws from which we have already quoted (893–9). We remember
that the Stranger says that some things are active and some are at

⸫st. Having said this he goes on to distinguish eight kinds of *kinêsis* or activity. Readers dispute about what the eight kinds are (his language is far from explicit).[1] The dispute is however not important, for he defines various of his eight items in terms of each other so that he is left with a list of three fundamental kinds of activity, namely motion, separation and combination, all physical activity being expressible in terms of these three (thus growth is combination, and so on). So far this account of physical change agrees with the *Timaeus*. Then the Stranger goes on to speak of things coming into existence (*genesis;* 894 a). He says that a thing comes into existence when a "beginning" (*archê*) grows to the second and then to the third stage and thus becomes perceptible; and this may or may not agree with the *Timaeus*. The Stranger's meaning seems to be that we do not call imperceptible particles things; one only has a thing when there is a sufficient aggregation of particles for the mass to be perceptible. The question is, why "beginnings" have to go through two stages of growth (i.e. presumably of combination with other "beginnings") in order to become perceptible. We can explain this in terms of the *Timaeus*; for Timaeus' molecules are not individually perceptible, but only assemblages of them (see *Timaeus* 56 c). Therefore a triangle must combine with other triangles to form a molecule (first stage) and a molecule with other molecules (second stage) before you get a perceptible object. On the other hand many readers take the Stranger's language about "beginnings" and "stages" (*metabaseis*) to refer to some process whereby points accumulate to form lines and lines accumulate to form planes or solids; and it certainly lends itself to such an interpretation. On that interpretation it could be held that the Stranger is merely using very oracular language to tell us that points and lines (or points and lines and planes) are not perceptible.[2] But this hardly squares with the fact that he is supposed to be talking about the coming into existence of things. It would seem then that if we interpret" beginning" as "point" he must be supposing that physical things are built of points. In that case he would sympathise with Timaeus, in that both would build physical things out of geometrical entities, but the Stranger would now use simpler entities. At any rate Timaeus and the Stranger certainly seem to agree that ordinary common-sense things come into existence by the aggregation of some kind of particles, and diminish or change into something else by means of separation.

The Stranger's next point also conforms to the general attitude of the *Timaeus*; for the purpose of this discussion of kinds of activity

---

[1] I think they are: rotation, locomotion, separation, combination, growth, diminution, destruction and coming into existence.

[2] Sir David Ross seems to take this view; *Plato's Theory of Ideas*, p. 215.

is to maintain the priority of spiritual over physical beings, and this he does, as we know, by identifying spirit with self-activation, and arguing for the necessity of a "Prime Mover".[1] This established, he insists that the standard activities of spirits are prior to the activities of bodies, and that therefore such things as wishes and beliefs are the "fundamental activities", and that they "take over the activities of bodies and bring about all growth, diminution, separation and combination, and the warmths . . . hardnesses . . . whitenesses . . . sweetnesses . . . etc. which are consequent upon these latter processes". This is the familiar doctrine that sensible properties are dependent upon the activities of particles, and that these last are determined by mind.

The Stranger then contends that at least two souls are responsible for the activity of the world; for it contains disorder as well as order, and the Stranger is not prepared to follow Timaeus and allow to matter any independent activity. This is not necessarily a Zoroastrian doctrine about an evil cosmic principle. The Stranger does not say whether there is more disorder than could be accounted for by the souls of wicked men. But he does say that the question arises whether the Supreme Governor is good or bad. This question he proposes to settle by asking whether the movements of the stars resemble the activity of mind. But he is afraid that to try to look straight at mind in order to decide what its activity is like might be a case of staring straight at the sun; and so he asks us to look at an image of it, namely rotation. Rotation resembles (long-suffering word!) a circle, and is akin to the passage of thought, in that both thought and motion in a circle are always self-consistent (897–8).

This is a clumsy passage, but it has two noteworthy features. Firstly we recognise the familiar notion that a well-ordered universe will symbolise in its behaviour the features of intelligence. Secondly the argument is designed to show that this is a well-ordered universe, and to do this it must show that its behaviour does so symbolise these features. But the argument says nothing about the behaviour of the universe; it is content to show that rotation symbolises thought. But this proves nothing unless it is assumed that the universe does rotate. From the fact that this premise is presupposed but not mentioned we can infer that Plato by now took for granted that the universe rotates, which presumably means that celestial phenomena can be accounted for by a system of circular orbits.[2] He had always, I think, believed this; now he assumes it as a matter of course.

---

[1] Above pp. 329–30 of Vol. 1.

[2] Perhaps no more is implied than that the fixed stars "rotate". But it would be a more convincing demonstration of the goodness of the supreme soul if it could be assumed that all the heavenly bodies follow circular paths.

The conclusion of all this can be expressed in two propositions. Firstly that whatever goes on goes on by means of physico-chemical processes which come about through the volitions of spiritual beings; and secondly that, among these spiritual beings, at least the one which is responsible for the over-all behaviour of the stars is rational and therefore good. It is to be observed that it does not follow from this that the physico-chemical processes which go on on the earth are rationally disposed. They occur through the agency of spiritual beings, but the possibility is left open that some of these may be irrational. Whether or not Plato intended to leave this open is not at all clear because it is not at all clear what spiritual being or beings are supposed to be responsible for terrestrial processes—whether a supreme creator, an individual soul belonging to this planet, or what. On the whole the *Laws* does not seem to leave much work for a supreme creator. It allots a soul each to the heavenly bodies (the passage we have been considering concludes by speculating whether the soul which propels the sun is located inside or outside its body). However these individual souls are more obviously responsible for orbiting their bodies than for what goes on inside them. There are many loose ends. We must therefore leave it open how far detailed terrestrial processes are thought to be rationally disposed, recording merely the impression that Plato is less confident than he was in the *Timaeus* that the finger of God can be detected by a scrutiny of what goes on on earth. More than ever it is the heavens that are declaratory of reason's sway.

(*c*) *Cosmology in education*, Laws *and* Epinomis. How to educate the members of the supreme council is a question discussed in the Twelfth Book of the *Laws*. There is a passage (966–8) concerned with astronomy in education. The general drift is that the study of astronomy is only atheistical in tendency if one fails to realise the priority of spirit over matter. Given this truth, however, astronomy is essential to true piety. For the intelligence of things is declared in the stars[1] and can be apprehended by those who have studied mathematics. No man can really understand human goodness unless he has "studied mathematics and astronomy, seen the affinity which music has with these things, and used all this in order to be able to give account of whatever can be given account of in the sphere of conduct and elsewhere" (967 e, paraphrased).

As in the *Republic*, so here; one cannot achieve a full grasp of what goodness is without mathematics, astronomy and music, and without making use of these things in order to "give account". There are however certain differences between this position and that

---

[1] 967 e 1. Possibly "is declared" should be "is said to be".

of the *Republic*; or perhaps it would be better to say that certain things are clear here which were unclear in the *Republic*. Firstly there is no reason to doubt that "astronomy" here means astronomy —the study of how the stars do in fact move. Secondly astronomy is not treated as one of the mathematical studies; rather we do mathematics in order to be able to see how the stars move. The position here then, surely, is this. The movements of the stars symbolise or embody rational principles; so too does music. In order to grasp these rational principles we must grasp them in their symbolical embodiments. In order to see how the stars move we need mathematics, firstly no doubt to work out their complicated orbits, and secondly to understand the "harmony" of these motions. Mathematics is so to speak the grammar which we need in order to read the message of the stars. Perhaps a fair comment on the difference between this passage and the *Republic* is that Plato is by now more confident that the message is in fact spelt out by the actual movements of the stars, and at the same time less confident that we are able to grasp rational principles except in their embodments; for this reason there is less emphasis on the stage of pure dialectic following upon astronomy.

The subject is resumed in the *Epinomis*, the obscure and incoherent, but at times moving epilogue to the *Laws*, in which the Stranger discusses the education of the supreme councillors in greater detail. Its theme may be said to be the importance of mathematics and astronomy and, in some obscure way, of "always looking toward unity" (991 e 5).

The knowledge of what he calls number (but which includes the whole of pure mathematics) is given to us, says the Stranger, by the heavens; celestial phenomena teach us to reckon. But to those who accept the gift, and use it to study the revolutions of the heavens, a greater gift is given. This greater gift is presumably the message which can be read in the stars.

Mathematics however is only the preface to wisdom. Wisdom seems to consist in understanding the goodness and unity of the cosmos. This leads the Stranger to talk about the Gods; what he says about them we have considered in an earlier chapter.[1] He concludes his discussion by insisting on the regularity of all the heavenly Gods, including the planets. He says a little about their orbits, and then concludes with the familiar points that mathematics is necessary if one is to understand these matters, and that mathematics is also bound up with music. Finally the end of all this is (1) to study "the divine element in the physical world" (*theia genesis* 991 b 6) and "the noblest and most divine of visible natures";

---

[1] Vol. 1, pp. 386–8.

for which study "the things previously discussed" are essential. Then (2) after all this "that which is unified" (*to kath' hen*) must be brought up against "that which is diversified" (*to kat' eide*) in a process of question and answer. One must carefully observe (3) how accurately celestial happenings observe their seasons in order to be convinced of the truth that the spiritual is prior to the physical and that divinity is all-pervasive. All this is of value (4) only if it is studied rightly. To study it rightly is to look always towards unity and to see that there is complete agreement (*mia homologia*)[1] between geometry, arithmetic, harmonics and the movement of the stars; for all of these are bound together by a single bond (991 b–992 a).

This is not very coherent. The second stage seems to be a process of dialectic, that is to say of trying to see the common feature ("that which is unified") and also the distinctive features ("that which is diversified") of comparable things. In particular, it seems, we are to employ this process of dialectic on mathematics, music and astronomy, in order to detect the common bond which unites these diverse embodiments of rationality. Finally the end of all this is that we may see that the world is governed by reason and understand the principles on which reason proceeds. All this is familiar, the one noteworthy point being the importance attached to observing how accurately the stars keep time in order that we may be convinced of the supremacy of spirit. The *Republic* thought that no true geometer would think this possible.

VI. CONCLUSIONS

I shall try to sum up Plato's contribution to natural philosophy in a few simple (and therefore over-simplified) propositions.

1.1. The physical world consists of particles in motion. Its familiar features result from the effect of their motion upon our senses.

1.11. The material of these particles is space or the stuff of physical extension. Their shapes are regular and may be called "imitations" of the forms or principles of order. (This proposition is not to be found explicitly except in the *Timaeus*).

1.2. The stuff of physical extension is not by itself capable of regular shapes or behaviour. Its regularity must be attributed to intelligence.

1.3. Intelligence is also responsible for so disposing the ultimate particles that their interaction produces a rationally satisfactory world.

1.4. A rationally satisfactory world is primarily a world con-

---

[1] Perhaps "one common message" catches the meaning.

sisting of living creatures conforming in their behaviour to rational principles.

1.5. Certain of these self-activating or "living" creatures (namely the stars) are simple enough on the physical side (being made of fire) for it to be possible to make them visible embodiments of rational principles.

1.51. Therefore they have been made into such embodiments. (It is with respect to 1.51. that there is the most obvious development in Plato's view; from the position that it is too much to hope that the heavens embody the intentions of reason he moves to the position that you cannot be sure of the supremacy of reason unless you see that they do).

1.6. The existence of music shows that there is at least one other sphere in which it has been found possible to create manifest embodiments of rational principles; and there may be other such spheres.

2.1. It is of the utmost importance to the good life to understand the principles of rational order.

2.11. In order to do this it is necessary to study them through their manifest embodiments.

2.2. However many manifest embodiments there may be (astronomy, music, and however many others), a "harmonious" mathematical structure will be evident in all of them. Therefore we need to be mathematicians in order to grasp the principles of rational order.

(Throughout, it seems to me, there is some ambiguity about the status of mathematics. Is it merely the grammar which we need to learn in order to read the manifest embodiments; or does mathematics constitute a co-ordinate field of manifest embodiments alongside astronomy and harmonics? *Laws* Bk. 12 encourages the former view, the *Republic* and the *Epinomis* encourage the latter).

3.1. To discover what goes on in the natural world it is necessary to decide how reason would have ordered the field in question.

3.2. It is necessary therefore to know by what principles the activity of reason is determined. (Great stress is laid on 3.2. in the *Republic* in terms of the nature of goodness.[1])

3.3. In trying to discover how reason would have ordered some field it is necessary to ask what part the entities in question play in the overall plan—what their *logos* is. (We detected this chiefly in the *Phaedo*).

3.4. In so far as we cannot be sure by what principles the activity of reason is determined, and since we cannot know what precisely

---

[1] But we thought we found something like it elsewhere in the doctrine of recollection; see above, pp. 139-41.

are the brute facts with which reason has to contend, we cannot discover what goes on in the natural world (apart from reading off the manifest embodiments of rational principles), except by producing conjectures which (*a*) to justice to the phenomena and (*b*) represent reason as acting rationally.

3.5. Compared with reading the manifest embodiments, which has vital moral significance, the rest of the work of discovering what goes on in the natural world is no better than a harmless recreation (*Timaeus* 59 c). Science for its own sake is a leisure-time activity.

4. Finally a question. Given that physical extension is not by itself capable of orderly behaviour, can it be organised once and for all into orderly behaviour, or is it always liable to *nostalgie de la boue*? On this point we did not find agreement in our sources. The nearer you get to the latter view (as in the *Statesman*) the nearer you get to a "Zoroastrian dualism".

METAPHYSICAL ANALYSIS

I. THE "THEORY OF FORMS"

A. *Introductory*

PLATO believed in something that we may vaguely call a rational order. Without this rational order the world would be a chaotic place. It is therefore important to know the rational order. Conceiving of knowledge to some extent after the model of acquaintance, Plato would naturally think of knowing the rational order in terms of knowing its various components. He would therefore think it important to come to know beauty, triangularity, equality, justice and the other things which constitute the rational order. The criterion of knowing beauty would naturally be the ability to say what it is. Therefore it would be essential, for every important value of X, to be able to say what X-hood is.

That is one reason (historical accuracy may be another) why in so many of the early dialogues Socrates is made to ask what so-and-so is. But supposing I buttonhole you and press the question: "What is beauty?"—what is likely to happen? One thing that may well happen is what happens in the *Meno* when Socrates presses the question: "What is moral excellence?" This is that Meno protests that there is no single thing moral excellence; there are many excellences. What constitutes excellence in a man is different from what constitutes excellence in a woman, and so for every stage and position in life (*Meno* 71–2). If you are anxious to get rid of me you may work this up into a doctrine of general relativism. It is ridiculous, you may say, to insist on asking what beauty is; the whole business is shifting and relative. What is beautiful in one context is ugly in another, what is beautiful in one comparison is plain when compared with something else. There is no such thing as beauty sharply marked off from everything else. So it is, you may say, with hardness also and heaviness and honesty and everything else which you feel I may care to ask you to define. These things are not definite and therefore they cannot be defined.

How shall I meet this attack? I might first admit the truth of your examples. I might concede that a thing which is beautiful in one context may be ugly in another, an act right in one situation, wrong in another. But I might plead that this is irrelevant. "I do not deny", I might say, "that it is a relative question whether a given thing is beautiful, but I do deny that beauty itself is relative. When I call something beautiful I am saying something definite; if I were not, I should not have to retract it when you set the object in a different context in which it seems ugly. What I want to know is what it is that I am saying when I say of it that it is beautiful. I am ascribing to it a property; what is this property that I ascribe?"

"But," you might retort, "there cannot be any definite property that you ascribe to the thing, because you own that you may have to deny of it (if I move it or compare it with something else) the very 'property' that you are now disposed to ascribe to it. Surely it is an odd sort of 'definite property' which is both ascribed to and denied of the same thing. Why not simply admit that beauty is relative?"

"But why should I?" I reply. "Certainly, I cannot claim more for this object than that it is or seems beautiful in this situation; one never can claim more than that for any object, whether it is its beauty or hardness or fitness or whatever it may be that one is speaking of. But when one claims for an object that it 'seems X here and now' one is ascribing to it indeed something that you might call an indefinite property, namely that of seeming-X-here-and-now. But if a thing can have the indefinite property of *seeming to be X under certain circumstances*, then there must be also the definite property *X-hood* that it seems under certain circumstances to have. Let us say by all means that X-hood is never a property of actual things. Things *are* not X; they *seem* to be X under given circumstances. But one can still ask what X-hood as such is, the absolute and definite property of which one is put in mind when one sees an object which seems to be X under the given circumstances. It is beauty as such, the absolute property which things sometimes 'seem' in this way to possess that I want you to define. It does not perturb me in the least that things can both be and not be beautiful. Of course they can; this only means that in one context they exhibit beauty and in another they fail to do so. But it has no tendency to refute the evident truth that *beauty itself* just simply is itself and never seems to be anything but itself. Things are shifting and relative when it comes to classifying them as X or not-X; this does not in the least mean that there is anything shifting or relative about the natures which we ascribe to them in classifying them—which indeed we loosely ascribe to them; for as you rightly point out we ought never to make an unqualified ascription of a nature or property to a thing."

Enough of this dialogue. I hope it is clear that it keeps fairly close to certain passages in Plato's writings; for example to the passage in the seventh book of the *Republic* where he discusses the problem of turning men's minds from "what becomes" to "what is" (*Republic* 523–5; see above, p. 183). It is intended to depict a contrast which was, I am convinced, of great importance to Plato. In some of the dialogues (particularly the *Phaedo* and *Republic*) Plato goes out of his way to make Socrates claim that it is typical of himself and his intimates to "believe in" or "attach importance to" (*nomizein*, cf. *Republic* 476 c) such things as "beauty itself" or "the things which we indicate by the phrase 'the very thing which is X' in our questions and answers" (*Phaedo* 75 d). It is this belief or attitude of mind which forms one side of the contrast I have just referred to. It amounts, I think, to the belief that it is essential, for discourse, to ascribe to things definite properties, and that it is vital, for understanding, to ask what these properties are. That is one side of the contrast. On the other side of the contrast is a more easy-going attitude to the use of words. It derives from the observation that we often find ourselves affirming and denying the same predicate of the same thing, and it supports this, perhaps, on a general Heraclitean denial of fixity in things. If everything is anyhow fluid, and a thing is often just as much P as not-P, why should we expect that there should be something fixed and unchanging called P-hood for which "P" stands? The practice of Socrates and his circle, according to Plato,[1] is to admit the partial truth of this, and to counter by using such phrases as "the very thing which is X" when they debate about the nature of X-hood, in order to make it clear that they are not talking about the nature common to the things which are commonly said to be X, but about the pure form of this nature.

This is of course the contrast between forming concepts counter-inductively and forming them inductively, in the language I have used; and we know that it constitutes the distinction between knowledge and belief. As we have also seen, the man whose concept of, say, justice is inductive uses a set of examples of just behaviour to give himself the meaning of "just". The man whose concept is counter-inductive, on the other hand, does not do that. His practice is to understand the meaning of "just" in terms of a grasp of the nature of justice. For this reason the abstract noun "justice" is more fundamental to him than the adjective "just", and he must take steps

---

[1] And why not also in fact? Why should Plato make Socrates claim this practice if he did not follow it?

to show that he is concerned to talk about justice rather than about just things.

But this is just the difficulty. One naturally takes P-hood to be the features common and peculiar to P things (where this means: "the things that we call P"). But this is just what Plato does not want us to do. He wants P-hood to be an "intelligible" (definite and sense-making) nature which is reflected by P things in so far as they are genuinely P, but which is belied by them in so far as they are not genuinely P. It is, if you like, the common nature of things which are P without qualification; but this does not help because there are no such things, and the adjective derives its meaning, for most of us, from the things that we do in fact use it of; and none of these is P without qualification.[1]

Therefore emphatic linguistic manoeuvres have to be carried out to make it clear that P-hood is not the common nature of standard P things. This was the more important, and the more difficult, for two reasons. One is the normal Greek idiom for abstractions, and the other was a lack of sensitivity to the logical traps which abstract expressions set.

The Greek language did contain abstract nouns, and indeed it contained a termination (analogous to the English "-hood" or "-ness") whereby one could form new ones at need. But for all that it also contained a very common idiom, namely that whereby (as in German) the definite article and the neuter of the adjective is made to do duty for the abstract noun. Thus *to kalon* or "the beautiful" is commonly used in place of *kallos* or "beauty". But *to kalon* can also be used to stand not for beauty but for the class of beautiful objects, or of course for *the* beautiful object. But it is easy to see that this idiom is a positive obstacle to the formulation of the doctrine. For it invites us to assume that to talk about beauty is the same as to talk about the class of beautiful objects, or some standard set of these. No doubt if Plato could have known what his views were before he thought them out he could have avoided this difficulty by avoiding this locution. But this of course is impossible, and we have to think of him[2] doing two things *pari passu*; one of these is to coin uncouth phrases such as "the very thing which is X" to express his meaning, and the other to isolate the thought which these phrases were to express.

This trouble was enhanced, as I say, by the insensitivity, inevitable at this stage, to the logical difficulties involved in handling abstract nouns. This could be illustrated from almost any of the earlier

---

[1] This requires more precise statement. See the discussion of imperfect embodiment below, pp. 284–305.

[2] Or of Socrates.

dialogues. It is clearly to be seen in the *Euthyphro* where in a short compass the word *hosiotês* or "piety" bears three different meanings (what is common to pious men, what is common to pious things, and religion), the oscillation between these three meanings being almost certainly inadvertent.

Another linguistic point (conjectural, but to my mind soundly based) is that there seems to have been a feeling that "is" ought strictly to assert identity—that just as "Scott is the author of *Waverley*" identifies Scott with the author of *Waverley*, so "Scott is bald" ought strictly to identify Scott with "the bald".

It is in the light of these points that we ought to understand the odd phrases which are used about forms "The X itself " and "the very thing which is X" (*auto ho esti . . .*) and even "the real X" (*to on . . .*) all serve, as I have argued, to show that what is being discussed is not the (fluctuating) common nature of X things, but the definite nature which that reflects. Again when X things are said to "resemble" X-hood it is this relation of reflecting-and-belying which is to be conveyed. The same relation is also referred to when things are said to "partake in" or "have a share of " the appropriate form, though I think that this metaphor is also intended to deny identity. Scott cannot strictly be said to be the bald, though he can be said to partake in it. This avoids one particular trouble. If Scott is said both to be and not to be bald (as he may, if he has a few strands), then if it is felt that this identifies him both with baldness and with not-baldness, it will seem to follow that these two predicates are identical with each other (if A=B and A=C, then B=C). This argument might indeed be used to show that baldness is not-baldness, and that therefore there are no definite properties. The participation-metaphor destroys this argument; using it, one says that it is strictly inaccurate to say that Scott is bald, and the strict formulation: "Scott partakes in the bald" does not cause trouble—for he can partake both in the bald and in the not-bald without these being thereby identified. The other common metaphors for the form/particular relationship, namely "presence" and "agency", have a simpler function than "participation". To say that X-hood is present to the X things and is that "through which" they become X is surely as much as to say that it is the discernibility (under appropriate circumstances) of X-hood in an X thing which makes it natural to call it an X thing.

It can be seen I hope from this discussion how this odd language came to be used and how it is to be taken. In particular I hope it can be seen that although these metaphors (similarity, participation, presence and agency) have in a sense different meanings, the use of one rather than another does not indicate a difference of doctrine;

it may indicate a mere desire for variety,[1] or perhaps it may indicate that a common doctrine is being thought of predominantly under a different aspect.

I do not believe therefore that Plato developed from an "immanent" to a "transcendent" conception of forms (nor the other way round), as some have thought. But I will conclude these introductory remarks with an *a priori* reflection upon the possibilities of development in the doctrine. The doctrine started (we thought) under the influence of a belief in a rational order. Such a belief was available for Socrates, let alone Plato, to learn of it from the teachings of Anaxagoras; and without such a background the doctrine of forms hardly seems to make sense. For why should one bother to dispute the "Heraclitean" denial of definite properties except under the influence of such a view? Initially however the thing to do would be to isolate the notion of an X-hood which is not the common nature of standard X things; and this would occupy Plato's energies for some time. But when this work had been accomplished it would become natural to ask further questions. For if forms are not the common natures of physical things, how ought they to be conceived of ? If they are in some sense independent of physical things, what kind of existence should they be supposed to have? How are they related to each other, and in particular is it necessary to postulate a form corresponding to each common feature of physical things; or can some programme of reduction be carried out whereby some can be dispensed with by being exhibited as functions of others? Questions like this would crowd in as soon as there was leisure to entertain them.

B. *The chronology of the theory of forms*

Plato always believed (I think) that nature is a product of rational ordering, and that therefore there is something which is more fundamental than the actual order of nature. This is, of course, the principles of rational order, to which mind looked, in terms of the myth, in ordering the chaos. Of these intelligible principles the actual properties of things are in some way images. All this, I think, was a permanent part of Plato's thought.

However in describing this attitude I have used the vague phrase "principles of rational order" without specifying what a principle of rational order may be. This I have done intentionally, because the truth seems to be that Plato was always more satisfied that there exist such principles, and that all ordering must be done in terms of them, than that any particular account of them is correct. However

---

[1] cp. *Phaedo* 100 d "presence, participation or whatever".

there seems to have been a period in his life during which he was prepared at least to give the impression of holding a fairly detailed account of their nature; and it is to the doctrines of this period that I shall apply the name "theory of forms" or "classical theory of forms".

The classical theory of forms, then, is prominent in the *Cratylus, Phaedo, Symposium, Republic* and *Timaeus*. It is prominent also in the *Phaedrus*, but in this dialogue the passages most characteristic of the theory occur in the myth, and are therefore possibly not to be taken seriously. It is subjected to critical discussion in the *Parmenides*, and so is some version of it in the *Sophist*. The mutual relations of universals or classes are an important topic in the *Phaedrus, Sophist, Statesman*, and *Philebus*; if we assume that whenever Plato talks about universals he means us to interpret his language in terms of the theory of forms, then we shall have to say that the theory is prominent in these four dialogues; but this assumption seems to me more than doubtful. Finally there are passages in the *Theaetetus* and in the *Philebus* in which the reader of the *Republic* is constantly expecting a mention of the forms, and in which his expectation is disappointed.

What then is the classical theory of forms? The essential characteristic of it seems to be the belief that there are such things as the very thing which is X, and that this is so for every value of "X". That is to say, for every "common name" there exists a "common nature". The beautiful, the equal, the large, fire, the bed, the shuttle; for each of these there exists a single form, and it is in the form alone that the common nature fully exists. In so far as the common nature exists also in things, it does so because they "partake" in it, or because it is "present" to them. Furthermore the form is not only the sole pure case of the common nature; it is also *nothing but* the beautiful, or whatever it may be. The beautiful is the only thing which *is* the beautiful (beautiful things *partaking* in it and not *being* it), and it is simply and solely the beautiful and nothing else (whereas every beautiful thing is a good deal else; a statue, perhaps, and made of marble, and so on).

That is what the forms are in terms of the classical theory. Of the forms we are also told that one can come to know them, and that the man who fails to believe in them thereby confines himself to the level of *doxa*. We are told also that they are changeless and self-consistent entities, and can be said to be (*einai*), whereas physical particulars are changeable and not self-consistent, and can only be said to become or happen (*gignesthai*). We are told also that forms are intelligible objects (*nöēta*), and that it is possible to define or give a *logos* of them. To them is applied the counter-inductive principle, that one cannot be sure that a given S is P until one can give the

253

logos of P-hood; the operation of this principle however is modified, as we know, in practice by the *prima facie* conflicting principle that the adequacy of an attempted *logos* can be tested by asking whether the range of application of the *logos* is identical with the range of application of the predicate whose *logos* it is.[1] Finally it is emphasised that whereas there is no blurring of the lines between forms (each being just precisely itself), there is considerable blurring of the lines between the properties of things; the same thing can be both P and not-P by participating in P-hood and in not-P-hood.

I hope that that is a fair account of the theory. We saw above that the dialogues in which it is most prominent are the *Cratylus, Phaedo, Symposium, Republic* and *Timaeus*. Of these five dialogues it would be generally agreed that the *Phaedo, Symposium* and *Republic* belong to Plato's middle period. The *Cratylus* is commonly thought to be rather earlier than this, but its date can easily be disputed. The *Timaeus* again is commonly thought to be considerably later than the *Republic*, though this too can be disputed; or we could dispose of the *Timaeus* by remembering that it is mythical in form and that its treatment of non-cosmological topics is on the whole summary. However that may be, if we neglect the *Cratylus* and *Timaeus* we can say that the classical theory of forms seems to be characteristic of Plato's middle period.

One might hold therefore that Plato inherited from Socrates an interest in definition; that he developed this in middle life into the classical theory of forms; and that after a while he repented of it, giving expression to his repentance in the *Parmenides* and perhaps the *Sophist*. We must ask whether this hypothesis seems satisfactory.

(i) *Early traces of the theory*

(a) *The imputation of it to Socrates.* In the *Phaedo* and the *Republic*, as we have seen, Plato makes Socrates claim that it is typical of himself and of his friends to attach importance to forms. On the other hand Aristotle says[2] that whereas Socrates was interested in defining universals, he left it to Plato to treat them as "separable" things. What exactly this means is not clear. On the whole in Aristotle's language a "separable" thing seems to be a "substance" —something like the Cheshire Cat (as opposed to its smile) which can exist on its own. It seems then that in Aristotle's opinion, presumably got from Plato, Socrates did not treat the forms as "substances". Since Aristotle implies that Plato did so treat them, and since it is very difficult to put a credible interpretation on this charge,

---

[1] We cannot accept as a *logos* of the just a formula which represents unjust acts as just or *vice versa*.

[2] *Metaphysics* M 1078 b 30–2.

one is forced to say that Plato went beyond Socrates in some un-identifiable way. However it is difficult to believe that Socrates was *simply* interested in seeking definitions in a common-sense twentieth-century manner. Undeniably Plato makes him claim that a belief in the existence of forms is a pecularity of himself and his friends; and a belief in the existence of forms, whatever exactly it may be, must at least be more than an enthusiasm for definition. Nor is it easy to see why Plato should have gone out of his way to make Socrates say that the belief was characteristic of his circle unless this were the case. Socrates could have been made to express the belief without claiming it as his trade mark.

It seems then reasonable to attribute to Socrates some kind of belief in forms; a belief, let us say, in the importance of distinguishing properties from the things which manifest them, and in treating the former counter-inductively. To this we may suppose that Plato added the doctrine that the existence of properties is somehow prior to and independent of the existence of instances. On this view then a good part of the theory of forms was to be found in the original deposit of Socratic teaching, and we should expect to find traces of it in Plato's earlier writings. We must now look to see whether there are such traces.

(*b*) *Traces in the earlier dialogues.* There are I think such traces. One possible indication, to which one cannot attach very much significance, is that the counter-inductive principle is commonly assumed in the earlier dialogues: i.e. that one cannot tell whether a given S is P until one knows P-hood. This we can find, for example, in the *Euthyphro* (6 d; cp. *Laches* 190). The counter-inductive principle, however, though part of the theory of forms, is not peculiar to it. As we saw in an earlier chapter,[1] the counter-inductive principle makes sense without the theory of forms in the context of the kind of properties discussed in these dialogues; for these are ethical properties such as courage or piety. In connection with such pro-perties it does make sense to say that we need to know what we (or "the deviser of language"; cp. *Charmides* 175 b 3) are getting at in distinguishing temperance, or whatever it may be, from its opposite, before we can decide what conduct deserves to be called temperate; and we could put this by saying that we need to know first what temperance is.

A more positive indication is the existence in the earlier dialogues of what looks like technical terminology bound up with the theory of forms. I will give three instances of this.

1. The *Lysis* (217–18) goes out of its way to express "the fact that S is P" in the form "the presence of P-hood to S", and to distinguish

[1] Vol. 1, pp. 59–60.

two different ways in which a property may be "present to" a thing (namely temporarily and permanently). The point Socrates wants to make could very easily have been made without using the notion of *parousia* or presence, and it looks very much as if Plato introduced it on purpose in order to point out its ambiguity (such points are commonly made *obiter* in this fashion in the early dialogues). But the notion of the presence of a property to a thing smells strongly of the theory of forms. The natural conclusion therefore is that Plato expected the *Lysis* to be read by people who were accustomed to use the language of the theory, and that he took the opportunity to warn them of an ambiguity.

2. The same impression can be got from the *Hippias Major*. (Some doubt the authenticity of this dialogue, but on grounds which seem to me weak).[1] A good part of this dialogue is taken up by the discussion of possible misunderstandings of the nature of Socratic definition. Socrates tries to make Hippias understand what he means by the question: "What is the beautiful?" First Hippias takes this to be a request for a standard beautiful object, and answers: "A pretty girl." Then (289 d 2) it is made clear to him that what is wanted is "that by which all other things are adorned, so that they seem beautiful when this kind (*eidos*) is present to them". Having got the idea that this is what he is being asked, Hippias solves the riddle at once; that from whose presence everything else draws its beauty is of course gilding! Hippias clearly is being made a fool of here for comic purposes; but the joke depends on the possibility of describing beauty as "that whose presence adorns everything *else*"; it depends in other words on treating beauty as a *thing, by whose agency* other things are beautiful, and the comedy consists in Hippias' gross materialistic interpretation of such language. The joke therefore could not be perpetrated except among those who were accustomed to using the notion of agency metaphorically in speaking of the relation of properties to their instances, and who could feel superior to those who took the metaphor literally. But this surely means people who accepted all or most of the theory of forms.

3. The third instance comes from the *Euthyphro*. In this dialogue as we saw the counter-inductive principle is clearly stated (6 d–e); and indeed strong language is used, for Socrates speaks of "looking away from" (*apoblepein*) particular pious acts towards the form (*idea*) by virtue of which pious acts are pious in order to judge the piety of allegedly pious behaviour. The use of "looking away from" particular instances, rather than, e.g., "looking more carefully at" them seems to me significant. Possibly more significant however is

[1] Chiefly that Aristotle used the phrase "the *Hippias*" to refer to the *Hippias Minor*.

the distinction drawn later in the dialogue (11 a 7) between the *ousia* and a *pathos* of piety. The *ousia* of something is its "essence", and a *pathos* (literally: "something which befalls it") is used for something which may be universally characteristic of it, but which is not part of its essence. This bit of terminology is used here as if its meaning were obvious; but it would only be obvious to readers whose thoughts about the definition of properties were fairly sophisticated. It is also true that the distinction between what is and what is not of the essence of a property could not be drawn on the "Heraclitean" view that there are no fixed properties. People therefore to whom all or most of the classical theory of forms was familiar would be just the people to understand this distinction at once.

It seems to me reasonable to conclude from these indications that Plato expected that some at least of those who read his earlier dialogues would be people who were accustomed to speak of the presence of P-hood to S, and of S being made P by the agency of P-hood, and who would appreciate the drawing of distinctions and the making of jokes concerning such metaphors. But if P-hood by its presence causes S to be P, then P-hood is responsible for the P-hood of S; in other words properties *tout court* are somehow more fundamental than the properties of things. But this distinction between "P-hood itself" and "the P-hood of P things" is the heart of the theory of forms. Let us conclude then, undeterred by Aristotle, that at any rate a large part of the classical theory of forms was inherited by Plato from Socrates. What we might perhaps say, to keep ourselves right with Aristotle, is that Plato hardened into a positive doctrine something which was implicit in Socrates' practice.

(ii) *Did Plato repent of the theory after his middle period?*

The view which we are considering holds that the theory of forms was invented by Plato in his middle period, and that he repented of it subsequently. We have disputed the first half of this proposition; what of the second?

That Plato repented of the theory of forms is a doctrine which rests chiefly on two supports. It rests firstly on the criticisms of something like the classical theory in the *Parmenides* and the *Sophist,* and secondly on the absence of any reference to the theory in places where it might have been expected, especially in the *Theaetetus* and the *Philebus.*

But the doctrine that Plato repented of his belief in forms conflicts with the Aristotelian evidence. Aristotle says nothing of any such change of mind. We gather from Aristotle that Plato never ceased to believe in forms. This is of course compatible with the view that Plato's ideas on these matters developed considerably, but hardly with the view that there was a drastic repentance. The most that Aristotle says about a change of mind is conveyed in the following words (*Metaphysics* 1078 b 9 sqq.): "Concerning the forms (as opposed to the entities involved in mathematics), we must now examine the doctrine of forms on its own. We shall examine it without attaching to it any considerations concerning the nature of numbers, but rather in the form in which the doctrine was originally understood by those who first asserted the existence of forms." It is fairly clear that "those who first asserted . . ." means Plato, and that therefore Aristotle is here implying that there was an earlier version of the theory in which it was not bound up with reflections about numbers, and a later version in which it was. This however is all we learn from Aristotle about earlier and later versions, or changes of mind, and this does not imply that the earlier version was given up, but that it was elaborated. Aristotle believes that he can refute Plato's views on the nature of mathematical entities, and thus destroy the elaborations, but it still remains for him to refute the belief in forms. But this surely means that the belief in forms had not been given up, or Aristotle would not need to refute it. He is carrying out a two-stage refutation: "Plato is wrong about numbers, and anyhow the whole notion of forms is a mistake." The second stage of this would not be necessary if the enemy were no longer in the field.

What then about the two supports on which the belief in repentance rests? The criticisms contained in the *Parmenides* and *Sophist* will require detailed discussion later. Here I will briefly anticipate. First, then, we shall find that the discussion in the *Parmenides* is intended to do two things. It is intended to deny certain doctrines which had at least seemed to be implicit in the classical theory of forms, and it is intended also to show that the classical theory must not be interpreted in certain ways. But it does not amount to an outright attack on the notion of forms. Next, with regard to the discussion in the *Sophist*, it must be conceded that the Eleatic Stranger speaks of forms in a disrespectful manner. He says (246 b 6 sqq.) of those whom he is criticising that "they defend themselves [against the materialists] with great discretion by drawing a defence from somewhere on high, from the invisible realm; they draft certain intelligible and incorporeal forms for the role of genuine being". However it is commonly Plato's custom to make his chief speakers use mocking language for the statement of Platonic doctrine, so that we cannot attach too much weight to the tone of the Stranger's remarks. And apart from that, his chief purpose, as we shall see later, is not to deny that there are forms, but to contend that "to be" does not mean "to be changeless".

The other support of the view that Plato changed his mind was the absence of the forms from places where mention of them might have been expected in the late dialogues, particularly in the *Theaetetus* and *Philebus*. The short answer to this argument is that there were really no good grounds for expecting to find in these dialogues anything but what one does find. The reason for expecting mention of the forms in the *Theaetetus* is that the dialogue discusses knowledge, and that in the *Republic* and elsewhere "knowledge is of the forms". But I hope I have shown in an earlier chapter[1] that "knowledge is of the forms" is an over-simplification, and that Plato in the *Theaetetus* is troubled by certain fairly specific doubts about knowledge which do not involve a rejection of forms. The reason for expecting a discussion of forms in the *Philebus* is that that dialogue divides "that which now is" into four classes, and that some readers assume that the forms will be one of the four classes, and are disappointed to find that they are not. But this as I shall argue later[2] is a mistake. To expect that the forms should appear as one of the four classes in the *Philebus* is to bring the discussion in that dialogue down to too low a logical level, to assume that Plato is distinguishing the formal and the material element *in things*, whereas in fact he is distinguishing the formal and the material element *in universals*.

The position then is as follows. According to the Aristotelian picture Plato always "believed in forms", where this means believing something which Aristotle thought wrong-headed. It must therefore involve more than, for instance, simply believing in universals. Furthermore there is nothing in the dialogues which can be set against this Aristotelian picture. There is evidence of a retreat from some parts of the classical theory of forms, but that is as far as it goes. I think that perhaps the following gives a correct account of the development.

Plato always believed that the organisation and differentiation of the world are the product of intelligence. Or if you prefer to put it less cosmologically, he always believed that the organised and differentiated world is intelligible. This seemed to him to entail that the features of the world are due to the presence in things of certain intelligible natures. But the features of actual things are blurred and indistinct, whereas reason demands clarity, distinctness, and lucidity in its objects. One must therefore distinguish P-hood itself from the P-hood of P things; the P-hood which the mind can grasp cannot be identified with the P-hood which the senses discover in things.

This is I think the continuous theme of Plato's belief in forms. What converts this continuous theme into the classical theory can perhaps be characterised as follows. Firstly Plato's struggles to force the language to give expression to the notion of an abstract entity

---

[1] See above, pp. 128–35.   [2] See below, pp. 423–36.

were not always successful, and he sometimes wrote as if P-hood were itself a concrete thing. This is a misinterpretation against which the *Parmenides* warns us, but it is one of which Plato himself may have been partially guilty at the time of the classical theory.

Then secondly at the time of the classical theory Plato was concerned to emphasise the importance of recognising the existence of forms, and not particularly concerned with their inter-relationships, nor with the question how many intelligible natures it is necessary to postulate. There is a form corresponding to every respect in which things may resemble each other. But this may have come to seem increasingly unplausible, especially perhaps as Plato turned his mind more seriously towards cosmology. If the forms are that to which mind looks in ordering the chaos, then does it make sense to regard bed-hood as a form? Surely that whose "presence" is responsible for the characteristics of good beds is not an independent intelligible nature, but something to do with the fact that there are men and that they need to sleep in a certain position. But the fact that there are men is due to the two facts that there ought to be terrestrial living creatures, and that the given nature of the physical realm imposes certain restrictions upon the designer. Following this line of thought it would seem that there is nothing ultimate about bed-hood; what is ultimate seems to be firstly living-creature-hood, secondly the regular figures and so forth whose imposition upon the given constitutes the terrestrial environment, and thirdly such properties as hardness and flexibility which the designer of a bed tries to blend with each other in order to make an efficient sleeping-machine, and which are dependent upon the shapes of the molecules of the materials he uses. In this way it would seem that the list of ultimate intelligible natures need only contain highly abstract entities, such indeed as are fit to be contemplated by the eternal reason even "before" the world was made. *Pari passu* with this development would go an increasing attention to the inter-relationships between universals. On the whole the picture presented by the classical theory was that whereas particulars are no more than meeting-points of universals, each universal is just simply itself and different from every other. But the attempt to represent comparatively concrete universals as functions of comparatively abstract ones would make this picture seem very misleading. For now it would be necessary to say that some universals are meeting points of others. Just as formerly cows have been cows by partaking in cow-hood, so now cow-hood would be what it is by partaking in animality and in whatever differentiates cows from other animals. Not only would particulars partake in universals; universals would also partake in each other.

Then thirdly I said that it was part of the continuous theme of

Plato's belief in forms that the P-hood which the mind can grasp cannot be identified with the P-hood which the senses detect in things. I say this is part of the continuous theme because it is to be found in late documents, e.g. the *Philebus* (62) and the *Seventh Letter* (342–4; see above pp. 122–6). But I would also say that this seems to me to have become less important to Plato as time went on, and that *emphasis* on it is characteristic of the classical theory. One might conjecture two reasons for this. Firstly, as we have seen,[1] the contrast between the P-hood itself which the mind grasps, and the P-hood which the senses detect in things depends on a misguided contrast between the mind and the senses, one which is much improved upon by the *Theaetetus*. Then secondly the more abstract the forms become, the less there is any temptation to talk of the senses grasping their reflections in things, and the less need to insist that the image must not be mistaken for the original. The properties of things are no longer images of forms, on a one-to-one property-to-form basis. Rather, things owe their properties to the ordering activity of mind, the forms which reason looks to in the work of ordering being of a highly abstract kind.

To sum up I would suggest that there are three points of difference between the classical theory of forms and Plato's later beliefs on the same subjects. Firstly in the classical period there was a tendency at least to seem to treat the forms as things; and in the later period it is clearly seen that this tendency must be resisted. Secondly in the classical period Plato on the whole ignores questions which later seem to him important concerning the number and the inter-relationship of the forms. Thirdly in the classical period there is an emphasis on the difference between "P-hood itself" and the P-hood of P things, this emphasis becoming less important later. Finally I would add that none of these three points of difference seems to me to involve a recantation, unless perhaps Plato recants the principle that forms do not partake in each other (the *Parmenides* perhaps suggests that Plato would at one time have asserted this principle). Apart from this, it is all a matter of tendency and of more and less, of things becoming clearer and of old points losing their importance.

Let this serve as a conjectural account of the place taken by the theory of forms in Plato's development. The classical theory is a primitive phase of a permanent attitude.

C. *Problems about the nature of forms*

The form of, say, beauty is something which is distinct and intelligible, whose presence is responsible for the shifting and relative

[1] Above, pp. 183 sqq., 247 sqq.

beauty of all beautiful things. That is all very well, but what sort of an entity is this? We shall be concerned in this section with the problems, whether real or verbal, to which the attempt to answer this question gives rise.

(i) *The forms as perfect particulars*

It is commonly thought that Plato at the period of the classical theory took forms to be perfect specimens of their own kind. To put this interpretation at its crudest, it amounts to accusing Plato of believing that the form of a bed is itself a perfect bed. There are some phrases and passages in the dialogues on which this very damaging accusation is based, and we must consider the correct interpretation of these in order to assess the validity of the charge. The conclusion that we shall come to is that the charge is slanderous; but I shall ask the reader to treat this conclusion circumspectly, in the following way. At its crudest, the charge is absurd. No sane man could people "the intelligible realm" with perfect beds, perfect equals, perfect elephants and perfect greater-than's. But of course the charge could be made a little less absurd than that by importing the confused but not impossible notion of an absolutely schematic object. I mean this. We are all familiar with schematised mock-ups. One might take a pump and some tubes and some foam rubber to make a mock-up of the human heart, arteries, capillaries and veins, and one might pump some red liquid through this apparatus to demonstrate the "intelligible principles" of the circulation of the blood. Such a mock-up would be "more intelligible" than Jones's cardiovascular system because it would involve only the bare bones of the system. Now however let us try to imagine the schematisation carried several steps further so that we have a *perfectly* schematic object which consists of nothing but its own principles. When it is something like the blood-system, the absurdity of trying to imagine anything of the kind is manifest. It is less manifest if we suppose that we are trying to imagine an object which is simply and only an embodiment of beauty or equality.[1] Take beauty, and suppose that we think that beauty is a matter of proportion. It does not seem absurd to suppose that a man might think that he could imagine an object which was simply and only proportionate in the required ways. But such an object would be a perfectly schematic, perfectly beautiful object, and every beautiful physical object would be an elaboration of it, a body built upon, and obscuring, its skeleton.

Now if the view that Plato took forms to be perfect particulars amounts to the view that he believed in the existence of perfectly

[1] And does not a piece of mathematics consist of almost nothing but its own principles?

schematic objects of this kind, then it seems to me to be mistaken, but not patently absurd. Indeed perhaps to call it positively mistaken is to go just a fraction too far. For as I have already urged Plato was developing the notion of an abstract entity or universal at the same time as he was developing the language for conveying the notion. He was developing it moreover against the resistance of people like Hippias in the *Hippias Major* who were inclined to take for granted that "the beautiful" must mean the, or a, standard beautiful object. More seriously he was developing it against the force of the human propensity (of which he himself warns us in the *Timaeus*)[1] to suppose that whatever exists exists in space, or, in other words, to suppose that to say that something exists is to say that it is extended. In this state of affairs it is plain that he would have found it difficult to convey, even perhaps to himself, the notion of a universal as a totally abstract non-physical entity. For something which is in no sense an extended object (however schematic) would seem to be unreal, a fiction of the mind or something of the like. This would make it natural, certainly for his readers, and possibly for himself, to suppose that the emphasis on the reality of the forms must carry with it an admission that they are extended objects, even though (inconsistently) they have also to be perfectly schematic and their extension must not be in physical space.

I am not prepared to concede that Plato ever thought that "the very thing which is beautiful" was in fact a concrete though non-physical thing. What might however be conceded is that it was necessary for him to struggle in order to keep away from notions of this kind; and the struggle may not always have been wholly successful. With this preface let us turn to consider the phrases and passages which support the perfect particulars interpretation of the forms.

(a) *"The very thing which is P" and related expressions*

Plato certainly sometimes uses of a form the phrase *auto ho esti . . .* or "the thing itself which is . . ."; and such a word as "just" or "shuttle" goes in the place of the dots. Undeniably this is an odd phrase for justice or shuttle-hood. Surely, it may be said, the thing itself or the very thing which is just, beautiful or a shuttle must be an individual. For justice cannot possibly be just, nor can the common nature of shuttles be itself a shuttle. The very thing which is shuttle can only be a pure and quintessential shuttle.

Again there is the passage at the end of the fifth book of the *Republic*[2] where it is said that none of the "multifarious beautifuls" is beautiful without qualification, from which it is natural to draw

---

[1] *Timaeus* 52 b; see footnote to p. 218.
[2] Discussed above, pp. 53–70.

the corollary that there is something which is beautiful without qualification, and that this must be the form. Here too then we seem to get the implication that forms are "self-reflexive"—i.e. that that whose presence makes P things P can itself be said to be P. And again critics argue that the one thing that can plainly never be said to be P is P-hood. Therefore that whose presence makes P things P cannot be the universal P-hood.

On the whole I do not think that very much significance can be attached to phrases such as this. The primary purposes of such language, I believe, is to insist that the forms are definite properties with no blurring of the lines between them. In other words we ought not to interpret "the very thing which is beautiful" as "the very thing which *has* the property beauty", but as "the very thing which *is* the property beauty". Difficulty arises because "is beautiful" is written instead of "is *the* beautiful". Nor is this use of the plain adjective rather than the phrase consisting of the adjective and the definite article at all surprising. Throughout the passage in the *Republic* of which we are speaking there is, we may remember, an ambiguity in the meaning of the phrase *polla kala*. Sometimes as we have seen this phrase is used to refer to the many classes of objects which the plain man will cite in answer to the question: "what is the beautiful?"; and in this use the phrase almost means "many beauties" ("many the beautiful's"). Sometimes on the other hand the reference of the phrase is to the many objects or classes of objects which are beautiful, not considered as so many different beauties or kinds of beauty, but simply as so many different things or sets of things; and in this use the phrase means "many beautiful things".[1] This ambiguity can be quoted as a further instance of the difficulty created by the use of the phrase "the P" for P-hood. Once, no doubt, a man becomes conscious of what he is doing, he will be careful always to say "the P" and never "P" when P-hood is what he means. Before that, however, he is likely not to see the importance of this rule. Perhaps a barbarism might be helpful; bearing in mind the idea that "is" connotes identity (predication being strictly conveyed by the notion of participation) we might render "the very thing which is beautiful" as "that which is identical with beautiful". The state of mind which would fail to see that this is a barbarism in the state of mind I am imputing to Plato.

It is, in fact, far from clear that Plato would at this time have found it odd to say that beauty is beautiful. Ask a plain man whether loyalty is loyal or colour coloured; what, I wonder, is the probability of getting the answer: "Yes"? Independent support for this can be

[1] For discussion of this see above p. 70. See *Republic* 479 a 3 for a fairly clear case of the first meaning of the phrase.

drawn from an argument in the *Protagoras* (330–1) where Socrates argues against Protagoras that "nothing else would be pious if piety (*hosiotês*) itself were not so". No doubt this can be given a good sense ("the disposition to do what the Gods desire is itself desired by the Gods"), but what is significant is that Socrates takes it as *obvious* that piety is pious. This supports the view, not that Plato took the forms to be perfect particulars, but that he felt it to be natural to predicate of an abstract noun the adjective from which it is formed.[1] The reason why it supports that view is that Socrates should not be talking in this place of a form, but of the piety of pious men—in fact, plainly a common quality.

Why precisely is it wrong to say that piety is pious or that colour is coloured? If there is difficulty in finding a lucid answer to this question, then it is easy to believe that Plato might have fallen into this manner of speaking and to discount the significance of the fact that he did so.

(b) *The form of goodness in the* Republic

The things said about goodness in the *Republic* are sometimes held to support the view that universals are perfect particulars. Can a universal, it is asked, create and illuminate other universals? But I hope that I have answered this question by attaching sense to the things said about the status of goodness;[2] and anyhow this argument proves too much. If anything it proves that the form of goodness is God; and then if the other forms are to be perfect particulars on the same basis, they will have to be Gods too—created ones at that.

(c) *The form of beauty in the* Symposium

The things that Socrates says about beauty in the *Symposium* (210–12) argue more powerfully than anything else for the view we are criticising. But in the end they do not argue powerfully enough. What Socrates says (in an after-dinner speech, it might be well to remember) is that a man can be led from love of one beautiful body to love of all beautiful bodies; and from there to a love of beauty or the beautiful (both expressions are used) in behaviour and in knowledge; and from there eventually to the very thing which is beautiful, which is always and in all respects beautiful, and which exists "simple, pure, unmixed, not full of human flesh and colour and other mortal nonsense, which is the beautiful, divine and single (*monöeides*)" (211 e 1–4).

Now, it is argued, this final vision must be of something which

---

[1] This might be helped out, subliminally, by the feeling that one must either say that piety is pious or that it is impious.

[2] See pp. 171–82; and also pp. 558–62 below.

gives aesthetic satisfaction—not beauty, but something beautiful. You cannot contemplate beauty, the universal; you can discover what beauty is, but you cannot love it;[1] and to discover what it is is to solve a problem, but not to do something likely to produce ecstasy and sublimate sexual passion. Or at least such ecstasy as discovery has to offer can be derived from the discovery of anything. Socrates cannot be urging us to seek the *logos* of beauty, he must be promising us the vision of a perfectly beautiful object.

But must he? It would be surely an odd way of putting oneself in train to receive this vision to proceed (as Socrates advises) by generalising one's affections. He says that the initiate must be led "to see that the beauty which exists at one body is the brother of that which exists at another; and that if one must pursue the beautiful which exists at a human form, it would be very unreasonable not to think that the beauty which exists at all bodies is one and the same". This—surely—is a deliberate pun on *eidos* or "form" ("from beauty of form to the form of beauty") and the implication of the pun is that the form is that which is present to all instances. This is not decisive either way, for no doubt the view that forms are schematised particulars can make sense of the "presence" of the form to its particulars. But it does seem to be strongly suggested that we are to become less and less devoted to a single instance in order to become, first, more and more devoted to the whole class, and then to the common quality which unites the whole class, at the last step shedding the "mortal nonsense" and fixing our affections on the common quality in abstraction from all embodiment.

But if this vision of the common quality is the culmination of a process of broadening out, this surely suggests that to see the form of beauty is to see what is common to whatever is beautiful—to grasp a universal, an intellectual and not a mystical achievement. But if this is the end of the journey, is it conceivable that it should produce ecstasy? Not perhaps in us; but the *Symposium* labours to show that Socrates was very different from us; and it is noteworthy that his proposals become unacceptable to the vulgar not at this point, but at the very beginning when he suggests that when we fall in love with one beautiful body we should spread the passion thin by converting it into an equal love of all beautiful bodies. And indeed if to contemplate beauty is to know what beauty is, is it inconceivable that that knowledge should be thought capable of producing ecstasy? Socrates, after all, believes that the man who knows what beauty is will hold the key to a large part of the design of the universe; he will be in a position to contemplate and take delight in the

---

[1] Except in the sense in which "loving beauty" means loving beautiful objects. This sense is not in point here.

harmony and excellence which reason has striven to reproduce in nature; in the course of his discovery he will no doubt have acquired the necessary mathematical techniques which shall enable him to enjoy harmonies in astronomy and elsewhere which are concealed from "those who cannot calculate". It is in comparison with delights such as these that the philosopher of *Republic* 6 despises carnal satisfactions. It seems perfectly credible therefore that what Socrates is telling us is something like this:—When we see a beautiful object, it excites us. It excites us because it stirs in the mind a "memory" of something which belongs to the mind by reason of its "kinship with universal nature",[1] namely a grasp of the nature of beauty. This makes us desire to recapture a full memory of beauty, and for this the single instance before us is very inadequate. For it is only one embodiment of the principles which constitute beauty, and it is an embodiment of much else besides. Therefore we must widen our range of instances, bringing in non-physical instances ("the beautiful in behaviour and in knowledge") as well as physical ones. We must widen the range in order to get as close as possible to the position in which we have before us a set of instances such that nothing but beauty is present to the whole set of them. The last stage of this process of "ostensive definition" is the leap by which we abstract the common quality from its instances, and know it in independence of them. Needless to say we do not naturally respond to the sight of beauty in this way; even the best of us, left to himself, does not understand that this is why it excites him.[2] But we can so respond, and Socrates, taught by the priestess, is urging that we should.

From the fact that this interpretation of the *Symposium* seems perfectly possible, I conclude that this dialogue cannot be invoked in defence of the view that the forms were perfect particulars.

Is there any thing—apart from its intrinsic absurdity—which can be urged against this view? I think that there is at least one very significant passage. It comes in the Tenth Book of the *Republic* (597). Socrates is speaking of the form of a bed. He says that the carpenter does not make "the form, or what we call that which is bed", but a particular bed, which is not that which is really bed (a 2–5). God makes the form, for each class of objects making one only. Why one only? Socrates dismisses the question whether some necessity constrained the divine will (c 1), but he is emphatic that one bed only has been made by God, and that no more ever will be. He gives the reason for this in the following words: "Had he made only two, even,

---

[1] See above, pp. 140 sqq.

[2] cp. *Phaedrus* 250 b 1. The whole passage *Phaedrus* 249–56 supports this interpretation of the *Symposium*.

then another would have appeared such that both of these had the form (*eidos*) of this third, and then it and not they would have been that which is bed." Therefore, desiring to be the maker of the real bed, God made one which is one by nature (d 3).

The significance of this passage is that it uses strong theory-of-forms language ("real beds" and so forth), and indeed perfect-particulars language (God makes that which is bed, and indeed he is said to make a *bed*); and yet the argument hinges on not taking this language at face value. We know, and I am not going to repeat the arguments here, that talk about the reality of forms and the un-reality of their particulars is not to be taken literally; it is also important to see that the talk about God making an archetypal bed is not to be taken seriously either. We shall consider later[1] what is the significance of the fact that in this passage (alone in Plato's works) a form is made by God. Meanwhile we must notice that what is made by him cannot be an archetypal bed, but must be that which is common to whatever beds there be. Suppose God to make two perfect beds or schematised beds; why should there at once arise a third bed whose form they both possessed? If I make two schematised motor engines, does there have to exist (even "laid up in heaven")[2] a schematisation of my two schematisations? But if God or anybody else makes two beds, they have to share a *common nature*, and this *eidos* or structure which they both have to have is "that which is bed". In other words Socrates is here saying, in a somewhat clumsy way, that the form is a universal. That which God made is "one by nature" (*mian phusei* d 3); that is to say Socrates is trying to distinguish that of which there can be more than one from that of which it is logically impossible that there should be more than one, the former of these being instances, and the latter their common nature. We might understand Socrates to be saying: "God could not make the same form twice over, because the form would be that which is common to the two instances, so that they would not be forms"; and this is a *reductio ad absurdum* method of saying that it does not make sense to speak of two cases of the same form; and this implies that the form is a common nature or universal.

Thus we see that a passage whose language lends itself to a perfect-particulars interpretation is in fact inconsistent with such an interpretation. This instance came from a dialogue belonging to the period of the classical theory of forms. We might for the sake of its similarity consider here an argument drawn from a much later dialogue, namely the *Philebus*. In this dialogue (15 a, b), Socrates

[1] p. 354.
[2] Not that I endorse this interpretation of this phrase. See above, p. 138 of Vol. 1.

says that it is a very real problem whether one should believe in unitary forms, and whether, if so, one should suppose that "they are torn to pieces and their unity is destroyed by their existence in manifold particulars (*gignomena*); or whether (what seems absolutely impossible) each form exists entire apart from itself, remaining self-identical and unitary both in the single form and in the many instances".

Now it might be urged that nobody who realised that a form was a universal or common nature could possibly think that there was a real problem about how forms retain their unity throughout their many instances. The principle of individuation of a universal is such that there cannot be any problem about how one and the same universal can be present in many instances; it is only if a form is thought of after the model of a concrete thing that there can seem to be any difficulty. Here therefore we see that Plato, long after the time of the *Republic,* was still unable to escape from the idea that a form is a particular.

It will be argued later[1] that Plato has in mind in this passage not only the relation of a form to its particulars, but also the relation of a more generic form to its more specific versions. However he is also thinking of the relation of a form to its particulars, and he does seem to make heavy weather ("what seems to be absolutely impossible"—this is not of course a rejection of this alternative, but a comment on the strangeness of the truth) over the possibility that the form retains its unity throughout its particulars.

But would it not be better to say that Plato is quite clear what he means; he means that we have to postulate entities such that the truth about them *seems* absolutely impossible, this appearance being due to the fact that we all wrongly tend to represent these entities to ourselves as concrete things? Is he not, in other words, once again making use of a clumsy way (*verbally* clumsy at any rate) of making it clear that he is talking about universals? "The entities I am talking about," we might suppose him to be saying, "are entities such that the same one can exist in innumerable physical things." But if one asks what entities these are, the answer at once is that they are common natures or universals. What he lacks, then, is not a clear grasp of his own meaning, but a terminology in which to express it. And this is not altogether an impoverishment, as a matter of fact, because it keeps him alive to the fact that in using, as we have to use, a "thing-based" vocabulary in order to talk about universals we inevitably dig for ourselves logical pits. Aristotle had technical words for "universal" and "particular", and his talk about them is thereby blander than Plato's. But it is really no clearer what

[1] Below, pp. 364 sqq.

269

Aristotle meant by *katholou* ("universal") than what Plato meant by his more uncouth expressions—but unfortunately it *seems* clearer.

The conclusion then of this discussion is that the forms were not perfect schematised particulars, they were universals or common natures. Or, to put it more precisely, the concept of a universal was the concept that Plato was trying to isolate and give expression to when he wrote about forms.

Note on the Aristotelian evidence. It must be conceded that Aristotle sometimes treats Platonic forms as some kind of particulars. There is, for example, the passage in *Metaphysics* B 997 b 5–12 where he says: "The worst absurdity is the view that there exist certain things additional to those in the physical universe, the former being the same as the latter except that the former are eternal while the latter are perishable. There exists, they say, just like that, such a thing as man itself, horse itself, health itself. This is on all fours with those who say that there are gods, only they are in human form—which doctrine simply adds up to believing in eternal men, and the doctrine of forms likewise simply adds up to believing in eternal physical things." But there are also places (e.g. *Metaphysics* Z ch. 14, *Nicomachean Ethics* 1, ch. 6) where Aristotle makes it perfectly clear that talking about Platonic forms and talking about universals or common natures are at the very least concerned with the same kind of topic. When Aristotle is castigating "them" we seldom know whether he has Plato himself in mind or whether he is primarily attacking other Platonists; and it is perfectly possible to suppose that he did not mean to include Plato among the believers in eternal physical things. It is after all quite likely that Plato's opinions hardened into an orthodoxy among his disciples, and got coarsened in the process. But if we do not allow ourselves to make use of this loophole, there are two ways in which we can reconcile the evidence that forms were, in Aristotle's view, particulars with the evidence that they were, also in his view, universals. We can say firstly that Aristotle realised that what Plato was *trying* to do was to arrive at the notion of a universal or common nature (and that this is why Aristotle treats Platonic forms as if they belonged to the same stable as Aristotelian universals), but that at the same time it was plain to Aristotle that what Plato did in fact believe in was a kind of entity for which "eternal physical things" would be an apt description; and these would have to be particulars of some kind. Alternatively we can say that Aristotle was well aware that Plato did not think that the form of man was a sort of divinised eternal man (nor the form of health a sort of divinised eternal what?), but that he thought that this was what Plato *ought* to have thought, and that the reason why Plato ought to have thought this was that Plato made the forms independent of their instances; for that which can exist on its own is, for Aristotle, an individual. It will be plain that I should prefer this second way of treating the problem; in other words I hold that when Aristotle says (in effect): "They make humanity into a superman", what he is really saying (on the assumption that "they" includes Plato) is: "The things they say about humanity (viz. that it is ontologically prior to human beings) must lead to the conclusion that it is a kind of superman; for what can 'man itself' denote except either that which is common to men (which must be ontologically dependent on their existence) or else a transcendent man?". It may be objected that to argue thus is to make Aristotle into a somewhat careless and captious critic. It must be replied that we are often captious critics of ideas from which we are only recently emancipated, and that there is positive evidence that Aristotle was sometimes a careless and captious critic of Plato. Two examples of carelessness may be worth citing. (1) In *Metaphysics* E 1026 b 14 sqq. Aristotle commends Plato's statement in the *Sophist* that sophists deal in not-being without giving the reader any warning that what he himself means by the formula: "Sophists deal in not-being" is something very different from what Plato had meant by it. One gets the impression that he has, at the moment, little recollection what the *Sophist* is about. (2) In *Metaphysics* L ch. 6 and elsewhere he seems to complain that in Plato's cosmology the forms were supposed to set the world in motion, and he points out that they cannot do so; Aristotle's God, he seems to say, is a more efficacious prime mover than Plato's forms. But it is very difficult to see how he could have thought such criticisms apposite if he had reflected for a moment on the *Timaeus* or on the Tenth Book of the *Laws*. It must, I think, be allowed that Aristotle is often careless in what he says about Plato, and also that he seems to feel the need to stress, to the point of exaggeration, the differences between himself and his one-time master. Psychologically this is surely entirely credible. In view of this, and in view of (for example) what the *Parmenides* has to say about treating the form of knowledge as a kind of super-knowledge, I find it impossible to take without a pinch of salt the passages where Aristotle seems to tell us that the forms were eternal physical things. Doubtless they often became that in domestic discussions within the Academy, but it is not what Plato meant them to be.

(ii) *Problems concerning the relations between the forms and the properties of things*

(a) *Introductory discussion*

The classical theory of forms consists, more or less, of an attempt to convey to the reader an enthusiastic faith in two related doctrines. The first of these is an ontological doctrine, and it holds that if the world is intelligible, then the important features of the things which exist in it are, or conform to, intelligible natures, which the mind can grasp in themselves, in abstraction from the things which embody them, being as it were abstract recipes in conformity with which the things in the world are made. Beauty, equality, straightness are instances of such intelligible natures. The second and related doctrine is an epistemological or perhaps a pedagogical one, and it holds that it is impossible to acquire a grasp of these intelligible natures by direct, "inductive", observation of things. It is important to notice at this point that there is a gap between these two doctrines, which may be indicated by the question: what is the relationship between the P-hood of P things on the one hand and the form of P-hood on the other? We know that we cannot acquire a grasp of P-hood from observation of P things (the counter-inductive stipulation) but it does not strictly follow from this that we must draw a distinction between the P-hood of P things and P-hood itself. Helen's beauty might be a perfect case or instance or part of true beauty although it was impossible to acquire an abstract grasp of the nature of beauty from the observation of Helen and her sisters. Rather

271

similarly it may be as a matter of fact impossible to acquire a grasp of the principles on which a code is constructed from direct observation of messages written in the code, despite the fact that the latter perfectly embody the former. There are questions therefore about the relationships between the form of P-hood and the common property of P things (are these identical? or is one of them an "image" of the other?) which we shall have to consider in this section. This is a very tangled topic, and we may well come to the conclusion that these were questions which Plato never clearly answered—perhaps never clearly posed.

The forms are archetypes in the sense that anything which is well-ordered is ordered in conformity with one or more forms. Everybody knows indeed that the Platonic forms were archetypes, but there are difficulties in the notion of an archetype which are not always correctly dealt with.

Some people argue, for example, that because Plato conceived of the forms as archetypes or models he must have conceived of them as perfect particulars. In the sphere of beauty, for example, according to this argument, the ultimate fact must be the existence of a perfectly beautiful object. Beauty, the universal, will be a property perfectly possessed by this object only. The beauty of ordinary beautiful things will be the fact that they conform, to some extent, to this perfectly beautiful object. First comes the perfect exemplar, then the perfect property, which characterises the perfect exemplar only, and then finally the imperfect property which consists in the possession of a certain similarity to the perfect exemplar.

The conclusive argument, as we have seen, against this conception is that it must be on this view a mere matter of contingent fact that there exists *only one* perfect exemplar for each class of objects. If (as is surely clear) the form is conceived of as *essentially* singular, then it must be conceived of as a property, and the perfect exemplifications of it (if any) must be logically subordinate and not superordinate. However our immediate business is not to refute this interpretation, but to show that it is not inextricably bound up with the family of ideas for which the word "archetype" stands. To do this consider a new model of car, say the Armstrong Royce 650. Now it might be the case that there existed in the factory one original vehicle made with scrupulous care to the strictest specifications, not to be sold but to serve as the model to which all subsequent 650's were to conform. These latter, being mass-produced, might all be inferior to the original model, and the 650-hood of the 650 in the street might consist in approximate conformity to the perfect 650 laid up in Coventry. The latter would be the archetype and the rest its progeny.

This is perhaps the natural way of using the notion of a *paradeigma*, paradigm or archetype. But it is not the only possible way. For the perfect 650 laid up in Coventry embodies (perfectly, as it happens) a certain design, a certain complex theory of how to make a motorcar; and this design is something which might be called an archetype.

No doubt there may be objections to the suggestion that a design can be called an archetype. To overcome these I want to look briefly at two passages in which makers of objects are said to "look towards the forms".

(b) *Excursus on forms and craftsmen*

One of these passages is in the Tenth Book of the *Republic* (596–602), and the other is in the *Cratylus* (389). In the passage in the *Republic* the carpenter is said to make beds and tables looking towards the form, in contrast with the painter who looks towards the craftsman's product to make his imitation. Superficially the contrast between the carpenter and the painter does suggest no doubt that a painting stands to a physical object as a physical object stands to its form, and we might perhaps be inclined to take this seriously if we thought it at all plausible to say that carpenters contemplate perfect celestial specimens before getting out their tools. This is not plausible however, and I hope that the discussion of this passage in an earlier chapter[1] has made it clear that there is a close connection between that to which the carpenter looks and that which a bed is for, or more strictly those features which a bed ought to have in order to fulfil its function. Similarly in the *Cratylus* what the carpenter is said to look towards is "that which is naturally fitted" to do the work of the object that he is making (389 a 7–8); and this phrase means, I think, that the carpenter asks himself what the object has to be like to do its job, his problem being, as Socrates goes on to say, to "put the shuttle, which is naturally fitted for a given kind of weaving, into wood". Here the "shuttle" which has to be put into wood is clearly a design or kind of shuttle demanded by a particular job, and the point is that the carpenter has to use his skill to construct in his material a functionally efficient object. In both places the suggestion is that what is true of carpenters with respect to beds and shuttles is true also of any other kind of making, whether by man or by nature, so that we seem to have in these passages a general conception of the nature of forms (many or all of them) according to which the form of a P object is something like the specification which the client gives to the architect—that which is determined by the function of P things, and which the expert has to work out in terms of his knowledge of materials. What this would mean in terms of such forms as

[1] See above, p. 86 sqq.

273

beauty or equality I do not know; but it is obviously consistent with the notion that the forms are that by which reason is guided in producing order out of chaos. Also, in connection with our present discussion, it seems clear that that towards which the carpenter looks would naturally be called a paradigm or archetype, and that this is in fact something such as a design, something of an abstract, universal kind.

(c) *Resumption of introductory discussion*

It seems then that an archetype (as Plato employed notions belonging to this family) need not be a concrete exemplar; it can be something abstract or universal such as a design. But here we meet another objection: "A design," it will be said, "is something immanent. The design of my car is of course on a logically different level from my car itself, but the relation between them is not one of transcendence but of being embodied. The car embodies the design and so does every other car of the same design. The design indeed is no more than the features common to all cars of the same kind. But there is surely abundant evidence that the Platonic form transcends its particulars (at any rate at some periods in his life), and that it is by no means identical with their common features."

It is just here that we need to be extremely cautious. Sir David Ross has carefully catalogued and discussed those passages which seem to imply "immanence" and those which seem to imply "transcendence" (see his *Plato's Theory of Ideas, circa* p. 229). I do not propose to do this over again; but it is necessary not only to look at the texts, but also to consider *a priori* what kinds of "immanence" and "transcendence" Plato might possibly have believed in.

Let us begin by taking the first conception of the archetype as a concrete model. Here the archetype is *comparable* to its progeny. It might be said to be "present to" or "in" its progeny in the sense in which a parent can be "seen in" the features or bearing of a child, and this provides a, perhaps rather strained, notion of immanence. If moreover the archetype is in fact superior to its progeny, then it will transcend them in that way; and no doubt, if we can stomach the idea of a non-physical exemplar of something physical, it might also transcend its progeny simply by being non-physical, eternal, not subject to change and decay, and so forth. Again it would obviously *resemble* its progeny in a straightforward sense.

Turning now to the second conception of an archetype as an abstract design we can find a very natural sense for its presence in its progeny in the fact that a design is embodied in the things made in accordance with it. With regard to transcendence the position is a little more complicated. I have argued above[1] that it is not unnatural (though doubtless incorrect) to speak of an artefact resembling its design. Again a design is of course on a different logical level from a thing, and it is possible that language attributing some sort of superiority to the form might be employed to make this point. It is more serious for a cook to lose a recipe than a cake; given the recipe one can always make another cake, and in that sense the recipe is more valuable. It may be protested however that the Platonic form is superior not only in this sense; it is also the general impression that the form of P is the only pure case of P-hood; to what extent can this be fitted into the conception of a form as a design? Obviously the form of P cannot be more P than an ordinary P thing—the design of a car cannot be more of a car than your car or mine; since equality cannot be equal it cannot be more or less equal than any pair of things. However there may be something that we can do about this. Assuming that the texts support the general impression that the form of P is more P than ordinary P things, then while it is true that we cannot compare in point of P-hood the class of P things with P-hood itself, none the less it might be possible to compare the P-hood of P things with "true P-hood" and to say that the former falls short of the latter. The design of a car may be regarded as a stipulation that the cars built to the design shall have certain properties; and the cars which result may or may not have precisely these properties. If they fail to do so, there will be a discrepancy between the properties which the cars actually have and those which it was intended that they should have. If we speak of the actual common features of a batch of cars as their actual design, it may be that their actual design falls short of their intended design, or in other words of the rational plan which the designer meant them to embody. Since the discrepancy will be due to inaccuracy it is likely that in speaking of actual common features we are speaking of something indeterminate. It is unlikely that all the cars will depart from the design in precisely the same way; this cam-shaft will be over the true size and that one under, and so on. The actual design therefore will be a shifting matter of more or less whereas the intended design will be single and precise. It seems therefore that we can think of the form as something abstract and yet talk meaningfully of particulars falling short of the form.

Nevertheless there remain some difficulties, or at least logical traps, and if we suppose that the Platonic form was something like an "intended design", we ought to expect that these should have given trouble. This is especially so if we accept the view, for which I have argued, that it was necessary for Plato to create the distinction between a universal or property and a class—to disentangle P-hood

[1] See p. 54.

and the class of P things from within the meaning of the phrase "the P".

Take for example beauty and the class of beautiful things. As we have seen every beautiful object is in some respect not beautiful, and therefore what is common to the class of beautiful objects seems to be: that they are in some respects beautiful and in some respects not beautiful. But the property beauty ought to be identical with what is common to the class of beautiful objects. But "beauty" means "being beautiful"—not "being in some respects beautiful and in some respects not". Therefore the property does not seem to be identical with the common features of the objects which have the property. Thus we get a dilemma. On the one hand, what is beauty if it is not the property common to beautiful objects? On the other hand, if it is this, then beauty includes not being beautiful. Either a property can be pure, in which case it belongs to nothing, or it can belong to things at the cost of including its own contradictory. We can try to get out of this dilemma by postulating a pure property which cannot be exhibited by things, but which can be grasped by the mind, but this will be an uncomfortable solution. If this pure property is a property then it must be logically possible for things of some kind to embody it perfectly, so that the conception of a pure property might seem to carry with it the conception of perfect and therefore perhaps non-physical particulars in which the property could be perfectly embodied.

It seems possible therefore that we might get the following situation. First there is the pure property—true equality, say, which simply consists in being equal. Next there is the class of perfect particulars, members of which can be equal to each other and in no way not equal. Then next there is the impure equality which is the property common to equal physical objects, and then finally there is the class of equal physical objects, specimens of this class which are equal to each other being also in some respects unequal to each other, so that the property common to the members of this class is an equality which admits of inequality. We might call the four classes of objects listed in this paragraph respectively the form, its perfect particulars, the vulgar universal, and finally the physical particulars. It is sometimes held that Plato believed in the existence of all four items in this list; that is, that he thought it important to distinguish the form from the vulgar universal in every case, and to attribute existence to each of these and to their associated particulars. Before we consider how good the evidence is for this view we might pause to ask ourselves what it is to "believe in the existence of " something such as forms or vulgar universals.

There is a sense in which universals *obviously* exist. It is plainly true, for example, that there is such a colour as redness; and redness is a universal. To "believe in the existence of universals" therefore in the sense in which such a belief is controversial is to go further than this. What exactly it is would no doubt be hard to say. Perhaps for our purposes it will do to say that if we conclude (for example) that Plato "believed in the existence" of equality both as a vulgar universal and as a form, that is to be taken to mean that he believed that in any metaphysically accurate analysis of equal objects it would be necessary to mention not only the pure property of equality which they fell short of but also the impure property which they embodied. Whereas the nominalist would hold that an accurate account of equal objects will mention only these, and would explain the role of abstract expressions such as "equality" in relation only to these, the "believer in universals" would hold that mention of the general property is at least as necessary to a metaphysically accurate account as mention of the similar particulars. To assert controversially that so-and-so exists is to assert that mention of so-and-so is necessary to an ultimate account of some matter; for the sake of a phrase we might say that the philosopher who controversially asserts the existence of something "demands an exalted status" for that thing. Whereas therefore we must all admit that there are such things as universal properties, realists differ from nominalists by demanding for these an exalted status. The question therefore: "Did Plato believe in the existence of . . . ?" can be construed: "Did Plato demand an exalted status for . . . ?"

To recapitulate this discussion, the point which we have arrived at is this. We have rejected the view that forms are unique particulars of which ordinary particulars are inferior copies (or at any rate copies). We insisted that forms were meant to be universal properties. We have suggested however that it may possibly be the case that forms are to be conceived of as *pure* properties, and that for that reason the actual properties of things, being in fact impure, are not to be identified with forms. If that is so it is possible, we have further suggested, that we may have to reckon with two sets of particulars—non-empirical particulars capable of exemplifying the pure properties or forms, and empirical particulars whose common features constitute the impure properties or vulgar universals. We have therefore the following questions: Did Plato believe in the existence of pure properties? of perfect particulars? of vulgar universals? of ordinary particulars? Cutting across these questions and offering us pointers towards the answering of them we have the further question: Did Plato think that ordinary particulars cannot embody the forms? When he speaks of ordinary things somehow falling short of the forms is it this that he has in mind?

(d) *Forms and vulgar universals*

I shall begin with the question whether Plato demanded an exalted status for vulgar universals.

Since he certainly demanded an exalted status for forms, if "forms" and "vulgar universals" were synonymous, we could answer this question affirmatively at once. Vulgar universals, it will be remembered, are the common features of actual things. For these to be identical with forms two things would have to be the case. Firstly there would have to be a form for every respect in which things can or do resemble each other (for every such respect is certainly a universal). If this condition was not fulfilled, then although some vulgar universals would be forms, others would not be, and the expressions would not be synonymous. The second condition which must be fulfilled if the two expressions are to be synonymous is of course that the forms should be perfectly embodied in the features of things.

This second condition, however, should be amplified. Let us consider once more Helen and her beauty. Now there are certain respects, as we know, in which we shall have to admit that Helen is not beautiful. Therefore a man who believes that "Helen is the beautiful"[1] believes something very misleading; for there are aspects of Helen which have nothing to do with "the beautiful". One cannot form concepts inductively—we have said all this before. But we do not have to say, just because of this, that there is anything wrong with *Helen's beauty*. There is something wrong with *Helen* if she is used as an ostensive definition of beauty, but we could say that this is because her beauty rubs shoulders with plainness. *She herself* in the concrete is not an embodiment of beauty, but *her beauty* is beauty none the less. In so far as she is beautiful, the property which characterises her is simply beauty. She is an inadequate embodiment, because she is characterised by other properties as well, because her beauty is fleeting, and so on; but all the same, in the respects in which she is beautiful, beautiful is what she is.

Now if it is said that physical particulars do not perfectly embody the forms, and if this is to be understood in the sense of the previous paragraph, then it will not follow from this that forms are to be distinguished from vulgar universals. For this to follow, the doctrine of imperfect embodiment must be taken further. It must involve the doctrine that Helen's *beauty* is not true beauty. The sagacity of an animal, it might be said, is not identical with human sagacity. Behaviour which stands to the general level of animal behaviour in the

---

[1] See *Hippias Major* 287 e. Hippias in fact gives the type—a beautiful girl—rather than the token—Helen—in answer to Socrates' question.

relationship, in which sagacious human behaviour stands to the normal, will be held to manifest animal sagacity. This makes the sagacity of animals analogous to, but not identical with, the sagacity of humans. A doctrine to the effect that Helen's beauty was, in something like this manner, analogous to but not identical with true beauty (and so on for the other properties of physical things) would entail the consequence that forms are to be distinguished from vulgar universals. We might speak of the doctrine outlined in the previous paragraph as the doctrine that forms are imperfectly embodied by things, and of the doctrine outlined in this paragraph as the doctrine that forms are imperfectly embodied in the properties of things. We need the latter doctrine if we are to drive a wedge between forms and vulgar universals.

Our question is: Did Plato demand an exalted status for vulgar universals? We saw that this question would only arise if the class of vulgar universals was different from the class of forms. We saw also that this might happen in either of two ways. The class of vulgar universals might be more numerous than the class of forms, so that we might reasonably ask whether Plato demanded an exalted status for these vulgar universals which are not also forms. Or it might be the case that Plato held the doctrine that forms are imperfectly embodied in the properties of things, in which case we could reasonably ask whether he demanded an exalted status for any vulgar universals whatever. This shows that our question can reasonably be asked. In attempting to answer it in this section I shall leave aside the question whether Plato maintained any doctrine of imperfect embodiment, and, if so, which. I shall ask whether the arguments which Plato advances for the existence of forms are arguments designed to claim an exalted status for common properties as such.

Historically speaking there are two different levels on which realism, or the belief in an exalted status for universals, has been defended—the cosmological and the logical. Thus on the cosmological level the realists in the Middle Ages[1] wanted to maintain a thesis about the role of the divine reason in creation, namely that God creates individual things in accordance with antecedently existing intelligible natures or "Divine Ideas"; and this the nominalists challenged in the interests of the divine freedom. It was because it was concerned with the relative importance of the divine understanding and the divine will that the medieval controversy had such vigorous life. But alongside cosmological considerations such as this, the controversy has also made use of arguments drawn from the level of pure logic (i.e. formal, though fallacious, arguments). Thus the realist is inclined to say that if A, B and C are alike in being, say,

---

[1] I owe this point to Dr. T. M. Parker.

red, then the redness in point of which they resemble each other *must* be something real. To this of course the nominalist retorts that the truth of the matter is simply that "red" is a word which can be used of any of an indefinitely large range of objects. Now if the argument is conducted on the cosmological level, the realist must attribute an exalted status to *some* universals, namely the intelligible natures in accordance with which creation is carried out. But I do not see why, so long as he remains on the cosmological level, the realist must demand a like status for *every single* common nature. It is when he buttresses the cosmological arguments with arguments of a purely logical kind that he incurs this consequence. "If A, B and C are alike in being P, then P-hood must be a real entity" retains what validity it has whatever P may be.

We could perhaps put it like this. If A and B are madeira cakes, then they will be in many respects alike. They will be alike because they are both baked to the same recipe, which will therefore be in a significant sense the cause of the similarities which hold between them,[1] and in this way the recipe has a superior ontological status with respect to the cakes. But there is no reason why any special status should be claimed for the consequential similarities, of taste, say, and colour, which hold between the two products. This example will perhaps show how it can be reasonable to claim an exalted status for some abstract entities but not for others. It is only if the claim for exalted status rests upon purely logical considerations that this becomes unreasonable.

It follows from these reflections that if Plato allowed force to the purely formal argument for realism, then he would have to demand an exalted status for vulgar universals as such; and that means that he ought (though of course he might fail to recognise this) to allow such a status to every single similarity between things. We will ask therefore whether there is any evidence that Plato did allow force to the purely formal argument for realism; and one of the questions we shall ask to help us decide this question is whether there is any evidence that he was prepared to assert that every single similarity is a real independent entity.

We may begin by noticing that in the *Timaeus* (51 c) he shows that he is aware of the possibility of a nominalist analysis. Timaeus is offering a confessedly summary argument for the existence of forms. He asks: "Are there such things as fire itself . . . and the other realities, each 'itself according to itself' as we say, or are sensible objects the only things to have this kind of truth? Is there nothing beside them, the belief in intelligible forms being an error, and forms

---

[1] We gather from Aristotle (e.g. *Eth. Nic.* 1096 b 25) that the forms were invoked to explain similarities.

nothing but speech (*logos*)?" Here he seems to say that unless there are forms, then nothing exists but particulars, and such things as fieriness and squareness are just "words"—a nominalist thesis. And it is interesting to see that he does not argue that this nominalist thesis is untenable on the logical level. What he says is that if there were no such things as forms there would be no such thing as knowledge as opposed to true belief, because knowledge requires the existence of intelligible kinds (*eidê*). To deny the existence of forms is to deny that we can apprehend intelligibles; the existence of forms is required by the existence of reason. This is much more like an argument for realism on the cosmological level. What it seems to say is that there must of course be forms, or there would be nothing for the intellect to know; with regard to the common natures of physical things it implies no more than that things are alike because the world has been rationally ordered. On the logical level the possibility of a nominalist analysis is at least not disputed.

There are certainly a number of places where the purely formal argument for realism seems to be deployed. In the *Parmenides* (132 a) Parmenides suggests to Socrates that he believes in forms because when he sees many things which share the same characteristic he argues that there must be one and the same form in all of them, and Socrates agrees to this.[1] But it is to be noticed firstly that Socrates evidently does not consistently concede force to this line of argument, for he has just expressed doubts as to whether there are forms of men, fire and water, not to mention hair, mud and dirt. Yet men at least are similar objects. It is to be noticed also that Parmenides puts this line of thought into Socrates' head in the course of getting him into difficulty. The suggestion is almost that Socrates should not have agreed that these were his reasons for believing in forms, and that in fact they were not.

Are there any places where Plato says that there exists a form corresponding to every similarity between things? We agreed that if there were this would show that Plato allowed force to the purely formal argument for realism. We must certainly admit that this was said by the Platonists, for Aristotle speaks of "the argument from the one over many" as a bad argument for the existence of forms.[2] Since he says of it that it would require the existence of forms even of negations, it is fairly obvious that the one-over-many argument must have been the argument that where several things are alike in any respect, there there must be a form to constitute the resemblance —i.e. the purely formal argument for realism. But Aristotle does not

[1] The *Parmenides* of course does not belong to the period of the classical theory, but it may be that the arguments of Socrates are supposed to represent it.
[2] *Metaphysics* 990 b.

tell us whether this argument was used by Plato himself, nor how important it was thought by whoever used it. It may have been one of those superficially clinching arguments which a philosopher is sometimes tempted to throw in for good measure, thereby spoiling his case.

It is certainly possible to find in Plato phrases which seem to suggest the argument from the one over many. Thus in the *Republic* (596 a), where Socrates is beginning the discussion of beds and bed-hood from which we have already quoted, he proposes to "follow our usual procedure and postulate a single form for each set of particulars of which we use the same name (*onoma*)". Wherever, in fact, there is a common name, there there is a common nature, and this is a form. But is this clinching? It depends surely on what would count as "using the same name" of a set of particulars. *Onoma* is certainly the standard word for a word, but it is possible to suppose that Plato had in mind only "classificatory names" such as "bed" and "table". In that case the "usual procedure" might be to suppose that where language distinguishes two different sets of things by classifying them under different heads, there there is an essential difference of structure between them and therefore a form corresponding to each.[1]

There is however just a little further on an argument which seems to invoke the "one over many", and this is Socrates' argument, recently quoted, to explain what would have happened had God made two forms of the bed. This, he says, would have generated a third. But why? Surely because they would have shared a common nature, and this would have been the form. This seems to involve the principle: "If A resembles B, their similarity is a form." We are of course dealing with a *reductio ad absurdum* argument, and strange things can happen when one extracts consequences from an absurdity; but probably we ought to concede that this is a place where Plato uses the purely formal argument for realism.

We saw that Socrates' position in the *Parmenides* was that forms are such that it makes sense to ask: "Is there a form of X?", where X is a respect in which things are alike. The implication of this of course is that not all universals are forms. It is not so clear, as we see, that this is the position of the *Republic*, but it is still arguable that this is the position that Plato *meant* to take up even in that dialogue. After all, if we put it the other way round, is it clear that *every* universal (being a poached egg, for example) is a form in the *Republic*, to be grasped in the light of goodness and all the rest of it?

It is perhaps legitimate at this stage to invoke antecedent proba-

[1] See *Sophist* 244 (discussed below, pp. 391–4) for a case where *onoma* means rather more than "word".

bility. If my account of Plato's main preoccupations is at all on the right lines, then we can see that he would have no reason to demand a special status for any universals except those which play a part in the rational order. But to persuade his readers to allow a special status to these universals he would have to overcome their reluctance to believe in the real existence of abstract entities. In zeal for this purpose he might be led to use arguments whose effect is to attribute a special status to all universals—and indeed he might find such arguments conclusive. He might therefore commit himself to the purely formal version of realism without truly intending to do so. That it was not his main purpose to do so may perhaps be supported by noticing an odd point. This is concerned with the examples which Plato tends to give when he is talking about forms. In any modern discussion of the existence of universals we are almost certain to encounter universals of colour—they are the stock examples. Plato, I think, has nowhere anything to say about "the red" or "the green". Similarity, straightness, equality, justice, beauty, the bed and the table are the kind of examples which he tends to use. In itself of course this proves nothing, but it is surely significant that the kind of forms which Plato mentions most often are not the most obvious of common characteristics (similarity for example is much more *récherché* than greenness), but that they are precisely the "intelligible natures" which would have some bearing on the cosmological activity of reason as it was described in the last chapter.

"But," it may be said, "what about such passages as *Republic* 5 475 e–476 a? Your thesis is that in Plato's primary purpose the status of forms is claimed only for the intelligible natures involved in the creation of order, and that if other universals get promoted along with them they get promoted almost through inadvertence. But in this passage the ugly, the unjust and the evil are specifically put on all fours with the beautiful, the just and the good. Nor is this a place where Plato is simply talking about universals without reference to their ontological status; on the contrary it is at the beginning of the passage in which he correlates knowledge with the forms."

I have reservations over my opponent's statement that Plato in this passage "correlates knowledge with the forms",[1] but I must concede that in this passage the ugly, the unjust and the evil get near to receiving the treatment due to forms. But I am not perturbed by this. After all the logical principle of non-vacuous contrast would almost require that in one way at least the ugly should have the same status as the beautiful. To know what a straight line is is also to know what a curved line is; if reason can deliberately impose the harmony which constitutes beauty, then it knows what proportions

[1] See above, pp. 53–70, for my account of this passage.

283

to avoid. In other words if beauty is an object of reason, then ugliness is so also.

This may seem evasive, but I hope that it will not seem so if I recapitulate my main point. This is that there is no evidence that Plato was primarily anxious to claim a special status for common characteristics *as such*. I concede that he used arguments which should have this consequence, that he used language that suggests it, but I do not believe that he would ever have postulated a form to correspond, say, to the common deformity of every letter *e* struck by my typewriter. On the other hand concern with the question whether to postulate a form for this or that does not seem to have arisen until after the period of the classical theory[1] and I do not therefore want to maintain the contrary of the thesis above; that is I do not want to say specifically that Plato would at this time have *denied* a special status to what we might call bye-product or consequential common characteristics. The truth probably is that he had not yet asked himself precisely what he meant by "common name" in the formula "to every common name there corresponds a common nature". The conclusion therefore is that the classical theory of forms does not primarily and explicitly claim a special status for every universal property. It is at least left open that the class of universals should be more extensive than the class of forms.[2] In the case of those universals which are not to be conceived of as forms presumably something like a nominalist treatment would be satisfactory. Paradoxical as it may seem, therefore, the suggestion is that Plato might have been willing to accept a nominalist analysis of at least some universals. If he believed that the properties of things do not perfectly embody the forms, then presumably every member of the class of vulgar universals could be handed over to the nominalists. If on the other hand he did not believe this, then the nominalists would have to confine themselves to those universals which were not also forms. To the topic of imperfect embodiment we must now turn.

(e) *Imperfect embodiment*

We all have a general impression that the doctrine that the properties of physical things are inferior versions of the forms is standard Platonic doctrine. When however we are challenged to say where this impression comes from, we are rather at a loss. This is the more

[1] See below, pp. 353–6.

[2] This was indisputably the case later on. For this reason I have not made much of the fact that the young Socrates in the *Parmenides* is made to ask the question: "Is there a form of X?"—for Plato might be guilty of an anachronism in implying that such a question could arise in connection with the early conception of forms. None the less I believe that a good deal could legitimately be made of this point.

so because some of the places we are inclined to point to seem on closer inspection to offer dubious witness. There are for example all those places where the physical world is contrasted unfavourably with the forms; but then in these places the point generally is that the physical world is a place of *change*; and of course change is the loss of one property and the acquisition of another, so that the fact of change is the fact that the *residence* of properties in the physical world is transitory, and carries no implications about their purity. Something which is *momentarily* white may be *just as* white as something which is always so.[1] Again when titles such as "the P itself ", "the very thing that is P" or "P itself according to itself " are used of the forms, it does not follow that nothing but the form is truly P; the proper interpretation of such phrases may be: "P-hood itself, abstracted from irrelevant features of P objects".

Indeed I cannot recall any passage in which it is said that ordinary P things are not perfectly P (as opposed to being also not-P). There are passages in the *Phaedo* and in the *Republic* which suggest that we never encounter the forms *unmixed* in physical things, but the point of such passages (e.g. *Republic* 476 a) may be the familiar counter-inductive point, that every P thing has many other properties as well, so that knowledge of P-hood cannot be derived from observation of P things. There are however three passages which are particularly relevant to the conception of imperfect embodiment, one from the *Phaedo*, one from the *Republic* and one from the *Timaeus*. These we must shortly examine. The two first passages do appear to say that everything which is P is also the contrary.

We must however at this point distinguish two different forms of statement—not because Plato necessarily distinguished them, but because they are distinct. These are:

(*a*) Whatever is P is also the contrary; and
(*b*) Nothing is ever perfectly P, not even the so-called P things.

The distinction between these two forms of statement lies in the context of thought in which each will naturally arise. The first could easily arise out of the ordinary counter-inductive thesis. The second however could hardly do so. To be prepared to assert the second form of statement one must be able to say in each case what P-hood is and how we come to be aware of it, if it is not the property common to the so-called P objects. This may seem a tall order, but an example will show that it is not out of the question that something of this kind should be said. Take for instance the statement that nothing is ever perfectly straight; this is the kind of statement that is sometimes

---

[1] Aristotle, for what it is worth, makes this point in the course of an argument *against* the Platonists in Nicomachean Ethics, 1, 6.

made. It is made of course because straightness is not the kind of property which must be defined ostensively. We seem to understand it intuitively and for that reason we are prepared to believe that it constitutes a standard that nothing can live up to. Or rather, that nothing *does* live up to; and this modification is perhaps important.

For let us suppose that Plato would have been prepared to make statements belonging to the second of our two forms in the case of suitable properties, namely those properties of which it is plausible to suppose that we have an intuitive grasp—"Nothing is ever perfectly straight/just/equal . . ." and so on, but not "Nothing is ever perfectly red". If he was prepared to say such things as these, then surely these would have been *contingent* statements of a hopelessly dogmatic kind. What good reason could he possibly have had for supposing that nowhere in the world is there a perfectly straight edge, or two peas of perfectly equal weight?

If we have to, I think that we can answer this point and rescue Plato from the charge of dogmatism. To do so however we shall have to impute to him ideas for which there is little textual warrant to be found, unless indeed it can be found in the Sixth and Seventh Books of the *Republic*.[1] It is therefore important to decide whether Plato was prepared to say that nothing is ever perfectly straight, just, equal and so on. Important, but also in my judgment impossible, for I know of no passage which unambiguously says something of the appropriate form (as opposed to the alternative form: "Whatever is P is also the contrary"). I know of no passage, in other words, which comes down unambiguously on the side of the view that the forms are not perfectly embodied in the properties of things.

Why then trouble to discuss this view? Firstly because it is traditional, and secondly because it is, when all is said and done, plausible. As I said just now, if one attributes certain doctrines to Plato one can understand how he could have said that nothing but equality is ever perfectly equal (etc.); and the doctrines which have to be attributed are all Platonic in ethos. If the reader will undertake to remember that I do not assert that Plato *did in fact* say things of this kind, we will consider hypothetically on what grounds he *may perhaps* have done so. I shall suggest four possible grounds.

1. *The recalcitrance of matter.* Up and down Plato's writings there are a number of passages which suggest the thought that matter is recalcitrant. There is a passage in the *Republic*[2] which seems to imply that nothing that human wit can do can prevent degeneration,

---

[1] In other words, unless my interpretation of these books is correct (above, pp. 70–103.)

[2] *Republic* 546 (esp. a 2); cp. also 530 b, discussed above, pp. 187–92.

which suggests that the physical realm has an inherent tendency towards backsliding. There is a remark in the *Timaeus*[1] to the effect that the materials which the Craftsman had to work on were second-rate, so that the ordering work was done only "as well as possible". It is said in the *Theaetetus*[2] that evil is and must be endemic on earth. Finally there is the myth of the *Statesman*[3] in which the world forgets its due order when left to itself. Pessimism about the possibility of ordering the physical world is expressed in all these places and was, no doubt, one of Plato's deep-rooted attitudes. Such pessimism would not entail that it is in principle impossible for the properties of things to embody the forms; but it might be thought to imply that perfect embodiments are so rare and transitory that the chance of meeting one is negligible. On the other hand, however, one might wonder whether the pessimism expressed in such passages is to be taken altogether seriously as philosophical doctrine.

2. *Errors about the copula.* Let us take as our text *Phaedo* 100 c 4: "If anything else is beautiful besides the beautiful itself, it is so on account of nothing but the fact that it partakes of that, namely the beautiful" (*ekeinou tou kalou*; it is perhaps significant that this phrase could equally well mean either "that, namely the beautiful", or "that beautiful thing"). We find in this text two significant points: first that "beautiful" is unhesitatingly predicated of the beautiful, and second that there seems to be some hesitation ("if . . .") about predicating it of anything else. Let me try to explain.

When we come to consider the *Parmenides*[4] we shall see that one thing that this dialogue may perhaps be trying to do is to clear away a certain confusion about what it would be for a particular perfectly to embody a property. Roughly, to anticipate, the confused idea which is possibly criticised in the *Parmenides* may be that if X is a perfect instance of P-hood, then X must be *nothing but* P. The point would be something like this. Begin with two subterranean assumptions, the one that "is" implies identity, the other that "P" and "P-hood" ("beautiful" and "the beautiful") are interchangeable. Given these two assumptions, "X is P" says that X is just what P-hood is. But nothing except P-hood is just what P-hood is. Therefore the form is its own perfect embodiment, and the only one that there can be. (If there were another it would be a second and identical form; which is absurd). It is easy to see that if Plato felt the force of this argument he would feel obliged to say that a property is predicable of itself, and hesitant about saying that it is strictly predicable of anything else. He would fear that there is a certain logical impropriety about the notion of a particular perfectly embodying a

---

[1] *Timaeus* 53 b 5.
[2] *Theaetetus* 176 a.
[3] *Statesman* 273 (esp. b 4).
[4] Below, pp. 326–53 (esp. 350).

form, without necessarily believing that there was anything of philosophical significance, so to speak, underlying the impropriety.

3. *How to decide whether S is P?* According to one possible interpretation of *Phaedo* 74 b[1] Socrates says of equal sticks and stones that they sometimes *seem* equal to one man and unequal to another. But this proves little (for one man might be wrong) unless one adds the rider: ". . . and who is to judge between them?" Perhaps in other words the point is that the form of equality, being something purely abstract, contains no reference to the manner in which objects affect the senses nor to the measuring processes by which we determine their size. This being the case, it is always in principle disputable whether A is equal to B, except where A and B are numbers or the like. Where A and B are physical objects one man's callipers may find them equal and another's unequal, and there can be no theoretical resolution of the dispute. When therefore I say that these two pennies are equal in size, what I *mean* by "equal" in this context is something like "*judged* by empirical techniques to have that relation which is *known* to hold between, say, 3^2 and $4+5$". In this way the equality which is predicated of physical objects is analogous to but not identical with the equality which is predicable of numbers. *Mutatis mutandis* something of the same kind might apply in the case of the other forms. This line of thought might be helped out by the paradoxes of the application of geometry to the world—e.g. the paradox that a tangent can be drawn to a circle, with the result that a straight line and an even curve must either run together for a finite distance (which is contradictory) or meet at a point (which is a meaningless evasion).[2] Such paradoxes seem to reinforce the thought that intelligible principles cannot be applied to the world.

4. *The irrelevance of extension.* This point is very closely connected with the last. If the reader will recall the general structure of the *Timaeus*,[3] he will remember that in that dialogue the forms are objects of contemplation of a totally disembodied reason. They cannot therefore essentially be recipes for the production of *physical* things, for the suggestion of the dialogue is that, if extension did not, unfortunately, exist, the Craftsman's contemplation of the forms would not have been interrupted by the episode of creation. There must therefore be a gap between the totally abstract intelligible principle of order which corresponds to, say, the property of fieriness on the one hand, and the common nature of fiery particles on the other; for the former, being totally abstract, cannot be a way of organising *space*. When, however, faced with the existence of space, reason derives from one of its totally abstract principles

---

[1] For a discussion of possible interpretations see below, p. 300.
[2] See above, p. 125.   [3] As stated above, pp. 197–237.

a way of organising space (namely, in our example, that of organising it into pyramids), what is thus begotten is an image or imitation of the totally abstract principle. The common nature of fiery objects would thus be an expression in terms of space of a principle which allows of but does not demand spatial expression.

This is closely similar to the thoughts which we found expressed in the central books of the *Republic*.[1] There too the relatively concrete entities which mathematicians handle, though abstract, are one degree less abstract than the forms. The end of the process of abstraction is always a jump beyond anything which has any reference to bulk or distance. If abstraction is conceived of as whittling away that part of a concept which is due to the physical status of that which the concept applies to, then it can be seen that the term of the process of abstraction is to arrive at the kernel which is a pure object of reason. If the latter is identified with the form then it can be seen that the forms cannot be identified with the common natures of physical things, which are a function both of the forms and of the conditions of physical existence. We have found this line of thought in the *Republic* and we shall find more hints of it in Aristotle's accounts of Plato's later teaching.[2] It seems therefore at least possible that embryonic ideas of this kind might have made Plato hesitate to say that any P thing ever has precisely the P-hood which is an object of rational contemplation. The essential point is that it is important to know the forms precisely because they are the alphabet of rational order and therefore the key to understanding whatever is ordered. To this end it becomes vital to distinguish the pure form from its physical expression; for concentration on the latter leads in the end up an intellectual blind alley.

The suggestion is that ideas like the four that I have outlined might perhaps have moved Plato to say, at the time of the classical theory, that nothing but P-hood itself is ever perfectly P. But we must remember that we have found no good evidence that he would in fact have said this. There is as we saw better evidence that he would have been prepared to assert the more modest doctrine that everything which is P is also the contrary. This is a more modest doctrine because it does not excite the question: "What then is P-hood if it is not the property common to P objects?" We do not have to try to drive a wedge between the forms and the world so as to bring it about that the one cannot apply to the other.

But if it is more modest, the doctrine before us is still paradoxical. It seems very odd that it should be possible to say of a thing which is, say, equal to a given thing that it is also not equal to that thing, of

[1] See above, pp. 70–103.　　　　[2] See below, pp. 459–71.

a thing that is beautiful that it is also not beautiful. There are however at least three ways in which it might seem right to say this.

1. *As a plea for counter-inductive definition.* This is a familiar point. This gilt spoon is fine to look at, but it is not fine for stirring porridge with.[1] Therefore it can be said to be fine and not fine, not just in order to tease, but to make the point that unless you already have some "recollection" of the nature of fineness you will not be able to derive an idea of it from the contemplation of fine objects, because you may always misdirect your attention towards the respects in which they are not fine.[2]

2. *By extrapolation from relational properties.* Where P is a relational property there is a crude sense in which that which is P is also the contrary. This penny is both equal (to that penny) and unequal (to that halfpenny). Properties like goodness and beauty may seem to resemble equality in this way; A is good for X but no good for Y. B is beautiful compared with C, but not compared with D. It might seem that what applies to equality, goodness and beauty applies to all properties, and in this way Plato might have come to say that whatever is P is also the contrary, without an implied restriction on the possible values for P. Against this view however (that Plato might have supposed that what applies to equality and goodness applies to all properties) we have the passage in *Republic* 7 (523) where Socrates distinguishes the predicate ". . . is a finger" from the predicates ". . . is large" and ". . . is soft" by saying that we can decide by inspection whether something is a finger whereas we cannot similarly decide whether something is large or soft, since *these properties involve comparison.* It seems unlikely therefore that Plato would inadvertently generalise to all properties from relational properties or from those which involve comparison.

On the other hand in the relevant passages from the *Phaedo* and the *Republic* in which the principle "Whatever is P is also the contrary" is stated Plato in fact confines his examples to properties such as equality, heaviness, beauty and largeness which are either relational or "comparative". It is possible therefore that the principle is meant to be confined to properties of this kind. We are however given no warning that this is so; we seem in both places to be concerned with a general contrast between the inductive and the counter-inductive approach.

It seems therefore unlikely that "whatever is P is also the contrary"

---

[1] This example is developed from *Hippias Major* 290. The word for "fine" is *kalon* or "beautiful".

[2] For a discussion of "recollection" see above, pp. 135–47. It is perhaps significant that the passage in the *Phaedo* which we shall shortly look at occurs in the course of an argument for "recollection".

was meant to apply only to a certain set of properties, and very unlikely that it was meant to apply to all properties by inadvertent extrapolation from what applies to that set. In fact I do not believe that it is very significant that Plato states his principle in terms of relational and comparative properties. This conclusion can be reinforced by the following reflection. These passages are concerned with some sort of contrast between forms and things. But the fact that equality is a relational property is not a fact about the equality of sticks and stones, but about equality as such. The proper conclusion therefore from the observation that A can be equal to B but not equal to C is not that things which are equal are also not equal, but that equality as such is a relational property; and this I believe to be the conclusion which Plato would have drawn.[1]

On the other hand relational properties do provide a good instance of the principle outlined in the section before this, the principle that unless you have some recollection of a character you cannot collect it from instances. According to one epistemological picture we acquire the concept of P-hood through observing P things which carry the property on their sleeves. This is plausible in the case of such properties as that of being a finger, not plausible in the case of such properties as equality, to ascribe which the mind must be active. If Plato is campaigning against this epistemological picture it would be natural that he should choose relational properties (and also, since something of the same applies to them, those which we called comparative) as instances with which to make his point, simply because the picture he is attacking is least plausible in the case of these. This may be the reason why he takes relational and comparative properties as instances of his principle.

3. *Because of the difficulty of deciding.* A third way in which it might have seemed right to say that whatever is P is also the contrary can be seen as follows. It is noteworthy that in those passages in the *Phaedo* and in the *Republic* from which we may perhaps extract this principle we encounter the verb *phainesthai*, "to seem" or perhaps "to appear as". "Is there one of the many beautifuls which will not seem ugly? . . . What of the many doubles? Do they not seem just as much halves as doubles?" Socrates asks in *Republic* 479 a–b. This puts us in mind of the point made in the Seventh Book of the same dialogue (*Republic* 523 sq.) to which we have recently referred about the impossibility of deciding by inspection whether something is soft or large. As we saw in an earlier chapter[2] Socrates is here

---

[1] I see no good evidence for the common belief that Plato was unaware of the peculiarities of relational properties; indeed the *Phaedo* seems to me to suggest the contrary; see below, pp. 311–13.

[2] Above, pp. 183–4.

making a general contrast between what he calls the senses and thought. His point seems to be something like this. For any pair of contrary properties such as hardness and softness the same sense which detects the one also detects the other; if an object is observed in suitable contexts (such as feeling a fairly soft object (*a*) after a hard object and (*b*) after a very soft object) it is possible that both of the opposed properties will be attributed to it. In this way whatever is hard is also soft. And the point of saying this would presumably be that there is no way of deciding which of these judgments is right unless we clarify our ideas about the nature of hardness and softness. So long as we remain on the common-sense level we shall find ourselves in the unsatisfactory situation of saying both that A is soft and that A is hard; and neither of these judgments will on that level be wrong. Likewise so long as we have no more than a common-sense understanding of "half" and "double" we shall find ourselves using these terms in similarly contradictory ways.

The suggestion that I am making is that Plato does not want to tell us that whatever *is* P *is* also the contrary, but that whatever *seems* P also *seems* the contrary; that is to say that so long as we remain on the common-sense level at which properties are ascribed to things on the basis of how they seem, so long we shall find ourselves saying contradictory things. According to this suggestion therefore the principle that whatever is P also is or seems the contrary has nothing to say about the relations between forms and things; it is concerned to contrast the accurate understanding of P-hood with the loose concept of it which we employ in ordinary life. Plato would not on this view be telling us that things are both P and its contrary; rather he would be assuming that this is absurd, and blackguarding the plain man's use of words by showing that he is bound to commit himself to absurdities of this kind.

To recapitulate, we have devoted much time to considering what we could understand Plato to mean if we found him to say either that nothing but P-hood is ever perfectly P, or that whatever is P also is or seems the contrary. We have found a number of ways (not all consistent with each other) in which one or other of these things might have been thought to be true. Our business now is to look at the three passages which most seem to support the conception of imperfect embodiment in some form in order to see what we can make of them in the light of our discussion of the possibilities. The passages are: *Republic* 479, *Phaedo* 74–5, *Timaeus* 50–2.

Imperfect embodiment in Republic *479*

We have looked at this passage before[1] and settled our opinion of most of it. The general point is that one cannot collect an adequate idea of a form by observing the appropriate particulars; and the reason for this is that each of the multifarious beautifuls (etc.) will also seem ugly (etc.).

The general point is that the plain man's conceptions of such things as beauty and weight, being derived inductively from the observation of beautiful and heavy things, are at best inadequate. This might be so either because there was something wrong with physical things, or because there was something wrong with the plain man's attitude towards them. If the heaviness of heavy things was not really true heaviness, itself according to itself and all the rest of it, then the observation of heavy things would be bound to give rise to the wrong idea of heaviness. But we should expect the same result if by the wrong method of concept-formation the plain man included in his conception of heaviness accidental features of heavy objects.

Can we decide which of these two points is in Plato's mind? One relevant consideration is the general context. Plato is arguing that *because* of their inadequate grasp of general properties plain men are unfit for a *practical* activity, namely ruling. Now in this context there is no point in saying that the heaviness of heavy objects is different from "true heaviness", because practical activity does not concern itself with the latter. The suggestion is that philosophers will get their decisions right, and plain men get them wrong, because philosophers alone know what justice and so forth really are. But this implies that what philosophers know is the justice which characterises just actions. It is no good their knowing the justice which is laid up in heaven if this is different from the justice which characterises what is done on earth.

Yet on the other hand the simile of the Cave does suggest that when the philosophers leave the life of contemplation to return to the practical activity of government, what they return to is in fact images, and that they handle these the better for having seen "the truth about noble and just and beautiful things" (520 c 5). In fact it seems to contradict the reasoning of the previous paragraph.

Yet I think that we can deal with this. If I release a heavy body outside the earth's gravitational field it will fail to fall towards the centre of the earth; and this will surprise me if I do not know what heaviness is.[2] Analogously in an odd situation I may fail to know

---

[1] See above, pp. 53–70.

[2] This example is not *entirely* anachronistic; see *Timaeus* 62–3.

what justice demands if my conception of justice is made up of wise saws. I shall in fact deal better with particular decisions if I am in Plato's sense a philosopher. But why call that with which I deal better "images" (*eidôla*)? Partly I think because the fact that in situation S it is just to do X is a "reflection" of justice in the sense that it is a consequence of its nature. Also perhaps because that which rulers have to deal with is in part people's claims to this or that as a just due; and these are images of justice in a more pejorative sense. I doubt therefore whether it is right to invoke the language of the Cave in defence of the view that Plato meant to tell us that the justice of a just decision is not true justice.

If we remember that we are trying to crystallise ideas which Plato perhaps never crystallised, I think it is fair to say that the main point of the present passage is that there is something wrong with the way in which the plain man's conceptions are built up. What in that case is the precise purport of such phrases as "Is there one of the many beautifuls which will not seem ugly?"

I suspect that the point is not quite precise, for Plato's range of examples is heterogeneous, and I doubt whether they can all be given precisely the same treatment. (He gives us *to kalon* or the beautiful or noble, the double, the small and the light). But a general formula which will blanket them all is as follows:—For any given object such that in one context it is right to say that it is P, it is always possible to find a context such that in that context it is right to predicate of it the contrary of P. And the implication is that P-hood is a function of the observable properties of the thing in terms of its relation to what we have vaguely called its context, and that this is what is ignored by the man who concentrates on the observable properties of things. Thus it is proper to call the gilt spoon *kalon* when it is thought of on the king's table, not when it is thought of as a kitchen utensil. Its nobility as royal cutlery is genuine nobility, but it resides not in its obvious feature (the gold) but in the fitness of its obvious feature to its function. The inductive error is to suppose that the feature which makes it noble is identical with its nobility. 8 again is double 4, but it is half 16. The fact that 8 contains eight units is not what its doubleness consists in, but the fact that it contains twice as many units as 4. The lightness of this object is not its ready portability, but the fact that its constitution makes it more readily portable than that lump of lead. In analogous but not, I think, strictly identical ways the correct ascription of these properties depends not upon observing the object but upon understanding its relation to its context. If this is the point it has no tendency to show that the object does not really and even perfectly possess the property in question, but that possession of the property does not consist in what the plain man takes it to consist in. This is shown by the fact that, on his conception of what it consists in, he will find himself ascribing and withholding the ascription of the same property to the same object, *and not being able to resolve the apparent contradiction.*[1]

Finally we may notice a self-contained point. It is only an enduring particular such as a gilt spoon which can be taken out of one context and put into another. A momentary particular such as a noble act exists only in the context in which it occurs. So if when Plato speaks of *polla kala* he includes such things as noble acts, then in the question: "Is there one of the many nobles (*polla kala*) which will not seem base?" he presumably refers to the noble act as a type (sacrificing one's life) and not as a token (Jones's sacrifice of his life on the 4th March); and the question must expand to: "Is there any type of generally noble action, instances of which cannot be found which are base?" In the case of Plato's other examples however it seems easier to construe that which is both P and not-P as a token rather than a type; and that is why I said in an earlier chapter[2] that in this section the type/token distinction is ignored.

To conclude, then, the point of this section of the *Republic* is not that things both possess and lack given properties, nor that they possess properties which fall short of the purity of the forms, but that the possession of a property (anyhow in many cases) is a more elaborate business than the plain man takes it to be. That the forms are imperfectly embodied in the properties of things is not therefore to be found in this passage. I must repeat however that in saying that this or that is the point of a passage such as this I mean that this is the point which does most justice to a line of thought that may not have been fully worked out.

Imperfect embodiment in Phaedo 74–5

Let us begin with a literal rendering of the passage 74 a 9–c 5. "Do we say," Socrates asks, "that equal is something?" (though the words could mean "that something is equal"). "I don't mean a stick to a stick or a stone to a stone or anything like that, but beside all these something else, namely the equal itself—shall we say that this is something or nothing?" Simmias chooses the first alternative—it is something. He agrees too that "we know the very thing which it is". "But where," asks Socrates, "do we get this knowledge from? From the things we've just mentioned? Do we see equal sticks and stones and so on and understand it from them, it being something other than them? Or don't you think it is something other? Look at it in

---

[1] As Socrates says in Book 7, we resolve the contradiction by calling in *logismos* or thought, thereby taking a step towards *to on* (*Republic* 524 b).

[2] Above, p. 70.

this way: surely equal sticks and stones sometimes, though they remain the same, seem equal to the one and unequal to the other?" Simmias says that of course they sometimes do. "Well then," Socrates goes on, "have the equals themselves ever seemed to you unequal, or equality inequality?" "Certainly not." "In that case," Socrates concludes, "these equals and the equal itself are not the same thing."

Equal sticks and stones often seem "equal to the one and unequal to the other", whereas the equals themselves never seem unequal, nor equality inequality. Therefore equal sticks and stones are not the same as the equal itself. This seems to be the argument, and it comes in the course of a discussion designed to show that we have some sort of inborn memory of the forms which is activated by experience of the appropriate particulars.

With regard to the appropriate particulars Socrates says some striking things in a passage (74 d 4–75 b 8) which we perhaps need not translate. His theme is that if I know that A, which I see before me, is like but inferior to B, then I must already have got to know B. Now when we see equal sticks and stones we are capable of realising that they "fall short of the very thing which is equal with respect to being of the same character as the equal" (d 6–7). Therefore we must have come to know "the equal" before we can do this. Since it is by the senses that we come to realise that "the equals derived from the senses" are striving to be like "the equal" but cannot do so and are more tawdry (*phaula*) than it, we must have acquired our knowledge of the equal before we began to see and hear.

Before discussing the significance of this passage as a whole we will notice a self-contained point, namely that the last step in the argument—that proving that we must have acquired our conception of equality before birth—is an obvious *non sequitur*. It depends on supposing that, because we have always been able to see, therefore we have always been able to notice what is there to be seen. This is a confusion of seeing, and therefore, indirectly, of what is there to be seen, with noticing the significance of what we see. The assumption involved in this is that taking in a situation is like taking a photograph of it. This is a piece of crude epistemology which may be important.

Now for the argument as a whole. We may begin by observing that the picture which Socrates' language tempts us to form is thoroughly "Platonic" in the conventional sense. Before our eyes there is a world of physical things; before our inward eye a world of ideal things. How much the physical things would like to conform to the purity of the ideal things and how miserably they fail! Take for example equality. In the ideal world things can be equal each to each; in the physical world, because of the nature of the physical, this is impossible. No two physical things however they strive can ever be equal to each other, nor perfectly manifest any other desirable property. Poor physical world; let us hasten from it with Socrates to Hades!

The poet in Plato likes painting such pictures even while the philosopher in him is writing arguments which in no way justify them. To enjoy the pictures we must read Plato; to get the philosophy we must dissect his arguments. So it is here.

Plato is concerned to make an epistemological point, namely that we cannot have derived our conception of equality from the senses since what our senses tell us is that the equals which they are competent to recognise fall short in some way of equality. I think that it would be illuminating to express the point in anachronistic terms by saying that Plato wants to tell us that we cannot have derived our conception of equality by observing how "equal" is used. I would justify this verbalistic re-formulation both as an expository device, and also by reference to the point which we recently noticed, namely the point that Plato confuses the taking in of the significance of a situation with taking a photograph of it. This is relevant because if you fail to see that there is a great deal more involved in understanding what is going on before you than is involved in having the appropriate sensations, you may well feel tempted to treat what is really a fact about how we talk about things as if it were a fact about the things themselves.

Take two men each exactly six feet high, but one of them very thin and the other very fat. There is no doubt that they constitute an instance of equality (in height), but also of inequality (in girth). So it is with most of the things which are said to be equal to each other—there is also some respect in which they are unequal. Even if you succeed in finding an object which is in your view equal in every respect to some other object, it is almost certain that you will be able to find somebody who will disagree with you. The ordinary use of "equal" therefore is one which tolerates its application to objects to which "unequal" can also be applied. The man who thought, therefore, that equality is "just what equals are" would think that equality and inequality are compatible, for it is in general true about equal objects that they are also unequal to each other, whether in some respects, or in somebody's opinion, or in some conditions. Nobody of course does suppose that equality and inequality are compatible, but this is because we do not suppose that equality is identical with the common nature of equal objects. We do not suppose this, because we have a prior understanding of the nature of equality, and are *therefore* able to abstract, from what is common

297

to pairs of equal objects, that feature in respect of which we call them equal. In the case of our two six-foot men we are able to fasten our attention on one particular aspect of the complex situation, namely their height, and by doing so to see them as a pair of equal objects. We can do this because equality, or agreement upon comparison, is a concept which we bring with us to the observation of the world. Antecedently able to seek for some respect in which, on being compared, they will agree, we are able to find such a respect and disregard the respects in which they disagree. We can do this because we know what we mean by "equality" before we start. If we were dependent upon the senses, or in other words on learning the meaning of "equality" by observing to what objects the predicate is awarded,[1] we could never learn how to use it. We would not, on being told that A and B are equal, be looking for a *respect* in which they are so, because we should not have the motive for disentangling one respect from another. We should just have two unassorted objects having various properties some singly and some in common, and no clue to tell to which of these properties "equal" refers. The argument is not damaged if you say that we might be *told* to direct our attention to their height, because we cannot arrive at the idea of a dimension if we cannot think of it as a respect in which things can be *equal*. We must already possess the idea of agreement upon comparison before we can form such notions as that of a dimension, and therefore before we can understand what is involved in calling things equal. The things themselves cannot teach it to us, because they are also unequal.

Much the same applies in the case of two objects which to you, who are equidistant between them, seem equal in some respect, say height, but to me, who am near to one of them, look unequal; though in this case we do not need to import the business of disentangling the respect in which the objects are equal. For you say that they are equal and I say that they are unequal. Why should I not conclude that they are equal to you and unequal to me just as lobster is digestible to you and indigestible to me? How do I know that the digestibility of lobster is not a fair analogy, and that one ought to say that they look equal from where you are and unequal from where I am, if I do not know that the equality of two objects consists in their agreement in some respect? Once again unless I know that equality is an abstract "rational" property, and not a matter of how things look,[2] I shall not see that the objects must be equal or unequal

---

[1] This is a *per impossibile* supposition, for the argument shows that in the situation described nobody ever would use the predicate, and hence the word would not exist.

[2] There is of course equality of look, but that is not a matter of how the looks look.

and cannot be equal-to-you and unequal-to-me. But this is some-thing which the things themselves could not have taught me; for the observable features of things rightly said to be equal are not, as such and *en bloc*, the same thing as equality.

I am not of course seriously ascribing all the details of this pseudo-Kantian argument to Plato. But I do seriously think that if we want to understand his argument we must suppose that he would have been prepared to develop it in something like this way. We must try to justify this from the text.

The text mentions four classes of objects: (*a*) physical equals ("equal sticks", "the equals derived from the senses" etc.); (*b*) "the equal itself" (also "the very thing which is equal"); (*c*) "the equals themselves"; and (*d*) equality (*isotês*).

It also makes two contrasts: (1) equal sticks "sometimes without changing seem equal to the one and unequal to the other", whereas "the equals themselves have never seemed unequal nor equality inequality"; and (2) "physical things are not equal in the same way as the very thing which is equal, but fall short of it with respect to being of the same character as the equal" (74 d 6; I take it that "the equals in the senses strive after that which is equal but fall short of it" in 75 b 1 makes the same point). In fact physical equals are contrasted with equality and with the very thing which is equal.

Now if somebody can produce a plausible version of the passage in which there are two contrasts, one for equality and one for the very thing which is equal, then one would have to consider the possibility that these two entities are distinct. But I do not believe that it can be done. There is therefore only one entity, namely equality, and only one contrast of the physical equals with this. What is the contrast? The statement that the equals in the senses fall short of equality suggests perhaps that physical things can never be equal, but I think that the earlier statement is the more precise, namely that physical equals are not equal in the same way as the very thing which is equal, but fall short of it *with respect to being of the same character as the equal* (74 d 6). But what this statement says, if one looks at it long enough, is that equality is of the same character as equality, and that it is in that respect that physical equals do not live up to its standard. Equality in other words is self-consistent whereas equal things in some way are not.[1] In what way are they not? Bearing in mind the two contrasts which we provisionally distin-guished, and noticing that the right-hand side of the former version (namely "equality has never seemed inequality") agrees with the right-hand side of the latter (namely, "equality is equality"), we can feel that our assumption that the two contrasts are identical is

[1] Or, better, "whereas the *common nature* of equal things in some way is not".

299

confirmed. In that case we can read the left-hand side of the former version into the left-hand side of the latter, with the result that the failure of physical equals to be self-consistent is identical with the fact that equal sticks often seem equal to the one and unequal to the other. This then is the only fact which Socrates cites to the discredit of physical objects and the only reason which he brings to show that our conception of equality is not of empirical origin.

But what is this fact? This is not easy to settle from the text. There are two important uncertainties. One is how far we are entitled to lay stress on the fact that the verb is "seem". We cannot answer this with confidence because the verb *phainesthai* could equally well mean "obviously are", "apparently are", or "look as if they were". The other uncertainty concerns the meaning of the words *tôi men . . . tôi de* which I have translated "to the one . . . to the other". Assuming that Plato wrote these words[1] they could mean "to one man . . . to another man", or they could mean "to one thing . . . to another thing". In fact the meaning of the passage may be either "equal sticks sometimes seem equal to Jones and unequal to Smith" or "equal sticks, or in other words a stick which is equal to a given stick, may sometimes be plainly unequal to a third stick".

One can advance arguments in favour of this or that interpretation of this tiresome passage, but in doing so one should not lose sight of the fact that Plato apparently did not think it important to be very precise about his exact meaning. It seems fair to say therefore that he thought it enough, in order to make the point that he wanted to make, to draw attention to the fact that there is some uncertainty or ambiguity attaching to the classification of physical things as equals. Since he does not tell us clearly which ambiguity is uppermost in his mind, perhaps we ought to conclude that it does not matter.

We may therefore import general considerations to help us decide what Plato's point was in the argument as a whole. On the one side we have the "conservative" view, that Plato wants to tell us that the nature of the physical world is such that it can contain no genuinely equal objects. The nearest approach that there can be to equality on earth is a substitute kind of equality which is compatible with inequality. "Equal" as used of physical things does not entail "not unequal". On the other hand there is the view which I am defending, which says that physical things can certainly be equal but that equality is not the same thing as the common nature of equal objects. This on the ground that while equality is a single self-consistent property and the antithesis of inequality, it is on the other hand common to any set of equal objects that it is always possible to find

[1] Some MSS. read *tote men . . . tote de*; this would mean "at one time . . . at another time".

some respect or context or something of the kind in which they can properly be called unequal, the result of this being that if a man supposes that to be equal is to have the relation which a given set of equal objects have to each other, his conception of equality will embrace a good deal of inequality.

Now Socrates' language may seem to favour the first of these two views. But against that there is the following fact. The immediate context—the proof that our knowledge of properties such as equality is due to recollection—certainly demands the doctrine that physical things do not *luminously* embody the forms, or the doctrine that a knowledge of the forms would not be bestowed upon an empty mind by experience of their instances. But the remoter context of the dialogue as a whole precludes the view that the properties of things are no more than makeshift imitations of the forms, inferior to the latter in that, where P and Q are incompatible forms, their make-shift copies P' and Q' are compatible with each other. For the crucial argument for immortality which closes the discussion is couched in terms which inevitably remind us of the present argument, and depends as we shall see[1] upon the principle that if P and Q are incompatible properties then the P-hood of a given thing is incompatible with Q-hood. This allows of course that a given object can be an instance of equality and of inequality in the way in which we should all allow that this is the case—as for example this penny is equal in size to that penny and unequal to this halfpenny. But it does rule out the view that no object can ever be genuinely equal to another, and that the spurious equality which is the most that physical objects can achieve is compatible with inequality. If therefore we find this latter view in the present passage we make Plato contradict himself in the most gross way within the same dialogue. It seems inevitable therefore that we must conclude that Plato does not mean to tell us that things can never *be* equal. He wants to remind us of the fact that things can never be *pure cases* of equality in the sense in which the number three is a pure case of three-hood,[2] and he wants to use this fact to prove that we have not derived our concept of equality from observation of its instances.

When therefore Plato speaks of physical equals striving after the equal and failing to attain to it, when in fact he appears to speak condescendingly of physical objects, we cannot take his language entirely seriously. We can attribute the depreciation of physical objects partly to the world-weary poet who often got hold of Plato's pen. We can attribute it also, I think, to the photographic conception

[1] Below, pp. 311–19.
[2] Being an instance of nothing but three-hood and the properties entailed by three-hood (e.g. oddness).

of thought which I mentioned at the beginning of this discussion. Plato's point is that equality does not correspond to the conception of equality which we should form if we had nothing but the experience of equal objects to go upon. What he says of equal objects is said in order to show us what that conception would be like. His contrast really is between the true concept of equality, which we have, and the concept which, on the "empiricist" view of concept-formation, we ought to have. But he tends to express this contrast as if it were a contrast between equality and equal objects, and as if the equal objects were to blame for the discrepancy. Is it not likely that the explanation of this is that he tends to take for granted that the conception of equal objects, which we would have formed had we nothing but the senses to go upon, would have been a photograph of them? If we suppose that at the back of his mind he thinks that an empirically formed concept will be a faithful picture of its object, then we can explain why he writes to some extent as if the deficiencies which would belong to an empirically formed concept of equality are due to the deficiencies of equal objects.

Appendix: "the equals themselves"

There is one problem in this section which we have not dealt with. Socrates says that equal sticks sometimes seem equal to the one and unequal to the other; "but *the equals themselves* have never seemed to you unequal, nor equality inequality" (74 c 1). What is the meaning of the phrase *auta ta isa*, "the equals themselves"?

Linguistically I suppose that it could mean something like "pure equals", or that in other words it could refer to some non-physical entities such as numbers. No doubt the conservative interpreter of the whole passage will be tempted to favour such a translation, on the ground that, since on his view equality has been extruded from the physical world, it would be convenient to find a reference to some ideal objects among which it would take refuge. But for myself I find such a translation very unplausible. *We* are inclined to associate expressions like *auto* and *auto kath' hauto* with "the ideal realm" because these phrases are used to refer to forms; and we have read books by Aristotle or others from which we have gathered the idea that Plato believed in the existence of non-physical entities such as numbers in which the forms were perfectly embodied. Therefore we can find it plausible that *auta ta isa* refers to such entities. But the first readers of the *Phaedo* had read no such books and I cannot see what there is in the context which should have put them in mind of perfect embodiments. Furthermore *auta* for them would have been a word of common language with no special correlation with "the ideal realm". For them, I conjecture, the phrase *auto to ison* would not have meant "the Form of Equality" with capital letters, but rather quite simply "equality itself" or "equality as such"—the word *auto* would have directed them to concentrate on equality and ignore what is irrelevantly associated with it.

Following that line of thought the plural phrase *auta ta isa* would naturally be taken to mean "the equals in themselves or as such"; and this translation is quite possible. Equals seem equal to one man and unequal to another; but the equals *in themselves*, or the things which seem to you equal, in the respect in which they seem to you equal, cannot seem to you unequal. An equal stick is also an unequal stick, but *qua* equal stick it cannot be unequal; for equality is not inequality.

But possible though this translation is, I find it rather forced. I would rather suppose that if one is habituated to referring to a property by a phrase of the form "the P" (which ought really to stand for the standard P object), then in the case of a property such as equality, a standard specimen of which would comprise more than one object, one would not find it awkward to use a plural phrase of the form "the P's" for P-hood. I think therefore that "the equals themselves" is a synonym for "the equal itself" and for "equality"; and that when Socrates says "the equals themselves have never seemed unequal nor equality inequality" he says the same thing twice over.[1]

Imperfect embodiment in the Timaeus 50–2

The conception of imperfect embodiment has one more chance of appearing unambiguously in the *Timaeus*. This we must now examine.

Timaeus is speaking of what he calls space (50 c). Of this he says that it is not predisposed to accept the shape or character (*morphê*) of any of "the things that enter into it" rather than any other. It is "activated and differentiated by the things that enter into it, and derives its apparent diversity from them. The things that enter into it and pass out of it are imitations of the realities (*onta*), printed off from them in a way which is not readily stated, into whose mysteries we must inquire later." The "things which enter in" are referred to as "that which becomes", and a little later on (52 c) he seems to speak of them as images which cannot be thought of as *onta* or ultimate realities, space, so far as I can see, being the reflecting

---

[1] *Philebus* 25 a 7 gives a fairly near parallel; here we get the phrase "the equal and equality" and this seems to be clearly a case of the same thing twice over. So far as I know these plural phrases only occur with relational expressions such as "equals".

medium on which the images occur, or possibly the material of which they are made.[1]

What does this mean? Physical extension, firstly, is in itself neither this nor that. If the physical world is differentiated into things of different kinds, this is because extension is moulded into imitations of the forms, which "enter into it and pass out of it" when, for instance, a pig of iron loses its hard character by being melted. Timaeus has recently told us that physical things are to be regarded as bits of extension temporarily characterised by specific properties, and therefore "the things which enter in" are not physical things but the properties or rather instances of properties whose occurrence in a given bit of extension creates what we treat as a physical thing. It is of these that he is speaking when he tells us that they are printed off from the ultimate entities in a puzzling manner which he will describe later, and that they have therefore the non-ultimate status of images.

If we assume that Timaeus fulfils his promise to describe later the manner in which the instances of properties are printed off, I suppose that its fulfilment is to be found in his account of the ultimate particles (triangles) and molecules (regular solids) out of which things are made. The ultimate realities will therefore presumably be such properties as fieriness (or the associated shape), and the printing-off of their images will be the bringing about of instances of such properties in space. The physical world therefore is being analysed into extension and property-instances, the latter being imitations or images of the forms.

How much is implied by "imitations" and "images", and why is it insisted that property-instances are not ultimate entities? Are we intended to suppose that the P-hood of P objects is an imitation of true P-hood in a sense of "imitation" which implies a difference of quality?

We saw above that such a conception would be perfectly intelligible in terms of the general pattern of the *Timaeus*. But I do not think that it is necessary to interpret Timaeus' language in this way. We must keep it in mind that he is talking not about properties, but about property-instances, not about P-hood in general, but about the P-hood of *particular* P things; and he is doing so in a context in which the emphasis is on transience—on the fact that a thing which is now P (e.g. hard) may shortly become Q (e.g. soft). When a thing changes in this way it may be said to lose P-hood, but of course P-hood itself is unaffected by this, and so are the many other instances of it elsewhere. Nothing happens to hardness as such when

[1] Timaeus speaks of images, not of mirror-images in particular. But it seems natural to take him to mean mirror-images—see for instance the use of "in" in this passage 52 c 4.

this bit of wax loses *its* hardness by melting. Now one might express this point by refusing to say that hardness characterises the wax at a given moment. What characterises the wax, one might prefer to say, is an *instance* of hardness. One cannot, after all, speak of a universal or common nature occurring at a given place. But just as one universal may have countless instances, so one original can have countless images. Therefore it seems that the language of images might well be chosen to convey the notion of instances; some metaphor would have to be chosen, there being as yet no dead metaphor ("instance" I suppose is a dead metaphor) to serve as a technical term. This logical point, that when one speaks of something happening to the P-hood of S one is not speaking of something happening to P-hood as such, would also I suggest be enough to explain why it should be said that property-instances are not *onta* or ultimate entities; it is not so much that they are not *onta* as that they are not *the onta*, or the properties as such. And this might be assisted by the following consideration. The desirable occurrences in nature take place as a result of the production in space of instances of the forms, and therefore as Timaeus says we can describe nature in terms of three items: the forms or properties which are the father, space which is the mother, and the occurrences themselves which are the progeny. It is because they are progeny that the occurrences of properties which constitute particular events are not ultimate entities. To put it another way, reason produces effects by moulding extension in conformity with principles of order. In this story the three ultimates are reason, the principles of order, and extension, or that which has to be reduced to order. Given these three, physical instances of properties are an inevitable product, and that is why they are not ultimate.

It seems possible therefore to deal with the *Timaeus* without importing the conception of imperfect embodiment, however consistent such a conception may be with the general pattern of the dialogue.

f. *Perfect embodiments*

We have discussed what seemed to be the three most convincing sources for the conception that the properties of physical things do not perfectly embody the forms, and failed to find it unambiguously present in any of them. However the reader may feel that a certain amount of special pleading has been necessary to purge this conception out of each of these passages. I do not think that this is altogether just, but I have already conceded that Plato may himself have thought that his arguments did entail the doctrine of imperfect embodiment even if in fact they did not. If the doctrine of imperfect embodiment was, so to speak, about in the air in his mind, that might be enough to tempt him to sympathise with its corollary, namely the doctrine that there exist non-physical entities whose properties perfectly embody the forms. It is our business now to look to see whether there are any traces of this corollary.

Traces have been detected by some readers. They can be divided into two classes, of which the first contains phrases such as "the P's themselves", and the second contains references to mathematical entities.

(i) *"P-hood" and "the P's themselves"*. We have just discussed the phrase "the equals themselves" in *Phaedo* 74 c 1, and we saw that on one possible interpretation this phrase refers to perfectly equal objects enjoying exalted status "in the intelligible realm" along with equality.

This passage is sometimes set alongside a long speech by Socrates in the *Parmenides* (128 e 5–130 a 2).[1] It seems to me however that careful inspection of this latter passage makes it less rather than more probable that "the equals themselves" refers to perfect embodiments in the *Phaedo*, for this interpretation is most unplausible in the *Parmenides*, as we shall see. Socrates is here protesting that it is not paradoxical that the same *thing* should be P and not-P, because things *partake* in forms. He means, I think, that since this penny is not *identical* with similarity, for example, there is no reason why it should not be similar (to that penny) and dissimilar (to that half-penny). But, he goes on to say, it would be really paradoxical if the *form* of P could be shown to be not-P. This is his theme. Now in the course of his speech he uses a remarkable variety of expressions, as the italics in the following quotations will show. He begins by saying that there is *"similarity,* and its opposite, *that which is dissimilar"*. He goes on to say that "things which partake in *similarity* will be similar, things which partake in *dissimilarity* dissimilar". Having said that things can partake in both, and thus be similar and dissimilar, he goes on to say: "It would be portentous if someone could show that the *similars themselves* become dissimilar or the dissimilars similar. . . . I shall indeed be surprised if someone can show that *the very thing which is one* is itself many, and that *the many* are one." And he continues in the same vein, with what seems to be a random mixture of abstract nouns and singular and plural phrases of "the P itself " form. Now it is conceivable that Socrates' meaning in all this is as follows:—Forms are just themselves. Likewise their perfect non-physical embodiments cannot embody the opposite form; but it is perfectly possible that their imperfect physical embodiments should do this.

---

[1] As was observed before, it is arguable that Socrates in this dialogue is meant to be a mouthpiece of the classical theory.

This is just possible but I think that it is most unlikely on grounds both of language and of sense. On grounds of language because Socrates gives no indication that he is talking about three sets of entities, unless the indication is given in his switches from abstract nouns and singular phrases to plural phrases. But there is no such indication. On the contrary it would be natural to assume for instance that the last two italicised phrases ("the very thing which is one" and "the many") refer to objects on the same level, despite the change of number. Moreover on grounds of sense, if Socrates meant to refer to three sets of entities, then it is very surprising that when Parmenides turns to tease him about what he has said he makes no play with the ambiguous status of the perfect embodiments. This is the more surprising in that Parmenides could make considerable difficulties for Socrates in connection with these latter. For Socrates has explained the co-predicability of contraries in the case of particular things by saying that they *partake* in the forms. But a perfect embodiment must also partake in the form which it embodies; why then would it be portentous if contraries were co-predicable of perfect embodiments? The fact that Parmenides makes no use of this damaging argument seems to show almost conclusively that he understands no reference to perfect embodiments in Socrates' speech. We too, then, should be wise to take such phrases as "the dissimilars themselves" as a synonym for "dissimilarity"; and this supports an analogous interpretation of "the equals themselves" in the *Phaedo*. Phrases of this kind are, as we have seen, a natural development of the common "the P itself". I conclude that phrases of this kind do not support the view that Plato believed in perfect non-physical embodiments of the forms.

(ii) *Mathematical entities.* It is characteristic of the logic of expressions such as "three" and "triangle" that they appear to stand for individuals (unlike "beauty", for example, they take the plural) which are nothing but instances of a single property. Therefore one might expect that mathematical entities would figure in any doctrine of perfect non-physical embodiments. Moreover we have seen in an earlier chapter[1] that forms are certainly "epistemologically embodied" in mathematical theorems; that is to say we have seen that to know mathematical truths is to grasp the forms indirectly. What we were unable to decide was whether an exalted status was claimed for the numbers and other mathematical entities mentioned in the theorems. We shall need to look at this question again later,[2] but if we suppose for the moment that Plato did at this time think it necessary to ascribe an exalted status to these entities, then it is clear that they could serve as perfect embodiments for at least some of the

[1] Above, pp. 79–85.   [2] Below, pp. 443–7.

307

forms—triangles for triangularity, numerical magnitudes for greater-than-ness or for equality. One might also perhaps imagine that Plato believed in pure beautifuls and pure beds to act as perfect embodiments of beauty and bed-hood.

Is there any evidence of all this? Very little. The Aristotelian evidence suggests that Plato postulated only mathematical entities in this intermediate status, and does not tell us at what time he did so. So far as the dialogues are concerned, if we dismiss phrases such as "the many" and "the equals themselves", then the most that could be said is that Plato believed in the existence of numbers as occupants of the intermediate status of perfect non-physical embodiments. No doubt this might be enough; for numbers could serve as embodiments of many non-numerical forms. One might for example say that squareness is embodied in n^2; and if beauty was conceived of as some kind of proportion then no doubt an algebraic expression could be found for it. It is conceivable therefore that there may have been a time at which Plato believed in the existence of pure numbers, as that in which the forms find their perfect embodiment.

But the evidence is very slender. The passages which may be cited are *Republic* 525–6 and (from a later period) *Philebus* 56. In both of these places it is said that pure mathematics is not concerned with unequal units such as cows and horses, but with equal units (of which the *Republic* says that they are, for that reason, intelligible only). This could express the belief that the intelligible realm contains pure numbers such as 11, made up of real, equal units, whereas the physical realm contains such things as football teams made up of unequal units. This interpretation is far from compulsory however. Another is that the word *arithmos* or "number" also connotes "group", and that one way of saying that one is talking about numbers rather than groups is to say "groups such that their component units are equal each to each". If this is the main purpose of these passages, then they need carry no implications about the status of numbers.

It must be concluded that there is no good evidence that Plato ever believed in perfect non-physical embodiments of the forms.

g. *Imperfect and perfect embodiment; conclusion*

There seems then to be no clinching evidence that Plato believed either that the properties of physical things cannot perfectly embody the forms, or that there exist certain non-physical particulars which can. Yet it remains true that the language of the dialogues does sometimes suggest otherwise, at least in the case of the first of these alternatives.

I have tried to offer some account of the aura of imperfect embodiment which hangs about the language of the *Phaedo* by saying that Plato may have projected on to physical things a defect which would (in his view) have been characteristic of empirical thought if we had nothing but the senses to go upon. When we come to consider the *Parmenides* I shall suggest that a certain hesitation about the logical propriety of predicating a property of any subject other than the property itself may perhaps have contributed to the aura. If it is strictly improper ever to say that S is P, then there will be a certain impropriety in the notion that S and its fellows constitute a class of P things. There will be a suggestion of shudder-quotes around class-names—"'equal' objects" will be the phrase for equal objects. But though this too may have contributed to the aura, it does not amount to a doctrine of imperfect embodiment. The fastidious man who puts shudder-quotes round the word "lounge" must not be accused of denying the existence of lounges.

But having waged war against the doctrine of imperfect embodiment I must now make some concessions. First, then, I do not claim that Plato would have asserted that there *are* any perfectly equal objects or perfectly just actions. All I have contended is that he is not committed to denying the possibility of their existence. On the whole I suspect that if proffered a pair of allegedly equal objects, he would have retorted "How do you know?" or "Momentarily equal perhaps, but no doubt their size fluctuates". I suspect that he would have chosen any device which came to hand rather than admit that there does in fact exist in the physical realm very much of that precision and definiteness which characterises abstract entities. He was temperamentally reluctant, on the whole, as I believe, to admit that you can make more than the best of a bad job of the physical world.

Secondly this would apply most strongly, I believe, in the case of substantival forms. By "substantival forms" I mean those such as man-hood and cow-hood which correspond to what Locke called our ideas of substances, as opposed to "adjectival forms" such as equality, straightness and so on, which correspond to our ideas of qualities. Roughly speaking whereas substantival forms are recipes for the making of relatively permanent objects, adjectival forms are ingredients mentioned in the recipes. If you asked Plato whether there had ever been a perfect embodiment of man-hood, cow-hood or equality, would he not have given an emphatic negative to the first two? If you had asked him whether men and cows in general were perfect specimens of the appropriate forms, would the negative not have been even more emphatic? Is not the *Republic* clear that however hard men try to make their city a true community, however well they know what is involved in a true community, nevertheless what they make will be imperfect at best, and subject to decay?

My attack on the doctrine of imperfect embodiment must not be stood on its head and made into a plea that Plato thought that there were all around us innumerable perfect instances of the intelligible natures which reason recognises. I claim no more than that the arguments which Plato uses do not commit him to the doctrine that it is in principle impossible that a physical object should ever perfectly embody a form. I cited earlier various possible grounds on which a doctrine of imperfect embodiment might have rested. None of these grounds seems to me un-Platonic and I dare say that he might have built an argument on any of them. All I contend on the other side is that, if so, that argument is not to be found unequivocally stated in the dialogues, and that whatever form such an argument is supposed to take it must not preclude the essential point of the *Phaedo* that the same incompatibilities and entailments hold between the properties of things as hold between properties in the abstract. Nor must it render unintelligible the emphasis which Plato lays on the importance of knowledge of the forms *for practical activity*.

h. *The status of property-instances*

We must now consider a different but related question, the question whether it is true that Plato thought it necessary to demand an exalted status for property-instances; that is, for entities such as Helen's beauty.

In considering the *Timaeus* recently[1] we saw that it had something to say about property-instances, and that so far from claiming an exalted status for them it spoke of them as images. But the last argument in the *Phaedo* seems to take the opposite view, and some will say that this appearance must be taken seriously.

It is indeed not difficult to see how Plato *might* have come to think it necessary to allow an exalted status to property-instances. He customarily said that X was P because it partook in P-hood. It is true that the *Parmenides* (131) warns us against taking such talk literally, and no doubt Plato never did take it literally. But he might all the same have been influenced by an implication of the participation metaphor. The metaphor suggests that there is a parcel of P-hood which X possesses, and while the picture of a parcel or nugget would of course be treated as a metaphorical picture, it might leave behind it the impression that the P-hood of X must be treated as an individual entity of some kind, enjoying some sort of exalted status. The preliminary appearances suggests that this is what has happened in the last argument in the *Phaedo*.

Before we investigate this we must notice that it does not cohere well with the conception of imperfect embodiment. For why should

---

[1] Above, pp. 303–5.

the P-hood of X be treated as a subsistent individual unless it were thought of as a part of P-hood? A conceivable answer is that one might be deceived by the behaviour of such expressions as "Helen's beauty" into thinking that, since they are grammatically substantival expressions, they must stand for substances; and then I suppose that one might think that, since Helen's beauty is not an instance of true beauty, such entities must be substances of an ambiguous kind like images. It does not help at all with the exegesis of the *Timaeus* to suppose that when Plato speaks of property-instances as images he wants us to treat them as subsistent individuals of a disreputable kind;[1] we must see whether anything of the kind helps with the exegesis of the *Phaedo*.

Phaedo *102–6*

In discussing *Phaedo* 74 c[2] I suggested that the phrase "the equals themselves have never seemed unequal" might mean that two objects have never seemed unequal in so far as they are equal. That is to say, in the case of these two pennies, that in so far as, and in what respect, Jones judges them to be equal, he cannot judge them to be unequal. He may know that they can lose their equality, or that Smith may judge them unequal, or that there may be some dimension in which they are unequal, and so forth; he may know, that is to say, that they are not pure cases of equality. But none the less he knows that the *equals themselves*, or the pennies under that aspect under which he has fixed on them as equals, cannot be judged unequal. For the same rules which are implicit in the nature of equality as such govern the use of this predicate when it is applied to things.

It is not at all clear that this meaning can plausibly be attached to "the equals themselves" in 74 c, but if it could be then this passage would be brought neatly into line with the section of the final proof of immortality which we are about to examine. For two things are characteristic of the latter, firstly that it appears to treat property-instances as if they were subsistent individuals, and secondly that it insists that if two properties are incompatible in the abstract, then they are incompatible in their application to things. Or, to put these two points together in what is roughly Plato's language, it insists that the entailments and incompatibilities which belong to P-hood as such belong also to "the P-hood in us". Socrates' argument is as follows.

He begins by offering an analysis of the familiar fact that a thing

---

[1] If we assume that whenever Plato uses a substantival expression he supposes it to stand for a substance, then of course we can find innumerable examples to support the view that he was "deceived by the logic of substantival phrases". But we can perform this trick on any author.

[2] Above, pp. 302–3.

can have each of a pair of incompatible predicates. P, he says, can truly be predicated of S when S partakes in P-hood; if however S partakes both in P-hood and in some incompatible property Q-hood, then S can paradoxically be said to be both P and Q. This he works out in terms of Simmias, who is taller than Socrates and shorter than Phaedo, and who can therefore be called both tall and short. He then goes on to say that Simmias is tall by virtue of the tallness which he possesses, and that Socrates is short by virtue of possessing "shortness in relation to Simmias' tallness". (102 c 3). *Mutatis mutandis* the same presumably applies to Simmias' relationship to Phaedo. So far this seems plain sailing. This looks like a common-sense explanation of the fact that "Simmias is tall" and "Simmias is short" can both be true, in terms of the relation *being greater than* and its converse, *being smaller than*. It is being said, we suppose, that the former of these holds from Phaedo to Simmias and from Simmias to Socrates, and that the latter holds in the opposite sense. It seems clear that Socrates is aware that *being greater than* is a relational property.[1] It is not quite clear whether, when he speaks of Socrates' being short because he possesses "shortness in relation to Simmias' tallness", he means that Socrates possesses "shortness-in-relation-to-Simmias'-tallness" (or in other words that he possesses the relational property of being-shorter-than-Simmias), or whether he means that Socrates possesses "shortness (in relation to Simmias' tallness)" (or in other words that he can be said to be short, when you compare him with Simmias). That is to say it is not quite clear whether Plato would call the property in question the relational property of being-shorter-than-X, or whether he would prefer to speak of it as the property of being short. But I do not think that this is an uncertainty of any substance, because it is evidently clear that Plato is aware that such predicates as "short" can only be awarded on the results of a comparison of the subject with something else.

This however is somewhat concealed by what happens next (102 d 5 and onwards). Socrates tells us that he has said all this in order to make the point that just as largeness itself cannot be both large and small, so the largeness in us cannot "accept the small and be exceeded", but must, on the approach of the small, either go away or be destroyed. The same barriers which hold between properties hold also between property-instances. A thing which has once accepted smallness remains small until it changes and thereby loses its smallness. Things can change, but when they do so what happens is not that a property-instance changes but that it is lost; the P-hood in us can no more change than the P-hood in nature.

[1] In the *Hippias Major* (294 b 2) that by which large things are large is said to be greater-than-ness (*to huperechon*).

Now if we attend to one vital point, this is still quite straight-forward. The vital point is the reason which Socrates gives in 102 d 5 for his explication of the paradox that Simmias can be both tall and short. He has analysed this, he says, *in order to* maintain the thesis that the smallness of a thing cannot become bigness, that properties which are incompatible in themselves are incompatible also in their instances. What Socrates must mean therefore is that Simmias *cannot* be both tall and short. He wants to maintain the general rule that a thing cannot be both P and -P (where -P is the opposite of P). But in order to maintain this rule he must first clear out of the way the *apparent* exception that, in those cases where P is a relational property, S can be more P than X and more -P than Y and is therefore liable to be called on occasion P and on occasion -P. It is most unfortunate that Plato has done no more to mark how the discussion of Simmias' height bears on the subsequent argument than to insert the easily overlooked phrase "I make this point for the sake of the following". For some readers have supposed that when Socrates says that the largeness in us cannot accept the small, but must on the approach of the small either go away or be destroyed, he means us to think that when Simmias is compared with Phaedo rather than with Socrates his largeness goes away or is destroyed. But this makes nonsense of Socrates' argument. Whatever the *property* in question may be called, Socrates is perfectly clear (102 c 10–d 2) that the *property-instance* X's tallness depends on the fact that X is taller than, say, Y. And of course it would be absurd to say that anything happens to the fact that Simmias is taller than Socrates when you compare him with Phaedo instead. Even if it is wrong to treat "Simmias' tallness" as equivalent to "the fact that Simmias is taller than Socrates" (and we shall see by the end of the argument that to treat a property-instance as a fact is to over-simplify), it remains true that Simmias retains the tallness which he has against Socrates even if you compare him with Phaedo.

If these observations are sound then Socrates has so far (*a*) explained the apparent paradox that Simmias can be truly called both tall and short, and (*b*) thereby salvaged the general rule that a thing which is P cannot also become -P, but must, if it becomes -P, thereby cease to be P, explaining the necessity of this by (*c*) the analysis of change according to which a change in a thing is not a change in a property-instance but the loss of one property-instance and the acquisition of another. Against a doctrine of imperfect embodiment which claims that Helen's beauty, for example, fades into plainness and that therefore beauty and plainness shade off into each other, this seems an excellent piece of clarification.

It is at this point however (103 c) that trouble begins to set in.

Socrates now takes two kinds of objects such that there is a property which essentially belongs to each of them—snow, which is essentially cold, and fire, which is essentially hot.[1] Of these he tells us that if snow is warmed or fire chilled they cannot become warm snow or cold fire; on the approach of warmth the "snow" (by which he means "snowishness") must go away or be destroyed, and so it is also with fire or the approach of coldness. The moral of this, he tells us (103 e), is that it is not only a property (*eidos*) which cannot have an incompatible predicate predicated of it; this is also true of "anything which has the structure of the property" (by which he means "any type of thing of which the property in question is an essential part"). He then offers a further illustration of the principle. The odd[2] is not the only thing of which "odd" must always be predicated; this is also true of every alternate number, 3, 5 and so on. An odd number is not identical with oddness, but it is always odd; and similarly an even number is always even. Odd and even numbers are thus analogous to fire and snow in that, although they are not essentially contraries, they essentially possess contrary properties, and an odd number cannot accept the property which belongs to an even number —3 cannot become even. Whatever therefore acquires the property three-hood must also become odd, and thus unable to accept the property evenness (104 d–e).

This being accepted, Socrates goes on to apply the principle to the soul. Just as three-hood brings oddness along with it and cannot for that reason become even, so the soul brings life along with it and cannot for that reason become dead (livingness and deadness being contraries). This shows that the soul is in a sense "immortal", or non-dying as we might put it (using the prefix "non-" to indicate "unable to become . . ."), just as three is non-even. But the fact that the soul is an instance of the non-dying is not enough to prove Socrates' point. It shows that a soul cannot become dead any more than three can become even, but it does not show that a soul cannot cease to exist. To indicate what is missing, Socrates goes on to say (106 a) that if the non-warm were necessarily indestructible, then, when snow is warmed, the snow would have to "go away undamaged", being *ex hypothesi* indestructible, and being an instance of the non-warm. We are evidently meant to infer that this does not happen. Socrates goes on to say[3] that if the non-cold were indestruct-

---

[1] Whether by "fire" he means burning material or the quasi-chemical element called by that name he does not make clear, and probably had not asked.

[2] *sc.*, in this case, oddness. It adds to the difficulty of the passage that "the odd" is used both for oddness and for odd numbers as a type (and so with other phrases).

[3] Using the counter-factual construction; i.e. the implication is that the fire is in fact quenched and destroyed.

ible then fire would not be quenched and destroyed on the approach of something cold. As things are, in other words, since neither the non-warm nor the non-cold is as such indestructible, we must suppose the snow and the fire to cease to exist when that which they previously characterised becomes warm or cold respectively. Likewise in the case of "the odd" (by which he must mean "something which is odd"—106 b 7–8). It is true that the odd (e.g. three) cannot become even, but there is no reason why we should say that it goes away on the approach of evenness, since there is no reason why we should say that the non-even as such is indestructible. If the non-even were indestructible, then no doubt we should have to say that "on the approach of the even, the odd and three go away" (106 c 5). It is only therefore if it can be shown that the non-mortal is indestructible that we shall have to say that the non-mortal goes away on the approach of death. It is then conceded that the non-mortal must surely be indestructible, so that it follows that we cannot, in the case of the soul, say what we can say in the other cases, that the fire is quenched, the three destroyed and so on, at the approach of the incompatible quality. In the case of the soul, alone of the cases considered, we have to say that it exercises the option of "going away undamaged".

What are we to say about this argument? The first and obvious comment is that it is extremely confusing, and that one cause of the trouble is that Plato seems quite insensitive to the ambiguities arising from the various Greek idioms for the abstract. He uses "the odd" to mean both oddness and that which is odd. He uses the neuter plural "the three" interchangeably with the abstract noun *trias*, which one might expect to mean three-hood.[1] This does not make it easy to decide what it is that "goes away or is destroyed". Verbally it is fire or three-hood or the three or the odd; but what are we to make of this? What indeed are we to make of the notion of evenness advancing on the three?

With regard to this case it has been suggested, probably rightly, that we should think of a group such as Brown's three children, the "advance of evenness" being brought about by the birth of a fourth. If this is right, what is destroyed by the birth of Brown's fourth child is not Brown's three children, but the three-ness of the group: Brown's children. By acquiring evenness the group consisting of Brown's children must lose its three-ness. In this case therefore what is "destroyed" is a property-instance, and we are naturally inclined to take the talk of its destruction as a metaphorical way of saying

---

[1] Though there is one place (105 c 6) where the analogous noun *monas* cannot mean unity, since it is not unity which makes numbers odd, but an odd unit.

that when a fourth child is born it ceases to be a fact that Brown's children are three in number.

That the tie-up between three-ness and oddness entails that any group which becomes even in number ceases to be a trio seems well enough, if a little obvious. Presumably we can work a similar analysis in the case of snow and fire. In these cases also we can find something (a parcel of H_2O in the case of the snow, and some sticks, perhaps, in the case of the fire) which survives the change, and also some characters (the frozenness and the burningness) which are destroyed when the snow is thawed or the fire put out. That the H_2O loses its frozenness when it is warmed seems an obvious truth, and if this analysis is correct we seem to have no more than a rather cumbrous statement of the general rule that a thing cannot be P and -P (where P and -P are contraries) and also that a thing cannot be Q and -P (where Q-hood entails P-hood).

But it is obvious that this analysis will not work in the case of the soul. So far we have treated the talk about things "going away or being destroyed" as a mere manner of speaking. We have said that when the three-hood of Brown's children is destroyed, all that happens is that it ceases to be the case that his children are a trio. But it is certainly not Plato's point that when Brown dies it ceases to be the case that he is alive—his soul literally goes away. Yet Brown's soul is treated as if it were something analogous to the three-hood of his children.

A possible answer to this can be worked out if we lay stress on the alternatives offered—going away or being destroyed. We might say something like this: Facts are destroyed, individuals go away. When Helen loses her beauty, it ceases to be the case that she is beautiful; when she loses her husband, he goes away. The two alternatives of going away or being destroyed were offered in the first place precisely because two different situations are under consideration.

In the first situation we have a subject which at one moment has a certain property and at another moment has a property incompatible with the first. In this case we can say metaphorically that the first property has been lost or destroyed, has ceased to exist. This simply means that it is no longer the case that the subject has the property. In the second situation we have a subject which contains at one moment an agent which causes it to have a certain property, and which at another moment has ceased to have that property. In this case we have to infer that the agent has literally gone away. Since it was always intended that "be destroyed" was to apply to the one type of situation and "go away" to the other, it is not surprising that the same analysis will not fit them both.

This certainly meets the point that the same analysis will not suit both situations, but it is hardly convincing. For one thing it draws a distinction between a property and an agent, and, as we saw in earlier chapters,[1] to draw that distinction clearly is to puncture the argument. For another thing it makes Plato wantonly combine in a single disjunctive expression a phrase to be interpreted literally and a phrase to be interpreted metaphorically. And thirdly Plato makes it almost indubitable that he did not see that he was dealing with things on different logical levels; for it is not so much that he treats Brown's soul as if it were analogous to the three-hood of his children, but rather the other way round. For he says that if the non-even were indestructible, then it would have to go away on the approach of evenness (106 c). But the fact that Brown's children constitute a trio (if this is a specimen of the non-even) is not the kind of thing that could be said to be indestructible in the literal sense. If Plato had seen that in talking of an instance of the non-even he was talking of a fact of a certain kind, then the protasis of the counter-factual conditional in 106 c just quoted would surely read something like: "If the non-even were a type of individual, *and* if individuals of that type were indestructible. . . ." But this is not what we find. All that the non-even lacks to make it able to choose the option of going away is indestructibility.

One must hesitate therefore about saying that that which "goes away or is destroyed" is a property-instance, and one must hesitate still more about saying that such language is metaphorical. On the other hand one ought equally to hesitate about saying that what we are talking about is property-instances raised to the status of individuals (nuggets of P-hood, destructible or indestructible as the case may be) and that "going away or being destroyed" is to be taken literally throughout. Surely it is better to say that the seeming analogy between such phrases as "the three" and "the soul" has concealed from Plato the fact that he is talking at the two different ends of his argument in two logically different atmospheres, and that it has concealed from him the fact that he himself would, if he reflected, want a metaphorical interpretation at one end of the argument and a literal interpretation at the other.

I suspect that the deceptions of language have worked the more easily because of a conceptual uncertainty concerned with the status of fire. Does "fire" stand for a quasi-fluid whose presence in the object gives it the appropriate properties (heat and so on), or does it stand simply for the fact that the object is alight? I suspect that

---

[1] Above pp. 321–3 of Vol. 1. The point is that an agent, being an individual, can lose its properties—a scent can lose its smell. There is no reason therefore why a soul, if it is conceived of as an animating agent, should not lose the properties which enable it to animate.

Plato did not, while writing this passage, ask himself this question. It is perhaps wrong to say that he took "fire", like "soul", to stand for an entity, because on that view one might expect the fire to flow out or "go away" from the object which loses its fire. But in fact Plato does not say this; rather he implies (106 a 9) that the fire is "quenched", almost as if he is using the word "fire" in the sense in which it is used when I say that there is a fire in the grate.[1] But if "fire" does not stand for an entity like the soul, nor yet simply for the fact that something is alight, that makes it easier for this un-examined concept to mediate between the individuals which figure at the end of the argument and the facts which figure at the be-ginning.

It seems therefore that we ought to say that Plato has been misled by the grammatical structure of such phrases as "Helen's beauty", and that it has been the easier for him to be misled because of his uncertainty as to what kind of an entity the expression "the fire" stands for—whether fire is an element in burning things or a condi-tion of them. But I do not think that he has been misled into thinking it necessary to treat "Helen's beauty" as the name of an individual entity. Rather he has been misled into thinking that the logical points which he has made about the nature of change in the first part of the argument offer valid analogical support for the substantial point about the soul which he makes at the end of the argument. The difference between thinking that Helen's beauty is a real individual entity on the one hand and overlooking the fact that "Helen's beauty" is not the name of an individual entity on the other may seem rather fine-drawn, but it is of considerable importance. It seems to me that Plato may be accused of the second of these, but not of the first. It is perhaps easier to believe that he could have been guilty of the second if one tries to put oneself in the position of one who has never discussed philosophy in any language but ancient Greek.

If this conclusion is rejected, if it is felt that Plato must have thought it necessary to accord to the threeness of Brown's children the same ontological status (apart from indestructibility) as he accorded to Brown's soul, then this will be one place where exalted status is claimed for property-instances. But it will, I think, be the only place, and therefore this claim should at most be regarded as an aberration and not as a permanent feature of the classical theory of forms.

Before we leave this passage we must underline the point that it is essential to the passage that a thing can be P without qualification

---

[1] On the other hand I suppose that the element could be quenched. The effect of a bucket of water might be to split Timaeus' pyramids into their component triangles.

and that so long as it is P it cannot be -P. Imperfect embodiment of the forms in the properties of things is not only not asserted here; it is almost in so many words denied. I suppose that a last-ditch defender of imperfect embodiment might make something of the fact that Socrates finds it *necessary to say* that the P-hood in us has the same entailments and incompatibilities as the P-hood in nature, because this implies a logical distinction between our properties and properties as such. But this is a last ditch, and I think that the defenders can be got out even of this. For we can easily suppose that Socrates is making this point against those who say:—"It is all very well to draw hard and fast lines between properties as you are always wanting to do; but you know, we don't ever meet with sharply demarcated properties on earth. Look at that little boy—his smallness changes gradually into largeness as he grows." "Distinguish if you like," Socrates can be supposed to retort, "between smallness as such and the boy's smallness; it is still true that if he gets large he must have *lost* his smallness; it does not make sense to talk of smallness changing into largeness, but only of small *things* changing into large ones" (cp. 103 a 11–c 2). Who is defending imperfect embodiments in this dialogue?

D. *The "classical theory of forms"; conclusion and application to the physical world*

The phrase "Plato's Theory of Ideas" suggests an established picture. According to this picture there exist both the physical world and the ideal world, and the objects to be found in the former are more or less poor copies of the objects to be found in the latter. That there is *some* justice in this picture it would be useless to deny. Aristotle himself (*Metaphysics* 990 a 33 sqq.) says that "those who postulated forms did so in the hope of explaining the objects around us, but merely provided us with an equal number of additional objects"— the theory has no explanatory force and merely doubles the number of entities calling for an explanation. This agrees with the view that "the ideal world" merely reduplicates the physical world at a higher level of purity.

But our argument has been that it was never Plato's primary intention to convey such a picture. According to our view the mainspring of the writings in which we find the classical theory of forms is the belief that the order which reason imposes is something which exists independently of the material on which it is imposed, and that the elements of this order (such things as equality, proportion and the like) are to be conceived of as timeless and independent objects of reason. In so far as we are ourselves rational beings we retain some "recollection" of these entities, and it is important for the proper conduct of our lives that we should recover a clear grasp of them. This we cannot do by attending to their physical instances for various reasons which we have examined. Therefore we must turn instead to the counter-inductive approach (based on Socrates' search for definitions) as it is roughly outlined in the *Republic* under the title of dialectic. The all-important contrast therefore is between two different approaches—the inductive and the counter-inductive—to the understanding of such entities as equality.

Entities of this kind are of course abstract entities; they are roughly what we mean when we speak of properties or universals. Yet Plato wrote (and perhaps spoke) in such a way that his readers (and perhaps his pupil Aristotle also) have got the impression that he wanted to postulate a world of concrete though non-physical entities, and that the essential contrast was not between two approaches to the understanding of universals, but between two worlds.

There are various explanations of this. I have laid stress on one of these already, namely that it was necessary for Plato to create the conception of an abstract entity. He had to labour to show the difference between giving an analytic definition of, say, beauty, and citing a range of beautiful objects. At the same time he wanted to say that beauty was in one sense at any rate not the same thing as the nature common to beautiful objects, in the sense that he wanted to claim that it would *exist*, as an object of reason, even if there were no physical objects for it to characterise; beauty was something *additional* to whatever beautiful things there may be. But in trying to claim independent existence for an abstract entity, it was very difficult to avoid giving (and perhaps himself succumbing to) the impression that he was speaking of something concrete but non-physical, the ghost of a physical thing.[1] In so far as this led to a concrete picture of the forms, the picture of the two worlds would tend to follow.

But I suspect that Plato wanted to say that beauty is something other than the common nature of beautiful objects, not only because it would exist even if there were no such objects, but also because he wanted the forms, as objects of pure reason, to be *de-physicalised* versions of common properties. I believe that he wanted triangularity, for example, to be an "abstract" entity, not just in the sense in which any property is an abstract entity, but in the further sense that it should be a purely "formal" property, involving no intrinsic reference to physical distance. He certainly seems to have arrived at a position

[1] Remember again Plato's own comment in *Timaeus* 52 b 4–5 on our propensity to believe that whatever exists must occupy space.

such as this towards the end of his life, and I believe that he was always conscious of the reasons for doing so. This would tend to make him lay emphasis on the difference between triangularity on the one hand and physical triangles on the other, and in the context of a concrete picture of the forms this would lead to the picture of two very different worlds.

Something quite different which may lie behind the picture of the two worlds is Plato's conception of the soul. He believed, after all, in another existence for human beings outside space and time, and he seems to have believed in some kind of divine beings whose enjoyment of this existence was continuous. He was in sympathy, on the level of the imagination at least, with the Orphic and Pythagorean conception of the two worlds, "here" and "yonder". This ought not in itself to have led him to people the spiritual world with the forms; one can believe in heaven without making the choir and furniture of heaven consist of goodness, equality and similar entities. But as we have seen in an earlier chapter[1] Plato was always inclined to conceive of the immortal soul as pure reason, so that he may naturally have been tempted to make its environment consist of the objects of pure reason. In the myths of the *Phaedo* and of the *Republic* Plato paints pictures of this environment, and in these pictures he does not make heaven consist of universals. No doubt the physical environments which he describes are meant to be regarded as mythological—we are to suppose some sort of spiritual equivalents for the meadows and gulfs and chasms which he speaks of; but there is no suggestion that these spiritual equivalents are to be forms. In the myth of the *Phaedrus* however it is different; in this myth the objects which the souls see as they journey round the heavens appear to be that which they afterwards recognise on earth as the common natures of things. The suggestion which I am making is this. Plato believed in the disembodied existence of the soul, and therefore in some spiritual environment in which this is carried on. This constituted a belief in another world. In so far as he also identified the disembodied activity of the soul with pure thought he would be inclined to make its "environment" consist of nothing but the objects of thought. But in doing so he might carry over from the older, more "personalist" conception, the notion of another world, and in this way the objects of thought might come to be spoken of as if they constituted another world, logically on a par with this world, but purged of everything physical.

Another possible source of the two-worlds picture is what I have described as the photographic conception of thought. According to my argument Plato wanted to contrast two methods of thought, the

[1] Vol. 1, Chapter 7.

inductive and the counter-inductive. The inductive method of thought is the formation of concepts by the observation of instances—the identification of P-hood with the observable features of P objects. The inductive conception of P-hood is thus what we arrive at by the use of the senses, as opposed to the true conception of P-hood which is arrived at by abstract thought. But if you take for granted that our concepts are a kind of photograph, then where you have two different sets of concepts you will tend to think that they faithfully depict two different sets of entities—empirical or inductive concepts depicting what is open to observation by the senses, counter-inductive concepts depicting what is open to observation by the mind. Thus we get two worlds, each experienced in a different way.

It may be protested at this point that I am being unreasonable. "You maintain," I shall be told, "that Plato did not want to paint the conventional Platonic picture of two worlds; but the texts force you to admit that he did paint it, and so you tease your wits to suggest how he might have come to paint it inadvertently. Why not simply admit that he painted it because he meant to?"

The answer to this is that the conventional picture of two worlds, with the forms constituting the upper world, agrees neither with the arguments which Plato puts forward nor with the recommendations which he bases upon them. It is Plato the poet, with a strong strain of religious pessimism, who paints the picture of two worlds; Plato the philosopher, seriously concerned to map and classify different levels of thought, never soberly justifies the picture.

The element in Plato's thought which receives least justice from the conventional picture is perhaps its strong practical bias. We ought not to forget that whereas Aristotle is prepared to recommend philosophy for its own sake as the noblest of human pursuits, in Plato we are always told to philosophise in order that we may know how to discharge our duty in those practical spheres for whose ordering we are responsible. Whereas Aristotle makes practical action the result of a type of thought which has no competence in the sphere of "things which cannot be otherwise", Plato would have us study the forms so that we may understand the nature of order and thus impose it better on our lives. The philosopher of the *Republic* needs to apprehend the forms in order to govern; the carpenter of the *Republic* looks towards the forms in order to make a table. There are places where the two-worlds picture is strongly suggested, for example *Philebus* 62 a–b where Socrates contrasts the knowledge of "the divine circle and sphere" with the knowledge of their "human" counterparts. But in such places it is incomprehensible either how we can ever come to know the former, or how it can be of practical importance to us to do so. Since Plato plainly did think that

322

we could come to know the forms[1] and that it was vitally important for us to do so, and since the whole scheme of his thought is built around these two tenets, we must refuse to take entirely seriously the flights of language which suggest otherwise. Plato's attitude to the natural world is not what it ought to be according to the conventional picture.

What then is Plato's attitude to the natural world at the period of the classical theory of forms?

The answer must be that from the period of the classical theory of forms there is very little evidence. As we saw in earlier chapters inferences can be drawn from the *Phaedo* and from the central books of the *Republic* about the status of physical things. The last pages of the *Cratylus* (a dialogue whose date must be left uncertain) seem to hand over the physical world to the Heracliteans; and of course from a number of places in the *Phaedo* and in the *Republic* we get the impression that the physical world is a theatre of change. But it is not until the *Theaetetus* that Plato tries to define his attitude to the Heraclitean doctrine of flux. There as we have seen[2] his position seems to be that, however much instability there is in physical things, the fact that we can describe them entails that the instability must conform to stable patterns of a relatively enduring kind. Since there is no substantial evidence either way it is best to assume that this is the position that Plato had adopted or was working towards at the time of the classical theory.

It is in the *Timaeus* that Plato offers a metaphysical analysis of physical things. Here we are told in effect that a thing may be analysed into a portion of space temporarily characterised by instances of properties, these latter being spoken of as imitations or images of forms. This table therefore is presumably a region characterised by solidity and flexibility, by that pattern of activity which is correlated with brown colour, and so forth. With regard to the persistence of the table through time very little is said. There is a passage in the *Symposium* (207–8) which offers a surprisingly Humeian analysis of identity, applying it even to the soul. A creature is called the same throughout its life not because it consists of the same material—this is continually being renewed—but because the material is renewed in such a way that the development of the creature is continuous. It is difficult to believe that Plato would always have wished to apply this doctrine to the soul, but so far as the body is concerned the *Timaeus* and *Theaetetus* seem to agree with the view that the persistence of a physical thing consists in the persistence of a pattern imposed on changing material. If it is asked what makes the pattern persist, there

---

[1] And that ordinary craftsmen "look towards them".

[2] Above, pp. 10–11, 27–33.

seems very little indication from which we can conjecture an answer. So far as the *Timaeus* goes the impression one gets is that the general laws of nature taken in conjunction with the initial disposition of elements at the moment of creation are responsible for everything which occurs subsequently, including the persistence of individuals (which can therefore be looked on as something like eddies in the flux).

At the opposite extreme from the picture of the two worlds there is another which we can offer. According to this picture a physical thing is nothing but extension differentiated from other bits of extension by the forms which characterise it—this penny is at the moment an instance or meeting-point of roundness, hardness, coldness and so forth (and all of these can be construed as forms or functions of forms, since such properties as coldness which are *prima facie* sensible properties may be thought of as resultants of certain patterns of physical activity). According to this analysis the picture of two worlds is done away with because the inferior world is reduced to extension characterised by the members of the superior world.

Does this analysis do better justice to Plato's thought than the picture of two worlds? In a way it does. The epistemological thesis characteristic of the classical theory—that one cannot learn of the forms by the observation of physical things—can be accommodated, on this view, if we say that it is because several forms are always co-present in any given thing that we are unable to grasp them from their instances. There is even a passage in the *Republic* (476 a 5–8) which can be quoted in partial support of this: "each (of the forms) is in itself single, but because they turn up in many instances each of them seems to be many by its association with acts and bodies and with other forms". If (as is not altogether impossible) one takes the last "and" in this quotation to mean "and, in a word", or "that is", then one has a place where Plato says that the forms seem to be diversified (and hence cannot be recognised) by reason of the fact that we encounter them mixed up in things and events, that is to say mixed up with each other.

However we remember that the *Timaeus* will not allow us to say that the properties of a physical thing *are* forms, but only that they are "images" of forms. We have not been able to decide how much is implied by this qualification, but at least it should make us cautious. It seems to me that the statement that the properties which constitute physical things *are* forms must be hedged by at least two cautions. The one is that the "are" must not be taken to imply identity, in the sense that the existence of a form must not be taken to be co-extensive with the existence of its instances. There exists such a nature as circularity, whether or not there has ever been a circular object. The other caution is that many of the properties of physical things are at the best remote resultants of forms. The taste of a lemon is not an eternal object of reason, but at most a consequence of the order imposed on the particles of lemons and of human tongues. Even in the case of such properties as roundness, I have already expressed the belief that the form is for Plato something with no explicit reference to space. Certainly therefore many of the properties of physical things cannot be said to be forms, and probably this is true of all of them. What we can say however is that the properties of a physical thing are what they are in consequence of the simultaneous application to a region of space of a number of principles of order, or in other words of forms.

With these two qualifications it seems to me that the doctrine that physical things are meeting-points of the forms is a good corrective to the doctrine of the two worlds. The truth lies somewhere between the two.

II. PLATO ON THE THEORY OF FORMS: THE *PARMENIDES*

It will be tedious to try to say what the *Parmenides* is about, but it would be cowardly not to try. The *Parmenides*, fortunately, is unique in philosophical literature, though the *Lysis* and *Euthydemus* foreshadow to some extent its method. This is to throw at the reader a piece of obviously tangled and fallacious argument, and leave it to him to untangle it. In a piece as slight as the *Euthydemus*, in which also the fallacies are mostly crude, one is not tempted to look for a general lesson which the dialogue is supposed to inculcate. The *Parmenides* is so long, so elaborate, and so boring if it be treated as a bed-side book (or even as a *Week-end Book of Puzzles*), that one is tempted to feel that only a lesson to be inculcated could have sustained its author in the work of writing it. Perhaps one ought to resist this temptation. Lewis Carroll adopts something of the same method, and it would be foolish to seek the philosophical lesson of the *Alice* books. Nevertheless it seems that a moral, or a number of morals, can be drawn from the *Parmenides*, and we shall try to draw them.

The dialogue is certainly concerned to discuss the theory of forms; indeed the first half of the dialogue is overtly devoted to discussing it, and is the only place in Plato's writings where the theory gets any sustained critical discussion. The second half of the dialogue is (less obviously, but still probably) occupied among other things, in giving an early airing to ideas which are to become important in Plato's later dialogues. It is therefore natural to date the *Parmenides* some time after the group of dialogues which put forward the classical theory of forms (especially the *Phaedo* and the *Republic*) and some time before the late group of dialogues (*Phaedrus, Sophist, Statesman* and *Philebus*) which seem to take up and develop ideas aired in the second part of the *Parmenides*.

Whether or not the *Parmenides* comes chronologically between these two groups, it looks as if that is its logical position. For it seems both to offer critical afterthoughts on the earlier writings and also to make feelers towards the later ones. Since it appears to occupy this midway logical position it would be satisfactory if one could discover some single theme which is the common source both of the critical looking backward and of the tentative looking forward. Without such a theme the dialogue becomes in effect two dialogues with two different purposes. I think that such a theme can be found—more easily found than expressed. I hope that it will emerge from our discussion. Roughly, to anticipate, it is that a mistaken conception of the self-identity of the forms has laid the writings of the classical theory open to misinterpretation, and has at the same time prevented the discussion of certain fruitful topics whose importance cannot be fully grasped until it is allowed that the forms can "partake in" each other without prejudice to their self-identity.

A. *The first part of the* Parmenides

We must now turn to the dialogue. The parties to the conversation are Socrates (in this case alone introduced as a very young man), Parmenides with his disciple Zeno, and another young man called Aristoteles. Parmenides is represented as elderly and authoritative; his attitude to Socrates is tutorial.

In what follows I shall number sections of exposition, and prefix a letter to sections of comment.

1. When the dialogue opens the company have just heard a reading of an early writing of Zeno's arguing that if there exist many things (as opposed to Parmenides' single all-inclusive substance), then they must be alike and un-alike. No doubt Zeno's purpose in this essay had been to show that it is even more absurd to say, with common sense, that there are many substances than it is to say, with Parmenides, that there is only one. But Socrates thinks that he can allow the force of Zeno's arguments, and yet retain a number of substances, if he is allowed to distinguish forms or properties from things. For Zeno has only shown that incompatible predicates are often co-predicable of *things*, and there is nothing impossible in this. If you allow that there is such a thing as likeness, or as unlikeness, in itself, and that things are alike or un-alike according as they have a

326

share in these natures, then likeness cannot be unlikeness, but things can be both alike and un-alike. Socrates is unimpressed by the demonstration that things can partake in a number of different, even incompatible, properties; he is himself, for example, obviously *one* man and *many* members. What would astound him would be a demonstration that properties themselves can be "blended or divorced among themselves". Let Zeno demonstrate, if he can, the same antinomy among the forms themselves, "showing in the things which are grasped by thought what he has already shown for the things revealed to sight". (128 e–130 a. This is the long speech from which I have quoted above, p. 306. I have assumed here the interpretation for which I have argued there).

A. The first point to notice here is that Socrates does not mind saying that things are alike and un-alike, so long as it is allowed that this means that they partake in likeness and in unlikeness. But it might have been felt that the statement that things partake in these two incompatible predicates is no more and no less paradoxical than the statement that they are alike and unalike. But Socrates does not feel this. If we pressed him to say why the "partake" formulation is not paradoxical he would presumably have to say that A can partake of likeness to B in one respect and of unlikeness in another. But similarly it could always be said that A is like B in one respect and unlike in another. Why then is the "is like" formulation paradoxical when the "partakes in likeness" formulation is not? The answer must be that, unless it is clearly stated that "S is P" does not mean "S is identical with the P", then "S is P and not-P" will seem to identify S with both of two incompatible predicates, thereby identifying the latter with each other. It must be this result (probably not clearly seen, but obscurely felt) that Socrates is trying to avoid when he invokes participation to deal with Zeno's paradoxes.

Next we must ask what it is that Socrates says cannot happen among the forms when he says (129 e 2) that they cannot be "blended and divorced among themselves". The answer seems to be this. Socrates has just allowed that he is himself an instance of unity and multiplicity, being one man and many members. Unity and multiplicity are therefore blended *in him*, and he allows that forms can be blended in this way *in things*, namely through the participation of S in more than one form. But he will not allow that they can be blended *among themselves*. What he must mean by this is that the apparent compatibility of incompatibles such as unity and multiplicity only arises through application of these predicates to a common subject. "Among themselves", or apart from such predication, properties cannot be blended. Two different predicates can co-exist in the same thing, but they cannot "co-exist" in any other way.

327

But the only ways in which they could "co-exist" seem to be either that the one predicate should be predicable of the other, or that there should be some third predicate of which both are predicable.[1] What Socrates is saying therefore is probably something like this, namely that although S can be both P and Q, so that a P thing is Q, it is impossible for P-hood to be Q, or for R-hood to be both P and Q (at least where P-hood and Q-hood are incompatibles). But how does he get to the phrase "blended and *divorced (diakrinesthai)*"? I suppose thus: if P-hood were said to be Q, then it would be made to fall under something other than itself, and hence would be separated from itself. If, for example, activity were said to be the same as itself, then by being "blended with", or made an instance of, sameness, it would be torn apart from itself. To this of course a reader of the *Sophist* will ask: "But why should we not say that 'activity is the same as itself' does not mean that activity is sameness, but that it partakes in sameness?[2] Why not repeat the 'participation' analysis at the level of properties, to deal with apparent paradoxes there, in the way in which similar paradoxes were dealt with at the level of things?" The answer must be that Socrates implicitly supposes that participation is a relation which things can have to properties but which properties cannot have to each other. Things can have characters, but characters *are* characters and cannot *have* any other character. It would impair the self-identity of a property to allow it to have any property but itself. It is fairly evident then that Plato is here attributing to Socrates a particular view of self-identity, and one which is the opposite of that which plays such an important part in his own later writings.

2. To return to the text, Socrates has brushed aside Zeno's antinomies by invoking the doctrine that things must be distinguished from forms or properties, and that the former partake in the latter. Parmenides does not take this lying down. He retorts by asking Socrates two sets of questions. The first are about the number and kind of forms which Socrates is prepared to believe in; the second are about the interpretation of the "participation" metaphor.

On the first point Parmenides asks Socrates whether he believes in the existence of forms of likeness, one, and many (using the indiscriminate collection of nouns and adjectives which I have reproduced). Socrates answers confidently that he does. Does he also believe in a form of justice, beauty and goodness? Yes. And of man, fire and water, apart from the familiar instances of these objects? Socrates says that he has never been sure about these. Then what of

---

[1] For there seems to be no point in saying that one predicate cannot be identical with another. No more can I be identical with you.

[2] cp. *Sophist* 256 b 1.

hair, mud and dirt? Here Socrates feels confident that these are "simply as we see them". Yet he admits that he has often been worried by the thought that there is something in common between their instances, but has so far felt unable to postulate a form in cases such as these, for fear of absurdity. Parmenides retorts that he is still beset by conventional notions of what constitutes absurdity (130 a–e).

B. We must notice first that Plato here imputes to Socrates (whether deliberately or otherwise) two distinct motives for believing in forms. Socrates is made to feel the force (in the case of mud, hair and dirt) of the reasoning that if things resemble each other there must be something of exalted status to constitute or account for the resemblance; and Parmenides seems to press this, the formal argument for realism, upon him. But on the other hand by hesitating over the existence of certain forms Socrates shows that he must have some other motive for belief in forms. It is not so much his hesitation over mud, hair and dirt that is significant (for these words might be thought to be vague words like "gadget" or "weed", so that there is really nothing in common between the whole range of objects to which they can be applied). What is significant is his hesitation over forms of man, fire and water, i.e., in cases where we are plainly dealing with things having common natures. Why is Socrates confident in claiming exalted status for similarity, unity and multiplicity, hesitant to claim it for the common natures of men and of parcels of fire and water?

The natural answer is that he feels (implicitly) the force of the reasoning that exalted status can only be claimed for these entities which *must* be mentioned in an *ultimate* account of nature. Conversely his second motive for "believing in forms" is that an exalted status *must* be claimed for these entities. But what are these entities? They are similarity, unity, multiplicity, justice, beauty, goodness, and so forth (no doubt the list given is incomplete). But why are these "more ultimate" than manhood and fieriness? The natural answer, consistent, as we have seen, with the structure of the *Timaeus*, is that men, fire and water are things which result from the ordering of nature in accordance with the totally abstract entities which the Craftsman can be supposed to contemplate "before the worlds".[1] I find therefore in the consideration of Socrates' confidences and hesitancies about which forms to postulate confirmation of my repeated claim that the cosmological function of the forms is paramount. It is those forms which must figure in the "alphabet of order"

---

[1] It may be said that justice, beauty and goodness are not "totally abstract". But the *Republic* has taught us that, if we really understand them, we see that they are.

that Socrates has no hesitation in postulating. In the case of those natural objects such as men which clearly possess a definite character, Socrates is uncertain whether a form must be postulated (or whether they can be treated as resultants of more ultimate principles of order). In the case of indeterminate objects like hair (which the *Timaeus* represents as a kind of excrement) he is clear that these correspond to no definite and intended character. They are, as Socrates says, "just what we see them to be"—matter left to its own devices.

The state of mind here attributed to Socrates is very Pythagorean in spirit. The Pythagoreans tried to reduce the natures of things to the mathematical elements of their structure just as Socrates, on my account, wonders whether they ought to be reduced to such elements as similarity and justice, of which he would probably believe that a mathematical expression can be given. The Pythagoreans also seem to have regarded *to apeiron* or the indeterminate as an element in nature; and with this we may compare Socrates' treatment of hair, mud and dirt. The theory of forms probably had Pythagorean ancestry, and Parmenides seems to have been an opponent of the Pythagoreans.[1] The late dialogues which make much of the mutual participation of forms have as their chief speaker a disciple of Parmenides. It seems fitting therefore to find Pythagorean opinions subjected to Eleatic[2] criticism in the *Parmenides*. Plato is confessing, we might suppose, that he has hitherto paid too little attention to the Eleatics.

3. Having accused Socrates of conventional ideas of absurdity, Parmenides proceeds to tease him on the subject of participation. He begins by asking what effect its numerous instantiations have on the unity of a property. Does he think that when a number of particulars participate in a property, the whole of the property exists in each of them, or that each has only a share? Socrates prefers the former, and illustrates it by the example of a day. A given day exists, as one and the same day in spatially separated places, and a property does so also. This seems a good illustration, but Parmenides will have none of it. "You don't seem to make many bones about having the same thing in several places. This is like saying that when a sail is covering a lot of men the whole of one thing is above several things. Or isn't that the sort of thing you mean?" Socrates says that perhaps that is the sort of thing that he means. (131 a–c).

C. Many readers seem to think that this bit of obvious sharp practice on Parmenides' part is not significant. I think that it is. Whatever defects Socrates' "one day in many places" may have as an illustration of the relation of a property to its instances, it has one

---

[1] See Cornford, *Plato and Parmenides*.   [2] i.e. Parmenidean.

immense merit which Parmenides' "one sail over many men" lacks; for the principle of individuation of a day is different from that of a physical object, whereas the principles of individuation of sails and human bodies are roughly the same in kind. For this reason the unity of a day in various places is fairly analogous to the unity of a property in its various instances. Socrates ought never to have accepted Parmenides' illustration in place of his own (his hesitant agreement shows that he himself had doubts), and it must surely be significant that he is rail-roaded into accepting it.

4. But once Socrates has accepted it, all is up with him. The bit of sail above me is different from the bit above Jones; so, if this illustrates the participation relation, it is only part of the form which exists in each of the particulars. But if the forms are divided in this way absurdities follow. For example the parts of bigness must be smaller than the whole of it, and so if this elephant is big because it possesses a part of bigness, it is big because it possesses something comparatively small—which is absurd. (131 c–e). (Others interpret this argument differently).

Parmenides then suggests that Socrates' reason for believing in forms is that when he sees a number of similar particulars, he finds himself thinking that there must be something common to them all. Socrates agrees to this (although as we saw he had doubts about the cogency of this line of reasoning in the case of men, fire, water, mud, hair and dirt). Parmenides then says that if you consider the very thing which is big (i.e. the form) along with all the other big things, there must be something common to all of them, or in other words, a super-form; and that this goes on indefinitely. (132 a–b).

Socrates then suggests that perhaps forms are only thoughts, or, I suppose, concepts. But Parmenides has two lethal answers to this. The first answer says that all thoughts are *of* something; thoughts of forms will have forms for their objects; therefore this only postpones the problem. The second answer says that if things participate in forms, and forms are thoughts, then things must participate in thoughts, or, in other words, think. (132 b–c).

Socrates now give up participation as the relation between particulars and forms, and tries resemblance instead. Let forms be exemplars or paradigms "set up in nature", and let particulars resemble them. But in that case, Parmenides retorts, the form must resemble the particulars; and since *ex hypothesi* all similars must "partake in" or in other words resemble a common form, once again we shall have to create a super-form for the set of similars consisting of the particulars and the form; and this goes on to infinity. (132 c–133 a).

Parmenides then adds what he says is the gravest of all the objections to the belief in forms. He allows that the objection can be met, but only by a very skilful man. The objection is roughly this. No supporter of forms would admit that they exist among us; their function is to transcend the vulgar world. But in that case they are unknowable. For in the case of pairs of correlatives, universals are correlated with universals and particulars with particulars; thus slavery is the correlate of masterdom, and a slave is the correlate of a master, but a slave is not the correlate of masterdom nor slavery of a master. Similarly then the form of knowledge corresponds to the form of truth, and only God can have true knowledge; the inferior knowledge which exists among men can only be of the truth which exists among men, which has been seen not to include the forms. Therefore the forms are unknowable by men. (133 a–135 a).

His destructive work done, Parmenides admits that Socrates is right to think that forms are necessary for dialectic (presumably because you cannot ask what P-hood is if you do not allow that there is such a thing). Since it seems that one both must and cannot believe in forms, Socrates is in a quandary. Parmenides advises him to submit himself to mental discipline if he wants to make progress. He was right to see that it is not difficult to show that things can be alike and un-alike; but he ought to make a practice of seeing not only what are the consequences of supposing that so-and-so is the case,[1] but also of supposing that it is not the case. (His meaning presumably is that Socrates has seen that the doctrine that things participate in forms solves certain problems, and has embraced it for that reason, but has not noticed that in certain other respects the contradictory doctrine has more satisfactory consequences. In other words one should never accept a philosophical doctrine just because it solves certain difficulties. If it creates more than it solves, that is if the consequences of the contradictory are more satisfactory, then it ought to be rejected). (135 a–136 a).

D. What is the significance of this attack on the doctrine of forms? It is very likely that part of Plato's purpose is to warn the young men of the Academy of some of the traps that an inexperienced defender of the doctrine is likely to fall into; but is there any general lesson that the passage is meant to teach us? Is it for example a recantation of the whole doctrine of forms?

I am confident that it is not. We may notice first of all that Parmenides allows that the "gravest" difficulty which he brings against the practice of "postulating a single distinct form for each of the things that there are" *is answerable* by "a very experienced and able

[1] Literally "that a given thing exists". But I think that the "thing" can be a fact.

disputant, who is willing to sustain a long and wide-ranging argument" (136 b).[1]

We may ask also just how much the argument may be thought to have shown. The just answer seems to be that it has shown (*a*) that it will not do to treat forms as concepts (*b*) that participation cannot be construed as strict similarity, at any rate if it is also maintained that for every class of similars there must exist a form which is not a member of the class; and (*c*) that forms must not be thought of in pseudo-concrete terms. The last of these three clauses may seem to need some justification, and I shall try to offer this. But before doing so I will record the conclusion that if this account of what the argument shows is correct, then it cannot be said to show either that it is wrong to postulate forms, or that it is wrong to say that things partake in them; it only shows that certain interpretations of "partake" will not do.

But is it fair to say that the argument shows that forms must not be thought of in pseudo-concrete terms? And, if so, is it likely that this is what Plato meant the argument to show? I would answer both questions affirmatively. The clearest indication that this is what Plato meant the argument to show is to be found in the way in which Parmenides is allowed to foist upon Socrates the concrete model of one sail over many men instead of Socrates' own model of one day in many places. Once this is done Parmenides' task is easy. He has led Socrates to think that it is proper to talk about forms as if they were concrete things; and all Socrates' difficulties arise from this assumption. Thus it is assumed that it makes sense to talk of parts of a form, to say that a part of bigness will be smaller than the whole (as if a part of bigness were like a part of my face), to wonder whether a form can resemble its particulars, and so forth. The proper answer to the question: "Does the whole of bigness exist in big things, or only part in each?" is that the question makes no more sense than the statement that justice is like a just act. A man has not learnt how to use expressions such as "bigness" or "justice" until he has learnt that such phrases as "parts of bigness" are simply bad language.

This same readiness to treat abstract nouns as if they were concrete nouns comes out also in Parmenides' "gravest" objection. For here Parmenides treats the form of knowledge as if it were a superior counterpart to human knowledge. He makes the form of knowledge stand to the form of truth in the relation in which human knowledge stands to terrestrial facts. But this of course makes no sense at all.

---

[1] Surely also if Plato were recanting he would not put the recanted heresy into the mouth of the *young and inexperienced* Socrates. More likely he would put it into the mouth of an over-ardent Socratic (*cp.*, Nicias in the *Laches*) and let Socrates tear it to bits.

This is to treat the form of knowledge not as that in which instances of knowledge partake, but as if it were the knowledge of a divine being: it is to treat a universal as if it were a superior member of the class of its own instances.

All Socrates' troubles, then, come from treating forms as if they were individuals or concrete entities. It must be, I believe, significant, both that the error is fathered on to him by Parmenides, and that he does not denounce it. That it is not what Socrates wanted to say signifies that it was never intended that forms should be concrete entities; that the young Socrates has no resistance to the view signifies that this is an error which the believers in forms had sometimes fallen into.

E. But just what error had they fallen into? Not, I think, that of treating forms as perfect particulars. For (where P is an adjectival property such as similarity or justice) a perfectly P object must have many properties besides P-hood. But Socrates insists that forms cannot be blended or divorced, that a form can have no property but itself. The error therefore was not that of treating a form as a thing which perfectly exemplifies a property, but as a *thing* which *is* a property. It is the error of making universals conform to the logical grammar of particulars. Perhaps it may have come about in this way. A word is commonly thought of as an *onoma* or name. Therefore a significant word names something. But "beautiful", for example, does not *name* beautiful objects, for there are many other words (even, in the limiting case, "ugly") each of which has an equally good claim to be regarded as the name of any given beautiful thing. The only thing which has a prerogative claim to the name "beautiful" is the thing which is just and only beautiful—the "very thing which is beautiful", or the form. This then is the only thing which the word "beautiful" really fits, and this it fits perfectly. To other things the word "beautiful" can only be applied by a kind of courtesy; this is marked by saying that they partake in the beautiful.[1] But the word perfectly fits the form, and the cause of the perfect fit is the fact that the form has no other properties except the one property that it is. Therefore a form cannot be blended; for if it could have any other property but itself then that, by destroying the perfect fit, would deprive the word of anything to which it could stand as the name. Therefore the form must be self-identical in the sense that it must be nothing but the *nominatum* of a name. A state of mind such as this would result from the isolation of the notion of a property, if this was combined with

---

[1] This should be borne in mind in considering the passages which seem to support the doctrine of imperfect embodiment. I do not think that it is the key to these passages, but it may have helped to make the things that are said in them seem plausible.

the view that to every significant expression there corresponds an entity which is both the *meaning* of the expression and also what the expression *names*. For the meaning of a general term is something abstract, whereas that which can be named is an individual. Hence we get the notion of an abstract individual.[1]

It may well be that the logical peculiarities of words for numbers helped to make plausible the notion of an abstract individual. For the number three, say, seems to be an individual (one can divide it or multiply by it for example) and yet it is an individual which (if we neglect oddness, primeness etc.) has no property but itself. The number three may thus seem to be an entity which makes a perfect fit with the word "three".

The suggestion is that the propensity to treat forms as "abstract individuals" or "named meanings" was the error into which believers in forms had sometimes fallen, and that it is through the influence of this propensity that Socrates can offer no resistance when Parmenides beguiles him into treating forms as things; for he was already half-inclined to think of them as things. We have seen that this view would preclude the belief that forms can partake in each other. It follows that if Plato wanted to maintain the latter doctrine as something contradicting what he had hitherto taken for granted, it might be natural for him to make Socrates insist that forms cannot be blended, and then get into trouble through adhering to the pre-supposition from which this insistence derived. This he does in the first part of the *Parmenides*. We shall see I hope that the conception of a named meaning is shown to be untenable in the second part of the dialogue and that this demonstration provides more than one way in which Parmenides' destructive criticisms can be met. The conception of a named meaning thus pulls together the two parts of the *Parmenides* and also explains its position in between the "theory-of-forms" and the "participation" dialogues. This encourages one to think that it is Plato's purpose to worry at the conception of a named meaning. If it be asked why, in that case, Plato does not say more clearly what he is at, two answers are available. One is that the dialogue is almost avowedly (through Parmenides' mouth) offered to us as something to sharpen our wits on. The other is that in all probability Plato, like many of us his commentators, found it easier to see than to say what the point was.

We must now turn to the second part of the dialogue.

---

[1] The belief in forms is sometimes said to rest on just this sort of reasoning. I would remind the reader that I do not subscribe to this view. This line of reasoning is responsible, in my view, not for the belief in forms but for deviations into which that belief sometimes slipped.

B. *The second part of the* Parmenides

5. Parmenides begins by repeating and amplifying the description he has given of the mental training which he advises Socrates to undergo. In the case of every hypothesis which he entertains, he is to make a practice of investigating the consequences both of the hypothesis and of its contradictory, the consequences both for the thing which the hypothesis is concerned with, and for each and every other thing. (Thus if the hypothesis were that there are tame tigers, we should have to investigate what is involved (1) in affirming and (2) in denying this, both (*a*) for the alleged take tigers themselves, and (*b*) for everything else). Parmenides agrees to play this "laborious game" in order to show them what he means. He will take he says "his own hypothesis, making a hypothesis about the one itself, and see what follows from saying that it is one and from saying that it is not one" (136 a–137 b).

F. It is important to notice the complete vagueness with which the topic to be discussed is introduced. What is meant by the (barely grammatical) sentence which I have translated at the end of the last paragraph? What is "the one"? Is it the single substance which Parmenides notoriously thought reality to consist of? Or is it unity? What do the two propositions "The one is one" and "The one is not one" mean? Neither here nor later are we given any clues towards the answering of these questions. Indeed there could be no clues, for as we shall see the meaning of the essential terms shifts as the argument develops. But it is most uncharacteristic of Plato to suppose that a topic can be clearly identified by stating it in one short and bald sentence. It is much more characteristic of him to try the readers' patience by the repetitions, illustrations and so on, by which he makes it clear what he is talking about.[1] The assumption that the reader can identify the topic "whether the one is one or not" from that description would be so un-typical of Plato that I cannot believe that he made it. But the only alternative explanation is that Plato did no more to isolate his topic because it was essential to his purpose that it should not be isolated. In other words the ambiguity is left because he intends to play upon it. This comes out also in a feature of the argument that we may as well notice here. This is that from Parmenides' advice to Socrates we ought to expect *four* extractions of consequences or deductions (how it affects (*a*) the one and (*b*) everything else if the hypothesis is (1) asserted and (2) denied). But in fact there are *eight* and not four, and each deduction in each pair

[1] It is sometimes *philosophically* unclear what he is talking about, but this happens, one feels, when Plato himself has not clearly distinguished two easily confused questions.

contradicts its colleague. Plato takes pains in this way to show that opposite consequences can be extracted from the same proposition *if* (he leaves us to work out this condition for ourselves) you do not fix the meaning of your terms.

None the less we can narrow down the meaning of Parmenides' hypothesis a little. It seems to me clear, to start with, that Parmenides' proposal is to discuss "a hypothesis about the one, that *it* is one", and not "that reality is one". It is not his monistic cosmology that he intends to talk about. (Possibly Plato thought that the hypothesis that the one is one in some way underlay Parmenides' monism, and that is why he makes Parmenides speak of it as "my own hypothesis". He might for example have thought that Parmenides' monist views could be traced to an argument of the following pattern: if there is only one universe, then the universe must be a unit, and therefore can contain no diversity. This argument seems to presuppose that "the one is one", understood in the sense "whatever is a unit is unitary"). We will suppose then that Parmenides' affirmative hypothesis is "that the one is one". However when he comes to consider the contradictory of this hypothesis in 160 b he says that they must consider what happens "if the one is not", where "is not" naturally means "does not exist". But to treat "the one is one" and "the one does not exist" as contradictories is to presuppose that either the one is one or there is no such thing as the one. This of course is a special case of the general rule: "Either the X is X or there is no such thing as the X." This general rule looks like Socrates' principle that properties are self-predicable.

If we read this presupposition into Parmenides' affirmative hypothesis we can exhibit the affirmative and negative hypotheses as near-contradictories thus:—the affirmative hypothesis becomes "there is such a thing as the one (and it is one)" and the negative "there is no such thing as the one". It seems to be clear that this is what Parmenides intends to discuss. What is not clear however is the meaning to be attached to *to hen* or "the one" (in what follows I shall write *to hen* to avoid begging this question). The following meanings at least are available: (1) unity in the sense of unitariness or complete lack of plurality. (2) unity in the ordinary sense—the oneness which can be attributed to anything which can be called *a* so-and-so. (3) units or unitary objects; objects characterised by unity in the first sense. (4) units in the ordinary sense, objects characterised by unity in the second sense. (We might use "unitary objects" and "units" respectively to stand for these last two possibilities).

6. *The first deduction.* Parmenides starts from the assertion "it is one", and argues that if it is one it cannot have parts. Therefore it cannot have shape, and therefore it cannot be in space. It cannot

move or change, and it cannot stay where it is. It cannot be the same as, or different from, either itself or anything else, nor like or unlike either itself or anything else, nor equal or unequal. Therefore it cannot be in time, and therefore finally it cannot exist, be known, spoken of or anything else whatever. (137 c–142 a; I have left out a good many of Parmenides' conclusions and almost all his reasons).

G. We must remember that Plato is playing on ambiguity throughout this part of the *Parmenides*, and therefore we cannot assume that *to hen* will maintain a constant meaning even throughout one deduction. We must also admit that there is more than one axe that Plato grinds in the course of these arguments. To ask therefore "What does he mean by *to hen* here, and what is he trying to show about it?" will be to oversimplify if we assume either that he means some one thing or that he is trying to show some one thing. With that proviso, let us ask if we can interpret this deduction.

If we ask what *to hen* is in this deduction we must answer either that its meaning varies, or that *to hen* is a "named meaning"; for it is treated both as a thing and as a property. It is treated as a thing when it is shown that it cannot change, move, be in space and so on; for it is not necessary to argue that a property cannot do these things. But it is also treated as a property in, for instance, the arguments showing that it cannot be other than something else, nor the same as itself (139 c–e). For these arguments depend on the principle that being different or being the same depend on difference and sameness, so that if *to hen* were different (or the same) it could not be so by *virtue of itself* and hence it could not be so *itself*; but it is only of a property that one can argue like this. John is not different from James by virtue of being himself, but he is himself different from James. But if beauty is not different from symmetry by virtue of itself, then it is not itself different from symmetry (and see 139 d 6: "But if unity (*to hen*) and sameness do not differ . . .").

However the conclusion of the argument does not apply exclusively to a named meaning, for a good deal of the argument would work equally well with "X" in the place of *to hen*. For a good deal of the argument simply depends on the principle that if anything is predicated of X, then X is complex, consisting of itself and whatever is predicated of it. This applies even if the predicate is existence. It follows that nothing perfectly unitary can exist. Since however it is in fact of *to hen* that this is said we can say that the conclusion of the argument is that not even *to hen* can be perfectly unitary. But the argument depends on the premise that *to hen* must be perfectly unitary, for it begins with the inference that, being *to hen*, it cannot have parts. It follows therefore that *to hen* is an impossible concept in the sense that there cannot be said to *be* anything which is perfectly unitary. There can be nothing which makes a perfect fit with the meaning of "unity". More generally, there cannot be anything which is just one simple property in the sense that nothing can be predicated of it. For any existent property is both the property which it is, and also existent; and this renders it complex.

7. *The second deduction.* Parmenides then suggests that they go back to the beginning again to see if they get a different result. He starts once more from the affirmative assertion that "it is one", and infers that it must in that case exist, and must therefore have parts (viz. existence and itself or *to hen*). It is also infinitely numerous; for both *to hen* and existence partake in each other, and therefore each of them has parts, and the same is true of their parts *ad infinitum*. But *to hen* is anyhow numerous, even without partaking in existence; for existence and *to hen* are different from each other, and therefore each of them has at least two elements, namely itself and being different from. Therefore if *to hen* exists number exists, for we have to have two entities, and from 1 and 2 all numbers can be generated. And if number exists, there is an infinite number of entities (each number being an entity); and since every entity is a case of *to hen,* there is an infinite number of cases of *to hen.* Moreover since *to hen* has parts it must have shape, and be in space, be in itself and in something else, be active and inactive, be the same as, and different from (and also like and unlike) both itself and other things . . . be in time . . . be knowable . . . come into being and perish, be separated and compounded, etc. (142 b–157 b. In 155 e Parmenides says "let us work it out the third time", but as he assumes what he has hitherto proved this concluding section does not really constitute a third deduction. I have left out a great deal of this deduction).

H. The first deduction showed that if unity has to be unitary it cannot exist. The second begins by showing that if unity has to exist it cannot be unitary. So far the two deductions agree together. The second deduction however does not content itself with making this point; it makes a great many others which seem to have little to do with this theme. Thus for a considerable part of the time Plato is creating logical paradoxes about the nature of space, time and process. These are of no immediate interest to us, and I cannot find any single moral which they might be thought to inculcate, unless it be the moral (suggested by the whole deduction) that it is possible to prove anything whatever so long as proving is simply a matter of manipulating words without reference to the realities which they concern. (I have no doubt that this is one moral that we are supposed to draw from the whole of the second part of the dialogue).

It is noteworthy that at the beginning of the deduction *to hen* is clearly unity (for existence is said to partake in it). This is almost

339

stated in 144 e 5 where Parmenides infers from the infinity of the numbers to the infinity of *to hen*, and uses words which I take to mean "not only is that which is one many, but also the one itself". Almost immediately however *to hen* becomes an object, and a physical object at that, for Parmenides proves that, since it has parts, it must have shape and be in space. Either therefore *to hen* is a named meaning, or the deduction breaks in half at this point. In the first part of the deduction, while *to hen* is still unity, it looks to the modern reader as if the following happens. First Plato accepts the converse of the conclusion of the first deduction, namely: if unity exists it must be in a sense complex, being both itself and also existent. He then shows that the complexity is greater than that, for whatever exists is also characterised by unity, sameness and difference. Existence, unity, sameness and difference in fact characterise every property (indeed every entity) whatsoever. Next however he produces a *reductio ad absurdum* argument to the conclusion that unity is many, the lesson to be derived from this being, we are inclined to suppose, that the fact that P-hood exists (is one, self-same, and different from everything else) does not entail that P-hood is something complex;[1] for if this counts as complexity, then P-hood will be infinitely complex. As I say, this is the lesson which the modern reader may well derive from this part of the argument; but I hesitate to affirm that this is the lesson that Plato meant us to derive.[2] If it is, however, the two deductions, so far, fit nicely together. The first has shown that unity cannot be perfectly unitary; the second, so far, says that you cannot, for all that, say that it is complex, for if you do you will be forced into the absurdity of saying that it is infinitely complex. It cannot perfectly fit the meaning of "unity", but that does not entail that it is complex, in the sense of having genuine parts.

After the break, when *to hen* becomes a physical object, what seems to happen, on the whole, is not that unity is illegitimately treated as a physical object (as in Parmenides' earlier argument about the "parts of bigness" etc.), but that the meaning of *to hen* changes from "unity" to "that which is one". From this point, in other words, the argument predominantly concerns itself with things which are units. Since however *to hen* has been shown to be complex, the units in question are complex entities. Therefore when Parmenides introduces "things other than *to hen*" these become things which are not units, and hence indefinite aggregations or something of the kind. Parmenides then succeeds in showing that the relations between the classes of units and the class of non-units are highly paradoxical.

[1] Is this also the moral of "Socrates' dream" in the *Theaetetus*? For a discussion of this see above, pp. 114–17.

[2] Partly because of an argument in the *Sophist*; see below, pp. 390–4.

8. *The third deduction.* This is the first of the pair of deductions which concern themselves with the consequences, for things other than *to hen*, of the hypothesis that it is one. First Parmenides shows that "the others" must have parts, or they would be perfectly unitary (whereas they are not one). Therefore, though not identical with *to hen*, they must partake in it, since parts must be parts of *a* whole; and so must each of their parts, and so on *ad infinitum*. But they must also be infinitely multitudinous; that is to say each of the parts must both partake in *to hen*, and hence be a unit, but it must also be an infinite multitude. The reason why it must be an infinite multitude is that, although it partakes in *to hen*, it cannot, at the moment of partaking, be a unit. But although infinite in this way, they must also be finite, as a result of partaking in *to hen*. The parts must be finite in the sense that any given part is different from any other, and from the whole. They are thus like each other (in being finite, and again in being infinite) and yet unlike each other (for in being both finite and infinite they partake in contrary predicates and hence are contrary). They are also identical with and different from each other . . . and they have every contradictory predicate. (For this Parmenides offers no argument. I suppose it is to follow from their being alike and un-alike). (157 b–159 b).

I. Zeno had criticised the Pythagorean notion that things are made up of units by arguing that a finite distance is infinitely divisible and thus contains an infinite number of components. This deduction is obviously concerned with this topic. It is also clearly concerned with the relation of participation. If S may be said to be P by participating in P-hood, then it may seem to be a fair question what S is like in itself, apart from its participation in P-hood. By the blatant argument that that which "takes a share of" unity cannot "at that moment" be a unit, Plato surely indicates that this is not a fair question, that you cannot treat the "subject" of properties as if it were itself a thing having properties of its own apart from the properties in which it "partakes". Partaking is not, like getting married, something which a thing does, and by doing which it changes its status.

What is *to hen* in this deduction? The discussion seems to be concerned with things which are not units, and these are called "things other than *to hen*". The class of things which are not unity is not the same as the class of things which are not units. Therefore *to hen* does not mean unity, but the class of units. Yet on the other hand the class of things which are not units partake in *to hen*, and here *to hen* does mean unity. *To hen* therefore seems at first sight to bear two meanings in this deduction, unity and the class of units. Perhaps however the truth is once more that *to hen* is the named meaning of "one". If the named meaning is the only thing which really *is* a unit (as opposed to partaking in unity), then everything other than the named meaning will fail to *be* a unit, and in this case "the things other than *to hen*" will be everything whatsoever except for the two-faced entity which is both unity and the only perfectly unitary object. This entity thus becomes identical with the class of units.

The discussion however is concerned with "the rest", and these *ex hypothesi* are not units. It is shown however that they must none the less "partake in unity", and this leads to the conclusion that these entities have very paradoxical features, which they owe to the fact that they are in a sense units, and therefore finite, and yet *ex hypothesi* non-units, and therefore infinite. This amounts to a demonstration that if unity is the only perfectly unitary entity then everything except unity has every pair of incompatible predicates. This constitutes a *reductio ad absurdum* of the proposition that unity is the only perfectly unitary entity. But it also constitutes a *reductio ad absurdum* of the proposition that there exist some non-units (for the absurdities would follow from this, whatever was comprised in the class of units). This of course reinforces the conclusion, hinted at in the second deduction, that unity characterises everything. By now therefore, if we add up our results, we are in something like the following position. (1) We see that the conception of a named meaning for "unity" is impossible. (2) We see (from the first deduction) that no thing can be unitary. (3) We see however, from the second and third deductions, that everything must be a unit. In fact a distinction is beginning to emerge between being unitary and being a unit, and we can see perhaps that if unity is not the property which belongs to a unitary entity (there being no such things), it can console itself with the status of the property common to units (i.e. to everything).

9. *The fourth deduction*, the counterpart to the third. As before, we now get the opposite result. First Parmenides proves that the things other than *to hen* do not partake in *to hen*, on the ground that *to hen* and the rest must be "apart from" (*chôris*) each other. They must be apart, because *to hen* and the rest together constitute all that there is. They are altogether apart, and neither is contained in the other. The rest must also be in principle innumerable; if they were numerable they would be a collection of units. Nor can they be alike or unalike, since in that case they would have to have at least one property (viz. alikeness, or unlikeness); and they are not allowed to partake in *to hen*. It follows that they can have no other properties either. (159 b–160 b).

J. One pictures a scene in the Academy. A group of students are exercising their wits on the *Parmenides*. One of them protests that from "*to hen* and the others are apart" you cannot infer "*to hen* cannot be in the others; therefore the others cannot partake in *to hen*", unless you treat "apart", and "be in" literally, as spatial concepts. Another protests that partaking in *one* property is not partaking in unity; and the students draw the conclusion that nothing remains of the argument of this deduction. What does Plato say? Does he retort to the first: "Yes, that is what I wanted you to see; but you must also see that Parmenides was wanting to treat partaking, in the first part of the dialogue, as if it were a physical relationship?" Does he answer the second objector similarly: "Yes, I wanted you to see that partaking in one X is not partaking in unity?" The trouble is that if Plato does respond like this he allows that the deduction has no force; it was no more than a fairly simple wit-twister. But then what happens to the contribution that this deduction might have made to a general and subtle point about the nature of forms?

For this deduction might have been regarded as complementary to the third. The third reduces the conception of non-units to absurdity by making non-units partake in unity, on the principle roughly that if they are things in the plural each of them must be *a* thing. The fourth deduction takes the alternative route of ruling that non-units cannot partake in unity, and thus comes to the same conclusion that there cannot be such a thing as a non-unit. This would be a very satisfactory result. Adding the two deductions together one could say: whether or not we suppose that non-units partake in unity, we reach the conclusion that there can be no non-units.

Are we entitled to think that these two deductions are meant to be added together in this way, in view of the fact that the second of the pair can be punctured by noticing two quite different, and fairly obvious, points which have nothing specially to do with the conception of a non-unit? I raise this question here because this deduction affords a convenient opportunity to demonstrate the problem, but it is a problem which faces one throughout the second part of the dialogue. On the one hand one feels that there must be some one general lesson which is meant to emerge and which allows one to see how Socrates could have met Parmenides' criticisms and retained his belief in forms. On the other hand one is continually saying to oneself: "But Plato cannot mean us to take *this* argument seriously; he must have written this whole passage as a logical exercise for the young men in the Academy to pull to pieces."[1]

Not knowing how to choose between these, I choose both. Whatever point Plato wanted to make in the *Parmenides* he has certainly failed to communicate it to us (some have even taken the dialogue to

---

[1] Cornford (*Plato and Parmenides*) maintains with great skill the thesis that all Plato's arguments are at least colourably valid. But at times even Cornford has to express doubts (see e.g. his comments on 145 e 7 sqq.).

be a serious essay in mystical theology). Perhaps the reason for this failure is that he tried to do two inconsistent things. He tried to bring out a point about the nature of forms by the method of teasing the reader's wits; but at the same time he decided to string on to this general thread a number of incidental logical puzzles having no essential bearing on the main puzzle. This was an injudicious decision, unless perhaps his main purpose in writing the dialogue was to use it in the class-room under his own supervision.

There is however a particular difficulty about the fourth deduction which might have forced Plato to rely on bad arguments. According to our interpretation he wants to make the point that non-units cannot partake in unity, because if they did they would be units. But in the language he is using this becomes: "things other than *to hen* cannot partake in *to hen*, because in that case they would not be other than *to hen*". But this (unless it is strengthened by dubious manoeuvres about *being apart* and *being in*) has the appearance of a *non-sequitur*; Helen is other than beauty, though she partakes in it. The point is of course that the formula we have just made up is ambiguous between: "things which are not members of the class of units cannot be units or they would not be non-members of the class of units" (which is true), and: "things other than unity cannot be units or they would not be other than unity" (which is false). So to make the point that non-units cannot be units (and therefore that there can be no non-units) it is necessary to distinguish between the extension of *to hen* (the class of units) and its intension (unity). But to do that would be to give the game away, for the game that Plato is at the moment playing depends on the notion of the named meaning, i.e. on the notion that the extension of a term consists, strictly speaking, of nothing but its intension; and Plato does not want to tell us in so many words that this is wrong. Since therefore he cannot validly make the subordinate point (that non-units cannot partake in unity) without first making the main point about the named meaning (and this he cannot or will not do) he relies on fallacies, the detection of which will anyhow be useful, to achieve the desired result. On the whole, then, I would conclude that the fourth deduction is designed to reinforce the third, and that the two together show that the conception of non-units is absurd.

10. *Concluding comment on the first four deductions.* Therefore, says Parmenides, if *to hen* is one it is everything (*or*: everything is *to hen*), and is not even one (*or*: is nothing), both with respect to itself and to everything else (160 b).

K. Parmenides does not in fact say that this sentence comments on all four deductions, but it seems that it does. It is an ambiguous sentence, but at least it draws attention to the fact that their results are very paradoxical. On our view, to recapitulate, the conclusions to be drawn from this fact are: that unity cannot be the named meaning of "unity"; that this is so because nothing can be perfectly unitary, and also because it is built into the conception of the named meaning of P-hood that only it *is* P; but the corollary of this in the case of unity (namely that there exist non-units) is absurd; therefore everything is a unit, though nothing is perfectly unitary.

11. *The fifth deduction: the first of the four deductions drawn from the contradictory of the hypothesis.* Parmenides argues that if we say that *to hen* does not exist, it must be something distinct to which we deny existence, and this distinct thing must be knowable. It must therefore have various properties, such as difference, this-ness, unlikeness, self-resemblance. It must also be unequal to other things (for it cannot be equal to other things, for that would involve its being). Other properties it must have are equality to other things, and also largeness and smallness (for various remarkable reasons); also existence "in some way". It must also be active and inactive, changing and unchanging; it must come into being and perish; and it must do neither of these things. (160 b–163 b, fairly heavily compressed).

12. *The sixth deduction* simply argues that if *to hen* does not exist, then it has no properties whatever, stands in no relation to anything, cannot be known, and in fact in no sense exists. (163 b–164 b).

L. These two deductions can be taken together. Plainly they are concerned with negative existential statements—statements of the form "There is no such thing as . . ." The first of the pair of deductions argues (in effect) that no such statement can be true; for every such statement must be about something, and that which it is about must exist. The second of the pair merely argues that what does not exist does not exist. Since the first of the pair in effect reduces to absurdity the idea that something which does not exist is nevertheless in some sense "there" (for it shows that a non-entity treated as something is an impossibly paradoxical entity) the lesson of the two deductions is perhaps that a denial of existence cannot be half-hearted. If (where "P" is the sort of expression which would be expected to stand for a property) I say that there is no such thing as P, then I deny myself the right to impute P to anything whatsoever. If therefore "P" is a significant expression, it must be false that there is no such thing as P. The point that a denial of existence must be wholehearted, is needed for the next two deductions, which depend on the total elimination of unity. The point that it cannot be true that there is no such thing as unity is wanted for the argument as a whole.

13. *The seventh deduction.* This is the first of the pair of deductions which consider the effect on "the others" of the elimination of *to*

345

hen. Parmenides begins by making the point that they cannot be other than *to hen* and must therefore be other than each other. This looks like a singularly feeble point about the title "the others", but what is probably Parmenides' real purpose emerges in his next move when he says that they must be other than each other "not by ones but by multitudes". That is to say, *to hen* being eliminated, the distinguishable "units" that there are cannot be real units but must be groups. Each of these aggregations must also be infinitely numerous, even though it *seems* to be one. It will *seem* as if the number of these aggregations is finite, and they will *seem* to have size, etc., and to be units, and to have the various contradictory properties which we have learned to expect. (164 b–165 e).

14. *The eighth deduction.* This argues that if *to hen* does not exist, nothing exists whatever; for there cannot be numerous things unless each of them is one, and there cannot seem to be. For if *to hen* is a non-entity, there cannot even be a semblance of unity, and therefore there cannot seem to be single things, and therefore there cannot seem to be things. Therefore if there is no such thing as *to hen*, there is nothing whatever. (165 e–166 c).

M. These two deductions, again, may be considered together. We may notice that in both of them the consequences of supposing that *to hen* does not exist are the consequences of supposing that unity does not exist. The difference between them seems to be this. The seventh supposes that unity does not "exist" in the sense that nothing in fact has the property, though it allows that it "exists" as a possibility, so to speak, so that things can seem to have the property. It then goes on to show that this supposition has paradoxical consequences, making in passing the important point that the numerability of a group depends on its unity.[1] The eighth on the other hand insists that whatever exists must be *a* so-and-so, so that the elimination of unity entails the elimination of everything. The effect of the two deductions taken together is to show that it is absurd to suppose that unity does not exist, and absurd to suppose that there are in fact no units. It is however brought out in the seventh deduction that a finite group will inevitably be *one* group, and it is natural for us to infer that conversely a unit may have parts.

15. *Parmenides' concluding comment.* "Therefore," says Parmenides, "we may say not only this" (viz. the conclusion of the eighth deduction) "but also, as it seems, that whether or not there is such a thing as *to hen*, both it and everything else both is and seems to be both absolutely everything and also nothing." "Very true," says Aristoteles (these being the last words of the dialogue).

[1] This point is made in 165 a–b. We shall see later (pp. 447 sqq.) that it is—rightly—important to Plato's theory of number.

N. The official result of the second part of the dialogue is that we incur impossible consequences if we say either that there is such a thing as *to hen*, and that it is one, or that there is no such thing as *to hen*. Plainly Plato did not mean us to take this result so complacently as Aristoteles takes it. We have argued that the lesson which we are meant to derive from the first four deductions is that nothing is perfectly unitary and that therefore there is nothing which makes a perfect fit with "unity", but that none the less unity characterises whatever exists. It now seems that the last four deductions support this result, for they seem to show that if we understand what is involved in a denial of existence we must see that it is absurd to deny the existence of unity, and absurd to deny that there are in fact units. The over-all conclusion then seems to be that while we cannot deny either the existence of unity or its instantiation, we cannot on the other hand maintain the existence of anything which is perfectly unitary or non-complex. Unity is a property of everything and it is compatible with complexity, but "unitariness" stands for nothing conceivable.

C. *The contribution of the second part of the* Parmenides *to the solution of the problems raised in the first part*

Parmenides has reduced to absurdity two propositions which he has treated as contradictories, namely:

> The one is one; and
> There is no such thing as the one.

Or, as we have decided to re-phrase these two propositions:

> There is such a thing as unity and it is unitary; and
> There is no such thing as unity.

This re-formulation of Parmenides' two propositions shows us how to escape from his dilemma, namely by asserting that:

> There is such a thing as unity, and it is false that it is unitary.

This then is a demonstration that unity is not unitary, and this shows that in the case of unity at least the conception of the named meaning, or the abstract individual which makes a perfect fit with the property, is untenable.[1] Since it is also shown that unity is a perfectly

---

[1] How does it show this? Not by showing that properties are not self-predicable (which is not indeed universally true; definability, for example, is perhaps definable). It is not shown that you cannot say that unity is one. What is shown is that you cannot say that unity (or anything else) is *unitary*. In fact there is nothing (not even the property unity) which is just and only one, and which is such that it is false that it is anything else whatever.

good property, being indeed characteristic of everything whatsoever, it follows that the existence of a property is not the existence of a named meaning.

How does this result (assuming that we are supposed to see something like this as the result of the second part) contribute towards rescuing Socrates from his difficulties in the first part? What light does this result throw on the question of the place of the *Parmenides* in Plato's writing?

1. We saw that Parmenides managed to reduce Socrates to silence on the subject of participation by foisting upon him a concrete physical picture of the relation of a property to its instances. We suggested also that the picture of a named meaning (though not precisely a physical picture) weakened Socrates' resistance to Parmenides' concrete models. In particular perhaps it may be supposed to have weakened Socrates' resistance to Parmenides' "gravest" objection, in which the form of knowledge is treated as God's knowledge, so that the relation of a form to its instances is treated very much as if it were the relation of an original to its reproduction. With the conception of a named meaning got rid of the way is clear to see that a property is something on a different logical level from its instances, so that Socrates' "one day in many places" is at least a possible model for the property-instance relationship, whereas Parmenides' "one sail over many men" is quite impossible.

2. Since a named meaning is an abstract *individual* the principle of individuation of a named meaning is the same as that of an ordinary individual. The principle of individuation of a property clearly is not. At the beginning of his cross-examination Parmenides tells Socrates that his views have the consequence that "one and the same form has to exist as a whole in numerous separate objects, and is thus separated from itself" (131 b 1–2; *cp.* also 131 c 9–11). But to regard this as paradoxical is to treat a form as if its principle of individuation were the same as that of an ordinary individual, as the conception of a named meaning implies. The destruction of this conception shows that no strain is put upon the unity of a property by its possession of numerous instances.

3. But Parmenides can retort:—"But if the concept of a property is such that one property can have many instances, then so much the worse for the concept of a property; for plainly what is one cannot at the same time be many." We can now answer this by saying that Parmenides is relying on an impossible conception of unity. Anything which is one so-and-so, is at the very least complex in the sense that it is both a so-and-so and an existent, and it is also the case that there is nothing wrong with the conception of the unity of a group, still less of an individual thing having parts.

4. These three points taken together would have enabled Socrates to meet Parmenides' criticisms by saying (*a*) (as he wanted to say) "Why should we not have one form in many instances? After all we have one day in many places"; and also (*b*) "But you cannot treat participation as a physical relationship; properties are not things." It would not however have allowed him to say positively what participation is. To answer this question he would have to say that for S to participate in P-hood is for S to be a P thing. But he could hardly give this answer so long as he felt (as we suggested above that he did feel) that participation is a special thing-to-property relationship which does not occur on the property-to-property level—so long, that is, as he felt that properties cannot be blended or divorced. For what underlies this is the confused grammar (responsible for the conception of the named meaning) according to which only the named meaning of "P" can strictly be said to be P. What is needed, in order to say what participation is, is the realisation that "participates in" is no more than a metaphor used to mark the predication as opposed to the identity sense of "is". It is therefore necessary to get rid of the conception of the named meaning in order to think clearly about participation.

These points emerge from the results of the second part of the dialogue in two different ways. The demonstration that unity is compatible with multiplicity emerges from what is said about unity as such. The destruction of the conception of the named meaning however emerges from a general conclusion about the nature of a property which derives from but goes beyond what is said about unity as such. It is demonstrated that it is not a necessary condition of the existence of unity that there should be a unitary thing; for the property does exist, and nothing could be perfectly unitary. This does not in itself show that a named meaning is an impossibility except in the case of unity.[1] It does show however that in the case of at least one property the named meaning is an impossibility, from which we can infer that a named meaning is not the same as a property. And since the whole point of a named meaning was to be the same as the property in question, this is in effect the death of the named meaning.

In destroying the conception of the named meaning the result of the second part of the *Parmenides* looks backward to the classical theory of forms. In discussing the *Phaedo*[2] we saw that Socrates tells us that physical things which are equal can also seem unequal. We

---

[1] Incidentally the same is conversely shown for the cases of existence, self-sameness, etc. For it can be inferred that nothing can be *purely* existent, since whatever is existent is also one, self-same, etc.

[2] Above, pp. 295–302.

suggested that his point was that you cannot learn what equality is from the observation of physical things, because unless you "remember" already what equality is you may fix your attention on an aspect in which they are unequal. But we noticed at the same time that Socrates spoke as if this were the fault of the physical things. We found an adequate explanation of this in the "photographic" conception of thought. Now however we can perhaps amplify this. Socrates speaks as if what he would like to have, as it were, is instances of equality about whose equality there *could not* be any dispute. But it is surely the case that if A and B have any other properties besides that of being equal to each other, then it will be possible to find a respect in which they are unequal. (I suppose that this is a version of the principle of the Identity of Indiscernibles; if A and B are different individuals then something must be true of one which is false of the other; therefore they are in this respect unlike; therefore they are in this respect unequal). Therefore what Socrates seems to desiderate is instances of equality which are simply and only instances of equality, and of which therefore there can in fact be only one (by the Identity of Indiscernibles once more). What he desiderates then is the named meaning. Since in the case of anything else he says of it that it is, or can seem, both equal and unequal, one feels that he would be willing to say "is equal" without reservation only of the named meaning of equality.[1]

In discussing this passage I did not say that it was to be regarded as putting forward the doctrine of imperfect embodiment on the ground that a property can only be predicated of itself; and I do not say it now.[2] The *Phaedo* does not teach imperfect embodiment; that is to say, it does not teach anything which implies that it is a false statement in modern English that things can be perfectly equal. This is the wrong account of the effect of the conception of the named meaning upon the theory of forms. But what I think is likely is that the conception of the named meaning may have predisposed Plato towards certain ways of talking. Nothing else has to the expression "equal" the relation of perfect fit which the named meaning has. Of nothing else therefore can the predicate "equal" be used with the same degree of strict propriety. If we, who have got over the conception of perfect fit, express this by saying "Plato believed that nothing but

---

[1] cp. *Phaedo* 100 c 4 "if anything is beautiful besides the beautiful itself" where the "if" suggests doubt about the propriety of saying that anything else is beautiful (p. 287 above).

[2] There is an equally good *apparent* case of imperfect embodiment long after the *Parmenides* had destroyed this putative ground in the *Seventh Letter* 343 a 5; cp. also *Philebus* 62 a. Whatever is responsible for the apparent cases of this doctrine survived the *Parmenides*.

P-hood can ever be perfectly P", we distort the facts. "Plato was inclined to say 'nothing but P-hood can ever be perfectly P' " may well be true, but if his reasons for saying this were concerned with perfect fit, then "Nothing but P-hood can ever be perfectly P", on his lips, must translate into "Nothing but P-hood can ever have perfect fit with 'P' " on our lips, and not into "Nothing but P-hood can ever be perfectly P"; for this latter, on our lips, would mean that allegedly P things have some property other than P-hood, and this is what Plato did not believe. Thus, if somebody says in modern English "Nothing is perfectly straight" he implies that so-called straight things are in fact slightly *curved*. This is the sort of thing that the *Phaedo* does not say. But because he wanted to deny that P things have perfect fit with P-hood, Plato was willing (in my view) to embrace any fair argument he could find whose conclusion could be represented in the form "Whereas P-hood is P without qualification, P things are also not P".

The *Parmenides*, then, represents a gain in understanding of the logic of general terms and (with it) of predication. As far as the earlier work is concerned this does not carry with it the abandonment of any of the earlier positions. What it does do is to open the door to investigation of the relations between universals—an investigation which is henceforth uninhibited by the conception that a universal is nothing but the named meaning of a general term. The *Parmenides* is therefore more important as an introduction to the later work than as destructive criticism of the earlier.

In this later work, as we shall see, Plato is interested in considering (without perhaps fully distinguishing) two topics. The first of these concerns itself with statements about properties (e.g. "Activity is different from existence"), the second with what we might call statements about classes (e.g. "The animal comprises the winged animal, the terrestrial and the aquatic"). Both of these topics seem to be referred to under the title "the sharing of kinds" (*koinônia genôn*).[1] If relations between classes are thought of as relations between the appropriate class-properties, then it can be seen that the *Parmenides* helps towards the discussion of both of these topics.

The conception of a named meaning is the conception of something which perfectly fits the meaning of a general term. P things do not perfectly fit the meaning of "P" because they partake in other properties beside P-hood. If P-hood itself partook in other properties beside itself that would impair its perfect fit with the meaning of "P". Therefore it partakes in no other properties—properties cannot be "blended among themselves". This argument shows how the

---

[1] A title which recalls Socrates' statement that forms or kinds cannot be "blended or divorced".

conception of perfect fit would inhibit the study of statements about properties. (I do not mean that the argument would have seemed convincing to Plato if he had expressed it. But one idea can inhibit another when there is in fact some logical connection between them even when this connection is not perceived. The suggestion is that when Plato perceived the connection he treated it as a *reductio ad absurdum* of perfect fit).

Perfect fit had to go before Plato could think clearly about statements about properties. In the case of the topic of statements about classes the important part of the results of the *Parmenides* is not so much this general point about the nature of a property, but rather the particular point about unity. The relation of generic properties to their specific versions—of the animal to the winged animal, the terrestrial and the aquatic for example—raise the problem of the unity of a property. Just as Parmenides worried Socrates to tell him how one form can be present in many instances, so, in the later dialogues, Plato lays frequent stress on the apparent paradox that one generic form can be present in many specific forms.[1] To accept this paradox as the truth it is necessary to see that forms can partake (and therefore to get rid, as we have seen, of perfect fit); but it is also necessary to see that something which is one so-and-so is not therefore unitary. It is important to see that it is not a metaphysical peculiarity of forms which allows them to be one-and-many, but a fact about the logic of "one" and of general terms.

If this interpretation of the *Parmenides* is anywhere near the truth (and I need hardly remind the reader that it must be highly speculative) then the dialogue does not express the abandonment of earlier opinions except perhaps the opinion that forms cannot be blended among themselves. Rather it is the culmination of the long process by which Plato succeeded in isolating the conception of a universal property and in learning what sort of language to use about these. It is the last wriggle by which the universal gets out of the chrysalis of the abstract individual. But it *may* after all be a treatise in mystical theology, or even, in Professor Taylor's view, a *jeu d'esprit*.

Perhaps I may make a personal statement. When I first seriously read the *Parmenides*, I found that a dim idea of Plato's purpose was forced upon me by the reading.[2] This dim idea has received abortive statement in many different forms in the course of preparing this

---

[1] As we shall see it seems that Plato confounded these two points and treated the property-instance relation as a special case of the genus-species relation. See pp. 366–8 below, also p. 295 above.

[2] A recollection of Professor Ryle's famous article (*Mind* for 1939) was doubtless subconsciously active.

section, the idea of an attack on perfect fit being the last and least incoherent of these. If then I am told that I am reading too much into the dialogue, that Plato cannot have meant anything which takes so much midnight oil to extract, then I would reply that the midnight oil has been burnt only on the work of rendering explicit an impression which the dialogue made on impact.

III. THE RANGE OF FORMS

When we discussed the relation between the concept of a form and the concept of a universal, we decided that a form was a universal for which exalted status was claimed. It follows that questions of the form "Is P-hood a form?" can be asked. In this section we must briefly investigate the range of the forms—for what sort of entities were forms postulated?

The evidence on this point is complex and difficult. It is mostly Aristotelian, the dialogues doing little more than to show that the question "Is P-hood a form?" can be asked. (I have suggested above that the formula "For every common name there exists a common nature" does not contradict this, for to this we can reply by asking what counts as a common nature). The evidence can be found in Sir David Ross's *Plato's Theory of Ideas*, Chapter 11. Ross's conclusion, with which I should not venture (and do not want) to quarrel, is that Plato probably "recognised" forms of "whatever exists by nature", where "nature" includes the useful arts. Or, in other words, there are forms of whatever is recognised[1] or contrived by divine or human reason.

This conclusion receives two bits of incidental support from the *Republic*—the dialogue from which comes the formula "For every common name there exists a common nature". In the Sixth Book, in the simile of the Line, when Plato wants to contrast seeing shadows with seeing things, he gives an oddly truncated list of things—animals, plants and manufactured articles. There seems no reason why bits of inanimate nature such as rocks should be left out of it; one can contrast seeing a crag with seeing its shadow. I suspect that Plato leaves out bits of inanimate nature from his list because he has it in mind that recognising an empirical object stands in some image-original relationship to grasping a form, and therefore he mentions only those empirical objects to which he is clear that forms correspond (510 a 5). Then again in the tenth book (601 d 4) in a context in which forms are anyhow much in his mind, he says that the "excellence, nobility and rightness of every manufactured article, living

[1] In the sense in which, e.g., equality is "recognised" to be an intelligible relationship.

creature, and action is determined by nothing but the use with reference to which it has been made by man or nature". This passage could almost be said to prove that Plato believed that there are forms for all these entities; it does not of course prove that there are no others. But it seems to me significant that Plato does not simply say "the excellence, etc., of *everything*", but gives a list. It looks as if the principle: "There are forms of whatever is made by man or nature" was in his mind when he wrote this sentence.

Perhaps a further argument can be drawn from the famous slip in the same book of the *Republic* (597 b), where Socrates says that the form of the bed was made by God. Everywhere and always, except in this one passage, forms are eternal objects, which stand as exemplars and not as products to the creative intelligence. Timaeus' Craftsman makes things, not forms. Yet one can see how the idea that God makes the form of the bed could slip out on the presupposition that exalted status belongs to the objects of reason as such. For men are products of creative reason; it is only when men are made that sleeping machines become necessary. Therefore the intelligible design which beds embody owes its existence, in a sense, to the creation of men, and therefore "God made the form of the bed". The status of forms of this kind, though exalted, is not exalted *in excelsis* as it were.

However this may be, we will assume that the position Plato eventually came to is that there are forms of whatever is recognised or contrived by divine or human reason. This list may possibly surprise us both in what it includes and in what it leaves out. For it presumably leaves out forms of undesirables such as ugliness, and we have already seen that the *Republic* seems to treat this and other undesirables as forms. But the answer which we gave to this was that if reason eternally knows what beauty is then *eo ipso* it eternally knows what ugliness is, since ugliness is the vicious absence of beauty. General terms such as "ugliness" would therefore have an ambiguous status. In certain contexts, especially in the context of "knowing what P-hood is", "ugliness" could go in the place of "P-hood" as naturally as "beauty". But in the context of the question: "To what general terms must we suppose an entity of exalted status to correspond?" "ugliness" might well be left out of the list. Ugliness is not an additional form alongside beauty, though in an epistemological context no harm is done by treating it as one.

So much for what is left out by "whatever is recognised or contrived by divine or human reason". But does it include too much? We saw in the *Parmenides* that Socrates hesitated over forms of men, fire and water, and we can see reason why he should hesitate. If Plato eventually came down on the affirmative side of this fence, is his decision consonant with the motives underlying the claim for exalted status for certain universals?

Locke said that our ideas of substances were complex ideas, built up out of simple ideas. Thus for instance our notion of an orange was made up of the ideas of a certain shape, a certain colour, savour and so on. Locke is talking in terms of concepts, but there is something in what he says on the objective side also. Thus a thing cannot be a table if it is soft or unstable beyond a certain degree, or if its dimensions and proportions stray outside certain limits. Table-hood therefore has certain liaisons with hardness, rigidity and a range of shapes and sizes. Might we not define table-hood in terms of these universals, perhaps by saying that to be a table is to be a movable raised surface capable of supporting objects and of being sat at? To put the point more generally could we not say that substantival forms such as table-hood are functions of adjectival forms such as hardness? Indeed *ought* not Plato to say this? From the beginning belief in forms has been correlated with defining them, and to define a universal is to provide a commensurate analytical formula which resolves it into its elements. It has therefore always been a part, and an important part of his theory that most universals are complexes of others; the emphasis on the "letters of reality" which we find in the later dialogues is laid on something which has always been entailed by the theory, and it seems that the letters (or highly generic universals) ought to be adjectival universals such as unity, equality and so on. If Plato had believed, in the Swedenborgian spirit of which he is sometimes accused, in the existence, as a matter of fact, of a repository of ideal objects, then of course its contents would be what they were; the repository being an arbitrary fiction, its inventory could be arbitrary too. But if the claim for exalted status for certain universals was based on the belief that exalted status must be allowed to the objects of reason as such, then surely substantival universals, or at any rate such as table-hood, ought to have been left off the list. God *ought* to have made the form of the bed, or in other words it ought not to have been a full-blooded form.

It seems to me that we have to admit that on Plato's view certain universals could be regarded as complexes or functions of others. But it also seems that he did not therefore eliminate the former from the class of forms. It seems to me that the *Timaeus* makes it obvious enough why not. One can distinguish within the *Timaeus* three levels of rational necessity. On the first level it is rationally necessary that there should exist living creatures—unions of soul and body. On the next level it is rationally necessary that space should be ordered in certain ways (viz. into regular solids). On the third level, given that there must exist living creatures and that space must be organised in certain ways, it becomes rationally necessary, or at least "best", that human beings and other creatures should have the design that they have. This gives us a kind of hierarchy of forms, in that the considerations of which reason is aware on the first two levels are in some way prior to those of which it is aware on the third. But in spite of this possibility of grading forms into the more and the less ultimate, and in spite of the fact that members of the less ultimate category can be regarded as products of members of the two more ultimate categories, nevertheless on every level we are dealing with intelligible natures. The design of a man may be some thing which is only intelligible in terms of the general ends in which reason is interested and of the way in which space is ordered, but nevertheless it is possible for an omniscient intelligence to see *a priori* that humanity is one possible mode of existence. For this reason the intelligible natures such as humanity which we encounter on the third level have a good claim to be treated as forms. For it can be seen *a priori* that objects which were instances of forms such as these (e.g. men) would be among the objects whose existence (unlike that of mud) would seem satisfactory to reason.

In a sense of course this is a matter of degree, and one can imagine a case in favour of a form of, say, hair. For after all Timaeus allows hair a function in human life, so that it is in this way in the same boat with chairs and tables. Whether or not Plato allowed it to be a matter of degree whether P-hood should count as a form we do not know. On the whole the Aristotelian evidence suggests that membership of the class of forms was settled, at any rate among "the Platonists". But whatever the truth may be about that, it does seem that the decision come to about the range of the forms is consonant with the motives for claiming exalted status for certain universals.

IV. RELATIONS BETWEEN UNIVERSALS

A. *Introductory*

We are now going to forget about the theory of forms, or the claim for exalted status for certain universals. As we have seen Plato never abandoned the theory of forms, but it seems that after a certain date (roughly that of the *Republic*) he ceased to find it expedient to direct his readers' attention continually to "the very thing which is so-and-so", or to urge the importance of "recognising the existence" of such entities. Universal properties continued to command a great deal of his attention, but there are a good many things which can be said about universal properties besides the things peculiar to the theory of forms, and it is with some of these that the later dialogues deal. This is what we are about to discuss. We shall know whether topics such as these are best called metaphysical or logical when we know whether turquoise is best called blue or green. I have included them in a chapter whose general heading is "metaphysical analysis" for various unimportant reasons. I hope that too much significance will not be attached to this. One of these unimportant reasons is that there is a continuity of language between the "metaphysical" topic of the existence of forms and the "logical" topic of the inter-relations of universals.[1] It is important to remember that Plato has no word for "forms". The words *eidos* and *idea* do not mean "form", in that no claim to exalted status is built into these words. Plato uses these words in passages which are concerned with exalted status and in passages which are not concerned with exalted status. Thus when he advises us to divide a class into homogeneous sub-classes, he refers to a homogeneous sub-class as an *eidos*, opposing it to a *meros* or "fragment". Predators which capture their prey by stealth and predators which capture their prey by violence constitute such homogeneous sub-classes; each is therefore an *eidos*. Does this mean that there is a form of the predator which captures its prey by stealth? Such questions are irrelevant. Plato is not always thinking of the theory of forms and we must not thrust such an obsession upon him. No doubt the whole topic of classes and sub-classes is bound up with the realisation, recorded in the *Parmenides*, that forms can be blended among themselves, and no doubt the later discussions of general terms and their inter-relationships have implications which can be read into the theory of forms. No doubt we could construct a "developed theory of forms" and contrast it with the "classical theory of forms". I shall not however attempt to do so. It seems to me that in the later dialogues Plato discussed the relationships between general properties without always glancing over his shoulder to the question of exalted status; and many of the things that he said can be appreciated in their own right without reference to this question. To mark this I shall abandon for many pages the use of the word "form" as a translation for *eidos* and *idea*, using various other words, but in particular the word "kind", instead. ("Kind" has an advantage over "class". We all know how a class is related to a property, but we are not so sure where to place a kind. Since an *eidos* seems to hover in some places between a class and a property, this gives "kind" an advantage).

The dominant, one might almost say the obsessive, theme of the group of later dialogues that we are concerned with (*Phaedrus, Sophist, Statesman, Philebus*) is what Plato calls the *koinônia genôn*,

---

[1] There is also of course a continuity of substance in that what is true about those universals which are forms is true about forms.

or "sharing of kinds". Let us briefly consider this phrase. The word *genos* in Aristotle came to be used for a genus, whereas *eidos* came to mean a species. In Plato however the two words seem to be used interchangeably outside the theory-of-forms context. The original meaning of *genos* is "tribe" or "race" whereas the original meaning of *eidos* is more like the ordinary English meaning of "form".[1] The interchangeability of these two words in Plato's later writings is therefore significant, for *genos* presumably connotes something like a class and *eidos* something like a class-property or distinguishing factor. It seems a fair inference that in these dialogues the general terms in which Plato is interested can on the whole be construed either as class-words or as class-property words. An *eidos* such as *to zôön* can be either animals as a class or animality, or perhaps something in between. To be willing to talk in these terms is to be a good distance away from the emphases of the earlier dialogues (though no change of doctrine as opposed to emphasis is involved if the earlier dialogues are construed as we have construed them).

The other member of the phrase *koinônia genôn*, the word *koinônia*, connotes sharing or having in common. The verb *koinônein* is one which Plato seems to use interchangeably (or at any rate without marking any differentiation) with verbs connoting mixing and with the old verb *metechein*, "to partake in". It seems therefore that the phrase *koinônia genôn* is one which could be used for a number of rather different relationships between either classes or class-properties. For if one class was a sub-class of another, the first could be said to share in the second, whereas if one property were predicable of another the second could be said to partake in the first, and it seems that so far as the words go both of these relationships could be called *koinônia genôn*.

We shall find, I think, that the phrase does comprise at least these two relationships within its meaning, and we shall have to ask how far Plato was aware of the differences between the various things to which he referred by a common title. Meanwhile we will notice that at least the following three kinds of propositions seem to come up for consideration in the dialogues we are concerned with, namely those illustrated by:—

Cats are animals
Activity is not identical with existence
Pleasure is worth pursuing.

To a very large extent what Plato has to say about the relations between classes and properties is stated in terms of how we ought to

[1] As in "beauty of form" *and* as in "another form of sponge-cake"—outward appearance, structure, type are all comprised in the sense of *eidos*.

set about discovering these relations, and this in turn is stated in terms of how the "dialectical" man proceeds. We have encountered the word "dialectic" in connection with the *Republic* and elsewhere, and we know that the dialectical man of the earlier dialogues is the man who "knows what each thing is". We meet a rather different emphasis in the later dialogues. Quite what the relation is between the earlier and later uses of the word "dialectic" is a question we shall defer to another chapter. Meanwhile we will avail ourselves of a useful conclusion of Mr. Robinson's,[1] namely that Plato tends to call "dialectical", as opposed to "eristical", any method of reasoning in philosophy of which he approves at any given time. "Dialectic" then means sound philosophical procedure. In considering what the dialectician does we are considering how philosophers ought to go about their business, and therefore, indirectly, what the world is like.

B. *Dialectic and Protarchus' Fallacy*

(i) *Protarchus' Fallacy*

Much of what Plato has to say about dialectic in these dialogues is intended to dispose of a pattern of reasoning which I shall call Protarchus' Fallacy. This name refers to the argumentation in a section of the *Philebus* (11–19).

At this stage of the *Philebus* Protarchus is defending the view that pleasure is "the good", or that which we ought to pursue, Socrates the view (which he later modifies) that this status belongs to intellectual activity. The position which Protarchus wants to maintain is that pleasure is worth pursuing as such; Socrates wants to meet this by saying that some pleasures are indeed worth pursuing, but not *qua* pleasures simply, but rather *qua* intelligent pleasures or something of the kind. To this end he claims that pleasures constitute a heterogeneous class. Protarchus retorts that since they are all pleasures they must constitute a homogeneous class, and this is essentially "Protarchus' fallacy". Socrates retorts that by parity of reasoning colours must also constitute a homogeneous class whereas in fact of course the "parts" of the class are as different as can be. He amplifies this by saying (in effect; 13 a sq.) that the hedonist treats pleasantness and goodness as co-extensive and has no warrant for doing this since "pleasant" and "good" are not synonymous. If it can be shown that pleasures are a heterogeneous class, the hedonist will have to demonstrate a feature common to them all in virtue of which they are all good, it having been shown that pleasantness is not such a feature. Protarchus falls back on denying that pleasures are heterogeneous "in so far as they are pleasures". Socrates tries to win

---

[1] *Plato's Earlier Dialectic*, p. 70. I do not altogether agree with this.

him round by allowing that his own candidate for the status of that which we ought to pursue, namely intellectual activity, is also a heterogeneous class. Protarchus is content with this equal handicapping of both candidates, but Socrates insists that the problem of unity and multiplicity (i.e. of heterogeneous classes) must first be cleared up. Evidently Plato thinks that there is here a major source of philosophical error. The treatment of unity and multiplicity which follows will have to be deferred for a moment.

Meanwhile there is another (no doubt earlier) place in which attention is drawn to Protarchus' fallacy, namely *Phaedrus* 265–6. Socrates has made a speech denouncing sexual love on the ground that love is to be defined as a kind of madness. But love is a god (*Erôs*), and Socrates feels guilty of blasphemy. He therefore makes a recantation in praise of love. In the course of this second speech he makes (implicitly) two distinctions. The first of these is that between divine and morbid madness, true love being, like poetry and prophecy, a form of divine madness. The second distinction is between true or platonic love and unrestrained carnal desire. Homosexual love is commonly condemned (he means) because men confuse the true and valuable relationship with its debased form.

It is not however on this confusion that he turns the theoretical spotlight in the passage in which we are interested (265–6) but the other, namely the confusion between two kinds of madness.[1] Socrates says that although in both his speeches he rightly discerned "a single kind", namely madness, he had wrongly overlooked the fact that madness has its left-handed and its right-handed members. In his first speech he had divided the left-hand kind of madness into its parts and so encountered carnal love as one of them and rightly condemned it; in his second speech he had likewise discerned platonic love as a specific version of right-hand madness and thus been able to praise it. He is, he says, a lover of these "collections and divisions" and practises them in order that he may talk and think straight; to the man who can turn his eyes on to one and many in this way he gives the title "dialectician".

Socrates' remarks are brief and picturesque. His meaning seems to be this. To decide such a question as the value of love you must define it or in other words subsume it under some more general notion. If however you do so without at the same time breaking up this more general notion into its specific kinds you are liable to be seduced (by Protarchus' fallacy in effect) into applying to the sub-kind under consideration an epithet which properly speaking belongs

[1] Why love is a kind of madness we have examined above, Vol. 1, pp. 183–6. Roughly it is because the lover's attitude is unmercenary, and this is also why love is valuable.

to another of the sub-kinds. You are liable to say: "Love is madness.
But madness is a bad thing. Therefore love is a bad thing." Or, to
expand this argument "Love is madness; so is ordinary lunacy.
Ordinary lunacy is a bad thing. But love and lunacy are alike because
they are both madness. Therefore if lunacy is a bad thing, love is
also." "Collection", or bringing together apparently disparate things
such as love and lunacy under the heading of madness, is an excellent
thing; the human intelligence is differentiated from the brutish by the
ability to "understand by kinds, to unify by the power of thought the
single kind which arises out of numerous perceptions" (249 b 6). But
such collection must be accompanied by division or distinction if
blunders are to be avoided.

Love is subsumed under madness and therefore condemned; it is
thought that, if some pleasures are worth pursuing, all must be. The
pattern of argument in both cases can be represented:

A and B are both P
Therefore they are alike
But A is Q (because it is P)
Therefore, since A and B are alike, B must also be Q.

(The parenthesis in the third line helps but is not essential to the
argument). The emphasis on the importance of collection and
division is designed to meet this kind of argument. As Socrates says
(*Phaedrus loc. cit.*) we must "divide" any common nature which we
discern in multifarious instances "at its joints, and not break off bits
like an incompetent cook". This is particularly so as he tells us (263)
in the case of what he calls "disputable" universals such as love or
justice as opposed to those such as iron or silver about whose
identity there is no dispute. This all seems plain sailing, but there are
a number of complications in detail which must be looked at. Some
of these will emerge if we look at what Socrates says to Protarchus in
the *Philebus*.

(ii) *Socrates on Protarchus' Fallacy*[1]

1. Socrates' advice to Protarchus stretches from *Philebus* 14 c to
19 c. He begins by characterising the problem as "the notoriously
troublesome paradox concerning the claim that many things are one
or one thing many". He goes on to say that under this heading there
are a number of problems which do not deserve to be taken seriously,
for instance the problem how one man can be both tall and short, or
how a single object such as a human body can also be regarded as a
number of members. These are vulgar paradoxes. The genuine

[1] Numbers prefixed to paragraphs of rough precis, letters to paragraphs of
comment.

problems arise not in the case of physical units, but when one postulates units such as the ox, the beautiful or the man. (The genuine
problems in fact concern the unity and multiplicity of universals).
About these units two[1] questions arise (they are in fact the questions
put to Socrates in the *Parmenides*): (1) whether we ought to say that
there are such units; and (2) if one does say so, whether we ought to
say that their original unity is disrupted when they are "torn to
pieces", and their unity destroyed, by their existence in manifold
instances; "or alternatively (what seems absolutely impossible) that
each kind exists entire, apart from itself, remaining self-identical and
unitary both in the one and in the many".

A. It is clear that we are to answer the first question "Yes", and
to accept the second alternative, "absolutely impossible" though it
seems, in the case of the second. We are to allow that there are common natures, which are torn "apart from themselves", or which, so
to speak, live a double life, in themselves and in their numerous
embodiments, without thereby losing their unity. But what are their
embodiments? Particulars (as this stoat is an embodiment of animality)? Or specific versions (as stoat-hood is an embodiment of
animality)? On the one hand Socrates' language is so reminiscent of
the *Parmenides* (131 a–b) that one feels that there is almost a cross-
reference, and in the *Parmenides* the topic was the relation of a universal to its particulars. On the other hand it is clear that what is
relevant here is not the relation of a universal to its particulars, but
the relation of a generic universal to its specific versions. Either then
Plato has confused or confounded these two topics, or else the apparent allusion to the *Parmenides* is misleading; for it is certainly the
second topic which is now uppermost in his mind.

2. Socrates goes on (15 d) to say that "the identity of one and
many is brought about by statements (*logoi*) and is a universal
characteristic of everything that we say". It is an inevitable consequence of statement-making, but it is exploited by the young, who
alternately confound together what should be distinguished and
make distinctions which should not be made.

B. The problem of unity and multiplicity, which leads the young
to draw distinctions in the wrong places, derives from a permanent
feature of statement-making. This feature (I think) is that most true
statements are not tautological. In Greek there is no indefinite
article, so that the complement of "Jones is a man" and "The
rational animal is man" consists of the same words ". . . is man".
This had led some philosophers to say that statements such as

---

[1] The MS text gives three problems (15 b 1 sq.), but I accept the suggestion
that we should read πρῶτον (or μὲν) for μίαν, and put a comma after ταύτην in
b 4. Otherwise the first two problems are the same.

"Jones is a man" are less than true—the only perfectly true statements are of the form "Man is man". This of course is the confusion of the copula with the identity sense of "is", against which Plato's weapon is the "participation" metaphor. Since the discussion is going on at the level of common natures, the feature of statement-making in question is the sharing of kinds. What happens to young men who are unaware that kinds can share (or that there are innumerable true propositions of the form "The P is Q") is that they either argue that if A and B are, say, kinds of pleasure then they must be alike (confounding what should be distinguished), or else insist that if A and B are distinct, then they cannot both be kinds of pleasure (distinguishing what should not be distinguished). This they do because they think that if A is P and B is P then P must be identical with A and with B. Socrates' diagnosis of Protarchus' fallacy therefore is that it rests at bottom on failure to accept the sharing of kinds.

3. After some facetious remarks about young men Socrates proceeds to recommend as the cure for this trouble the method which he has always loved and always found difficult to carry out (16 b). This method is later (17 a) said to be dialectic, and it is contrasted with "eristical" procedure, which seems to be roughly that attributed to the young men in paragraph 2. Socrates says that we are to accept a "heavenly tradition" to the effect that unity and multiplicity and also *peras* and *apeiron* are universal features of things (16 c).

C. "Of things" means "of universals". I shall offer some argument for this later.[1] That there is unity and multiplicity in every universal means primarily (see paragraph A) that every universal exists in many versions. The word *peras* and *apeiron* literally mean "limit" and "the unlimited", or "definiteness" and "indefiniteness", and one special case of definiteness and indefiniteness is denumerability and innumerability. This is the special case which Socrates has in mind (the argument for this too must be deferred).[2] To say that unity and multiplicity, and also *peras* and *apeiron*, are necessary features of all universals is to say the following things:—(1) that every one of the vast majority of universals (i.e. all except *summa genera* and *infimae species* (a) has its own subordinate versions (as cow-hood has Jersey-hood), and (b) is itself a version of a higher universal (as cow-hood is a version of animality); but (2) that this does not go on indefinitely, for reality has a finite number of joints—a point will come, in other words, when we have distinguished all the versions of a given universal, and when this point comes we may "invoke innumerability".

[1] Below, pp. 367–8. The argument essentially is, as in paragraph A above, that Plato is here talking at the level of universals.
[2] Below, pp. 367n, 424–6.

4. Things being dovetailed together in this way, Socrates continues (16 d), the proper procedure when dealing with any given kind is to seek for one common nature (*idea*), which will always be found. This common nature being found, we should try to divide it into two if it has two parts, or if not two, then three, or more, and we should go on doing this until "the unit we started with is not seen simply as one and many and innumerable, but as some definite number. Innumerability should not be thrust upon the multitude until some number between one and infinity (*apeiron*) has been detected in it. Then and only then that unit can be dismissed to infinity." (16 d 4–e 2).

D. The meaning of this is that one should not say that there are innumerable cases of P-hood until one has made all the sub-divisions that can be made, so that one is in a position to say just how many subordinate versions of P-hood there are. It is only when this has been done and we have arrived at *infimae species* that we may say: "Of course there can be innumerable instances of this." Take for example pleasure; divide it into, say, mental and physical. Divide mental pleasure into: of learning, of the exercise of the senses, of anticipation etc. Divide physical into: preceded and not preceded by appetite. Divide preceded by appetite into. . . . When and only when this anatomy (some of which is informally carried out later in the dialogue) is complete, then one may "invoke innumerability" or "dismiss the unit to infinity". But what is this? Is it that, when one has arrived at an *infima species* (say the pleasantness of some activity which counteracts some bodily disorder), one may say: "Of course there can be innumerable *occurrences* of this pleasure."? Or is it that, when that point is reached, one may say: "Of course there can be innumerable *different but not significantly different sub-kinds* of this kind. Thus scratching to relieve an itch is different but not significantly different from coughing to clear the throat, or rubbing the eyes when they smart. The type of pleasantness involved in all these activities should be treated as the same."? On the whole I think that Plato has his eye on the second of these things, but would probably include both of them. Finally we notice that we are told to "divide into two, or if not that, into three or some other number". We shall meet this point again later. Roughly it is that we are always to divide at genuine joints, but that in fact one usually hits on a joint if one divides something into two. Sometimes however it will be obvious that there are three or more versions of a given kind.

5. Socrates now (16 e–17 a) presents his point negatively. Contemporary thinkers "make one and many unmethodically and hence more quickly and more slowly than they should, and then proceed straight to innumerables, missing everything that comes in between;

and this constitutes the difference between dialectical and eristical argument".

E. He means, I think, that common natures are hastily identified, and therefore never really identified. All pleasures are lumped together as pleasure; but more haste is less speed, and this is a slow way of arriving at the goal or of discovering the unifying factor. What it is that makes all pleasures truly to some extent alike is not isolated (the Socratic question "What is pleasure?" is not asked). But having bundled classes together on the basis of apparent resemblance, the eristical man promptly "invokes innumerability" in the sense that he treats attempts at making distinctions as attempts at splitting hairs. The class has of course innumerable members, but, since it is a class of similars, to try to divide it into sub-classes is to break up what should remain united. The eristic thus commits Protarchus' fallacy because he fails to ask: "*What* is it that unifies the class?" If he saw that there is *some one* common nature which unifies the class, then (if he also realised that common natures can blend with each other) he might see that there may be *other* common natures which diversify the class into sub-classes. As we saw, at the level of *infimae species* it is right to refuse to make further distinctions, but it is not right above that level. An *infima species* might therefore be defined as a class such that no philosophical or scientific purpose can be served by dividing it into sub-classes. It is that, to split which is to split hairs.[1]

6. Socrates proceeds to illustrate his meaning by three examples, two from grammar and one from music. Finally he brings the discussion back to its starting point by saying that it is important to decide into what sub-kinds and on what basis pleasure and intellectual activity ought to be divided.

F. I do not find Socrates' illustrations very clear, but they seem to make the general point that one is not an expert in a field just by knowing that its elements are diverse; one has to know how many different kinds of elements there are (e.g. vowels, consonants and mutes in the case of letters) and what differentiates them from each other. What is more illuminating than the illustrations is that Socrates does not in fact, in the rest of the dialogue, commit himself to the place taken by pleasure or intellectual activity in the good life until he has performed upon them (roughly and informally) the kind of anatomy we have taken him to be recommending.

---

[1] Thus it would be unreasonable for a man to treat the pleasure of scratching a tickle as innocent but to adopt a different attitude to rubbing the eyes, unless he could find some relevant respect in which the class of activities whose pleasantness consists in relieving a bodily disorder ought to be divided, and which was such that one of these activities fell on one side of the division, the other on the other.

Three things are noteworthy about all this. The first is that Plato is on the track of a point of very considerable importance. This is that a common nature is not the same thing as a resemblance. All white objects are in one respect *alike*, but it is absurd to say this of all animals. All adult buck chinchilla rabbits perhaps (i.e. an *infima species*) are alike, but all animals are not. Nonetheless animality does constitute a genuine common nature—it is not arbitrary to treat animals as a class. This is of great importance in all disciplines, but especially (as the *Phaedrus* suggests with its talk of "disputable" common natures) in philosophy. (Alternatively, if one prefers to treat resemblance as the relation which holds between things which have a common nature, one can express the point by saying that some resemblances are tenuous and abstract). That Plato is aware of this point comes out in various ways. It comes out for example in Socrates' riposte to Protarchus: "If all pleasures are alike, then all colours are alike"—for the nature common to colours is very obviously not what would ordinarily be thought of as a resemblance between them. It comes out also in Socrates' language about the difficulty of believing that a common nature can preserve its unity. It comes out in the injunction to "*seek* for a common nature in each case—for it will always be possible to find one", and also in the charge against the eristics that they create unities and multitudes both too quickly and too slowly; for I think that this can only mean that they hastily treat every class as a class of similars, and *thereby delay* the discovery of the tenuous common factor which unifies the class, and which, being tenuous, has to be *sought for*.

But the second thing to notice in this passage is that Plato's own comments on his point are not very illuminating, for he diagnoses the trouble which he is combating as a failure to see that kinds can share (see paragraphs 2 and B). No doubt this is one way of putting it; it amounts to saying that a generic character, being combined with a number of specific characters, can constitute distinct classes which ought not to be confounded. But it allows one to suppose that the generic character is a sort of kernel of strict resemblance which persists in all the specific versions. On this picture to discover the common nature of animals might be represented as a feat of intellectual vision by which one discerns some hidden respect in which elephants, lizards and humming birds are all *exactly alike*. The doctrine that kinds can share needs to be complemented by the doctrine that a common nature is not a resemblance. I think that Plato always took this for granted and that it is implicit here.[1] If he had made it

---

[1] It is implicit surely in the notion, to be found in the *Republic*, that the same form can be embodied in mathematical entities or in human behaviour; see above pp. 80 sqq.

explicit he might have answered in advance some of Aristotle's criticisms (e.g. *Nicomachean Ethics*, 1, 6, 1096 b 25).

The third noteworthy feature of this passage is that Plato fails to distinguish the relation of a universal to its individual instances from the relation of a generic universal to its specific versions. Some readers, I am sure, will deny that Plato confused these two topics; but he certainly failed to distinguish them. Since any reader of the *Philebus* is almost bound to recall the *Parmenides* (see paragraph A) in which the former topic is discussed, and since the latter topic is the relevant one here, the failure to distinguish the two topics amounts to confounding them. I suspect that Protarchus' fallacy is responsible: Particulars partake in universals; a species partakes in its genus. Since both are cases of participation the two relations must be the same. Plato has "collected" but not "divided" participation. There is another conceivable explanation, namely that Plato seriously thought that the relation of Buttercup to the class of Shorthorns was in all respects the same as the relation of the class of Shorthorns to the class of cows, on the ground that Buttercup, being no more than the sum of her properties, is nothing but an absolutely specific nature. In this way the relation of an individual to its universal would *become* the relation of a specific to a generic universal. If however this line of thought was responsible for the confounding of the two relationships, then Plato did not pursue it consistently; for if an individual becomes an *infima species* then there is no point at which one can "invoke innumerability".[1] Plato's readers would have been helped very considerably if he had dismissed the pseudo-problem about how a single universal can be present in a number of instances as one of the vulgar one-many problems along with "How can one man have many sizes or consist of many members?" It would have helped also if, when he lists examples in 15 a of the kind of units whose multiplicity is genuinely paradoxical, he had not included ox-hood and man-hood in the list along with beauty and goodness. For the genuine paradox (that the possession of a common nature need not create a resemblance) is a matter of degree. At the bottom level (the *infima species*) there is no need to distinguish a class having a common nature from a class of similars; for at that degree of specificity a common nature *is* a resemblance. At the level of men and oxen there is nothing very unplausible in treating their common nature as a resemblance. It is when one comes to such universals as

---

[1] I find quite unplausible the idea that *apeiron* signifies "the indefinite" in the sense of Aristotelian "matter" or Lockeian "something, I know not what". If Socrates meant something of this kind, then the repeated use of the mathematical sense of the word in 16 d, e, could do nothing but turn the reader's attention in the wrong direction. It must mean "the innumerable".

animality, colour, pleasure, beauty, intellectual activity, wisdom that the difference between these two things becomes apparent. Therefore Plato's examples were ill-chosen to convey what we have taken to be his main point.

If neither Aristotle nor Plato noticed what point he was making, was he really making it? I think that he was.

(iii) *Collection and division*

In the *Phaedrus* (265 e–266 b) Socrates says that his two speeches about love "grasped imprudence of the mind as one kind in common", and that the first speech "cut off the left-hand portion of madness, and went on cutting that up into pieces until it found what is called left-hand love among them". He then goes on to remark that he is fond of these "collections and divisions" and thinks them necessary to intellectual rectitude. This is, I suppose, the earliest use of the terms "collection" and "division" in a more or less technical sense. We must have a look at this sense of these terms.

A. *Collection*

"Collection" or *sunagôgê* in the *Phaedrus* must refer to what Socrates did when he "grasped imprudence of the mind as one kind in common", the subsequent "cutting up" of this kind being what is called *diairesis* or "division". This suggests that to collect a kind is to discern a common feature which unifies a number of disparate things (as: that they all involve imprudence of the mind).

There is however a passage in the *Philebus* (25 d 5–9) where the word seems to refer not so much to discerning the common feature of a kind, but rather to something like giving a selection of specimens chosen to illustrate the range over which the kind extends.[1] It would however be rather disconcerting to identify collection with the giving of specimens to indicate the range of a kind, for the texts suggest that collection and division together constitute the whole of dialectic, and if we interpret collection in that way we leave no place for Socratic definition. But as late as the *Theaetetus* (146–7) Socrates reproves Theaetetus for attempting to define knowledge by illustrating its range, and tells him that what he wanted when he asked what knowledge is was *not many things but one*. Clearly this reference to "one and many" chimes with the description in the *Phaedrus* (*loc. cit.*) of

[1] For Socrates says that they have collected *apeiron* but failed to collect *peras*. Since he has given specimens to indicate the range of *apeiron* and stated the common nature of cases of *peras*, "collecting" would seem to refer to the former activity, not the latter.

the dialectician as the man "who can look at one and towards many", and clearly, again, "looking at one" refers to the same thing as "grasping one kind in common" or in other words to collection. Therefore unless there is a silent change of mind between the *Phaedrus* and the *Philebus* discernment of the common feature of a class must be part of the meaning of collection.[1]

The truth is surely something like this. In the mythology of the *Phaedrus* every human mind has seen at least some of the forms, and "remembers" enough of this experience to be able "to unify in thought what is presented in manifold sense-experiences" (*Phaedrus*, 249 b 6, paraphrase). We are all in fact able intuitively to recognise common natures, and it is this intuitive ability which allows the eristics of the *Philebus* to "create unities too quickly". But an intuitive awareness that there is something in common between the lunatic, the lover and the poet is not enough. It must be supplemented in two ways, and these two ways converge. It must be supplemented firstly by a *systematic* survey of the range of the property in question, and secondly by an ability to isolate the common factor. These two ways converge in that it is reasonable to suppose that an increase in the ability to say how far the property extends will go hand in hand with an increase in the ability to say what the property is. In my view "collection" refers to progress along these convergent paths, the emphasis falling sometimes on the one and sometimes on the other.

However, Plato was always chary of claiming that a definition had been achieved. It is taken for granted in the earlier dialogues that one knows more or less what is comprised in justice before one is at all able to say what justice consists in.[2] The two paths may converge, but one travels more quickly along the first of them. This is perhaps because a conception of the range of justice, for example, which is slightly incorrect will nevertheless be adequate for most of the time, whereas a Socratic definition, to be serviceable, must be exactly right. The first is a matter of degree, the second is black and white. After a kind has been to all intents and purposes successfully collected, both in that its extent is known, and in that the unifying factor has been discerned, it may still be the case that one cannot "give account" of the unifying factor. It has been, so to speak, grasped as a syllable, but not yet spelled out into its letters. More of this later. Meanwhile I assume that in the places in which Plato allows us to collect the

---

[1] In one sense every collection is a division. To collect madness is to divide it from everything else. But the *Phaedrus* seems to use "division" to mean "*sub*-division" or the breaking-up of a kind into its sub-kinds.

[2] The position of Cephalus in the *Republic*. He would no doubt be at sea in *novel* situations, but only in these.

impression that dialectic consists of collection and division he takes for granted that we will understand that collection *par excellence* includes the ability to "give account".[1]

In some places however Plato seems to use some word other than "collection" to refer to the discernment of the common feature. This he does, in my view, not because this discernment is excluded from the meaning of "collection", but because it is convenient sometimes to refer to this aspect of the complex. Thus in *Philebus* 25 d, as we have seen,[2] "collection" seems to refer to the giving of specimens of the range of a property (in this case *apeiron* or indefiniteness). A page further on however (26 c 9–d 2) he speaks of unifying *apeiron* by defining it as the class of more and less, and refers to this activity as "sealing" it. Here it seems that "collecting" refers primarily to grasping the range of a property, "sealing" being used to refer to the discerning of the common feature (perhaps because the grasp of the range is stabilised, and in that sense sealed, when the common feature is discerned). Again in the *Statesman* 285 a–b Plato uses another metaphor (this time "fencing") to refer to the act whereby the collected flock is prevented from dispersing again, and this is clearly the discernment of the common nature.[3] First, let us suppose, one gathers together a number of disparate entities by observing that they have some nature in common. At this point one will be vague both about the membership of the class and about the class-property. Then one finds a name for the class-property thereby determining its membership, collecting its members more securely, fencing and branding the flock. Beyond this there is still a third stage at which one spells out the class-property into its letters, and even perhaps a fourth stage at which, in the spirit of the *Seventh Letter*, one actually *sees* what the letters spell. It seems to me that this is the complete operation of unifying a kind, and that the word "collection" refers to this operation in general, but more particularly to its earlier stages.

---

[1] But not *just* in words. See our discussion of the Seventh Letter on "knowing what each thing is", above, pp. 122–6.

[2] See p. 368 footnote.

[3] Having accused those who believe that all things can be measured of confounding dissimilars and of making distinctions haphazardly, the Stranger outlines the dialectical approach. "Having first detected something in common among numerous things, one should persist until one has found all the differences which divide the field into kinds, and likewise when one sees unlikenesses among groups one should not be able to give up until everything which is akin has been surrounded and fenced with the essence of some kind." (*Statesman* 285 a 7–b 6). This is an obscure sentence, but "fencing with the essence of some kind" must refer to discerning the common nature of a group of similars. The *Statesman* also talks of "sealing one *idea* upon" statesmanship (258 c 5).

B. *Division*

Division or *diairesis* is intimately connected with collection, not only because Plato insists that collections without divisions are dangerous, but also because he requires divisions to be done "at a joint". But to discern where the joints come is to collect the two sub-kinds between which they come.

The operation of dividing at a joint is briefly contrasted in the *Phaedrus* (265 e) with "breaking off bits like an incompetent cook". This is amplified in the *Statesman,* where a bit or *meros* is contrasted with an *eidos* or kind. In this dialogue (*Statesman* 272) the Eleatic Stranger lays down two rules for division. The first is that the division should not leave one with one small portion on the one hand, and a number of portions on the other, and that the division should be done "with an *eidos*" (also *idea*). The second rule, or perhaps counsel, is that one should divide a kind into two, "down the middle", the reason for this being that one is more likely to encounter an *idea* if one complies with it. The Stranger briefly illustrates his point by saying that one should not divide mankind in such a way that one has Greeks on the one hand and the large and heterogeneous class of barbarians (non-Greeks) on the other; nor should one divide numbers into 10,000 and the rest. It is better to divide numbers into odd and even, men into male and female (these being divisions "down the middle"); the time to divide men into Lydians, Phrygians and so on does not arrive until it is no longer possible to make any further divisions such that each of the resulting portions is also a kind.

The meaning of this is easy to grasp intuitively though it eludes formal statement. It depends on the loose notion of an *eidos* or non-arbitrary class. The difficulty which the modern reader feels with it (as with the Aristotelian conception of essences which it foreshadows), is that we should want to say that no classification is ever arbitrary or non-arbitrary as such, but only for a given purpose. A distinction which is important in one context will be arbitrary and irrelevant in another. This reminds us of the ontological bones on which this discussion of classification rests. There are, for Plato, certain natures or ways of existence, and whatever can be classified owes its determinateness to the fact that it embodies a certain complex or syllable of these natures.

What does the Stranger mean by "dividing down the middle", and why does he think it expedient to do so? Again it is fairly clear intuitively what he means. The important point is not that the membership of the resultant sub-classes should be equally numerous, but that the properties which define them should be so to speak of equal weight, or of an equal degree of specificity, so that the two sub-classes are equally homogeneous. Thus one feels that if half the world's population were Mohammedans, a division into Mohammedans and others would still be like the division into Greeks and foreigners, on the ground that the second member of the division would consist of what the Stranger calls an "uncombinable and incongruous" group.

As to why the Stranger thinks it expedient to divide in this way, I think that the answer must be that he believes that it is as a matter of fact the case that a generic common nature is most often modified by two specific characteristics of equal weight rather than by some other number. Subsequently indeed (287 b–c) he[1] allows that it is sometimes impossible to divide into two (i.e. impossible to arrive at two genuine sub-kinds by a dichotomy) and proceeds to divide the topic he is dealing with "into limbs, like a sacrifice". (Thus for example a division of religions into theistic and non-theistic might be less correct than a four-fold division into pantheistic, monotheistic, polytheistic and non-theistic). If Plato had any reasons to offer why reality is such that a dichotomy is usually correct, he has not told us what they are.

In this discussion of division I have quoted from the *Statesman* and assumed that what is called division in that dialogue is the same as that which is called division in the general descriptions of dialectic in the *Phaedrus* and *Philebus*. This assumption however is disputable on the ground that the discussion in the *Statesman* is connected with a technique of definition by dichotomy, and that the relation between this technique and dialectic is not clear. It will be convenient to defer this particular topic for a while, and I will here only say that, whatever may be the relation of dichotomous definition to dialectic, it seems obvious that the Stranger's advice about division is meant to tell us what it is to divide reality at the joints.

C. *Dialectic as collection and division*

Two points remain to be made about collection and division taken together. The first concerns the relationship between collection and division on the one hand and the sharing of kinds on the other, both of these being notions with which that of dialectic is intimately connected. There is an obvious affinity between collection and division and ordinary classification or taxonomy. This is especially clear in connection with division in the *Sophist* and *Statesman* where it is discussed in the context of definition by dichotomy, an operation

[1] Like Socrates in the *Philebus*; above, p. 364.

which naturally suggests something like the animal kingdom set out as in a school biology book with a first division into vertebrates and invertebrates and so on. The anatomy of something like madness or pleasure is not a strictly taxonomic operation, and the notion of genus and species applies here in a less direct way. It applies, however, intelligibly enough (there is an obvious affinity between the two kinds of case); and if it is said that the possibility of performing either of these two kinds of classification is due to the sharing of kinds, then the type of sharing which is in point will be the sharing of what we can intelligibly call a "species" in a "genus". So far therefore to think of dialectic (*a*) in terms of collection and division and (*b*) in terms of the sharing of kinds will be simply to look at the same thing from two different points of view. If however the sharing of kinds includes (as it does) relations between properties which have nothing to do with the genus/species relation, then it will seem to follow that the sharing of kinds and dialectic conceived of as collection and division will be to that extent out of focus with each other.

The second general point which should be made about dialectic conceived of as collection and division is that there is no conflict between the emphasis on division in these later dialogues and the earlier emphasis on "knowing what each thing is". This can be illustrated from many places; let us take an example from the *Statesman*. In a passage already referred to above (*Statesman* 284–5) the Stranger makes one of those points-in-passing of which Plato had always been fond. This time the point is, in effect, that the Greek comparative is ambiguous, the same word doing duty for "too P" and for "more P than".[1] The actual topic is the word for "too long" or "longer than", and the ambiguity is worked out in terms of two kinds of measurement, one of which is to compare something with a given amount, the other of which is to compare something with the right amount. The first type of measurement of course produces results like "A is longer than B", the second results like "A is too long". The Stranger goes on to say that "various ingenious persons", who have said that all physical things can be measured, have confounded these two kinds of measurement and thus (this seems to be his meaning) have crudely inferred that if it is possible for an X to be too P then there must be a standard degree of P-hood, being more P than this being what it is to be too P. Thus (to adapt the Stranger's own example) what makes a speech too long is its being longer than necessary for its purpose, not being longer than some given length which is the right length for a speech. Unless you realise that in some

---

[1] This ambiguity is the origin of Aristotle's doctrine of the mean. "The mean" is that which the too aggressive man is more aggressive than.

comparisons the one term is the context-determined quantity *to metrion* or "the moderate", you will postulate in these comparisons a standard amount in order that that which is too P may be more P than this postulated constant. To the "ingenious persons" who fail to see this the Stranger reads the lesson on collection and division from which we have quoted the metaphor of "fencing", accusing them of lack of practice in dividing into kinds.

My purpose in quoting this is to argue that the "ingenious persons" might equally well have been charged, in the spirit of the earlier dialogues, with "not knowing what measurement is", or, as now, with "not being able to divide measurement into kinds". For a man will hardly be able to see what kinds of measurement there are unless he asks himself what kind of an activity measuring is, and he will hardly be able to see what kind of an activity it is without being at any rate well placed to see that it is a heterogeneous activity (for he will have to see that measurement is comparison, and this will suggest that the nature of the other term to the comparison may make a significant difference). I cannot divide into its kinds something which I do not understand, and I cannot come to understand something without getting hints about the position of its joints. Therefore the new emphasis on the importance of division supplements but does not supplant the old emphasis on "knowing what each thing is". The reason for the shift of emphasis is that Plato has seen that Protarchus' fallacy is a rich source of error in philosophy, and pleads the importance of division as the defence against it.

C. *Dialectic and the letters and syllables of reality*

(i) *Introductory*

In the last section we discussed dialectic in terms of Protarchus' fallacy, and therefore in terms of collection and division. In this section we are to discuss it in terms of a theme which is equally prominent in the later dialogues, the metaphor of the letters and syllables of reality.

These two themes are closely connected. I have already indicated the connection in one way when I said that the man who has collected a kind, even to the extent of fencing it with its common nature, may perhaps have grasped the common nature *only as a syllable* which he cannot yet spell out into its letters. The connection may also be indicated as follows. Protarchus' fallacy deludes a man into assuming that B is Q because A is Q and because A and B are alike in being P; that is to say it leads a man to predicate of a class as a whole something which is truly predicable only of part of the class.[1] As Socrates says in the *Philebus* (13 a 7 sq.) Protarchus' crime is lightly to "predicate of a heterogeneous class an expression which is non-synonymous with" the class-predicate. Protarchus' fallacy becomes important, in fact, when a man is trying to make a synthetic judgment about a class as a whole—e.g. the synthetic judgment that pleasure is good. In the earlier dialogues, for example the *Meno*, we remember that Socrates used to insist that it is dangerous to make synthetic judgments of this kind until one can first offer an analytic definition. "Make no synthetic judgments about P, until you know what it is", was his advice then; "make no synthetic judgments about P until you have divided it into its kinds" is his advice now. We have just seen, in the example of the *Statesman* on measurement, that these two pieces of advice do not conflict. As stated however they are negative cautions. There was a positive side to the earlier advice,[2] in that it was assumed that it was possible by inspection of the class-property to decide what synthetic judgments were true of the class as a whole. Thus if virtue were seen to be some kind of knowledge, it would be at least reasonable to conclude from that that virtue can be taught. This was the positive side to the earlier advice, and it seems to me that its counterpart in the later dialogues is the notion of spelling out a syllable into its letters; it is by doing this that we know what synthetic judgments are true of the class as a whole. The relationship therefore between division on the one hand and spelling on the other is that we must divide in order to resist Protarchan temptations to false synthetic judgments, but that we must spell in order to know what synthetic judgments are true.

I would not like to say flatly that Plato was conscious that this is the relationship between the two topics, for he never seems to discuss the relationship. In some places moreover he throws the weight on the one recommendation, in other places on the other. The *Philebus* is all for division, the *Statesman* all for spelling. Possibly the reason for this is that spelling can be subsumed under division, but with the important difference that spelling is division *down to*, whereas ordinary division is division *down from*. Thus to spell pleasure is to arrive at it by the sub-division of some more general nature (if there is one in this case); whereas to divide it in the ordinary sense is to arrive at its sub-kinds by sub-division of pleasure itself. We will return to this point later when we know more about spelling; meanwhile, if it seems that Plato did not clearly distinguish these two topics, this may be the reason.

---

[1] " Measurement is *always* the comparison of one thing with another thing", "Madness is *always* deplorable", "Pleasure is *always* worth pursuing".

[2] See pp. 563–7, 163–5.

(ii) *Letters and syllables in the* Cratylus

The *Cratylus* (421 sqq.) probably provides the earliest[1] example of the use of the metaphor of letters and syllables. The way has been prepared for this metaphor by the use of the word *stoicheion* to mean both "element" and "letter". The theme of the *Cratylus* is the relation between language and reality, and the theory which is being toyed with is that a word ought to depict its referent; that is to say, the natural interpretation of the meaning of the word (its *rêma*, or what it says) ought to imply a true theory about the things it is used of, as "shepherd" truly implies that shepherds herd sheep. But if one follows this line of thought one will soon get to basic words (Socrates uses the word *stoicheion* for these as well as for letters), such as "sheep" and "herd" in our example, which cannot be broken down into component words. These can only be broken down into letters, and so the theory goes on to suggest that certain letters "imitate" or have a natural affinity to certain basic realities. Thus for example the letter *r* might "imitate" motion, and a primitive word with an *r* in it might stand for the kind of motion indicated by its other letters. Plato is of course well aware that languages are not in fact constructed in this way; what he is exploring is the suggestion that it might be a good idea if they were. If they were, then, a well-constructed language would reflect the structure of reality on the assumption that there exists in reality something to correspond to the letters out of which words are built. This would have to be highly general natures such as motion, change, restraint and so on, out of which ordinary complex universals might be in some way constructed. Given that there are such letters of reality, the task of building a language, on this view, would be twofold. First the language-builder must classify his material—the available sounds—into its kinds (into vowels, mutes and consonants, and each of these classes into its component letters); then second he must classify the realities that have to be named, looking to see whether there are any "letters" or elements in reality to which everything has to be traced back, and if there are, into what kinds they are to be classified (424 d; I have paraphrased roughly for I am not sure in detail what text ought to be read, or how it should be construed).

Plato's views on language-building do not concern us here.[2] He certainly does not think that languages *are* built in this way, and it could be argued that he does not commit himself to the ontological part of the theory either—to the idea that there are letters of reality.

[1] The "conservative" view is that the *Cratylus* is an early dialogue. Some would argue however that the occurrence of this topic in it implies a fairly late date.

[2] See below, pp. 475–86.

Perhaps the correct account is that while this idea is not asserted it is also not criticised, and that it is treated as a natural assumption. With regard to the manner in which ontological letters (if there are any) would combine to form ontological syllables, nothing precise is said. Here however is one of the innumerable examples that the dialogue offers of a complex and its elements: the word *historia* or "enquiry", it is suggested, might be derived from *histanai* "to arrest" and *roê* "flux", so that enquiry would be that which arrests the flux of thought. The examples given in the dialogue are given in a frivolous spirit and one cannot put any weight on them, but for what it is worth we may notice that the relation between the elements in this particular complex is not the relation between a generic and a specific character (as for example animality and rationality in the rational animal or man). Enquiry is not the arrested species of flux (nor conversely) but the flux-arrester.

(iii) *Letters and syllables in the* Theaetetus

We have seen in an earlier chapter[1] that the metaphor of letters and syllables occurs in the part of the *Theaetetus* commonly called Socrates' Dream. We saw that there is one interpretation of this passage according to which the letters are universals. This would bring the use of the metaphor in the *Theaetetus* into line with the use of it in the other later dialogues. We preferred however another interpretation. If we were wrong to do so, then the *Theaetetus* contributes to the view outlined in the *Cratylus* the additional point that the letters of reality cannot be defined. This is a natural thought (indeed if definition is identified with resolution into components, it is almost an inevitable thought) and one which may well have occurred to Plato. On the other hand, if he did think that there are some indefinable universals, it is a little odd that he should not have said so, except rather obliquely in this one place; and I do not believe that he said it there. But whether he said it or not, it might be argued that he should have said it, or in other words that the doctrine that the letters are indefinable is a corollary of the notion that there are letters and syllables. This seems to me wrong. The doctrine that the letters are indefinable could have been evaded in either of two ways. Either it could be said that definition and spelling-out into letters are not, or are not always, the same thing. Or it could be said that nothing is a letter as such, but only a letter with respect to a given syllable. One can give account of any universal in terms of others, and to do this is to spell it into its letters. This would rather spoil the appropriateness of the metaphor, but otherwise it seems to be a possible view. The fact that the *Sophist* gets near to offering a

[1] Above pp. 114–17. The reference is *Theaetetus* 201–2.

definition of existence (247 e 3) could perhaps be used to suggest that Plato somehow evaded the view that there are any indefinable natures.

Possibly then the *Theaetetus* contributes the view that one cannot give account of the letters of reality, thus suggesting that "giving account of" and "spelling" mean the same. I do not however accept this interpretation.

(iv) *Letters and syllables in the* Statesman

Letters and syllables are mentioned in the *Sophist*, but the *Sophist* is so difficult that it must have individual attention. For the moment I shall pass it over and go to its sequel the *Statesman*. Letters and syllables come up in this dialogue in an important passage beginning at 277.

The general context of the dialogue is that they are asking what a statesman or ruler is, in order (in the spirit of the *Meno*) that they may be able to say how he should conduct himself, whether he should be subject to the law, and so on. Attempts at defining statesmen by the method of dichotomous definition have failed, and the Stranger tries a new approach, that of using a *paradeigma* or illustrative parallel.[1] Any important topic, he tells us, is best explained with the aid of a *paradeigma*; for the predicament of all of us is that we understand everything in a kind of dream, but not in a wide-awake manner. He then goes on to explain what he means by a *paradeigma* by giving what he calls a *paradeigma* of a *paradeigma*. In teaching a child to read, you enable it to cope with difficult syllables by setting alongside the difficult syllable a number of easy ones in which the same letters occur. An illustration or *paradeigma* has been effected when the child has been brought to identify the same letter in two different contexts, and is thus enabled to manage it in the difficult one.

Like children who cannot read certain syllables, although they know all the letters, so, it is said, we understand the letters of all things in certain combinations but not in others. In attempting therefore to understand something difficult like the nature of government, we should be well advised to proceed by looking first at some trivial parallel. As his trivial parallel, the Stranger (presumably by an intuitive perception of its analogy) takes weaving. In the course of a mock-pretentious and boring discussion he succeeds in finding a number of general relationships which hold in weaving and also in ruling. Thus:—

[1] He does not in fact say that the use of a *paradeigma* is alternative or superior to the use of dichotomous definition; but that is the impression one gets.

1. Weaving is *one* of the wool-handling trades; ruling is *one* of the man-handling trades.

2. Weaving is not self-sufficient, for its tools are made by *ancillary* trades; ruling too has its *ancillaries*.

3. Weaving *combines* materials which have *different* properties (tough threads in one direction, soft ones in the other) to form a *unity*; the ruler also *combines* men of *different* temperaments into a *unity*.

More generally put, one can distinguish a trade from trades which do different things to the same materials; one can distinguish a trade from ancillary tool-making trades; and one can classify trades as combining trades, separating trades and so on.

Since it is these general features which are common to the easy parallel and to the difficult syllable, it is presumably these that are, or are among, its letters. Such properties therefore as *having ancillaries*, or *being a combining activity* seem to be typical letters, and I suppose that *men* and *wool* are also letters or sets of letters.

The use of Plato's favourite dream simile at the beginning of the passage provokes the idea of clear definition as opposed to blurring. The man who "knows perfectly well" what ruling is, but cannot "give account of it", is like the man whose dream objects are blurred. What he needs to do is to focus the image, and this is what the *paradeigma* does for him. It is to be noticed that the Stranger suggests (278 c–e) that we can read *all* the letters of reality in simple syllables, and argues that if we could not we could never progress from false belief to understanding. Philosophical perplexity is an unclear vision of a complex entity. Clarity is achieved by identifying the members of the complex, and this can be done by recognising them in some simpler arrangement. There is never an unfamiliar element that has to be learnt, but only a complexity that has to be unravelled.

It is obvious how close this treatment of letters and syllables comes to the doctrine of the *Meno* and other early dialogues. It would, for example, be easy to fit on to this discussion the doctrine of recollection, by saying that the reason why all the letters are familiar is that we remember them. It is to be remembered also that the reason why the Stranger wants to be able to spell the syllable of ruling is that he will then be able to decide what synthetic judgments can be made about it. In this way spelling a syllable into its letters seems to play the part played in the earlier dialogues by giving account or saying what something is. Not to beat about the bush, spelling a syllable into its letters *is* giving account. The metaphor of letters and syllables, in this place at least, is a new presentation of the old topic of Socratic definition.

"Ruling is the trade which combines men of different character

379

into a unity." The *Statesman* suggests that this or something like it is how to spell ruling. How can this tell us what synthetic judgments to make about ruling? Roughly thus. Ruling is an *art*; the true ruler therefore will *know* his business; it is therefore unreasonable to subordinate him to law (for what skilled man will allow his hands to be tied by rules?). It is an art of *combination*; the true ruler has *different* materials and will use their different properties to give strength and cohesion to the whole. These materials are *men* who can be appealed to on the rational level and manipulated on the animal level; and so on. (This keeps reasonably close to the concluding pages of the dialogue). We can see from this that it is not to be thought that true synthetic judgments about politics can be *read off* from the letters of ruling. Spelling is not a magic process. It suggests analogies, but one still has to think to decide how they apply. It is a necessary condition of right judgments, but it is not a slot-machine for dispensing them. Plato *never* believed in slot-machines.

(v) *The relation of spelling to collection and division*

"Ruling is the trade which combines men of different character into a unity." To arrive at this spelling we must first see that ruling, properly speaking, is a trade, art or skill. We must next see that it is in particular an art of combination, and then that it is an art of combining men, and then that it is an art of combining different types of men into a cohesive unity. To do this is to subsume ruling under the genus art, and to discover its *differentia* within the genus by subdividing the genus into its kinds, the appropriate kinds being in turn sub-divided, and the process being repeated until the syllable is spelt. In this way it is evident that at least one way of spelling a syllable is to define it *per genus et differentiam*, and that what one does is to identify the genus, and then come down to the syllable which is to be defined by the process of division as we have described it.

(vi) *The relation of spelling to dichotomous definition*

It is also clear that if spelling is the kind of process we have described, then it conforms to the rules for dichotomous definition given in the *Sophist* and *Statesman*. The technique of dichotomous definition is introduced by the Stranger at the beginning of the *Sophist* (218 c). They want to "discover" (i.e. define in the Socratic sense) the sophist, or sophistry; and it is important that all parties to the conversation should be using the word to refer to the same man. To make sure of this the Stranger proposes to use a certain technique (*methodos*) which he proposes to demonstrate first on something which is more easily discovered than sophistry. The example chosen is a certain kind of fishing.

First it is agreed that the fisherman is a skilled man—fishing is subsumed under the genus skill. Then skills are divided into acquisitive and creative, and fishing is agreed to be an acquisitive skill. Then acquisitive skills are divided into those which capture and those which entice their prey, and it is agreed that fishing falls under the first of these heads. The fisherman so far is a skilled acquirer of unwilling prey. By a series of further dichotomies of the same kind a precise definition of the appropriate form of fishing is eventually arrived at. There could no longer be any doubt, in a discussion of the *aspalieutês*, precisely who was being discussed. He has been "tracked down".

The Stranger now turns the technique on to the sophist. He uses it in fact five times over producing five different definitions (or perhaps we should really say four, as the third is only a minor modification of the second). According to the first definition the sophist is a skilled hunter of tame land animals by persuasion in private for pay. According to the second he is (roughly) one skilled in the selling of spiritual food by instruction in virtue. According to the last definition he is one skilled in sifting better from worse in the soul—(etc., etc.); but the Stranger is worried about this last definition, and fears that it is really perhaps a definition of the philosopher.

The reader will have detected an ironical flavour in these definitions. The ironical flavour becomes stronger when the technique is reintroduced at the beginning of the *Statesman*. Here the ruler is defined as a skilled manager of gregarious featherless bipeds. (This is an abbreviated version of the definition; if it were set out in full there would be two or three complete versions according to the way in which the bipeds are identified). Various lessons are rubbed in during the course of arriving at this definition. Thus an attempted division of animals into men and brutes is met with the rebuke (from which we quoted above) that one should always divide down the middle. Later on also, when the animals in question have been defined as hornless, cloven-footed and incapable of cross-breeding, the Stranger takes time off to observe that so far the definition is satisfied by rulers and pig-keepers, and that this shows that his technique takes no account of the prestige of the objects it is used on. Its aim he says is truth (266 d). Unfortunately however it misses its aim, this time, for "skilled managers of featherless bipeds" does not define statesmen, but the divine rulers of the mythical golden age. It is not that the livestock with which rulers are concerned have been clumsily identified (as one might have thought), but that rulers under modern conditions are not managers.

One might have thought that this blunder would discredit the technique, but it turns up again a good deal further on. For when the *paradeigma* of weaving is introduced the technique is used to define weaving, and it or something like it makes further sporadic appearances while the application of the parallel is being worked out.

In plain English, it all seems very silly. Why, for example, one wants to ask, is a division of animals into horned and hornless allowed to count as a division down the middle, whereas a division into rational and irrational apparently is not? No doubt the management of horned animals is different from that of hornless—that is the argument for polling cattle. But the difference is much less than that which separates the management of rational and irrational animals. That his bipeds are featherless no doubt prevents one confusing a ruler with a chicken-farmer; but it hardly illuminates the nature of ruling.

What is the supposed purpose of this technique? Is it intended to identify its objects, or to throw light on them? It is officially introduced in the *Sophist* as a method for identifying a subject. But if it is really meant as a method of identification, then the Stranger's advice in the *Statesman* about dividing by kinds and down the middle is unnecessary. "The objects whose cards are not allowed to move in the game of Dover Patrol" identifies naval mines, but I am sure this definition does not conform to the Stranger's rules. Nor is the technique in fact used as a method of identification. The man who did not know what the word "sophist" stood for would be more, not less, in the dark, by the end of the definitions in the *Sophist*. The technique is in fact used to throw light (most of it ironical) on the objects defined.

One might ask alternatively whether the technique is intended to assist one in the *discovery* of a correct definition (whatever that may be), or in the *exposition* of one. If it is intended as a technique of discovery, then it seems to be a bad one, and it seems to be Plato's purpose to show that it is a bad one; for it seems that when one wants to define a sophist or a ruler one may find that the technique has allowed one to define a philosopher or a demi-god.

The following seems to me to be true. Plato uses this technique *as if it were designed* to illuminate the thing defined, but he does not use it *to* illuminate the thing defined. Both in the *Sophist* and in the *Statesman*, when he wants to get down to serious business, he drops the technique. In the *Sophist* (232 a, b) the Stranger has to complain in the end that they have not hit on the essential nature of the sophist, and must ask straight out what this is. In the *Statesman*, while the technique plays some part in developing the parallel of weaving and ruling, it is by hitting upon this parallel that light is found. Again while the technique is presented as if it were a technique of discovery, it is plainly not used as if it were one, for the

Stranger could not proceed in the way in which he does proceed unless he knew where he was going. It looks therefore as if somebody's leg is being pulled, somebody (actual or possible) who thought that such a technique could be used as a tool of philosophical discovery. At the same time, however, there is a more constructive side to Plato's account of the technique. For if it is regarded as a method of exposition only, then it makes sense. For if the Stranger's rules are adhered to, and if one is allowed to be sensible about what counts as dividing down the middle, then the *result* of a definition by dichotomy is in fact a spelt out syllable. The *process* is far from infallible, and it seems to be part of Plato's purpose to point this out; but if it is conducted skilfully then the form which the result takes is the form of a correct definition in which something is first subsumed under its genus and then spelt out by a process of dividing down until it is reached. I suspect that the Stranger is allowed to play about with the method and get the wrong answers out of it because it is Plato's purpose simultaneously to illustrate the form which division takes and also to show that mere knowledge of the form cannot impart skill in dividing.

Skill in dividing will of course depend very largely on a pretty accurate idea of the nature of the thing to be defined, but it will also depend on having a stock of ready-made divisions. "Skills may be divided into: creative and acquisitive." "Constitutions may be divided into . . ."; the Stranger produces propositions of this kind off his cuff, and one feels that he has thought it all out before. There is some evidence[1] that the Academy manufactured ready-made divisions of this kind, presumably so that its pupils should have a filing-system available for the definition of anything. Possibly we are meant to infer the desirability of such a filing-system from the use that the Stranger makes of his. But I am sure we are also meant to see that it is not a substitute for thought.

The conclusion is that the things that are said about dichotomous definition are seriously meant although the examples of it are conducted so as to show that as a dodge it is fallible (and to make some hits at rulers and sophists). We may therefore safely take the Stranger's advice about division, given in the context of dichotomous definition, to apply to division as a component in dialectic.

(vii) *A general problem about the metaphor of letters and syllables*

A surgeon is skilled at cutting living animal matter. This makes him look like a cousin of a carpenter who is skilled at cutting dead vegetable matter. On the other hand a surgeon is skilled at curing disease by making appropriate modifications in the body by the

[1] See e.g. Ross, *Plato's Theory of Ideas*, pp. 143–5.

agency of hands and tools. This makes a surgeon look less like a carpenter and more like a physician. According to the first definition a surgeon is like a carpenter except that he cuts different things; according to the second definition a surgeon is like a physician except that he cures in different ways. It seems to be possible to spell a syllable in various ways and in so doing to set it in various lights. Even so the Stranger makes his sophist look now like a kind of hunter, now like a kind of merchant, now like a kind of psychiatrist.

This excites the question: Is there *one correct* way of spelling a given syllable? On one side of the metaphor, of course, there is. Greek orthography, so far as I know, was pretty well settled in Plato's day, and *P l a t ô n* was the one correct way of spelling Plato's name. Are we meant to carry over this feature of literal spelling to its metaphorical counterpart?

Two extreme views can be stated. On one view a complex nature or syllable is what it is because it is a complex of just those letters, rather as a chemical compound is what it is because it results from those elements in this proportion. Thus the complex nature manhood would be what it is simply because it is animality modified by rationality (or whatever the truth may be). This view has the advantage that it keeps close to the metaphors: for *c a t* spells "cat" because of the phonetic value of the letters.

The other extreme view is that this part of the metaphor ought to be totally disregarded. Spelling out complex natures has nothing to do with discerning the factors whose inter-action makes the complex nature what it is. Spelling out complex natures is simply a method whereby we either identify the thing under discussion, or throw light on it or both. Since there are many ways in which any given thing can be identified, and often several lights in which it may usefully be placed, there is no one correct way of spelling a given syllable. Surgeons and carpenters after all have common problems, just as surgeons and physicians, and we shall not understand all about surgery unless we make all the linkages of this kind that we can. The letters of an ontological syllable do not *cause it to be* the syllable which it is; they are not constituting factors. Rather they are identifying factors in that they serve to identify the syllable, and to suggest comparisons with other syllables which can be spelt so that they share some of the same letters.

This is of course bound up with the view that we take of the relation between dichotomous definition and spelling. If there is one correct way of spelling a syllable, namely that which gives its constituting factors, then (if dichotomous definition is an attempt at spelling) most or all of the Stranger's spellings of the sophist must be wrong. So also must be his spelling of men as featherless bipeds, and as cloven-footed . . . gregarious bipeds; for it is difficult to believe that these letters have combined to make human nature what it is. No doubt our lack of feathers and our upright posture have done something to make us what we are; but intelligence has done more. So if we take the view that there is only one correct way of spelling a syllable, and also the view that the Stranger was trying in his dichotomous definitions to spell syllables, we shall have to conclude not only that the technique is fallible, but that he used it very, very badly.

This conclusion is quite feasible. As we have seen he does not in fact make any use of his spellings except to offer them as illustrations of a method whereby one ought to be able to do something which he in fact fails to do. One is also inclined to favour this conclusion on the ground that it is difficult to avoid it without giving up the idea that there is only one correct way of spelling a syllable; for it is difficult to cut the links between spelling and dichotomous definition. The idea that there is only one correct way of spelling a syllable is difficult to abandon if one remembers that the whole business is stated as if it were part of dialectic, and "dialectic" seems to mean philosophical method. But unless Plato has abandoned altogether the view that things are as they are because of the universal properties which they embody, surely philosophical method will still consist in the attempt to see clearly the universal properties whose presence in a given class of things *makes them what they are.* But that means that the goal of philosophical method is the discovery of the *one correct* method of spelling a syllable.

Nor is the "chemical compound" view hopelessly unplausible (that is to say the view that a given syllable owes its nature to the natures of the letters of which it is a function). If we remember the structure of the *Timaeus* it seems reasonable to say that human nature is animality modified by rationality, given that this specification has to be realised in given materials. The equation

"Humanity=animality× rationality× the given materials"

seems to be a reasonable statement of Plato's view.

But there is something to be said on the other side. What Plato has to say, now, about dialectic, is dominated by the shadow of Protarchus' fallacy. If you vaguely see that love is madness you will condemn romance; and inconclusive arguments may spring up between Lysias who thinks that one kind of love is one kind of madness and Socrates who thinks that another kind of love is another kind of madness. Before you start discussing, you must decide *what* kind of love and *what* kind of madness. Identification is vital; it does not matter how the topic is identified. Any spelling which pinpoints the syllable will do.

I do not know how to settle this question. Perhaps the following will serve. Plato is not very serious about dichotomous definition, not very clear how the spelling metaphor is to be taken. He assumes that good philosophers will proceed by imagination and insight, and that bad philosophers cannot be turned into good ones by techniques. He has in his mind two ideas. The first is that every complex nature is constituted by certain simpler factors whose interaction makes it what it is, and that we cannot make synthetic judgments about a given kind without finding out what these are in its case. The second is simply that it is vital always to isolate the topic under discussion. Both of these point to definition of some kind, some sort of subsumption under a genus coupled with statement of a *differentia*. In the light of the first idea it matters how the definition is effected; in the light of the second it only matters that the definition should uniquely identify. He is not too clear that there is this difference, and he is not too serious about the examples he offers because he does not really believe in techniques. In the course of offering identificatory definitions, which do not have to be correct "essential" definitions, there is plenty of scope for irony; he makes use of it, and in doing so forgets how much the reader will be puzzled by the oddity of the examples if they are thought of as essential definitions. I feel reasonably confident only of the general point of this paragraph, which can be expressed as follows. There is an ontological aspect in what Plato has to say about letters and syllables, and therefore also in what he has to say about definition by dichotomy. But there is also a purely logical aspect (after all dichotomous definition is officially introduced as a technique for fixing the reference of a word); and Plato is confusing and probably confused about the relation between these two aspects.

D. *Conclusion of this account of the relations between universals*

The principle of Socratic definition had always implied that some sort of relations hold between universals. For Socratic definition can be regarded as the detection of elements within a complex. It need not however be so regarded. The model of a complex and its elements is not the only one available. One might alternatively make use of a geographical model. Take for example two definitions of shape which are given in the *Meno* (75):[1] "Shape is that which is invariably concomitant upon colour", and "Shape is the boundary of a solid". We might regard these definitions as telling us where

[1] They are offered to Meno as patterns of the kind of definition Socrates wants. He does not claim that they are perfect; in fact he implies perhaps (75 c 1) that the first at least is no more than "adequate".

shape lies, so to speak, with reference to colour and to solidity. Since neither of these is precisely a definition *per genus et differentiam* the geographical model would fit these more happily than the model of a complex and its elements; for colour is hardly an element in shape. So long as Plato felt that universals cannot be blended, I daresay that he would have felt the geographical model a better account of definition than the other; for he might surely have felt that there was something uncomfortably near to blending in saying that P was the Q version of R.

So soon as he became reconciled to the idea of blending, any hesitations of this kind would disappear, and the model of a complex and its elements, or of definition *per genus et differentiam* would become the natural model to adopt. The emphasis on dichotomous definition suggests that something like this took place, though we have already seen reason to doubt whether Plato drew the logical conclusion that there are *summa genera* which cannot be defined. We ought not therefore to say that Plato held that definition *is per genus et differentiam*, but only that he came to look on it in this way.

The removal, then, of inhibitions about blending may have led to the crystallisation of a certain picture of the nature of definition. This would chime in with an interest in classification in the sense of taxonomy in the natural world. There is evidence that classification was an interest of the Academy. I have already referred to this in connection with "divisions". There is also a Comic fragment which represents the young men of the Academy trying, under Plato's benevolent eye, to classify a pumpkin. Interest in classification might tend to conflict with the view that a correct definition should give pointers to the synthetic judgments which can be made about a kind. Any gardener who has been irritated by changes in botanical names will agree that classification and illumination do not always go hand in hand. Illumination however is not particularly in point in connection with such universals as pumpkin-hood. It is when the taxonomic model moves over into the sphere of "disputable", or philosophically interesting, universals such as pleasure that the interest in classification and the pursuit of illumination may well conflict. The more it is felt that the purpose of classification in these fields is to avoid Protarchan confusions, the more likely is it that the interests of illumination will fall into the background.

We find then three motives in the writings which we have examined. There is the old interest in the illumination to be got from a correct essential definition. There is the new emphasis on the importance of distinguishing one version of a given kind from another. Finally there is a new interest in classification for its own sake. In so far as there are confusing features in these writings, an uncertain balance between these three interests is probably responsible for them.

V. THE *SOPHIST*

A. *Introductory*

The doctrine of the *Sophist* is continuous with that which we have been examining. The fact that I have relegated the *Sophist* to a section of its own must not be allowed to give a contrary impression. I have given the *Sophist* a section on its own partly because it is very difficult, and partly because it adds something to the doctrine sketched in the *Cratylus* and common to the *Phaedrus*, *Statesman* and *Philebus*. There are two parts to this additional material. One of these parts deals with matters which are perhaps more properly called logical than metaphysical, namely the meaning of the verb *einai* or "to be", and the nature of negation. The discussion of these topics is entangled with that of the others and can only be separated by violence. I shall use violence, however, and postpone the detailed consideration of these topics to the next chapter. The other part of the additional material can perhaps be described as follows. So far the "kinds" whose "sharing" we have been considering have been, on the whole, material or limiting properties. I call, for example, animality a limiting property, because there are certain limits which cannot be transgressed by anything which is to have the property. We recall however that the discussion in the *Parmenides* was concerned with the formal or non-limiting property unity—non-limiting in the sense that to be told that X is one is to be told nothing whatever about the nature of X. It is clear that the relation of non-limiting to limiting properties was an important question in Plato's latest phase, and it is in the *Sophist* that this is first discussed in connection with the sharing of kinds. This is the special material with which this section will be primarily concerned. I may add that it will be impossible in a discussion of this—perhaps of any—length to justify an interpretation of the *Sophist*.[1]

B. *Analysis of the relevant section*

In what follows I shall use the practice of prefixing a number to paragraphs which purport to give the gist of a section of text (it will

---

[1] Some readers will want to protest that it is wrong to treat unity, existence, etc., as properties; they will want to deny the existence of my class of "non-limiting properties". No doubt this is right, but it would probably be un-Platonic (that is something we must consider), and it is certainly cumbrous to speak always of "the adjective 'one' " rather than " unity".

often be more that than a *précis*), and a letter to paragraphs of comment. The ground to be covered is *Sophist* 241–60.

A. The Eleatic Stranger wants to say that sophists are purveyors of fakes, of semblances of knowledge but not the real thing. But he knows that, if he says that, the sophists will retort that there are no such things as semblances; for a semblance is something which is-not[1] what it sets out to be, and, since there is no such thing as nothing, it is impossible for anything to not-be. Therefore the Stranger must explain how things can not-be. Not-being must therefore be allowed some kind of existence; it must be shown to be a genuine "way of existing", or a genuine predicate. This is done by demonstrating that not-being is the same as being different from. This obviously makes not-being something real. But the statement that not-being exists must be distinguished from the statement that not-being is identical with being. (The chance of confusing these two statements seems remote in English, but we must remember that in Greek the use of participial phrases and the lack of an indefinite article makes it natural to express the former: "*mê on estin on*" or "not-being is being"). Plato's traditional device for distinguishing predication from identity is "participates", and therefore he expresses what he wants to say in the form "Not-being participates in, but is not identical with, being". Since, however, not-being, or difference, and being are universals this statement makes the participation relation hold between universals as such, in contravention of the old principle that universals "cannot be blended among themselves". In other words the solution of the problem of giving a logical analysis of negation gets tied up with the principle of the sharing of kinds, and that is how the *prima facie* very different topics of dialectic and of negative statements get entangled with each other.

(The commonest verbs for the participation relation have been *metechein* and *metalambanein*. In this dialogue we also encounter *meignusthai* or "to be mixed", *koinônein* or "to share", and various other verbs. I do not think that Plato's choice of a verb is significant —four are used in the four lines 251 d 5–9 for example—but I will use "partake" or "participate" for the first two, and "share" for *koinônein*).

1. It is to be shown that not-being in a sense is, and being in a sense is-not. The Stranger begins by examining the views of those who have put forward theories about the nature of *to on*, "being" or "the real". His complaint is that they have left the notion obscure. Perhaps, he suggests, being is just as puzzling as not-being, and the

---

[1] Where convenient I shall hyphenate "is" and "not". This has no special significance. I shall also have to make barbarous use of "is", where "exists" would be correct, to preserve the Greek ambiguity.

Eleatic tradition has been wrong in supposing the contrary (241–3). Of those who have "ventured to decide the number and kinds of beings that there are", the Stranger first considers various kinds of pluralists, for example those who say that the hot and the cold constitute everything. Of those who identify *to on* with any such set of properties the Stranger demands that they should say what they mean by "is" in their statements (e.g. "The hot is."). If you predicate being of the hot and the cold ("Being is the hot and the cold" for example), then you seem on the one hand to say that there exist two kinds only, while on the other hand, by predicating being of them, you apparently commit yourself to the existence of a third (viz. being). (243–4).

B. Presumably these thinkers meant to say that some set of properties, P, Q . . . constitutes the class of ultimate properties in terms of which everything can be explained. Undertaking to explain all phenomena in terms of, say, the hot and the cold, they identify the hot and the cold with the real. In effect the Stranger's reply is that since one can say that the hot is, and that the cold is, being must be a further property over and above those specified. He is making a general point against "Parmenides and anyone else who ventures to decide the number and kinds of beings that there are" (242 c 4–6); this is that, since being is not identical with any other universal, if there are said to be n universals, then being must be the $n+1$ th. The doctrines the Stranger is examining are of the form "The real is P, Q . . .". If such doctrines are taken (as they are intended) to mean that everything can be explained in terms of the properties P, Q . . ., then the Stranger does not commit himself to an opinion about the truth or falsity of these views. His point is directed against such doctrines taken not as pieces of physical science but as pieces of metaphysical analysis, to the effect that there are no ultimate properties except P, Q . . ., and to this interpretation of such doctrines his rejoinder is that being must feature in any list of ultimate properties, and cannot be identified with any set of properties.

2. He next considers Parmenidean monism—the view that being is one. His arguments are obscure but they seem to come to something like this:—The monist believes in nothing but "the one". But he must believe in being. Therefore *prima facie* he believes, despite his protestations, in two things, being and the one. He can hardly say that these are two names for the same thing. He can hardly allow that there are two names, for he would thereby commit himself to the existence of two entities. Indeed he can hardly allow that there exist such things as names (244 d 1); for a name must be something distinct from the thing named, thus begetting a plurality of entities. A further difficulty for monists concerns "the whole" or wholeness.

It seems that the one must be identical with the whole. But in that case it must have parts. It is true that its parts can be unified ("can suffer the one") so that it is in that way one; but it cannot be "the one itself: for that which is truly one cannot have parts".[1] If one says that being is unified, and thus preserves its wholeness, then there will be two entities, being which is unified, and unity which does the unifying. If on the other hand one says that being is not a whole, but allows nonetheless that wholeness exists, then being will not include wholeness, and this too means that there must exist more than one thing, namely being and wholeness, "each having its own nature apart from the other". It is, finally, impossible to avoid this conclusion by denying the existence of "the whole", for nothing can exist or come into being except *as a whole*. (244–5).

C. On the face of it these criticisms are very childish. As in the *Parmenides*, so here one gets the impression that the counters are being pushed about without any serious attempt to ascertain what they mean. What, for example, can be meant by conceding, or questioning, the existence of wholeness? Worse than this, perhaps, what can be meant by the argument about the existence of a name? Yet these criticisms are not childish, though their expression is certainly unsophisticated. Take for example the apparently absurd argument about names. One is inclined to protest than a monist who is prepared to say that there is only one substance is not likely to be moved by the thought that words exist. If the sun, moon and stars can be boiled down into one substance, surely the addition of language to the pot will make little difference. But this misses the point. Parmenides said that nothing exists but *to hen on*, "the one being". Everything else (the obviously plural empirical world) is appearance; "the one" is the only reality. He allowed certain properties to "the one"; for example it was changeless and spherical. But how did he know that reality or "the one" had these properties? The answer is that he endowed it with those properties which seemed to him to follow from its reality and its unity. It had to exist and therefore it could contain no non-existence or empty space (nor therefore could motion occur in it); and it had to be one. But it had to be one not in the harmless sense in which anything is always one so-and-so, but in a sense fertile of consequences. It had to be unitary in the sense in which we used that word in our discussion of the *Parmenides*— non-complex. It had in fact to satisfy the conditions for the named

---

[1] 245 a. This looks like a reappearance of the named meaning of *to hen* which we thought that the *Parmenides* was getting rid of. A possible answer to this is that (as the *Parmenides* implies) Parmenides' views depended on something like the named meaning—Parmenides speaks of "my hypothesis" that the one is one— and that the Stranger is arguing against Parmenides on the latter's terms.

meaning of "one".[1] Because it had to be unitary Parmenides' views can be refuted if it can be shown that the existence of the one entails that there exists something complex. This the Stranger does; but why does he do it? Why does he refute Parmenides' views when he is not supposed to be showing that reality is not a well-rounded sphere, but rather that being is an obscure notion? The answer must be, I think, that Plato thought that Parmenides' views amounted to the identification of existence and unity. Parmenides has to get somehow from the truism that there is only one reality to the startling doctrine that reality is not complex. The belief that to exist is to be unitary would enable him to do this;[2] for reality or that which certainly exists would thus become that which certainly is unitary. Given this diagnosis of the origin of Parmenides' monism, a demonstration that there exists something complex would both refute Parmenides and also bring out the falsity of the presupposition on which his views were thought to rest, or in other words of the equation of existence with unity. Therefore the Stranger goes so far with Parmenides as to leave unchallenged the doctrine that only the one exists, proving (along routes sketched out in the *Parmenides*) that this is enough in itself to prove that there exists something complex. The upshot of this is that even Parmenides (who is prepared to dismiss everything except the one as appearance) must allow that something complex exists and that therefore existence does not preclude complexity and is therefore not identical with unity in the sense in which Parmenides uses the term. We are inclined to be more bewildered even than we need be by Plato's argument through failing to observe the level on which Plato thinks it necessary to meet Parmenides. We feel inclined to say that Parmenides could be refuted by being told that it is plainly false that nothing exists except the one. On the whole Plato also tends to be content to bring a common-sense answer of this kind against high metaphysical views —consider for example his treatment of Heracliteanism in the *Theaetetus*. But he seems to have been mesmerised by Parmenides, and to have felt in consequence that the thesis that nothing exists but the one must be treated as a possible view, which can only be refuted if it is shown to contain internal contradictions.

We must allow then that Plato's purpose is to find internal con-

---

[1] For this use of "unitary" see p. 337. For the notion of a "named meaning" see pp. 334-5.

[2] So of course, in fact, would the belief that what is one is unitary. But this belief itself might depend, a little, on the view that existence is unity. If you accept the converse of Plato's view that not-being is diversity (namely that diversity is not-being) you will come to think that what is cannot be diverse, and that therefore the one reality is unitary, and also that to exist is not to be diverse; so "the one is unitary" and "the being is the one".

tradictions in the doctrine that only the one exists, and that the immediate reason for doing this is to show that existence is not the same as unitariness. He begins by suggesting that the doctrine "only the one exists" is to be taken as an ordinary subject–predicate statement in which one nature (existence) is predicated of another (the one). This would mean at once that that which exists is complex, consisting of the one and existence.[1] Therefore the Stranger knows that the monists will not accept this version of their doctrine. He suggests that they will treat it as a kind of tautology in which the subject term and the predicate term are different "names" but do not stand for different "realities". To this he retorts that to have to allow the existence of two "names", or even the existence of one "name" (*onoma*) and one "reality" (*pragma*), is fatal because either of these entails the existence of something complex. Now it is certainly true that Plato normally uses the word *onoma* to mean "word", but he cannot be doing so here. It would not worry the monist to admit that there exists both the one and also words, because it does not worry the monist to admit that there exists both the one and also mice, thunderstorms and so on. The existence of mice and men is "appearance" and the existence of human speech would have the same status. "That there exist two 'names' " must mean something like "that there exist *grounds* necessitating the use of two non-synonymous words", or "that the one substance contains two aspects". How Plato comes to use *onoma* in this way I do not know (it is not an incomprehensible use, but it is not customary in Plato). But unless we allow that he does use it in some such way we cannot rescue the argument from triviality. Perhaps he was conforming to some Eleatic usage. However that may be, the suggestion that the monist is supposed to put forward is that there exists only one substance, the one, but that it has two aspects. To this the Stranger's retort is that if you have to distinguish two aspects, or even one aspect from its substance, you concede the existence of something complex. You cannot get out of this by identifying the aspect with its substance because then the substance becomes an aspect so that the aspect is an aspect of an aspect, which is absurd. Unless the Stranger is descending to pure sophistry his meaning must be something like this. (See note on page 472)

The argument about wholeness is more convincing on the surface but perhaps more complicated. It begins from the fact that Parmenides admits that the one is also the whole. Indeed he must admit

[1] This might seem to, but does not, conflict with my interpretation of Socrates' Dream (above pp. 114–17). The point there is not that "P exists" mentions only one entity (namely P), but that this *logos* can be a *logos* about an element, because it is about P (and not about P and existence); and P may be elementary.

this, because nothing can exist or come into being except as a whole. In less crabbed language, the notion of something which is not in principle divisible into parts is a contradiction. This means that whereas Parmenides insisted that the properties of reality must be such as follow from its unity, one can equally well insist that its properties must be such as follow from its wholeness, viz. it must have parts. The Stranger then supposes that the monist will defend himself by saying that the real may perhaps have parts, but may none the less "suffer unity upon its parts", or in other words that reality may be unified even if it is not unitary. If the monist did make this move he would in fact be giving up the claim that reality is one in the challenging sense of "one", and his views would collapse to the truism that there are not two or more realities. However the Stranger does not make this point against him, but says that in the case where reality is a unity of many members it will not be *auto ge to hen* (245 a 5), which seems to be the property unity conceived of as a named meaning; for this must be non-complex. In a series of arguments whose details do not concern us the Stranger goes on to show that once wholeness is brought into the story that which ultimately exists must be complex, consisting of reality and the one which unifies it, or of reality and wholeness. The conclusion of the whole argument could be put by saying that since "the one", "the being" and "the whole" are not synonymous expressions that which exists must be complex, unity, existence and wholeness being ultimate properties which cannot be reduced to each other. The consequence of this is that unity and existence cannot be identified, and that the failure of the Parmenideans to see this shows the slipperiness of the notion of *to on* or being.

The position now arrived at is that one cannot identify existence either with some set of physical properties such as the hot and the cold, or with the "metaphysical" property unity. Even if it is true in a sense that *to on* is the hot and the cold or that *to on* is the one, existence is something distinct from the kinds which can truly be said to exist. (The *verbal* point that *to on* is sometimes used to mean "that which exists" and sometimes as a substitute for *einai* or "existence" is not made. Plato seems insensitive to the dangers of this phrase, as he is to those of other phrases of the same form. But though he fails to make the verbal point, he does I think want to make the substantial point. A clear statement of the verbal point would have given great help).

3. The Stranger now goes on to consider the views of those whom he calls the less rigorous thinkers, still with a view to showing that being is no clearer than not-being. There are two classes of these less rigorous thinkers, materialists and those described as "partisans of

the forms". The materialists deny the existence of non-corporeal entities. They admit that there are souls, but make them honorary physical objects by saying that they are, or can only exist in, bodies. They are however embarrassed by the status of entities like virtues which exist in souls. They cannot plausibly deny that virtues are non-corporeal entities, and if they admit this they can be asked to say what is common to non-corporeal and to corporeal entities such that both can be said to exist. If they cannot answer, the Stranger offers them the following formula (247 d 8–e 4):—"Whatever has the capacity to affect in any way, or to be affected by, anything else . . . may be said to be; I lay down capacity as the criterion (*horos*) of being". (246–7).

D. Unless this is intended as no more than an irrelevant attack on materialism, the point of it surely is the same as the point of the two previous criticisms, namely to prevent the identification of existence with some other property, in this case with that of being corporeal. Being less rigorous thinkers these persons are not told that their doctrine "Only the corporeal is" must, if it is to be non-tautological, predicate one kind of another; they are dealt with on a level more suited to their grosser intelligences.[1]

Ought we to say that the Stranger's formula about capacity (*dunamis*) is meant as a Socratic definition or "spelling" of existence? It is called a *horos* or boundary and not a *logos* or account, so that it is not compulsory to say so. It might be said that in a section devoted to showing that existence must not be confused with any other property it would be tactless to define existence. If existence were identified with the capacity to affect or be affected, what would happen to the statement that this capacity exists? Could we not argue that "The capacity . . . exists" is analogous to "The one exists" and that it must predicate one kind of another? Perhaps we might argue in this way, but Plato might conceivably retort that "The capacity . . . exists" predicates a kind of itself. If the Parmenidean demanded similar treatment for "The one exists" Plato would have to rely in the end on the obvious difference of meaning between "the one" and "existence". I do not know what the answer to this question is. On the whole I incline to the view that the Stranger is not interested in saying that existence is indefinable and that he would not be shocked to hear his formula described as a provisional definition. (I say "provisional" because the word with which he "lays down" his *horos*, namely *tithemai*, is commonly used to describe the putting forward of a hypothesis). At *Phaedrus* 270 d Socrates has implied that to investigate any "nature" is to ask what it can do or undergo. A specific nature is a specific pattern of doing and undergoing. If

[1] Their position incidentally reminds us of that sketched in *Timaeus* 52 b.

a specific nature is thought of as a way of existing, existence in general would naturally be thought of as doing and undergoing in general. The Stranger's formula seems therefore to be the kind of account of existence which we might expect Plato to give. But however that may be, the main purpose of this section is to deny that to exist is to be material.

4. The next class of less rigorous thinkers whose views are criticised are described as Partisans of the Forms. It is said of them that they believe that being consists of "certain intelligible and non-physical forms", which are not susceptible to change, and that they relegate changeable physical things to the status of becoming. Against them the Stranger argues firstly that there is reason to suppose that something which is known thereby undergoes something, and that therefore that which cannot undergo change cannot be known; and secondly that it is intolerable to deny that change and life and soul and intelligence are "present to *to on*". Reality cannot be said to be "without life or thought, existing in holy dignity, without intelligence, unchanging and inert". Nevertheless it is also impossible to maintain that everything always changes in every respect; for that too will make knowledge impossible. (246 and 248–9).

E. The Partisans of the Forms sound very like Platonists. Is Plato here criticising his own views? I shall defer this question to a later section. For our immediate purposes the significance of this section is that it shows that there must be both some changing things, and also some stability in things, and that the consequence of this is that existence cannot be identified either with passivity or with activity. This however is not made clear at this stage any more than in the previous cases.

5. The Stranger goes on to argue that activity and inactivity can both be said to be, but that they cannot both be said to be active; nor, in saying that they both exist, does one mean that they are both inactive. Therefore being is some third thing which embraces activity and inactivity, and in which they both share. Therefore according to its own nature being is neither active nor inactive. But this is paradoxical, since one would have thought that whatever is not active would be inactive, and *vice versa*. Therefore, he concludes, the problem of what "being" is to be taken to be the name of is at least as puzzling as the analogous problem about "not-being". (250).

F. The demonstration that being is neither active nor inactive, and thus breaks the Law of the Excluded Middle, is obviously fallacious. "To be" does not indeed mean the same either as "to be active" or as "to be inactive".[1] It follows from this that from the

[1] But it might be suggested that "to be" does mean the same as "to be active *or* inactive".

statement that X exists you cannot infer that X is active, nor that it is inactive, but it does not follow that there is anything which is neither active nor inactive. From "Existence is not activity and it is not inactivity" we cannot derive "Existence is not active and it is not inactive". But this is not a criticism of Plato's argument, for this is the point which he is trying to make. For it will seem that the latter statement can be derived from the former so long as it is thought that the attribution of a property to a subject is a statement of identity between subject and property. The Stranger's argument is assisted by the dangerous practice of using *to on* to mean both "existing" and "that which exists", and also by the equally dangerous practice of saying that A is not B when one means that "A" does not mean the same as "B". Plato does not warn us against the danger of these practices, but he does go on to make the point that a predication is not a statement of identity; and this is enough to clear away the Stranger's paradox. Thus the function of the paradox is to show that the distinction is necessary, as the Stranger goes on to say.

6. The Stranger says that we must consider the mechanics of the practice whereby we use "many names of the same thing"—or in other words, of non-tautologous statement. There are those who say that many things cannot be one nor one many, and that therefore a man can only be a man and cannot also be for example good. Since to be tall is not the same as to be Jones, they infer that it is false that Jones is tall. Yet we are all happy to defy this and say that Jones is tall; and if we were not thus prepared to assert non-identical predicates of a subject we could not say anything. Indeed we could not even say that being tall is not identical with anything else (the "tautologies only" thesis), since even this is a combining of different things —being, non-identity and everything else are combined with tallness in this proposition. Unless things can combine with, share or partake in each other, nothing at all can be said. Given that things can combine, activity and inactivity can be said to exist although they are not the same as being. (251–2).

7. Some combinations must be possible, then, and the question is whether all combinations are possible, or whether some are impossible. It is obvious, the Stranger and Theaetetus agree, that some combinations are impossible, for if all combinations were possible, then "Activity is inactive" and its converse would be true. (252).

G. It is not clear why it is thought to be obvious that "Activity is inactive" is false (252 d). For if Plato is in complete command of the point which he is making, then he must see that "Activity is inactive" does not mean the same as "Activity is inactivity". Indeed in 256 b 6 the Stranger does observe (in effect) that propositions of the pattern of "Activity is inactive" can in principle be true. We shall have to return to this point later. Here we will observe that there is an ambiguity in "activity". The word could stand for the general property of being active, or it could stand for a particular case of it, such as the sun's activity. If it stands for the general property then one might have thought that there is a case for saying that this *is* inactive (though the Stranger has disputed this in connection with properties in general in his argument against the Partisans of the Forms; see paragraph 4). If it stands for particular cases of activity, then one might have thought that the earth's rotation about its axis is a case of inactive activity, or of change which does not change.[1] It is possible that "Activity is inactive" is being interpreted as "All change is constant", whereas the most that can be maintained is that some is. However that may be, the alleged falsity of "Activity is inactive" and its converse is used to show that some combinations are impossible.

8. It has been shown, then, that some kinds can be combined whereas some cannot. This, it is said, resembles the situation with regard to letters and musical notes;[2] here too some combinations are possible and others are not. Vowels in particular constitute a bond running through all the other letters. It takes a grammarian or musician to know what combinations of letters or notes are possible; it takes an analogously skilled person to know: (*a*) what kinds can and cannot combine with what; (*b*) whether there are any kinds which are to be found "running through all things, and which hold them together so as to make them able to blend"; and (*c*) whether "in divisions there are other kinds which turn up throughout the combinations and are responsible for division". The Stranger goes on to remark that this skill is of course dialectic, for to be a dialectician is to be able to divide by kinds, and not to think the same kind different, or a different one the same. He then lists four things that a dialectician can do (or at any rate uses four phrases to describe his activity); and goes on to conclude the passage by saying that they will know whereabouts to find the philosopher if they should subsequently want to define him. (252–3).

H. This section contains hints of the greatest importance and utmost difficulty which we shall have to consider later. Meanwhile the position is that it has been informally shown that being is not

---

[1] The *Theaetetus* has surely shown that a process of change can be constant, see above, pp. 10–11. I think that it was Mr. Gosling who drew my attention to the ambiguity in "activity".

[2] These are different situations, for certain combinations of letters (e.g. *d r m*) are downright impossible, whereas no combination of notes is more than nasty. I welcome this assimilation of the two situations by Plato, for it fits well with my contention (see e.g. pp. 167–8), that he thought of logical impossibility as the limiting case of offensiveness to reason.

identical with any other kind, but that nevertheless any kind can be said to be. There are therefore true synthetic propositions as well as statements of identity. It has also been suggested that there may be certain factors which are responsible for the possibility of certain combinations, and certain other factors which are responsible for divisions. The Stranger is now about to discuss these possibilities and impossibilities in terms of examples without further reference to cohesive and differentiating factors. If it is asked whether these factors are to be looked for in the examples chosen, it must be answered that the text does not make this clear. (It is a fault of the dialogue method that, in so far as it reproduces the rambling course of ordinary conversation, one is never certain how close the connection between one passage and another is supposed to be. A fault? Perhaps a virtue rather for an essentially exploratory writer like Plato, who is probably never certain himself).

9. The Stranger proposes to pursue further the question of possibilities and impossibilities of combination among kinds by taking three of the "very great" ones, namely being, activity and inactivity. It has already been shown that both activity and inactivity can be said to be, or in other words that they can combine with being. It is now added that each of the three is the same as itself and different from each of the others. But this is taken to show that there are two more very great kinds, namely sameness and difference, which can combine with each of the original three, but which cannot be identified with any of them. Sameness for example cannot be identified with inactivity (it might have been thought that for a thing to be the same as itself it must be inactive); for self-sameness can be predicated both of activity and of inactivity, so that if self-sameness were identified with inactivity, that would mean that inactivity could be predicated of activity; and this has been deemed impossible. (254–5).

I. It may be noticed in parenthesis that the arguments devised to show that sameness and difference cannot be identified with any of the other three very great kinds make it very clear how difficult it is to conduct such a discussion in the terminology available to Plato. I have quoted the only one of these arguments which is superficially lucid. The argument designed to show that being cannot be identified with sameness, though valid, looks at first sight like a feeble pun, and it needs a good deal of careful scrutiny to see that the point both of this argument and of its successor (designed to show that being is not identical with difference) is to bring out the valid point that sameness and difference are relational properties whereas being is not. But at any rate the conclusion is that sameness and difference are two further very great kinds, and that they "run through" the three others. (The phrase for "run through" is *dia pantôn*, 255 e 3. This is the same phrase as that used for the factors responsible for cohesion and division 253 c 1; see paragraph 8).

10. The Stranger now proceeds to state the relations between activity and the other four. (*a*) Activity is different from inactivity, and therefore it is not inactivity. (*b*) It partakes in being and therefore is. (*c*) It is different from the same (*sc. sameness*) and therefore is not the same. (*d*) It partakes in the same (as does everything else) and therefore it is the same. (*e*) It is different from the different and therefore is and is not the different (*sc. it is an instance of the different, but it is not identical with it*). (*f*) It is different from being and therefore is not being, although (*g*) it partakes in being and therefore is. After making points (*c*) and (*d*) the Stranger comments that such apparent contradictions are easily generated and should not worry us; for "when we say that activity is the same and when we say that activity is not the same we are not talking in the same way. It is the same by virtue of partaking in sameness with respect to itself; it is not the same by virtue of sharing in difference, whereby it is separated off from sameness, and thus becomes not sameness, but something other than it." He goes on to add the remark already referred to (paragraph G) to the effect that if activity could partake in inactivity one might quite well find oneself saying that activity is stable. (255–6).

J. I have added the parentheses in italics above. They bring out the fact that the paradoxes which the Stranger creates and explains depend upon the fact that an adjective can be used in Greek both as an adjective and as an abstract substantive.[1] The Stranger's cure for this is to express a denial of identity in the form "A shares in difference with respect to B" (or "A is different from B" for short) and to express a predication in the form "A partakes in B". It seems reasonable to suppose that an assertion of identity would be expressed in the form "A partakes in sameness with respect to B" (the form used for "Activity is the same as itself" in 256 b 1). However a distinct formulation for denials of identity and for predication is all that the Stranger needs for his immediate purposes, which are to show how a thing can be said both to be and to not-be, or in other words how it is that one can say that A is not B without thereby saying that A does not exist.

11. Activity has been shown to be different from being and yet to be. This is generalised. Difference renders every kind different from being, though by participation in being each exists. Not-being in the ordinary sense is difference or antithesis (the question whether sense

[1] Incidentally in English we say "A is *the same* as B", but not "C is *the different* from D".

can be made of the notion of not-being as the opposite of being is dismissed). It is added that there exist any number of terms, each of which can be one term in an antithesis, just as there exist any number of realities each of which may be grasped by a mind. And just as the latter means that knowledge is divided into many branches or parts, so the former means that difference is divided into many, many parts. Thus the non-beautiful, for example, is "Separated off from some one class of beings, and again contrasted with one being". (256–7).

K. The Stranger now proceeds to apply the notion that not-being is difference to the definition of the sophist as a vendor of fakes. Essentially the point is that when "S is P" is significant but false, and hence "S is not P" is true, then P is a real property though different from those which belong to S. This explains how there can be significant but false propositions, and from this the possibility of sophistry follows. We will not at the moment inquire into the details of the Stranger's application of his results to the problem with which he is ostensibly concerned, the problem of false or negative propositions. It is enough to say here that the application is not straightforward since we have been given an analysis only of "A is not identical with B" and not of "S has not got the property P". We are therefore left thinking that "Jones is not rich" says that Jones (though existent) is a different existent from "the rich", or in other words from wealth. But this would be so, even if Jones *was* rich. But these enticing topics must be left for another chapter. We are here concerned with the contribution of the *Sophist* to the topics of the relation between universals and of dialectic. This concludes our analysis of the relevant section.

C. *Problems in* Sophist 241–60

(i) *The nature of the general terms discussed and of the relations said to hold between them*

Probably every reader of this section of the *Sophist* has been worried by the difficulty of deciding what sense the notion of *participation* is to bear, and what are the entities between which it is said to hold. We must now consider this matter.

An answer of a kind to the second question is that the entities discussed in this passage are forms. But this is a very inadequate answer. It is, I suppose, true, to the extent that Plato thought that the things that he said in this passage had application to entities of exalted status; but it is very obvious that he does not direct his readers' attention, during his discussion of identity and participation, to the topic of exalted status, and that he does on the other hand expect his remarks to be illuminating with respect to logical puzzles encountered in the discussion of the most mundane topics. His view is that we cannot understand the logic of negations unless we realise that "kinds can share". But we cannot tell what precisely we are to realise until we can settle what a "kind" is in this context, and what "sharing" amounts to.

Plato's purpose in the discussion of the very great kinds is to isolate the class of assertions and denials of identity, and to argue that not all statements about general terms are to be construed as assertions or denials of identity. In order to make the point that "A is B" need not mean "A and B are the same thing" he employs the formula "A partakes in B" on occasions when this meaning is not intended. "A is B", then, is bifurcated into "A is identical with B" (expressed either by "is" or by "partakes in self-sameness with respect to") and into "A partakes in B". It is the meaning of this latter formula which causes especial difficulty. When Socrates is said to partake in ugliness the meaning is that he himself is ugly. But when one general term, S-hood, is said to partake in another, P-hood, two interpretations are possible, which we will call respectively the "pure property" and the "class-inclusion" interpretation. According to the pure property interpretation "S-hood partakes in P-hood" says that S-hood is *itself* P. According to the class-inclusion interpretation P-hood belongs to S-hood distributively, so to speak, or in other words, the meaning of the sentence is that every S thing is P. Our problem is to decide whether the doctrine that kinds can share amounts to the doctrine that there are class-inclusions, or to the doctrine that properties can themselves have properties. After some preliminaries we will look to see what light the text sheds on this. The answer that we shall come to is that Plato does not clearly distinguish these two points.

For the first preliminary we may remind ourselves that there are three facts of Greek idiom which do not help in this matter. (1) There is the form "the A" which can be used indifferently for A-hood and for the class of A things. Plato uses this form throughout (though not universally, for in the case of activity and inactivity he usually uses the abstract nouns *kinêsis* and *stasis*). (2) There is the fact that Greek has no indefinite article. (3) There is the fact that one can often omit the definite article. As a result of these idioms the phrase *taúton estin on* (for example) whose verbatim translation is "the same is existent" could be used to mean

(a) Everything which is self-same exists
(b) The property of self-sameness exists
(c) (at a pinch). Self-sameness is existence.

Against ambiguities of this kind the Greek language has of course measures of self-defence in ordinary conversation, but such devices do not help us in abstract thought until we have seen that the ambiguity is an ambiguity; and it is this perception in part that Plato is struggling towards.

In accordance with the usage adopted a little way back, let us call a statement like (*a*) in our three examples above a class-inclusion statement, and a statement like (*b*) a property-statement.[1] Now commonly to a true class-inclusion statement there corresponds a true property-statement to the effect that the common property of the first or included class is a kind or version of the common property of the second or including class. Thus to "All cats are animals" there corresponds "Cat-hood is a version of animality". Similarly it is often the case that to a true property-statement there corresponds a true class-inclusion statement. Thus (to change the example) to "Whiteness exists" there corresponds "White things are among existing things". Normally therefore it is not important to distinguish between property-statements and class-inclusion statements, and "The A partakes in the B" can be harmlessly used without troubling to ask whether it is to be taken as saying something about A-hood (that it is a version of B-hood) or something about A things (that they are a sub-set of B things). However this is rot always the case. Thus for example the statements that goodness is non-natural or that vagueness is definable do not entail that good things are non-natural or that vague things can be defined. In these cases the statement is intended to apply to the property and not to the things which have the property. They are what we might call pure property-statements, i.e. property-statements to which class-inclusion statements do not correspond. We may notice that the number of predicates which can occur in pure property-statements is limited (properties cannot for example be said to be coloured) so that the pure property interpretation of a participation-statement cannot always be given ("The red partakes in the coloured" would have to be a class-inclusion). Unfortunately however the predicates which can occur in pure property-statements certainly include "existent", "self-same" and "different" from among Plato's very great kinds, and might be held to include "active" and "inactive" also. It is

---

[1] A property-statement is to be any statement whose subject-term designates a property. Where we get a property-statement which is such that in the sense in which the statement is meant by the speaker a class-inclusion statement does not correspond to it in the way shortly to be indicated, we get what I shall call a *pure* property-statement. Thus "The S partakes in the P" is certainly a property-statement, and it is also a pure property-statement if it is intended only to say that S-hood is P, and not intended also to say that S things are among the P things.

therefore likely on the face of it that both interpretations of the property-statements in this passage will be possible.

Finally we may notice that a special case of class-inclusion is that of mutual class-inclusion or class-coincidence, and that some statements of identity (e.g. "The rabbit is the farmer's worst enemy") can be interpreted as mutual class-inclusion statements.

With these preliminaries let us turn to the discussion of the very great kinds and ask how we are to understand the terms and relations which occur firstly in the identity-statements and secondly in the participation-statements which it includes. Since it is Plato's main purpose in this passage to distinguish these two types of statements from each other, we cannot assume that the general terms in the one type are to be construed in the same way as those in the other.

(*a*) *The case of identity-statements.* It had of course always been taken for granted by Plato that identity-statements can be made about general terms. The Socratic question "What is the A?" includes in its meaning the directive: Find a value for "B" such that "the A is the B" is true. But it is also true that nothing had ever been laid down about what would constitute a successful definition, or what the criterion of identity between the subject and the predicate is, though the failure of mutual class-inclusion to hold (the discovery of an A thing which is not a B or *vice versa*) had been taken as a criterion of non-identity.

Here, where identity-statements are being isolated, the criterion of identity becomes important. It is clear from the way the argument goes that mutual class-inclusion does not constitute identity. Every existent thing, for example, is the same as itself and different from everything else, and the converse is also true; but this does not allow us to identify being with sameness or difference (see paragraphs G and I). If the criterion of identity is not coincidence of classes, then, what is it? It becomes clear that when two expressions "A" and "B" turn out to be identical in meaning, then one can say that the A is identical with the B. Thus not-being is identified with difference; and this, the Stranger says (258 d 6), is not only to say what not-being is but also to give its *eidos*. This means, I suppose, that a successful answer has been found to a Socratic "What is X?" question. Again when it is suggested that perhaps sameness and difference can be identified with some two of the three original very great kinds, the Stranger says that "we may conceivably be failing to notice that we are speaking of one of them when we speak of the same and the different" (255 a). The suggestion here clearly is that two expressions which are *prima facie* non-synonymous may none the less stand for the same property. In such a case an identity-affirmation could be made; and it is presumably in terms of this that the identity-denials which are to be found in our passage are to be understood. "Activity is not self-sameness" means that "activity" and "self-sameness" do not refer to the same property. There are questions which can be asked about this criterion of identity (is triangularity, for example, to be identified with trilaterality, or are these distinct but mutually entailed properties?). But at any rate it is clear that identity-statements in this passage are not about classes. We would be inclined to say that they are in fact about the synonymity of expressions; if such language seems anachronistic we had better say that their subjects are properties.

(b) *The case of participation-statements.* Although the relation of identity clearly is to hold or fail to hold between general terms as such, so that one would expect that the general terms occurring in participation-statements are to be construed in the same way, there are nevertheless also reasons for expecting the contrary. For Plato prefaces his discussion of the very great kinds with a discussion of dialectic which puts one in mind of standard examples of dialectical discovery, such as that lovers are lunatics, or vowels letters. But discoveries of this kind are of course class-inclusion discoveries. Every lover is a lunatic and every vowel a letter; the property of being a vowel is not itself a letter. This is not a conclusive argument, for a sentence such as "The vowel partakes in the letter" could be taken as telling us that the former nature "has a share in" the latter in the sense that it is a specific version of it. I dare say that it is indeed probable that Plato thought of the discoveries of dialecticians as discoveries of relationships of this kind between properties and not of inclusion relationships between classes. But discoveries of this kind are such that they *can* be construed as class-inclusions. If therefore such a sentence as "Activity partakes in existence" was meant to be construed as, *and only as,* a pure property-statement ("There is such a thing as the property activity" rather than "Active things are among existing things") there would be a certain awkwardness in prefacing the discussion in which such sentences occur with a general account of dialectic. We ought perhaps to say that if Plato clearly intended such sentences to be construed as pure property-statements *and not* as class-inclusions, then he has misled us by associating this topic too closely with that of dialectic in general.

An argument which may be thought slightly stronger (but which may be dismissed as depending on a slip) is provided by the fact that it is twice taken as obvious by the Stranger and by Theaetetus that activity cannot be inactive, and *vice versa* (252 d and 256 b). This does not mean (and in the second place the Stranger makes it clear that he knows this) that activity cannot be identical with inactivity, which is indeed obvious. It means that activity cannot be inactive. But the subject of this statement could either be the property of activity, or the class of active things, or (the hybrid mentioned in paragraph G) the class of property-instances correlated with the property of being active. Now what sorts of things are obviously true of the first of these three possible subjects, the property itself? Is it obvious that the property activity cannot be inactive? Not, surely, obvious; for the Partisans of the Forms thought that all properties were inactive. And if it is argued that Theaetetus and the Stranger are relying on the refutation of these persons, then we shall find it difficult to explain how it could be obvious (or even true) that the property inactivity cannot be active; for if the view of the Partisans that properties are not subject to change is to be thought of as having been refuted, then it has been shown that properties are subject to change, or, in other words, active. It seems clear therefore that the subject of the *obviously* false proposition "Activity is inactive" cannot be the property as such. What happens then if we suppose that the sentence is to be construed as conveying a general statement about instances of activity—the sun's activity, the moon's and so on? In that case the meaning would be something like "All change is constant". But surely we shall be reading in altogether too much if we suppose that this is what is being dismissed as obviously false—obviously false though it is. It seems clear, then, that Theaetetus and the Stranger take the statement that activity cannot blend with, share or partake in inactivity to be a statement about active things, to the effect that none of them can be inactive. This argument is not irresistible. One might reply to it that Plato has for the moment taken it for granted that "active" and "inactive" are predicates which cannot meaningfully be predicated of properties, so that no good sense can be found for "The property activity is inactive" or its converse. In the light of the recent passage about the Partisans of the Forms it would be odd that Plato should take this for granted, but not impossible. But unless some such solution is adopted we shall have to allow that we have here two places in the discussion of the very great kinds where a participation-statement is to be construed as a class-inclusion.

So far as they go the two arguments which we have considered support the view that the participation-statements in this passage are to be construed as class-inclusions, or as the kind of property-statements to which class-inclusions correspond. "The A shares in the B" is to be taken as saying that A-hood is a kind or version of B-hood. This would drive a further wedge between identities and participation-statements, since the former are pure property-statements and the latter, apparently, are not. There are however a number of indications which suggest that the position is not like this.

One indication is as follows. If it were the case that identity-statements were pure property-statements whereas participation-statements were not, it would be important not to confuse the two kinds. Yet Plato in fact employs a participation formula to deny identity.[1] He uses "A partakes in difference from B" to say that A and B are not the same thing, and he would no doubt be willing to use "A partakes in sameness to B" to identify A and B. It seems clear from this that he at least has not any sharp distinction in mind between the manner in which general terms are used in identity-statements and in participation-statements. Plainly some of the statements in this passage are pure property-statements; and others it seems are not. But if we try to make this difference correspond to the difference between identity-statements and statements of participation we run into the difficulty we have just noticed. It seems that we must say that the former difference has not been clearly apprehended.

Another indication that Plato has not made up his mind whether he is discussing relations between properties or relations between classes is to be found in his rather perfunctory treatment of negative terms such as the not-beautiful (257). He lays down the rule that to prefix "not" to a word or phrase is to "indicate something other than the words that follow it, or rather than the things with which the words following the negative have to do" (257 b 10–c 3). To say then that something is not P is to say that it is other than P. This may seem satisfactory at first sight, until we remember that to say that S is other than P is to say that S and P are not the same thing. This is what we do indeed say when we say that bright colouring is not beauty, for example; but how does it apply to the negation of a participation-statement, e.g. to "Gorillas are not beautiful"? The odd thing is that Plato does not tell us anything about how his analysis of negation in terms of difference is to be applied in the case of participation-statements. Various possibilities suggest themselves. For example, "Every property in which the gorilla partakes is other than beauty", or "The gorilla is other than that which partakes in the beautiful", or "The gorilla partakes in difference with respect

---

[1] This can be shown from 256 a 11–b 4. We read there that activity is not the same (*sc.* is not self-sameness) *because it partakes in difference from self-sameness.* Here it might be thought that the clause in italics is a class-inclusion statement giving a reason why activity is not self-sameness. But this will not do; for if it is a class-inclusion it can only say that active things are among the things which are different from self-sameness, and this is not a reason for denying that activity is self-sameness. For active things are also among the things which are different from activity. Therefore the clause in italics must be a reformulation of "Activity is not the same", i.e. of an identity-denial.

407

to the beautiful". It is in itself strange that Plato does not tell us which analysis he intends. It is more strange when we realise that the first of these analyses is a fair distance away from Plato's formula that "to prefix a negative . . . is to indicate something other than . . . the things with which the words following the negative have to do"; and that in the case of the second and third further analysis is needed. For example in the case of the third, and perhaps likeliest, candidate we must ask what "the beautiful" signifies. It cannot be beauty; for to say of gorillas that they partake in difference with respect to beauty is to say of them something that could equally well be said of Helen of Troy; for she is not identical with the property in which she partakes. Does "the beautiful" then mean the class of beautiful objects, so that the meaning of the sentence is that the race of gorillas partakes in difference from the race of beautiful objects? But this is not to say that no gorilla is a beautiful object; for the race of prime numbers partakes in difference with respect to the race of numbers, and yet every prime number is a number. It is not enough, in fact, to say that the class of gorillas is not identical with the property beauty, nor to say that it is not identical with the class of beautiful objects. We need the notion of class-exclusion ("For all values of x and y, if x is a gorilla and y is beautiful, then it is false that x is identical with y"), and it is not clear how this is to be got out of the notion of difference. This same criticism applies also to the second candidate ("The gorilla is other than that which partakes in the beautiful"); for two classes may well fail to be identical without its being the case that no member of the first is also a member of the second. It would obviously be captious to complain that Plato has not given us an analysis of negative participation-statements which conforms to modern standards of explicitness; and it is not my purpose to do so. What is significant is not that Plato's account is a little blurred, but that there is no account. It looks as if Plato has simply not noticed that to say that S is other than P means two substantially different things according to whether "P" stands for a property or for a class. For, if he had noticed this, then he would surely have told us which he intended, and would probably have seen that the treatment of negative participation-statements involves complications about which something would have to be said.

There is indeed one place in which Plato shows that he is aware that properties and classes both come into the story, though he does not seem to feel that it is necessary to distinguish the rôles that they play. In 257 e 2–4 he says of the not-beautiful that it is something real by virtue of the fact that it is "separated off from some one kind (*genos*), and then again (*au palin*) set over against one of the things that are".[1] The relatively emphatic phrase "then again" suggests that two points are made in this sentence and not the same point twice over. If this is correct, the two points probably are that the class of not-beautiful things is a different class ("separated off") from the class of beautiful things, and that it is unified by contrast with ("set over against") beauty, i.e. by the fact that the common feature of its members is the lack of beauty. If this interpretation is correct, then we must say that in this passage Plato shows an awareness of the fact that he is using both the class of beautiful things and also the property beauty as positive terms in the contrast which generates the not-beautiful, but that he wrongly thinks that they can be treated as to all intents and purposes the same term, the different relationships which the not-beautiful has to each of these terms requiring no more notice than that which is given by a casual change of verb in a single sentence.

So far, then, the conclusion is that Plato's treatment of "The S partakes in the P" fails to distinguish the case where P-hood is a property of S-hood from the case where P-hood is a property of S things; and moreover that whereas some indications suggest that the first case is being discussed, others suggest that our concern is with the second. The hypothesis which would account for this, and explain the somewhat defective treatment of negative terms, is that Plato was operating with a pictorial conception of the terms whose relations he is discussing according to which they were simple units, neither properties nor classes but something in between. We must suppose that in thinking this passage out he had in his mind a picture in which one counter, so to speak, represented "the gorilla" (i.e. the class of all gorillas), whereas another indifferently represented "the beautiful" in the sense of the property beauty and also in the sense of the class of all beautiful objects. With such a pictorial conception he might well fail to see that an account of negation worked out in terms of identity-denials such as "Bright colouring is not beauty" cannot be simply taken over without modification to become an account of negative participation-statements such as "Gorillas are not beautiful"; for it would seem that in both cases the statement that the one counter was not the same as the other would do the trick.

(I am not of course saying that Plato actually *believed* that "Gorillas are not beautiful" means that "the gorilla" is not identical with "the beautiful"; nor am I saying that he would have said that the property P and the class of P objects are one and the same thing.

[1] There is some dispute about the translation of this sentence, but it should not infect the sense of the words quoted. The question is whether the first τῶν ὄντων is governed by ἄλλο or by γένους.

On the contrary, now as always, I believe, he would have denied that this identification can be made. What has happened, in my opinion, is that he has thought that in this immediate context it is not important to distinguish P-hood from the class of P things, and that accordingly he has allowed himself to use phrases of the form "the P" to stand for both of these entities, thereby failing to observe certain complications. It is incidentally noteworthy that, if this is correct, he is not in the least preoccupied in this passage with the topics characteristic of the Theory of Forms).

We have failed, then, to decide whether statements of the form "The S partakes in the P" are to be construed as predicating P-hood of S-hood or of the class of S things. I believe however that the former construction is primarily intended in this passage. The reason for this cannot be fully expounded at this stage, for it is connected with the relation between sameness and difference on the one hand and the rest of the very great kinds on the other. This relation is that the latter partake in the former. On the class-inclusion interpretation this would mean that active things (for example) are self-same. In itself this is perfectly satisfactory. But when we consider what is meant by what is said about cohesive and disruptive factors in the discussion of dialectic (253, paragraph 8) we shall find reason to say that "Activity partakes in the self-same" is meant to tell us that the property activity is self-identical. If this is correct we shall be forced to conclude that there is a twist in the notion of participation as a whole. The introductory reference to dialectic in general puts us in mind of dialectical discoveries such as that the lover partakes in the lunatic. But this tells us that lovers are a sub-class of lunatics, or, at best, that the property of being a lover is a specific version of the property of being a lunatic. It does not tell us that the property of being a lover is itself a lunatic thing. That activity partakes in self-sameness, however, is meant to tell us that activity is a self-same thing. Plato is introducing a class of "formal properties" of which existence, sameness and difference are instances. These properties characterise all entities whatsoever, and therefore they characterise the entities which fall under other properties such as activity. But Plato's purpose is not to tell us that these "formal" properties characterise the instances of "material" properties such as beauty or activity, but that they characterise the properties themselves. Unfortunately he has failed to see that this kind of "participation" is not the same as that which commonly crops up in his discussions of dialectic. Sometimes "The A partakes in the B" means that A things are among B things, sometimes that A-hood is itself a B thing.

(ii) *Problems in the* Sophist *241–60; the "vowels of reality"; cohesive and disruptive factors*

We shall now consider a problem arising out of the passage condensed in paragraph 8 of our analysis (252 e–253 c; see above p. 398). The question is whether the subsequent discussion of the very great kinds is intended to throw light on the statement that the dialectician has to know what kinds can and cannot combine, and that in order to do this he must ask whether there are any kinds which act, like vowels, as bonding factors, and any others which are responsible for divisions. I have already observed that it is not necessary to suppose that the later passage is meant to throw light on the earlier, but the opposite hypothesis is probable enough to be worth exploring. A caution is however necessary. It is suggested in *Sophist* 253 e 8 and made clear at the beginning of the *Statesman* that Plato projected a dialogue the *Philosopher* which he never wrote. In it no doubt he would have worked out the hints which he dropped about the nature of dialectic in this part of the *Sophist*. But it is possible that the reason why the *Philosopher* was never written is that Plato came to repent of these hints. We may therefore be considering ideas which he came to think bad ones.

We will take these risks. The Stranger suggests that dialectic is comparable to grammar and music in that these studies also enable us to know what elements can and what cannot be combined. He then goes on to suggest that there may be certain natures which run through all combinations and hold them together, thereby doing what vowels do among the letters, and also some disruptive natures which are responsible for divisions. Since the "vowels" run through everything, and since the very great kinds are very great, it is natural to expect that the very great kinds (or some of them) constitute the "vowels". This natural thought is however less attractive when one asks how it is possible for the very great kinds to enter into combinations.

For such properties as existence, self-sameness and difference are formal or non-limiting properties; and activity and inactivity are almost such. But a formal property can surely make no contribution to a combination that it enters into. To say of something that it is (*a*) an organism and (*b*) self-identical is simply to say that it is an organism. It is only material or limiting properties, such as that of being an organism, which can do any work in combinations. In fact, whatever can be present in all combinations can make no contribution to any. This presents us with a difficulty. We get the impression (from the *Cratylus* and from the *Statesman* as well as from the present passage) that syllables are made up of letters, and that this

411

means that relatively specific properties such as humanity are, or may be, somehow built up out of highly generic properties or relationships such as activity, solidity or the relation of containing (to quote examples of what the *Cratylus* seems to have in mind).[1] But it is also natural to suppose that the vowels are among the letters, and therefore are among the ingredients of syllables and play a part in the building-up of more specific properties. But if the vowels occur in *all* the syllables this seems to be impossible. Properties which are all-pervasive like existence or self-identity cannot contribute to the building-up of anything. They are not features of reality, pervasive or otherwise; reality could have what features you please and still everything in it would be existent and self-identical. It does not follow of course that Plato did not think of the relationship between vowels and other letters in the way which is troubling us; he may well have done so. We observe that among the letters (the syllable-builders) of the *Cratylus* activity figures; and activity is highly dubious as a syllable-builder. It is true that animals are organisms which can move about and that plants are organisms which cannot—i.e. that the ability to move oneself about can differentiate one kind from another. But it is not clear that the same is true of activity. For to say that something is active is in no way to say what features it has; it is merely to say that not everything that is true of it at one moment is true of it at every other moment. But if Plato did think of letters and vowels in the way suggested, then one wonders if he had not deceived himself by a simple fallacy:—Many things partake in the animal, more things still in the organism, and everything whatsoever in the self-same; being an organism therefore is a more pervasive feature of reality than being an animal, and being self-same is a more pervasive feature still. One wonders in fact whether Plato did not mistakenly think that being *all*-pervasive is merely a matter of being *more* pervasive than highly generic properties such as that of being an animal.

Having observed this difficulty let us stand back from it and ask the following question. It is suggested that certain kinds act like vowels in making syllables possible, and that there are others which contrariwise cause divisions; and that the dialectician, by knowing what these bonding and disruptive factors are, knows what combinations are possible. Now the question is whether the knowledge of the vowels and disrupters gives the dialectician a stock of general information which enables him to decide *a priori* whether S can partake in P, or whether this is not the case, but the dialectician simply knows the right answer for every S and every P.

Since the dialectician is compared to the grammarian we may

---

[1] See above, pp. 376–7.

begin by asking whether the grammarian decides which combinations are possible by referring to a stock of general information. There seem to be three possibilities:—

1. That the grammarian merely has a lot of *ad hoc* information —e.g. that one can sound *ct* but not *gc*.
2. That he knows general principles—e.g. that two gutturals next door to each other cannot be sounded.
3. That he knows the *one* general principle that every syllable must contain a vowel.

About these questions one gets a number of discrepant impressions from the text. On the one hand Plato talks as if he had some kind of general principles in mind, as if his dialectician would know *a priori* various truths of some such form as: Any property which is an A-type property can combine only with a B-type or C-type property. On the other hand whether or not the *dialectician* can decide that a certain combination is or is not possible by reference to principles of this kind, the *Stranger* certainly has to decide such questions *ad hoc*. He has to settle by inspection the question whether activity can combine with inactivity. No principles of the kind that we are imagining emerge from the discussion in the *Sophist*. Perhaps they were to be stated in the *Philosopher* and it was because Plato never managed to think of them that that dialogue was never written. At any rate so far as the *Sophist* is concerned we seem to be left with the bare point that it is important for the dialectician to know the "vowels" and "counter-vowels" or disrupters.

In what way does a vowel "bind its syllables together"? How does *a* unify *c a t*? Presumably by making the three sound-factors which constitute the syllable soundable as one sound. Since there are a number of syllables—*c a t*, *b a t*, *b a g* and so on—all of which could be thought of as different modifications of the same fundamental sound (the *a*-sound), one is tempted to try out something like the following. The "vowels" of reality are very general natures which can turn up in many forms, their various forms being due to modification by the "consonants" of reality. Thus a "substantival" nature like animality might be a "vowel", an "adjectival" nature like carnivorousness a "consonant". It seems, after all, natural to think that an adjectival nature can exist only as a modification of a substantival nature, whereas a substantival nature (like an Aristotelian second substance) can exist on its own; and this would reflect the fact that consonants cannot, and vowels can, be sounded on their own. But although this line of thought is tempting, there is the difficulty, already noticed, that the very great kinds do not seem to be highly generic substantival natures, and there is also the difficulty that Plato contrasts his vowels not with consonants but with counter-vowels or disrupters.

If we give due weight to this last point, then (on the assumption that the vowels feature in the discussion of the very great kinds) we shall find it difficult to resist the conclusion that sameness is the vowels or bonding agents and difference the counter-vowels. (If it is objected that we are looking for bonding agents and disrupting agents in the plural, we may perhaps remind the objector that difference has "many, many parts"; and presumably the same is true of sameness). The argument for this conclusion is that we are to look out for things which create divisions (*diaireseis*). Yet in the sequel it is more than once said that it is by participation in difference that A is different from B. It is therefore difficult to resist the suspicion that difference (or the parts of difference) are the disrupters.[1] But since the disrupters are paired with the vowels, and since difference is paired with sameness, it is natural to go on to the further inference that sameness (or the parts of sameness) are the vowels.

But if we try to ask what this conclusion can mean, it seems absurd. It is because A is different from B and the same as itself that it can enter into the wholes, syllables or complexes that it can enter into. It is because being an animal is the same as being an animal and different from being, say, a triangle, that animality can be combined with aquaticity in the complex : aquatic animal. The mountains seem to have brought forth a mouse of a high order of trivial absurdity.

But is this judgment just? Take a physical volume whose contents are completely unstable. In such a world "same" (*numero*) and "different" would have no application to physical objects but only to places. In our world "same" and "different" have application to physical objects; and to say that this is the case is to say that our world is not completely unstable. To say then that physical objects are self-identical is not to say nothing; it is to say (in the language of Mr. Strawson's *Individuals*) that we can re-identify particulars.

In the light of this analogy we see that the doctrine that general terms are self-identical and different from each other is not vacuous either. It is the fundamental postulate of the classical theory of forms, that general terms have sharp edges. Let us take once more the example of the general term the soul. Now souls are a heterogeneous lot. There is plenty of the indefinite in them. But there is also enough[2] of the definite, for every soul is a soul. There are limits to the variety. For the general nature *the soul* is self-identical. It is one definite kind, not a congeries of more or less similar natures.

---

[1] When the dialectician makes a *division* he does so by detecting a *difference*.
[2] "Plenty", "enough"; see *Philebus* 30 c 4, discussed below, p. 434.

Being identical with being a soul is being an animating agent (*Phaedo*) or a self-activator (*Phaedrus* and *Laws*), and it is being different from everything which is not that. And this does determine the syllables in which the letter *soul* can figure. It allows there to be good souls and bad souls, wise souls and foolish souls, but it rules out the syllable *dead soul*. For *dead*, being identical with *de-animated* and hence incompatible with *animating*, cannot combine with *animating agent*.

That, then, which determines that a given letter can enter into given syllables, and which binds these syllables together, is sameness, or the class of facts having the form of Socratic definitions:—to be X is the same as to be Y. Conversely what prevents a given letter from entering into certain syllables is difference, or the class of facts having the form of rebuttals of Socratic definitions:—to be A is not the same as to be B. This does not mean (where X is the same as Y) that XY is a syllable, nor (where A is not the same as B) that AB cannot be. XY is a tautology ("self-activating soul") and AB *may* be a perfectly good syllable ("rational animal"—for rationality is not the same as animality). It means that it is the fact that souls are what they are and not what they are not that brings it about that there can be good souls and bad souls but not dead ones. Which syllables it is that are ruled out by sameness (or sameness-and-difference) is something that has to be decided by direct inspection in each case; and this is what we rather expected to find. It is the knowledge *that there are* these vowels which tells the dialectician that *some* combinations will be possible and *some* impossible. *Which* are possible he has to find out by using his intelligence. The view that Plato is combating is the eristical view (251; paragraph 6 of our analysis) according to which *either* combinations are impossible (men are simply men, and not animals, good, mortal or anything else), *or else* anything can be anything. To this Plato's answer is that there can be true synthetic statements but that there are also logical impossibilities.

If this interpretation is correct, the point that Plato is making is an old one. It is very much what he had argued in the Seventh Book of the *Republic* (523–5). There he tells us that we are inclined to think that there is no absolute difference between unity and multiplicity, or largeness and smallness, because whatever we see as the one we also see as the other. But if we forget about how we see things and reflect on the nature of largeness we are forced to realise that the property of being-larger-than is quite different from that of being-smaller-than. Again the stress on self-identity reinforces the old belief in the importance of Socratic definition. For if the point is that no letter can be forced into a syllable membership of which would violate its self-identity, then obviously it is important to know in what the self-identity of any given letter consists.

If this interpretation is correct (and I must remind the reader that it must be highly conjectural) then we may notice that to say of a general term that it partakes in sameness is to say something about the property and not about the class. It is because the property of being a soul is a definite property having a definite nature that there cannot be dead souls. Therefore a statement of the form "P-hood partakes in the self-same" is intended as a pure property-statement. This is the consideration (mentioned above) which makes us say that the primary sense of "participation" in the discussion of the very great kinds is that according to which a participation-statement is a pure property-statement.

Finally we may observe that the pre-occupation with the role of formal properties such as unity and multiplicity in other properties is characteristic of Plato's later years. There is no immense gulf between what is said of sameness and difference in the *Sophist* and what is said of *peras* and *apeiron* in the *Philebus*.[1]

(iii) *Problems in the* Sophist *241–60; participation*

That kinds can be blended, can share or partake in each other is the battle-cry of these late "dialectical" dialogues. We have seen already that this relation of participation or whatever we prefer to call it is a somewhat vague one. At times it seems to be little more than the notion that there can be true synthetic propositions such as "Some men are bald". At other times it is nearer to a conception of the species/genus relationship—"Cats are animals" or "Love is lunacy". At other times the reference is to the fact that properties themselves can have properties. The truth seems to be that Plato advances participation as the cure for a somewhat vaguely conceived syndrome of errors diagnosed as due to the failure to see that kinds can blend with kinds other than, and even incompatible with, themselves.

We can see this more clearly if we glance back at the *Parmenides*. We remember that the young Socrates is made to tell Zeno that he would be very surprised if somebody who was prepared to distinguish kinds from particulars could go on to show that "likeness and unlikeness and multitude and the one and inactivity and activity and other such things can be blended and divorced among themselves" (*Parmenides* 129 d 6–e 3). We saw that his meaning was that kinds can be blended and divorced *in things*, in that a thing, by participation in opposed forms, can have contradictory predicates, kinds

---

[1] See below, pp. 423–40. The reader is also asked to recall what is said about sameness and difference in the account of the soul of the world in the *Timaeus* (see above, pp. 202 sqq.).

being thereby forced into what seem to be unnatural unions; but that this cannot happen to kinds *among themselves*. We can now see that what Socrates is denying is (in terms of the *Sophist*) that it is possible to show that, for instance, not-being is, or that activity is the same and not the same. That the young Socrates is wrong to think this, is brought out by the rest of the dialogue where it is made clear that you have to say that unity is not unitary and many other things of this kind. You cannot argue from the fact that unity is indivisibility either that a thing which is one so-and-so is in all respects indivisible, nor even that unity itself is indivisible (for if it exists it must have properties and thus be complex). Unity and complexity are thus blended even "among themselves".

There are two consequences of bringing the *Parmenides* and the *Sophist* together in this way. One is that the suspicion that the participation-statements in the discussion of the very great kinds are intended as pure property-statements is increased, with the result that the internal inconsistency of the *Sophist* (the suggestion that the discussion of the very great kinds is an example of run-of-the-mill dialectic) is sharpened. The other is that any inconsistencies that there may be in the *Parmenides* can fairly be imported into the *Sophist*. But one cannot help suspecting that in the *Parmenides* the demonstration in the second part of the dialogue that general terms can partake in each other is supposed to ease the paradox stated in the first part, the paradox of supposing that particulars can partake in general terms. But these relationships are not the same.

It seems then that "participation" refers to three things: to the fact that a particular S can have the property P; to the fact that all P things can be Q things; and to the fact that the property P-hood can itself have the property R. Of these three things it is the second that is most obviously the odd-man-out. Nor can it be brought into line by substituting for "All P things are Q things" the alternative form "P-hood is a version of Q-hood"—for this is not the same as "P-hood is Q" (cathood is not an animal). It seems that we must say that Plato was not clear of the importance of "dividing participation at its joints".

(iv) *Problems in the* Sophist *241–60; what the dialectician can do*

In paragraph 8 of my analysis of this passage I said that the Stranger gives a brief description of what the dialectician has to be able to do. I gave no detail of what he says, because the exegesis of his meaning constitutes a difficult problem. This we must now consider.

The passage in question is to be found in 253 d. The Stranger says that it belongs to dialectic to divide according to kinds without either driving a wedge between identicals nor identifying non-identicals. This is clear enough; but the Stranger goes on to say that the man who can do this can do the following things:—

(*a*) He can sufficiently discern the one universal (*idea*) which permeates many things, each of which is different from the others;

(*b*) He can sufficiently discern many universals which are different from each other but are all embraced from without by a single universal;

(*c*) He can sufficiently discern one universal which is joined together throughout many wholes; and finally

(*d*) He can sufficiently discern many universals which are everywhere sundered.

What are we to make of these four phrases? The oddity of them is that there seem to be three phrases descriptive of the positive side, three for seeing that A and B can combine, one for seeing that they cannot. Why three to one?

I find it rather tempting to say that we have a reference here to a fact of which I have already claimed that Plato was aware, namely that some common characteristics do and some do not constitute positive similarities. For it seems fair to say that the three verbs in the three positive phrases represent three degrees of increasing tenuousness. What is said of the more generic universal in each case is: in the first that it *permeates* others; in the second that it *embraces* them; in the third that it *is joined together*—a passive phrase. Might it not be that the meaning is something like the following? Being a vegetable permeates being a carrot, being a turnip, being a cabbage; and, permeating them all, it creates a positive resemblance between them. Being an organism however is a more abstract kind of common character, more extrinsic to what it characterises, in that it merely surrounds or embraces being a vegetable and being an animal. Such common characters create a measure of similarity if you like, where they hold, but a small measure. The most abstract common characters, however, such as existing, being one, being self-same, create no similarity at all. They neither permeate nor embrace, they merely are joined together or preserve their identity in the many wholes, complexes or syllables in which they are to be found.

If this suggestion is correct it confirms the suspicion that Plato thought of formal properties as properties which are merely more universal in their application than generic material properties such as animality. Since it is these formal properties which occur in the pure property-statements that we are concerned with, whereas it is material properties which occur in class-inclusion statements, the treatment of formal and material properties as if they were on all fours is consistent with the analogous treatment of pure property-statements and statements of class inclusion. Once more we find ourselves saying that Plato's treatment of dialectic at this period is infected by uncertainty about the difference between relations between classes and relations between properties.

(v) *Problems in the* Sophist *241–60; who are the "Partisans of the Forms"?*

We come now to another self-contained question, the question who are the *eidôn philoi* or Partisans of the Forms whose views are criticised in 246–9.[1] This is one of the passages on which they rely who tell us that Plato repented in his later years of his belief in forms.

We must ask then how much is involved in the attack on the Partisans of the Forms. It is not perfectly clear what the quarrel with these actual or fictitious persons is. The essentials of the argument are as follows.

1. The Partisans identify being with certain non-corporeal forms to which they allow no kind of activity.

2. But if to be known is to undergo something, then, if being cannot do or undergo, it cannot be known.

3. But surely activity and life and soul and intelligence must be "present to being". (In other words it is intolerable to deny that spiritual beings are among the ultimate entities).

4. But on the other hand it cannot be true that everything moves and changes, for that would equally render knowledge impossible; for understanding requires self-consistency,[2] and self-consistency requires inactivity.

5. Therefore the philosopher must deny (*a*) that the all is inert, and (*b*) that being changes in every way.

The conclusion of the argument seems familiar enough. One cannot deny to spiritual beings the status of ultimate entities; whatever else can be "reduced" they cannot. The all, therefore, is not inert. But at the same time every thing which deserves the title of an *on* or ultimate entity must be in some ways unchanging. It cannot be denied that some ultimate entities are active; perhaps indeed all are, in certain ways. Nevertheless every ultimate entity must at the

---

[1] The title of these persons seems to be one of the few places where *eidos* is used almost as a technical term for "form".

[2] The phrase for "self-consistency" is "the according-to-the-same-things-and-in-the-same-way-and-about-the-same-thing". In fact understanding (*nous*) has to proceed according to the same principles, and therefore the nature of intelligence has to be unchanging; and its objects must be self-identical, and therefore they too must stay put.

same time be unchanging in some respects. There is nothing in this conclusion which reads like a recantation of anything that Plato has ever written. The only sign of recantation so far is the contemptuous language in which the Stranger speaks of "certain intelligible forms" being drafted for the role of genuine being (246 b).

What is the purpose of the argument? The purpose of all this string of criticisms of philosophical schools is to show that existence cannot be identified with any other property. To do this it is necessary to disentangle the sense of *einai* in which it means "to exist" from certain other senses—in this case from the sense in which, by being contrasted with *gignesthai*, "to become", it acquires the connotation of changelessness. This is done by two arguments. First it is suggested hypothetically that for X to be known is for X to undergo something. It is true that this suggestion is made hypothetically, but the Stranger must think that it cannot plausibly be denied. For if it could be, then the Partisans will retort: "Well, the forms can be known, and they cannot undergo; therefore to be known is not to undergo something." The Stranger must think that his opponents cannot make this retort. In that case presumably his point is as follows:—That which can be known can be said to be without qualification an *on* or ultimate entity. This is agreed on all hands. But that which can be known can (surely) thereby undergo. Therefore complete impassivity cannot be characteristic of ultimate entities. But the existence of these cannot conceivably be denied. Therefore existence cannot entail impassivity.

The second argument is stronger. It depends on the premise, introduced with a rhetorical outburst, that ultimacy cannot be denied to souls. But souls are active. Therefore some ultimate entities are active. Therefore existence cannot entail inactivity.

The following debating point can be made against those who find a recantation in this passage. If there is a recantation here, there must be a denial of the existence of self-consistent forms. But there .is no such denial. For such a denial could be derived only from the Stranger's first argument. But the first argument depends on a premise which is not asserted but left hanging hypothetically. Therefore it is the second argument which bears the weight; and the second argument has no tendency to deny the existence of forms. A more cogent point however which can be made against the recantation view is that the Stranger's conclusion forbids us to infer that his first argument is meant to deny the existence of changeless objects of knowledge. For his conclusion must be that that which can be known is *both* changeless in some ways, and *also* (if the first argument is cogent) changeable, not of course in the same ways but in others. It cannot be inferred from this that there are no changeless forms, but only that, if there are, it must be conceded that they can undergo whatever change may be involved in becoming known.

I conclude, then, that the purpose of the argument is not to deny (or assert) the existence of forms, but to deny that existence entails inactivity. The purpose of the first argument which leads to this conclusion may be to forestall a possible objection to the activity-language which the Stranger intends to use later about his kinds (they partake in each other, they are divided into pieces and so on). If an opponent protests that properties, being inactive, cannot "do" things in this way, then it can be retorted that by parity of reasoning they cannot be known; for being known is just as much "under-going" as partaking is "doing". This may be why the argument is put forward hypothetically. Plato does not want to assert that the fact that general terms can stand as subjects to active and passive verbs entails that they do and undergo things; but if this sort of inference is going to be drawn then he will reply that this can only be used as an objection to the things that he says at the cost of allowing that it is objectionable to say that general terms can be known. General terms cannot be so passive that they cannot engage in "notional activities" like partaking, unless they are also so passive that they cannot be known.

How much self-criticism is there in all this? Those who are being criticised are those who have inferred from the contrast of *einai* "to be" with *gignesthai* "to become", that if a thing is in any sense a *gignomenon* then it is in no sense an *on*. They are those who have identified inactivity with existence. It seems to be impossible to tell whether Plato included himself among their number. Whether he did or not, whether or not he is to that extent criticising himself, there is no reason to say that he is here repenting of the belief in unchanging forms in the only sense of "unchanging" to which he had ever intended to commit himself. This is that they are unchanging in the ways in which a thing must, as this passage itself reiterates, be unchanging if it is to be an object of understanding.

In conclusion.

The *Sophist* contributes to the conception of dialectic which we have encountered in the other "dialectical" dialogues the notion that there are certain pervasive factors which enable letters to combine in syllables, along with certain other pervasive factors which create divisions; and at the same time it introduces into the discussion of dialectic certain *formal* properties (existence, sameness and difference), the possession of which by ordinary material pro-perties is thought by Plato to be important. As we have seen these two contributions appear to be at least closely related, and, in closely relating them, Plato seems to have confused together such logically different statements as

The lion partakes in the animal; and
Activity partakes in existence.

VI. THE *PHILEBUS*

A. *Introductory*

The *Philebus* is a difficult dialogue; and it is often misunderstood. One reason, perhaps, for these misunderstandings is that Plato introduces into the dialogue, in a somewhat cursory and off-hand manner, notions which can only be understood in the light of pre-occupations of his later years of which we learn only from Aristotle. He who reads the *Philebus* in the light of Plato's earlier writings only is almost bound to be baffled by it. Very briefly, the metaphysical questions discussed in the earlier dialogues concerned the relations of universals to particulars and of universals to each other. The new element which we encounter in the *Philebus* (prefigured indeed in the *Sophist* and even in the *Republic* if my interpretation of these dialogues is correct) is the question of the relation of the formal to the material element in any given universal. No doubt this is obscure, but I hope that it will become clearer as we go along.

To be sure, in some parts of the *Philebus* we seem to be treading on familiar ground. The account of dialectic seems in many of its features to be identical with that sketched in the *Phaedrus* and common to a whole group of later dialogues. Nevertheless there are other features of the account of dialectic, and of Socrates' subsequent discussion, which are less familiar.

One of these unfamiliar notions we considered in an earlier chapter,[1] and decided that it did not entail a startling change of opinion: I mean the notion that *genesis* or becoming can develop into *ousia* or being. We saw in that discussion that *ousia* in this use denotes a stable condition, and that the *genesis* which issues in *ousia* is the process whereby such a condition is brought about. We may now observe that although these concepts entail no startling change of opinion, nevertheless they suggest a development which is of interest to us. What is novel in the notion of *gegenêmenê ousia* ("stable conditions, resulting from processes of becoming") is that *genesis* and *ousia* are no longer *contrasted* with each other as the transient with the eternal. The transient is thought of as developing into conditions of sufficient permanence to deserve the honorific

[1] Above pp. 238–9.

title *ousia*. To my mind this reflects the increased confidence of Plato's cosmological views in his old age. That which he hesitated to affirm in so many words in the *Republic*, he now takes for granted —namely that reason does bring about in the physical world states of affairs which are rationally satisfactory. It is of some importance to remember that the metaphysical discussions of the *Philebus* take place within this cosmological framework.

The novel concepts which occur in these metaphysical discussions are the Pythagorean concepts of *peras* and *to apeiron*. We shall have to discuss in detail the use to which these concepts are put by Plato. In the course of this discussion I shall use where convenient the word *peras* (plural *perata*)[1] and the word *apeiron* (plural *apeira*) without translation. The reader is asked to bear in mind that etymologically speaking *peras* means "limit" whereas *apeiron* means "unlimited". It is because there is considerable uncertainty, not about the meanings of these words, but about the realities that they stand for, that I shall not, on the whole, translate them.

B. *The concepts of* peras *and* to apeiron

There are two distinct passages in the *Philebus* which talk about *peras* and *apeiron*, namely 16–20 and then again 23–30, with a cross-reference between them (23 c). We will call the first of these passages the Heavenly Tradition and the second the Anatomy of Entities. We have already considered the Heavenly Tradition in our discussion of Protarchus' fallacy (above, pp. 359–68).

In the Pythagorean cosmology *to apeiron* seems to have been a spatially boundless vapour which did something of the work of absolute space in the cosmology of Newton, whereas *peras* stood for the configurations of physical units of which things were made; and things were made of *peras* and *apeiron* in the sense that this penny is a portion of space limited or marked out by the units which compose it. At first sight this Pythagorean use of the two concepts might seem to agree with that which occurs in the Anatomy of Entities, in which also things seem to be made of *peras* and *apeiron*.

The Pythagorean *apeiron*, one might argue, was something rather like space; and did not Plato in the *Timaeus* describe the physical world as a work of reason, looking to the forms and moulding *space* into conformity with them? Why, then, should we not suppose that *peras* in the *Philebus* corresponds more or less closely to the forms in the *Timaeus*, *apeiron* to *chôra* or space? But a glance at the *Philebus* is enough to provoke doubts about this. A different idea

---

[1] Plato's plural is *peras echonta* ("things which have *peras*"). I use *perata* for simplicity.

seems to be at work from any of those in the *Timaeus*. The difference is roughly this. The *Timaeus* seemed to be a serious attempt to reduce everything to geometry. Physical properties are represented as resultants of geometrical properties; the sensible properties of fire (its warmth and so on) and also its causal properties (its power to burn) are ascribed to the shape of its particles. In such a serious attempt to make geometry the foundation of all things it is natural that space should become the only "material"[1] element in things. But this is not what we find in the *Philebus*. Here *apeiron* seems to stand not just for space, but for such quality-ranges as warmth-to-coldness, wetness-to-dryness and so on. If then we try to make the *Philebus* parallel to the *Timaeus* we must at least allow that Plato has changed his mind concerning the nature of the material element, the datum with which creative intelligence must cope. This will now be more than simply extension. If the problem for reason in the *Timaeus* was to create order out of disorderly motion in three dimensions, the problem here seems to be to create order out of *given types* of material in a three-dimensional world. The datum has become more complex.

This perhaps is not very conclusive, and indeed the difference between the two dialogues is exaggerated in this account, for as we have seen the *Timaeus* is not so whole-heartedly "geometrist" as I have just represented it as being. But a stronger argument can be found against the view that *peras* and *apeiron* in the *Philebus* are doing something like the same work as the forms and space in the *Timaeus*. This is that when Socrates introduces *peras* and *apeiron* at the beginning of the Anatomy of Entities (23 c) he explicitly identifies this use of the terms with their use in the Heavenly Tradition. But however well the idea which we are examining may seem to fit the use of *peras* and *apeiron* in the Anatomy of Entities, it fits not at all their use in the earlier passage. Here it is I think quite plain that these words are being given an arithmetical application. The *peras* in things is the fact that a generic universal has a *definite* number of specific versions, the *apeiron* in things the fact that a specific universal has an *indefinite* number of variants, or instances, or both. It is true that on any view a certain amount of quick thinking has to be done to bring the use of *peras* and *apeiron* in the two passages into full accord; but the difficulties are greatly increased if we interpret the Anatomy of Entities in the sense which we have been considering.

In a moment we shall look at the text of the *Philebus* to see what it says; first, however, I shall state my main conclusion. This is that the crucial error which can be made in interpreting the *Philebus* is to

---

[1] This use of "material" is meant to be more or less Aristotelian.

suppose that it is Plato's purpose to tell us that *peras* and *apeiron* are elements in *individual things* such as this penny. On the contrary he is not here interested in discovering a formal and a material element in individual things, but in universals. In both of our two passages, when Plato says that there is *peras* and *apeiron* in things, "in things" means "in universal properties". That Plato was interested in his later years in distinguishing the formal from the material element in general terms is clear from the Aristotelian evidence which is to be briefly glanced at in the concluding section of this chapter. Thus we learn from Aristotle that Plato spoke of a "masculine" and a "feminine" element in numerical properties and apparently in others also. The masculine element was either unity or some other numerical property, the feminine element having several names, "greatness-and-smallness" and "the indefinite" (*ahoristos*, not *apeiros*) "duality" being two of them. We learn also that he was prepared to speak, for example, of linearity (one-dimensionality) as "two-ness in length", and of discursive knowledge also as "two-ness"—presumably "in" something else.

This all sounds very queer; but if it is not to be dismissed as dotage, it must be regarded as an attempt to analyse universals—linearity, knowledge and so on—into a formal and a material element. Duality is a formal element which can be embodied in different material; duality in terms of spatial extension is linearity, in terms of, say, intellectual grasp it is discursive knowledge. We have found thoughts belonging to this stable in the *Republic*, and it is clear from the Aristotelian evidence that they occupied Plato's mind towards the end of his life. I am confident that this is the background to the discussions of the *Philebus*. What Plato has in mind, and what we must keep firmly in mind, is general terms such as health. It is in general terms such as this that he detects an element of *peras* and an element of *apeiron*. This is my main conclusion. The argument for it is chiefly that it makes excellent sense of the text, as I shall now try to indicate.

We have already discussed the Heavenly Tradition. As we saw, the statement in that passage that "there is *peras* and *apeiron*[1] in whatever is said to exist" (16 c 8–9) *refers to* the fact that a general term in some way comprises a definite number of versions and an indefinite number of variant cases. Since that is what it refers to, it can be said to *mean* that there is definiteness and indefiniteness in things. The meaning of the terms, then, in the Heavenly Tradition is "definiteness" and "indefiniteness". I make this point about the meaning and reference of the terms because I want to argue that

---

[1] He actually uses the word *apeiria*, the abstract noun. I do not think this significant.

whereas the reference of the two terms may seem to differ between the two passages, their meaning remains the same.

So much for the Heavenly Tradition. The Anatomy of Entities opens in the following way. Protarchus has been convinced that the best life is not a life of pleasure nor a life of intellectual activity, but a mixed life. He insists however that pleasure and intellect should contend for second prize. For this dispute Socrates says that he will require new tools. The new tools turn out to be a four-fold classification of "the things that now are" (*ta nun onta*; this means, I think, "that which exists in the physical world"). Socrates begins with his "recent statement that a god had shown that a part of the things that are is *apeiron* and a part *peras*" (23 c). These are two of the tools Socrates requires. The third is "a single thing made of the mixture of these two",[1] and the fourth is "the cause of the mixture". Each of these four entities (*peras, apeiron,* the mixture of *peras* and *apeiron* and the cause of the mixture) is, I think, a class—entities may be divided into those which are *perata*, those which are *apeira*, those which are *meikta* or mixtures, and those which are causes. Furthermore in my opinion any member of each of the first three classes is itself a general term—health for example is a *meikton* or mixture, the ratio 2 : 3 is a *peras*. The fourth class, the class of causes, will be seen to be the class of intelligences, so that the members of this class are presumably individuals. We have then three classes of general terms of which the third is some kind of function of the first two, and one class of intelligences which are responsible for creating instances of the general terms which constitute the third class. But this is to anticipate.

Having briefly introduced his four classes Socrates turns his attention to *peras* and *apeiron*. Each of these he tells us is one and many (23 e). In other words there is a class of *perata* and a class of *apeira*, various things are alike in having *peras* as their common feature,[2] various others in having *apeiron* as theirs. Bearing in mind the meaning which these terms bore in the Heavenly Tradition, we can say that various things are alike in that they are definite, various other things in that they are indefinite.

Socrates then proceeds to introduce the class of *apeira* by making use of the comparative adjectives of "warm" and "cold". (I speak of "the comparative adjectives" and not simply of "warmer" and "colder" because it may be significant that the same word in Greek can mean "warmer" or "too warm"; i.e. the comparative perhaps

---

[1] It is also called *genesis eis ousian* ("process leading to a stable condition") or more accurately *gegenêmenê ousia* ("a generated stable condition").

[2] Socrates seems to speak of "being *peras*" and of "having *peras*" indifferently. That which *has peras* is *a peras*, I suppose.

carries with it an association of *excess*). He points out that "warmer" and "colder" necessarily contain more or less[1] and have no terminus. (Does he mean by this that temperature is a range which can in principle be extended indefinitely in either direction?). Being able to receive more and less, and having no terminus seems to be the defining character of an *apeiron*; the class property *apeiron* or indefiniteness is the property of being able to receive more and less and having no terminus. Shortly afterwards (25 c) more instances of *apeira* are introduced, namely drier and wetter, more and less in the adjectival sense, faster and slower, bigger and smaller. Socrates also seems to introduce more defining characters (24 e–25 a), namely being able to receive intensely and mildly and excessively; and he implies that there are others. (It is all done very informally, with no clear distinction between instances and defining characters. I can only hope that I have correctly disentangled Socrates' meaning).

As for *peras*, it is said (25 a, b) that we would do well to gather into this pigeon hole those things which can receive the opposites of more and less, namely the equal and equality and the double and every ratio of number to number or measure to measure. The class property of *peras* or definiteness, then, is the ability to receive the equal, the double, ratios, and in general that which is the opposite of more and less, intensely and mildly, and the other defining characters of *apeiron*. Having told us in this oracular way what definiteness is, Socrates fails to give us any instances of *perata* or things which exhibit this characteristic. Presumably it is this omission which he refers to a page further on (25 d) when he says that "the *peras*-like was not collected into one in the way in which this service was performed for *apeiron*". He must I think mean that whereas instances of *apeira* have been given, instances of *perata* have not. In this place therefore the notion of "collecting" (*sunagein*) must refer to the giving of instances designed to illustrate the range of a general term.[2] However, Socrates goes on to say, it is to be hoped that when they collect *apeiron* and *peras* together (i.e. when they collect the third class of mixtures) the race of *peras* will become clear, "the race of the equal and the double, the race which in general arrests the strife of opposites by introducing number and making them proportionate and harmonious" (25 d 11–e 2). He then, as it appears, proceeds to "collect" his third class, or to give instances of mixtures, citing such things as health, good weather, virtue and other things which depend on order, law and the absence of excess.

The failure to "collect" *peras* is of course deliberate, and the hint which is thereby conveyed is that *peras* is a difficult notion to grasp

---

[1] Or (the same ambiguity being present) "too much and too little".

[2] I have referred to this passage in discussing collection above, p. 368.

other than intuitively and that if we want to understand the passage we should concentrate our attention on the third class. We may therefore interpret what Socrates says thus:—I gave you some instances of things which have the defining characteristics of *apeira*. I have not given you instances of *perata*, but perhaps if I say what kinds of things have the characteristics of being mixtures of these (health, good weather, etc.) you will be able to see what *perata* are. For the mixtures are things which depend on law, order and the absence of excess; from this you will conclude that law, order, etc. are typical *perata*.

Let us now try to see what *apeiron* and *peras* stand for. Taking *apeiron* first, we will forget the conclusions which we have already enunciated and ask what the first-sight possibilities are. There seem to me to be three. Of these one makes *apeiron* a material element in things, while the other two make an *apeiron* something which you might encounter in the world, not something discovered by metaphysical analysis.

1. The first possibility. When a carpenter takes a bit of wood to cut it to length for a table it is an *apeiron*, a random length. He imposes *peras* on it by cutting it to length. *Apeira* are objects which are of random size, length, temperature, etc., mixtures are objects whose size, length, temperature, etc. is determinate with respect to some purpose of human or cosmic intelligence.

2. If we bear in mind the possibility that an individual *apeiron* may be itself a general term we shall be able to think of another interpretation. According to this interpretation an *apeiron* is any *class* of objects members of which can be called warmer or too warm (etc.) but which have (qua *members of that class*) no definite temperature (etc.). Gales would thus be one *apeiron*, and fevers another, not in that any given gale has no determinate wind-velocity, but in that there is no determinate wind-velocity of "the gale as such". Gales are windier than calms, and indeed too windy, fevered patients are warmer than healthy ones and indeed too warm; but you cannot ask "How windy is a gale?" or "How hot is a fever?", though you *can* ask "What is normal blood-heat?" The case for this interpretation is "that which can receive more or less"; for one way of taking this is "those things which can be said to be more P or less P, but which cannot be said to be equally P as, twice as P as, etc."

3. The third interpretation is also based on the phrase "that which can receive more and less". This is now taken to mean "that which is meant by those adjectives which can properly form comparatives". An *apeiron* thus becomes what we may call a pseudo-quality or quality-range. Some adjectives, for example "triangular", stand for definite qualities, and everything that such an adjective can be used

of manifests that one quality. "Warm" and "wet" however do not stand for definite qualities; they represent respects in which things may be compared. A cannot be more triangular than B though it can be warmer than B. Contrariwise C cannot strictly be just warm, but, rather, warmer than is comfortable, warmer than is usual, warmer than it was, and so on. Warmth, we might quite well say, is essentially an *indefinite* notion, and this natural form of words is an apt commentary on *apeiron*. An *apeiron* then on this view is a pseudo-quality or quality-range, something like warmth, size, hardness, wetness or anything else which constitutes a respect for comparison. It is a fact about the world that things can vary in respect of warmth, of size, of wetness and so on, and it is this fact about the world which constitutes its *apeiria* or indefiniteness.

Subject to a complication to which I shall draw attention shortly, I believe that the third interpretation of *apeiron* is correct. Reflection on the complication will convince us that in fact the term is ambiguous and that the second interpretation is, though recessive, also correct. The dominant use of *apeiron* however is to refer to a pseudo-quality. Having thus provisionally settled *apeiron* we should naturally like to find a corresponding sense for *peras*. To find such a corresponding sense we remind ourselves that the defining character of *apeiron* was the ability to take more and less, whereas the defining character of *peras* was the ability to take the opposite of more and less such as the equal, the double, all ratios and so on. But we have understood "that which can take more and less" as that for which stand those values of "P" which make sense in "more P than". Surely then "that which can take the equal and the double" will be that for which stand those values of "P" which make sense in "equally P as", "twice as P as" and so on. Very well—until we realise that any value of "P" which makes sense in "more P than" also makes sense in "equally P as", and *vice versa*. In fact if we interpret "that which can take more and less" in the way in which we have been interpreting it, it is impossible to find an interpretation of "that which can take the equal and the double" which is (*a*) parallel, but also (*b*) produces something different. If the two phrases are taken to be parallel, then whatever satisfies either satisfies the other. This unfortunate result may make us turn back towards the second interpretation of *apeiron*; perhaps we can achieve parallelism with this. On this interpretation an *apeiron* was a general term S (such as fever) which can be said, as a general term, to be *too* P or *more* P than T, but which cannot be said to be *just so* P. *Apeira* are those conditions which are essentially too P or not P enough, but which are not in general something definite such as 32° Fahrenheit. What must a *peras* be to be something parallel to this? Presumably it will be something which is essentially equal to, twice, two-thirds of,[1] and so forth—in other words a quantity. This is satisfactory, for it is obvious that *peras* is at any rate something very like quantity. But before the reader decides that this is a conclusive argument for the second interpretation of *apeiron* I must observe that it is in some respects too satisfactory. For if an *apeiron* is something like a fever, then its antithesis is something like health or in other words a member of the third class of mixtures. *Meikta* are the sheep, *apeira* the goats on this interpretation. But if the antithesis is between these two terms, then there does not seem any reason to expect that there should be parallelism between *apeiron* and *peras*. Nor indeed can one imagine how in any sense of "mixture" health could be a mixture of something like fever with something like quantity. A perfect cake is a function ("mixture") of its ingredients and of the proportions which hold between them; it is the ingredients "rendered harmonious by the introduction of number". It is not a bad cake restored to grace by the introduction of number. If we are to make sense of the notion of a *mixture* of *peras* and *apeiron* it seems plain that *apeira* must be those things of which there are the right amounts in conditions such as health, and the wrong amounts in conditions such as fever; *apeira* therefore cannot be such things as fever, but rather such things as run riot in such conditions as fever. These are the pseudo-qualities, and that is why *apeiron* predominantly stands for these.

But in that case we have already shown that there cannot be the parallelism which we naturally expect between the two occurrences of "that which can take" (*ta dechomena*) in the account of the defining characters of our two terms in 25 e–26 a. This is a pity but we cannot help it; we remember that Socrates seemed unable to offer us a clear account of *peras*. We shall have to forget about parallelism with *apeiron* and work out the meaning of *peras* on its own. Fortunately this is not too difficult.

First of all a natural interpretation of "that which can take the equal and the double" is "those values of 'A' and of 'B' such that 'A is equal to B' or 'A is twice B' makes sense". What are these? Surely they are quantities. 2 is half 4, three feet are equal to one yard, a quart is twice as much as a pint. Numbers and dimensions then are *perata*. But before we settle for this it would be as well if we took Socrates' hint and tried to gather the nature of *perata* from his examples of mixtures. Now the point about the mixtures is that they are all *ousiai* or stable and in general admirable conditions. But *peras* is said to be that which composes the strife of opposites and, by introducing number, renders them proportionate and harmonious

---

[1] Fractions were thought of as ratios.

(25 d–e). "Due sharing" (*orthê koinônia*) of *peras* and *apeiron* is said to be responsible for health, music and (we may infer) for *ousiai* in general. In fact it is evident that either *peras* or due *peras* is responsible for the goodness of the members of the third class. But in speaking of *hubris* and vice Socrates observes that the goddess "when she saw that there is no *peras* in pleasures and satisfactions, imposed law and order, which are things that have *peras*" (26 b). In other words in human life pleasures and satisfactions are among the *apeira* and law and order constitute the element of *peras* the admixture of which creates virtue. In virtue then (and no doubt in other *ousiai* as well) the element of *peras* is law and order, and this is not precisely the same as numbers and dimensions. The situation is, then, that when we looked at the defining character of *peras* we thought that the class of *peras* must be numbers and dimensions; when we took Socrates' hint and looked at his examples of *ousiai* or mixtures, we thought that *peras* must be something wider.

This should not alarm us too much. We recall that Socrates failed to "collect the race of *peras*" and we suspected that this meant that he found it difficult to grasp this class other than intuitively. I suspect that the reason for this is that the class of *peras* does not consists of numbers and dimensions, but of whatever has the precision which is pre-eminently displayed by numbers and dimensions. Law and order "have *peras*" in the sense that they depend if not on numerical, then on para-numerical properties. I say "para-numerical" because I suspect that Plato wishes to tell us that whatever is admirable depends on such properties as proportionateness, but I would not like to say categorically that he would wish to tell us, for example, that the proportion which ought to hold (as we learn in the *Timaeus*) between the soul and the body can be stated in numerical terms. Proportionateness, then, is perhaps a para-numerical property.

I conclude that the class of *peras* consists of the whole range of law, order, recipe, harmony, proportion and so forth of which such things as virtuous living, music and precise numerical magnitudes are in some way diverse functions. A *peras* is anything the presence of which "introduces number" into that to which it is present, where "number" is, as I suspect, to be interpreted in a rather generous sense. It is because *peras* is this sort of a concept that Plato (like ourselves) is unable to be very precise about it and leaves us to catch an intuitive understanding of it from reflection on members of the third class of mixtures or stable conditions.[1]

---

[1] In 26 d 4 it is said that the class of *peras* "had not many members". This must mean "not very many", because it has already been said that *peras* is "one and many". Even so this remark is inapposite in context, and I think (following many scholars) that the text should be emended.

We must now say something about this third term. Socrates sometimes speaks of the contents of this third class as *meikta* or "mixed things", sometimes as *genesis eis ousian* or "process leading to stability", once as *meiktê kai gegenêmenê ousia*, or "stable being which has come about through mixture" (*sc.* of *peras* with *apeiron*). Of these phrases the last is the most accurate. This is shown both by the instances which Socrates cites and also by the fact that the fourth class, the "cause of the mixture", is the class of intelligences. It is I think clear that Socrates' conception is that intelligence (human or divine) produces stable and admirable conditions, or *ousiai*, such as health, temperate weather, moral virtue or the ordered sequence of the seasons, by imposing *peras* on *apeiron*. A "process leading to stability" is a *mixing*, the resultant *mixture* being the stable condition to which the process leads. The position is, then, that intelligence by imposing proportion upon the diverse quality-ranges which exist in the world brings about stable conditions of an admirable kind. This seems an entirely Platonic doctrine, and one which is extremely apposite to the ethical theme of the *Philebus*, which is essentially that the good life depends for its goodness on the proportionate, ordered, harmonious disposition of its ingredients. For this reason one would like to say that Socrates' four terms have now been identified. The fourth is intelligence, the third the good states which intelligence contrives, the second the proportions, recipes or what you will whose imposition brings these states about, the first the quality ranges upon which these proportions, etc., are imposed.

But before we can say this we must look at the difficulty which I mentioned above. In a sense it is one difficulty though it is perhaps best stated twice over, once in terms of *apeiron*, once in terms of *peras*. In terms of *apeiron* the difficulty is that there is no name in Plato's four which can stand for that class of "things which now are", of which fever and storms are instances, unless that name is *apeiron*. And yet as we saw above we want to reserve *apeiron* for that which is rightly ordered in such *meikta* as health, and therefore not to use it for disordered conditions. Yet there ought to be a name for conditions such as fever and storms, for when Socrates first introduces his categories (23 c 4) he seems to say that "*everything* that now is" can be fitted into them. Furthermore there is some evidence that things such as this are to be classed as *apeira*. In a short passage from 27 d–28 a Socrates tries to classify the contending "lives" in terms of his categories. First he decides that the best life (which contains a mixture in some sense of pleasure with intelligence) is obviously a *meikton* since it consists of "all the *apeira* kept in check by *peras*".[1]

[1] In saying this Socrates is going far beyond anything that Protarchus has conceded. Protarchus has admitted that some intellectual activity is necessary for

Next he asks how to classify the life of pleasure un-checked. He does not answer this question directly, but says that pleasure and pain must be *apeira* apparently in the sense that any given amount or intensity of either can always in theory be exceeded, so that it is never impossible to desire more pleasure than you are having or to fear more pain. From this we are presumably meant to infer that the life of the uninhibited pleasure-seeker (which is something which is from Socrates' point of view disordered and therein analogous to fever and storms) is an *apeiron*. It seems then that undesirable and unstable conditions are to be classed as *apeira*. But if this is so there must be an ambiguity in *apeiron*; it must mean that which is rightly ordered *in* the sheep (*sc.* the *meikta*), but it must also be used to refer to the goats themselves; it must be both an element in good things, and also it must be bad things.

Now to state the difficulty from the point of view of *peras*. We will begin with an odd sentence (26 a–2–4) in which Socrates says that "in the case of pitch and tempo (which are *apeira*) the due sharing of *peras* and *apeiron* accomplishes *peras* and thereby constructs most perfectly the whole of music". It is true that the words "the due sharing of *peras* and *apeiron*" do not actually occur in the sentence (but must be understood from two lines back); nevertheless it is very striking that the *right combination* of *peras* and *apeiron* can be said to *produce peras* and thus create music. One feels inclined to say that *peras* has two meanings in this sentence. In the first sense (where you have to have it in *right* combination) it means "proportion"; in the second sense it means "due proportion". "The correct ordering of pitch and tempo begets the orderliness of music"; this paraphrase will perhaps make the point clear. But whatever is thought about this particular sentence, the following point remains: if *peras* means no more than proportion, ratio and things of this kind, then these things are present in fevers, storms and in general in *apeira*, in the recessive sense of that word, as much as in *meikta*. If I play two notes with a concordant interval, then a stateable proportion holds between their vibrations; the presence of proportion has created proportion as Socrates says in the sentence we have just noticed. But proportion is also present and creates disproportion in the case of a discord. If the ratio of the octave is 1 : 2, nevertheless some ratio holds between the successive notes of a cat's yowling. We are often told that *peras* means no more than something definite, so that 32° Fahrenheit is a mixture of *peras* and *apeiron*. But this really will not do, for anything whatsoever whose temperature can be measured

---

happiness, and Socrates is foisting upon him the assumption that this entails an *ordered* life.

has some definite temperature, everything whatsoever whose size can be measured has some definite size and some definite ratio between its dimensions. If *peras* is not an evaluative concept, then the imposition of *peras* upon *apeiron* will not uniquely produce stable and admirable conditions, but, equally, unstable and bad ones. If *peras* means something like proportion, ratio and so on, then it must be *due peras* which produces good results. Yet Plato normally speaks as if stable conditions were produced simply by *peras*, not *due peras*. What are we to say then? Should we suppose that Plato has in mind only arithmetically elegant ratios and proportions? Yet he himself says (25 a 8) that *every* ratio of number to number and measure to measure may be included under *peras*.

I think that we can solve both of these difficulties if we keep in mind the cosmological setting of the discussion. Socrates goes on to argue that the human body, which is derivative from the physical universe, is superintended by a soul and cannot without that superintendence achieve any good thing; and that it is unreasonable to deny that the physical universe also is superintended by a soul. He then adds the revealing sentence (30 c): "There is then in the universe plenty of *apeiron*, sufficient *peras*, and over them a grand cause which orders and disposes the years and seasons and months, and which deserves the title of wisdom and intelligence." The cosmic intelligence, by imposing *peras* on *apeiron* produces from their admixture the *ousiai* of the astronomical regularities. But what is revealing in this sentence is the adjectives "plenty . . . sufficient". The picture suggested is that of a mass of potentially disordered material, to cope with which reason has at its disposal a barely adequate supply of order; one thinks of *peras* as a rather under-manned cosmic police force.

The serious point here is that the *apeiron/peras* distinction is not *just* logical. One can distinguish quantitative factors from qualitative factors (or something of the kind) and the distinction can be purely logical. An architect might draw up a specification of materials for some job in two columns. On the right go the names of the materials (cement, softwood, bricks), on the left go quantities, dimensions, etc. (5000 ft, 4 in. $\times$ 2 in.). The right-hand column will be "essentially non-quantitative" simply in the sense that all quantities go in the other column; it will be "essentially disorderly" in the same way— for anything which could count as "order" goes on the left. Yet such a table could be drawn up completely at random and could be such that no reasonable building could be made from what it specified. But the *apeiron/peras* contrast is not this kind of purely logical distinction between something like quality and something like quantity. There underlies it a presupposition according to which the qualitative aspect of the world is essentially disorderly in a more genuine sense, liable to get out of hand except where it is constrained by a *rightly* proportioned disposition of its elements. There is, if you like, a presupposition according to which "that which can take more and less" is always liable to become "too or not enough". Yet the terms *apeiron* and *peras* are introduced as if it were no more than a logical distinction between quality and quantity (or something of the kind) that Plato wants to put before us. The question is: how does Plato get from the logical distinction according to which *apeiron* is more or less equivalent to quality and *peras* to quantity, to a more cosmological distinction according to which *peras* becomes *due* quantitative factors and *apeiron* can be states of affairs which are disordered?

The answer, I believe, is that Plato is thinking at the level of general terms, at the level of things like health and fever. Now in health there exists a ratio between the bodily elements; in fever there does not, for the expression "fever" does not stand for some one determinate state but for an infinite number of deviations. One can go right in only one way, one can go wrong in infinitely many as Aristotle said. Similarly there is *an* interval between the notes in a cuckoo's song, and you can write down in musical notation *the* song of *the* cuckoo. You cannot likewise write down *the* yowl of *the* cat. Of course you could score the notes of any given yowl, but that is not the point. There is no such thing as the cat's yowl as there is such a thing as the cuckoo's song. Similarly there is one pattern or recipe (in a loose sense) to which the good life conforms, but there is no pattern or recipe in the life of pleasure, for the uninhibited pleasure-seeker acknowledges no recipe except the "open" recipe: accept as much pleasure as you can get. Therefore there are in the world only a certain number of recipes, ratios, proportions, patterns or what you will such that each is the pattern of the so-and-so (where "the so-and-so" is a general term). Furthermore each of these patterns is a "good" pattern. The reason for this is that the quality-ranges which constitute the material element of the world are essentially disorderly and do not in consequence throw up recurrent patterns on their own. It is only where intelligence in pursuit of its intelligent purposes has disposed the qualitative material in due proportion that one gets recurrent pattern. Therefore the only pattern that there is, cosmologically speaking (that is, the only pattern that recurs), is good pattern. That is why *peras* is due *peras*. For the members of the class of *perata* are not just anything which can logically be described as a pattern (as the shape of a man whose trunk was ten times as long as his legs could logically be called a pattern). The members of the class of *perata* are such things as the pattern of health or of good weather; they are the patterns that recur. It is of course contingent that the only patterns that are to be found in nature are good patterns—there might have been a class of recurring cacophonies, whereas in fact cacophonies are as multifarious as evil, and only euphonies are as uniform as goodness. But since this is contingent upon the fact that intelligence is intelligent and does not dispose things foolishly on principle, this need not disturb us. We see now why *peras* and due *peras* are the same thing; it is because by *peras* Plato means "those orderings which recur in nature". We can see also how *apeiron* can be extended from its dominant meaning (quality-ranges) to its recessive meaning (undesirable conditions). For such an expression as "fever" does not stand for some one condition; it covers the whole range of what happens when the relevant *peras* is disturbed and the quality-ranges are left to their own devices; fever is no more than temperature moving towards excess. (I need hardly say that I do not ask the reader to believe all this; only to believe that Plato believed it). We can see also that it would be wrong to ask such a question as: where are we to classify such general terms as fever? For there is no such general term as fever. We can see also that I am in a sense wrong to distinguish the dominant from the recessive sense of *apeiron*. There being no such thing as the gale (but only infinitely various conditions in which the *peras* which creates fair weather is inoperative) the gale cannot be said to be one of the things for which *apeiron* stands.

Nature then is a turbulence of qualities. Upon that turbulence reason imposes certain patterns which are quantitative or quasi-quantitative in nature, and which have the effect of producing stable states of affairs. In so far as there are in nature any "things" (stable, determinate and recurrent conditions) it is the imposition of pattern upon the turbulence which creates them. In so far as the turbulence reasserts itself nature falls back into the "infinite sea of dissimilarity" (*Statesman* 273 d 6. It is significant that the word for "infinite" is *apeiros*). This is the doctrine of the Anatomy of Entities in the *Philebus*.

C. *Some questions*

Three questions remain to be discussed. The first is the relation between the use of *peras* and *apeiron* in the Heavenly Tradition and their use in the Anatomy of Entities. We saw that in the Heavenly Tradition the element of *peras* in things was the subdivisibility of universals into subordinate versions—of animality into cow-hood, cat-hood, etc.; and that the element of *apeiron* was the fact that unclassifiable variations (or perhaps just uncountable members) still turn up in the smallest kinds which it is scientific to discover. In that case the word *peras* not only means the same ("definiteness") in both passages, but it also refers to the same things, namely to the common natures which reason has produced in the world. It is true that in the Heavenly Tradition the element of definiteness is so called because the number of subordinate versions of a kind is finite, and that this is not the case in the Anatomy of Entities where the pattern exhibited by health, for example, is definite in the sense that it is one self-consistent pattern. Nevertheless there is a satisfying affinity between the two uses of the word. The same is true, if less clearly so, in the case of *apeiron*. For, after all, the fact that there occur infinitely many insignificant variants within any genuine kind, no matter how small, must be a manifestation of *apeiron* in the sense in which the word is used in the Anatomy of Entities. For if it is unscientific to regard the similarity which happens to obtain between, say, seven individual cats as constituting a subordinate version of cathood, this must be because the similarity in question is not one which reason has produced; but in that case it must be an accidental similarity thrown up in the course of the random turbulences of *apeiron*. That there are such insignificant variations is evidence that nature, though organised by the imposition of a finite number of self-consistent intelligible patterns, is not tightly organised to the last nut and bolt; and the reason why this is so is that the "plentiful *apeiron*" is only sufficiently policed by the "sufficient *peras*". There is therefore an adequate affinity between the uses of *peras* and *apeiron* in the two passages.

Our second and third questions will glide into one another. The second question is one which is commonly asked, namely: what is the position of the forms *vis-à-vis* the four terms mentioned in the Anatomy of Entities? Are they identical with some one of the terms, or do they in some way fail to make contact with the Anatomy? Or is the Anatomy a substitute for the theory of forms? Our answer to this question will depend on certain questions concerning the theory of forms. For the *meikta* which constitute the third class of the Anatomy are common natures of "things that now are". They are such things as health, fair weather and virtue. Now are we to say that general terms such as health *are* forms or that there are forms *of* such general terms? If we say that health *is* a form, how precisely are we going to deal with the "other-worldliness" of forms, with the fact that forms are eternal *onta* and all the rest of it, whereas the physical world is a theatre of *genesis* and instability? On the other hand if we say that there is a form *of* health, what is it like? The *Parmenides*[1] has warned us against the vulgar "Platonist" error of

[1] See above, p. 332.

437

supposing that the form of health is a sort of ethereal counterpart of human health. Is it then something like the intelligible structure which is "imitated" by the structure of the elements in healthy persons? In that case the form of health must be something very like the *peras* whose imposition upon the *apeira* of the body produces the *meikton* health. In fact the position seems to be that if we take an "immanentist" view of forms according to which there is no gulf between "the P-hood which is in" (or "among") "us" and the form "P-hood itself", then we can say that the *meikta* are forms; for, being general terms, the *meikta* are the common natures of these physical things and states which reason has produced. If on the other hand we take a "transcendentalist" view of forms and insist on a gulf between "the P-hood which is among us" and "P-hood itself", then we shall perhaps be able to identify the forms with the class of *peras*. If we still feel that a *peras*, being a structure possessed by a thing that recurs in nature, is too earthy to be a form, then perhaps we can compromise and say that *perata* are imitations of the forms. When we discussed the Classical Theory of Forms the conclusion that I hope we came to was that Plato's language was at that time always more "transcendentalist" than his arguments seemed to warrant, and that he was perhaps in some uncertainty as to what his position was. However, in one document belonging to the time of the Classical Theory we found something which agrees well with the view that associates the forms with the class of *peras*; I mean the doctrine in the Sixth and Seventh Books of the *Republic* according to which the forms are something like totally abstract principles of order which are embodied both in mathematical relationships and also in the common natures of rightly ordered things.

One hesitates then whether to identify (or closely associate) the forms with the class of *meikta* or with the class of *peras*. One is drawn in both directions. This is significant, and its significance can best be seen when we remember that Plato has abandoned the old contrast between *genesis* and *ousia*—the world and the forms. He still uses the old contrast—one can find it in *Philebus* 59—but it is no longer the only contrast. The meaning of this surely is that Plato no longer wishes to distinguish sharply between P-hood itself and the P-hood which is among us. *Genesis* no longer implies simply transience; it is also used to stand for "becoming" in a better sense of that word—something like "progress towards"; and correspondingly the title *ousia* is no longer denied to the stable conditions towards which the progress is. I have already argued that this does not involve a wholesale change of doctrine, but it is an interesting change of emphasis. The significance of it is not, however, that Plato is now prepared to identify the forms with the class of *meikta*, the eternal objects of reason with the common natures of ordered physical things. Intelligence *produces meikta*, whereas the forms are always co-eval with intelligence. The significance of it is that Plato is now clearer about what it is for which he wants to claim transcendence. I suspect that it was because he was not clear about this at the time of his earlier writings that we derive from them conflicting impressions on the subject of transcendence. Roughly speaking it is clear that Plato wants to tell us that the forms are transcendent, but not clear why he does so. So long as he is prepared to talk of "the form of X" where X is a concrete physical thing it is difficult to see why one should deny that X-hood is immanent in X things. The doctrine that there are no genuinely X things would of course provide a reason, but we have seen that he is never prepared to assert the doctrine of imperfect embodiment whole-heartedly.

The new element which appears clearly in the *Philebus* (though it is foreshadowed in my view in the *Republic*) is that *in any general term of which there are physical instances there is a formal and a material element*. (This incidentally answers the third question which I wanted to ask, namely the question what I meant by saying that the *Philebus* reflects Plato's interest in disentangling a formal and a material element within universals). This is no doubt a development of the conception of the datum in the *Timaeus*. Health is a disposition (formal) of certain *apeira* (material). The *apeira* which have to be disposed constitute the datum which intelligence must take for granted in contriving health.

Does this mean that Plato would or should allow that the class of forms and the class of *peras* are identical (or perhaps that the latter are "copies" or something of the former)? Not necessarily; the matter is complicated by a question about the nature of forms which we have several times raised but never settled. The question is whether the form of P is that to which the Craftsman looks in creating P things, or merely the formal element in that. Let us put it like this. If we say that the form of, say, health is one of the things to which the Craftsman looks in the work of creation, then we shall have to say that the form will comprise a material element. For that to which the Craftsman looks will have to be something like the fact that if *apeira* E, F, G . . . are disposed according to pattern P, that will produce health. Forms will have to be something like general hypotheticals about which *peras* imposed on what *apeiron* will produce the state of affairs in question. This is a little disconcerting if forms are the eternal objects of pure reason. If on the other hand one says that the form is nothing more than the *peras* which occurs in the fact, then the form will hardly suffice as that to which creative reason looks. If I am arranging something I cannot just pull an

439

arrangement out of the hat and make the objects conform to it. I must tell myself that *these* could be rendered orderly in *this* way. The organiser cannot ignore the things that he has to organise. There seem then to be reasons for saying that a form must be something of a purely formal nature, but there seem also to be reasons for saying that it must be something like an eternal truth which contains a reference to empirical material. That the forms are to be objects of abstract reason pulls in one direction, that they are to play a part as archetypes in the ordering of the physical world pulls in the other. If we go in the first direction the forms will be very closely associated with *peras*; if we go in the second direction they will be something more like archetypes of *meikta*.

We shall discuss towards the end of this chapter the question which of these directions Plato took. My impression is that he was at any rate strongly drawn towards the former. But our immediate purpose is to settle the relation between the *Philebus* and the theory of forms. Our answer to the question how this is to be done is that it cannot be done. To draw attention to the fact that in such a general term as health there is a material element and a formal element will settle the question of what it is that is transcendent, but it will raise the question what a form is. That for which it is worth while claiming transcendence will be the formal element, the *peras*; it is this which is congenial to pure reason. But that only provokes the question what to say about the form, the archetype of physical things. Is the *peras* alone the archetype, or must the archetype itself be (in the appropriate sense) a "mixture" of *peras* with *apeiron*? The *Timaeus* draws attention to this question by introducing the concept of the datum, the *Philebus* makes it more urgent by employing the correlative concepts *peras* and *apeiron* of which the one is purely formal and the other purely material. This is why attempts to bring the Classical Theory of Forms into relation with the Anatomy of Entities never get anywhere; for the latter provokes questions the overlooking of which was essential to the former.

VII. THE UNWRITTEN DOCTRINES

We have now examined all those passages from the dialogues which seem to contain important contributions to what I have called metaphysical analysis. There remain however certain doctrines ascribed to Plato by Aristotle (and others) which are not to be found in the dialogues and which must have formed part of what Aristotle called Plato's "unwritten opinions". The evidence for these opinions comes almost entirely from polemical writings of Aristotle's (largely from the *Metaphysics*), and it cannot be said that his sketchy and hostile observations give one anything like a sound basis for reconstructing these doctrines. It is like trying to guess what the defence was by reading the concluding speech for the prosecution. Nevertheless it is necessary to say something about these doctrines. I am not competent to assess the Aristotelian evidence (a most admirable account of it can be found in Sir David Ross, *Plato's Theory of Ideas*). Nor could the opinions of a competent scholar about the bearing of the evidence be more than guesswork. But if the Aristotelian accounts of the doctrines are thrown at one, as they often are, as accounts of what Plato thought in his later years, they tend to create in a candid mind the impression that Plato must have outlived his sanity. What I shall try to demonstrate therefore is that it is possible to put a sane interpretation upon these doctrines. I make no claim to a correct interpretation; I only want to show that sense can be made of these uncouth sayings. If there is one reasonable interpretation, no doubt there may be others more reasonable and more correct. That a reasonable interpretation can be found has of course been shown before; but there is no harm in trying again.

Our problem then is to make head or tail of the doctrines which I shall list in a moment, each of which is ascribed by Aristotle either to Plato or to some Platonists among whom scholarly considerations are held to show that Plato must be included. Aristotle's source for these doctrines must be in most cases Plato's oral teaching, conversation, and in particular the famous course of lectures on goodness which so disconcerted its audience by containing no moral exhortation and much mathematics. In the table of doctrines which follows I have roughly divided them into two kinds: those which primarily concern the philosophy of mathematics, and those which concern the relations of forms and numbers. Comments of my own I shall put within brackets; everything else is meant to be what rests on Aristotle's authority. Plato then is said to have believed in the following doctrines.

A. *Mathematical*

1. There are two kinds of numbers, formal numbers (*eidêtikoi arithmoi*) and mathematical numbers. Formal numbers are not "comparable" or "addible" (*sumblêtoi*), whereas mathematical numbers are. (This is thought to mean that no formal number is e.g. half or twice any other). Mathematical numbers are the objects of mathematics, and are "in between" forms and things in that they are not changeable like things, but there can be any number of each (e.g. one can talk of seven threes). (Presumably the formal number 2

is two-ness, and the mathematical number is that which is mentioned in 2+2=4. It is generally assumed that formal numbers are forms).

2. Formal numbers can be "generated" by two parents, one of which is unity and the other something which is called by various names, the *ahoristos duas* ("the indefinite pair" or "indefinite duality"), the *mega kai mikron* ("the great-and-small" or "greatness-and-smallness"), the unequal, or possibly plurality (*plêthos*).

2.1. Of these two parents the job of the male parent unity is to "equalise", and of the other parent, the unequal, the function is to double. (This may be no more than Aristotle's interpretation of Plato's meaning).

2.2. "The one" is the middle unit in the case of odd numbers.

3. Points are "geometers' fictions". It would be better to speak of "indivisible lines".

4. The (formal) number 2 is correlated with the line, 3 with the plane, 4 with the solid.

4.1. But the line is not two-ness, but two-ness in-length, and so with the others.

4.2. (There are thus four classes of objects, namely forms or formal numbers such as two-ness; geometrical entities such as the line, the objects of mathematics such as the number 27 or—I suppose—a given triangle; and finally physical things such as this circular table top).

B. *Metaphysical*

5. Forms are numbers. (Aristotle takes this for granted, though he does not state it in so many words. On the other hand Theophrastus, Aristotle's colleague and successor in the Lyceum, puts what must be the same doctrine rather differently: he says that Plato made those forms which are numbers—i.e. formal numbers—*more fundamental* than the other forms. This would suggest that e.g. animality was in some way derived from numerical properties but not itself such a property. This clash between Aristotle and Theophrastus is interesting; for if Theophrastus' carefully worded statement is correct it looks as if Aristotle has not always troubled to be fair to what he has deemed the details of Plato's views).

6. Particular numbers can be assigned to particular forms, e.g. to humanity. (This too Aristotle takes for granted). In particular intellectual grasp (*nous*) is unity, the ability to demonstrate something (epistêmê)[1] is two-ness, opinion three-ness and sensation four-ness.

---

[1] I have translated *nous* and *epistêmê* as if Aristotle were using the words in his own sense. But Plato may have used them in the same sense. We have met

7. Goodness is unity (unity apparently being the more fundamental aspect).

8. (*a*) Since the forms are the causes of all things, their elements are the elements of all things. (*b*) The material element is greatness-and-smallness, the formal element unity; (*c*) for numbers come from greatness-and-smallness by participation in unity.[1] (Numbers, then, are functions of unity operating on greatness and smallness. Aristotle probably means that individual things are functions of the forms—not of unity—operating on greatness-and-smallness. The analysis of individual things is therefore not the same as the analysis of forms; things are functions of forms and greatness-and-smallness whereas forms are functions of unity and greatness-and-smallness. Unity and greatness-and-smallness thus become the only ultimate elements that we encounter anywhere. This comment so far presupposes that the relation between clauses (*a*), (*b*) and (*c*) above is as follows:—the elements of things are unity and greatness-and-smallness (*b*); for these are the elements of numbers (*c*); and forms are the formal element in things (*a*); *and of course forms are numbers.* The clause in italics explains the relation of (*c*) to what goes before it. But this may perhaps be wrong. It may be that this is a place where Aristotle shows his awareness of the more precise account of the relations of forms and numbers which Theophrastus offers. Thus: The elements of the forms are the elements of all things; for the elements of things are forms and greatness-and-smallness, and the elements of numbers are unity and greatness-and-smallness; *and the elements of forms are numbers and greatness-and-smallness.* Again the clause in italics is supplied to explain the relation of clause (*c*) to what has gone before. Either way unity and greatness-and-smallness become the only ultimate elements, but whereas the first way takes for granted the identification of forms and numbers the second way makes numerical properties into the element of *peras* in forms).

9. That which participates (*sc.* in the forms) is place.

A. *Theory of number; mathematical numbers*

We will begin to try to make sense of this series of uncouth sayings by seeing whether we can create for Plato an intelligible theory of number. We must first decide what we are discussing. In ordinary

---

[1] In this passage (*Metaphysics* 987 b 18–22) Aristotle speaks of "the great and the small" as if they were two things. Ross has cogently argued however that this is a mistake; Plato did not use two material elements, greatness and smallness, but one, greatness-and-smallness. I take this to be established.

---

epistêmê used for something not quite first rate in the *Seventh Letter* (see above, pp. 122–6).

Greek usage the word *arithmos* which we translate "number", connotes a group, and hence 0, 1, $\sqrt{2}$, -3, $4\frac{1}{2}$ are not *arithmoi*. The only numbers in the Greek sense are the integers from 2 upwards. Fractions are treated as ratios; if I have four and a half apples I have four apples and something which stands to an apple as 1 stands to 2. No doubt the other kinds of numbers (in the modern sense) which are not *arithmoi* would be dealt with in similar ways.

I make this point about the word *arithmos* not because Plato's usage conformed completely to this standard Greek usage, but because the latter is a clue to the way in which he conceived of numbers. In fact Plato seems to have felt the pressure of the reasons which have created the wide concept of number in the modern sense; for many arithmetical purposes $2\frac{1}{2}$, -3 or $\sqrt{2}$ are on all fours with 6 and 7, and Plato seems to have divined this. There is a passage in the *Epinomis* (990–1) in which Plato[1] speaks of "that which is absurdly called geometry" (i.e. "land-measurement") "but which is really the process by which the similarity of numbers[2] which are not naturally similar is made apparent in terms of plane figures", and goes on to make analogous remarks about solid geometry. What this must mean is as follows. It is impossible literally to obey the directive: "Find the number whose product by itself is 2." Therefore it seems that $\sqrt{2}$ and $\sqrt{4}$ are "not naturally similar"—that these expressions stand for entities different in kind. But a square whose sides are 1 in. long has a diagonal which is $\sqrt{2}$ in. long (by Pythagoras). Hence the directive to construct such a square gives the use of the expression "$\sqrt{2}$ in."; and shows in what sense $\sqrt{2}$ is similar to 2. In being prepared to use the word *arithmos* of both of these entities, Plato has evidently seen the ways in which they are and are not similar, and this amounts to seeing the utility of using a concept of number which is wider than the common Greek one, and which is such that surds are a species of numbers. In his own language he has seen the unity of surds and whole numbers.

But although Plato came in this way to a wider concept of number, it is important to remember that *arithmos* connotes a group, for this fact is or may be the explanation of those passages in which he finds it necessary in the dialogues[3] to distinguish vulgar from mathematical "numbers"—vulgar numbers being such that their members are not pure units (but entities such as oxen which are neither indivisible nor equal each to each), mathematical numbers being such that their members are pure units.

---

[1] Or his disciple, if it is felt that Plato did not himself write the work.

[2] The noun is not used, but the gender of some of the adjectives in the passage shows that it must be understood.

[3] *Republic* 526 a, *Philebus* 56 d–e in particular.

It is natural to suppose that these mathematical numbers which are "intelligible only"[1] are transcendental entities and that they are identical with the mathematical numbers whose existence Plato is said to have professed in his "unwritten doctrines". We must however be rather cautious here. Formal numbers in the unwritten doctrine seem to have been such entities as threeness and fourness, mathematical numbers those, five of which are mentioned in the statement "Four threes are twelve". Now there exist in the world trios, quartets and in general groups of various numbers of members. These are, perhaps, vulgar *arithmoi*. There exist also threeness, fourness and in general the properties of such groups. These are formal *arithmoi*. These do not also exist entities such as the threes any three of which are said to make nine in the formula "$3 \times 3 = 9$". There do not, in other words, exist mathematical numbers. Nevertheless it does not appear to make sense to talk of multiplying or adding formal numbers. Threeness is one property and it does not make sense to talk of two threenesses. Nor (so long as addition is thought of as some kind of putting together) does it make sense to talk of adding threeness and twoness to produce fiveness. The mathematical logicians of the last century have shown that it is possible so to define the mathematical operations that one numerical property can quite intelligibly be spoken of as the "sum" or "product" of two others. Such definitions provide something that Plato plainly wanted, namely a clear distinction between physical and mathematical operations; as early as the *Phaedo* (101) he makes it clear that he realises that addition is not putting together nor division dissection (not even "ideal" dissection). Still, he may perhaps have been unable to hit on such definitions of the mathematical operations, and in default of them he may have felt that it is necessary to say that there exist mathematical in addition to formal and to vulgar numbers. Indeed in a loose sense of "there exist" it is no doubt correct to say this. Now the passages in the dialogues which we have referred to do not necessarily imply the existence of mathematical numbers. In one sense vulgar numbers are in fact the subject matter of arithmetic. "$2+2=4$" tells us something about pairs and quartets; we can infer from this that the group consisting of the two groups Marshall and Snelgrove and Dickens and Jones is as numerous as the group consisting of Matthew, Mark, Luke and John. Nevertheless we can say that $1+1=2$, and that $1=1$, whereas we cannot say that Marshall = Snelgrove. Nothing physical, in other words, is a unit in the sense required by arithmetic. This is strictly wrong; for anything whatever is a unit (this is one house, and London is one city) provided that you are counting things of that kind. Nevertheless one cannot infer

[1] *Republic, loc. cit.*

445

from "1 = 1" that this one house is equal to that one city in anything except number. We need in fact to interpose an inference-stop between "1 = 1" and statements of the form "Any one . . . . . equals any one . . . . . ." (where a name of some object goes in place of the dots). This can be done by saying that arithmetic is not about physical objects, or not about vulgar numbers. This can be said provided it is taken as supplying the inference-stop which we have just spoken of. But it provokes the question "What then is arithmetic about?". To this we may answer: "Numerical properties"; but on the other hand we *may* answer: "Special transcendental entities." Now when we have to interpret the passages in the dialogues which say that arithmetic is concerned with "intelligible units", and not with physical things, we have to ask what Plato intended by such statements. Did he merely wish to draw attention to the fact that such *arithmoi* as this group of five apples are not perfect exemplifications of the mathematical concept of *arithmos* (for the members of such groups are not indivisible nor equal each to each); or did he wish to say positively that the *arithmoi* with which mathematics is concerned are groups of special kinds of entities? So far as the passages in the dialogues are concerned it does not seem to be possible to answer this question.

So far as Aristotle's statements about the "unwritten doctrines" are concerned the position is rather different. For here we have some people denying, and Plato on the other side asserting, that it is necessary to say that there exist mathematical entities which are intermediate in status (changeless but plural) between the forms and things. This looks like something more than an attempt to insist on the abstract nature of mathematics. Nevertheless it is still possible to suspect that Aristotle misinterpreted the spirit of the argument which he reports. We might be inclined to say in the formal mode of speech that we have a use not only for the abstract noun "threeness" (defined by Frege and Russell) and for the adjective "three" (as in "three cats") but also for the noun "three" (as in "four threes are twelve"). Now in the material mode of speech this would have to become "There are such things as threes in addition to threeness on the one hand and to trios of objects on the other". Did Plato want to go further than this? Again it seems impossible to say. It is however a relevant comment that although he asserted "that there are" mathematical numbers, he gave his attention chiefly to formal numbers. Mathematical numbers existed, but they do not seem to have been an important part of the story. It seems therefore reasonable to say that even if Plato felt compelled to postulate entities to be denoted by number substantives, he did not make much of them, and would perhaps have been glad to dispense with them if he could.

That Plato was not eager to multiply entities beyond necessity is perhaps shown by the dictum that points are a geometers' fiction and that it is better to speak of indivisible lines. It is not clear how this dictum is to be taken. Even in antiquity it was taken to be a silly remark, implying the discontinuity of space. But this seems unlikely. Plato was well aware that space is a continuum. It seems to me much more likely that "indivisible lines" was a deliberate paradox whose serious purpose was to eliminate points as a special class of mathematical entities by treating them as the vanishing case of a line— "that part of a line which is so small that it cannot be divided". There is of course no such part any more than there can be something which has position but no magnitude. The reason, I suppose, for the traditional Euclidean definition of a point is the view that position is an intuitive notion. It might be contended however that distance is a more fundamental concept, and that a point is therefore best treated as a minimum distance or "indivisible line". However this may be Plato certainly seems to have applied Occam's Razor to points, which suggests that he was not eager to multiply entities in mathematical philosophy.

To return to the theory of number, the paradox of the mathematician in the *Theaetetus* (198) illustrates the point which I am trying to make about the concept *arithmos*. The paradox is that, if a mathematician counts something, he is seeking to know that which, as a mathematician, he must know already, namely how great a given *arithmos* is. But what the mathematician is seeking to know is how numerous a given group is; what he knows already is the position of (say) 52 in the number series. The paradox is created by using *arithmos* to mean something like "the tale of a given group" as well as to mean an integer. This illustrates the close connection between *arithmos* and given groups. It was necessary for Plato to draw attention to the fact that arithmetic is completely general, that it is not concerned with tales of given groups. In the course of making this point the notion that mathematics discusses the relations between special sorts of entities may possibly have hardened from being a manner of speaking to being an embarrassing piece of doctrine. So much for mathematical numbers.

B. *Theory of number; formal numbers*

The formal numbers are the numerical properties two-ness, three-ness and so on.[1] These properties as Socrates says in the *Hippias*

[1] It is true that Aristotle criticises Plato (*Metaphysics M*) for treating numbers as self-subsistent entities or substances. But this is a special case of Aristotle's general complaint that Plato treated all properties as substances.

Major (301–2) are properties which can only be possessed by groups. If I have two aunts, what is two is neither Aunt Jane nor Aunt Lucinda, but the class or group of my aunts. In "five aunts" therefore and in "sainted aunts" the relation of the adjective to the noun is quite different.

The emphasis which Plato laid on the formal numbers was perfectly proper, indeed important. But it was ill-understood by Aristotle, and it was left for the moderns to re-discover the truth that numbers are fundamentally the common features of sets of groups which can be paired off, member for member, with each other (as five is the common feature of all groups which can be paired off with the fingers of my left hand). The existence of number is the existence of properties of this kind.

So far so good. What is much less readily intelligible is the things that Plato seems to have said about the possibility of "generating" number from unity (the male parent) and the indefinite pair (the many-named female parent). Before we attend to the evidence on this matter we ought to ask ourselves first what can be meant by the biological metaphor of "generating" numbers, and second what can be the point of attempting to "generate" them. We ought to explore the possibility that Plato was considering some real problem and not just playing with fancies. The thought of a real problem in this area puts one in mind inevitably of such philosophers of mathematics as Peano, Frege and Russell. It is therefore worth exploring the possibility that Plato was attempting to do something like that which Frege and Russell attempted, namely to show that the concepts of mathematics can be derived from simpler and more general concepts. If this is correct, then to say that numbers can be generated from unity and greatness-and-smallness is to say that any given number can be analysed into or exhibited as a function of these two terms. I am going to interpret the doctrine in this spirit. It may be objected that this is plainly not how Aristotle conceived of it; to that one might retort that many of the criticisms levelled against Russell were equally wide of the mark.

I believe that there are three important clues that we must bear in mind. The first clue is a fact about the relation between numbers and numerals. We are inclined to think that every number is an independent entity, one greater than its predecessor, one smaller than its successor. But this is a misleading way of expressing the fact that every numeral has a position in a certain series, i.e., that it comes after its predecessor and before its successor. There are two important facts; one is that groups can be more and less numerous, the other that in order to tell how numerous a given group is we pair off each member of it in turn against successive members of a standard series of sounds. It is not essential that we should count in this way. If I was only interested in enumerating collections of less than twenty-one members, and if in counting I always flexed my digits in a standard order, I could manage without numerals by flexing my fingers and toes. The essence of counting is to pair off the members of one group against the members of another group, the latter group being such that one knows already how large it is. It is in order that one may know how long a string of numerals has been consumed in counting a given group that the numerals consist of a set of different sounds which succeed each other in a standard order. This ensures that if, for example, I conclude a count by uttering the numeral "six", I know at once that the group of objects which I am counting can be paired off with the group or string of numerals from "one" to "six". That is how I know that there are six objects before me, or rather that is what knowing that there are six objects before me is. If one group is larger than another, as the apostles are more numerous than the evangelists, then more numerals will be consumed in counting the first group than the second. Since we learnt at school that the string of numerals from "one" to "twelve" can be enumerated by using the string of numerals from "one" to "four" three times over, as soon as we know that the last numeral uttered in a count of the apostles is "twelve" and that the last numeral uttered in a count of the evangelists is "four", we can infer that the group of the apostles can be correlated with the group of the evangelists by pairing one of the latter against three of the former. This is a crude account of how the numerals work. The purpose of this account is to show that strings of numerals are groups of standard objects which can, like other groups, be more and less numerous. What is logically fundamental is not that the integers succeed one another, but that groups can be more or less numerous. Numerals succeed each other because by making them do so in a standard order we can tell whether one group is greater than another. The relation of *being more numerous than* (which holds between groups) is more fundamental than the relation of *succeeding* (which holds between numerals). The purpose of saying this in this context is that it seems clear that Plato treated (formal) numbers as properties of groups, so that in order to understand what he is saying, and the value of it, we want to divest ourselves of the picture of numbers as entities which come after each other in a series. It may also help us to understand some of the things that Plato is supposed to have said if we recall that *being more numerous than* is a special case of *being greater than*, another special case of which is *being longer than*. It is natural to speak of groups of numerals as "strings", to say for example that the string consumed in counting the apostles is three

449

times as long as the string consumed in counting the evangelists. It is easy in other words to think of a linear representation of the relations of *exceeding* and *being exceeded* which hold between the numerousness of groups, or in other words between numerical properties. I hope that the significance of these remarks will emerge as we go along.

My first clue then is a fact about the nature of numbers (that they are fundamentally properties of groups) of which I believe that Plato was aware, coupled with the fact that by thinking of longer and shorter distances we can create a pictorial representation of the relationships between numerical properties. The second and third clues are things that Plato is alleged to have said. The second is that 2 is the number of the line. I shall argue that this is connected with the fact that a line is essentially dual because it is a section cut from something which tends in both of two directions; there is *this* way and *that* way along it, and no more.

The third clue is the identification of unity with goodness and its association with intellectual grasp. I suggest that the thought underlying both these strange sayings is that unity is essentially unifiedness. If one asks how unity could be identified with goodness and made the dominant partner, one answers that the thought surely must have been that whatever is good is coherent and as such exhibits *one single* nature. A bad man is two or three things—a man, a lion, and a many-headed monster (*Republic* 588)—whereas a good man is at unity with himself. Again I suggest that the essential difference between *nous* (which is correlated with unity) and *epistêmê* (which is correlated with two-ness) is that whereas *epistêmê* is the ability to demonstrate the entailment of *q* by *p*, *nous* is the apprehension of the *pq* complex as what it is, namely one single complex fact. In *epistêmê* one grasps the premises and the conclusion and that they are connected; in *nous*, the theory is, the complex fact is seen as *one* fact with its "consequences" comprehended as indissoluble parts of it. There is therefore an essential duality in *epistêmê* as there is an essential duality (or three-ness) in an ill-governed man or city. Two (or more) elements are held together so that the entity in question is *one twofold* (or *manifold*) *entity*. The degree of unification in things which are correlated with the property two-ness is thus a lower degree than that which is present in things which are correlated with unity. The bad city is one indeed but it is one uneasy combination of several cities (*Republic* 422–3), whereas the good city is *one* city without qualification, being unified by the unanimous acceptance on the part of its members of a single principle. Unity is present therefore in that which is manifold, but in that which is manifold it is present only in that the elements are united. This is to be distinguished from the way in which unity is present in that which is not manifold, in that which is *unitary*.[1]

To sum up these three clues, the first invites us to conceive of a number as a stretch, something which can be imagined as a line. The second reminds us that a line can be conceived of as essentially *dual*. The third reminds us that whereas anything whatsoever is *one* so-and-so, it may nevertheless be one by the holding together of any number of members from one upwards. Our business now is to show that with the notions of a stretch, of duality and of unity we can create the notion of numbers.

Let us first try to do it pictorially. We will begin by thinking of a continuum, a line if you like stretching indefinitely in either direction, or if you prefer an axis such as East–West. Such an axis is obviously indefinite, and it is also in a sense a duality in that it is constituted by its two directions. It is made *one* axis by the fact that it is the unification of *two* terms, hither and thither. But the unity of two terms is duality, or the property of a pair; therefore such a line could be called an *ahoristos duas* "indefinite duality or pair". Being essentially a dimension, or something along which greater and smaller measurements can be made, we can see how such a line could be said to represent "greatness-and-smallness".

Let us next take this indefinite line and mark off against it definite stretches by putting against it objects of different lengths. Each of these would be *a* stretch, and what would unify it would be the fact that it was so much of the line as was marked off by a certain object. We have already seen that numbers can be pictured as stretches. It is also true that any given number, say 3, is the number of any group which contains as many members as a three-fold group or trio contains members. Therefore when we picture larger and smaller numbers as longer and shorter stretches of our indefinite line, we can imagine each of these stretches as marked off, or being made into one definite stretch, by being as long as a group to which it corresponds. The group therefore which marks off some definite stretch of the line, by being as long as it, unifies that stretch, or creates a piece of unified plurality.

The *Parmenides* seems to have suggested that it would be possible to derive from the notion of the named meaning standards of unity so rigorous that nothing could ever be a unity. For everything whatsoever is at least what it is and also an existent; so that, if that kind of complexity constitutes plurality, everything whatsoever, including unity, will be a plural entity. To avoid this conclusion we must drop

---

[1] This does not conflict with the *Parmenides*. That which is unitary in this sense is not non-complex in the sense in which the *Parmenides* (and *Sophist*) demonstrate that nothing can be non-complex.

451

the view that unity or unitariness excludes all complexity whatsoever. A unitary entity may be complex in the ways in which it is logically necessary that every entity should be complex. If we allow this we shall find that it is possible to divide entities into those which are unitary and those which are plural. Within the field of cities, for example, Socrates' Republic would have been unitary, whereas an ordinary community, being an association of dissident groups, and hence several "cities" bounded by a common wall, will be plural. (Socrates' Republic would of course have been many men as well as one city, but the *Philebus* tells us that such paradoxes are vulgar; as a city it would have been unitary in a genuine sense whereas other cities are unitary only by courtesy). There are therefore unitary entities and plural entities, the most obvious example of plural entities being groups such as that consisting of Marshall and of Snelgrove. Now the Greeks did not think of 1 as an *arithmos*, and unitariness is not, therefore, a numerical property. Two-ness is the simplest numerical property. But obviously nothing but a group can have the property of two-ness; and the same is true of every other numerical property. Nothing therefore can have a numerical property unless it is plural. To put it rather differently, plurality is an essential "moment" in every numerical property.

But unity is another essential moment. For that which can be counted is always a specific group. Therefore that which can have a numerical property is always a single entity of a special kind, namely a plural entity or group. We cannot just count; we must always count something, and there is a sense in which it is right to say "something" and not "some things". To count is to discover how numerous some group is. If we specify some group, such as the cups on this table, or the cars which we shall meet on this journey, we can proceed to count them. If we complete the work of counting by uttering, say, the numeral 5, then the group has five members; but what is five-fold is not the members, but the group. It is *one* group, which has *many* members, and is therefore *plural*. Numerability is a property always of *one manifold* entity. Therefore every numerical property is a function in some sense of unity and plurality.

It may be convenient at this point to reflect upon the dictum that the function of unity in numbers is to "equalise" (2. 1). The clue to the meaning of this may be perhaps as follows. The "female" feature in numbers (plurality, the "great-and-small" and so on) is sometimes called "inequality". Inequality and indefiniteness are thus associated in its titles—for it is also "indefinite duality". This suggests that perhaps *isazein*, to equalise or to balance one thing with another, may bear the sense of "to render definite". This is not so far-fetched as it may seem. For an indefinite plurality is not the kind of thing which can be equal to anything, nor unequal either. It is only when it is rendered definite that it can stand in one of these relationships. To put it more clearly in the formal mode, a subject expression such as "Some Englishmen" cannot meaningfully be followed by such words as "are as numerous as . . ." It is only when a group is specified (those Englishmen who wear stiff collars, for example) that one can go on to say that that group is equal or unequal to some other. But as we have seen (and as the seventh deduction in the *Parmenides* has hinted)[1] it is unity which constitutes a group; or in clearer language a definite group is *one* class—to talk about the Englishmen who wear stiff collars is to talk not just about *many* entities but about *one set* of entities. Nothing can be equally numerous with something else unless it has some definite number; nothing has some definite number unless it is one set; therefore unity "equalises" in the sense that the subject of an assertion of equality must always be one set. This seems a reasonable explanation of the statement that the function of the male parent is to balance or equalise.

The argument so far is as follows. In discussing numbers we are not discussing special sorts of entities but special sorts of properties. (That Plato claimed exalted status for numbers is not inconsistent with this; for it is notorious that he claimed exalted status for at least some properties). In each of these properties, that is to say in every numerical property, a part is played by unity and a part by plurality. Of these two factors plurality can be spoken of as indefinite duality because the simplest model of it is that which we have described as a dimension. This is essentially dual because it consists of nothing but two directions—East and West, say; in general, hither and thither. It is also indefinite because a dimension is not a definite distance, but that along which a definite distance is measured. For the same reason it is great-and-small—it (so to speak) accommodates great distances as well as small ones. Finally and very conjecturally the motive for speaking of plurality in such terms may perhaps have been the thought that the notion of a dimension or stretch is more primitive than the notion of plurality. "Some", Plato may have thought, seems to presuppose number, whereas the notion of a dimension is a spatial representation of the abstract notion of a respect in which things may be compared, this latter notion being prior to, and not dependent upon, the operation of counting. It may be added that the presupposition of this last suggestion (to which I attach more importance than I attach to the suggestion itself) is that Plato's purpose in all this (like Russell's) is to exhibit mathematical properties as functions of properties which are as primitive as possible.

So far then *n*-hood (any numerical property) is a function of unity

[1] See above, p. 346.

and plurality. That which has a numerical property is always a unified plurality, and the numerical property which characterises, say, all trios is the specific plurality-of-a-unity which makes them all trios—namely threeness. This however is not entirely satisfactory, for Plato's remarks are not concerned with what it is to be a number, but with what it is to be a specific number. He is not telling us what makes something countable, but what makes something five or seven or whatever it may be. Indeed these remarks ought to be stiffened; for we are told that the Platonists "did not posit a form of number" on the ground, it seems, that numbers essentially succeed each other. This would seem to mean that they did not think of threeness and fourness as distinct kinds or versions of a generic property "numericality" or "numerability"—the property of having a definite tale. Threeness and fourness were not different kinds of number but different numbers. Unity and plurality are not to be conceived of as "begetting" once and for all a generic property of which the various numerical properties are specific versions. Aristotle speaks as if there were repeated "begettings", and he complains that the masculine feature, or unity, uses the same feminine feature, plurality, each time, whereas when the masculine feature tabularity begets tables it uses a different female (different bits of wood) each time. He complains in fact that the relation between the "formal" and the "material" element in Plato's account of numbers is anomalous.

This is not perhaps surprising since Plato is talking not about the analysis of individual things into "form" and "matter", but about the analysis of properties into elements which can only be described as formal and material by analogy with Aristotle's use of these terms.[1] However that may be, the denial of a form of number perhaps amounts to saying that the countability which is exhibited both by trios, for example, and by sextets does not constitute a common nature which they share, but a basis upon which they may be compared. Countability is perhaps in the language of the *Philebus* an *apeiron*, a pseudo-quality or range, and not a common nature or form. This however does not alter the fact that for a thing to be countable it must be one set having many members, and remarks to this effect are not invalidated by the denial of a form of number as such. Nevertheless to be countable a thing must be one set of a *specific* number of members, and for that reason countability is posterior logically, and not prior, to the various numerical properties. Therefore the primary function of unity and plurality will be to "beget" the specific numerical properties, two-ness, three-ness and the rest.

---

[1] That is with Aristotle's primary use of these terms (i.e. that according to which the wood is the matter of the table). Aristotle himself also uses them at a higher logical level.

How then can one analyse particular numbers simply into unity and plurality? It is obviously no good saying that three-ness is the property of any one threefold group; but how can one manage without this kind of circularity? How, in effect, can one derive the specific numerical properties from the notions of "an" and "some"?

It is fairly evident that one cannot; but at the same time it seems to me fairly clear that this is what Plato tried to do. With regard to the details of his method rational confidence is impossible. Many suggestions have been made; I shall try to set out that which commends itself to me as the most probable. We will employ once more the spatial picture of a dimension. We will begin by reminding ourselves that the function of the male parent, unity, is to equalise, whereas that of the female parent is to double. We conjectured earlier that to equalise is to render definite, to select from the plurality of things some one set. The role of unity in numerical properties consists in the fact that that which can have a numerical property is always one complex entity. Applying this to the generation of numbers we may suppose that we are to render definite our continuous line or dimension by selecting from it a finite stretch or distance. By imposing unity upon (or, in simpler words, by selecting *a* bit out of) the "indefinite duality" of our dimension, we have created something finite, which we will call a distance. But, for the same reasons for which a dimension can be called an indefinite duality, a distance can be called a definite duality. A distance, we might say, is as simple or abstract an object as we can find which has the property two-ness; and two-ness is the property of such a distance. He who can form the idea of a finite stretch of a dimension can thereby form the idea of the number two, for two-ness is the property of such a stretch; a distance is a spatial representation of the simplest case of unified plurality, which is duality. We have therefore generated the number two.

The elements of a distance are its two ends[1] and the holding of them together. If we now imagine the same relation of *holding together* obtaining not between two ends, but between two such distances, we get a spatial representation of the property of being fourfold.

●◄┄┄►●

FIG. 1. Two-foldness

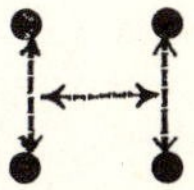

FIG. 2. Four-foldness

We can see now in what sense the element of distance might be said to "double". To think of a distance is, so to speak, to unite, and

[1] The two ends being, so to speak, created out of the two directions constituting the dimension by the selection of a definite stretch out of it.

yet to hold apart, its two ends; there are the two elements, from–which and to–which; and they only stand in that relation to each other in so far as they are conceived of as creating one distance. A distance therefore is essentially dual; and as such, whatever the complexity of its terms, the complexity of the whole figure is double the complexity of each of its ends. Therefore by the same process by which we generated four-foldness out of two-foldness we can obviously go on to generate all the powers of 2.

Next suppose that in Fig. 1 we have, not only the two ends, but a third intermediate point, so that we have the distance "from A to C through B" as in Fig. 3. We now have a picture of three-foldness.

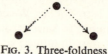

FIG. 3. Three-foldness

By "holding together" two such distances we can depict 6; by complicating Fig. 2 in an analogous manner we can produce 5; and

FIG. 4. Five-foldness

it can now be seen that we can similarly produce every number. The intermediate point which is related in odd numbers gives sense to the dictum (2.2 above), that the one is the middle unit in odd numbers.

I am afraid that these diagrams look complicated, and I would not like them to be taken very seriously. I do not suggest that Plato developed his generation of the numbers in spatial terms. Indeed the attempt at pictorial representation of the notion of unified plurality produces complications once we get beyond the simplest case of unified plurality, namely twofoldness. The notion of a distance, therefore, is to be taken as an abstract pictorial representation of duality, and fourfoldness is to be thought of not in terms of an impossible picture of a distance whose ends are themselves distances, but simply as dual duality.

Let us say then that the simplest case of unified plurality is that which can be depicted as a distance—a "unity of two moments" or a "twofold unity"—something such as Marshall and Snelgrove. In this complex object there is just that much complexity which there is in a distance—the two termini and the holding of them together. This is

the simplest case of complexity, and this simple case can be complicated in two ways. One is to have another object in addition to, or
"between", the two terms which constitute a pair; the other is to
make the pair itself a pair of pairs. Combining these two complications we can of course have a pair of pairs with an additional object
between them, or a pair of pairs-with-an-additional-object-between-
their-terms . . . a pair of pairs of pairs and so on. (We have thus
"generated" 2, 3, 4, 5, 6 and 8, and we only left out 7 because it
would have required a very cumbrous phrase; obviously we can
"generate" all the numbers in this way).

This is all very obvious and indeed trivial; but it is not without
point. If we continue to toy with the supposition that Plato's generation of numbers was somewhat along these lines, then we can say
that it was a serious (though unsuccessful) attempt to derive arithmetical notions from the more primitive notions of "an" and "some".
But why is it necessary or desirable to try to do this? The fundamental answer to this question is, I suppose, Plato's realisation that
the numbers are not "comparable" or "addible" (*sumblêtoi*); in
particular, I think, that n is not n-1 and one more. There is a primitive picture of numbers, which we all tend to have, according to
which they are a series of entities each of which is one bigger than its
predecessor. But numbers are not such a series of entities, and this,
as I maintain, is what Plato had realised. The numerals constitute a
series, but the numerals are not a set of objects. They are a set of
words or ciphers which we utter in a standard order and which we
use as a set of standard objects (more convenient than fingers and
toes) with which to count and compute. What there is beside the
numerals is the fact that there are varying degrees of complexity
which groups can manifest, and that these degrees of complexity are
inter-related. In particular any given degree of complexity can be
regarded *either* (1) as the simplest case of complexity (duality), *or*
(2) as an instance of the simplest case of complexity (duality) holding
between terms each of which is of some other degree of complexity
(as 84-hood is dual 42-hood), *or* (3) as such an instance complicated
by the presence of an intermediate term (as 85-hood is 42-hood not
just doubled but doubled *via*, so to speak, an additional unit). Any
degree of complexity can be thought of as standing to some other
degree of complexity in such a way that the former can be depicted
as a distance and the latter as its two termini, the distance being
either the simple distance *A to B* or the complex distance *A to B
through C*. Whatever the value of n may be, if a group is n-fold, there
is always some other degree of complexity,[1] m-foldness, such that the
n-fold group is either a two-fold grouping of m-fold terms or else a

[1] Treating unity as the limiting case of complexity.

two-fold grouping of *m*-fold terms grouped *via* a middle unit. It is this extremely simple and yet extremely important fact that makes it possible to order the various degrees of complexity in a series; and it is the fact that the various degrees of complexity can be ordered in a series which constitutes the series of numbers; for the series of numbers is nothing but the set of facts one instance of which is that fourfoldness is a group-property one degree more complex than three-foldness. This is something of fundamental importance in the philosophy of mathematics, and it is out of this, I suggest, that Plato's rather uncouth-sounding generation of numbers arises.

If this is correct, Plato's attempt at generating the numbers is something important and not fanciful. It is an attempt to get back to the logical bones of arithmetic, to isolate the fundamental features of reality which underlie our use of numerical language and explain the rules by which we govern this. We may illustrate this by asking a question which is commonly asked. Why, it is said, was Plato not content to generate numbers by multiplication and addition out of 1 and 2, as he did in passing in the *Parmenides* (143–4)? The answer that suggests itself to this question is that a "generation" of numbers in this fashion is not a "generation" of them in a philosophically interesting sense. For if we do this we take for granted the terms upon which we perform our operations (1 and 2) and the mathematical operations of multiplication and addition which we perform upon them. When I say that $(2 \times 2) + 1 = 5$ what I say has no meaning except in an arithmetical context. It does nothing, so to speak, to show what the arithmetical context is there for. Plato's "generation" of numbers is not meant to tell us how to construct sums in such a way that the various integers appear successively as the answers to them; it is an attempt to get back behind the notion of a sum or of a mathematical operation and to tell us what we are talking about when we count or compute—his answer being that it is the complexity of groups that we are comparing. This means that, whether it is successful or unsuccessful, the generation of numbers is philosophically important.

Criticisms can of course be brought against Plato's theory of number on this interpretation (as indeed on any other). One such criticism would be that Plato does not seem to make clear to us in what order the degrees of complexity are to be ordered. I say he "does not seem" to make this clear, for we must of course remember that all that we know of this part of Plato's work is derived from polemical sayings of Aristotle's which do not even claim to offer us a complete and systematic account. But on the data that we have got, if we ask the question "How do we know that four-foldness is a complexity of greater degree than two-foldness?" we get an answer (for four-foldness is, roughly, two-fold two-foldness). But if we ask instead the question "How do we know that four-foldness is a complexity of greater degree, and indeed just one degree greater, than three-foldness?" I do not know what answer we shall get. We *do* of course know this, as we know that 4=3+1; but it does seem to be a valid criticism of Plato's attempt to exhibit number as a series of increasing degrees of complexity (assuming, still, that that is what it was) that he apparently fails to tell us how the series is ordered. There may however have been some subtleties that Aristotle did not catch or at any rate failed to report.

A further criticism which can perhaps be justly brought is that Plato paid too little attention to the way in which we talk about arithmetical matters, and in particular to the numerals, to the system of signs wherewith we count and compute. For there is an element of "convention" in arithmetic which is dependent upon the characteristics of the system of numerals which we employ—in particular upon the fact that it is a decimal system. For the clarification of the nature of arithmetical operations it is essential that this conventional element should be understood; we must see that in computation we are operating purposively with a system of signs having certain properties, that we could achieve the same purposes with signs having rather different properties, and that our operations would look rather different if we did. The unnecessary contention "that there are mathematical numbers" is perhaps partly due to Plato's failure (so far as we know) to pay sufficient attention to arithmetical signs. As we have seen it is harmless to say that there are mathematical numbers in the sense in which this is an indisputable truth, i.e., in the sense in which it maintains no more than that entities such as "threes" receive apparent mention in arithmetical discourse. It appears however that Plato maintained the existence of mathematical numbers as if it were a disputable doctrine; and for this error attention to the manner in which we talk about arithmetical matters might have been the cure. But when these criticisms have been made the impression remains that Plato's discussion of numbers represents a very considerable achievement.[1]

C. *Mathematical properties and the world; things, forms and numbers*

We must now consider those of Plato's unwritten doctrines which concern the relationship to each other of forms, numbers and things.

[1] Aristotle tells us that Plato only "generated" the numbers up to 10. It is fairly generally agreed however that the only truth that could underlie this statement is that Plato did not trouble to show that his method could "generate" numbers outside the first decade. No great weight therefore need be put on this statement.

The problem that we have to tackle is set by the remarks of Aristotle reported in paragraph 8 of our table of unwritten doctrines, and by the impression conveyed by Aristotle, here and elsewhere, that forms are more or less to be equated with numbers. We have to try to find an account of what Plato may have been attempting to do such that we can represent it as something which was at once philosophically serious and also capable of being summarily reported in the terms in which Aristotle reports it.

We will begin by remembering that Aristotle makes free use of the notions of form and matter in his discussion of Plato's views. He complains, as we saw above, that Plato's account of the generation of numbers is anomalous in that the same material element is used many times over, whereas in the generation of tables different pieces of wood are employed for each table. That Aristotle makes this complaint shows that he thought that Plato was attempting to do the sort of thing which could be justly represented in terms of Aristotle's own concepts of form and matter. He assumes that the model of the craftsman having on the one hand his design and on the other hand his random lengths of timber is a fair model to apply to Plato's discussion of number. It is probable indeed that Aristotle may be forcing Plato's teaching into an unduly rigid Aristotelian mould in so doing, but if we are cautious we shall surely be right in accepting the hint that the notion of a formal and of a material element can illuminate this topic.

The notion of a formal and of a material element inevitably reminds us of the notions of *peras* and *apeiron* in the *Philebus*, and also of the contributions of reason and of brute fact in the *Timaeus*. It is perhaps sufficiently obvious that the model of the craftsman, his design and his materials, is relevant to both of these pairs of ideas. Let us therefore tentatively think of the formal element as that which reason contributes, and of the material element as that with which reason has to contend. Let us also employ the model given in the *Timaeus* according to which we have reason on the one side confronted with a formless chaos on the other. Now if we apply this model to the "generation" of numbers we shall have to think that "greatness-and-smallness" or plurality, being the *apeiron* or the material element, is something which is, so to speak, imposed upon reason from outside. Continuing to make use of the model of reason over against the chaos, we can say perhaps that reason is intrinsically simple and unitary (*habitués* will probably agree that this has a Platonic sound), and that its apprehension of manifoldness is an apprehension of something which does not arise out of its own nature but out of that which confronts it. But reason can do nothing with the notion of that which is simply plural, for this is a notion of something which is *apeiron*, boundless or indefinite, something, in the language of the *Philebus*, which is just "more" or "too much" and not of any definite degree. Reason cannot, so to speak, do anything with what we might call brute plurality. Reason can only apprehend definite degrees of plurality (in other words the numerical properties), and these as we have seen are attained by the "imposition" of unity. In terms of the model which we are employing, we can think of reason as being aware that it is confronted with something to which "more" and "less" are applicable, something within which comparisons of various kinds can be made, something which is thus "great-and-small". So that it may be able to handle this amorphous entity reason forges suitable tools, namely the definite degrees of plurality or the numerical properties; and in the forging of these tools it makes use of its own tool, namely of unity.

This of course is fanciful; and it has the additional drawback that it represents the numerical properties as something which reason forges for the sake of understanding the world, unity being the only implement with which reason is initially provided. Let us try again without the model of reason and its amorphous *vis-à-vis*. Let us say that reason is the potentiality of understanding whatever there may be to be understood. But understanding is achieved through definiteness, whereas that which is to be understood is complex. Therefore the essential tools of understanding are definite degrees of complexity. Reason, as the potentiality of understanding, must contain an awareness of these definite degrees of complexity, and the latter must therefore exist in order that reason may apprehend them. For reason does not create what it apprehends, any more than the senses create what they apprehend. We have therefore three sets of terms: we have reason, we have the definite degrees of complexity which reason apprehends, and we have finally "the world" or that with which reason has to contend, that which can be understood in so far as it manifests, or can be made to manifest, definite degrees of complexity.

This is a familiar triad; for the numerical properties are at least a sub-class of forms, so that what we have here is in conformity with the essential triad of the *Timaeus*: Craftsman, forms, and brute fact or "space". Within the numerical properties we can say that the element of complexity derives from the fact that that which is to be understood is complex whereas the element of unity derives from the fact that understanding proceeds by drawing its material together into a condition of unity. Metaphorical as it is, such language perhaps explains why unity is the formal element, greatness-and-smallness the material element, in numerical properties.

If we forget about the world, we can say that the numerical

properties constitute a field for rational understanding, namely the field of pure mathematics. But they are also capable of application. They are so to speak structural properties which anything can manifest. They are of course capable of direct application in the sense that a group of three pigs manifests the property of three-ness; but they are also capable of indirect application within other properties in a manner which I shall try to elucidate. To do this let us consider what are sometimes called "the things after the numbers" (paragraphs 4, 4.1, above).

The things after the numbers

The "things after the numbers" are "the line, the plane and the solid". It appears that at one time Plato had talked of numbers and forms (whether or not these are identical), of mathematical numbers and other mathematical entities (pure non-physical triangles and so forth), and of physical things; but that at some late stage this scheme had been complicated by the introduction at the second logical level (i.e. presumably super-ordinate to mathematical entities) of "the line, the plane and the solid". Aristotle speaks of these last as if they were the same kind of entities as his own *eidê enhula* or "en-mattered forms". An en-mattered form was a general term such that in defining it it is necessary to mention the material in which it is embodied (as snubness cannot be defined without referring to noses, whereas concavity can be defined without referring to any particular material). It seems therefore that the things after the numbers are to be construed as general terms, but as general terms which involve a reference to something material. Since they are general terms we must take it that "the line" means finite one-dimensional extension or distance, "the plane" finite two-dimensional extension or area, and "the solid" finite three-dimensional extension or volume; not particular lines, areas and volumes, but the general terms ("linearity" etc.) of which these might be thought to be instances. Now with each of these entities a number is correlated and also a type of greatness-and-smallness. One-dimensional extension was duality embodied in the long and the short, two-dimensional extension three-ness embodied in the broad and the narrow, three-dimensional extension four-ness embodied in the deep and the shallow. Aristotle implies that there was some disagreement about the numbers said to be embodied in these entities, and also that some Platonists wished to maintain that linearity was simply duality; Plato however, it appears, insisted that it was duality *embodied* in *the long and the short*.

The purpose of this insistence looks clear enough. It is the same as the analysis of general terms into an element of *peras* and an element of *apeiron* in the *Philebus*, the same as the analysis of numerical properties into unity and greatness-and-smallness. It might perhaps be made clearer by the introduction of names for two distinct relationships; "instantiation" and "embodiment" might serve as these names. A particular may be said to "instantiate" a general term as this round plate instantiates roundness and platehood. "Embodiment" however is to be a relation which holds not between a particular and a general term, but between two general terms A and B. We might begin to define this relationship by saying that B embodies A when any instance of B is also in some respect an instance of A, and the nature of B is such that an instance of B must have certain properties which are not necessary to an instance of A. Thus triangles are three-fold entities, but they are also extended. Triangularity therefore is an embodiment of threefoldness.

Now the picture that is borne in upon one is as follows. Plato is anxious to begin with properties which are as "pure" or as "abstract" as possible—with properties that reason can contemplate without being thereby committed to contemplating general terms whose instances must be physical things. But he is also aware that unless such properties are "embodied" by being imposed upon a material element, one will never progress from pure properties to the common natures of physical things. To put it cosmologically, if that to which reason looks in ordering the chaos is simply a range of pure properties, reason will have no exemplars to determine its creative work. The purest of all properties is unity. By being embodied in greatness and smallness it "generates" an infinite range of properties—the numerical properties—which are pure in the sense that they have no necessary application to physical things. But it is necessary to get from such properties to properties which are less pure. A step in this direction is taken in the doctrine of the things after the numbers. Take duality and feed into it, so to speak, the possibility of linear motion. This gives one a distance. A distance is that which is twofold, if the two terms are to be spatial entities. Distance is twofoldness embodied in one-dimensional extension. Since the line ABC is, if straight, really the line AC, a "line" which is genuinely threefold defines a plane figure, namely a triangle. Therefore if three-foldness is to be given a spatial embodiment one must feed into it the possibility of motion in two dimensions. Three-foldness embodied in the possibility of motion cannot be understood except in terms of motion on a plane. Three-foldness imposed upon extension generates a plane figure. Similarly, perhaps, to understand what four-foldness amounts to in terms of space one must feed into it the possibility of motion in another dimension; for one of the possible fourfold spatial entities is a tetrahedron. It was perhaps in something like this way that the numerical properties were assigned. I am not entirely happy with this

463

since the assignment of 3 to the plane and 4 to the solid seems to depend upon counting points, and "points are geometers' fictions". (One can assign 2 to the line by counting not its ends but the directions along it). It would be pleasant to find some other way of correlating 3 and 4 respectively with planarity and solidity, but I cannot do it. However I feel reasonably confident that what this doctrine is concerned with is the analysis of what might be thought to be the fundamental entities of geometry into a purely formal, numerical element, and a material element, the imposition of the former upon the latter "generating" distance, area and volume after the fashion whereby the imposition of number upon greatness-and-smallness "generated" numerical properties. The aim is to show what must be added to the notion of numerical properties in order to construct the notion of figures in space—the answer, roughly speaking, being "Space". The doctrine of the things after the numbers is a first step away from pure properties such that the contemplation of them is not the contemplation of exemplars of physical things towards properties which are impure in that the contemplation of them is the contemplation of such exemplars. A bridge is being built between two *desiderata*: the *desideratum* that the forms should be the correlates of pure reason, and the *desideratum* that they should be exemplars usable in the ordering of physical chaos. The *Timaeus* has made it clear that much of the *detail* of the common natures of physical things will be due to the nature of the materials of which they have to be made (in the creation of which material the Craftsman's hands are to some extent tied); but the *Philebus* has also begun to express the realisation that even so the forms to which the Craftsman looks in creation will have to contain some measure of physical commitment. They will not be, so to speak, the architect's working drawings (these are worked out in terms of the available materials), but rather the client's specification; but a client cannot specify what sort of building he wants without at least making it clear that what he wants is a system of enclosed spaces of such and such a kind. (This analogy is not to be taken too seriously).

Thus we get the following:

Rank 1 Numerical properties (two-ness etc.).
Rank 2 Linearity etc. (the "things after the numbers").
Rank 3 Mathematical entities (triangles, mathematical numbers, etc.).

The relation of the things after the numbers on Rank 2 of the hierarchy to the mathematical entities on Rank 3 will presumably be rather complicated. Mathematical *numbers* look like being straight instances of the numerical properties on Rank 1, whereas other mathematical entities such as pure triangles will only be instances of numerical properties *via* their Rank 2 spatial embodiments. This might seem to entail a complication in the hierarchy, a division of Rank 3 into 3.1 and 3.2 so to speak. Since however all the mathematical entities on Rank 3 were presumably particulars (although non-physical), that perhaps is enough to keep them together on the same logical level.

Numbers and forms

Our problem now is to make sense of the impression which Aristotle leaves with us that the class of forms and the class of numerical properties are more or less identical; or at the very least that numbers could be assigned to such general terms as man, belief, the horse and so forth. The clue that I shall follow first is the same that we have used so far; that is to say, that to proceed from pure properties to exemplars of the common natures of physical things it is necessary but also sufficient to feed in a *substratum* such that the imposition of the pure properties upon the *substratum* "generates" the exemplars. "Feeding in" and "generating" will still bear the sense that they have borne hitherto. That is to say we are not talking about the cosmological work of creating physical particulars which are instances of general terms, but about the logical work of progressing from properties which do not presuppose that their instantiations inhabit the kind of world that we inhabit, towards properties in whose definition this is presupposed. This clue is so consistent with the spirit of the *Timaeus* and of the *Philebus*, and also, as I believe, of the central books of the *Republic*, that I am reluctant to give it up. It must be confessed however that it does not work out as neatly as one would wish. It is difficult to resist the impression that there are complications which either Plato failed to notice or Aristotle failed to report.

Aristotle tells us that since the forms are the "causes" of all things (i.e. since forms are that by virtue of which things are as they are) their elements are the elements of all things; and that these elements are greatness-and-smallness and unity (paragraph 8 of our table above). This seems to imply that forms are numerical properties, since it is numerical properties that are generated out of these elements, and since it is not easy to see what else could be generated out of them. We have already seen however that if you feed into that which unity generates upon greatness-and-smallness (viz. numerical properties) a *special form* of greatness-and-smallness (viz. great-and-small extension in space), it is possible for numerical properties to generate embodiments of themselves. This suggests the possibilities (*a*) that the formal element in all things is unity only because unity is the formal element in the numerical properties which are in turn the

465

formal element in other general terms; and (*b*) that "greatness-and-smallness", like *apeiron* in the *Philebus*, may perhaps be a class-expression standing for a number of ranges or scales, or in other words that there may be a number of material elements different in kind but alike in that each is "indefinite" in some sense until a numerical property is imposed upon it. If we are allowed to make these suppositions this would get us to a position which would square with the statement of Theophrastus (see paragraph 5 of our table) according to which numerical properties are not identical with but *logically prior to* other forms. For this is what they would be if they were the formal element in the latter. Let us see if we can work this out.

The numbers 2, 3 and 4 belong not only to "the line, the plane and the solid", but also to *epistêmê* (demonstrative knowledge), *doxa* (belief) and *aisthêsis* (perception) respectively. In this assignment of numbers to general terms (the only such assignment which can be confidently cited) *nous* or intellectual apprehension is correlated with unity; and the reason why *epistêmê* is allotted the number 2 is said to be that it goes straight from premise to conclusion (i.e. it is like a line). Now Aristotle speaks of *doxa* having "the number of the plane" and so on; and it is difficult to resist the impression that the cases of line, plane and solid and of *epistêmê*, *doxa* and *aisthêsis* are actually analogous. That is to say, it is difficult to resist the impression that the reason for assigning a given number to a member of the first list is the same as the reason for assigning the same number to a member of the second. Moreover it is not difficult to guess at a possible analogy. Aristotle gives us the hint that *epistêmê*, the second best of the four states, is like a line in that in it the mind travels from one proposition to another. Now it is easy to imagine that in the supreme state *nous* the two "moments", which appear separated in *epistêmê* as premise and conclusion, are to be thought of as unified into one complex whole. Such language is reminiscent of idealistic logic, but it does not follow that it is un-Platonic. *Nous*, let us say, is a unitary state in that in it we grasp a complex fact as a unitary whole; it will have the sort of unity of Socrates' Republic. By contrast *epistêmê* is dual in that the two elements of the complex fact are seen to be respectively premise and conclusion but are no more unified than this. I do not know how to develop this so as to cover the other two states in the list, but the thought that *doxa* is a looser form of apprehension than *epistêmê* with a third term coming in somewhere seems to be a Platonic kind of thought; and clearly, from the point of view of understanding, sense-perception is looser still. Just as in a solid figure four (or more) points are held in relation to each other but not identified, so, one imagines, it might well be that in sense perception there are four or more terms somehow entering in. This would give one an embodiment of fourfoldness since four-foldness is that which characterises something which is *a* so-and-so of *four* elements.

This tempts one to form the following picture. There is an indefinite, a field or range, which we might call cognition for the sake of a name. Like the possibility of motion it is a material element. If it is fed into duality one gets demonstrative knowledge; demonstrative knowledge is how duality is expressed in terms of cognition, just as distance is how duality is expressed in terms of space. So too with the other numbers. This is attractive; it fits with the general analytic technique of the *Philebus*; it gives us an analogy between the correlation of numerical properties with the cognitive states and their correlation with the things after the numbers; and it is easy to imagine that the principle on which the correlation is done might look as if it were able to be indefinitely extended over any number of other forms of greatness-and-smallness, and hence might be able to generate the whole range of general terms. But there is a difficulty. Whereas it is easy to imagine that Plato might describe "the long and the short" as a version of "the great and the small", it is not easy to see that "cognition" could be spoken of in such terms. Therefore if we are to accept the account that we have been toying with we shall have to try to prop it up. We might perhaps argue that Plato used the phrase "greatness-and-smallness" so loosely that he did in fact allow it to cover cognition. If he did however surely Aristotle would have had something to say about it: "In what sense is cognition great and small?" one imagines, but does not find, him asking.

Ought we then to drop the clue that we have so far been following? It must be admitted that Sextus Empiricus[1] gives a quite different reason why numerical properties were said to be logically prior to other forms. This is, very roughly, that whereas every form is in one sense a unity, it may also be dual, threefold etc. in that it includes other forms within itself (in the manner, I suppose, in which man-hood may be said to include rationality and animality); and that since there are therefore many true propositions of the form "S-hood in *n*-fold", the numerical properties which occur as predicates in such propositions are logically prior to the forms of which they are predicated. This would certainly give us a basis on which to assign numbers to general terms. But it is at first sight not very convincing. It does not seem to explain the assignment of numbers either to the cognitive states or to the things after the numbers. It is much easier to see that *epistêmê* might be said to be dual on the ground that every *case* of it is a unity of two elements than it is to see how *epistêmê*

---

[1] *Adv. Math.* 258, cited Ross, *op. cit.*, p. 216.

itself is a function of just two other forms. And the fact that in the case of any given general term one can count the number of other general terms of which it is a function gives us only a very weak reason for making numerical properties logically prior to other forms, still less for saying things that could be summed up in the slogan "Forms are numbers".

However it is possible that we might find a compromise somewhat as follows. We might observe, for example, that in the case of the cognitive states the series begins with a unitary entity, *nous*, which is the supreme state within its field. (Unity is goodness). We might suggest therefore that *epistêmê* is so to speak the first falling-off from *nous*, the two-fold entity which comes in the same field as *nous*, *doxa* the threefold entity and so on. Nor is it impossible to imagine other such series. There are in the dialogues passages which suggest that within the sphere of living creatures those which have bodies of fire (stars) are unitary entities in a sense in which men are by comparison complex; for in the case of the star the fiery body offers no resistance to the motions of the soul. As a piece of *epistêmê* is one thing consisting of two not entirely integrated elements, so a man is a unity of potentially conflicting parts. Since *n*-foldness is the unification of *n* elements, this would be a ground for saying that manhood embodies a numerical property. One might indeed develop this along the lines suggested by the passage from Sextus. An amphibious animal for example includes within itself two divergent ways of life; and therefore the general term *the amphibious animal* might be said to be one degree more complex than *the land animal*. Possibly this could be generalised. Any two "natures" it might be said are potentially conflicting, so that any entity which instantiates more than one nature will be a complex and not a unitary entity. Any general term therefore which "includes within itself" two or more general terms will be such that its instances are complex entities, and such a general term will in this way embody some numerical property. This would be in accordance with Sextus' account.

The upshot would be that the class of general terms would be divided into "fields" in the sense in which the four cognitive states constitute one field. In any field there might be one term which was the supreme realisation of the field and which was such that its instances were unitary entities. Such a term would embody unity. Below it there might be one or more terms in each of which the field was less perfectly realised, and whose instances were dual entities. Such terms would embody duality. Below them again we might find three-fold terms on the same basis, and so on. This would give us a fair degree of analogy between the assignments of numerical properties in the case of the things after the numbers and in the other cases. For in each case the ground for the assignment would be derived from what we have taken to be Plato's theory of number. A given numerical property is possessed by an entity which is irreducibly complex to a given degree; and both lines and cases of *epistêmê* are irreducibly dual for reasons which we have seen. This is enough to make the general terms, of which these are instances, embodiments of duality. This account can also be squared with Aristotle's statement that unity and greatness-and-smallness are the elements of the forms, if we take this simply to mean that they are the elements of the numerical properties which the forms embody.

But there is still a fly in the ointment; for after all this is a rather lax way of taking Aristotle's words. To put it in another way, while we may have found a basis on which it could perhaps have been said that forms *embody* numerical properties, we do not seem to have found anything which could lend itself to the slogan "Forms are numbers". For even if *the aquatic animal* embodies n-foldness there is obviously a great deal more to aquatic animals than that. At the very least they are expressions of n-foldness in terms of life or something of the kind. We should be better off if we could say, as we tried to say earlier, that "fields" such as life or cognition are *cases* of greatness-and-smallness. For then we could say that *the aquatic animal* is the embodiment of n-foldness in this particular kind of greatness-and-smallness, as we tried to say in the case of the cognitive states. This would give us unity, as the ultimate formal principle, begetting n-foldness in greatness-and-smallness, with n-foldness in turn begetting *the aquatic animal* upon one particular case of greatness-and-smallness, namely life. But it is difficult to be happy with this.

The difficulty might be expressed as follows. If you set out to make an n-fold entity there is no special reason why you should make an aquatic animal. For low values of n at least, one imagines that there must be very many other kinds of n-fold entities, there being some other factor presumably to which they owe their diversity. This being the case it seems perverse to identify *the aquatic animal* with the numerical property which it shares, we imagine, with many other forms, rather than with the factor which differentiates it from them. It would however be less perverse if it were thought that there was something of great metaphysical significance in the numerical property. Is it possible to find such a thing? There might be an answer along the following lines. The *Sophist* says that the true dialectician must be able to tell what kinds can combine and what cannot. It is probable that in the *Sophist* itself Plato does not envisage any general theory from which possibilities or impossibilities of combination can be deduced in particular cases. But he might perhaps have cherished a belief that it is the numerical properties embodied in the forms which somehow determine the relationships into which they can enter. If this were the case it would mean that mathematics decides in the end how the system of forms is organised—a conclusion that Plato would probably have found congenial. On this line of thought the justification for more or less identifying a form with the numerical property which it embodies would be that it is the latter which determines the combinations which it enters into, so that the philosopher who wants to understand the reason of things needs above all to attend to the numerical properties of the forms. That is perhaps one way by which "Forms embody numerical properties" might have been exaggerated into "Forms are numbers".

There are other possible ways in which numerical properties might perhaps be correlated with forms which we have not considered in this discussion. For example it is thought that the Pythagoreans said that justice is 4 on the ground that justice is reciprocity and that 4, being the first square, is an arithmetical expression of the relationship: A does to B what B does to A. (For in "2×2" each factor doubles the other, whereas in "2×3" the first doubles the second whereas the second triples the first. 2 and 3 do not contribute equally to the making of 6). I have argued[1] that the *Republic* is sympathetic towards ideas of this kind, and it is quite possible that Plato retained such sympathy. But the *Republic* does not say that forms are numerical properties; rather that the entities and relationships which mathematicians study are images through which the forms can be discerned. It seems dubious therefore whether this treatment of the relation between forms and numerical properties could be taken far enough to account for what we hear of the unwritten doctrines. But it may have contributed to them.

For there is a consideration of general probability with which we may conclude. This is that it is surely likely that Plato's thoughts on this matter were more tentative, exploratory and confused than we have so far granted. Making all allowances that we can for Aristotle's defects as a source for Plato's views, it is surely likely that if there was one simple doctrine we should have a clearer account of it from him. The most reasonable belief is that Plato persisted in maintaining that there was an intimate relationship between numerical properties and other forms, with the former dominant in the partnership; and that he may well have used a wide variety of arguments hinging on a number of different relationships between numerical and other properties in the hope of giving substance to this conviction. I have tried to indicate one line of thought which might have given rise to the conviction. I do not want to suggest that no others were pursued.

[1] See Chapter 1, pp. 80–3.

Forms and things

Aristotle says that the material element in all things is greatness-and-smallness; but he also says that "that which participates is place". (paragraphs 8 and 9). He makes it fairly clear that the reference of this last saying is to the *chôra* or space which the *Timaeus* depicts as that with which reason has to contend. Since the *Philebus* employs the notion of *apeiron* in much the same way as that in which the *Timaeus* employs the notion of space, there is no necessary conflict between these two dicta of Aristotle's. For *apeiron* and greatness-and-smallness are concepts out of the same stable. But it is possible, as we have seen, that "greatness-and-smallness", as the name of a material element, refers only to the material element in the numerical properties which the forms embody. In that case talk of unity and greatness-and-smallness would be appropriate in the context of the logical analysis of forms into their elements, the analysis of things being into forms as their formal, "space" as their material element.

However that may be, it seems likely that the forms which Plato treated as intimately connected with numerical properties were something much more abstract than the common natures of physical things, in so far as the latter phrase includes a reference to the details of the structure of physical things. Forms, we have suggested, stood to common natures in roughly the relation in which the client's specification stands to the architect's working drawings. All men have hair on their heads and livers in their bellies not because these details are comprised in the form of manhood, but because the nature of the materials which the properties of "space" make it possible to construct is such that to realise instances of the form of manhood it is expedient to employ these devices.

VIII. CONCLUSION

We have seen that in some of Plato's earlier writings much is made of the claim for exalted status on behalf of certain general terms. We have seen also that in certain later writings themes reappear which make no sense except in terms of the range of ideas which also provides the motive for the claim for exalted status in the earlier writings (I am thinking in particular of the treatment of *peras* and *apeiron* in the *Philebus*); and we have seen that the same applies to the Platonic doctrines which we hear of in Aristotle only. It is also true however that, so far as Plato's later *writings* are concerned, the discussion of general terms and their relationships is often carried on without any reference to exalted status. It is a mistake therefore to suppose that Plato was obsessed to the point of monomania with

471

what we may call the topic of Forms with a capital F, though it is also a mistake to suppose that he ever abandoned belief in such entities.

Belief in Forms is belief in objects of reason; that is what Forms are. To discuss the nature of Forms; to ask whether P-hood is a Form; to claim that there is a relation between Forms and numerical properties—all topics of this kind are concerned with the question: If Reason is something which is eternal and which is prior to the ordered cosmos, what must we posit as the objects of its contemplation? The urge towards the highest degree of abstraction, which is evident throughout the treatment of Forms from the *Republic* to the unwritten doctrines, is due to the thought that if reason is independent of the cosmos and yet responsible for its order, there must be objects which it apprehends which are not implicated in the details of physical existence, which can serve as principles capable of being *brought to* physical nature in order to impose upon it an orderliness which it does not possess in its own right. The key to the topic of Forms is the doctrine of *Laws* 10 that mind is prior to bodies. There is however a good deal of discussion of general terms for which we do not need this key.

"(*Note on p. 393; Second Impression*). What is said in the text on p. 393 is clearly wrong. The point that Plato is making against Parmenides may well be that names have to be mentioned *even in the last analysis*, whereas other things do not. It is, Plato may well be suggesting, supposed by the Eleatics to be metaphysical truth, reached by "the way of knowledge", that "only the one exists; all else is mere names". But to say this is to say that names figure in the ultimate account of reality, alongside unity and existence."

4

LOGIC AND LANGUAGE

I. FORMAL AND INFORMAL LOGIC

The established doctrine that Aristotle invented formal logic has sometimes been disputed, rather unwisely, on Plato's behalf; but the truth is that there is nö evidence in Plato's writings that the notion of formal logic ever occurred to him, and he made no contribution to it. The formal logician investigates the force of certain words (the so-called logical constants such as *all, some, a, none, not, if, and, or*) and he exhibits the force of these words in terms of each other by constructing models of statements and saying how they are related. Thus he tells us that "All S is P" entails "Some S is P" and is incompatible with "This S is not P" and so on. The idea of doing this first occurred to Aristotle (though he would not perhaps have described it in the terms we have used). It does not seem to have occurred to Plato.

Among Socrates' contemporaries and also probably among Plato's there were those who exploited the practice of argument in such a way as to bring discredit on it. The plain man, clearly, was in danger of coming to think that argument can prove anything. It was necessary, if logical reasoning was not to be discredited, that somebody should show that it is only by invalid reasoning that we can prove that black is white. It is obvious that Plato believed in logical reasoning and that he also believed that it can be done well or badly. It is not clear to me, however, that he was altogether emancipated from the view that demonstration is a kind of persuasion (though it is certainly true that he sometimes—e.g. *Timaeus* 51 e—distinguishes between demonstrating and persuading). I suspect that he retained to some extent the view that the sovereign defence against the solicitations of invalid argument was the practice of keeping one's eye on the realities which are being discussed rather than on the words or concepts which are used in discussing them. Nevertheless he was plainly conscious of the fact that some pieces of fallacious reasoning depend upon failure to observe the logical peculiarities of the concepts we employ—though he might have described this as a failure to notice the peculiar features of the entities which we mention in our discussions.

There are in the dialogues a fair number of places where the fallacy-provoking features of certain concepts (or entities) are pointed out or hinted at. There is however nothing that could be called the beginnings of a systematic classification of the sources of fallacy, and there is very little that has to do with the fallacies that arise from the misuse of logical constants. In so far as Plato's interest in what we now call logic was to warn us of the pits that we may fall into, he was largely right to devote relatively little attention to the logical constants. Fallacies do not often depend on failure to use such notions correctly. A common fallacy which does do this is that of inferring "All P is S" from "All S is P", and Plato does in fact warn us against this in the *Protagoras* (350 c 6 sqq.). But our fallacious reasonings depend much less often on the mishandling of logical constants, much more often on things like simple ambiguity, or the assumption that if two notions behave in the same way part of the time they behave in the same way all the time. Thus, to take an example of ambiguity which is exposed in the *Euthydemus* (276–8), *manthanein* in Greek means "to learn" and "to understand", and this can be used to show that it is impossible to learn anything; for we can only *manthanein* (understand) what we understand, but we can only *manthanein* (learn) what we do not understand. Or, to take an example of the assumption that notions of similar must be of identical behaviour, "brave" and "numerous" are both predicates, yet if the Greeks are brave it can be presumed that this Greek is brave, whereas if the Greeks are numerous it cannot be presumed that this Greek is numerous (cp. *Hippias Major* 301–2 where approximately this point is made).

There are a good many instances of the detection of ambiguity and of similar fallacy-sources in the dialogues. The *Euthydemus* contains several, some of them depending on technical terms like *parousia* ("presence", a name for the relation of a universal to its particulars), some on ordinary terms like *manthanein*, some on peculiarities of Greek syntax.[1] The *Lysis* has a good deal to say about the ambiguity of a particular notion, namely *philos*, a word which can mean "friend of", "fond of" and "dear to", though it conveys its message not be explicating the ambiguity but by entangling the reader in it. There are also a number of places where the idiosyncrasies of

---

[1] *Parousia Euthydemus* 301 a, cp. *Lysis* 217 c sq.; for a syntactical equivocation see *Euthydemus* 301 d, where the trick depends on the fact that the subject of a verb in the infinitive is in the accusative case.

particular kinds of notions are pointed out or at least hinted at, though there is nowhere any systematic treatment of such topics. There is the distinction quoted above from the *Hippias Major*; in the *Charmides* (167–9) a distinction is drawn between reflexive and irreflexive relations, not of course in these words; in the *Theaetetus* (154–5) Socrates draws attention to those properties (such as *being greater than B*) which a subject can acquire without thereby undergoing change. The *Parmenides* contains a large number of arguments the main purpose of which, perhaps, was to draw attention to the logical peculiarities of certain concepts. (See for example *Parmenides* 152 a where the slipperiness of comparative adjectives such as "older" and "younger" is exploited to produce the conclusion that what gets older must get younger).

It seems to me that if a collection was made of all the places where Plato makes contributions such as these to what is sometimes called informal logic the total bulk would be impressive; and to fail to make such a collection must somewhat distort the overall picture of Plato's philosophical activity. I do not however intend to make such a collection, and the reader is asked to correct the picture accordingly.

II. THE *CRATYLUS* ON LANGUAGE

In the *Cratylus* Plato is very much in his Lewis Carroll vein. Socrates is asked to intervene in an argument between Cratylus and Hermogenes. Hermogenes maintains a conventionalist view of language. The proper meaning of a word is what it is used to stand for: to have meaning is to be used consistently. This Cratylus disputes, though the grounds on which he disputes it are not very clear. Socrates seems to favour a compromise solution according to which conventional usage is all that is *strictly necessary* for signification, but certain sounds are none the less *naturally* suited to carry certain meanings, so that it is *better* that these sounds should be used for these meanings. To this he adds the stipulation that in a well-made language the relations between sounds should reflect the relations which hold between the types of things they signify. Thus "dogfish" should not be used for dogfish unless they are, as it implies, in some way a doggy kind of fish.

But this discussion is used, Carroll-wise, as a thread on which to hang a great many light-hearted allusions to philosophical views. Thus the stipulation that the structure of language should mirror the structure of the world leads to a (frivolously conducted) discussion of derivations; for it is assumed that complex poly-syllabic words stand for entities of complex "poly-syllabic" nature. In this discussion a striking tendency towards the Heraclitean doctrine of flux is detected in the authors of the Greek language. And in some of the particular derivations Socrates manages (often by gross and admitted *tours de force*) to represent particular words as condensed statements of philosophical positions, sometimes Platonic and sometimes not. Thus the word "Hades", to take a Platonic example, is found to show that its coiners believed the after life to be a condition of glad purification and not of terror.

It is incidentally interesting, in view of the fact that Aristotle tells us that it was Cratylus who persuaded Plato of Heracliteanism, that he is treated in this dialogue as a noodle.

The essentials of the dialogue are as follows.

Words throughout are referred to according to standard Greek usage as names (*onomata*), and the view underlying this usage, that all words signify by standing for realities, is influential at least to the extent of determining the way in which things are said; though as we shall see Plato is already coming to see that even if all words are names, words are not always *used as* names.

Socrates begins with an antinomy. There are true and false propositions, and propositions are composed of names. A true proposition "says what is", a false proposition "says what is not". Therefore it would seem natural to say that, as a true proposition represents, through a string of names, something which is the case, therefore each name in it truly names some feature in the existing situation; and hence there would seem to be true (and false) names. (I have expanded the argument to give what seems to me to be its point. Socrates simply says that the parts of a true statement must themselves be true). And yet, as Hermogenes urges, it would seem reasonable to say that if I consistently call men horses, then "horses" is the name for men in my language. So on this view Humpty Dumpty would be right and there would be no true names.

This leads Socrates to consider the function of language. They begin by agreeing that even if man is master of words he is not master of facts. Protagoras' view that "what seems to a man, is to that man" is refuted along the lines of the refutation in the *Theaetetus*.[1] There are, then, ineluctable facts to which speakers must conform themselves; and there are, similarly, right and wrong ways of doing things. Speaking being an activity there will be a right and a wrong way of doing it; and since "naming" or word-coining is a part of speaking, the same will apply to it: there will be a right and a wrong way of doing it, and the right way will be determined by the purpose of the activity.

The purpose of shuttle-making is to enable weavers to weave. The purpose of word-making is to enable speakers to distinguish one

[1] See above, pp. 8–10.

thing from another. The existence of the word "table" for example enables me to single out tables and make statements about them. Words or names therefore are a sort of tools, their function being to distinguish what is being talked about from what is not. A carpenter must make a shuttle with its function in mind ("looking to the form"); he must make the kind of thing which is naturally suited to do the work a shuttle has to do, and furthermore the particular kind of work that this particular shuttle is required for (apparently there were different sorts of shuttles for different sorts of work). Tool-making in general is a matter of giving the material the properties which it needs for the work it has to do, the user of the tool being the judge of whether this has been correctly done.

Likewise the word-maker must keep his eye on what it is to be a name, and in particular must know how to shape his material (namely sounds) into a set of names, each of them naturally suited to the thing whose name it is. What sounds he uses is immaterial (and will differ, it is implied, in different languages) provided that each object is given the kind of name suitable to it. (390 a). Since the general function of words is to discriminate, and since the discriminator *par excellence* is the dialectician, it is the dialectician or philosopher who can judge whether a language has been well made.

There is, then, an analogy drawn between shuttles and words. Each is a kind of tool and has a general function, and within each kind there are sub-kinds with special functions within the general function. In each case the form that the tool takes depends on its function. The obvious criticism of this analogy is that whereas the function of a shuttle does determine its form, the function of a word does not. A shuttle (I believe) has to be carried backwards and forwards between a lot of crossed threads, and therefore has to have a certain shape; whereas a word has merely to distinguish, and therefore can be any sound you please provided the same sound is not used for two different words. Shuttles therefore have their form determined to some extent by their general function whereas words do not; *cat* and *felis* serve equally well to distinguish cats from other things.

So the analogy applies badly at the level of the general function; how about the special functions? Here the implication is that just as there are special kinds of shuttles for special kinds of weaving so there are special kinds of names for special kinds of distinguishing. At first sight this seems to express true and important doctrine. If we call the relation between any word and reality "naming", then it is true to say that within this general relation there are many special relations, and therefore many kinds of naming. An ordinary noun such as "cat" has corresponding to it a special class of objects, for each of which the word "cat" answers the question "What is it?".

To an ordinary adjective such as "grey" there corresponds a class of objects, for each of which the word "grey" answers the question "What is it *like*?". An abstract noun such as "cat-hood" or "grey-ness" does not mean the same as the corresponding ordinary noun or adjective; and yet insofar as there is any class of objects corresponding to "cat-hood", it is the same class of objects as corresponds to "cat". The abstract noun is not the name of a special thing or class of things: it relates to the same things as the corresponding concrete noun or adjective, but it is used when we want to speak of them in a different way. There are then different relations in which words stand to reality (the three illustrated by "cat", "grey", and "cat-hood" and many more) and therefore different kinds of naming. And it could easily be said that these different special functions do or should affect the forms of words. Thus it should be possible to tell at a glance whether a given sound is used for a noun, an adjective, an abstract noun, or something else; and in an inflected language such as Greek this is on the whole possible to a large extent.

So far so good. Such doctrine is wholesome and it would seem to follow from the analogy between kinds of shuttles and kinds of words if we pressed it. But I doubt whether it is plausible to say that Plato intended it. From the way the dialogue goes it is much more likely that he has something quite different in mind. The leading idea seems to be that things are related to each other, and that names ought to reflect these relationships. Thus for example male and female lions are alike though not identical, and there ought to be in any language a sound which singles out the whole class of lions of either sex, and also sounds which single out male lions and female lions; and the relationship between the sounds ought to indicate the relationship between the things they "name". If this illustrates the kind of thing Plato has in mind, we shall have to say that the analogy is misleading: for naming lions and naming tigers are not different kinds of naming, but merely naming of different things; and nothing follows from the nature of what is named concerning the form of the name except the general rule that the names of different things must be different.[1] The function of the dialectician as a judge of language will be simply that of deciding whether the range of coverage allotted to a given sound confounds dissimilars. We shall have to leave to Aristotle the credit of having distinguished different "kinds of naming"—for example the substantival and the adjectival use of sounds.

---

[1] Unless it is assumed—as subterraneously it is—that certain sounds *naturally* evoke certain notions. In that case a sound to be used to refer to cats would have its form determined by the fact that certain sounds are naturally appropriate for the work of putting us in mind of these animals.

478

At any rate Socrates is not made to press the analogy. It has been established that naming has a function—discrimination—and that there are special functions within that general function, and hence that word-coining is a skilled business; a name has only been rightly given if the giver has "looked to what is the natural name of each thing, and succeeded in expressing its form in letters and syllables" (390 a). *W* is only the right name for something if *W* is naturally suited to be the sound for that thing. This establishes that there is such a thing as "rightness of names", but not what it is, and they turn to the Greek language for insight into this latter question.

We will not follow the details of this investigation, but we will observe that it is assumed from the start that rightness of names is a matter of mutual relations between words, and not of the relation of a single word to what it stands for. I mean this. It could be held that when a word is the right word for something its rightness depends on some sort of natural affinity between the word and the thing—say between "horse" and horses. This would make rightness a sound-thing relationship as we will call it. On the other hand, and of course much more reasonably, it could be held that no word can be called right or wrong considered by itself, but only by relating it to other words. Thus if a sixth child is born into a family the parents can give it any name they wish, except a name which already belongs to one of the other children. To have two Johns in the family would defeat the object of naming, which is to distinguish. Similarly it would be wrong to use "horse" for cows as well as for horses though there is nothing in the sound "horse" which makes it in itself an improper sound to use for cows. This would make rightness and wrongness of names a sound-sound relationship (as we will call it). For the moment at any rate Socrates discusses the rightness of names in sound-sound terms.

This comes out for example in his meditations about the names of Hector the champion of Troy and his son Astyanax. Each of these names seems to imply that its bearer is a protector of the city; and this is perfectly proper. For if Astyanax followed (as might be expected) his father he too would in time become the champion of Troy and so it was right that he should be given what is in one sense the same name as his father. Just as doctors disguise the active principle in their medicines with all kinds of flavours, so the word-maker is at liberty to allow euphony and many other considerations to influence his construction of sounds provided that the final product means what it ought to mean, in the sense that the combined meaning of its components does accurately describe what it is used for, as "Hector" and "Astyanax" accurately describe anybody who is or may be expected to become a champion in his city.

Proceeding on these lines Socrates conducts, in frivolous vein, what is I suppose the earliest extant discussion of the derivation of words. He has indeed little to say about such topics as consonantal changes (how *p* in Greek often becomes *qu* in Latin and so on) though he does recognise the existence of such processes in the development of languages; but his attention is chiefly given to derivation in the sense in which "shepherd" may be said to be derived from "sheep" and "herd". As we said earlier he amuses himself by finding a number of philosophical morals pointed in the derivation of words.

However all talk of derivations brings one in the end to the subject of roots; and as we saw in the last chapter Socrates enunciates a theory according to which there are elements of reality with elementary sounds corresponding to them, so that the rightness of names consists in most cases in the correspondence between the elements in a complex sound and the elements in the complex reality it is used to name.

The theory is stated in the following terms (421–6). They have been seeking the meaning of names (the word for "meaning" is *rêma* or what the word says), and such an investigation cannot go on indefinitely. A compound word whose parts are themselves words (e.g. "shepherd" or "catfish") can imply a theory about the nature of the objects it is used to name. But if one goes on to ask what theory is implied by a simple word whose parts are not themselves words (e.g. "sheep" or "cat"), either one will have to say that no theory is implied by such a word concerning the nature of the things it names, or one will have to resolve the word into elements (e.g. the *sh* sound in "fish" might signify a gliding motion, so that "fish" would imply the theory that fishes glide). But at any rate at some point one would have to come down to elementary words or sounds whose use is to be explained not as the use of "shepherd" is to be explained (i.e. where the word implies an obvious theory about the nature of its referents) but in some other way. As to the nature of this other way, Socrates says that if we had no speech we should indicate objects, or in other words discharge the function of speech, by imitative gesture; it would seem then natural, he argues, to suppose that the elementary parts of speech are imitative gestures with the voice. On this Socrates sets the qualification that what we imitate in speech is the essence (*ousia*) and not the obvious sensible properties of things; we do not bellow when we want to speak of bulls. Nor (he seems to imply) would imitation of this kind indicate "*what* each thing is", even though it might succeed in conveying the intended reference. Ideal imitation would reproduce in the sound each of the factors which make the object referred to what it is, so that in a language which consisted of ideal imitations we should be able to tell from an inspection of a word the nature of the objects for which it stood—not perhaps how they would look, sound or smell, but their essential constitution on which no doubt their sensible properties in some way depend. (423–4. In 423 e Socrates seems to confuse imitating the *ousia* of forms, such as what it is to be a colour, with imitating the *ousia* of things which are, *inter alia*, coloured. At any rate he passes from speaking of imitating, as painters do, the colours of things, to imitating the *ousia* of colour. Imitating the *ousia* of the things whose appearances painters imitate —such as bulls—would seem to be a half-way house).

Therefore to construct an ideal language (Socrates speaks for the moment as if he assumes that Greek is such) one would have to do the following things: (*a*) resolve sounds into their elements or letters, classifying these into their kinds; (*b*) discover whether there are any elements in reality, and, assuming that there are, classify these also; finally, (*c*) put letters together into syllables, syllables into words and words into statements (which consist of *onomata* and *rêmata* or names and things said) in such a way that the completed statement is like a portrait of the fact which it conveys. (424–5).

(It is interesting to observe that Socrates speaks as if a statement were merely a more complex picture than a word; "fish" depicts or should depict the essence of fishes, "salt fish" the essence of salt fish, and "There is salt fish for dinner today" depicts presumably in like manner the preparations now going forward in the kitchen. The idea that statements are very long complex words underlies the view that there can be no meaningful false propositions; for a false proposition would have to depict what is not, or in other words nothing, and so would be meaningless).

Socrates admits that this theory of ideal imitation is a very odd one, but holds that it is implied by the notion that there is such a thing as rightness of names—that the relation of words to things is not purely conventional (425 d). But in fact Socrates is going to retreat from the theory that language is essentially a system of ideal imitations.

He begins (426 b) by bringing the theory down to brass tacks by making some tentative identifications of elementary notions and the sounds which convey them—*i* for example might signify lightness, *l* smoothness, *r* motion and so on. What he intends to do is to show that even if the origin of language is to be explained in terms of the natural affinity or "resemblance" which holds between sounds and basic constituents of reality in this way, so that words were built up out of the sounds which portray what were thought to be the essential features of their referents—even if this is true, the fact remains that a badly constructed word (according to these standards) can be just as effective in speech as a well-constructed one. From this it would

481

follow that affinity or resemblance between word and reality cannot be a necessary feature of language though it may be a desirable one. Thus the Greek word *sklêros* which means "hard" or "harsh" contains the *l* which is supposed to portray smoothness; one can say that the word *ought* to be *skrêros*, but one cannot deny that *sklêros*, however ill-formed, is universally understood. *Sklêros* may be a *bad* name for hardness, but it *is* its name.

To substantiate this however Socrates has to meet an objection from Cratylus to the effect that there can be no bad names; there can be names, and sounds which are not names, and that is all. This view Socrates treats as part of the familiar view that there can be no false propositions. Cratylus is not a conventionalist; he is not saying that any name which is generally used is the right name and therefore cannot be a bad one. His view is that if a name fails to portray what it is used of, as "Hermogenes" ("scion of the god of good luck") fails to portray Hermogenes, then it is the name of something else; so that if Hermogenes is addressed or introduced as Hermogenes the speaker has not correctly or incorrectly addressed or introduced him; he has simply made a non-significant noise. For (I think this is what is implied) the gesture, or whatever effected the act of addressing or introducing, made it clear that the accompanying sound was intended to refer to Hermogenes, whereas the meaning of the sound makes it clear that it could not refer to Hermogenes as he is not the scion of the god of good luck. Therefore the sound must be regarded as something that should not have happened, like a hiccough, and not as a piece of significant speech. Cratylus applies this doctrine to ordinary words as well as to proper names. (429–30).

This sounds silly, but there is a real difficulty which is being got at. Consider the phrase "the morning star", and imagine that there is a rigid distinction between stars and planets. Now the object which is called the morning star is not a star but a planet. Evidently therefore if somebody, hearing the phrase, looked for a specially matutinal star for it to refer to, he would not think of the planet Venus and therefore he would not stumble upon the object to which the phrase does in fact refer. For the meaning of the phrase is inappropriate to its reference. Again, if hearing splashing sounds from Brown's bathroom, I say "Brown is having a bath" when in fact he is shaving, the meaning of the expression I use is inappropriate to its reference (if I may stretch the sense of that phrase). A false proposition can therefore be regarded as a kind of misnomer of a fact. But in the case of misnomers the question can be asked: How, since the expression in question cannot *mean* what it misnames, can it be said to *refer* to that thing or situation? Since what it means is something which is not the case, it must mean nothing and hence be a mere noise.

The question how a misnomer can refer to that which it misnames is not of course a difficult one, though the assumption which provokes the question, namely that expressions refer solely by virtue of their meaning, is one that still sometimes gives trouble. Forgetting for the moment about propositions, a phrase which misdescribes what it refers to can be said to refer to that thing provided it is in some way known what that phrase is commonly, or is on this occasion, used to refer to. Thus a man who knows that Venus is a planet has no trouble with the phrase "the morning star" because he knows that it is conventionally used for Venus; and when you point at a rabbit and say "Look at that cat" it is your gesture which tells me what it is that you are misdescribing. Reference is not fixed solely by meaning and hence misnomers are possible and can indeed function perfectly efficiently in communication.

Socrates says that he is too old for such subtleties, but in effect he makes the correct answer. (*Socrates* nowhere dissects the problem in detail, though it is mentioned more than once. It is left to the Eleatic Stranger to treat it at length. Perhaps it would have been too anachronistic to allow Socrates to do so). He says that a name, like a picture, is an imitation; it is easy to see that I may pair off pictures and originals and furthermore may do it wrong. I can give George a picture of Jane and tell him it is a picture of himself. This, Socrates says, is exactly analogous to calling a man a woman (430–1). This is of course a highly informal solution, but by invoking the notion of *pairing-off* it makes the essential point that expressions can be allotted to objects and that the allotment need not be done by virtue of resemblance or fitness.

He has not however fully grasped the point and he goes on to spoil it. Cratylus will not have it that a non-complex word could be (through faulty combination of elements) a bad imitation, contending that if I leave out some of the letters in a word or put wrong ones in, I do not spell that word incorrectly; I spell something else. Misnomers would be, like mis-spellings, not incorrect representations but representations of something else. To this Socrates retorts that an imitation does not have to be a reduplication of its original (that would be a second original); it only needs to have the *tupos* or stamp of its original; in other words it must resemble it just sufficiently for it to be possible to discern what it is an imitation of. If that much life-like-ness is given, we know what it is meant to resemble and can go on to decide whether it does it well or ill. This retort is fair enough in the case of pictures, but to use it to explain the possibility of words which imply erroneous theories, but which carry in practice the meaning they are intended to carry, is to under-estimate the force of convention and other such factors in the use of language. (431–3).

However, Socrates has established that there can be misnomers and can return to the ideal imitation theory of language. The function of words being to indicate things there are two possible views of the origin of non-complex words. Either they are attempted reproductions in sound of the realities they stand for, or we must suppose that realities were first distinguished without the aid of language (433 e 4) and that a word was then allotted to each by convention. The former view seems the more plausible but it has to meet the objection that words containing the wrong elements can do their work perfectly well (the *l* in *sklēros* does not impair its efficiency as the name for hardness). Furthermore it would be impossible to imitate all the numbers in sound. Therefore resemblance may be a desirable feature in words but it cannot be necessary to their significance. For that, convention is enough, in the sense of a habitual recognition that when a certain sound is being uttered a certain thing is being thought of by the utterer.

Socrates then (435 d) rather abruptly widens the scope of the conversation by asking again what language is for. He thus brings to the surface something which has been going on beneath the surface of the dialogue and which underlies the view that resemblance is a desirable feature of words. For earlier the function of words had been said to be to *distinguish* entities; but "distinguish" has gradually given way to "declare" (*dēloun*) and there has been building up the idea, which Cratylus now espouses, that when a word is used it ought to be possible not only to know *what* precisely is being talked about, but also what the thing which is being talked about *is* (i.e. what its essence is). The resemblance which ought to hold between words and things should make it possible from an inspection of a word to know what the thing it stands for is like. Indeed Cratylus makes himself the first (and perhaps the only true) "linguistic philosopher" by declaring that there is no other way of studying reality but the study of it in its names. To this Socrates very reasonably retorts that it seems a very dangerous method of philosophising; for if the father of language has made a mistake or two in his depiction of realities we may be led seriously astray, especially in the case of complex expressions, in which an initial error might be heavily multiplied. (435-6).

This thought makes Socrates reconsider the derivations of common words. His previous investigation had uncovered a Heraclitean slant in the views of the father of language; now of course he detects a number of words with an anti-Heraclitean tendency; there would seem to be some cross-currents at the fount. Without however pressing this point, Socrates attacks Cratylus' view with a dilemma which is fatal to it. Either it is impossible to study reality directly, in which case the father of language could never have studied it, found out what things are like and given them appropriate names; or it is not impossible to study reality directly, in which case it is silly to confine one's attention to names, which are only reproductions, when one might attend to the originals, and learn of them by direct inspection and comparison one with another. (436-8).

This disposes of Cratylus' linguisticism, and the dialogue ends with an attack on extreme Heracliteanism which closely parallels that in the *Theaetetus*, but which I will briefly reproduce. Socrates begins by inviting Cratylus to agree with his "recurring dream", that there is such a thing as goodness and beauty and all the other universal natures. Cratylus does so. Socrates then proposes that they should dismiss the question whether perhaps beautiful faces may be in a state of flux (Heracliteanism as a physical theory is not in question), and ask whether beauty itself does not always remain the same. It is agreed that it does. If it did not it would have no properties; nor could it be known, for "on the approach of the knower it would change" so that one could never characterise it, and what is character-less could not be known.[1] Again the view that everything changes would directly entail that there is no such thing as knowledge, independently of the fate of its objects; for knowledge would have to change also, and would not be a distinct state. Therefore it must be allowed that that which knows and that which is known (beauty, goodness etc.) are unchanging (*estin aei*). Whether or not Hera-cliteanism is acceptable as a physical theory, it certainly seems that it cannot be extended to the point of saying that there are no such things as stable properties. This however, Socrates concludes, is a baffling problem, and one which certainly cannot be settled from an inspection of language.

It will be seen that this is a less bold attack on Heracliteanism than that in the *Theaetetus*. In the latter dialogue Socrates seems to want to say that stones and sticks can be said to be white or whatever it may be and that this implies some persistence in physical objects. Here he dismisses the question of physical objects and confines him-self to saying that there must be stable properties without reference to the question how far they can be ascribed to things.

The *Cratylus* has been an inconclusive dialogue. It has canvassed a number of important notions but has sat on a good many fences. It shows a liking for the view that speech is a form of imitative gesture

---

[1] 439 e–440 a. It might be thought that this passage *could* mean (with *Sophist* 248) that an unchanging thing cannot be known, since knowing it must change it. I do not believe it does mean this however as the passage is too short for the making of such an unexpected point.

at bottom which develops into articulate language through the joining together of imitative vocal gestures into syllables which do or should correspond to the syllables of reality. But at the same time it is conscious of the fact that, for the distinguishing of objects which is the essential purpose of speech, convention will suffice. The additional advantage of an ideal imitation language—that it is declaratory of the nature of reality—is shown to be no real advantage in that to know that one was dealing with such a language one would already have to know what reality is like, and hence would not need the illumination language offers. Likewise it develops the notion of derivation, and assumes that it is natural to suppose that the reference of a complex word is fixed for it by the force of its elements; but it is aware of the fact that the existence of perfectly significant misnomers makes this a notion which must be carefully handled. It has not got rid of the view that a proposition is a very long and complex word; but in using the simile of giving a man what you suppose to be his portrait it has made the essential first move towards understanding what a proposition is. It is the development of this which is the great contribution of the *Sophist* to which we will shortly return.

Meanwhile there is one final comment to be made on the *Cratylus*, and that is that Plato operates the notion of imitation according to very lax rules. He cannot suppose that a man rolling his tongue to the letter *r* can plausibly be said to be *imitating* movement. What he wants here (as he also wants it in the discussion of music and dancing in the *Laws*)[1] is a vaguer notion of "expressive affinity" or something of the kind. The point is that there is some kind of affinity —though not resemblance—between certain sounds and certain realities, such that it is natural to utter the former when one's mind is full of the latter. This makes Plato's aesthetic theories seem less peculiar.

III. THE PARADOX OF FALSE BELIEF

The Paradox of False Belief consists of a family of arguments which appear to show that there can be no meaningful false propositions and therefore no false beliefs. This has of course the consequence that the ordinary view that some beliefs are false cannot be true and must be dismissed as incoherent babbling.[2] This consequence might be treated (as perhaps Parmenides treated it) as a further instance of the fact that all opinions which do not rest on *a priori* reasoning are

[1] See Vol. 1, pp. 188–91.
[2] If you say that it is logically true that all propositions are true, you do not have to allow that "Some propositions are false" is true; for this might be a contradictory form of words and hence not a proposition.

486

vanity, not even candidates for the epithet "true", and their expression mere empty sound having no reference to reality. Or one might attempt (with Protagoras) to render plausible the view that all opinions are true including, perhaps, the opinion that this is not the case.[1] (Each of these solutions would amount to a proposal to abandon the ordinary *true/false* classification of beliefs). Or a more robust reaction would be to treat the Paradox as a further instance of the fact that reliance on abstract logical argument can induce us to believe what is patently absurd. Plato took the fourth of the possible responses to the Paradox, that namely of assuming that if the arguments purport to prove that there can be no false opinions there must be something wrong with the arguments. He several times recurs to the Paradox without solving it to his satisfaction before he disposes of it in the *Sophist*. There is some reason to think that he began by supposing that it would be fairly easy to solve the Paradox if one gave one's mind to it and ended by realising that considerable conceptual readjustments were necessary if it was to be avoided. It seems impossible to say whether his abiding interest in the Paradox was due to a desire to restore faith in abstract argument in those who thought the Paradox obviously silly, or to a dislike of the conclusions extracted from it by those who thought it valid. Probably it was due to both of these factors. We must now look at the passages which discuss the Paradox.

A. *Inconclusive discussions of the Paradox*

1. *The* Republic. We have discussed in an earlier chapter[2] the brief appearance which the Paradox makes in the Fifth Book of the *Republic*. We saw there that the paradox depends essentially (*a*) on treating *that*-clauses as names of states of affairs; and (*b*) on assuming that epithets such as "non-existent" which properly belong to states of affairs can harmlessly be transferred to the *that*-clauses which, *ex hypothesi*, name them. In a word it depends essentially on failure to use the notion of a proposition in the analysis of belief. This diagnosis of the trouble will be drawn upon in the discussions which follow. Meanwhile with regard to the passage in the *Republic*, it is to our immediate purpose to remember that while Plato does not scruple to use an argument belonging to the Paradox, it is not at all his intention to deploy the Paradox; and that he fails to see that the resolution of the Paradox will require a change in his terminology for

---

[1] The discussion in the *Theaetetus* suggests that Protagoras did not in fact face this consequence (see above, p. 9). I do not mean to say that Parmenides and Protagoras took the views that I say they might have taken.

[2] Above pp. 59–63.

the discussion of cognitive states. This may perhaps be taken as showing that he has not at this stage taken the problem seriously. He uses the language which leads to the problem, and he uses an argument which begets the paradoxical conclusion without intending that conclusion. This looks as if he felt that he could resist the passage from the argument to the conclusion without reforming his terminology.

2. *The* Euthydemus. The passage in the *Euthydemus* runs from 283–7. In the dialogue as a whole the two sophists, Euthydemus and Dionysodorus, who tease Socrates and his friend Ctesippus, maintain a number of silly paradoxes, most of them resting on very obvious fallacies. But among their paradoxes are: that there can be no false statements, and that contradiction is impossible. (The latter is of course a corollary of the former, for if neither "Jones is drunk" nor "Jones is not drunk" is false, clearly they cannot be contradictory).

That there can be no false statements is contended on the ground that even a false statement must "say the thing that the statement is about" (283 e 9), and this must be some existing thing, some *on*. But any statement that says some existing thing says the truth. In other words if a statement refers to (*legei*, "says") something, e.g. today's weather, it must state today's weather and therefore it must state something which is. To the retort that a false statement, none the less, does not state what is, it is replied that in that case it must state what is-not (or rather the latter formulation is surreptitiously substituted for the former, 284 b 1–3), that what is-not is a nonentity, and that, since nothing can be done to nonentities, they cannot be stated.

The second part of the argument, as presented, may have seemed to Plato to depend on the surreptitious substitution mentioned above. So far as the first part of the argument is concerned, it is obvious that there is an ambiguity in the word *legein* as we have indicated. That however is not quite the whole story. The ambiguity is not an accidental ambiguity but one which depends on treating a proposition as a representation of the state of affairs to which it refers; what the statement *legei* (says, states or mentions) is what it puts into words. We cannot get rid of the trouble until we see that a proposition mentions a subject and says something of it. If we think that "It will be fine today" is about, not today's weather, but the clemency of today's weather, then we shall have to think that if it rains all day there will be nothing for it to be about. So long as "S is P" is a picture, not of S, but of S's being P, we are in trouble where "S is P" is false. Ctesippus half-sees the difficulty, for he says that a false statement "says things which are . . . but not *as* they are". This could be developed into the view that a false statement mentions realities but misrepresents them. Dionysodorus however takes it to mean, e.g., that a true statement states warm things warmly (this being "as they are"), and the argument dies away into abuse.

The abuse leads on to the next paradox (285 d 7), namely that contradiction is impossible. This is contended on the ground that each thing has its statement or account, and that any other statement is not an account of that thing. Only the true statement about X, in other words, belongs to X; any other statement belongs to something else and hence cannot conflict; for to conflict two statements must belong to the same subject and assert different things about it. Here again it is evident that it is the distinction between subject and predicate that is needed to clear the matter up. Socrates however merely says that he has a crude mind which cannot understand such arguments, and asks Euthydemus and Dionysodorus how, if there is no such thing as false beliefs, they can offer to teach anything; for if there are no false beliefs any opinion should be as good as any other.

It is not clear how seriously Plato took these arguments at this stage. What is clear however is that these paradoxes occur among others of a very low level, and the presumption perhaps is that Plato thought that these also were of little account. It seems evident to us that we shall not get rid of them without employing the notion of reference, but it may not have seemed so to him; he may have thought that they depended on simple ambiguity like many others in the same dialogue.

3. *The* Cratylus. We have recently examined the account in the *Cratylus*.[1] It is only necessary to remind ourselves that the *Cratylus* both makes very clear how the trouble arises and also takes the essential step towards getting rid of it. It does the former by treating all significant expressions, including sentences, as names, and by using for them the analogy of a picture; and it does the second by introducing the notion of reference under the guise of the act whereby I give George Jane's picture and tell him that it is a picture of him. This makes the point that, somehow, an expression which belies something can nevertheless refer to the thing which it belies.

4. *The* Theaetetus. As we have seen in an earlier chapter, the Paradox is glanced at in two places in the *Theaetetus* if our understanding of that dialogue is correct.[2] It appears first in a somewhat psychological version in the passage where Socrates is discussing, not so much the question how there can be false propositions, as how we can believe them. We remember that his difficulty essentially is: error would seem to be impossible since we cannot believe anything,

---

[1] Above pp. 482–3.   [2] See above Chapter 1, pp. 107–20.

erroneous or otherwise, about something of which we are ignorant, and we cannot believe something erroneous about something which we know. As we saw above, the difficulty in this form invites us to introduce the notion of degrees of knowledge and ignorance, of being in and out of touch with something. I cannot refer to something which I am completely out of touch with, but to intend my statement to refer to it I do not need to be so intimately in touch with it that I become infallible about it. This solution of the difficulty, though it has a psychological flavour, is not unconnected with the more logical solution in terms of reference and of the distinction between subject and predicate. Let us allow that in order to refer to something we do not need to know all about it, we only need to know, so to speak, where to find it. This will still not solve our problem by itself, so long as we fail to see that that to which we refer is that which is "named" by the subject term. If I wrongly believe that Jones has a moustache, the doctrine of degrees of acquaintance will solve our difficulties so long as we realise that "Jones has a moustache" refers to Jones and not to Jones's possession of a moustache. All we need say is that I know whom I mean by Jones, but do not claim to know everything about him. But if "Jones has a moustache" refers either to the actual state of the topic as a whole (viz. Jones's clean-shaven-ness) or to the alleged state of the topic (viz. Jones's possession of a moustache) then in either case I must be totally out of touch with what I refer to, since in the first case I totally traduce it and in the second it is non-existent.

This comes out clearly in the section (188–90) in which Socrates roughs out part of the solution which is advanced in the *Sophist* and then creates difficulties for it. He begins by posing a logical version of the Paradox, in a form similar to that which it bears in its brief appearance in the *Republic*. The argument is:—Granted that he who believes what is-not believes something false, how can one believe what is-not? If one sees, hears, or touches one must see, hear or touch something which is, and surely the same ought to apply to believing. But what is-not is nothing. Reflection on the case of hallucination shows that this argument could be partially met by distinguishing the truism that a cognitive act must have a content from the proposition that it must always be directed upon something real. When Macbeth saw a dagger he saw something, but something which did not exist. As we saw in discussing the *Republic* the difficulty depends on confusing the content of a belief-state, which must exist but may be false, with the state of affairs which it alleges, which may not exist; and in the present passage, as in the *Republic*, certain features of the word *doxazein* may have assisted the confusion.[1]

[1] See p. 33, pp. 46 sqq. and pp. 60 sqq. for further discussion of these two points.

Socrates however does not attack his problem in this way. He concludes, rather, that one cannot believe what is-not and suggests that false belief is "the exchange of one reality for another in the mind", "the supposing that a thing is something else and not itself". This however leads to the conclusion that a man who believes what is false must be doing something very preposterous such as believing beauty to be ugliness or a cow to be a horse.

The difficulty which Socrates thus creates clearly bears upon the topic of reference. When I wrongly say that Jones has a moustache there must be something that I am referring to and am therefore at least to some extent in touch with. It might be either of two things: the alleged state of affairs (Jones's possession of a moustache) or the actual state of affairs (Jones's clean-shavenness). It cannot be the former, for that does not exist. Therefore what I am talking about must be the actual state of affairs, that Jones is clean-shaven. But if I am talking about this, how indeed can I represent it in the form of words "Jones has a moustache"? The answer of course is to see that what I am talking about is neither Jones's moustache, nor his lack of one, but Jones.

So far then the discussion of false belief in the *Theaetetus* has made it clear (whether or not this was Plato's intention) that to get rid of the Paradox we need to introduce the notions (*a*) of degrees of acquaintance and (*b*) of the subject term. The proposal that false belief is *allodoxia* or exchange of realities (a proposal which is to be worked out in the *Sophist*) is not rejected. The rest of the discussion is devoted to trying to meet the difficulty which we have just looked at. The attempt is unsuccessful, but it is not concluded that the enterprise is impossible. Rather the subject of false belief is shelved in favour of a resumed attack on the definition of knowledge. *Allodoxia* therefore remains in the field if its possibility can be demonstrated, a demonstration which depends as we have seen on the second of the two key points made in the *Sophist*, namely the isolation of the subject term.

The Paradox (or the presupposition which it rests on) appears again in the *Theaetetus*, if our interpretation is correct, in the passage called Socrates' Dream.[1] The theory which Socrates claims to have dreamt maintains that a simple element cannot have a *logos* or proposition which is *oikeios* or private to it; for a *logos* is a complex of "names", and belongs (this is the assumption) to the complex of entities named in it. Plainly Plato intends to cast doubt of some kind on this theory, and in the present context it is obviously tempting to think that what he wanted us to abandon was the view that a statement is a complex "name" and "belongs" to the entities which it

[1] See above, pp. 114–17.

names. The full contrary of this view would be the doctrine of the *Sophist* that a statement is not a name nor a string of names and that it belongs to its subject term. (It is not of course a necessary part of this interpretation that Plato was already willing to assert this).

B. *The* Sophist *on the Paradox of False Belief*

The discussion in the *Sophist* is of great complexity. We will consider first the solution of the Paradox of False Belief which Plato offers and then return to deal with some of the complexities. The section with which we are immediately concerned runs from 257 to 264. It has been established that there is such a thing as the *koinônia genôn* or "sharing of kinds",[1] and in particular that every property shares in difference with respect to every other. Every property therefore is-not every other, and every negative property such as not being beautiful can be said to be a part of difference. As we saw in our earlier discussion Plato seems to think that this allows him to deal satisfactorily with negation, though he appears to tell us explicitly only how to deal with denials of identity and not with negative predications (with "A is not identical with B" but not with "S has not got the property P"). But Plato seems to be satisfied that he has shown us how to analyse negative statements in general in such a way as to avoid the suspicion that a negative statement imputes a kind of non-existence to something which exists; what it imputes to it is merely difference from something else. (257-9).

The Stranger now goes on to say that the results so far obtained must be applied to the topics of belief and statement-making. He observes (259 e) that *logos* or speech comes about through the combination of entities which are not identical. In other words a flat tautology of the form "S is S" is not a real statement; we only get a statement when we say something like "S is P" where "S" and "P" are not synonyms. He then observes that although it has been demonstrated that there is such a thing as not-being (namely difference) it does not automatically follow that thoughts and statements can combine with it; the sophists may deny that this is possible, "for one cannot think or say what is-not; for not-being in no way partakes in being" (260 d 2).[2]

It is not immediately obvious why he says this; one had thought that it had been shown that not-being, since it is difference, does partake in being. Why then does it have to be specially shown that statements and thoughts can "combine with not-being"? The text

[1] For this see above, pp. 357-8, 397 sqq., 407 sqq.
[2] For a statement to "combine with" (or "partake in") "not-being" is for it to be false; this becomes clear as we go along.

does not make the answer to this question very clear, but the point I think is this. It has been shown that an ordinary negation ("Jones is not bald") does not impute to its subject a kind of non-existence. But when I say that some proposition is false I say that some state of affairs is not the case. But a state of affairs which is not the case is not just a state of affairs which is different from some other; it is a state of affairs which does not exist. If it is false that Jones is bald, Jones's baldness is simply a nonentity. But it has yet to be shown how one can say of something that it is a nonentity. This is what the Stranger is about to do for the case of assertions of falsity. The difficulty is of course this: that it seems contradictory to ascribe non-existence to something which you succeed in mentioning. And the solution must be: that you do not, when you say that *p* is false, mention a nonentity. You do not mention the nonentity Jones's baldness, but the two entities, Jones and baldness.

This is the solution which the Stranger proceeds to offer to the problem how a statement can combine with not-being, or in other words how non-existence can be predicated of something that somebody has said. Before we attend to his solution however we will briefly notice the statement of his problem. In our language his problem is: "Can an opinion or statement be false?" In his language it is "Can opinion and statement combine with not-being?" In a language which compromises between ours and his, his problem is: "Can we predicate non-existence of opinions and statements?" To this one feels inclined to retort: "Who wants to? It is falsity that one predicates of statements." In other words, even when on the point of solving his problem, Plato retains, without apparently noticing that he is doing so, one of the habits which (as we saw in discussing the *Republic*) generates the problem, namely that of predicating of the proposition the predicate ("non-existent") which ought to be used of the situation which the proposition alleges rather than the predicate ("false") which properly belongs to the proposition. There are two things which I might say of some opinion, say Jones's statement that Smith wears spectacles. I might say of it that it *is* a *mê on* or nonentity, or I might say of it that it *asserts* a *mê on* or nonentity. So far as the Paradox is concerned it does not matter which I say because I can be caught either way. If I say the first I can be asked how anything can be a nonentity; if I say the second I can be told that Jones's statement cannot assert a nonentity, because Jones certainly said something, and a nonentity is not something. But the Stranger's language about statements combining with (*meignusthai* 260 b 11) *to mê on* suggests that he has in mind the first kind of comment, whereas what he actually deals with is the second, where what the false statement is accused of is the offence not so much of combining with *to mê on* as of doing something to it. The Stranger tacitly passes from the form "*p* is a nonentity" to the form "*p* asserts a nonentity" and analyses this: "*p* ascribes to an entity an entity which does not belong to it." This is harmless enough so far as our present purposes go, but the tacit passage obscures the fact that Plato has not dealt with one of the problems which he seemed to be about to deal with, namely the problem how we can say that something does not exist. (We do not want to say this of false statements, but there are other things of which we do want to say it, including the states of affairs whose existence false statements allege). Indeed he leaves the impression that this is impossible. We shall return to this topic later. Meanwhile it is instructive to notice that one of the sources of the Paradox of False Belief has not been explicitly dealt with, namely the lack of a clear distinction between statements and states of affairs which gives rise to the habit of transferring the predicate "non-existent" from the former to the latter, and thus to one version of the Paradox.

The problem then is: "How can a statement be a nonentity?", where these words are construed as "How can a statement assert a nonentity?". The Stranger begins his solution by asking whether there is any special combination of words which constitutes a proposition (261 d). His answer is that not every string of words or "names" (*onomata*) constitutes a statement; a statement must consist of two factors, which he calls an *onoma* and a *rêma*.

We ought to be a little careful about this terminology, and we may begin by resisting the common translation "noun" and "verb".[1] If we put a sufficiently elastic interpretation upon these English words they will no doubt serve the purpose, but their strongly grammatical flavour obscures the point. Plato's terminology is unfortunate because he retains the word *onoma* as the general word for a word while also introducing it as a special word for a word which is being used in a certain way. The point is, I suppose, that any word can be regarded as a name (even a word such as a participle occurring in the *rêma* of a sentence), but that not all the words in a sentence are discharging the indicating function which is characteristic of a name. Thus in the sentence "Jones is running" "Jones" is the only word which is functioning as a name, and is therefore the *onoma* in the new, special sense, "is running" being the *rêma* or thing said of him. But in the old sense "running" can still be spoken of as an *onoma* because what this participle does in the sentence is to name the activity of which Jones is accused. Aristotle's terms "subject" and

---

[1] Every *rêma* must contain a verb, in that a form of words is not a predicate unless it is somehow shown that it is being used predicatively. That which shows this is the verb.

katêgoria, "charge" or "predicate", are preferable so long as *onoma* retains its old general sense; better still perhaps would have been to follow the hint contained in the new use and to cease to speak of words as names. However the point is clear enough; there are two factors in every indicative sentence; the first indicates some entity and the second says something about it. That the distinction between *onoma* and *rêma* is logical rather than grammatical is suggested by the use of these words in the *Cratylus* (421 d, e). There, it will be remembered, a word is called an *onoma* and the theory which the word implies is called its *rêma*, or what it says about the things that it names. Plato's point here, then, is that there are in a statement factors fulfilling each of two functions; the pinning-down function discharged by the *onoma* he calls *onomazein* or "naming", the function of the *rêma* *dêloun* or "declaring".

This being established the Stranger goes on to say that every proposition (*a*) must "belong" to something (this is what the *onoma* ensures: a proposition "belongs" to that which its *onoma* singles out); (*b*) must have what he calls a "quality", i.e. must be true or false; and (*c*) is effected by joining a thing to an activity by means of an *onoma* and a *rêma*. ("Activity" here must bear a wide sense; every expression containing a verb will stand for an activity). Thus "Theaetetus is sitting down" and "Theaetetus is flying" are both propositions (as opposed to "lion stag horse" or "walks run sleeps" which are merely strings of words), the former, we will say, being true and the latter false. And the point is that the false proposition accuses the object that it belongs to of an activity which is a real activity, but which is other than the activities of which that object is in fact guilty.

So much for false statements. Since thought, opinion and fancy are merely variant ways in which statements occur inwardly in the mind (thought being inward conversation, opinion inward assertion, and fancy the pictorial version of these), what applies to statements applies, *mutatis mutandis*, to thought, opinion and fancy, and hence the whole subject of falsity has been covered. This includes the Stranger's resolution of the Paradox of False Belief; he now feels free to say that sophists teach falsehoods.

It is plain that we could construe what we are here offered as a criterion of significance. It is the answer to one problem raised by the Paradox of False Belief—how do we distinguish the case where a man who utters words is "saying something" from the case where he is "saying nothing"? It tells us to ask of any utterance whose significance is in doubt two questions. Firstly does it succeed in indicating some object as that which it is about? Secondly, does it ascribe to that object some "activity" (in a wide sense) such that instances of that activity do or could exist? If the answer to these two questions is affirmative then the utterance is a significant statement, true if the indicated object is guilty of the alleged activity, false if it is not. This is indeed an admirable criterion of significance. We might want to add to it something to the effect that the indicated object and the alleged activity must be logically suited to each other (the condition infringed by "Saturday is in bed"), but it might nevertheless have been studied with profit by the verificationalists when they were worried about the application of the verification principle to statements about the past and other such topics.

It is also of course the key to the Paradox of False Belief. As we have seen all along, that Paradox chiefly depends on treating a proposition as a long name. Once that assumption is tacitly made we cannot help asking how a succession of sounds which does not depict something which is can possibly have meaning. For a succession of sounds which does not depict something which is is essentially a meaningless succession of sounds. The answer is of course that a proposition does not stand for something in the way in which a word may (albeit dangerously) be said to stand for something. Roughly speaking, that which is *composed* of words (whether it is a proposition or a many-word description) is not itself a word and does not derive its significance from standing for something, but from the fact that its component words each stand for something. This rescues both the proposition "Theaetetus is now flying" and the long substantival phrase "The flying which Theaetetus is now doing" from the charge that they are meaningless because the state of affairs which they would name does not exist. No proposition nor many-word description need be ashamed of standing for nothing; a proposition cannot stand for anything and a many-word description need not (except of course in the sense in which an expression can be said to stand for what it means). Therefore the essential first step towards dissolving the problem of falsity is the one that Plato takes, namely that of saying that a proposition is not a name, and does not depict an entity or a nonentity; rather it selects an entity and ascribes to it another entity.

It is unfortunate however that Plato does not rightly estimate the importance of the points which he makes in the *Sophist*. He labours the sharing of kinds and lays little stress on the analysis of a proposition into *onoma* and *rêma*. No doubt as he saw the problem it was important to show that kinds can share, or that predicates can be predicated of non-identical subjects. No doubt (as we shall see later) it was also important to show that not-being is difference. But neither of these points will dissolve the Paradox without the distinction of *onoma* from *rêma*. For what is the contribution of the doctrine that not-being is difference? The point seems to be that, when we say that "Theaetetus is flying" is or asserts something that is-not, we do not mean that this proposition asserts something unreal, intangible, not there to be described; we only mean that it asserts something which is real but different from what is going on. As the Stranger says (263 b 11–12) it asserts of Theaetetus realities which are different from the realities which belong to him. But this solution is no good until we have seen that a proposition asserts a predicate of a subject—until we have distinguished *onoma* from *rêma*. For as we have seen, the realities are Theaetetus and flying, and Theaetetus'-flying-now *is* an unreality. So long as we suppose that a proposition ought to stand for something as a word stands for something, so long shall we be worried by the fact that there is nothing for a false proposition to stand for. Once we see that it is the components of a proposition which have to stand for something, and that a proposition must be broken up into its components before questions of reference are raised, then the problem is solved. To say that flying is a reality which is not one of Theaetetus' is just as clear as to say that flying is a reality which is different from any of Theaetetus'; the point is that flying is a reality though Theaetetus' flying is not.

Therefore the key to the solution is the *onoma/rêma* or subject/predicate distinction which is adumbrated in the *Cratylus* when it is said that to say something false is like offering somebody as his portrait what is in fact the portrait of somebody else. For this simile makes the two essential points. That a proposition must identify its subject is taken care of by the fact that the portrait is offered to somebody, and that he is told that it is his. That the predicate of a false proposition must ascribe a real activity to the wrong subject is taken care of by the fact that what is offered is a portrait, though of somebody else.

It is clear that Plato by now sees that the Paradox of False Belief is one whose solution requires considerable conceptual readjustment, but it is not clear, as we have seen, that he is equally conscious of each stage in the process. The doctrine of *allodoxia* or exchange of realities, conceived in the grand framework of the *koinônia genôn*, takes up too much of his attention. Beyond this he lays stress on the notion of the subject of a proposition. He does not however tell us in so many words that the analysis of belief will defeat us until we introduce the notion of a proposition; or, if this is thought to be contained in what he says about the relation of thought, opinion and fancy to statement, he does not lay enough stress on this point. He poses his problem in the form "How can not-beings be?" and solves it as if the question were "How can a statement assert a not-being?" He uses the notion of a proposition in arriving at his solution, but he does not demand our attention to this feature of his analysis. Nor does he ask us to remember that non-existence is something that we predicate of states of affairs and not of opinions. Certain fag-ends of the Paradox are therefore still left lying about, and I dare say there were those who, having read the *Sophist*, still thought that they could reinstate it in some such form as this:—Yesterday's forecast forecast fine weather; but the fine weather did not happen. Therefore it forecast nothing real; therefore it forecast nothing.

But the justice of some of these comments will perhaps be seen more clearly when we look at some of the other details of the account in the *Sophist*. Meanwhile perhaps it would be more fitting, instead of carping at Plato for not laying emphasis on the utility of slippery notions like *proposition* and *state of affairs*, to pay tribute to a remarkable logical achievement. If however a further criticism were wanted of the passage which we have just examined, it would be that it is to be regretted that Plato did not abandon the dangerous habit of speaking of words as "names". You can say if you like that ordinary common nouns derive their significance from being correlated with classes of objects, and in this respect resemble names, and you can extend the analogy a little if you are very careful. But it breaks down when it comes to words such as "I", "this", "not", "if", "all", "and", "good" and so on, which make a difference to the sentences they occur in, and hence are significant, but do not derive their significance from standing for realities. Significance therefore cannot be equated in general with standing-for, and there was a chance that Plato might have seen this (had he been miraculously long-sighted) when he drafted the word *onoma* to stand for a word or expression used in a certain way.

IV. SOME FURTHER PROBLEMS ARISING OUT OF THE *SOPHIST*: THE COPULA
AND EXISTENCE, ETC.

We have already discussed the doctrine of the *Sophist* in two places. In the discussion just concluded we have directed our attention to what it says about the analysis of a proposition, and the contribution of this to the Paradox of False Belief. In an earlier chapter we considered what it has to say about existence and the very great kinds in the context of the notion of dialectic; and this entailed some attention to its analysis of negation.[1] This has not however exhausted the themes contained in the *Sophist* and a further discussion will be necessary. In particular we have not fully dealt with what it has to say about the ambiguities of the verb *einai*, "to be".

We have seen in earlier chapters that *einai* has a good deal of

[1] Above pp. 407–10.

work to do. It is equivalent, firstly, both to "to be" and to "to exist"; and in doing the work of "to be" it is already discharging two functions—the "is" of identity and the "is" of predication. In addition to this it is used in philosophical Greek in contrast both with "to become" and "to appear", and in such usage it conveys the sense (depending to some extent on the other term with which it is contrasted) of something like stability, ultimacy or reality. There are furthermore a number of passages, in the *Republic* and elsewhere, where one wonders whether the argument depends on confusion between some of these senses, in particular between existing and being so-and-so or between existing and being real.

Whether there are in fact such confusions in Plato's own work we have discussed in connection with the passages which excite the question. But whether there are or not, the possibility of them undoubtedly exists, and perhaps one of the main purposes of the *Sophist* is to get rid of them by trying to disentangle the various senses of *einai*. I would not claim that Plato saw with perfect clarity what he was doing; rather he was aware of a nest of confusions and took some of the steps necessary towards clearing them up.

We have already seen how the *Sophist* distinguishes the identity from the predication sense of "is". When we turn back to the details of the Stranger's argument with the sophists we shall see that some of it is obviously designed to show that "X is not genuine" (in Greek "X is not an *on*") does not entail "X does not exist". In addition to this, though less obviously, we shall observe from certain details that he seems also to want to show that an ordinary negation of the form "X is not so-and-so" does not entail the non-existence of X.

This additional point amounts to an analysis of negation in terms of the assumption that the "is" of the copula asserts existence, and that the "is not" of the negative copula might be expected to assert non-existence. The traditional doctrine says that a proposition consists of a subject, a predicate and a copula, and that the copula does not imply existence. The "is" in "Jones is a bachelor" does not assert that Jones exists, it merely serves to link him with bachelordom. Consequently, we are told, it is important not to confuse the "is" of predication, nor indeed the "is" of identity, with the "is" which asserts existence. Plato's analysis of negation in terms of difference could be regarded as doing much the same work as the traditional doctrine of the copula. It would however, I think, be a mistake to suppose that we find in Plato the doctrine that the verb "to be", when functioning as a copula, does not assert existence. Rather it is taken for granted that it does (though at the same time it is taken for granted that existential import can also be carried by other verbs, or at any rate that a denial of existence might be mistakenly inferred

499

from the use of other verbs in the negative, just as from the negative copula "is not"). I feel sure that Plato would have said that "Jones is a bachelor" says that Jones exists as a bachelor, and that being a bachelor is a part or way of existence. This will seem objectionable to those who cleave to the traditional doctrine of the copula, and also to those who think it important to maintain that existence is "not a predicate"—not the sort of thing there can be parts or ways of. But the assumption that "Jones is a bachelor" says that Jones exists is not seriously objectionable so far as affirmative statements are concerned. Certainly something in this sentence commits its utterer to the existence of Jones. It is no doubt clearer to say that the commitment is carried by the use of his name as a referring expression rather than by the use of "is". But nothing disastrous results so long as it is not supposed that "Jones is *not* a bachelor" implies that Jones does not exist (or to some extent non-exists), nor that not being a bachelor is a part or way of non-existence. Plato avoids these dangers by saying (in effect) that "Jones is not a bachelor" says that everything that Jones is is different from being a bachelor.[1] Nor is it disastrous in itself to say that existence is a predicate, and that being a bachelor is a way of existing, provided it is realised that existence is a very odd predicate, in that we cannot encounter or imagine instances of the lack of it. Plato's realisation that existence is a predicate of everything whatsoever will serve to make this point. The analysis therefore of negation in terms of difference is designed to obviate the dangers which are involved in the assumption that the copula implies existence, and the assumption, given this analysis, does no great harm, unless perhaps it induced Plato to think too highly of the metaphysical status of such entities as existence, sameness and difference; but for that charge I see no clear evidence.[2]

There is indeed a problem with which Plato's doctrine cannot deal as it stands, namely that of the correct analysis of denials of existence (e.g. "The King of Portugal is non-existent"). For such statements appear to assert that something exists ("is") as a nonentity. Plato is

[1] We saw in our first discussion (pp. 407–10 above) that Plato does not explicitly tell us how to understand negative predications but only denials of identity. But the formula in the text will probably do.

[2] The analysis of negation in terms of difference is not the only way of saving the assumption that the copula asserts existence from the disasters that await us if we say that the negative copula denies it. The contradictory of "asserts" is "does not assert", not "denies". We could treat "Jones is a bachelor" as a conjunction—"Jones exists and bachelorises". The denial of this conjunction (viz. "Jones is not a bachelor") would be true if either conjunct were false; e.g. if Jones existed but did not bachelorise. It is to some extent a question of taste or idiom whether we may say "Jones is not a bachelor" when our reason for saying this is that there is no such person as Jones.

concerned to avoid the paradox that statements such as "X is a fake" appear to assert that something exists as a nonentity, and he does this by showing us that such statements are not denials of existence, despite the contrary appearance that Greek idiom gives rise to. But he does not consider the case of genuine denials of existence, and it is true that the doctrine that the copula does not assert existence does dispose, after a fashion, of the contradictory appearances of these; for it tells us that "The King of Portugal is non-existent" does not assert the King's existence, but only his non-existence. But the doctrine of the copula does not do this very lucidly, for it does not dispose of the related troubles which arise over those false statements which owe their falsity to the non-existence of their subject terms (e.g. "All my gold-mines are in full production"). For both a statement of this kind and its contradictory (e.g. "My gold-mines are not all in full production") do in some sense imply the existence of the subject term and may therefore both be false (or at least mendacious) whatever we say about the existential implication of "is".

We know well from recent discussions what to do in order to deal at one blow with denials of existence and also with statements the existence of whose subjects ought to be denied. This is to ask, as Plato could have asked: "What happens when the *onoma* of a proposition apparently stands for something which does not exist?" Once this question is raised it can be seen that to use a name or descriptive phrase as a referring expression is to claim that the thing named or described exists. When this is seen we can see further, firstly that both of the above statements about my gold-mines commit me in some sense to the claim that I have gold-mines, as well as to whatever I say about their productivity, and that this is how they can both be mendacious; and secondly that "The King of Portugal is non-existent" must be turned into some such form as "No man rules Portugal" or " 'The King of Portugal' refers to nobody" if its logical form is to be made evident. What is needed to dispose of both of these difficulties, in fact, is that we should reflect on the function of the subject in a proposition rather than on that of the copula. Plato did not indeed ask what happens when the *onoma* of a proposition apparently stands for something which does not exist, and perhaps the question could hardly have occurred to him so long as he retained the expression *onoma* or "name" to stand for the subject-term; for names in the literal sense are normally only given to existents, fictional or otherwise. Nevertheless, so far as the failure to distinguish the existential "is" from the "is" of the copula is concerned, this failure does not prevent the raising of the question and is not therefore responsible for the fact that Plato's doctrine does not show us how to deal with denials of existence.

To sum up then, the discussion in the *Sophist* seems to attempt the following things: to distinguish the sense of *einai* in which it means "exist" from various other senses which the word bears; to deal, as we have seen, with the Paradox of False Belief; and to deal with the (related) problems raised by negation on the assumption that a sentence which does contain, or could be re-phrased so as to contain, the copula "is" asserts the existence of its subject and that its negation might be thought to assert its non-existence, or at least to attribute to it a measure of non-existence. I hope that this will become clear in the following account of the argument in which, as before, I shall prefix a number to paragraphs which purport to give the gist of the text and a letter to those which contain comment.

(*To on* is that which is, an *on* is something which is; *to mê on* is that which is-not, a *mê on* is something which is-not; *einai* means "to be").

1. The relevant section begins in 236 d, when the Stranger, having said that sophists pursue apparent rather than real wisdom, goes on to say that there has been, and still is, a serious puzzle about "appearing and yet not being, and about saying something and yet something which is not true". Arguments implying the possibility of false statement or false belief "venture to say that not-being is; for there could not otherwise be such a thing as falsity" (237 a 4).

A. The Stranger does not, I think, mean that a false statement (e.g. that Jones has a moustache) alleges the existence of something which is in fact non-existent (Jones's moustache). A false statement does not say that not-being is; it says *of* a not-being *that* it is, and I see no reason to say that the Stranger has missed this point. "Venturing to say that not-being is" is not what you do when you make a false statement, but what I do when I say that your statement is false. This clearly envisages some such comment on my part as: "What you said is a *mê on*." Such comments were doubtless made in these words infrequently, but we see from the arguments in the *Euthydemus* and elsewhere that it was felt that "What you said is false" entailed "What you said is a *mê on*". (You said something, but, if something false, then not an *on*; therefore a *mê on*. This seems to imply that a not-being can be something).

Notice that the Stranger brackets together "appearing and not being" with "saying something which is not true". These are rather dissimilar matters. When I say that what Smith possesses is only apparent and not real wisdom, I do not obviously say that not-being is. I assert the existence of something that is not an instance of wisdom, but not of a nonentity. It is partly because the Greeks used the participle of the verb "to be" for "real" and the adverb formed from it for "really"' that the trouble in this case arises. In other words

502

the topic of appearances or fakes requires that the uses of *einai* and its parts to connote genuineness be isolated. This could be done by showing that *ontôs* ("being-ly" or "really") means the same as "truly". The reason why Plato does not take this simple path is, I think, that "Smith is not truly wise" is still a negative statement, and Plato is, subliminally to some extent, worried about the analysis of negation. This is probably partly due to the fact that a negative statement asserts the falsity of its contradictory, so that the topic of negation and therefore of fakes is bound up with the topic of false belief after all, partly also, I think, because of the fear that "is not" may be taken to assert non-existence. This is why Plato is not happy until "Smith is not really wise" has been got into the form "Everything in which Smith partakes is other than real wisdom".

2. The Stranger then says that Parmenides always warned his pupils not to say that not-being is, and offers as the reason for this ban the argument that "not-being" cannot be the name of anything which is, and therefore cannot be the name of anything. But a man who says something must say some one thing; therefore the man who does not say something must say nothing, and therefore perhaps we ought to say that the man who tries to utter what is-not not only says nothing, but does not even say at all. (237 a–e).

B. I think, though I am not certain, that the man who "tries to utter what is-not", is not the man who makes a false statement, but the man who uses the expression *mê on* in condemning someone else's statement as false. Judgments of the form "*p* is false", in other words, being equivalent to "*p* is a *mê on*" are meaningless. This incidentally would explain how an Eleatic could maintain that there are no false propositions without being deterred by the apparent consequence that in that case it must be false that there are false propositions. For this apparent consequence, being of the form "*p* is false" would not be a real consequence of the premise that every proposition must be true, but a meaningless noise which we are inclined to utter when we become convinced of the premise. This would leave us with an exhaustive division of the things which we are inclined to say into propositions which report pieces of reality and meaningless utterances which we are tempted to make whenever we depart from the strait paths of *a priori* reasoning. We can see from this another reason why Plato might have been worried about negation. For the view that all true utterances report pieces of reality is anyhow very congenial to an extreme picture or correspondence theory of truth, and a theory like this is inclined to create in those who hold it anxiety about the status of negative facts. "A is B" pictures the B-hood of A but "C is not D" can hardly picture the non-D-hood of C, for what on earth is that?

3. It has been shown so far that not-being is a baffling notion. On the one hand we often have occasion to use it; on the other hand Parmenides has good reason to forbid us to do so. The Stranger goes on to find further difficulties in the notion of not-being. That which he calls the chief of them is as follows. Something which does not exist cannot have any properties. But if one is going to speak of non-entity at all one must either use the singular or the plural ("not-being" or "not-beings"). Not-being, therefore, cannot be spoken of nor thought of at all. Furthermore, and worse, even to say that much about it is to treat it as if it were some one existing thing. (238 a–239 c).

C. In fact if we want to say anything about something, even that it does not exist, we have to pretend that it exists because we have to use a referring expression to indicate what we are talking about. The demonstration that not-being is a baffling notion has thus brought up what we might call the problem of the proposition whose referring expression has nothing corresponding to it, "not-being" being one instance of such an expression, "the present King of France" another. I said above that Plato offers no analysis of these propositions, perhaps because he did not notice that the problem is not confined to statements about not-being, and these he has taught us how to avoid. But he is certainly aware of the difficulty. Thus the whole of the fifth argument in the second section of the *Parmenides* (160–3; see above, p. 345) depends on the assumption that anything about which statements can be made must exist. In the course of this argument Parmenides propounds the following ingenious tongue-twister (161 e–162 b). If "the one" is-not it must partake in existence in a sense. For if what we say about it is true, then it must be as we say it is. Therefore if we say that it *is* not, it must *be* in not-being. Being therefore as a not-being is what makes it not-be, just as not being not-being is what makes being be. Being therefore partakes in the being of being being and the not-being of not being not-being, while not-being partakes in the not-being of not being being and the being of being not-being! It is incidentally interesting to notice that Parmenides in this section ascribes a good many properties to "the one" (on the assumption that it does not exist) simply on the basis of the fact that statements about it have it and not something else for their subject; but does not venture to ascribe existence to his non-existent until his argument is well advanced, and then does so on the ground that it has been said that it *is* a not-being. It is not in fact until he draws attention to the use of the copula in statements about not-being that Parmenides ventures to assert the paradox that a non-existent exists in some sense, with the corollary that being partakes in not-being and not-being in being. It is perhaps fair to infer from this that Plato was sensitive to the logical tricks that the copula can play.

To return to the *Sophist*, the difficulties which arise about statements with not-being as their subject do not bear very directly upon the question of the genuineness of the sophist's teaching. It has been sufficiently shown that we cannot accuse the sophists of purveying not-beings, and Plato's purpose in adding more arguments is not only, perhaps, to punch the nail right home, but also, as we saw above, to show that not-being is a baffling notion. He is in fact on the point of raising corresponding difficulties about being. We could say (though doubtless this would be to put it too baldly) that the reason why Plato wants to show us that not-being is a baffling notion is that he wants to show us that we must distinguish between the use of *einai* to mean "to exist" and its other uses, such as "to be genuine" or "to be the case". For when we in fact need to use the phrase *to mê on* we do not need it to refer to what he later calls the opposite of *to on* or "that which exists", for we do not need to talk of that which does not exist. Parmenides is right in saying that there is no such thing. We need the phrase *to mê on* to refer to that which is a fake or a semblance or to that which is not the case. There are thus legitimate uses of a phrase which, from the meanings of the words which compose it, we might expect to have none but an illegitimate use; and this is why the phrase is baffling.

4. The Stranger goes on to conclude from the difficulties he has raised about not-being that it will be embarrassing to say that sophists create semblances (*eikones*). For the sophists will ask what an *eikôn* is, will refuse to accept an ostensive definition, and will force you to admit that a semblance is something which is not the genuine thing. And since the genuine thing is really a being, and the non-genuine its opposite, a semblance will have to be something which "is not really a being, but exists in a way, though not genuinely, except that it really is a semblance", and therefore "not really being, it really is". And thus we shall have to say that a not-being in a way is. (239 c–240 b).

D. This brings near to the surface the fact that part of the difficulty depends on confusing non-genuineness with non-existence. Notice also that at this stage what Plato is concerned about is the condition of not being genuine (*alêthinos*), not just the condition of not being so-and-so. It is only certain negations, namely those which deny genuineness, which have been shown to cause trouble. Later we shall see cause for thinking that Plato is worried, as we have said, about negation in general.

5. The Stranger then says that he is unable to see how to define sophistry without contradicting the conclusions that they have come

to in their discussion so far. He wants to say that sophists make us believe what is false, but he sees that the sophists will retort that this is impossible because a false belief must be one that asserts what is contrary to what is, either by holding that not-beings are, or by holding that beings are not. Therefore if we say that there are false propositions we shall, as Theaetetus puts it, "be forced to tack being on to not-being, which we have agreed to be impossible". (240 c– 241 b).

E. At first sight at any rate the Stranger appears to be deploying a new argument in this passage. He seems to be saying that, from the premise that false propositions say that not-beings are, we can directly infer the conclusion that to say that there are false propositions is to tack being on to not-being. This seems to be a new argument, because the premise seems to depend on a mistake which the Stranger has not hitherto exploited. No false proposition (except the proposition "There are not-beings") says that not-beings are. False propositions say, if you like, that certain things exist (when these things do not exist), or *vice versa*, but they do not say that certain things which exist also non-exist. We only get this impression if we make the mistake of including within the *oratio obliqua* a relative clause which properly belongs outside it. We had not hitherto seen reason for thinking that the Stranger's account of the Paradox depended on making use of this mistake. Hitherto his argument has seemed to be that "What you said is false", being equivalent to "What you said is a *mê on*", is without meaning, with the corollary in the background that if I say that it has meaning I must intend that something (viz. what you say) can be nothing. This is a more formidable argument than the new one which the Stranger appears to be introducing, the argument namely from the premise that false propositions are contradictory to the conclusion that it is contradictory to say that there are false propositions. The arguments are not indeed disconnected. In the case of the new argument we should get presumably from the premise to the conclusion by means of the reflection that if false statements are contradictory they cannot say anything, and hence are not propositions, so that the notion of a false proposition is a contradiction in terms. This depends on the rule that a proposition must say something; and the earlier argument (that "Your proposition is a *mê on*" entails that something can be nothing) also depends on the use, or misuse, of this rule. While therefore there are logical connections between the two arguments, the suspicion remains that the Stranger is introducing in this passage a new argument of a more specious kind than the old one. The Stranger is of course entitled to introduce any bad arguments that he wishes in building up his Aunt Sally; and this one has the advantage that, in order to see what is wrong with the premise that a false statement says that a not-being is, we need to make the point, which he is going to make, that a proposition has an *onoma* and a *rêma*; it is this that allows us to offer the correct analysis, that a false proposition names an entity and attributes to it an activity of which it is not guilty. This form therefore of the Paradox of False Belief deserves an airing, and hitherto, so it seems, has not had one. But it is difficult to resist the impression that Plato is not aware that the Stranger is now using a new argument; nor indeed does he make it clear either how the Stranger gets the premise that false propositions say that not-beings are, or how he thinks that he can pass from this to the conclusion that it is contradictory to say that there are false propositions. One is inclined to say that Plato is feeling his way through the tangles of the Paradox without a perfectly clear view of them. Indeed it could hardly be otherwise.

6. The Stranger then says that they must come to terms with Parmenides, and show that not-being in a way is, and being in a way is-not. This leads him to the criticisms of various philosophical and cosmological schools which we have examined in an earlier chapter, the professed aim of these criticisms being to show that being is just as difficult a notion as not-being. He criticises (*a*) those who say that *to on* is two or three things, such as the warm and the cold; (*b*) Parmenides who says that it is *to hen* (which could mean either "unity" or "the one substance"); (*c*) the materialists who say that *to on* is what we can see and touch; and (*d*) the Partisans of the Forms who say that *to on* is utterly changeless. Showing, from this last criticism, that activity and inactivity both are (i.e. exist), and yet are not being, he concludes that it is as difficult to say what "being" is the name of as it is to say what "not-being" is the name of. (241 d–251 a).

F. The apparent purpose of the Stranger's criticisms of the various schools is to show that existence is a distinct property which is possessed by everything else, including every other property, but which is not identical with anything else. Everything else partakes in, but is-not, being. As we have already said this demonstration corresponds, more or less, with the difficulties which were raised about not-being. These showed, we thought, that since we want to say of some things that they are "unreal", false, or in some other way not-beings, without thereby denying them existence, we must distinguish the senses of *mê einai* in which it means "to be unreal" (etc.) from those in which it means "not to exist". What we are now being shown is that there are, correspondingly, affirmative uses of *einai* in which it does not mean "to exist". You may say if you like that the real is what you can see or touch, or that reality is unity or changelessness, but in so saying you cannot equate "to be real" with "to exist". If you did so, you would be saying that there is nothing which lacks whichever property it is that you believe to constitute being real. Parmenides probably did try to argue that there was nothing whatever which lacked unity and that that was why there was only one substance; he really meant to equate unity with reality and thus with existence, and that is why the criticism of his views has to go on at such an abstruse level. The other schools did not intend to deny the existence of that which they differentiated from *to on*; and they are easier to deal with. The underlying point is that there are no properties which are incompatible with existence, and therefore any theory which contrasts a property called "being" with some other property (so that if X possessed the latter property it would not be a being) cannot mean existence by "being", but must mean something else—being an ultimate element, being able to affect the senses, being changeless. The corollary of this is that one cannot convey any information about a thing's nature by saying that it exists, and conversely that to say of something, with descriptive intention that it is a not-being cannot be to say that it does not exist, but to contrast its status with some other (say that of being a fake with that of being genuine).

7. The Stranger continues his argument by way of drawing attention to the fact that in every predication something other than the subject is predicated of it, and that this shows that kinds can share. Then follows the passage about dialectic and the discussion of the very great kinds—being, activity, inactivity, sameness and difference—in which it is demonstrated that all of these are, but that none is identical with any of the others. From this it is concluded (256-7) that activity (for instance) is not being, and that therefore "not-being must exist with respect to activity and in accordance with all the kinds". Since none of them is identical with being they can all be called not-beings while at the same time they are beings. "Every kind has much being and infinite not-being" (256 e 1). Even being itself is-not everything else. (251 a–257 a).

G. When the Stranger says that every kind has much being and infinite not-being he means, I think, that it is everything that can be predicated of it, and is-not everything that is not identical with it. (The latter class is the larger; hence the change from "much" to "infinite"). In 256 e 1 the Stranger seems to imply that the reason why some kind (he is speaking of difference) is a not-being is that it is-not being; but further on when he says that every kind has *infinite* not-being the reason why it has not-being must be, as we have seen, that it is-not each of the infinitely many things that are not identical with it. Being, at least, could not owe its not-being to not being identical with being, and must owe it to not being identical with other properties (cp. 259 b 6). Given the Stranger's analysis of predication, that which has or partakes in not-being can have not-being predicated of it, i.e. it can be called a not-being. Difference, therefore, being and every other property can be called a not-being. As the Stranger says (257 a 8) this is not objectionable if we grant the *koinônia genôn*, i.e. if we see that in calling P a not-being I am only predicating not-being of P, I am not identifying P with not-being. But what is interesting here is that a thing can be called a not-being not only because it is-not being, but also because it is-not any you please of the infinitely many things with which it is not identical. At the beginning of the Stranger's discussion a not-being seemed to be something which was not a being. "Not-being" seemed to bear a fairly specific sense as the negation of "being" in certain senses of that word. "Not to be" meant "not to be a being", and that was a phrase which could intelligibly be used, Plato seemed to argue, of such things as fakes, false propositions, and so on. At this stage it looked as if "having not-being" would be the characteristic of things which lacked truth or genuineness. Now however it looks as if the truth of any negation is enough to make its subject a not-being. That scholarship is not pedantry is enough to make scholarship have not-being. This means that things can now be said to "have not-being" which would not idiomatically be described as *ouk onta* or not-beings. The reader's attention is therefore distracted from what he took to be one of Plato's main purposes in this discussion, namely to explain how fakes and false opinions come to be described as not-beings. He is asked instead to see how it is the case that this description *could* be extended from things that are not beings (in this idiomatic sense) to things that are not so-and-so—in fact to everything whatsoever. But this seems to miss the important point that *not being a cat* (for example) is a very different matter from *not being a being*. This point could have been preserved had the Stranger said that whereas everything had infinite *not-being so-and-so*, it was only certain things which had the property of *not-being beings*. Why does Plato not do this? One answer could be as follows. Plato has failed to see that *einai* has certain special uses. He thinks that "not to be a being" would have to mean "to be non-existent". He is convinced that we can never predicate non-existence of a subject which we have succeeded in mentioning; therefore he cannot draw a distinction between *not-being so-and-so* and *not-being a being*, because he thinks that the latter property does not exist. This is an answer which I cannot give without some embarrassment since I have argued that the discussion of the puzzling nature of *einai* and of *mê einai* shows that Plato *is* aware that this verb has certain special uses; and this ought to mean that he sees that "not to be a being" has a meaning other than "not to exist".

How can I get the best of both worlds? It seems to be necessary to concede that Plato is not fully and explicitly conscious of the fact that he has shown that *einai* has certain special uses. This I shall allow while still maintaining that he has in some sense intended to make this point.[1] This blinds him to the fact that it would be useful to distinguish *not-being a being* (which in fact produces the paradoxes) from *not-being so-and-so* (which does not). But I shall add to this the suggestion that another reason why he does not see this is that he is now thinking of a wider range of paradoxes than that with which he started: he is now thinking of the paradoxes connected with negation in general as well as those connected with that class of negations which deny genuineness or "truth".[2] These are the paradoxes which result if we think that if X is not Y it must be a *mê on*, and fail to see that "being a *mê on*" only means "partaking in difference with respect to . . .". A desire to deal with these paradoxes, to dispose of the view that if A is-not B then A partakes in non-existence, would lead Plato to treat of all negations on all-fours, and thus distract his attention from the importance of distinguishing denials of genuineness from denials of other kinds, even if he had been fully in the position to make this distinction.

This incidentally throws a little more light on something that we glanced at earlier in this chapter,[3] namely that in his solution of the Paradox of False Belief Plato does not lay his emphasis where we would wish him to, and that he makes too much, in particular, of the formula that not-being is difference. For how does this formula help us to deal with the statement that something (some fake or false opinion) is not an *on*? To say of something that it is different from an *on* hardly seems to deal with the difficulties that may appear to arise if we say that it is not an *on*. For if "different from an *on*" means "different from *some on*", this is something which could be said of anything and hence does not represent what we meant when we said that a fake is not an *on*;[4] whereas if "different from an *on*" means "different from *every on*", this re-formulation does not seem to help; for what is different from every X *is not* an X. Nor can we solve the problem by saying that Plato's analysis of "S is not an *on*" is:

---

[1] One might explain this by saying that he thought of the point in the material mode (that being is a property which is difficult to comprehend) rather than in the formal mode (that *einai* is ambiguous).

[2] Following Plato I am here lumping together the problem of false propositions and the problem of fakes. As we have seen these problems are not identical, but this does not affect the present point.

[3] Above pp. 496–8.

[4] The same is true of "different from every *on* except itself".

"Everything in which S partakes is different from *to on.*" For that too makes S not exist (until we distinguish *to on,* the existent, from *to on,* the genuine). The formula that negation is difference does not seem helpful in the case of "S is not an *on*", however useful it may be in the case of "S is not an animal" (etc.). It is the paradoxes of negation in general rather than that of false belief in particular which are dealt with by the formula that not-being is difference, and it is because Plato has these paradoxes in mind that he attaches so much importance to this formula.

8. The Stranger now concludes that when we speak of not-being we do not speak of the *opposite* of being, but only of something different from it. Negation does not "signify the opposite". To prefix "not" to a word is to indicate something different from the thing that the word stands for. There are many parts of difference, or in other words many contrasts, such as that between the beautiful and that which is different from it; and the contrasted term (such as the not-beautiful) is just as much a being as the other term, since the former does not signify the opposite of the latter, but only something different from it. This, he says, deals with the problem of the sophists' teaching. Not-being is difference. It is not the opposite of being. We are not "venturing to say" that the opposite of being exists. The question whether there is such a thing as not-being conceived of as the opposite of being, and if so whether any account can be given of it, is not one which arises in this connection. It is sufficient for the present purpose to show that the kinds can share, and that though difference (or "not-being" in the ordinary sense of that phrase) is not being, it *is a* being, in which all other beings, including being itself, partake. (257 b–259 b).

H. It has been pointed out in an earlier chapter[1] that this does not, as it stands, give us an adequate account of negation. Meanwhile we may notice that this section of the argument obviously reinforces the claim that Plato is by now interested in the paradoxes arising out of negation in general. We may observe in particular that he passes from "when we speak of not-being we speak of something different from being" (257 b 3) to the mention of negative properties in general such as *not being large* and *not being beautiful,* making the point that these are just as much beings as their contrasting positive properties. This is to pass from *not-being being* to *not-being so-and-so,* and the passage, made as it is without comment, amounts to a subsumption of the former under the latter. Further support for the view that we have taken of this can perhaps be got from the details of the argument. We notice that a particular negative property is called a part of difference and therefore of not-being, and it is natural to infer from this that a particular positive property would be called a

[1] Above pp. 407–10.

511

part of being (after all, all properties *partake* in being).[1] This makes it easy to imagine that Plato has in mind an argument which conceives of the possession of a property as a part or way of existence and concludes from this that not to possess the property is a way of non-existence. This is the conclusion which would seem to follow from the premise if we thought that negation "signified the opposite" (as opposed to "something different") and applied this to the case of those negations which do not deny existence. For when I say that cabbages are vegetables, I say, according to the premise of the argument, that they exist as vegetables, and it might seem that the opposite of this is to say that they non-exist as vegetables, or that they partake in a kind of negativity, namely non-vegetable-hood. But we sometimes want to say that things are not vegetables without imputing to them some mysterious kind of negativity. I suggest that it is because Plato sympathises with the premise of this imaginary argument (viz. that "Cabbages are vegetables" says that cabbages partake in that part of existence) that he feels it necessary to say that negation does not signify the opposite, but only something different. He means that when I say that cats are not vegetables I say that they partake in the not-vegetable but that this is not a part of non-existence, but rather an existent which is other than vegetable-hood. The view that affirmations and negations signify each other's opposite is the view that existence and non-existence are the opposed terms and that under the first comes existence as P, existence as Q`. . ., under the second non-existence as P . . . non-existence as Q. . . . The view that negation signifies not "the opposite" but "the different" is the view that all statements assert that their subject partakes in existence, the function of negation being to locate the subject in some region of existence other than that part of it specified by the negated term. We might put this by saying that "not" is logically hyphenated, not to the copula, but to the rest of the predicate; and that is what Plato almost does say in 257 c when he speaks of "not" signifying the opposite of the words to which it is prefixed and then goes on to take examples such as "not large".[2] It is difficult

---

[1] There is a certain a-symmetry here. All properties partake in being and in not-being, and also in sameness and in difference (see pp. 411–16 for the significance of the latter). Not-being is difference, but being is not identical with (self-)same-ness, as we might have expected. This is because the existence of a thing is logically prior to its self-identity. On the other hand a property could not exist if it were not self-identical, so that "P-hood exists" entails, though it is not synonymous with, "P-hood is self-identical".

[2] In Greek one commonly says *ouk esti mega*, i.e. "not is large", the "not" coming before the copula. This is why one cannot say that Plato actually makes the point which I say he almost makes, for the copula commonly is one of the words to which the "not" is prefixed.

to see how we could understand the contrast which Plato draws between "the opposite" (*to enantion*) and "something different" (*ti tôn allôn*) unless we understood it roughly as above. Plato cannot for example mean to tell us that the contradictory of a proposition is not the same as its contrary (that to deny that Jones is very silly indeed is not to say he is very wise indeed); for this, though true, seems to be quite irrelevant.

To say then that something is not P (where P is any property, including "being") is to locate it in some part of existence other than that occupied by P. We see that this is so by seeing that negation does not, normally, "signify the opposite". Plato suggests however (258 e–259 a) that there might be such a thing as the opposite of *to on*, but dismisses the questions whether there is such a thing, and, if there is, whether it is *logon echon* or *alogon* as questions which need not be raised. (I take the second question to mean: "whether it could or could not enter into discourse"). His language suggests to me that he is against holding that there is such a thing as *to mê on* where this is the opposite of *to on*. It is not immediately obvious, however, what such a view would amount to. It is probably a little too simple to say that the view is that there is such a thing as non-existence. It seems more likely that *to on* is what we get if we add together all the parts of *to on*, where the latter are things like being large, being beautiful and so on. *To on* would thus become something like the sum of all possible positive predicates, characters or ways of existing. The idea, then, that *to on* might conceivably have an opposite would be the idea that there might be something left if one went on subtracting predicates until one had subtracted them all. If *to on* stands for the sum of all positive predicates, *to mê on* in the sense in which Plato does not want to commit himself to the meaningfulness of this phrase would stand for the absence of all positive predicates; it would be, to express it in abstract terms, total characterlessness. If we understand "the opposite of *to on*" in this way it will be easier to see why Plato does not deny its existence straight out. It would not be altogether impossible to wonder whether we might not need to postulate the existence of that which totally lacks character to be that in which character inheres. *Chôra* in the *Timaeus* comes dangerously near to this.[1] Indeed in the *Physics* 192 a 6–16 Aristotle says that Plato spoke of that in which properties inhere as *to mê on*. If he is speaking of the *Timaeus* Aristotle is verbally inexact, but it is conceivable that Plato used the phrase *to mê on* in conversation to do something like the work done by *chôra* in that dialogue. This then may be why Plato does not dismiss the notion out of hand. Perhaps however he could hardly have done so even if he had no idea of the

[1] See above, Chapter 2, pp. 222–4.

use to which he might want to put the notion. For the idea that there might be a state of desperate ontological impoverishment, total negativity, non-existence, *le néant*, seems to be a corollary of supposing that *to on* is something in which everything else partakes, at any rate if this is taken to mean, not that *to on* is the collective name for everything that there is, but rather that existence is a property that everything has. For if existence is a property then it ought to be logically possible that there should *be* something which lacked the property (even if this logical possibility is somehow metaphysically excluded). I have argued that participation is not for Plato a very clear notion,[1] and it seems likely that "S partakes in *to on*" is ambiguous between "S is a member of the class: what there is" and "S has the property: existence". In so far as Plato attached something like the latter meaning to the statement that everything partakes in *to on* he would tend to think that existence was a property and that there ought to be such a thing as the lack of this property, as there is such a thing as the lack of any other property.

9. The Stranger continues his argument by warning his hearers against the frivolous production of antinomies. The fact that *logos* or the making of statements involves the interweaving of different kinds means that it will always be possible to produce apparent antinomies out of innocent statements if one fails to attend to the sense of what is said. But to exploit such antinomies is to render discourse impossible. He then alarms his hearers by telling them that though the existence of not-being has been established, the sophists will still be able to contend that statements and beliefs cannot partake in it, and meets this with the analysis of a proposition into an *onoma* and a *rêma* with which we are familiar. (259 b–264 b).

We may sum up this discussion by saying that the main theme of this part of the *Sophist* is falsity and ungenuineness, the fear that is to be exorcised being that to say that something is a not-being is to "join being and not-being". This fear arises primarily from the fact that denials of truth and genuineness appear to be denials of existence; but the discussion of this point gets entangled with a discussion which is really addressed to the possibility that all denials whatsoever might appear to be denials of existence. In so far as Plato is concerned with the difficulties which arise from the idiomatic uses of "is a not-being" to describe falsehoods and fakes, he deals with them (*a*) by an analysis of falsity which makes us no longer want to call a false proposition a not-being, and (*b*) by a discussion of the uses of *einai* and *mê einai* which make it intuitively clear to us that "exist" is not the only meaning of *einai*. In so far as Plato has also his eye

---

[1] See Chapter 3, pp. 416–17.

on the problems apparently engendered by negation in general, he deals with these by the doctrine that negation does not signify the opposite but only something different.

Plato's handling of the notion of existence is not above criticism. Nobody, perhaps, has given an unexceptionable account of this topic. We, perhaps, will find the notion that positive predicates are parts of existence unhelpful. We may possibly suspect that the notion of being a part of, or partaking in, existence is ambiguous between being a member of what there is and having the property of existence. We should like, in other words, a clear distinction between the use of *to on* to mean "that which is" and its use to mean "existence", just as we should like an analogous distinction in the case of other phrases of the form "the X". No doubt we should also be willing to exchange, for the criticisms of the various philosophical schools, a clear statement in the formal mode that *einai* does not always mean "to exist" or its negation "not to exist".

But the most tangible criticism of Plato's discussion is that, by rescuing ordinary negations from the charge of contradictoriness by showing that they do not deny existence, he leaves us with the impression that he has proved too much. For this leaves us thinking that if ordinary negations did deny existence they would be contradictory; and this would be unfortunate in view of the fact that we sometimes need to deny existence. Plato's analysis of negation not only does not deal with legitimate denials of existence; by continually edging away from the notion of a denial of existence it suggests that such a thing could not legitimately occur. But of course it can, and indeed it occurs in a more puzzling form in Greek than in many other languages. We seldom say that fairies are not; we say that there are no fairies. The German idiom *es gibt* is even better than the English *there are*; it—the universe, or what-not—has no fairies to give to those who would like to meet them. But in Greek one must say "Fairies are not" or "Fairies are not-beings" (the Greek word-order in "Fairies are not" may be different, commonly, from what it would be in "Fairies are not pachydermatous"; but word-order is fluid). This creates the impression that we are predicating non-existence of something which we have succeeded in mentioning, and this might lead us to think that fairies must *exist* at some minimal level at which they also non-exist, since statements about them (as with the non-existent "one" in the *Parmenides*) are evidently about *them* and not about something else. Plato's discussion of negation does not of course make it impossible for us to deal with denials of existence; if it did, that would put it out of court. Indeed, as we have seen, the *onoma/rêma* analysis opens the way to a correct analysis of denials of existence in that it shows us just why statements such as "Fairies are not" must be recast if their logical form is to be made apparent. As it stands however Plato's account leaves us with the impression that he thinks that there are no true statements of this form. He is right to say that ordinary negations are not denials of existence, wrong to leave us with the impression that they would be self-contradictory if they were.

5

PLATO'S CONCEPTION OF PHILOSOPHICAL METHOD

I. GENERAL CONSIDERATIONS

WHY do we call Plato a philosopher? What did he conceive of himself as doing? By what methods did he think that that which he was doing ought to be done?

We call Plato a philosopher, and we give the same title to some of our contemporaries; for instance to G. E. Moore. Is there any common feature which justifies the common title; and, if there is, what is it? In this chapter we shall try to answer questions such as these by reflecting on Plato's work, both on how he practised and on what he preached.

In one sense of the word, Plato was the first philosopher to put his work in writing. If his picture of Socrates is correct, then Socrates was the first philosopher in history; if the Platonic Socrates is Plato's figment, then the invention of this peculiar branch of intellectual activity is the work of Plato. This may seem a paradoxical statement when we remember the "pre-Socratic philosophers"— such men as Pythagoras, Heraclitus, Parmenides and Protagoras. But in one important sense of the word these men seem not to have been philosophers. If philosophy were a subject-matter, so that anybody who discoursed, no matter how dogmatically, about that subject matter was a philosopher, then Heraclitus and Parmenides, for example, would undoubtedly deserve the title. But philosophy is not primarily a subject-matter; primarily it is a manner and only secondarily a subject-matter, namely that subject-matter to which the manner is appropriate. Essentially, as we are now using the word, a philosopher is not one who discusses abstract questions, but one who tries so to discuss abstract questions that men may not become entangled in conceptual confusions in attempting to answer them.

Philosophy arises from a number of causes, and its origins determine both what we can expect of it and how it should be done. It arises sometimes out of practical activity. We wonder, for example, whether it is just that one who has stolen more should be punished more heavily than one who has stolen less; and this may lead us to ask what justice is, what it is that we are trying to do when we try to make our decisions just, and whether it is something that we should still want to do if we saw clearly what it is.

Philosophy arises also because men have theories about life and about the world. Some of these theories arise in answer to the questionings we have just considered. Thus a man may say that what we are trying to do in the law-courts is to preserve the rights of property and that justice is the rule of the privileged. Or a man may deny the existence of the gods, or assert the immortality of the soul. Or again, perhaps in the course of argument about topics such as these, one man may confess or evince a belief that nothing is real but what he can see or touch, another may incline contrariwise to a belief in the unique reality of minds and their experiences.

Such theories can be put forward and the resources of poetry and rhetoric can be used to commend them. But such theories are not in themselves philosophy. Nor do they become philosophy, in the sense in which we are using the word, just because their author attempts to prove them by bringing forward what seem to be logically cogent arguments, as Parmenides tried to prove his strange conclusions. Proof of conclusions indeed is out of place in philosophy. For a proposition can only be established by proof on the basis of another; establishment by proof requires axioms. But at the level of fundamental questioning at which philosophy arises there are no axioms to be had; for why should certain propositions be regarded as sacrosanct when others are being questioned? Theories such as those we have mentioned are not philosophy in themselves, then, nor do they become philosophy by being represented as the conclusions of cogent arguments. They only become philosophy in so far as they are critically handled, whether by the man who puts them forward, or by another. This means that the discussion of such a theory only becomes philosophy in so far as it is designed to show just what is involved in the theory, what would be entailed by its acceptance or rejection, and whether it does or does not offer an increase of illumination with respect to the area of life with which it deals.

A philosopher therefore is essentially a critic of theories and not a propounder of them. This does not mean that he is essentially a champion of common sense against those who put forward revolutionary new ideas. "Common-sense", in any epoch, is the name of a theory or set of theories, and there is no reason why these should be immune from philosophic criticism any more than any others.

Nor is it the duty of a philosopher to be neutral just because it is his duty to be critical. The greatest philosophers, generally speaking, have been partisans; some of them have been partisans of the outlook called among their contemporaries common-sense, others have supported what have seemed to them to be new insights of their own, or of some religious or scientific doctrine, or something of the kind. A philosopher may have a view and he may try to recommend it. But he must not become a propagandist for it, for philosophy is essentially an attempt to see what is involved in accepting or rejecting some opinion. It is the attempt to impart scientific standards of clarity and reasonableness into the discussion of matters, the final arbitration of which must be an act of judgment; its objective is to prevent people from swallowing theories, whether novel or commonsensical, without first taking a good look at them to see what they are made of. It uses deductive reasoning, for it is concerned to draw out the consequences of propositions, but it is not a deductive science like mathematics and logic. It refers to the facts of experience, because it has to ask what system of concepts makes the best sense of them, but it is not an empirical discipline. It is the critical advocacy and the critical discussion of possible answers to the abstract questions which arise out of our experience of the world.

So far however we have spoken mostly of the kind of philosophy which interests the plain man. But there is also a more exclusively technical kind of philosophy which arises out of the first kind. For in the course of the arguments, clarifications, distinction-drawings, and so forth which are made by those who critically discuss such problems as the nature of justice or the freedom of the will, there will be certain recurrent features. Certain concepts, such as objectivity, reality, probability, causality, truth, will continually turn up, certain patterns of argument will be continually met with. The discussion of these is the origin of disinterested technical philosophy, which is a tool-making activity, not directly concerned with the discussion of theories about life and the world, but with the forging and refining of notions which will be employed in any such discussions, and with the diagnosis of the type of pit into which such discussions are liable to fall.

Such a conception of the nature of philosophy would be challenged from two sides. It would be challenged by the positivists who hold that there are no questions in the decision of which progress can be made by the philosophical method of conceptual clarification. There *seem* to be such questions ("Is the will free?" "Are material objects independent of our experience of them?" and so on) and we *feel* that there is more than one answer to them, and that we must philosophise, or work out the implications of these answers, before we can choose between them. But this is only because the questions are themselves confused. It is not that we need to see more clearly before we can decide which answer to give; the work of clarification is to be done at an earlier stage, and if it is done properly it will show us why the questions do not really arise. The purpose of philosophy is not to help us to answer such questions rationally, but to save us from asking them. The only questions which really arise are those which "science" (in a broad sense) can answer.

Our conception would also be challenged by the deductive metaphysicians. We have described the philosopher as one who helps men to judge rationally on matters which are essentially matters of judgment because they cannot be settled by empirical investigation. The positivist says that there are no such matters, because all real questions can in principle be answered by empirical investigation. We agree with the positivist that it will often be the case that when an issue is clarified, the settling of it will be an empirical matter, but we do not agree that this is always so. The deductive metaphysician will agree with the positivist that there are no matters which are essentially matters of judgment, but not for the reason that all real questions can in principle be settled empirically. The deductive metaphysician will agree with us that this is not so, but he will hold that all or most of the questions which cannot be settled empirically can be settled metaphysically. For there are in his view certain propositions which are both self-evidently true and also fertile of consequences which are of practical significance. The business of philosophy is to hunt for these indisputable axioms, and, by deducing their consequences, and the consequences of their consequences, to settle finally and conclusively the questions which we want to ask, but cannot determine by empirical investigation.

It is my intention to claim Plato as the begetter and a practitioner of the conception of philosophy which I outlined first. He was neither a positivist nor a deductive metaphysician.

Nobody would call Plato a positivist, but he is commonly deemed to have been the arch-druid of deductive metaphysicians. This impression I shall try to combat. It derives partly from the fact that he does indeed discuss "metaphysical" topics (God, immortality, the status of the material word), and that his outlook is "metaphysical" rather than commonsensical. This however is not enough to make him a deductive metaphysician, for his discussion of his chosen topics and his advocacy of his standpoint are not done in the metaphysical, but in the genuinely philosophical manner; and philosophy, once more, is a manner and not a range of topics or a set of opinions.

So far as Plato's practice is concerned, it is fairly obvious that it is not the practice of the deductive metaphysician. The deductive metaphysician and the positivist, as I have described them, are no doubt ideal creatures not represented in the real world; but if we take someone like Spinoza as an approximation to the deductive metaphysician, it is fairly clear that Plato is in practice a very different kind of thinker. The deductive metaphysician begins with clearly defined terms, and proceeds to deduce the consequences of the propositions which he constructs out of these terms. Definition and demonstration are the essence of his method. But in all of Plato's writings how very few definitions there are, how very few conclusions are proved. Many of the dialogues are unsuccessful attempts at producing definitions; it is Plato's constant lament that we use words without really understanding what we mean by them, and that the work of coming to understand this is of the greatest difficulty. We are indeed offered definitions of terms like *speed* and *shape*, terms of no great philosophical significance. But perhaps the only philosophically important term of which Plato offers what seems to be a definition is *the soul*, which he defines as self-activating activity.

Again there is a good deal of refutation in the dialogues; for example the thesis of Theaetetus that knowledge is sensation is refuted. This particular refutation is indeed offered as conclusive; yet even with negative conclusions it is characteristic of Plato not to say that A *cannot* be B, but rather to use some formula which expresses a measure of uncertainty—"it does not seem so" and the like. But while there are a fair number of more or less tentative negative conclusions in the dialogues, the number of positive conclusions which are put forward as if they had been definitely established is very small. The most important instance of a doctrine which Plato claims to have established conclusively is the doctrine that spiritual activity is the uncreated source of all activity, a doctrine for which there is a demonstrative argument in the *Phaedrus* and the *Laws*. But the doctrine that there are forms is nowhere the object of what purports to be a deductive argument. Usually it is put forward as an article of the Socratic faith. There is indeed an argument for it in the *Timaeus* (51–2), but it does not pretend to be conclusive. It rests on the admittedly controvertible fact that understanding is not the same thing as right opinion, and this might be said to rest on the fact that to be persuaded of something is not the same as to come to understand how it must be true.

Very typical is the position of the final argument for immortality in the *Phaedo*. Here, having shown that souls cannot die, Socrates does not attempt to show that they are therefore indestructible, for it is conceded by all the company that things which cannot die must be among the indestructibles. But it is not suggested that this is logically necessary; rather, the opposite hypothesis is dismissed as not worth considering. The reason why it is not worth considering, as we have suggested in earlier chapters, is that a situation in which things which cannot die were nevertheless destructible would be an absurd situation; and Socrates and his friends are convinced that absurd situations of this kind are not to be met with in nature. If you replied that nature in your opinion was full of absurdities then Plato would undertake to wean you of this opinion. The *Republic* and with it the *Timaeus* can be construed as a kind of manifesto of the sort of intellectual discipline which he would make you undergo. He would teach you enough mathematics to enable you to find order in what had hitherto seemed disorderly. He would try to make you share his conviction that the world can be seen as rationally ordered if one thinks hard enough about it; and he would rest this conviction no doubt on the doctrine of the primacy of spiritual activity already alluded to. He would undertake to change your outlook if you would submit yourself to the appropriate kind of training; but this is not the same thing as producing a demonstrative argument.

Plato had of course a view of his own, and it was not the view of common-sense. He was convinced that the world owes such definiteness and tractability as it possesses to the activity of reason which is prior to and independent of the physical world. This is his fundamental tenet. Much of his mature work is in one sense an attempt to work out the consequences of this doctrine. But this is not to say that Platonism is an axiomatic system *ordine geometrico demonstratum* with this doctrine as one of the axioms. The philosopher who has a personal conviction which he wants to recommend will not get very far if he tries simply to deduce its consequences in the mathematical manner. He must work squint-wise. He must keep one eye on the conviction which he is recommending, while allowing the other to range over the facts of experience. The problem all the time is not: "What follows from my fundamental postulate?" but something more like: "How, in the light of my fundamental postulate, am I to describe or account for the facts which one encounters in this or that department of experience?" To say therefore that all of Plato's mature work derives from a fundamental conviction is not to say that he does nothing but reiterate that conviction and deduce its consequences. In fact he seldom mentions it, and practically never explicitly derives anything from it. He earns the title of a philosopher not because he has an opinion, but because he attempts to clarify the issues which will have to be discussed in the accepting or rejecting of that opinion. A man does not gain the title by sticking mulishly to common sense, nor does he forfeit it by recommending a personal insight. He earns it by the work which he does to render clearer what is involved in the choice between different accounts of the world. He earns the title of a great philosopher not by the skill with which he forces us to agree with him but by the extent to which he exposes the difficulty, complexity, and ramifying nature of theoretical questions.

I said earlier that one of the causes which give rise to philosophical activity is the co-existence in the same man of the philosophical temper as we have just been describing it, and of a personal conviction about the world. It seems to me clear that Plato had both a philosophic temper and a personal conviction. But we saw also that there are other causes which give rise to philosophical activity. One of these is the tangles which arise out of the theoretical discussion of practical matters. Some philosophers have given a good deal of their time to trying to solve puzzles which have arisen in the course of such discussions. On the whole Plato does not do very much of this. When he asks such questions as "What is piety?" or "What is justice?" we do not feel that he is offering his services as an un-raveller of confusions to the practical man. Before very long either he is pulling some theory to pieces (as in the *Laches, Meno, Char-mides, Lysis*) or he is delineating more of the positive Platonic outlook (as in the *Republic* and to some extent in the *Euthyphro*). In fact if we want to find Plato working as an under-labourer at the clearing away of thickets, we shall probably be best advised to look at the *Laws*. Here we shall find, for example, a long discussion in the Ninth Book of matters connected with responsibility under the criminal law. To some slight extent this discussion is provoked by the necessity of reconciling the doctrine that no man willingly does wrong with the conception of criminal intent, but in general it is fair to say that Plato is here doing what Aristotle did again along much the same lines in the Third Book of the *Nicomachean Ethics*, namely laying the foundations of jurisprudence by distinguishing some of the essential concepts.

Philosophy also arises, as we have seen, as a sort of second-order activity concerned to elucidate the concepts which are used and the patterns of argument which arise in first-order philosophical dis-cussion. Of this kind of technical philosophy we do not find very much in Plato—naturally enough, since he was hardly in a position to know what the technical problems of philosophy were going to be. We shall look in vain for discussions of such topics as truth or probability, the nature of obligation or causality, and the others which have occupied so much of the attention of philosophers in recent times. Plato has of course views on many of these matters, sometimes views which he takes for granted and which we have to state for him, at other times views which he was sufficiently conscious of to give a brief statement of them. But in general Plato has little to say on those problems which only arise in the course of philosophical discussion, in response to questions which do not arise out of practical activity or from a conflict of attitudes to life, but which are rather questions which only somebody who had done some philosophy would think of asking.

But it would be a very incomplete account of Plato's philosophical activity which omitted to stress his critical work. Philosophy is the antidote to propaganda, and there was a good deal of propaganda about in ancient Greece. Especially in his earlier writings Plato's determination that received views should not be accepted without scrutiny is very pronounced. Nor, so far as we can tell, does Plato confine his criticism to views with which he is unsympathetic. Being human, he may have argued more energetically against views of which he disapproved. But when he says that the worst form of ignorance is to suppose that we know when we do not, it seems that he means what he says. We cannot progress so long as we wrongly believe that we understand something, even when the doctrine we uncritically subscribe to happens to be true. Thus in the *Laches* Nicias is attacked because he is eager to propose a view along the lines of the Socratic doctrine that virtue is knowledge without asking himself just what the view involves. A true proposition, swallowed whole, cannot be digested and may do as much damage as a false one. Understanding does not consist, as the *Seventh Letter* make clear, in the propensity to utter true propositions, nor is teaching the communication of this propensity. Teaching is a matter of conveying the vision in which understanding consists, and "friendly refutation" plays a large part in the long process which is needed to bring this about. Consistently with this Plato spends a good deal of his time raising difficulties against plausible views. It is significant that there is only one place in which the theory of forms is subjected to discussion, namely the first part of the *Parmenides*; and here the discussion is distinctly unfriendly. We are indeed told that Parmenides' criticisms can be met, but we are left to work out for ourselves how to meet them. It is not valuable that we should believe true propositions, but that we should understand their truth.

I hope that I have done enough to remind the reader that the things that Plato does are characteristic of the activity which has since come to be called philosophy and that he does not do them in the manner of the deductive metaphysician or rationalist. It is of course possible that Plato's practice as an oral teacher was a good deal more rationalistic than his practice as a writer. We know that he had a low view of the importance of written philosophy, and it might be that he had a metaphysical system of a rationalist kind which he was prepared to expound orally but not to expose to the misunderstandings to which written works are subject. This is possible, but there seems to be no reason to believe that it is true. The belief that Plato was a deductive metaphysician, therefore, rests neither on his practice as a writer nor on theories about his practice as an oral teacher, but rather on his preaching. But it cannot rest on a consistent body of preaching for as we know there are many places where Plato preaches things that are not at all rationalist in temper. It must indeed rest on one passage only, namely the Seventh Book of the *Republic*.

We have discussed this passage elsewhere. Here we need only remind ourselves of the conception that we can attain to an *anhupothetos archê* or non-provisional starting point, from which we can proceed "downwards" establishing with certainty what has hitherto been hypothetical. For this conception has at least a superficial resemblance to the conception of the deductive metaphysician that we can attain to a set of axioms from which we can derive the answers to all the questions of philosophy.

But the resemblance is a superficial one. For one thing, as we have seen in earlier chapters, there is no very clear suggestion even in this passage that philosophy should be done in the rationalist manner. Much the greater part of the time of those who are trained in accordance with the curriculum which Socrates describes will be occupied with what he calls the "way up", or the search for the non-provisional starting-point. On the question what sort of intellectual activity follows upon the vision of the nature of goodness Socrates is even vaguer than he is on the question what sort of intellectual activity precedes it; and it is at least left open to us to suppose that the "way down" consists of little more than the setting out in logical order of that which has been discovered on the "way up". In that case practically all the real work would consist of the process of finding out "what each thing is", which precedes the acquisition of the non-provisional starting-point. The truth is surely that Plato believed in the existence of a coherent system of rational principles and that, in the *Republic* at any rate, he believed that the nature of goodness was in some sense the keystone of the system. This amounts to saying that there exists to be discovered a body of truths, whose validity reason will recognise, which depends in some way on a single truth, whose validity also will be apparent in the same way. But it does not amount to saying that the derivation of consequences from self-evident axioms plays any part whatever in the discovery of these truths. If we distinguish the two questions: "How do we know that we have attained to the truth?" and "How do we set about attaining to it?" it appears that there will be some similarity between the answer to the first question which the Seventh Book of the *Republic* suggests and that which the rationalist metaphysician would give; for both will agree that the truth will consist of a starting-point which will commend itself to the mind and of a remainder which will cohere with that starting-point. But it does not appear that there will be any similarity between the two answers to the second question. In so far as we can extract from the passage in the *Republic* any doctrine about the process of invention, it appears to consist of a kind of contemplative activity whereby we attempt to "give account" of general terms; that is to say it appears to consist of an attempt to render explicit the understanding which we in some sense possess of the various general terms which we employ. Either as metaphor or as sober doctrine the model of a man trying to recapture a memory, though absent from the text of this passage of the *Republic*, seems to be an important part of Plato's account of the process of discovery.

But furthermore there is really no reason to think that the non-provisional starting-point consists of anything like an axiom or a set of axioms, or that the other members of the system stand to it as its logical consequences. According to the account that we have given, some conception of the nature of goodness has been presupposed in all the conclusions that have been come to on the upward path, and these conclusions must remain provisional until we have somehow come to see that this account of the nature of goodness is correct. But there is no clear suggestion that the process of coming to see that this conception is correct consists in discovering that it can be stated in a self-evident or logically true proposition. The suggestion is rather that we simply know that we are contemplating a reality. As to how we can know this kind of thing, Plato no more tells us than Descartes tells us what he means when he speaks of the clear perceptions of an undoubting mind. The conception of logical truth imported implicitly by Spinoza and explicitly by Leibniz is one way of making precise what was adumbrated by Descartes. In its application to Plato it is not a particularly plausible way of interpreting his apophthegms. Nor is there any reason to suppose that when we have attained to a proposition of the form "Goodness is a.b.c." (assuming that the vision of goodness can be expressed in a proposition) we are to think that this proposition confirms the other propositions of the system by entailing them. According to the interpretation that we have followed this is not the case. Rather, the position is more like this. We have rejected, on the way up, any account of a general term which does not seem to us to make sense. To use once more an example which we have already used too often, we have rejected the conception that souls are perishable things because it does not seem to us to make sense that things which cannot die can perish. In doing this however we have presupposed a certain conception of that which commends itself to reason, or in other words of goodness. Until we can satisfy ourselves that this conception is correct, the "accounts" which we have arrived at in the light of it cannot be regarded as established. It is a little as if I had worked out some problem (say about the rate at which a cistern will become depleted if it is supplied by two pipes of a given diameter and emptied by a third pipe of some other diameter) on the assumption that a pint of water occupies a cubic foot. I cannot be confident of my answer until I have checked this (erroneous) assumption. The assumption about the nature of goodness is indeed more intimately connected with the rest of the workings than this example suggests; for the doctrine seems to be that we are in no position to discover what goodness is until we have used a conception of its nature to give account of everything else, whereas we can find out the equivalent of a pint in cubic inches by looking it up at any time. This however only reinforces the point that it is Plato's belief that we have in some sense possessed all along any knowledge which we can come to possess explicitly. It does not alter the point that the final discovery "confirms" what has been discovered before it not because it entails it but because it has been assumed in it.

It seems then that the conception of philosophical method which is vaguely outlined in the Seventh Book of the *Republic* has little to do with the rationalist conception of metaphysics as a system of logically necessary truths. It is indeed perhaps worth suggesting that Plato's *picture* of philosophical knowledge is far removed from that of someone like Spinoza. For it is probably true that Plato did not conceive of the matter very much in terms of the acquisition of true propositions; the goal was something much more like really getting to know one's general terms. There are relations like equality or conditions like virtue, and in a sense we are all familiar with entities like these. Yet just as I, being familiar with Piccadilly Circus, would nevertheless not score very high marks in a contest in which one had to detail the lay-out of its buildings, so we are most of us unable to give account of equality and virtue; and just as it is frequent and observant visiting of Piccadilly Circus which will better our ability to describe it, so it is by frequently and critically giving our attention to equality and virtue that we shall come to understand them.

The goal of philosophy, then, is the critical understanding of those general terms, the concepts answering to which are crucial to the conceptual system which we employ; and one of Plato's main emphases is upon the difficulty and precariousness of the process of acquiring this understanding. Since something like this goal and something like these emphases are common to many contemporary philosophers, and carry with them a distrust of systems and formulas, it is perhaps a little surprising that it is Aristotle, the systematiser and formularist, who is still often thought to be on the side of the angels, Plato on that of the apes.

II. HYPOTHESES AND DIALECTIC

We must leave these pleasant generalisations for a discussion of two terms which seem to have some technical flavour, namely "hypotheses" and "dialectic". The two terms are interconnected, in that the position seems to be that you have to use hypotheses so long as you have failed to achieve that which you are trying to achieve when you do dialectic. It is success in dialectic which will make hypotheses unnecessary.

Some scholars have made much of what they call the hypothetical method. In their view Plato attached considerable importance to a technique of hypothetical argument. It was, they say, one of his main recommendations that we should treat hypotheses in a certain manner. In an earlier draft of this chapter I worked out a fairly elaborate methodological doctrine which I described as the hypothetical method, claiming that it was put forward by Plato as a technique of invention. On reflection however I have come to think that too much can easily be made of the rather scarce and slender remarks that Plato makes about hypotheses. It would be a mistake, all the same, to go to the other extreme and deny that there is any such thing as the hypothetical method. Both in the *Meno* and in the *Phaedo* the concept of *hupothesis* seems to be somewhat gratuitously introduced into the argument, and in both of these places and also in the *Republic* the term is used as if it were something of a technical term. It seems then that there is some technical doctrine connected with this word that Plato is anxious to communicate to us. Unfortunately it is also true that in all three places Plato tells us less than we should like to know about the meaning that he puts upon this word and upon some of its associates. It is almost as if he has in mind some body of teaching on the subject of *hupothesis*. It may be that he had in mind some private doctrine of his own and that he failed to notice that he had not given us enough clues to enable us to follow him with confidence; or it may be that he is referring to something which was familiar to his contemporaries, but which is lost to us.

Verbally it seems that a *hupothesis* primarily ought to be an act of supposing or of putting forward for the sake of argument or of taking for granted, and that secondarily it ought to be the proposition supposed, put forward or taken for granted—just as a *propositio* ought to be a putting forward, and thus the thing put forward, or proposition. "Hypothesis" therefore will do as a translation of *hupothesis* if one discounts the element of explanatory power which "hypothesis" tends to connote and if one also bears in mind that a *hupothesis* may sometimes be the act of supposing. It is probably also true that the word "hypothesis" has too strong a flavour of tentativeness to do as a perfect translation of *hupothesis*. The *hupotheseis* of mathematicians in the *Republic*, namely oddness, evenness, the shapes and three kinds of angles, are probably not so called because mathematicians either do in fact or should in principle put forward propositions about these entities as tentative hypotheses; the point is rather that they take their concepts of these entities as basic and do not attempt to "give account" of them or "ask what they are". Again in the Fourth Book of the *Republic* when the principle, that A cannot simultaneously have to B both of two opposed relationships, is called a *hupothesis*[1] it is not an important part of Plato's meaning that the principle is dubious. Some tentativeness is indeed connoted by *hupothesis*; it is probably true to say that Plato sometimes chooses this word or its cognates as part of his general programme of insisting on the tentativeness of all philosophical speculations put forward by a judicious mind. But it would be wrong, I think, to suppose that when he uses it he always intends to mark the special tentativeness of that which he uses it of.

A. *Hypotheses in the* Meno *and* Phaedo

In the passage in the *Phaedo* which is concerned with *hupothesis* (*Phaedo* 99–102) Socrates is about to embark on his final argument for immortality, and therefore is discussing the conditions under which things can come about. He has described his dissatisfaction with the types of explanation currently offered in science and mathematics. In particular he has expressed his sympathy with the type of explanation which explains a fact by showing how it is best that it should be as it is, and regretted his inability either to find such explanations in any one else's writings or to invent them for himself. In view of this inability he has "worked out a 'second voyage' to the search for explanation" (99 d). Having failed in the contemplation of realities, he has made up his mind not to stare at them, but to look at their images in *logoi* (statements, accounts or definitions).[2] His procedure is to suppose (*hupotithesthai*, "hypothesise") on every occasion the *logos* which seems to him the strongest, and to suppose the truth of everything which accords with it and the falsity of everything which conflicts with it. He then asks whether this is understood;

---

[1] The participle *hupothemenoi* is used *Rep.* 437 a 6.
[2] On this, and indeed on the whole passage, see above, pp. 156–71.

he is told that it is not, and he goes on, not to explain what he means by "supposing the strongest *logos*", but to give what appears to be the *logos* which he has decided to suppose on the subject of explanation. He cites his hypothesis, in other words, rather than tells us what a hypothesis is, or what makes one stronger than another. (*Phaedo* 100 b, c. On any interpretation this passage seems to be rather elliptical and inelegant). His hypothesis is, he says, a very familiar one; it is that there are forms and that nothing comes to acquire a property except through the presence of a form to it— nothing is beautiful except by virtue of beauty, nothing is greater than anything else except by virtue of greater-than-ness.

The use that Socrates makes of this obscure hypothesis does not concern us here.[1] What is to our immediate purpose is that after various applications of the hypothesis Socrates goes on to make some methodological remarks which are gratuitous with respect to the main purpose and which must have been written for our instruction. He says (101–2) that he presumes that Kebes will agree that the number 2 cannot be created by addition or division, but only by participation in duality. Anything "subtler" than this is best left to the wiser (this is presumably ironical). Socrates and Kebes will "hold on to the safety of the hypothesis". They will stick to the rule that only two-ness makes 2, and hence avoid talking nonsense. However Socrates now envisages the possibility that somebody may challenge the hypothesis, and he advises Kebes how to proceed when this happens. The remarks which Socrates makes are hardly self-explanatory, and I find it easy to suppose that Plato has something in mind on which he is consciously or unconsciously relying to make his meaning clear. So far as his own writings go the only passage to which he could be referring us is the discussion of hypotheses in the *Meno*; but as we shall see shortly this will hardly give us all we want. Meanwhile we must ask what the general significance of this passage is.

It is possible to attach to it very little significance. We could begin by saying that when Socrates contrasts looking at things in *logoi* with looking at them in *erga* (*sc.* in sense-experience?) he does not mean to suggest that the former method is any more indirect than the latter; indeed he says as much himself (100 a 1). All that he means to tell us, on this view, is that he decided that the collection of data would not solve problems; what was needed was thought about general principles. In describing his decision to do some of this thinking as a "second voyage" (a phrase which seems properly to mean a slower and more laborious way of getting to the same place, but which can mean no more than "second best") he is being ironical, as he certainly is at various places in this passage.[1] Similarly the description of his principle as a hypothesis is no more than a piece of modesty. Socrates is really telling us that he came to the conclusion that scientific investigation would make no sure progress until somebody could establish some general principles as to what can count as a valid explanation of a phenomenon. His "hypothesis" is such a principle. His concluding methodological remarks far from having any reference to some special "hypothetical method" of reasoning, add up in fact to the humdrum advice to take things by stages and not to try to find grounds for accepting a proposition before you have first discovered whether it has, so to speak, passed the qualifying examination, or in other words whether it is free from paradoxical consequences.

I confess that I do not find this rather deflationary interpretation of this passage incredible. It is certainly true that when Socrates first speaks of "hypothesising" he is more interested, as we have already seen, in the content of his hypothesis than he is in the question what he means by calling it a hypothesis. This is consistent with the view that "hypothesising whatever I judge to be the strongest *logos*" simply means "taking the view that seems to be right". It is only the methodological remarks at the end of the passage that seem to be ill catered for on the deflationary interpretation. On the other hand I do not feel tempted to go the whole way in the other direction. That is to say I do not think that Socrates is giving the outlines of a method of investigation which is specifically put forward as inferior to some other method of investigation which he is incompetent to follow. That might be his meaning if he represented his procedure as "second voyage" to dialectic; but in so many words at any rate this is not what he does. He represents it as "second voyage" to the methods of Anaxagoras and others whom he has just been ridiculing. The implication surely is that Anaxagoras and other early scientists had been trying to go too fast because they had failed to lay adequate theoretical foundations; there is no clear suggestion that Socrates intends to use a method which is slower than some ideal method.

Nevertheless that might be what he has in mind, though it is not what he clearly brings out. We shall turn now to the discussion in the *Meno* to see what light we can get from there. The passage which is is specially concerned with hypotheses is *Meno* 86–9, but we must also take account of the general shape of the dialogue.

The official subject of the *Meno* is the question whether virtue can be taught. Socrates however protests, when Meno poses this question, that he does not know what virtue is and hence cannot know whether

[1] e.g. 97 b 7.

it is teachable. In general he says (71) that unless one knows what (*ti*) a thing or person is, one cannot know what it is like (*hopoion*). In accordance with this principle Socrates tries to get Meno to offer a satisfactory definition of virtue.

The contrast between knowing what a thing is and knowing what it is like is important and recurs in various contexts which have to do with dialectic. It refers to what we have called the counter-inductive stipulation that one must be able to offer an analysis of P-hood before one can say what is in general true of P things. It is defended in this place by an unfortunate, not to say sophistical, analogy—namely that I cannot say what sort of person Meno is if I do not know who he is. This suggests that Socrates' meaning is that if I cannot identify that which "virtue" stands for, if I do not know what the word means, I cannot make true statements about the thing. This however is not the point; Socrates can perfectly well, to this extent, identify virtue. What he refers to as "knowing what a thing is" is the condition which we described earlier in this chapter as the critical understanding of a general term; it is a state of mind which goes far beyond the mere ability to perform successfully with the corresponding concept, and it is the only state of mind which enables us to make general statements about the term in question, or in other words to "know what sort of a thing it is". We must first see clearly what we are doing in classifying states of character as virtue and vice before we are in a position to decide by what means such states are acquired.

To return to Socrates' discussion with Meno, Meno fails to offer a satisfactory definition of virtue. He then complains (79–80) that Socrates is notorious for stunning those who talk with him, for inducing in them a condition of *aporia* or of not knowing how to proceed. For he, Meno, who has often listened with approbation to his own discourses on the nature of virtue, is unable to tell Socrates what it is. This indeed, he adds, seems to be a hopeless condition; for how can a man ever learn what something is? If he knows already, then there is nothing to learn; but if he does not know what he is enquiring into, how will he know what he is looking for or recognise it if by chance he encounters it? (80 d–e). Socrates treats this as a well-known sophism, but takes it seriously. His answer to it is the doctrine of *anamnêsis* or recollection. Of this he specifically says (86 b) that the only part of the doctrine of which he is quite confident is that it is worth while seeking for that which one does not know. In other words the relevance of the doctrine of *anamnêsis* in this context is that somehow or other we possess a latent understanding of the general terms which we employ, and that this latent understanding can be drawn out by discussion and questioning. This amounts to saying that the attempt to see "what something is" is not hopeless.

This disposes of Meno's attempt to show that it is futile to try to discover what virtue is. Nevertheless he is not enthusiastic for this enterprise and says that he would prefer to discuss the question whether virtue is teachable. With some show of reluctance, Socrates agrees to discuss this question *ex hupotheseôs*, "from a hypothesis", and he illustrates the meaning of this phrase by a geometrical analogy (86 e–87 b). The analogy is not altogether easy to interpret. A paraphrase of what he says is as follows. "By *ex hupotheseôs* I mean the method of investigation which is sometimes followed by a geometer, for example when he is asked about some area, say whether a given triangle can be inscribed in a given circle. He may reply that he does not know as yet whether this is so or not, but that he thinks that he has a hypothesis which is relevant; this is that if the triangle has a certain property so and so seems to him to follow, whereas if it lacks that property the consequences seem to be other. He is willing therefore, he says, to make a hypothesis and say what follows with respect to the inscribability of the triangle." It is not clear here whether the hypothesis is meant to be: "That the triangle has a certain property", or whether it is meant to be: "That if the triangle has a certain property certain consequences follow, whereas if it lacks the property certain other consequences follow." Moreover if (as seems the more probable) the latter is the meaning, the possibility seems to arise that this is called a hypothesis not because it is "put forward" but because it is an *if-then* statement, or hypothetical. On the whole I incline to the view that the hypothesis is the hypothetical, but that it is not because it is hypothetical that it is called a hypothesis. It is noteworthy that the geometer is represented as saying that if the triangle has a certain property, then it *seems to him* that certain consequences would follow; the hypothetical is advanced, not as a theorem, but as something probable.

Similar doubts encumber the hypothesis about virtue which Socrates goes on to produce and which is supposed to be analogous to the geometrical example. It is not clear whether this is meant to be: "That virtue is knowledge", or: "That if virtue is knowledge it is teachable." On the whole, again, I incline to the view that the latter is intended, despite the fact that when this proposition is introduced it is not at all put forward in a tentative fashion. What Socrates does, having given his geometrical analogy, is to say: "So let us, since we know neither what virtue is nor what sort of a thing it is, make a hypothesis and thus investigate whether it is teachable or not, saying as follows: If it fell into what category of psychical endowments would it be teachable. . . . ? Firstly, if it were of a different character from that of knowledge would it be teachable (or rather, as we have just said recollectable). . . .? Or is it obvious to everybody that nothing is taught to a man but knowledge? This is obvious, surely. Then if it is knowledge obviously it would be teachable" (87 b 2–c 6). If it were essential to a *hupothesis* that it be put forward tentatively or for the sake of argument, then the "obviously" which occurs in it would disqualify the last sentence for the status of a *hupothesis*. If however something which seems obvious can be called a *hupothesis* so long, perhaps, as its truth has not been formally demonstrated, this disqualification would not apply.

At any rate, having said that virtue will be teachable if and only if it is of the same character as knowledge, Socrates goes on to ask whether it is indeed of this character. He argues first in favour of this view. His argument is based on another *hupothesis*, this time that virtue is a good thing. Of this *hupothesis* he says (87 d 3) that it *menei*, which probably means that it will not be overturned. He then contends that virtue can only fail to be knowledge if there are good things which do not depend on the latter. Everything however which is sometimes beneficial is also sometimes harmful; its beneficial character depends on its right use. The "courage" which does not consist in right understanding (*phronêsis*), but is rather a kind of boldness of temperament, is sometimes disastrous; and so on. If then, as has been agreed, virtue is always beneficial, it must contain some built-in principle of right use; it must therefore be right understanding.

Having thus stated a case for the view that virtue is knowledge (a case for the view that virtue is right understanding is at least a partial case for the view that virtue is knowledge),[1] Socrates proceeds to examine whether virtue is in fact teachable, as it should be if this view is correct. A long discussion reaches the conclusion that those who may be presumed to try to teach it fail to do so, from which it is inferred that it is not teachable. Since however it has been agreed that virtue is always a good thing, and that this means that the right use of it is somehow guaranteed, a connection between virtue and right use more tenuous than that which was supplied by the view that virtue was knowledge must be sought. This is found in the suggestion that virtue is right belief, and this suggestion is tentatively adopted. Socrates ends the conversation however by saying that we cannot expect to get clear about the question how men acquire virtue until we first try to find out what it is "itself according to itself".

It is very obvious that philosophical method is a main theme of this dialogue. One could indeed say that the questions what virtue is

---

[1] In fact it seems to me that *phronêsis* and *epistêmê* are used as synonyms in this passage; see for example 97 a 6 where *phronimos* seems to mean the same as *eidôs*.

and how we acquire it are only discussed for the sake of example. The real purpose of the dialogue (we might argue) is to insist on the importance of critical understanding of key terms, and to explain by the doctrine of *anamnêsis* how this is possible. It is probably always a mistake to find some one purpose only in a Platonic dialogue, but it is undeniable that this is one of the purposes of the *Meno*. In this light it is tempting to wonder whether what is said about hypotheses may not be intended to suggest a technique of philosophical invention. We remember that Meno complained that Socrates had the habit of paralysing those whom he talked to by demanding Socratic definitions. The sophistical paradox which purports to show that discovery is impossible is refuted by the doctrine of recollection; but this only shows us that discovery is possible, it does not tell us how to achieve it. The suggestion that we proceed "from a hypothesis", we might say, is meant to tell us what to do when, in our frailty, we have failed to "give account of what something is itself according to itself". We might indeed suggest that the very word *hupothesis* is only chosen to reinforce the general principle that until we have achieved a critical understanding of a term we have no right to regard any proposition containing that term as established.

If we were confident that the hypothesis that Socrates suggests were "That virtue is knowledge" we could represent him as saying something like the following:—"You can't say what virtue is? Never mind; have a shot. Say for the sake of argument that it is knowledge. This will give you something to go on. There is a familiar connection between knowledge and teachability, and also a connection between goodness and knowledge. The latter supports the hypothesis that virtue is knowledge, whereas the former gives you something that you can test. Ask whether virtue is teachable. Apparently it is not. Therefore it does not seem to be knowledge. Yet it ought to have some connection with knowledge because of the link between utility and knowledge. How would it be then if virtue were a kind of cousin of knowledge, namely right opinion? This suggestion would be enough to explain why virtue is always useful without running into the difficulty that it does not appear to be teachable; for opinions do not come and go by teaching. Thus you see that by supposing that virtue is knowledge you have made progress towards discovering what it is. You have eliminated provisionally one answer which seems to be untenable (namely the one that you tried out), but the process of putting it forward has suggested to you considerations about the presence in virtue of some factor guaranteeing right use, which in turn has led to the suggestion, so far unrefuted, that it is in fact right opinion. We haven't tested this properly and it may well be wrong (I'm not sure for example whether virtue isn't something more secure than

535

right opinion); but at least we can claim to have established reasonably firmly a vaguer principle to the effect that some kind of right understanding is somehow essential to virtue. This will give us something to go on next time we meet to resume the discussion of what virtue is."

This gives a rather attractive reconstruction of the argument of the *Meno*, and I am not sure that a train of thought like this was altogether absent from Plato's mind. But if this was his meaning he has not made it clear. The trouble with this reconstruction is that it overlooks the fact that Socrates agrees to consider Meno's question, whether virtue is teachable, from a hypothesis, whereas on this reconstruction he is all the time interested only in his own question, what virtue is. The question whether it is teachable is not considered "from a hypothesis"; it is simply considered by asking whether in fact people do succeed in teaching it.

To be candid, however, this fact seems to constitute an obstacle to any reasonable interpretation of this part of the dialogue. We are inclined to think that what the geometer to whom Socrates likens himself says is something like this: "I cannot answer your question on the data you give me, but I can tell you something that may help. If the figure that you are concerned with has a certain property, then it can be inscribed; if not, not. Your next step therefore is to see whether your figure has this property." But if that is how the geometers are meant to proceed, it is not how Socrates proceeds. For to proceed in that way would be to advise Meno to settle whether virtue is knowledge, because the answer to that question is necessary in order to answer the question whether it is teachable. The form of the argument would have been (for example) the following: "If p ('virtue is knowledge') then q ('virtue is teachable') and if not-p then not-q; but p; therefore q." But in fact the argument has the form: "If p then q and if not-p then not-q; but not-q; therefore not-p." "Not-q" ("virtue is not teachable") is established without any help from the introduction of p, and is used to discredit p. Meno's question is answered by empirical investigation into the success which people have in teaching virtue, and the nature of virtue has no bearing on the investigation. Therefore the supposition that virtue is knowledge does nothing whatever to assist in answering Meno's question, and it is hard to see what Socrates meant by saying that he would only attempt to answer this question if he was allowed to do so "from a hypothesis".

Therefore unless we suppose (what is by no means incredible) that Plato has lost his grip on the structure of the dialogue at this point, we shall have to conclude that the introduction of hypotheses is not intended to help in answering Meno's question; for it does not in fact help. Is it then an irrelevant intrusion? Not necessarily. It is possible to suppose that the function of the hypothesis in Socrates' mind is, not to help in the answering of Meno's question, but to bring it about that the giving of a provisional answer to Meno's question shall contribute something (negatively) to the answering of Socrates' own. In other words Socrates is saying: "I am not going to go chasing hares about whether virtue can be taught, when we ought first to be deciding what it is. But if you are prepared to let me link up the question whether it can be taught with the prior question what it is, then I don't mind paying some attention to your question. It will after all get us somewhere. If the appearances suggest that virtue can't be taught, that will at least give us an idea of what it isn't. The whole thing will be provisional and unsatisfactory because we can't be sure that we are looking for the answers to your question in the right places until we have answered mine. I mean, if we are going to look at reputable Athenian citizens to see whether they managed to make their children reputable, and if we regard this as asking whether virtue can be taught, we shall be taking it for granted that virtue is that which stuffs the shirts of Pericles and Themistocles; and it may very well not be. Still, if we bear in mind that the whole discussion is on a provisional level, it will do no harm to ask whether, if virtue is the quality of men like these, it is a quality which can be taught." In other words Socrates is prepared to consider the particular, practical question whether virtue can be taught only if it is explicitly bound up with the general theoretical question what virtue is, in such a way that the practical question can be made to give some help, of a provisional kind, to the attempt at "recollecting" virtue, or at seeing what we are really doing when we divide men into good and bad.

Is there, then, any methodological advice offered in this section of the Meno? As we saw above, it is tempting to link together the introduction of hypotheses and the paralysing effect of Socrates' habit of demanding that we should say what something is before we say anything else about it. So far as *Socrates* is concerned he insists to the end (*cp. Meno* 100 b 5) that this is the correct order; but it is possible that *Plato* intends to tell us that we can sometimes make better progress if we make the kind of departure from Socrates' order that he might have been induced, once in a way, to tolerate. In that case the methodological advice that Plato is offering us could perhaps be along the following lines. It cannot be (surely) that there is *nothing* in so well established a habit as that of distinguishing virtue from vice. But unless we understand the *rationale* of the distinction it may well be that we draw it badly. The slave had reasons of a kind for his wrong answers to Socrates' geometrical questions as well as for his right ones; but they were confused reasons, and he could not tell the good ones from the bad. Similarly we may well divide virtue

from vice in a confused and incoherent way; conventional evalua-
tions, which we could not uphold if we saw that we were making
them, may lead us to include in the class of virtuous persons members
who have no real right to be there. Socrates is right therefore in
thinking that we cannot settle questions about the teachability of
virtue by examining the performances of virtuous parents; for, as we
have seen, we may be wrong about who these are, and we may indeed
be burdened with any number of other confusions. We must first
understand the *rationale* of the distinction between virtue and vice
before we can settle any questions about them. But what Socrates
overlooked, perhaps, is that a rigid insistence on this principle may
have a paralysing effect upon us. We cannot indeed *settle* subsequent
questions without settling the prior one, but it may well be helpful to
raise subsequent questions so long as we do two things, namely so
long as we realise that what we are doing is provisional, and so long
as we keep the discussion of subsequent questions explicitly in touch
with the prior question. Thus in the present case we can take for
granted what seems to be a reasonable hypothesis, namely that there
is an invariant connection between something's being knowledge and
its being teachable, and in the light of this reasonable assumption we
may find that an investigation of the question of teachability may
relieve the paralysis induced by the prior question and may even give
us some clues which can be used in attempting to answer it.

I am inclined to think that this is not entirely unlike the point
which Plato meant to make by introducing the notion of *investigating
from a hypothesis* into the *Meno*; in particular I feel fairly confident
that he wanted to indicate that it may be fruitful to make an oblique
kind of approach to the question what something is by permitting
oneself to *raise* subsequent questions at a stage in the argument at
which it would be logically improper to think of *settling* them. In that
case the *Meno* could be construed as giving notice that Plato did not
intend to conform to the Socratic rule that prior questions must be
tackled first; and the legitimacy of this departure from the strait
path would be the first of its methodological recommendations. Two
further methodological recommendations would be, the one that
during the discussion of subsequent questions we should try, so far
as possible, to keep their bearing on the prior question in mind, the
other that the discussion of subsequent questions before the settling
of the prior question must inevitably be of a provisional character.
It would be this last point with which the words "from a *hupothesis*"
would be specially connected.[1] The connotation of *hupothesis* in the
Meno would be tentativeness.

---

[1] The *Meno* comes tentatively to a conclusion (that virtue is right opinion) that
we naturally regard as un-Platonic. Perhaps Plato's contemporaries would also

If this is right, what help can we get from the *Meno* towards the interpretation of the passages concerning hypotheses which we have already looked at in the *Phaedo*? The answer seems to be, not very much. Presumably, as in the *Meno*, so here words like *hupothesis* are used to mark the tentative nature of the thoughts which Socrates is describing. Beyond that however we shall not get much help of a direct kind from the *Meno* and must consider the problems raised by the *Phaedo* on their own merits.

In *Phaedo* 100 a 3 Socrates speaks of himself as "regularly supposing (*hupothemenos*) whatever seems to be the strongest *logos* on any matter", and says that he "accepts (*tithêmi*) as true whatever seems to agree with it, rejecting as false what does not". The word for "agree" here is *sumphônein*, a (perhaps dead) metaphor from music. We shall have to suppose that Plato was not very clear about the logical relation which he intended *sumphônein* to mark in this sentence; for we cannot find a logical relation R such that Socrates could reasonably accept as true whatever has R to his selected hypothesis and reject as false whatever fails to have R to the latter.[1] Clearly Socrates' meaning is that he accepts as true whatever the hypothesis that he is currently assuming plainly points to, and rejects as false whatever conflicts with it. Furthermore it seems to me obvious that, just as Socrates does not choose the word *sumphônein* with great nicety, so we have no right to suppose that he intends to say (what his words could be taken to mean) that it is the chosen hypothesis on its own which points to some things and conflicts with others. That is to say, we need not suppose that the things which Socrates "takes as true" are things which can be derived from the hypothesis alone without the aid of other premises, or that the things which he "rejects as false" are things which contradict the hypothesis in isolation. I see no reason to deny that Socrates is taking it for granted that, on any occasion on which he adopts a hypothesis, he will have in his mind a number of relevant beliefs which he will consider at least as credible as the hypothesis, and that these other relevant beliefs plus the hypothesis will constitute the grounds for accepting the propositions that they plainly point to, taken together, and for rejecting the propositions which plainly conflict with them. Thus if he were on some occasion to adopt the hypothesis that virtue

---

[1] Mr. Robinson has sufficiently shown this in *Plato's Earlier Dialectic*, pp. 126–9 (Clarendon Press edition). I am much indebted to his discussion though it will be obvious that I do not entirely agree with it.

---

have regarded it as un-Platonic, and this might have served to make the point to them that prior discussion of subsequent questions must be provisional and may go wrong. The intelligent reader might have seen that what the *Meno* shows is that there is *some connection* between virtue and right understanding.

involves right understanding, this hypothesis would be admitted, so to speak, into an outlook which already includes the observation that worthy citizens do not regularly succeed in communicating their worthiness to their children; and some of the propositions which the adoption of the hypothesis would force Socrates to accept would follow not from the hypothesis alone but from the hypothesis taken together with this observation and with other relevant bits of his existing outlook on the matter.

This will be disputed by those who want to say that in this part of the *Phaedo* Socrates is telling us that he turned his back on all ordinary methods of thought and adopted some completely mysterious method of his own which involved a kind of Cartesian purge of all existing beliefs; for in that case there would be no "outlook" for a hypothesis to be accepted into. I have argued in an earlier chapter[1] that we need not accept such a drastic interpretation of this part of the *Phaedo*. If we may suppose, then, that on any given occasion there would be a corpus of existing beliefs for a hypothesis to be added to, that will throw some light on the otherwise somewhat mysterious question how Socrates decides which is the strongest *logos* on some matter. For just as the adoption of a hypothesis *h* may make me abandon some proposition *p* which I was tempted to believe, so if I am strongly tempted to believe *p* I shall not adopt *h*. Presumably therefore the strongest hypothesis on any given matter is the hypothesis which fits best with the things which I am already disposed to believe.

It is, then, really rather a small mouse which is emerging from so much disputation. For all that Socrates is telling us is that, being uncertain what the right answers are, he has made it his practice to embrace hypothetically that answer to any question which seems to him the most probable, extending of course equal credence to the consequences that it seems to carry with it (and which are among the reasons why it is the most probable answer). It is not a special method that he is adopting, except in so far as it is special to make up one's mind as to what is most probable and to abide by that decision until one sees grounds for changing it.

We come now to the somewhat cryptic remarks about hypotheses that Socrates makes in *Phaedo* 101 d–e. He begins by telling Kebes that if somebody challenges his hypothesis (viz., that only the presence of P-hood can make P things P) he is not to answer until he has looked at the things that emerge from the hypothesis to see if they agree or disagree with each other. "And when you have to give account of the hypothesis itself, do it thus: posit another hypothesis, whichever of the higher ones seems to you the best, until you come to

[1] Above, pp. 165–71.

something which is good enough (*hikanon*); and do not muddle it up together like the people who argue to confute their opponents, discoursing both about the starting point and about the things that emerge from it. Avoid this if you want to find one of the realities."

Obscure as some of this is, it seems to contain three methodological recommendations. (1) First scrutinise the challenged hypothesis for inconsistencies; (2) next back it up by resting it on a "higher" hypothesis; and (3) do not confound these stages together. It is implied moreover that conformity to these recommendations may enable one to "find one of the realities". Let us look at these points one by one.

Taking the last point first, we must agree that the suggestion that compliance with Socrates' advice may enable one to "find one of the realities" would fit well with the notion that here, as in the *Meno*, Socrates is describing not a method of proof, but a method of invention, a method which we can use when we are trying to find "what something is" and have got ourselves into an *aporia* or *impasse*. Since however the question under discussion is whether the soul is immortal (i.e. not specifically a question of the form "What is X?") it would probably be unwise to press this point.

We come then to Socrates' first recommendation, namely that, when a hypothesis which one is relying on is "grabbed hold of", one should not answer until one has first looked to see whether the things that have emerged from it agree with each other or disagree. (The word for "agree" here is *sumphônein* which we also encountered in the earlier passage, and "disagree" is its opposite *diaphônein*). There are perhaps three ways of interpreting this recommendation. Firstly we may suppose that "the things that have emerged" from the hypothesis are the logical consequences of the hypothesis on its own; and that we are to investigate whether these are consistent. In other words we are to try *reductio ad absurdum* on the hypothesis—which would therefore presumably have to be more than just one proposition. Secondly[1] we may suppose that (as is anyhow likely) the hypothesis is a general proposition, and that the things that have emerged from it are its applications. Thus if the hypothesis were that virtue is instilled by teaching, one of the things that emerge from it would be that courage is instilled by teaching, and also, perhaps, that Jones's courage was instilled by teaching. On this view when we look to see whether the emergent propositions agree or disagree with each other what we are to do is to see whether the applications of the hypothesis are all true. The metaphor in *sumphônein* and *diaphônein* could be, on this view, alive; when the applications are all true, they shout in unison in support of the hypothesis; when some of them are false

---

[1] I owe this suggestion to Mr. M. C. P. Dunworth.

their voices are discordant. (We need not trouble perhaps with the case where they are all false, for we should never have entertained a general proposition all of whose applications are false; nothing would have suggested it to us). On this view then the first thing to do when a general idea is challenged is to see whether it seems to work out in terms of particular cases. Does the assumption that only P-hood can make P things P work in the case of beauty? of two-ness? of largeness? . . . and so on. This is an attractive interpretation. Perhaps however the third interpretation is the most plausible simply because it is the least stringent. According to this interpretation we are to assume, as we did in the earlier passage, that every hypothesis is admitted into an existing corpus of beliefs, and that the things which emerge from it are the propositions to which we find ourselves committed if we add the hypothesis to that existing corpus; they are the consequences not of the hypothesis alone but of the hypothesis plus existing beliefs. (It may be observed however that in so far as *hupothesis* retains the meaning "act of supposing" they will be the results, and in that sense the consequences, just of the *hupothesis*). What we are to do on this view is to make sure whether, if we assert the hypothesis in question, we shall not find ourselves asserting things which contradict other propositions which we wish to assert. Thus the hypothesis that virtue can be taught will have consequences that disagree with each other if, in combination with other beliefs which seem to us equally plausible, it commits us to saying that all worthy citizens try to teach to their children something that can be taught, and that they all fail; for these two opinions, though logically compatible, might be said to disagree.

According to the first of these three interpretations the first move when a hypothesis is challenged is to inspect it for internal self-consistency only; both of the other two interpretations require, or at least allow, the hypothesis to be confronted at this stage with the facts. Those who believe that Socrates is here advising us to turn our backs on the facts will prefer the first interpretation for this reason. To me however this is a reason for rejecting this interpretation. I find the second the neatest of the three, but there is little doubt that the third is the simplest and that there is no cogent reason for rejecting it; that it imputes to Plato a certain laxity of expression is not a reason. It does not seem to me that it is safe to take anything more precise than the third interpretation.

So much for the first of Socrates' recommendations. The second comes into force when we have to "give account" (*logon didonai*) of the hypothesis. Whether "having to give account of the hypothesis" is part of what one has to do when "someone grabs hold of it", or a necessity which confronts one on other occasions, is not made quite clear. On the whole my impression is that the grabbing hold is hostile, and that the opponent holds his fire while we comply with the first recommendation; but that when that stage is over he is still waiting to be given a *logos* or account of why he should accept the hypothesis; in other words, I think that the second recommendation has to be complied with as soon as we have dealt with the first. The second recommendation is that we should "hypothesise another hypothesis, whichever of the higher ones seems best, until we come to something adequate". What does this mean, and in particular what is the sense of "higher"? Many readers think that "higher" here means "more general". If this is the relationship in which "All animals are carnivorous" stands to "All cats are carnivorous" I think that this translation is too restrictive. We need a vaguer notion, something perhaps like the following. Presumably we never put forward a hypothesis to the effect that all S is P unless we have an idea, perhaps at the back of our minds, of the connection that holds between S and P. Thus a man would not think it worth while trying out the idea that virtue is knowledge unless he felt that he could see that the two terms are connected. As the *Meno* suggests, the connection might be that virtue is invariably useful, and that nothing is invariably useful except you know how to use it; having therefore a guarantee of right use virtue must surely be knowledge. In this argument the premise that virtue is invariably useful and the premise that everything can be harmful if it is wrongly used do not entail that virtue is knowledge, but they do support it. They would be, of course, enunciated before the conclusion that they support in a formal exposition of the argument, and indeed they would be written "above" it in a written exposition. Either therefore of these premises, or the conjunction of them, might be described as "higher" than the conclusion that virtue is knowledge. It seems to me that this example illustrates the relationship that Socrates has in mind. When a hypothesis is challenged, he is telling us, ask yourself why you thought it worth supposing.

The next question is what is meant by "until you come to something adequate". "Adequate" presumably means "that your opponent will accept"; but there are two different understandings of the process of arriving at this. According to one it is a vertical process of getting back to first principles. I support a hypothesis by a higher one, that in turn by one yet higher, and so on until I come to something that my opponent and I both accept. I then try to show him (presumably) that if he accepts this *archê* or starting point he will have to accept my hypothesis. But it is also possible that Socrates has a horizontal process in mind, whereby I choose the likeliest of the various grounds which could be advanced in support of my hypothesis, and try it out, either by enunciating it to my opponent or, perhaps, by obeying the first recommendation and scrutinising the things that emerge from it. However, my first attempt may be unsuccessful; my opponent may show me that it will not do, or I may see for myself that its consequences disagree. When this happens I abandon this argument and look for something else which will give equal support to my hypothesis; and I go on doing this until I come to "something adequate", or in other words to an argument which satisfies both my opponent and myself. Which of these two Socrates means it is difficult to decide. Memories of the Seventh Book of the *Republic* incline many readers to take the former for granted; perhaps however the latter is the more natural interpretation of this passage as it stands in isolation. But whichever we adopt it will be the case that Socrates' second recommendation advises us to seek grounds for a challenged hypothesis not by an inductive process of citing favourable cases but by something more like setting out the reasons which made the hypothesis seem antecedently plausible.

Socrates' third recommendation is that we should keep these two steps separate "and not confuse them together like those who argue to confute their opponents,[1] discoursing both about the *archê* and about the things that have emerged from it". According to Aristotle[2] Plato attached great importance to keeping apart arguments towards an *archê* or starting point and arguments from it; he "frequently used to ask: 'Are we going to or from the *archai*?' ". The present passage seems to be an instance of this habit. What is however a little paradoxical about this present passage is that it appears that we are advised first to consider what comes from the *archê*, and only then to see what arguments lead to it. (It is true that Plato does not say in so many words that Socrates' first recommendation is to be complied with first and the second only subsequently; but this is certainly the impression that one gets). It seems likely that if we can see the reason for this apparently paradoxical order, that will give us the clue to the whole passage.

Perhaps the first point that we need to see is that Socrates is not telling us how to prove things, but how to find things out. Probably we ought also to remember that he is not concerned with ordinary empirical hypotheses; his interest is in making philosophical progress, not in detecting murderers, ascertaining the functions of bodily organs or reconstructing bits of history. Perhaps if we look at what happens in the *Meno* we shall see what Plato is cautioning us against. It may be that Socrates' hypothesis in the *Meno* is, as we thought, that if virtue is knowledge it is teachable. But the view that virtue is

---

[1] Or perhaps "like contradiction-mongers". The word is *antilogikoi*.
[2] *Nicomachean Ethics I*, 4 (1095 a 32).

knowledge is also put forward, and we can call it a hypothesis, even if it is not the hypothesis that Socrates refers to. Now the hypothesis that virtue is knowledge is supported at an early stage of the discussion by the consideration that virtue can never be wrongly used. But the assumption that if it is knowledge it must be teachable seems to show that virtue cannot be knowledge, because it does not appear to be teachable. This produces an *impasse*; it must be, and it cannot be, knowledge. By good fortune Socrates finds his way out of the *impasse* when he remembers that right opinion is equally effective with knowledge; but the discussion has been circuitous, and it is only by good luck that it does not break off in a plain contradiction. This circuitous path could have been avoided if the things that emerge from supposing that virtue is knowledge had been scrutinised before, rather than after, the production of arguments in favour of this view. For if that had been done the view would have been ruled out from the start. It seems, then, reasonable to suppose that why we are told to scrutinise the consequences of a hypothesis before we produce arguments for it is that this is a kind of qualifying examination which can eliminate opinions which are untenable and therefore not worth supporting by the production of grounds.

The point that must be seen clearly is that a higher hypothesis, such as one would cite in defence of a lower hypothesis, may be as good grounds for an untenable as for a tenable lower hypothesis, and that this may be so even though the higher hypothesis is true. The reason for this, of course, is that the higher hypothesis does not entail, but merely supports, the lower. Therefore an eristic could easily confuse his opponent by first producing what seemed to be a clinching argument in defence of some view, and then showing the view to be untenable. Such practices could easily induce in their victims *misologia* or distrust of argument, a condition which Plato deplores in the *Phaedo* (89 d) and which is, he says, incurred by putting excessive trust in an argument which subsequently turns out to be untrustworthy. Such excessive trust will be prevented if we first make sure that there is nothing against an opinion before we consider what there is to be said in its favour.

We can see this more clearly if we set out formally the skeleton of the argument which commands the temporary assent of Socrates and Meno in the *Meno*. It might run like this.

1. Virtue is always a good thing.
   Therefore
   either (*a*) Virtue involves understanding, or (*b*) Some invariably good things do not involve understanding.
   1.1. But (*b*) begets paradoxes and (*a*) does not.

2. Therefore virtue involves understanding.
Therefore
either (c) Virtue is right opinion *or* (d) Virtue is knowledge.
2.1. (d) begets paradoxes and (c) does not.
3. Therefore virtue is right opinion.

We can see from this tabulation that the conclusion which follows logically from each premise is disjunctive, and that it is only by showing that one of the two disjuncts is untenable that we establish the conclusion of each step. But of course we can only set the argument out deductively in this way when we have discovered it; and Socrates' concern in the *Phaedo* is not with how to set the argument out but with how to discover it. This, I suggest, is why he recommends that we should do the destructive work first; we are to eliminate all the untenable members of the disjunction before we try to render explicit the consideration that made us think them reasonable.

Three comments on these proposals suggest themselves. Firstly, if they were advanced as an infallible prescription we should have to say that Socrates is assuming that of the disjunctive conclusion to which a true higher hypothesis points we shall always be able to eliminate all but one of the disjuncts at the stage at which we scrutinise their consequences. There seems to be no reason why we should be so fortunate, but this is not a criticism of Socrates, for we have no right to say that he regards his recommendations as infallible. Secondly, there is something to be said for recommendations which keep closer to the "confused" order of the *Meno* than these seem to. It was in fact because considerations had already been adduced in support of "Virtue is knowledge" that Socrates was able to think of the tenable disjunct "Virtue is right opinion" when the former showed itself to be untenable. (For he thought of the tenable disjunct by reminding himself of the grounds for its untenable colleague). Therefore we might suggest the following procedure. "When somebody challenges what has seemed to be a likely hypothesis, first make sure that it is tenable. Then, whether it is tenable or not, ask yourself what was the higher hypothesis which made it seem plausible in the first place. If the lower hypothesis has turned out to be untenable, ask yourself what other lower hypothesis would do equal justice to the force of the higher, and then check the tenability of that. If the lower hypothesis has turned out to be tenable, so far so good, but do not omit to ask whether there is any other hypothesis on the same level which is equally tenable and which does equal justice to the force of the higher. If there is, you will have to seek further afield to try to decide between them." However, although it cannot be said that Socrates recommends the procedure which we have just outlined, it equally cannot be said that he denies its utility; for he does not suggest that he has given a fully articulated account of how to proceed in philosophy. He throws out a few sentences which describe the course which he himself follows, and we shall generate quite unnecessary problems if we insist on viewing these sentences as purveying a complete methodology.

Thirdly, we may observe that Socrates' recommendations, as we have understood them, have nothing specially anti-empirical about them. Socrates is not outlining a method whereby we can deduce things from self-evident first principles, but a technique whereby we can render explicit trains of thought which lie at the back of our minds. Nor is he denying that philosophical theories ought to be confronted with the facts. He does not indeed say that they should, but there seems every reason to suppose that this confrontation will occur at the stage at which we test the consequences of a theory for agreement or disagreement. What he tells us is little more than that what he does, when he is groping for the truth, is to adopt the likeliest assumption, along with all that goes with it; to see whether this requires him to believe anything inconsistent; and, if it does not, to see what grounds he can bring forward in support of the assumption which shall seem adequate to himself and others. Finally we may make a comment which perhaps hardly deserves making. This is that, if we asked Socrates explicitly whether it is right to wait until somebody challenges a hypothesis before we test it for consistency and seek for grounds for it, he would presumably reply that of course this is not the case. While we are actually using a hypothesis to solve some problem we cannot simultaneously be testing it for consistency (though a revelation of inconsistency may emerge), and in this way the stages are distinct; but we cannot believe that Socrates means us to defer the second of them until we encounter someone who disagrees with our hypothesis. Presumably we ought sometimes to be our own challengers and to dispute our own assumptions.

We may conclude the discussion of the notion of *hupothesis* in the *Meno* and *Phaedo* by observing that in both dialogues the word connotes the tentativeness which ought to characterise our procedures when we do not see clearly. Since the condition of seeing clearly is the condition elsewhere ascribed to the dialectician we may say that it is so long as we fail to reach the dialectical goal that we are obliged to reason hypothetically; and to reason hypothetically is to try to approach to the dialectical goal by trying to render explicit the logical liaisons between distinct notions of which we retain some "memory" and which we are trying to "recollect". Finally we may observe that the *Phaedo* is a little more enthusiastic than the *Meno* about the utility of hypothetical reasoning, in that in the earlier dialogue Socrates agrees with reluctance to discuss a subsequent question from a hypothesis without first settling the prior question, whereas in the *Phaedo* he tells us that hypothetical reasoning is his habitual practice. It seems likely that Plato became increasingly convinced that we cannot in practice spend our philosophical lives asking "what each thing is", and that we are therefore forced to reason hypothetically.

B. *Hypotheses and dialectic in the* Republic

The use of the notion of *hupothesis* in the *Republic* is intimately connected with the use of the notion of *dialektikê*, and we shall have to take them together.

The essential passages in the *Republic* are the simile of the Line at the end of Book Six, and a short passage in Book Seven. It would be wearisome to summarise once more the simile of the Line; I shall therefore cite only the crucial points.[1]

1. The Line contrasts *nöêsis* with *dianoia* (or the kind of intellectual activity characteristic of the mathematician), likening the relationship between them to the relationship between *epistêmê* and *doxa*, and therefore to the relationship between seeing a physical thing directly and "seeing it indirectly" when one looks at a reflection or shadow of it. *Nöêsis* is the direct vision of the forms, and *dianoia* is the vision of their shadows or reflections. In describing *dianoia* Socrates says that in this condition we have to do the following things: (1) use physical things as images of what we are thinking about; (2) search "from hypotheses", and (3) travel towards the end, not towards the starting point. Of *nöêsis* he says that in this condition we do the following: (1) we go towards a non-provisional starting point; (2) we go "from a hypothesis" and (3) we dispense with images, "making our way through the forms themselves by the forms themselves".

2. Socrates explains as follows: Mathematicians (1) hypothesise "the odd, the even, the figures, three kinds of angles and so on"; (2) treat these as if they knew them, making them hypotheses; (3) think these to be clear to everyone and that they need not give account of them, but start from them; and (4) talk about visible shapes, although they are really thinking about the things the visible shapes resemble, such as "the square itself". He then repeats the three points made in his description of *dianoia* above, explaining the third point (that *dianoia* does not travel towards the starting point) by the fact that in *dianoia* we do not get out above the hypotheses.

3. He then explains his statements about *nöêsis* in the following

[1] A fuller account can be found above in Chapter 1, pp. 73 sqq.

terms: Here the *logos* itself (I suppose this means "the account we give", though it almost means "pure reason") gets into touch with its objects, treating its hypotheses not as starting-points, but as hypotheses (or in other words as things to stand on and jump off from) until it arrives at the non-hypothetical starting-point of everything; and then, having got into touch with this, it comes down again by holding on to the things which hold on to the starting-point, right down to the end, at no point making use of anything empirical.

4. Glaucon says that he more or less understands what Socrates means, and offers his own version. According to him the point is that that part of the real and the intelligible which is contemplated by dialectic is clearer than that part which is contemplated by the "sciences" (by which he must mean mathematics);[1] that in the "sciences" hypotheses are starting-points; that in the "sciences" we do not "understand" the objects we are discussing although they are objects which can be "understood" given the starting-point; that the reason why we do not "understand" is that we are going from hypotheses and not to the starting-point; and that the word *dianoia* is appropriate because the condition is in between *doxa* and understanding (*nous*), being an intellectual activity, but one which does not achieve understanding.

The following comment should perhaps be made at this stage. Glaucon's remarks in paragraph 4 leave the impression that he believes in two kinds or levels of "understandables" (*nöêta*), only one of which is fully "understandable". It seems to be fairly clear however that he does not mean to say that there exist in nature two distinct kinds of understandables, those of *dianoia* and those of *nöêsis*. The objects of the inferior state are shadows of the objects of the superior; and I think this means that ontologically speaking the inferior state has no objects of its own; its "objects" are indirect perceptions of the objects of *nöêsis*.

The other essential passage about hypotheses and dialectic comes in the Seventh Book, 532-4. Socrates has been describing the lengthy training of his rulers in the mathematical sciences which appear to constitute *dianoia*. He then says that all this work is valuable only if a man can be brought to see how all these things fit together. All this however is only the prelude. For the purpose is to make the pupil "dialectical", and this is a virtue mathematicians seldom possess in that they can seldom "give or receive account" of the things they say, and hence cannot really understand them.

Accordingly Socrates continues by giving some hints as to the

---

[1] The word is *technai*.

nature of dialectic (he expressly says that Glaucon would not be able to follow a full exposition). His hints are as follows (532–4):—

1. Dialectic is a kind of intellectual sight and its business is to see what each thing (i.e. each universal) is. This is to be carried through until one reaches the goal of the intelligible, or in other words sees what goodness is.

2. The preparatory work, without which this insight cannot be had, is done by the mathematical sciences. Only dialectic can give the insight and it can only give it to one trained in mathematics.

3. The difference between dialectic and all other mental activities is that the latter are either empirical, or else, if they have some contact with intelligible realities, have no more than dream-contact with them. The reason for this is that they use hypotheses which they allow to lie undisturbed, and of which they cannot give account. They thus achieve coherency but not knowledge.

4. "Dialectic is the only path which travels to the starting-point in order that it may be confirmed, destroying hypotheses" (533 c 7–d 1). It uses the mathematical sciences as its helpers in raising the mind out of the mud.

5. Finally the dialectician is the man who grasps the *logos* of the *ousia* of each thing (i.e. of each form).

So much for the summary of the crucial passages. In trying to interpret them perhaps the first point to make is that the *Republic* speaks of hypotheses in two different ways, one pejorative and the other not. There is nothing intrinsically wrong with conjecturing, yet "You are only conjecturing" may be a hostile comment. This is so when what I mean is that although your opinion lacks solid grounds and hence must be classed as a conjecture, you fail to realise this. What is bad is a conjecture which is not admitted to be conjectural. Similarly thought which depends on hypotheses is to be condemned if the hypotheses are not recognised and treated as such; there is nothing wrong with making use of hypotheses if they are used in the right way, that is as "things to stand on and jump off from". The *Republic* neither condemns nor commends the use of hypotheses; it condemns their abuse while allowing that their proper employment is essential to progress as it was in the *Meno* and *Phaedo*.

The main theme of this part of the *Republic* is that the entities, relationships and so on which mathematicians study are embodiments of the forms or rational principles which it is essential that the rulers should come to understand. These principles in some way converge upon the chief of their number, namely goodness; and since all abstract thinking is done by the light shed by goodness it is perhaps fair to infer that the understanding of these principles will be a kind of recollecting along the lines laid down in the *Meno*; for it will be the explicit re-capturing of truths of which we are already sufficiently possessed for our thought to be determined by them. The objective then is to gain, or regain, an explicit understanding of the rational principles which converge upon goodness and whose application constitutes thought; and the method is to start from those embodiments of these principles which contain the smallest amount of irrelevant material, namely those which mathematics studies.

These embodiments will be the elementary notions of mathematics, notions such as equality, odd and even numbers, right, acute and obtuse angles, squares, parallelograms and so on. It is such notions that Socrates speaks of, I think, as the hypotheses of the mathematicians. It is at first sight somewhat surprising that Socrates should cite a list of terms rather than a list of propositions to exemplify the hypotheses of the mathematicians; for we are used to the idea that a *hupothesis* is the supposing of a proposition. Correspondingly with this, "giving account" of a hypothesis in the *Phaedo* seemed to mean finding a reason for believing it, whereas in the *Republic* the phrase seems to mean something more like stating the analysis of a term—doing that which it is not necessary to do in the case of a term which is "clear to everyone".

That this is not really surprising can be seen if we reflect on what the mathematicians are said to do. They take their hypotheses, refuse to give account of them on the ground that they are clear to everyone, and proceed "towards the end". (This must surely refer to the derivation of theorems). In the course of this derivation the mathematicians are obliged to make use of empirical material. The only account which seems to make sense of all this is the following. The mathematician takes such a notion as oddness. For his purpose it is not necessary to attempt the kind of analysis of such a notion which a philosopher of mathematics might wish to attempt. For the purpose of proving theorems about odd numbers it is clear enough to everyone what oddness is; it is the characteristic in virtue of which some numbers cannot be divided in half without remainder. But if you refuse in this way to reflect on the nature of oddness you will be forced to make use of empirical material in the sense that you will fail to achieve an abstract understanding of such notions as "division" and "remainder", and hence will be forced to picture them to yourself as physical processes or products. You may protest that you do not make any use of such physical pictures, as Socrates' geometers protest that they do not depend on their diagrams; but the fact remains that you have nothing to put in their place. That you can perform efficiently a non-physical arithmetical operation of which you have no conception but a physical picture shows only that you can see by the light shed by goodness, or in other words that you already possess implicitly the understanding that you refuse to try to recapture explicitly.

The hypothesis of the odd therefore is the hypothesis that there is a characteristic in virtue of which some numbers cannot be divided in half without remainder. In this way there is no real difference between hypothesising, or taking for granted, a single term on the one hand and a proposition on the other, and there is no discrepancy here between the *Republic* and the earlier dialogues. On the other hand there is a difference between what makes such terms as "taking for granted" applicable here and what makes them applicable in some other places. Mathematicians may be said to take oddness for granted not because there is any doubt of the truth of the proposition that there exists a characteristic in virtue of which some numbers cannot be divided in half without remainder, but because this proposition, as the mathematician treats it, is opaque in the sense that he has nothing better than a physical picture or some operational rules to tell him what it means. Therefore the kind of "giving account" which the mathematician declines to bother with is not the same as the kind which Socrates advises Kebes to do with the aid of a higher hypothesis; for what the mathematician lacks is clear understanding rather than grounds. This difference however is probably one of emphasis, and should not be made too much of. As we have seen in earlier chapters it seems to be part of Plato's general outlook to believe that it is when and only when I achieve a clear understanding of a general term that I can see why the things that are true of it must be so. When I see what the soul is I see that it must be immortal, and I cannot be sure of the latter until I achieve the former. Certainty and clarity go hand in hand. If I saw what oddness is I would see why every other number must have this characteristic. Conversely in considering the *Meno* and the *Phaedo* we saw that hypothesising in the sense of putting forward a dubious proposition is something that one does when one does not see clearly; a dubious proposition will therefore be always to some extent an opaque one, and an opaque proposition doubtless always to some extent dubious.[1]

The hypotheses of the mathematicians then can be regarded as single terms or as propositions about those terms; and they are hypotheses not so much because they are put forward without adequate grounds as because they are put forward without adequate attention to what they mean. To treat these terms or propositions as the mathematician treats them—that is to use them to derive theorems—

---

[1] In philosophy, that is. There is nothing specially opaque about dubious propositions in history, for example.

is no doubt a legitimate activity, but it is illegitimate to think that it constitutes understanding. It is for this offence that the mathematicians are accused of relying on hypotheses in a pejorative sense. It is a peculiarly damnable offence just because the entities which mathematicians discuss are outstandingly "understandable given the *archê*"; that is to say they are the jumping-off points from which to recover an explicit understanding of rational principles.

Dialectic does not start until a man has learnt mathematics and brought his mathematical knowledge together. It proceeds by trying to say what each thing is, by trying to give account; and it starts from hypotheses, although it proceeds by destroying hypotheses. Or at least *nöêsis* starts from hypotheses (treated as hypotheses), and while Plato is not explicit about the relationship between *nöêsis* and the *dialektikê methodos* I take it that they must refer to the same process. It would be too much to have two processes both leading upwards to the un-hypothetical starting-point. Dialectic then starts from hypotheses, and I presume that it starts from the hypotheses of the mathematicians; that is why one must do mathematics first. What the mathematicians fail to do to their hypotheses is to give account of them, and what dialectic tries to do is to say what each thing is. It seems reasonable to bring these two phrases together and to conclude that dialectic is the attempt to do that which the mathematician fails to do, and that dialectic starts from hypotheses in the sense that it takes some such notion as oddness and tries to achieve an abstract understanding of it. (It seems to me that it is very clearly brought out in 533 c that the things which the mathematicians do not trouble to attempt, and hence fail to achieve, are identical with the things which dialectic attempts and may hope to achieve).

The purpose of seeking an abstract understanding of such a notion as oddness is, as we saw before, that mathematical entities such as this are peculiarly clear embodiments of abstract principles or forms. By what means, however, are we to achieve this purpose? It is all very well to adjure us to ask what oddness is, but, as the *Meno* has shown, such questions have a paralysing effect on the mind. How does Plato expect us to achieve answers to such questions; and how does he expect that the asking and answering of such questions will conduct us upwards to the unhypothetical starting-point or source of all things, namely goodness? Perhaps the reason why Socrates is made to tell Glaucon that he would not understand a full account of the nature of dialectic is that Plato has no answer to this at his finger tips. He could presumably say that he had already said something, explicitly in the *Meno* and *Phaedo*, and by example elsewhere, of the hypothetical procedure which is legitimately followed when we are trying to achieve understanding.

A question which is not unrelated to this one is the question whether there are discriminable stages in the dialectic path. There seems no doubt that many readers derive from this section of the *Republic* the impression that the forms constitute a sort of pyramid with goodness at its apex, and that the dialectical journey is an ascent of this pyramid. It is not so clear to me where this impression comes from—perhaps from the fact that we start with many problematical terms and at the last stage have only one, namely goodness—but I confess that I share it. If it is correct some sort of content could be given to it in the following way. In trying to give a lucid account of such a term as *oddness* or *equality* we should very likely find that we were relying on more general notions such as that of a *number* or a *quantity*; and if *number* figured in the analysis of *oddness*, it would figure in that of *evenness* also. In this way if we started with a batch of fairly specific terms we might find that the analysis of these left us with a smaller number of more generic terms still requiring analysis; and that, as we dealt with these in turn, the number of opaque terms would be reduced still further until we were left with two or three highly general notions such as *unity* and *multiplicity*, and at last with one only, namely *goodness*. In this way it would not be possible to say that the analysis of any term had been completed until the analysis of them all had been done (for the higher and more general notions which would come up for analysis at any given stage would be residual blocks of opacity at the stage below), and at the same time it would not be possible (or at least it would be unnatural) to attempt the analysis of more abstract terms until we had achieved the analysis of their more concrete progeny. A conception such as this would represent dialectical activity as a steady journey by stages upwards, and it would explain why goodness was the last term which we could tackle. An objection to such a structure however is that it is difficult to see how the manner in which goodness is involved in all subordinate notions would be the same as the manner in which number is involved in oddness, or in which unity and multiplicity are involved in a wide range of mathematical terms. Still we could always suppose that this was a point which Plato had overlooked.

It seems to me possible that Plato had some such structure as this in mind. Still, while he speaks several times of journeying upwards until the single *archê* or starting-point is reached, and while he makes it clear that no certainty is achieved until the *archê* is attained, he does not so far as I can see say anything which makes this pyramid structure inescapable. The objective is to understand the nature of goodness by understanding the nature of order, and the method is to start, primarily at any rate, from the embodiments of order in ordered quantity. But such an objective could be realised in more than one way. It seems clear that Plato intended us to start from the hypotheses of the mathematicians in the manner described, that is to say to try to understand these entities and relationships in abstract non-sensuous terms. But the next step in the process might be to turn to the non-mathematical analogues of these quantitative embodiments of order and to try to see the latter in the former. We might for example reflect on equality as this notion applies in the sphere of justice, and try to divine in it the abstract scheme which we found in its mathematical counterpart. We might then move on to circularity, attempt to achieve an abstract understanding of this principle as one capable of non-spatial application, and then try to see how it applies to the self-consistency of rational thought. It might be that we were intended to travel horizontally in this way over the range of mathematical embodiments, bringing each of them into relationship with the non-mathematical embodiment of the same form; and that when we had covered the whole ground we should be ready to divine the nature of goodness as that which was somehow involved in everything that we had so far seemed to understand. It would perhaps be less natural to describe such a process as a journeying upwards. Travelling over the range of mathematical embodiments would seem to be a horizontal rather than an upwards journey. It is true that the horizontal journey would be undertaken for the sake of the upwards leap which would only be possible at the end of it, but the notion of an upwards journey seems to require that we are all the time gaining height and achieving a wider view. No doubt we could use such language to describe what happens when we add one new notion to the stock of those which we have provisionally analysed, but this does not seem a very satisfactory explication of the metaphor of ascent.

However it is no doubt possible to work out various pictures which combine the notion of a pyramid structure with the notion of travelling over the range of mathematical embodiments of the forms and bringing their non-mathematical correlates into relationship with them. For example it is easy to imagine that various mathematical terms can be subsumed in some way under others of a higher order, and that the same is true on the non-mathematical side; oddness and evenness both presuppose number, as justice and courage both presuppose virtue. But since Plato deliberately refuses to tell us how he supposes us to travel up the dialectical path it would be temerarious to assert that this or that must be precisely what he had in mind.

What he does want to tell us is that dialectic proceeds by destroying hypotheses and that its purpose is to see what each thing is. The phrase "destroying hypotheses" (533 c 8) has given a good deal of

555

trouble to interpreters. It seems to me that if we pay sufficient attention to the obvious parallelism between what Plato says of mathematics and what he says of dialectic in this passage, his intention becomes clear enough, even if we remain uncertain just why he chose those particular words. The mathematicians "allow their hypotheses to remain undisturbed and cannot give account of them" (533 c 2), and because of this they cannot be said to possess *epistêmê* or knowledge. Dialectic seeks to achieve knowledge by seeing what each thing is, and it progresses destroying hypotheses. Surely it must be that destroying hypotheses is the opposite of allowing them to remain undisturbed; and since (as we have decided) the trouble with the mathematicians is not primarily that they do not try to prove their axioms (how could they?), but that they do not try to achieve an abstract understanding of their basic principles, it surely must be precisely this that dialectic does try to do. Verbally it seems to me probable that "destroying hypotheses" should be translated" destroying supposals" and that the explication of this is "breaking up this indolent habit of taking oddness and so on for granted as clear to everyone".

There is a further problem of translation in this same sentence. Dialectic travels towards the starting-point destroying hypotheses as it goes, "in order that it may be confirmed". What is the "it" here? Is it dialectic that is confirmed, or is it the starting-point? I do not know which noun Plato intended to be the subject of the verb; but there is one interpretation of this sentence which ought to be ruled out. This is that dialectic somehow by travelling upwards confirms or establishes an unhypothetical axiom from which the whole body of truth is then derived. The conception that dialectic is a method of establishing first principles seems to make nonsense of the whole passage, and indeed to require us to suppose an intellectual activity which could not conceivably be carried out. Therefore I take it that the words "in order that it may be confirmed" are to be understood as meaning either that dialectic goes right on to the *archê* in order that it may achieve certainty, or perhaps that the dialectician goes right on to the *archê* in order that his conception of it (*his* starting-point) may be confirmed. Either way, that which gets confirmed on arrival at the starting-point is the journey which has led to the starting-point; we know that we have taken the right road when we see that we have got to our destination.

It may be objected that if we say this we make the starting-point into a finishing-post; and that Socrates speaks not only of a way up but also of a way down. The first objection is easily met. It is a familiar idea that that which is logically fundamental, and which is in that sense the first principle, may be the last to be discovered.

Goodness is the source of everything else (and "source" is an equally good translation of *archê*) in that everything else is as it is because goodness is what it is; but although goodness is in this way that from which everything comes, it is not that from which we start. We start, as the Cave makes clear, from the murk, and climb out of it by accustoming our eyes to entities which become progressively less and less derivative, until finally we see the sun; and there our progress stops. The whole paradox on which the Cave simile depends is that that which is the source of visibility, and itself supremely visible, is that which we are last able to gaze at. The first shall be last; and that is the same as making the starting-point into a finishing-post.

I am not therefore perturbed about the use of the word *archê* for the end of the journey; it is a paradox but the paradox on which the whole passage hinges. But this does not dispose of the way down. The view that I am combating can do a good deal with the way down. This view says that the way up is essentially preparatory; it is concerned with achieving a starting-point, and it is not until we have achieved this that we can start doing constructive philosophy. This constructive philosophy is what "the way down" refers to, and this is the *philosophia* in which, as Socrates tells us, those who have been brought to the vision of goodness spend the greater part of their time (540 b 2). This certainly gives plenty of content to the way down; but it is too much. Plato nowhere effaces the impression which the simile of the Cave creates, that the vision of goodness is the culmination of the process of illumination, not just the end of a preparatory stage. In the simile of the Cave itself what we do when we have visited the outside world is to go down into the Cave again and help its inhabitants with the recognition of the simulacra whose originals we have seen; we turn our illumination to practical use. That we do this is repeated in the passage which we have just referred to. It is indeed said that the *illuminati* delightfully employ the greater part of their time in *philosophia*, but this need not mean that it is they who are at last getting down to the real work. Indeed it cannot mean this, because it is clearly implied that as soon as a man has seen goodness he is ready "to use it as an exemplar (*paradeigma*) whereby to order his own life and that of his city" (540 a 9). The essential work is already done. The *philosophia* in which those who are off duty pass their time is presumably intellectual activity of a general kind—for example "harmless conjectures" such as those which take most of the space in the *Timaeus*. There is a good deal to be done after general principles have all been established.

It follows that the way down contributes nothing which has not been contributed by the way up; there is no subsequent intellectual activity for "the way down" to refer to. What then does Socrates

mean when he says that *nöêsis*, having arrived at "the non-hypothetical *archê* of everything and made contact with it, comes down
again to the end (*teleutê*), holding on to the things which hold on to
the *archê*, making use of nothing sensible, but only forms themselves,
travelling through them and to them and terminating at them"
(511 b 6 sqq.)?

It seems to me that it is possible to give in one sentence the answer
to this question, though that one sentence may need many to elucidate it. The key sentence is: that the order of invention and the
order of exposition are opposites. When, after the injunctions given
in the *Phaedo*, I find a higher hypothesis wherewith to defend a lower,
I move upwards, but what I get is an argument in which the order of
logical dependence is the other way round. I start from the thought
that virtue is knowledge; this idea commends itself to me. The
reason why it does so is that I am dimly aware of the considerations
which I only render explicit when the original idea is challenged. The
challenge to my hypothesis makes me seek for its grounds. When I
find them I have an argument, in the discovery of which my hypothesis has been the springboard, and in the exposition of which it
becomes the conclusion. If I am satisfied with the grounds which I
discover, and if I am satisfied also that my hypothesis alone does
justice to them, I proceed to derive my hypothesis from its grounds.
In this way what is a step upwards from one point of view is a step
downwards from another, for it is a climb on to the premises from
which the hypothesis depends. Going up from the lower hypothesis
is discovering how to go down to it; and I cannot be sure that I have
gone upwards to a higher hypothesis which is genuinely above my
initial hypothesis until I satisfy myself that I can validly descend from
the former to the latter. Every time therefore that I reconstruct or
"recollect" the reasons why something seems to me to be the case I
discover a route by which I can descend. There is however no pro-
bative force in such a descent from grounds to conclusion unless I
manage to ascend to "something adequate". It is therefore only a
complete ascent to something which is indisputable which enables
me to make a cogent downwards journey and establish the disputed
hypothesis. I test every step in the ascent by making sure that it allows
of a valid descent, but it is only when I have got to something which
can serve as a summit that I can journey downwards with any force.
I have to get to the top before I can come down, and I get to the top
in order to come down, but in a sense the coming down adds nothing
to what the ascent has achieved.

In this way the way down is the *raison d'être* of the way up without
adding anything new to it. We can apply this to what Socrates says in
the *Republic*. Being human and imprisoned in the cave of sense-

experience, we start, both in the mathematical and in the practical sphere, with notions of a fairly down-to-earth kind, with distinctions which we draw for practical purposes and work with without understanding their *rationale*—for example that alternate numbers are not divisible by two without remainder. These notions, distinctions and so on reflect intelligible principles, distinctions or what you will, in the sense that it is a "memory" of the latter that has made us create the former; but as they stand the notions of good and bad, odd and even, fair and unfair that we start from are notions which we just have to take for granted and which we have to conceive of in empirical terms. We have to take the existence of oddness or of unfairness as matters of fact, brute, given, no more intelligible than the fact that John has cut his finger. Gradually however the philosopher begins to see reason for these truths or to gain insight into these terms—it does not matter which we say, for to see why some conduct is unfair is the same as to see what unfairness is. In some way, as we have seen, it is the special message of the *Republic* that the mathematical embodiments of rational principles are of crucial help to us in this progress. Gradually we become able to see sense in what we have hitherto accepted as brute fact, and *pari passu*, I think, we purge the empirical element out of our concepts. But when we have attained the level at which we can see fairness and unfairness, courage and cowardice and so on as special cases of virtue and vice, it may very well be that we still lack insight into the *rationale* of the distinction between these last two. Virtue and vice are still *hupotheseis* in the sense that we cannot yet give account of them. If we accept them as a starting-point we can travel downwards from them to the more specific concepts which lie below them; but of course it is wrong to rest content with this achievement. We need to go on until the distinction between virtue and vice is no longer something given, conceived of in terms of its instances, but something which we understand. We shall probably make many false starts in finding higher level concepts which give sense to the distinction between virtue and vice; but in due course we may come to some which seem promising—it might be, for instance, order and disorder. If we were provisionally to pause here we should find that we had constructed, and could "descend" through, a small hierarchy of concepts; from order to virtue as its application to the human organism, and from virtue to justice as the application of virtue in certain fields. But we could do no more than pause here, for nothing is to be accepted as a *datum*; we must understand and not just accept the distinction between order and disorder. So we go on upwards, getting further and further away from concepts which are of a high degree of specificity and therefore of direct practical application, improving our insight into our system of concepts by seeing more and more of them as special cases of increasingly abstract notions. But what guarantee have we that we are achieving insight rather than deluding ourselves as we go along? A partial guarantee is presumably provided by the context of friendly discussion in which we must assume that the dialectical activity is carried on; as we shall see, "dialectic" implies discussion. A further guarantee is provided by the fact that we are trying to re-discover what we in some sense knew all along, the criterion of success in this being, I suppose, whether at each stage it is evident to us that we have achieved a better understanding of the stages below. But there might still be false starts and blind alleys despite these guarantees. What would however certify us that we were on the right track would be if all our various investigations converged upwards on the one *arché*, the nature of goodness, or of that which is congruent with reason, so that the existence of goodness remained the only thing that we had to take for granted. This of course is the stage at which Plato must have believed in a sort of flash of illumination whereby we should somehow come to know the light by which all our steps hitherto had been guided. When this had happened what would the situation be? Every conception that we have, every distinction that we draw, would fall into place as something which we have to have or draw in the light of that which is congruent with reason. Whereas hitherto, the nature of goodness being unknown, all our concepts would still have owed their meaning to their empirical application, now this would no longer apply. Hitherto the system would have rested on its base (the readily applicable concepts of every day); now it will hang from its apex. We shall have at our disposal a system of pure concepts all deriving from the nature of goodness. Indeed it will be misleading to speak of them as concepts, if a concept is the representation of something in the human mind. For he who understands, for example, the distinction between virtue and vice in the light of the nature of goodness will be apprehending a distinction which is there in the nature of things, whether we notice it or not, a distinction which is ultimately responsible for the concepts of virtue and vice which men form, dimly apprehending it, and represent to themselves in terms of practical instances, but which is in no way dependent upon such recognition for its validity. Thus the man who ascends to the nature of goodness thereby transforms a system of concepts which more or less accurately reflect the forms into an apprehension of the system of forms. He is in a position to turn round and to descend (and the process I suppose might take a little time) purging out the empirical element which remains in his concepts; knowledge of goodness having taken the place of a conception of goodness, the same substitution would spread downwards from the apex until the most commonsensical distinctions such as those between odd and even numbers or fair and unfair actions were seen as differences that there have to be, goodness being what it is. This, I suggest, is what Plato means when he says that *nöêsis* comes down again from the unhypothetical source of all things, holding on to the things which hold on to it (i.e. the terms whose universality is only less than that of goodness) and journeying from forms through forms to forms, terminating in forms, and making use of nothing sensuous. When we get the key to the solution of some problem, and see in a flash how the key unlocks the door, I suppose that the process of making sure that the key unlocks the door takes a measurable amount of time even in the case of simple problems. In one sense however you cannot distinguish knowing that you have got the key from checking that it unlocks the door. My impression is that Plato did not think that the process of seeing how everything depends upon goodness took very much time; I suspect that he thought that we should achieve this in a flash as we sometimes see in a flash how the key solves the whole problem. This however is not very important; the point that I want to lay stress on is that this is the logical relationship between the way up and the way down; the way down is the moment or process or whatever it may be in which we see what we have achieved on the way up.

Our next question is already answered—the question in what sense the *archê* is unhypothetical. The answer is that we know that we have arrived at the end of our journey because the nature of goodness was the last thing that we did not understand, and we know that we have ascertained the nature of goodness because nothing that we do in the intellectual life now remains a matter of brute fact. We now understand why we had the concepts and made the distinctions that we did because we now see the whole of the system of intelligible principles to which these concepts and distinctions roughly and readily correspond. Nothing is any longer taken for granted, and therefore we are making no more *hupotheseis*.

Perhaps it would be expedient to remind ourselves at this point that this part of the *Republic* records a vision which Plato never succeeded (and never could have succeeded) in working out in humdrum detail. Parts of his vision he appears to have abandoned. What is permanently Platonic in the doctrine of this part of the dialogue is that philosophy is not an attempt to prove things but an attempt to understand why we do the things which, as thinkers and men of rational action, we do find ourselves doing. That mathematics is specially helpful in this enterprise, and that the key to it is the divination of the nature of goodness, Plato does not repeat, and perhaps ceased to believe, in the form in which these doctrines appear in the *Republic*; he did not abandon belief in the value of the enterprise.

It has taken us a long time to decide what Plato meant by *noêsis* and dialectic. Now that we have decided we see that the aim of the process to which these words refer is nothing novel. As to the manner in which the process is carried on, we have seen that Plato says nothing about this. But I think that there is every reason to suppose that the search for understanding would be essentially conversational. It follows therefore that the activity described as dialectic would have been something very like the activity of which the *Meno* —and indeed the other early dialogues—give examples. It would have been the attempt to achieve, by means of argument, an understanding of the terms, concepts, distinctions or what you will that we employ in thought.

The conclusion is then that, despite its mystifying and hierophantic language, this section of the *Republic* does not detract from the point that Plato did not conceive of philosophy as the acquisition of axioms from which a system of new truths could be deduced. Rather, the philosopher is engaged in trying to understand, and thus to do better, the things which he already does, though haltingly, whenever he thinks.

III. THE CONCEPT OF DIALECTIC

The notion of dialectic is very prominent in Plato's writings whenever he is talking about philosophical method. A little must be said here about the concept or concepts for which the word stands.

First for the word itself. In trying to understand it we must banish completely all associations with Kantian, Hegelian or Marxist usages, and those derived from these. The word "dialectic" (*dialektikê*) is an adjective, and the noun that accompanies it, or that is to be understood with it, is "knowledge" or "art" or "method"; and the dialectic art is the art of doing something for which the related verb *dialegesthai* is used. To have dialectic art is to know how to *dialegesthai*.

Dialegesthai is a verb in what is called the middle voice. The middle voice is so called because it comes "between" the active and the passive, in that the general sense of the middle is that the agent is the person affected or benefited by the action. In the case of a good many verbs, however, the active voice and the middle voice constitute in practice two distinct active verbs; and so it is with this one. The common meaning of *dialegesthai* is "to converse" (the meaning from which the noun "dialogue" derives). But a common meaning of the active voice *dialegein* is "to sort". To discriminate things into their kinds is to *dialegein*. Xenophon tells us (*Memorabilia* IV, 5, 12) that Socrates connected dialectic with *dialegein* in the active voice; he said that the *dialektikos* or dialectician is the man who can sort good from bad, and that dialectic is the practice of sorting things into their kinds by taking counsel with each other. The theory which Xenophon here imputes to Socrates would be roughly along these lines. To *dialegesthai* is to engage in the sort of conversation that is courteous, serious and concerned with the truth.[1] When men are thus seriously conversing, each trying to learn from the other, they are sorting things for themselves; and roughly the only way in which a man can sort things for himself is to expose his ideas in this way to another's criticism. Thus the colloquial meaning of *dialegesthai*, namely "to converse as one should", can be seen to be equivalent to the meaning which etymology might lead us to put upon the middle voice of *dialegein*, namely "to sort for oneself".

I suspect that no modern etymologist would accept this derivation of *dialegesthai*, and I do not know whether Plato accepted it. Xenophon's witness however suggests that Socrates thought it at least a significant point; and I believe that we ought to allow that for him and for Plato *dialegesthai* and *dialektikē* carried the connotation, not only of conversation which is sincere and characterised by give and take, but also that the purpose of such conversation is to see each thing separately in its true nature. Mr. Robinson has suggested that Plato tended to use "dialectic" to stand for the ideal method of philosophy, whatever, at any time, he conceived that to be. This is true, but I think that it is also the case that the objective remains throughout: that we should attain a clear vision of realities as they are in themselves, not confusing one with another. This remains the objective of the dialectician. His methods change at different times in Plato's life, or at least different sides of his activity receive the emphasis at different times; but the change is entirely intelligible in the light of Plato's general development, as I shall try to show.

We may begin by reminding ourselves that, whereas we tend to picture the philosopher as a man who tries to find out truths, Plato tended to picture him as a man who tries to become better acquainted with realities. The philosopher, for Plato, does not immediately ask whether all S is P; he asks what S and P are. If he succeeds in answering these questions, the answers will tell him whether it must be the case that all S is P, or that no S is P, or, perhaps, that it is contingent whether or not any S is P; but it is from his acquaintance with the entities involved that the philosopher derives the truths about them.

[1] In his admirable discussion in *Plato's Earlier Dialectic* Mr. Robinson has shown that Plato's usage of the verb is along these lines.

Knowledge is a kind of vision. It comes about when an objectively real entity is seen by the mind precisely as it is without any distortion whatever, or *auto kath' hauto*, "itself according to itself", as Plato so often puts it. The general terms which the philosopher wants to know better are all perfectly intelligible. This emerges clearly in the later dialogues when Plato speaks of the letters and syllables of reality, and says that we are familiar with all the letters; but I think that we may also reasonably claim that this doctrine underlies the earlier writings as well. Socrates always chides himself for his stupidity when he fails to say what something is. But if the entities which we want to know better are all perfectly intelligible, why do we not understand them perfectly? The answer, so far as such earlier writings as the *Phaedo* and the *Republic* are concerned, tends to be given in terms of the body. It is the senses which inhibit our knowledge of general terms. We have seen in earlier chapters[1] that when Plato speaks of the senses in this way he does not mean literally the senses; he means rather the impression that we should get if we looked and listened and felt quite uncritically. The absurd view that we should all be wonderful philosophers if we had no sense-organs should not be imputed to Plato, though his language sometimes asks for it. But it is not because we can use our eyes that we fail to understand the nature of equality or triangularity or justice. It is because we tend to form what I have called inductive conceptions of these entities; that is to say we tend to think that the important features of K-hood are the most evident features of a representative set of familiar K things. We thus fill our minds with *doxai* or inductively-based impressions, and these obscure our ignorance from us. We get along well enough with our *doxai* for practical purposes most of the time, and therefore we think that we understand.

This being the case, the emphasis in those of the earlier dialogues which ask a dialectical or "What is X?" question is on *elenchos* or refutation. People must be shown that they do not understand. And in the *Republic*, when Plato is talking specifically about dialectic, he does so in language which blackguards the use of the senses, emphasises that *noêsis* is a pure grasp of the forms without the assistance of any empirical material, and puts mathematics in between philosophy and ordinary *doxa* as a kind of plateau on which we pause to become accustomed to the rarefied air which we shall have to breathe on the peaks. There is in the *Republic* a harsh antipathy between dialectic and anything that we get from the senses, just because at this stage in Plato's thought what a man must do, who wants to become better acquainted with justice, equality, triangularity and so on, is to abandon the habit of thinking of these things in sensuous terms,

[1] See above, pp. 86 sqq.; also pp. 297 sqq.

that is as if they were identical with the evident features of their instances.

Nevertheless there is another side to the dialectician in the *Republic*; he is *sunoptikos*, his view is synoptic, he sees things in relation to each other. This points forward to later emphases, but it is not inconsistent with the truth that the dialectician of the *Republic* sees each thing as it is. For the entities which the dialectician tries to see are of course related to each other. It had always been implicit in the practice of Socratic definition (or in other words dialectic) that one general term can be analysed in terms of others; and we saw in an earlier chapter[1] that the *Phaedo* probably adumbrates the conception of syllogising, or of discovering what must necessarily be the case by investigating the entailment relationships which hold between general terms. One cannot see what the soul is without seeing also that its nature entails immortality and probably also indestructibility.

In the earlier period, then, the dialectician, in trying to see what each thing is and to understand, through this, how things are related to one another, will take care to purge out of his conception of general terms anything that does not belong to them as they are "themselves according to themselves", but rather to their instances. In the later writings this anti-empirical emphasis disappears, either because Plato ceased to believe in it or because he thought that he had sufficiently made the point. We have seen in earlier chapters that the main shift of interest in Plato's writing occurred when he began to attach importance to the *koinônia genôn* or to the mutual relationships of general terms. The way in which the descriptions of the dialectician change between the earlier and the later writings is entirely consistent with this. Plato begins to see clearly that philosophical blunders can arise not only because people stuff their minds with inductive *doxai* but also because they mis-classify things, and commit what we have called Protarchus' fallacy. We condemn passion because we think it is madness, and because we attach to madness as a whole the blame which properly belongs to a part of it only. We ought to have seen that the affinity which holds between love and lunacy contains a difference, and that the simple undifferentiated concept of madness masks the difference. To avoid this kind of blunder a man must be skilful at *sunagôgê* or at surveying the range of possible instances of a common nature and drawing together those that belong together, and also at *diairesis* or the drawing of distinctions that need to be drawn.

General terms can "combine"; and where they combine we get sub-classes whose members must not be lumped together. Therefore

[1] Above, Chapter 2, pp. 161–5.

it is necessary to "draw together" with discretion and to "divide" with nicety, making use only of those divisions which are not arbitrary. Evidently to recognise the importance of this is not to deny the importance of purifying our concepts of their sensuous elements. The new emphasis does not entail the abandoning of the old. Philosophy for Plato had always had its practical relevance; one did dialectic in the *Republic* in order to set to rights one's own life and that of the city. There was therefore always the problem (though Plato may not have realised this) of how the man who has come to understand what virtue is is to apply his understanding to life. To apply it he would have to be able to distinguish, for example, one kind of madness from another. He would also be starting from a confused and incoherent *hupothesis* if he started from a conception of justice or virtue whose empirical representation was a range of disparate instances. It will not be fruitful to seek the rational principle which underlies a concept which assimilates dissimilars. To have the sort of notions whose origin it is worth trying to "recollect" we must first practise *sunagôgê* and *diairesis*. Socrates in the earlier dialogues ignores the importance of this. He assumes much too readily that if we have a single word (for example *sophrôsunê* in the *Charmides* and the *Republic*) it is worth while enquiring without further ado into the single thing for which the word stands. He places unreasonable trust in the skill at *sunagôgê* and *diairesis* shown by the makers of language.[1] It is this that the later descriptions of dialectic correct. It would be possible however to combine the point that we must become nice in our use of concepts before we have something whose *rationale* is worth seeking with the point that to seek for the *rationale* of our concepts we must turn our attention away from their instances. We must first gather together instances which have a genuine common nature, but when we come to ask what this common nature really is we must think of it as something to which embodiment in these instances is not essential. It seems then that the earlier and later emphases in the description of dialectic can be combined. Whether Plato intended them to be combined in this way it is not perhaps possible to decide. It may be that at one time he was conscious of one source of error, subsequently of another; and that he posted warning notices against each without explicitly asking himself what path that left open to us.

"Dialectic" then throughout Plato's writings stands for the attempt to discover or re-discover the true nature of the rational principles which we dimly recognise in our thought; to discover the true nature of each as it is in isolation from its embodiments and in

[1] I wonder whether the reckless and frivolous etymologies in the *Cratylus* show Plato's awareness of this?

relation to all the others. What changes in Plato's description of the dialectician is his account of the steps which we have to take if we are to achieve this purpose.

IV. CONCLUSION

Let me begin this section with a piece of self-defence. I have argued against the notion that Plato conceived of philosophy as an attempt at discovering self-evident axioms and deducing from them a body of metaphysical knowledge. I have argued also against the notion that he conceived of philosophy as some kind of vision of quite special and peculiar things called forms. My contention has been that he thought of philosophy as the re-discovery of knowledge which is in some sense our birthright but which it is nevertheless arduous to re-possess; and I have said that what we hope to re-discover is the true nature of the rational principles which we dimly recognise in our thought.

Such an account of Plato's conception of philosophy, with its emphasis on "recollection", is perhaps best suited to his middle period—but a middle period which stretches from the *Meno* to the *Phaedrus*. But I shall be told that even so far as this middle period is concerned I have purchased a plausibility which I do not deserve by the dissolute use of phrases such as "rational principles". Plato talks of forms, of common natures, of the odd and the even, of the triangle itself; he nowhere talks of rational principles. This is true; Plato never talks of rational principles, and indeed I do not know what the Greek for such a phrase would be. But when you have to put into Greek a phrase for which there is no equivalent, you recast the sentence so that it is more congenial to Greek thought-forms. My claim is that this is what I have been doing the other way round. Plato talks of discovering what justice is; to us such language suggests an investigation which he does not in fact mean to carry out —for example deciding whether it is just to do this or that. You cannot discover what justice is in Plato's sense without deciding what are the characteristics the possession of which makes some men more laudable in this respect than others; and to decide this is to state articulately a rational principle according to which one may classify men. To every term corresponds a proposition, in the sense that to hypothesise a term such as "the odd" is to suppose the truth of the proposition that there exists a characteristic such that certain entities do or might possess it, and would be thereby significantly different from those which lack it. To Plato it is more natural to talk of investigating the term, asking what the odd is. To us it is more natural to talk of questioning the proposition, of investigating the *rationale* of a principle of classification. This is my *apologia* for making use of phrases like "rational principles".

In one of C. S. Lewis's books for children the world in which his young heroes find themselves comes to an end, and they with it. But after it has come to an end, it and they are reborn more gloriously. The children marvel; but an aged professor who is sharing their experiences rebukes their wondering. They ought to have expected a new heaven and a new earth, that this corruptible should put on incorruption. But the reason why they ought to have expected it is not that it is in St. Paul or the Book of Revelation. No; the professor's comment is: "What do they teach them in these schools? *It's all in Plato.*"

It is not in Plato that the natural world is a transient image of an eternal and more glorious archetype so far as this book has been concerned. But the time has come to make amends. This book has offered a more "Aristotelian" account of Plato than that which has often been adopted by people who are called Platonists. It has put Plato more into the company of philosophers like Aristotle, Hume, Kant or Russell than into the company of mystical thinkers like Plotinus with whom he is often linked. I do not repent of this, but there is a characteristic of Plato's manner of philosophical writing which must be acknowledged. He had an almost unequalled stylistic gift; he could do, it seems, whatever he put his writing hand to. He could be absolutely lucid. On the whole however he disdained lucidity as he also disdained logical rigour. He thought perhaps that an undue attention to the exposition of an argument or to the precise words which were chosen to convey an opinion would distract attention from the realities which were under discussion; and he thought also that an eye fixed steadily on realities was the only sure defence against the deceptions of words. At any rate it is his habit, for whatever reason, to suggest his points rather than to state them; and it is commonly the case that he uses his unique gift of prose-poetry to set them in a certain emotional atmosphere. For this reason there is not one Plato but many; you find in him, to some extent, what you are looking for, and if the plain sense of the words does not support your interpretation, perhaps you will be able to base it on the general feeling of the passage, or *vice versa*.

It may be, and I suggest that to some extent it is the case, that all the various Platos are authentic. It was perhaps the chief of his several philosophical purposes to convince us of the reality of transcendent entities; and I dare say that he did not suppose himself to know too clearly of what character they were. It is also I believe the case that his conception of the transcendent was rendered ambiguous by the tension which I have tried to describe in earlier chapters[1] between the personalist and the rationalist strains in his religious outlook. The personalist requires for the dwelling place of the purified soul something like the world which is described in the myth of the *Phaedo*—a world which is a world like ours, only altogether more glorious. Its air is so pure that ours, by comparison, is fog; its colours are more brilliant than anything that we have seen, its trees and plants more vigorous and resplendent, its rocks are emeralds, jaspers and sardine stones. In fact it is utterly satisfying to the senses, an ideal environment for human life, and the archetype of this imperfect earth. But the rationalist strain in Plato will not allow that this is a mythical representation of eternity. Even in the myth of the *Phaedo* there is a higher realm, said to be difficult to describe, for those who can live entirely without the body; and one suspects from earlier passages in the dialogue that this higher realm, being the soul's true home, will be a rather depressing place furnished, like the heaven of the *Phaedrus*, only with forms. For the soul in its true nature is pure reason, and philosophy its one preoccupation, truth its only nourishment. In so far then as Plato gave scope to his imagination he became the poet of the new heaven of which this earth is the transient and imperfect image; in so far as he restrained his imagination his account became increasingly abstract, rationalistic and prosaic.

[1] Chapters 7 and 8 of Vol. 1.

INDEX

All references are to this volume. Certain of the more important references are in heavy type. See also the Table of Contents.

Ackrill, J. L.   31 n
Aesthetes   86 sqq
Aisthêsis   1–33; see also *Sense-perception*
Anamnêsis   133 sq, **135–47**, 290, 296 sqq, 526, 532, 551 sqq
Anaxagoras   157, 252, 531
Apeiron   176 n, **359–68, 422–40**
Archê anhupothetos   556 sqq.
Aristotle   48, 66 n, 151, 163, 200 n, 254, 257 sq, 269–70, 270–1, 280, 281, 319, 367, 440 sqq *passim*, 478, 513, 544
Astronomy   159 sq, 167 sq, 185 sqq, 207 sqq, 241–6

Causal Theory (of perception)   19 sqq, 130 sqq
Cave (simile of)   **85–9**
Charmides   255, 475
Connaître (*vs. savoir*)   41, 45, 107, 111, 113, 119, 121
Copula (existential import of)   499 sqq; see also *Identity*
Cornford, F. M.   220, 223 n, 330 n
Counter-inductiveness   55 sq, 59, 67–70, 98, 128, 184, 249 sqq, 255, 271 sqq, 285 sqq, 290, 293 sqq, 322, 532, 564
Craftsmanship   86 sqq
Cratylus   199 n, 238, 273 sq, 323, **376–7, 475–86**, 495, 497, 566 n

Descartes, R.   133, 218
Dialectic   37, 154, 180, **359–422**, 477, 553 sqq, **562–7**

Dunamis (cognitive function)   57 sq
Dunworth, M. C. P.   541

Eikasia   66 n, 75 sq, 91
Eikôn; see *Image*
Eleaticism   33, 125, 390 sqq, 484, 503
Elements (and complexes); see *Letters*
Epinomis   37, 243–4, 444
Eudoxus   188
Euthydemus   474, **488–9**, 502
Euthyphro   251, 255, 256 sq

Fallacy   473–5
False belief, paradox of   59, 62, 476, 482 sq, **486–516**
Frege, G.   446, 448

Gorgias   51–2, 81, 82
Gosling, J. C. B.   ix, 53

Hare, R. M.   ix
Heracliteanism   **4–33**, 238–9, 247 sqq, 323, 475 sqq, 485
Hippias Major   67 n, 256, 290 n, 312 n, 448, 474
Hypotheses   528 sqq; "destroying hypotheses"   555 sq

Idea   174 n
Identity (copula construed as)   251, **401 sqq**, 499
Image   47, 49 sq

Induction; see Counter-inductiveness

Kant, I. 218 n
Koinônia genôn 357 sqq, 389 sqq

Laches 255, 524
Laws 25, 81, 189, 227, 238–43, 486, 521, 523
Leibniz, G. W. 119, 182
Letters (and syllables) 109, 115 sqq, 411 sqq
Leucippus 151
Lewis, C. S. 568
Line (simile of) 73–85, 89–102, 548 sqq
Locke, J. 15, 19, 217 n, 355
Lysis 255–6, 474

Mathematicals 97, 307–8
Mathematics 77–85, 183–93 passim, 207, 210 sqq, 242–5, 307–8
Meno 50–2, 105 sq, 136–41, 146, 531–9
Mitchell, B. G. ix
Music 186 sqq, 207 sqq

Naïve Realism 16 sqq
Negation 407 sqq
Neutral Monism 22 sqq
Nominalism (vs realism) 279 sqq

Objects (of cognitive functions) 41–50, 57 sqq, 93 sqq
Observation; see Sense-perception
Owen, G. E. L. 27

Parker, T. M. 279 n
Parmenides 126, 258, 260, 261, 281, 287, 306–7, 326–53, 362, 391–2, 416–17, 451, 458, 475, 515, 524
Parmenides 486
Peras 359–68, 422–40
Phaedo 7 n, 50 n, 124, 129, 134, 141–4, 146 sq, 156–71, 172–8, 182, 236 sq, 249, 287, 288, 295–303, 310–19, 349–50, 415, 445, 521 sq, 529–31, 539–48

Phaedrus 144–6, 360–1, 368 sqq, 395, 521
Phenomenalism 19 sqq
Philebus 37, 126, 176 n, 238–9, 259, 261, 268 sq, 308, 350 n, 359–70, 422–40, 444, 454, 460 sqq
Photographic conception of thought 96, 103, 292, 296, 302, 322, 350
Physical world, knowledge of 36 sqq
Points 240, 442, 447
Predication; see Copula and Identity
Propositions 45 sqq, 58, 61, 111 sq, 116 sq, 121, 476, 481, 486, 487 sqq passim
Protagoras 265, 474
Protagoras 4–12, 59, 476, 486
Protarchus' fallacy 565
Pythagoreans 197, 223, 330, 423 sq

Qualities, primary and secondary 24 sq, 192, 221 sq, 241

Realism (vs nominalism) 279 sqq; see also Naïve Realism
Recollection; see Anamnêsis
Reference 110 sq, 116
Republic 53–104, 148–52, 171–97, 199 n, 234–6, 242–3, 249, 263–5, 267 sqq, 273 sq, 286, 290, 291–2, 293–5, 308, 324, 353–4, 415, 425, 438, 444, 450, 465, 470, 487–8, 522, 525–7, 548–62
Robinson, R. 359, 539 n, 563 n
Ross, W. D. 240, 274, 353, 441, 443 n
Russell, B. 22, 446, 448
Ryle, G. ix, 117 n, 120 n, 352 n

Sensation; see Aisthêsis; also Sense-perception
Sense-perception (sense-experience) 54 sqq, 86 sqq, 128, 129, 130 sq, 133, 154, 167 sqq, 170 sq, 183 sq, 190 sq, 195 sq, 228 sq, 232 sqq, 261, 296 sqq, 322, 540, 559 sqq, 564

Seventh Letter **122–7**, 261, 350 n, 524
Sextus Empiricus 467
Socrates 249, 250, 252, 254–5
Socrates' Dream **114–17**, 377–8, 491 sq
Sophist 63, 202, 258, 271, 328, 380 sqq, **388–422**, 451 n, 469 sq, **492–516**
Space (*chôra*) 217–19, 222–8
Spheres of competence (of mental functions) 63–4, 148–52
Spinoza, B. 521
Statesman 153, 155, 237, 287, **370–6, 378–80**, 380 sqq, 436
Syllables; see *Letters*
Symposium 23, 62 sq, 265–7, 323

Theaetetus **2–33**, **105–22**, 126–7, 146–7, 259, 261, 287, 323, **377–8**, 447, 475, 485, 489–92
Theophrastus 442, 466
Third man 331
Timaeus 1–2, 17, 21, 24, 31, 35 sq, 38 sqq, 55, 186, 190, **197–237**, 280 sq, 287, **303–5**, 323 sqq, 355 sq, 423–4, 439 sq, 460 sqq, 513, 521 sq

Xenophon 563

Zeno (the Eleatic) 125, 327 sq
Zoroastrianism 227, 241

International Library of Philosophy & Scientific Method

Editor: Ted Honderich
Advisory Editor: Bernard Williams

List of titles, page two

International Library of Psychology Philosophy & Scientific Method

Editor: C K Ogden

List of titles, page six

ROUTLEDGE AND KEGAN PAUL LTD
68 Carter Lane London EC4

International Library of Philosophy and Scientific Method
(Demy 8vo)

Allen, R. E. (Ed.)
Studies in Plato's Metaphysics
Contributors: J. L. Ackrill, R. E. Allen, R. S. Bluck, H. F. Cherniss, F. M. Cornford, R. C. Cross, P. T. Geach, R. Hackforth, W. F. Hicken, A. C. Lloyd, G. R. Morrow, G. E. L. Owen, G. Ryle, W. G. Runciman, G. Vlastos
464 pp. 1965. (2nd Impression 1967.) 70s.

Armstrong, D. M.
Perception and the Physical World
208 pp. 1961. (3rd Impression 1966.) 25s.
A Materialist Theory of the Mind
376 pp. 1967. about 45s.

Bambrough, Renford (Ed.)
New Essays on Plato and Aristotle
Contributors: J. L. Ackrill, G. E. M. Anscombe, Renford Bambrough, R. M. Hare, D. M. MacKinnon, G. E. L. Owen, G. Ryle, G. Vlastos
184 pp. 1965. (2nd Impression 1967.) 28s.

Barry, Brian
Political Argument
382 pp. 1965. 50s.

Bird, Graham
Kant's Theory of Knowledge:
An Outline of One Central Argument in the *Critique of Pure Reason*
220 pp. 1962. (2nd Impression 1965.) 28s.

Brentano, Franz
The True and the Evident
Edited and narrated by Professor R. Chisholm
218 pp. 1965. 40s.

Broad, C. D.
Lectures on Psychical Research
Incorporating the Perrott Lectures given in Cambridge University in 1959 and 1960
461 pp. 1962. (2nd Impression 1966.) 56s.

Crombie, I. M.
An Examination of Plato's Doctrine
I. Plato on Man and Society
408 pp. 1962. (2nd Impression 1966.) 42s.
II. Plato on Knowledge and Reality
583 pp. 1963. (2nd Impression 1967.) 63s.

Day, John Patrick
Inductive Probability
352 pp. 1961. 40s.

2

International Library of Philosophy and Scientific Method
(Demy 8vo)

Edel, Abraham
Method in Ethical Theory
379 pp. 1963. 32s.

Flew, Anthony
Hume's Philosophy of Belief
A Study of his First "Inquiry"
296 pp. 1961. (2nd Impression 1966.) 30s.

Fogelin, Robert J.
Evidence and Meaning
Studies in Analytical Philosophy
200 pp. 1967. 25s.

Gale, Richard
The Language of Time
256 pp. 1967. about 30s.

Goldman, Lucien
The Hidden God
A Study of Tragic Vision in the *Pensées* of Pascal and the Tragedies of
Racine. Translated from the French by Philip Thody
424 pp. 1964. 70s.

Hamlyn, D. W.
Sensation and Perception
A History of the Philosophy of Perception
222 pp. 1961. (3rd Impression 1967.) 25s.

Kemp, J.
Reason, Action and Morality
216 pp. 1964. 30s.

Körner, Stephan
Experience and Theory
An Essay in the Philosophy of Science
272 pp. 1966. 45s.

Lazerowitz, Morris
Studies in Metaphilosophy
276 pp. 1964. 35s.

Linsky, Leonard
Referring
152 pp. 1967. about 28s.

Merleau-Ponty, M.
Phenomenology of Perception
Translated from the French by Colin Smith
487 pp. 1962. (4th Impression 1967.) 56s.

International Library of Philosophy and Scientific Method
(Demy 8vo)

Perelman, Chaim
The Idea of Justice and the Problem of Argument
Introduction by H. L. A. Hart. Translated from the French by John Petrie
224 pp. 1963. 28s.

Ross, Alf
Directives, Norms and their Logic
192 pp. 1967. about 25s.

Schlesinger, G.
Method in the Physical Sciences
148 pp. 1963. 21s.

Sellars, W. F.
Science, Perception and Reality
374 pp. 1963. (2nd Impression 1966.) 50s.

Shwayder, D. S.
The Stratification of Behaviour
A System of Definitions Propounded and Defended
428 pp. 1965. 56s.

Skolimowski, Henryk
Polish Analytical Philosophy
288 pp. 1967. 40s.

Smart, J. J. C.
Philosophy and Scientific Realism
168 pp. 1963. (3rd Impression 1967.) 25s.

Smythies, J. R. (Ed.)
Brain and Mind
Contributors: Lord Brain, John Beloff, C. J. Ducasse, Antony Flew,
Hartwig Kuhlenbeck, D. M. MacKay, H. H. Price, Anthony Quinton and
J. R. Smythies
288 pp. 1965. 40s.

Science and E.S.P.
Contributors: Gilbert Murray, H. H. Price, Rosalind Heywood, Cyril Burt,
C. D. Broad, Francis Huxley and John Beloff
320 pp. about 40s.

Taylor, Charles
The Explanation of Behaviour
288 pp. 1964. (2nd Impression 1965.) 40s.

Williams, Bernard, and Montefiore, Alan
British Analytical Philosophy
352 pp. 1965. (2nd Impression 1967.) 45s.

4

International Library of Philosophy and Scientific Method
(Demy 8vo)

Wittgenstein, Ludwig
Tractatus Logico-Philosophicus
The German text of the *Logisch-Philosophische Abhandlung* with a new translation by D. F. Pears and B. F. McGuinness. Introduction by Bertrand Russell
188 pp. 1961. (3rd Impression 1966.) 21s.

Wright, Georg Henrik Von
Norm and Action
A Logical Enquiry. The Gifford Lectures
232 pp. 1963. (2nd Impression 1964.) 32s.

The Varieties of Goodness
The Gifford Lectures
236 pp. 1963. (3rd Impression 1966.) 28s.

Zinkernagel, Peter
Conditions for Description
Translated from the Danish by Olaf Lindum
272 pp. 1962. 37s. 6d.

International Library of Psychology, Philosophy, and Scientific Method

(Demy 8vo)

PHILOSOPHY

Anton, John Peter
Aristotle's Theory of Contrariety
276 pp. 1957. 25s.

Bentham, J.
The Theory of Fictions
Introduction by C. K. Ogden
214 pp. 1932. 30s.

Black, Max
The Nature of Mathematics
A Critical Survey
242 pp. 1933. (5th Impression 1965.) 28s.

Bluck, R. S.
Plato's Phaedo
A Translation with Introduction, Notes and Appendices
226 pp. 1955. 21s.

Broad, C. D.
Scientific Thought
556 pp. 1923. (4th Impression 1952.) 40s.

Five Types of Ethical Theory
322 pp. 1930. (9th Impression 1967.) 30s.

The Mind and Its Place in Nature
694 pp. 1925. (7th Impression 1962.) 55s. See also Lean, Martin

Buchler, Justus (Ed.)
The Philosophy of Peirce
Selected Writings
412 pp. 1940. (3rd Impression 1956.) 35s.

Burtt, E. A.
The Metaphysical Foundations of Modern Physical Science
A Historical and Critical Essay
364 pp. 2nd (revised) edition 1932. (5th Impression 1964.) 35s.

International Library of Psychology, Philosophy, and Scientific Method
(Demy 8vo)

Carnap, Rudolf
The Logical Syntax of Language
Translated from the German by Amethe Smeaton
376 pp. 1937. (7th Impression 1967.) 40s.

Chwistek, Leon
The Limits of Science
Outline of Logic and of the Methodology of the Exact Sciences
With Introduction and Appendix by Helen Charlotte Brodie
414 pp. 2nd edition 1949. 32s.

Cornford, F. M.
Plato's Theory of Knowledge
The Theaetetus and Sophist of Plato
Translated with a running commentary
358 pp. 1935. (7th Impression 1967.) 28s.

Plato's Cosmology
The Timaeus of Plato
Translated with a running commentary
402 pp. Frontispiece. 1937. (5th Impression 1966.) 45s.

Plato and Parmenides
Parmenides' *Way of Truth* and Plato's *Parmenides*
Translated with a running commentary
280 pp 1939 (5th Impression 1964.) 32s.

Crawshay-Williams, Rupert
Methods and Criteria of Reasoning
An Inquiry into the Structure of Controversy
312 pp. 1957. 32s.

Fritz, Charles A.
Bertrand Russell's Construction of the External World
252 pp. 1952. 30s.

Hulme, T. E.
Speculations
Essays on Humanism and the Philosophy of Art
Edited by Herbert Read. Foreword and Frontispiece by Jacob Epstein
296 pp. 2nd edition 1936. (6th Impression 1965.) 32s.

Lange, Frederick Albert
The History of Materialism
And Criticism of its Present Importance
With an Introduction by Bertrand Russell, F.R.S. Translated from the German
by Ernest Chester Thomas
1,146 pp. 1925. (3rd Impression 1957.) 70s.

7

International Library of Psychology, Philosophy, and Scientific Method
(Demy 8vo)

Lazerowitz, Morris
The Structure of Metaphysics
With a Foreword by John Wisdom
262 pp. 1955. (2nd Impression 1963.) 30s.

Lean, Martin
Sense-Perception and Matter
A Critical Analysis of C. D. Broad's Theory of Perception
234 pp. 1953. 25s.

Lodge, Rupert C.
Plato's Theory of Art
332 pp. 1953. 25s.

The Philosophy of Plato
366 pp. 1956. 32s.

Mannheim, Karl
Ideology and Utopia
An Introduction to the Sociology of Knowledge
With a Preface by Louis Wirth. Translated from the German by Louis Wirth
and Edward Shils
360 pp. 1954. (2nd Impression 1966.) 30s.

Moore, G. E.
Philosophical Studies
360 pp. 1922. (6th Impression 1965.) 35s. See also Ramsey, F. P.

Ogden, C. K., and Richards, I. A.
The Meaning of Meaning
A Study of the Influence of Language upon Thought and of the
Science of Symbolism
With supplementary essays by B. Malinowski and F. G. Crookshank
394 pp. 10th Edition 1949. (6th Impression 1967.) 32s.
See also Bentham, J.

Peirce, Charles, *see* Buchler, J.

Ramsey, Frank Plumpton
**The Foundations of Mathematics and other Logical
Essays**
Edited by R. B. Braithwaite. Preface by G. E. Moore
318 pp. 1931. (4th Impression 1965.) 35s.

Richards, I. A.
Principles of Literary Criticism
312 pp. 2nd edition. 1926. (17th Impression 1966.) 30s.

Mencius on the Mind. Experiments in Multiple Definition
190 pp. 1932. (2nd Impression 1964.) 28s.

Russell, Bertrand, *see* Fritz C. A.; Lange, F. A.; Wittgenstein, L.

8

International Library of Psychology, Philosophy, and Scientific Method
(Demy 8vo)

Smart, Ninian
Reasons and Faiths
An Investigation of Religious Discourse, Christian and Non-Christian
230 pp. 1958. (2nd Impression 1965.) 28s.

Vaihinger, H.
The Philosophy of As If
A System of the Theoretical, Practical and Religious Fictions of Mankind
Translated by C. K. Ogden
428 pp. 2nd edition 1935. (4th Impression 1965.) 45s.

Wittgenstein, Ludwig
Tractatus Logico-Philosophicus
With an Introduction by Bertrand Russell, F.R.S., German text with an English translation en regard
216 pp. 1922. (9th Impression 1962.) 21s.
For the Pears-McGuinness translation—*see page 5*

Wright, Georg Henrik von
Logical Studies
214 pp. 1957. (2nd Impression 1967.) 28s.

Zeller, Eduard
Outlines of the History of Greek Philosophy
Revised by Dr. Wilhelm Nestle. Translated from the German by L. R. Palmer
248 pp. 13th (revised) edition 1931. (5th Impression 1963.) 28s.

PSYCHOLOGY

Adler, Alfred
The Practice and Theory of Individual Psychology
Translated by P. Radin
368 pp. 2nd (revised) edition 1929. (8th Impression 1964.) 30s.

Eng, Helga
The Psychology of Children's Drawings
From the First Stroke to the Coloured Drawing
240 pp. 8 colour plates. 139 figures. 2nd edition 1954. (3rd Impression 1966.) 40s.

Jung, C. G.
Psychological Types
or The Psychology of Individuation
Translated from the German and with a Preface by H. Godwin Baynes
696 pp. 1923. (12th Impression 1964.) 45s.

International Library of Psychology, Philosophy, and Scientific Method
(Demy 8vo)

Koffka, Kurt
The Growth of the Mind
An Introduction to Child-Psychology
Translated from the German by Robert Morris Ogden
456 pp. 16 figures. 2nd edition (revised) 1928. (6th Impression 1965.) 45s.
Principles of Gestalt Psychology
740 pp. 112 figures. 39 tables. 1935. (5th Impression 1962.) 60s.

Malinowski, Bronislaw
Crime and Custom in Savage Society
152 pp. 6 plates. 1926. (8th Impression 1966.) 21s.
Sex and Repression in Savage Society
290 pp. 1927. (4th Impression 1953.) 28s
See also Ogden, C. K.

Murphy, Gardner
An Historical Introduction to Modern Psychology
488 pp. 5th edition (revised) 1949. (6th Impression 1967.) 40s.

Paget, R.
Human Speech
Some Observations, Experiments, and Conclusions as to the Nature, Origin, Purpose and Possible Improvement of Human Speech
374 pp. 5 plates. 1930. (2nd Impression 1963.) 42s.

Petermann, Bruno
The Gestalt Theory and the Problem of Configuration
Translated from the German by Meyer Fortes
364 pp. 20 figures. 1932. (2nd Impression 1950.) 25s.

Piaget, Jean
The Language and Thought of the Child
Preface by E. Claparède. Translated from the French by Marjorie Gabain
220 pp. 3rd edition (revised and enlarged) 1959. (3rd Impression 1966.) 30s.

Judgment and Reasoning in the Child
Translated from the French by Marjorie Warden
276 pp. 1928 (4th Impression 1966.) 28s.

The Child's Conception of the World
Translated from the French by Joan and Andrew Tomlinson
408 pp. 1929. (4th Impression 1964.) 40s.

Piaget, Jean *(continued)*

The Child's Conception of Physical Causality
Translated from the French by Marjorie Gabain
(3rd Impression 1965.) 30s.

The Moral Judgment of the Child
Translated from the French by Marjorie Gabain
438 pp. 1932. (4th Impression 1965.) 35s.

The Psychology of Intelligence
Translated from the French by Malcolm Piercy and D. E. Berlyne
198 pp. 1950. (4th Impression 1964.) 18s.

The Child's Conception of Number
Translated from the French by C. Gattegno and F. M. Hodgson
266 pp. 1952. (3rd Impression 1964.) 25s.

The Origin of Intelligence in the Child
Translated from the French by Margaret Cook
448 pp. 1953. (2nd Impression 1966.) 42s.

The Child's Conception of Geometry
In collaboration with Bärbel Inhelder and Alina Szeminska. Translated from the French by E. A. Lunzer
428 pp. 1960. (2nd Impression 1966.) 45s.

Piaget, Jean and Inhelder, Bärbel
The Child's Conception of Space
Translated from the French by F. J. Langdon and J. L. Lunzer
512 pp. 29 figures. 1956 (3rd Impression 1967.) 42s.

Roback, A. A.
The Psychology of Character
With a Survey of Personality in General
786 pp. 3rd edition (revised and enlarged 1952.) 50s.

Smythies, J. R.
Analysis of Perception
With a Preface by Sir Russell Brain, Bt.
162 pp. 1956. 21s.

van der Hoop, J. H.
Character and the Unconscious
A Critical Exposition of the Psychology of Freud and Jung
Translated from the German by Elizabeth Trevelyan
240 pp. 1923. (2nd Impression 1950.) 20s.

Woodger, J. H.
Biological Principles
508 pp. 1929. (Reissued with a new Introduction 1966.) 60s.